Praise for Kirstin Downey's

ISABELLA

"Downey has crafted a capable, thoroughly researched account of Isabella's life that clearly conveys her crucial role." —*The Boston Globe*

"From *Game of Thrones* to *Pillars of the Earth*, popular culture offers up medieval stories where royal blood grabs for power, where crucial alliances are built between church and state, where important people suddenly fall over dead after a sumptuous meal, poisoned by a hidden rival. But this world did, in fact, exist, and the subject of Kirstin Downey's new biography, Queen Isabella of Castile, maneuvered through it with unlikely and thrilling success." —*BookPage*

"A strong, fascinating woman, Isabella helped to usher in the modern age, and this rich, clearly written biography is a worthy chronicle of her impressive yet controversial life." —*Kirkus Reviews* (starred review)

"Kirstin Downey makes medieval history read like a modern-day thriller. Queen Isabella's life unfolded at the pivotal moment when the old world was astonished by the discovery of the new, and this graceful and insightful biography reveals her crucial role in making it happen."
—Deirdre Bair, National Book Award–winning
author of *Samuel Beckett*

"Kirstin Downey triumphantly restores Isabella to her rightful place in history. This is an engrossing new portrait of one of the most fascinating and controversial women who ever lived." —Amanda Foreman,
author of the *New York Times* bestseller
Georgiana: Duchess of Devonshire

KIRSTIN DOWNEY

ISABELLA

Kirstin Downey is the author of *The Woman Behind the New Deal*, which was a finalist for the 2009 Los Angeles Times Book Prize. She was one of the writers of the *New York Times* bestselling *Financial Crisis Inquiry Report* and was previously a staff writer at *The Washington Post*, where she shared in the 2008 Pulitzer Prize for its coverage of the Virginia Tech shootings. She was a Nieman Fellow at Harvard University in 2001. She is married to Neil Warner Averitt, and together they have five children.

www.kirstindowney.com

ISABELLA

ISABELLA

THE
WARRIOR
QUEEN

KIRSTIN DOWNEY

ANCHOR BOOKS

A DIVISION OF PENGUIN RANDOM HOUSE LLC

NEW YORK

FIRST ANCHOR BOOKS EDITION, NOVEMBER 2015

The Library of Congress has cataloged the Nan A. Talese/Doubleday
edition as follows:
Downey, Kirstin.
Isabella : the warrior queen / Kirstin Downey.—First edition.
pages cm
Includes bibliographical references and index.
1. Isabella I, Queen of Spain, 1451–1504.
2. Queens—Spain—Biography.
3. Spain—History—Ferdinand and Isabella, 1479–1516.   I. Title.
DP163.D69 2014   946.03092—dc23   [B]   2014003895

Anchor Books Trade Paperback ISBN: 978-0-307-74216-2
eBook ISBN: 978-0-385-53412-3

Author photograph © Michael Lionstar
Maps by Gene Thorp
Book design by Pei Loi Koay

www.anchorbooks.com

Printed in the United States of America
10   9   8

To Laura Gregg Roa, who sat on the seawall with me in
Coco Solo, Panama, dreaming of sailing ships and distant
lands, and the queen who sent the explorer to our shores

1957 – 2009

CONTENTS

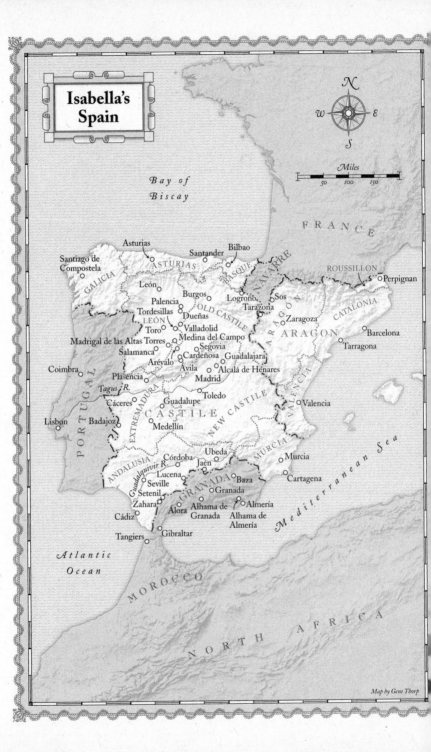

Isabella's Spain

Bay of
Biscay

FRANCE

Santiago de
Compostela

GALICIA

Asturias
ASTURIAS
Santander   Bilbao

BASQUE

NAVARRE

ROUSSILLON
Perpignan

León

Palencia
Tordesillas
LEÓN   Dueñas
Toro
Madrigal de las Altas Torres
Salamanca
Arévalo
Plasencia

Burgos
Logroño   Sos
OLD CASTILE   Tarazona
Valladolid   Zaragoza
Medina del Campo
Segovia
Cardeñosa   Guadalajara
Ávila   Alcalá de Henares
Madrid

ARAGON
ARAGON

CATALONIA

Barcelona

Tarragona

Coimbra

PORTUGAL

Tagus R.
Cáceres
EXTREMADURA
CASTILE

Toledo

NEW CASTILE

Guadalupe

VALENCIA

Valencia

Lisbon   Badajoz
Medellín

Córdoba
ANDALUSIA
Guadalquivir R.   Lucena
Seville
Setenil
Zahara
Cádiz   Álora
Tangiers   Gibraltar

Ubeda
Jaén
GRANADA   Baza
Granada
Alhama de   Almería
Granada   Alhama de
Almería

MURCIA
Murcia
Cartagena

Mediterranean Sea

Atlantic
Ocean

MOROCCO

NORTH AFRICA

Miles
50   100   150

Map by Gene Thorp

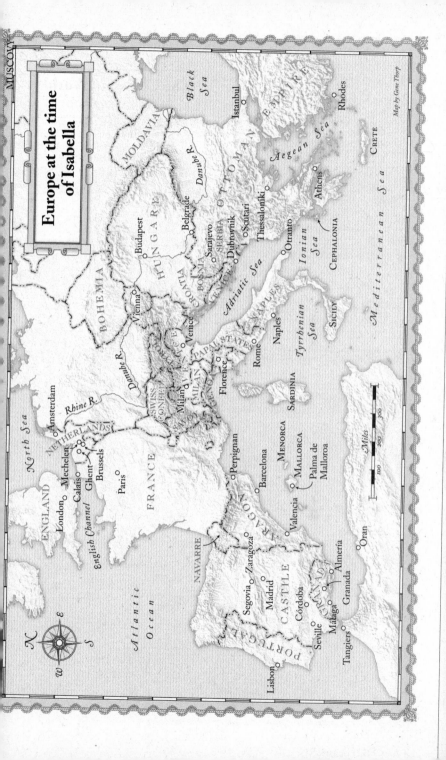

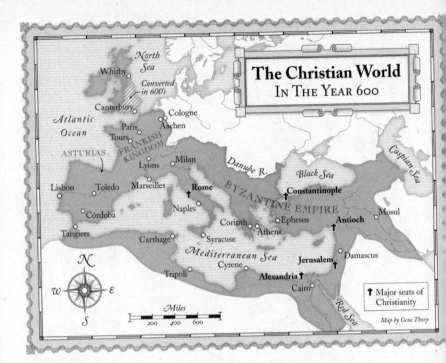

The Christian World
IN THE YEAR 600

North Sea
Whitby
Converted in 600's
Canterbury
Cologne
Atlantic Ocean
Paris
Aachen
Tours
FRANKISH KINGDOM
ASTURIAS
Lyons
Milan
Danube R.
Black Sea
Caspian Sea
Lisbon
Toledo
Marseilles
Rome
BYZANTINE EMPIRE
Constantinople
Mosul
Córdoba
Naples
Antioch
Tangiers
Corinth
Ephesus
Carthage
Syracuse
Athens
Damascus
Mediterranean Sea
Jerusalem
Cyrene
Alexandria
Tripoli
Cairo
Red Sea

N W E S

Miles
200   400   600

✝ Major seats of Christianity

Map by Gene Thorp

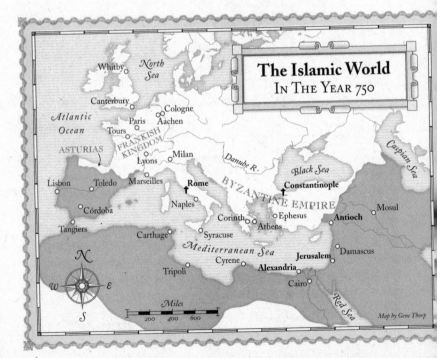

The Islamic World
IN THE YEAR 750

Whitby
North Sea
Canterbury
Cologne
Atlantic Ocean
Paris
Aachen
Tours
FRANKISH KINGDOM
ASTURIAS
Lyons
Milan
Danube R.
Black Sea
Caspian Sea
Lisbon
Toledo
Marseilles
Rome
BYZANTINE EMPIRE
Constantinople
Mosul
Córdoba
Naples
Antioch
Tangiers
Corinth
Ephesus
Carthage
Syracuse
Athens
Damascus
Mediterranean Sea
Jerusalem
Cyrene
Alexandria
Tripoli
Cairo
Red Sea

N W E S

Miles
200   400   600

Map by Gene Thorp

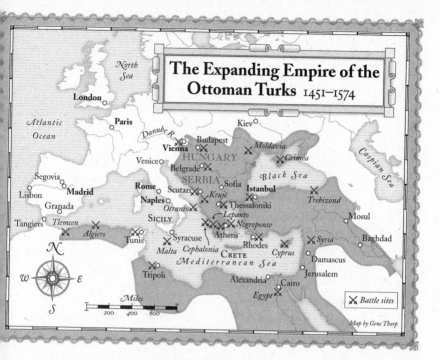

The Expanding Empire of the Ottoman Turks 1451–1574

North Sea

London

Atlantic Ocean

Paris

Danube R.

Vienna

Budapest

Kiev

Moldavia

Crimea

Venice

HUNGARY

Belgrade

SERBIA

Sofia

Black Sea

Segovia

Lisbon

Madrid

Granada

Rome

Naples

Scutari

Krujë

Istanbul

Thessaloniki

Trebizond

Tangiers

Tlemcen

SICILY

Otranto

Lepanto

Negroponte

Mosul

Algiers

Tunis

Syracuse

Cephalonia

Athens

Rhodes

Cyprus

Syria

Baghdad

Malta

CRETE

Damascus

Mediterranean Sea

Tripoli

Alexandria

Cairo

Jerusalem

Egypt

N W E S

Miles
200 400 600

✕ Battle sites

Map by Gene Thorp

N W E S

CASTILE AND LEON

Segura R.

Baeza

Ubeda

Córdoba

Jaén

Vélez-Blanco

Guadalquiver R.

Seville

Écija

Lucena

GRANADA

Moclín

Vélez-Rubio

Genil R.

Marchena

Íllora

Guadix

Almanzora R.

Antequera

Loja

Santa Fe

Granada

Guadalete R.

Zahara

Ronda

Álora

Alhama

Vélez-Málaga

Almería

Coín

Málaga

Almuñecar

Marbella

Atlantic Ocean

Gibraltar

Mediterranean Sea

Ceuta

Miles
20 40 60

Granada

Map by Gene Thorp

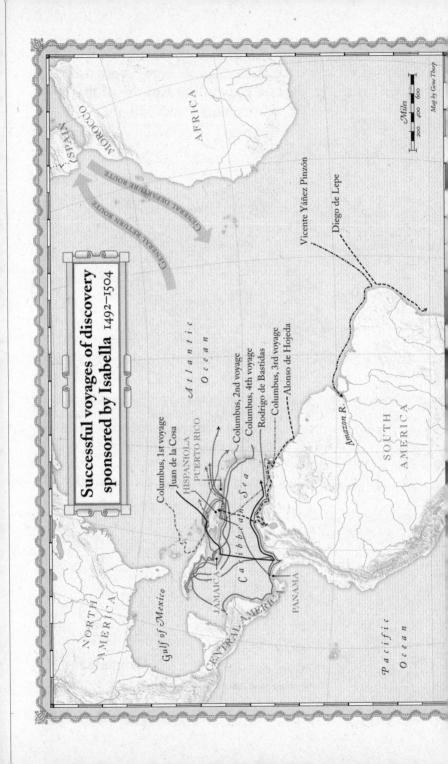

Successful voyages of discovery sponsored by Isabella 1492–1504

Map by Gene Thorp

Columbus, 1st voyage
Juan de la Cosa
Columbus, 2nd voyage
Columbus, 4th voyage
Rodrigo de Bastidas
Columbus, 3rd voyage
Alonso de Hojeda
Vicente Yáñez Pinzón
Diego de Lepe

GENERAL DEPARTURE ROUTE
GENERAL RETURN ROUTE

SPAIN
MOROCCO
AFRICA

Atlantic Ocean

HISPANIOLA
PUERTO RICO
JAMAICA
Caribbean Sea
CENTRAL AMERICA
PANAMA

NORTH AMERICA
Gulf of Mexico

Pacific Ocean

SOUTH AMERICA
Amazon R.

Miles
200 400 600

ISABELLA

PROLOGUE

I n a castle on a steep promontory overlooking the windswept plains of north-central Spain, a slender red-haired princess finalized the plans for a ceremony that was likely to throw her nation—already teetering toward anarchy—into full-fledged civil war.

Her name was Isabella, and she had just learned that her older brother, King Enrique—known as Enrique El Impotente, which symbolized his failings, both administrative and sexual—had died.

King Enrique's lascivious young wife, who had occupied her time bestowing her favors on the other gentlemen of the court, had produced a child, but many people doubted that the king was actually the child's father. Isabella had decided to end the controversy over the succession by having herself crowned queen instead. The twenty-three-year-old woman was essentially orchestrating a coup.

No woman had ruled the combined Kingdoms of Castile and León, the largest single realm on the Iberian peninsula, in more than two hundred years. In many European countries, it was illegal for a woman to rule alone. On the rare occasions when women reigned, it was usually as regent for a son who was too young to govern. Isabella had a husband, Ferdinand, who was heir to the neighboring Kingdom of Aragon, but he had been traveling when the news of Enrique's death arrived, and she had decided to seize the initiative. She would take the crown for herself alone.

On that bitter-cold morning in December 1474, Isabella added the finishing touches to an ensemble intentionally designed to impress onlookers with her splendor and regal grandeur. She donned an elegant gown encrusted with jewels; a dark red ruby glittered at her throat.

Observers already awed by the pageantry now gasped at an additional sight. On Isabella's orders, a court official walked ahead of her horse, holding aloft an unsheathed sword, the naked blade pointing straight upward toward the zenith, in an ancient symbol of the right to enforce justice. It was a dramatic warning gesture, symbolizing Isabella's intent to take power and to use it forcefully.

Acknowledging nothing out of the ordinary, Isabella took a seat on an improvised platform in the square. A silver crown was placed upon her head. As the crowd cheered, Isabella was proclaimed queen. Afterward she proceeded to Segovia's cathedral. She prostrated herself in prayer before the altar, offering her thanks and imploring God to help her to rule wisely and well. She viewed the tasks ahead as titanic. She believed Christianity was in mortal danger.

The Ottoman Turks were aggressively on the march in eastern and southern Europe. The Muslims retained an entrenched foothold in the Andalusian kingdom of Granada, which Isabella and others feared would prove a beachhead into the rest of Spain. A succession of popes had pleaded in vain for a steely-eyed commander, a stalwart warrior, to step forward to counter the threat. Instead it was a young woman, the mother of a young daughter, who was taking up the banner.

The means she used were effective but brutal. For centuries to come, historians would debate the meaning of her life. Was she a saint? Or was she satanic?

As she stood in the sun in Segovia that winter afternoon, however, she showed no trace of fear or hesitation. Inspired by the example of Joan of Arc, who had died just two decades before Isabella was born and whose stories were much repeated during her childhood, Isabella similarly began to fashion herself as a religious icon. Inwardly infused with a sense of her own destiny, a faith that was "fervent, mystical and intense,"[1] Isabella was confident to her core that God was on her side and that He intended her to rule. The questioning would only come much later.

ONE

A BIRTH WITHOUT
FANFARE

Throughout most of Spanish history, and particularly in the Middles Ages, when bloodlines determined who would rule, the birth of a prince or princess in Castile was a cause for national jubilation. The child's arrival was breathlessly anticipated and often intimately observed by the nation's highest-ranking families, who competed for the right to attend the delivery. Street festivals were orchestrated; gifts were exchanged; the child's baptism was a particularly reverent celebration.

But when Isabella, the daughter of King Juan II, arrived in this world in late April 1451, this was not the case. Castile already had a male heir, Isabella's older half brother, Enrique, born to Juan's first wife, and the line of succession seemed set. Prince Enrique was twenty-six, married, and already had a court of his own. Enrique's children, when they came along, would presumably rule when Enrique died.

Isabella's own mother, who was twenty-three years old, was Juan's second wife, and King Juan had not been there when the baby was delivered. Isabella was born on a Thursday afternoon "in a small alcove of an airless second-floor bedroom," in an unprepossessing brick palace built around a Roman-style central patio.[1] There was not even a fireplace in the room; a smoky coal brazier supplied the only heat. The birth occurred in Madrigal de las Altas Torres, an out-of-the-way farm town in the north-central part of the Iberian peninsula, in a place where the men of the family frequently stashed unwanted female relatives. Just a few thousand residents lived there, huddled behind walls that protected them from attack. The baby's mother, Juan's wife, was Isabel of Portugal, and her mother in turn was Isabel of Barcelos, also from Portugal, and so the baby was named Isabel, or Isabella, after her mother and grandmother—Isabel in its Spanish and Portuguese forms, or Anglicized as Isabella. The baby was therefore half Portuguese. It was long-established custom among the ruling families of Iberia, whether Portuguese, Castilian, or Aragonese, to name children after their grandparents, and so Isabella was named after the Portuguese side of the family.

Several days after his wife gave birth, King Juan sent out messengers to several large cities telling officials the news of the delivery, but he did so in such an offhand way that it has been difficult to determine the exact date. It was probably on April 22. In a letter dated April 23, sent from Madrid, Juan informed officials in Segovia that his wife had borne a princess "thanks to the grace of Our Lord," on the previous Thursday.[2]

Archivists are equally unsure where the child was baptized. Royal baptisms tended to be freighted with both political and religious significance. The baptism of an heir to the throne was generally performed with ritual splendor in one of the finest cathedrals in the land. No chronicle reports the king's attendance at this ceremony, however. It was probably held in Madrigal at the local Church of St. Nicholas. The fact that nobody knows where Isabella was baptized underscores the general lack of interest in the baby's arrival.

Isabella's birth was in many ways almost a distraction, for her parents were preoccupied by the political intrigue swirling around them. Her father was approaching an acrimonious, fatal parting of the ways with his closest friend and adviser, Álvaro de Luna, a man who was both brilliant and ruthless. Isabella's mother was prodding her husband along toward this split. The consequences were likely to prove significant. Álvaro had orchestrated the marriage between Isabella's parents, possibly after nudging King Juan's first wife along to the afterlife by poisoning her. That first wife, María of Aragon, who had once ordered Álvaro de Luna to leave the court, had suddenly developed swollen purple marks all over her body and collapsed; her sister, an ally who lived in a distant city, died the same week from the same strange affliction.[3] Queen Isabel had reason to believe that she too might be at risk if her actions were seen to be jeopardizing Álvaro's steely grip over her husband and his administration. Yet she sought that outcome nonetheless.

She may have believed she had no choice. The circumstances of Juan's young queen had been precarious from the start. It had been difficult to win the king's heart. Juan had preferred to take a luscious French princess for his second wife, but Álvaro, "secretly and without the knowledge of the king," had decided that a Portuguese alliance was more advantageous for the realm.[4] He negotiated the terms of the marriage without informing Juan, and the king had been miffed when he learned he would have no further say in the matter. The king's displeasure had been common knowledge inside the court.

Isabel, the unwanted bride, arrived in Castile in 1447, accompanied by a Portuguese retinue, and set about doing what she could to secure her husband's love. Juan, forty-two, was a cultivated and sophisticated man who read philosophy and literature and was an avid enthusiast of the early Renaissance painting techniques being pioneered in Burgundy. Tall, blue-eyed, and ruddy-skinned, he was also worldly and pleasure-loving, with a roving eye. The nineteen-year-old bride soon found herself having to compete for her husband's affections. She tried to make herself as agreeable as possible, doing as she was asked, but worried when she did not quickly become pregnant.[5] If she failed to conceive, her husband might attempt to have the marriage annulled or have her sent away into seclusion and disgrace. Most women then were valued primarily for their ability to produce offspring, an obligation even more pronounced among royalty. If she failed to produce a child, she would be viewed as almost worthless.

Not surprisingly, the queen felt threatened by the young and beautiful women at court. Even one of her own ladies-in-waiting, Beatriz de Silva, had attracted the king's attention. Isabel must have been at the limits of her patience, because she had the offending woman seized and thrown into a cupboard in the basement, without access to food or drink, for three days. The woman finally emerged, claiming she had had a religious conversion during her imprisonment, kept her face covered for the remainder of her life to conceal her beauty, and went on to found a religious order. Queen Isabel's furious reaction to a woman she perceived as a rival indicated that the marriage was on a rocky footing. As time went on, however, Juan became more fond of his wife. After baby Isabella was born, Queen Isabel bore the king a second child, the prince Alfonso, two years later, a birth that attracted considerably more favorable attention. King Juan now had a male heir and a spare.

Queen Isabel's testy relationship with Álvaro de Luna complicated the process of strengthening her marriage. Álvaro and King Juan were in the custom of going off together on debauched revels, with a nunnery-turned-brothel one of their favorite destinations. Álvaro maintained tight controls over Juan's comings and goings, even dictating to the couple when they were permitted to enjoy conjugal relations. He held remarkable sway over the king, whom he had manipulated into transferring vast properties and honors into his hands, making him by far the wealthiest man in the kingdom. Álvaro had been appointed constable of Castile, which made him the kingdom's leading military officer, and was also named grand master of the Order of Santiago, Castile's wealthiest order of monastic knights. In that role alone, Álvaro controlled more than sixty towns and castles and commanded 100,000 vassals.[6]

King Juan had given him almost total control over the kingdom. Wits in Castile joked that thanks to Álvaro de Luna, Juan "had no other task except to eat."[7]

Queen Isabel was understandably unhappy with the situation, and even more so after she made a surprise visit to her husband in the important Castilian city of Valladolid and slept with him in his chambers that night. Álvaro was furious when he learned she was there and hastened over to the palace, where he pounded on the bedroom door. "Were you not told that you were not supposed to come?" he shouted angrily at her in front of a circle of court observers, who were astonished by the ferocity of the exchange.[8] On another occasion, he made an explicit threat to the queen: "I married you, and I'll unmarry you," he said.[9]

Queen Isabel was not the only person who viewed Álvaro de Luna with enmity. His privileged position stirred envy among many of the other nobles, particularly the king's relatives, who thought they should be receiving King Juan's bounty, instead of Álvaro de Luna. The man's high-handed tactics and greed were widely criticized almost everywhere. Six years into his second marriage, King Juan finally summoned the courage to face down Álvaro and ordered him executed. The courtier was beheaded in 1453 in a humiliating public ceremony in the main square of Valladolid. This bold demonstration of royal power sent ripples of shock across the kingdom. Almost immediately, however, Juan regretted the decision, because it meant he needed to shoulder the burdens of rule on his own, something he had never wanted to do. He fell into depression and, within a year, died at the age of forty-nine.

This loss of her husband was another blow to the unhappy young queen. She slipped into what chroniclers called *profunda tristeza,* or a deep sadness, speaking only seldom and staring vacantly into space, perhaps at first as a result of postnatal depression and then from loneliness and grief.[10] She believed that she was being haunted by Álvaro de Luna and sometimes fancied she could hear his mournful cries in the wind on bitter nights. The young Isabella was left virtually parentless, observers noted, a condition that bound her tightly to the younger brother who shared her tenuous childhood. The two children clung to each other.

The fateful breakdown in the lifelong political alliance between the king and Álvaro de Luna came at a bad time for Castile, which was already at a low point in its history. The kingdom was splintered by political squabbles between nobles and by even more dangerous rivalries between the king and his cousins in the adjacent Kingdom of Aragon, who were forever hoping to take control of Castile themselves. The countryside was wracked with crime, but its rulers were distracted by a nearly constant string of civil wars.

Isabella's older half brother Enrique took the throne at King Juan's death, when she was three. The first few years of his royal administration were successful, but then many of the same problems that had haunted their father's reign reemerged.

The personal and political tumult reverberated in Isabella's life. Enrique had many good qualities but also a number of character flaws, which were exacerbated in relation to Isabella because of tensions within the stepfamily. As ruler of Castile, King Enrique now possessed complete power over his stepmother, Queen Isabel, who as a dowager queen deserved to be viewed with maternal respect but was in fact three years younger than her stepson. The emotions among the siblings were a boiling cauldron of love and resentment. King Enrique did little to nurture his younger sister and brother, and instead their relationship with him became a source of tension and fear.

With such an unpredictable childhood, it was not surprising that Isabella took consolation in an institution that provided the greatest single source of stability to her daily routine: the Catholic Church, whose rituals dominated the lives of European Christians during the Middle Ages. The tick-tock clock of life in the medieval world was the church and its ecclesiastical calendar. Church bells tolled to the schedule of services—matins, vespers, vigils at midnight; each day of the year belonged to a particular saint, who was due special reverence and specific forms of veneration. Religion played an even bigger role in Isabella's life than for most people of the age, because the Castilian court was essentially itinerant, moving from palace to palace around the kingdom. Each residence also served as a monastery or convent to house priests and nuns who maintained the houses in the absence of the royal family and so were present in the homes whenever the family visited. Isabella grew up surrounded by clerics.

This child who had lost her parents so early turned to the church and its teachings for moral guidance, and Isabella became extremely susceptible to influences from church officials, particularly those who gave evidence of living lives of abstemious self-denial. Cleaning and building the church, purifying it from corruption, causing it to grow, and maintaining it without a taint of stain or heresy became a primary life preoccupation for her. Sin and punishment were recurring motifs for Isabella, who believed that all humans were descended from the surviving sons of Noah, who had sailed to safety when God drowned the rest of mankind in anger over human wrongdoing. She loved the New Testament, but she lived by the rigid morality of the Old Testament. She was always more inclined to claim an eye for an eye than to turn the other cheek.

Her worldview and religious perspective had been shaped by events that had happened on the other end of the Mediterranean Sea many hundreds of years before her birth. Four men in particular, three men from the Levant, and a fourth, Muhammad, born on the Arabian peninsula, had reported they heard God speaking to them, and each had said and done things that had had repercussions for centuries. The first three were Abraham and Moses, both Jews, and Jesus, born and raised a Jew, who went on to announce a new religion. The lives and actions of these first three men were vividly depicted around her, in the paintings, tapestries, sculptures, books, and illustrated manuscripts that filled the churches and palaces where she spent her days and nights.

Abraham was a prophet who rejected the worship of idols and embraced the concept of a single, all-powerful God to whom submission in all things was required. He is viewed as the forefather of the Jewish people. Moses was a prophet who introduced the Ten Commandments, a basic code of conduct for moral living, which were words he said came directly from God. Jesus was a Jew who proposed a group of variations on Judaism and called for his followers to proselytize and seek out new converts to their reform faith, which came to be known as Christianity.

Conflicts from that ancient time would still be felt in Isabella's Spain. The Christians were angry that the Jews did not accept Jesus's teachings and their account of the resurrection. Moreover, they believed that Jewish rulers had played a role in Jesus's death by crucifixion and had later persecuted the followers of Jesus. Jews, on the other hand, believed that Jesus had been executed by the Romans and that they had been unfairly charged with complicity. They did not want to change their beliefs. Obsessing over these different perspectives meant that innocent people born many years after these events had occurred could become scapegoats for religious fanatics and anti-Semites, even as far away as Spain.

Spain itself made several appearances in the New Testament. At one point Saint Paul said he planned to visit there; Saint Jerome later described the route Paul had taken. Another apostle of Jesus's, Saint James—or in Spanish, Santiago—was also believed to have traveled to Spain, and although evidence for this journey was scanty, his arrival and burial in northern Spain became an article of faith to the pious Christians of western Europe and made the town of Santiago de Compostela one of the most important pilgrimage destinations in Christendom.[11] That meant that many Christians in Europe traveled to the north of Spain, through the region known as Galicia, and problems inside Spain during the Middle Ages had political and religious reverberations elsewhere.

Spain also continued to feel the influences of classical Greek and Roman civilization. Isabella and her family believed themselves to be descended from Hercules, the legendary warrior, half-God and half-mortal. They believed the hero had personally founded the cities of Arévalo, Segovia, Ávila, and Salamanca, places that Isabella knew well. Hercules was particularly associated with an ancient lighthouse, more than 100 feet tall, dating from the Phoenician era, overlooking the coast of Galicia in northern Spain, in an area notorious for shipwrecks. Its construction would have been viewed as a remarkable engineering feat, even in Isabella's day. It was a surviving illustration of the ways in which Greek mythology and biblical tales intermingled in the Spanish mind. A history book that Isabella commissioned and helped edit, Diego de Valera's *Chronicle of Spain,* published in 1493, highlighted the kingdom's ties to Greece. The dedication even pointedly referred to Isabella's ancestral title of Duchess of Athens through her marriage to Ferdinand.

The belief that magical or mythological figures such as Hercules played a role in Spain's past would not have seemed terribly far-fetched, for awe-inspiring Roman ruins were everywhere. In Segovia, the gemlike town that would prove so central to Isabella's formative years, the old Roman aqueduct transported clean mountain water from more than twenty miles away, in its last stages bridging a valley ninety-four feet deep. Many other cities in Spain had once been flourishing Roman centers as well, including Seville, Salamanca, and Zaragoza. Some of the most famous Roman writers hailed from Iberia, including Martial, Lucan, and Seneca the Elder; the emperors Hadrian and Trajan are believed to have been born near Seville.[12]

The land then known as Hispania had been reorganized as a Roman province by Emperor Augustus in 38 B.C., and for the next six centuries the peninsula's history was intermingled with that of the great Roman Empire. "The Romans built not only highways, theaters, circuses, bridges, aqueducts, and temples; they also brought their political and juridical institutions and their concepts of social and family life," wrote the French historian Jean Descola.[13]

Isabella's birthplace, the palace in Madrigal, with its chambers facing a central area or patio, was not unique in its Roman-style design. Many homes were similarly built in that fashion, with rooms opening onto an arcade around a central atrium. The inhabitants of the Iberian peninsula adopted Greco-Roman customs and manners, and in time, Spaniards were sometimes referred to as Greeks themselves. In the age-old pattern, religious observance followed political power. The pantheon of Greek and Roman gods held sway until the Roman emperor Constantine made Christianity permissible in 312, beginning a new era of cooperation between church and state. As Christianity became ascendant over pagan forms of worship, the persecutions of Christians by the Romans finally stopped. The imperial endorsement ushered in an explosive expansion in the number of followers of Christianity. Even small villages built their own churches. An ecclesiastical hierarchy linked all the Christian churches throughout the Roman Empire. Five major religious seats developed: Antioch, Jerusalem, Alexandria, Rome, and Constantinople. Christianity became the primary religion in Europe and throughout the Near East and North Africa.

As the centuries passed and Rome's power disintegrated, corruption and persistent waves of foreign invasion weakened the western half of the old Roman Empire. When the Visigoths, people of a Germanic stock, surged down from the Pyrenees into the Iberian peninsula in the fifth century, they quickly asserted dominance in the new power vacuum. Coming from the north, they tended to be blonder and taller than the dark-haired peoples of the Mediterranean. They crafted beautiful jewelry and created their own signature architectural styles. They made their capital in Toledo, in the heart of the peninsula, and eventually declared Christianity to be the official religion. The kingdom ruled by the Visigoths was the place that the historian Isidore of Seville proudly described as the "ornament of the world."[14] Isabella, who possessed the red-blond hair and gray-blue eyes of the Visigoths, saw herself as a descendant of that lineage, and the princess read Isidore's account of the Visigothic era with avid interest, collecting several copies of his published work.

The Roman heritage and Christianity became interwoven, with the empire's cultural and literary legacy preserved in various forms across Europe. By now the Roman Empire had split into two parts. Eastern Europe, with its capital in the great metropolis of Constantinople, became the heart of Christianity and the cultural center for the classical tradition, the home of the Byzantine Empire. Western Europe was politically fragmented by the barbarian invasions but retained its religious capital in Rome. Eventually the two branches of Christianity became estranged and developed doctrinal differences. The Orthodox Church in Constantinople viewed itself as maintaining the ancient traditions. In western Europe, including Spain, the Roman Catholic Church had primacy. The two branches of the Christian Church feuded with each other, adherents of each believing they were religiously superior to the other. Snubs became insults.

Spain was also home to a significant Jewish population, whose ancestors had been dispersed around the Mediterranean as part of their own persecutions by the Romans. They prospered, however, and among the Visigoths, jealousy and anti-Semitism arose. In the 600s, King Chintila ordered all the Jews expelled or forcibly converted. The seventeenth council of Toledo in 702 ordered the Jews enslaved and forbade them to marry. The Spanish did not fully enforce these harsh laws, however, and many Jews managed to carry on in Spain. Some declared themselves Christian for survival, not by choice, and deeply resented their mistreatment at the hands of the Visigoths.

By the early eighth century, the post-Roman, Germanic kingdoms of western Europe had grown weak and disorganized, leaving the area open to raiding expeditions by a new generation of outside invaders. To the north, the Vikings, explorers and pirates from Iceland, Greenland, and

Scandinavia, surged into England, France, and Ireland and murdered, robbed, and terrorized the people living there.

In Spain, the threat came from the south, in the form of a new religion that built on the Jewish and Christian belief in the existence of a single God but added some notable features. It had been founded by the prophet Muhammad, a merchant who believed that religious truth had been revealed to him. Born in 570, he preached from about 613 to 632. He honored Jews and Christians for their precursor teachings but believed that Islam was the true faith, given to him directly as the final revelation from God. The new religion, called Islam—from an Arabic word that means "submission" or commitment to God—attracted scores of believers, and its burgeoning popularity threatened the existing social order in the Arabian peninsula.

Muhammad lived in Mecca, but as opposition to him grew, he moved to the nearby city of Medina. From there he turned and began a campaign against his former hometown. He launched raids against trading caravans, seizing valuable booty and hostages. While some Christians and Jews supported Muhammad, those who opposed him or cooperated with his enemies were exiled with loss of their lands, enslaved, or executed. By the time of his death, Muhammad was ruler of western Arabia. The Muslims spread the faith by evangelization and also by sending armed bands of believers to attack centers of opposition. Most of Palestine and Syria were seized in the 630s; Egypt was taken in 642. It was a wholesale colonial expansion. The Muslims occupied the southern half of the Byzantine Empire and replaced its leaders with people of Arabic origin. "Property and wealth ... were redistributed on a grand scale," writes the historian John Esposito.[15]

Islam presented unique challenges to Christianity. It was a competing religious philosophy, another proselytizing faith that established set patterns of worship and codes of behavior that followers found satisfying and helped their societies function more smoothly. "From its birth, the Islamic religion was the chief contender with Christianity for the hearts of men; Islamic civilization was the nearest neighbor and deadliest rival of European Christendom," wrote the historian Bernard Lewis.[16]

Modeling their behavior on that of their warrior prophet Muhammad turned out to be an excellent blueprint for territorial expansion. Muhammad in fact had urged his followers to expand their dominions, calling on them to seize property and wealth through force of arms.

Many captives were taken in these raiding excursions and distributed into the tribes and families of their captors. The female family members of defeated rulers were turned into wives or concubines. This process created an administrative and military machine that allowed Islam to explode into many areas almost simultaneously. Many men were eager to join the marauding forces, to expand the faith, to enrich themselves, or to find adventure.

Timing was also key to the Islamic successes. The Byzantine and Persian Empires had just finished fighting in prolonged conflict to the point of exhaustion. When the Muslim insurgency developed, they lacked the will and the resources to defend themselves.

The Muslims' conquest of Spain came with blinding swiftness in 711, just twelve years after they vanquished North Africa. Full details of the conquest have been lost to time because the Visigothic civilization was destroyed and the Muslim culture superimposed, and as ordinarily occurs, history is told by the victors. A rare surviving Christian document, called the Chronicle of 754, blamed the almost-instantaneous disintegration of the Visigothic state on internal tensions that had left the kingdom unable to mobilize in the face of an outside threat. A new king, Roderic, had climbed to power in 711, but he was unpopular and inexperienced at ruling. A rival leader, angry at Roderic, aided and encouraged the Muslim invasion. The Christian chronicler described the invasion as horrific, with cities burned to the ground, men crucified, children killed, and looting everywhere. He compared the invasion to the great disasters of history, to "Adam's fall, to the fall of Troy, to the Babylonian capture of Jerusalem and to the sack of Rome," writes historian Roger Collins.[17]

Muslim accounts mirror that story but present the facts from a triumphant perspective. To them, the attack was religiously justified because Muhammad had said it was divine will that "every one of the regions . . . shall be subdued by my people."[18]

The fullest account of the invasion comes from the Arab historian Ahmad ibn Muhammad Al-Maqqari, who wrote that events began with a preliminary foray by two vessels of soldiers who raided Andalusia, in the south of Spain, and came home "loaded with spoil." They reported that they found a "a country with delightful valleys, and fertile lands, rich in all sorts of agricultural productions, watered by many large rivers, and abounding in springs of the sweetest waters."[19] The leaders of the foraging trip marveled at how close this bountiful land was to North Africa.

"It's not an ocean, but only a narrow channel," one said to another, explaining the likely ease of conquest.[20]

Then a Berber warrior named Tarif Abu Zarah launched a larger raid with between five hundred and one thousand soldiers and returned with "a rich spoil and several captives, who were so handsome that Mu'sa and his companions had never seen the like of them." And when word of his successful expedition spread, "everyone wished to go to Andalus," Al-Maqqari wrote.[21]

A third and even more devastating raid was soon on its way, again led by Abu Zarah. He laid waste what fell in his path, burning down the homes of residents and destroying a church "very much venerated" by the residents, according to Al-Maqqari. "He then put to the sword such of its inhabitants as he met, and, making a few prisoners, returned safe to Africa."[22]

Now plans were made for a large-scale invasion and permanent conquest. These were put in the hands of a warrior named Tarik ibn Zeyad ibn Abdillah, who entered southern Spain with thousands of soldiers, ferrying them across the eight-mile strait in four boats that shuttled back and forth until all the men had reached Europe. During the passage, Tarik was reported to have had a dream in which Muhammad promised him military success in the invasion. This mystical experience filled Tarik with confidence, and as soon as he arrived, he swept across the land and "began to overrun and lay waste the neighboring country," wrote Al-Maqqari.[23] They had entered Europe close by a giant rock formation in the south of Spain; the spot came to be known as Jabal Tarik, "Mountain of Tarik," and in time, Gibraltar.[24]

Probably about fifteen thousand Arab and Berber soldiers participated in the invasion. The role of the Berbers, from Africa, seems to have been crucial. The Arab historian Ibn Khallikan said Tarik was a Berber and that his troops were primarily Berbers.[25] Generally speaking, the Spanish men were killed and the women and children were enslaved. The interest in taking women and not killing them suggests that few of the Arabs had brought their wives and families with them. The speed of movement of the Arab armies also suggests they traveled unencumbered.[26]

The Iberians were dumbstruck by the unexpected attacks. They attempted to respond, but their troops fell apart in chaos. Roderic was in the far distant north when the first major assault occurred. He quickly moved south and summoned troop reinforcements from all over the kingdom. Tarik similarly called for reinforcements from North Africa, and additional thousands of Muslim soldiers rallied to his side, in what seems to have been the first instance of Muslims reaching back to Africa to seek reinforcements against the Christians.

Tarik urged his soldiers to fight bravely, in the name of Allah, according to Al-Maqqari. "Know that if you only suffer for a while, you will reap in the end an abundant harvest of pleasures and enjoyments," Tarik told his troops. "You must know how the . . . maidens, as handsome as houris, their necks glittering with innumerable pearls and jewels, their bodies clothed with tunics of costly silks sprinkled with gold, are awaiting your arrival, reclining on soft couches in the sumptuous palaces of crowned lords and princes."[27]

The men roared their approval and rushed into battle. Roderic was killed, the Visigothic forces collapsed, and the Christians ran helter-skelter in disarray, fleeing in all directions. Roderic's body was never found; he was believed to have drowned in a stream. "The Christians were obliged to shut themselves up in their castles and fortresses, and quitting the flat country, betake themselves to the mountains."[28]

Now Tarif led attack after attack, conquering city after city. "God filled with terror and alarm the hearts of the idolaters," Al-Maqqari wrote, for the Christians had originally believed the Muslims would invade, steal booty, and then depart for their homes in North Africa. Now they realized they were coming to seize and occupy the kingdom.[29] Some cities quickly capitulated; others fought feebly to defend themselves.

Tarik, Al-Maqqari wrote, endeavored to increase the terror of the Christians by means of the following stratagem:

> [H]e directed his men to cook the flesh of the slain in the presence of the Gothic captives in his camp, and when the flesh had thus been cooked in large copper vessels he ordered it to be cut up, as if it were to be distributed to his men for their meals; he after this allowed some of the captives to escape, that they might report to their countrymen what they had seen. And thus the stratagem produced the desired effect, since the report of the fugitives contributed in no small degree to increase the panic of the infidels.[30]

The Muslims spread out across the countryside, riding horses they had taken from the Christians, with the existing Roman roads making quick progress very easy. A Muslim soldier named Mugheyth Ar-rumi was ordered to attack Córdoba, a large city in the south of Spain, while other battalions went toward Málaga and Elviria. Tarik headed toward Toledo, the Visigothic capital, located near the center of the peninsula. In Córdoba, Mugheyth's army surprised the sentries and overpowered the garrison stationed there. Some of the troops and the governor eluded capture and took refuge in a church near the city. The Muslims besieged the church for three months and finally grew tired of waiting, according to Arab historians. They ordered the refugees to convert to Islam or agree to pay tribute, and when they refused, the church was set on fire and the people within perished in the blaze.[31]

"After the taking of Córdoba," Al-Maqqari wrote, "Mugheyth assembled all the Jews in the city and left them in charge of it, trusting them in preference to the Christians, on account of their hatred and animosity toward the latter." Mugheyth then took possession of the palace as his own home and turned over the rest of the town to be inhabited by the Muslims.[32]

The same strategy was used in another town, Elviria, on the peninsula's Mediterranean coast: "The citadel of this latter place they entrusted to the care of the Jews, and this practice became almost general in the succeeding years; for whenever the Muslims conquered a town, it was left in the custody of the Jews with only a few Muslims, the rest of the army proceeding to new conquests, and where Jews were deficient a proportionally greater body of Muslims was left in charge."[33]

Tarik took a party of Jews with him to gain control of the capital city of Toledo, Al-Maqqari wrote. There they seized many items of great value, including

> 25 gold crowns, one for each of the Gothic monarchs who had reigned over Andalus, (It being the custom of that nation that each of their kings should deposit in that sacred spot a gold diadem, having his name, figure, and condition, the number of children he left, the length of his life, and that of his reign, engraven on it,) one and twenty copies of the Pentateuch, the Gospel, or the Psalms; the book of Abraham; and that of Moses, several other books containing secrets of nature and art, or treating about the manner of using plants, minerals, and living animals, beneficially for man; another which contained talismans of ancient Greek

philosophers, and a collection of recipes and simples and elixirs; several gold vases filled with pearls, rubies, emeralds, topazes, and every description of precious stones; many lofty rooms filled with gold and tissue robes, and tunics of every variety of costly silk and satin, without counting gilt armor, richly set daggers and swords, bows, spears, and all sorts of offensive and defensive weapons.[34]

They also found a bejeweled table made of gold and silver, and encrusted with gems, which they were told had been owned by King Solomon. This became a highly coveted trophy of war and the soldiers broke it into pieces and fought over who should get each part.

The Christians fled northward, and those who stayed behind were permitted to remain only by paying tribute, Al-Maqqari wrote. The abandoned homes were occupied by the invaders. "The Arabs inhabited the towns deserted by the Christians; for whenever, an Arab or a Berber, received orders to settle in a spot, he . . . established himself with his family in it without reluctance, by means of which the words of Islam spread far into the country, and the idolatry of the Christians was destroyed and annihilated." More North Africans and Arabs surged across the straits:

> When the news of the mighty conquest had spread over the countries inhabited by the Muslims, great numbers of the population of Syria and other distant regions felt a strong desire to visit Andalus and take up their abode in it. Accordingly many individuals of the best and most illustrious among the Arabian tribes left the tents of their fathers and settled in Andalus.[35]

Many important cultural and religious sites were destroyed in the process; holy relics were discarded. The famous mosque of Córdoba was "lighted with bronze lamps made out of Christian bells," Al-Maqqari wrote, "and [a] great addition . . . was built entirely with the materials of demolished churches brought to Córdoba on the heads of Christian captives."[36]

This series of events was seared into the memories of many residents of Iberia. The history of Spain commissioned by Isabella contained many details of the conquest from the perspective of the defeated Iberians. "The land was depopulated and filled with tears and blood," wrote the chronicler Diego de Valera. The women were "forced" and "children were killed," and in some cities, "the major portion" of civilian residents were slaughtered.[37]

The Muslim advance into western Europe was finally halted at the Pyrenees Mountains, the rocky border between France and Spain, after the Frankish ruler Charles Martel defeated the Arab forces at Tours in 732.

* * *

Ultimately only a small remnant of an opposing Christian force remained active in Spain, in the far northern enclave of Asturias. "A despicable barbarian, whose name was Pelayo, rose in the land of Galicia, and having reproached his countrymen for their ignominious dependence and their cowardly flight, began to stir them up to revenge the past injuries, and to expel the Muslims from the land of their fathers," Al-Maqqari wrote.

> From that moment the Christians of Andalus began to resist the attacks of the Muslims on such districts as had remained in their possession, and to defend their wives and daughters; for until then they had not shown the least inclination to do either. The commencement of the rebellion started thus: there remained no city, town or village in Galicia but what was in the hands of the Muslims with the exception of a steep mountain on which this Pelayo took refuge with a handful of men; there his followers went on dying through hunger until he saw their numbers reduced to about thirty men and ten women, having no other food for support than the honey they gathered in crevices of the rocks which they themselves inhabited like so many bees. However, Pelayo and his men fortified themselves by degrees in the passes of the mountain until the Muslims were made acquainted with their preparations; but perceiving how few they were, they heeded not the advice conveyed to them, and allowed them to gather strength, saying, "What are 30 barbarians, perched upon a rock? They must inevitably die."[38]

These remnants of the Visigoths survived, however, and eked out a living in the rainy, chilly provinces of Galicia and Asturias, far from the comfortable prosperity they had enjoyed as masters of the peninsula. Al-Maqqari's account depicts them struggling for existence. In fact, Pelayo's son Favila was killed by a bear while hunting, which suggests they were reduced to hardscrabble survival. The heirs of the Visigoths spent the next twenty-four generations recovering the peninsula, inch by inch, mile by mile, mostly in fits and starts, until by Isabella's birth the remaining Muslim stronghold in Spain was in the South, in the Kingdom of Granada. The Christian survival and advance were based on an intense collaboration between church and state that allowed them to remain a community through the long fight back to recover what they had lost. On the Iberian peninsula, church and state thus grew "closely united."[39]

The story of Pelayo became central to Isabella's frame of reference. She believed herself to be a direct lineal descendant of that stalwart Visigoth and the inheritor of his mantle. In the palace where she spent much of her childhood, the Alcázar of Segovia, statues of her ancestors stood in niches all around the walls, and Pelayo was presented as the first of her line. A statue of him stood in the throne room, making him a mute participant in every event that took place in the administration of the government.

In much of the rest of Spain, however, for the Christian and Jewish people who agreed to accept domination under the Muslims—also known in Spain as the Moors because of their arrival from Morocco—conditions were generally not particularly harsh. Many lived their lives with comfort. They were allowed to follow their own religion, as long as they paid extra taxes for the privilege. In the years following the conquest, many Spaniards converted to Islam. Some of the converts, known as muladíes, were sincere. But others only pretended to convert in order to curry favor with the ruling class. Similarly, some of the invading Berbers had themselves been reluctant or conflicted converts. The same was true of some Jews who converted.

The defeat of the Visigoths could not have been so complete or quick without the assistance of this mistreated minority, the Jews, some of whom welcomed the new arrivals and assisted them in governing their new possessions. For the Jews, life under the Muslims brought a marked improvement over the abuse they had suffered under the Visigoths. In time it allowed them to develop a golden era of literature, science, medicine, and poetry.

For the Christians, however, the role of the Jews in the defeat of the Visigoths, combined with old grievances over the treatment of the early Christian martyrs in the Holy Land, became dark and painful memories. Over the next seven hundred years, even as the three faiths coexisted and celebrated each other's artistic, literary, and culinary achievements, angry hurt was a corrosive burr just under the surface.

"The time during which the Muslims and Christians, along with Jews, lived in proximity in the Iberian peninsula has often been cited as a kind of ideal era of interfaith harmony," writes the historian Jane I. Smith.

> To some extent that claim may be justified, but if so the era was fairly short and was soon supplanted by the tensions, prejudices, and treatment of minorities by both Muslims and Christians that more often has characterized relationships between the communities. By the tenth century the chaos of earlier invasions had settled, and the Iberian peninsula was pretty well split between the Christian Kingdom of Leon in the north and the considerably larger Muslim al-Andalus (known as Andalusia) in the south, with a thin frontier zone between. During the rule of Abd al-Rahman III in Córdoba (912–961), the Spanish Islamic state reached the height of power and fame. It was a time of great opulence and achievement, in which intellectual circles of Muslims, Jews and Christians under Abd al-Rahman's patronage contributed to a flourishing of the arts, literature, astronomy, medicine, and other cultural and scientific disciplines. Muslim tolerance of the so-called People of the Book was high, and social intercourse was easy and constant. It was also a period during which a significant number of Christians chose to convert to Islam, although Christians continued to outnumber Muslims in Andalusia until the second half of the tenth century.[40]

Many Christians and Jews adopted Arab customs and styles of dress during these years.

Tolerance faded in the late tenth century during the rule of Abu Amir Al-Mansur, "who began a series of ruthless campaigns against Christians, including the plundering of churches and other Christian sites."[41] Social interactions grew strained, Smith writes:

> Pious Muslims refrained from speaking to the infidels except at a distance. If a Muslim and a Christian met on a public road, the Christian always had to give way to the Muslim. Houses of Chris-

tians had to be lower than those of Muslims. An "infidel" Christian could never employ a Muslim in service. . . . Christians were buried in their own cemeteries, far from Muslims. . . . A Muslim who converted to Christianity was immediately sentenced to death. . . . Thus the era of harmonious interaction between Muslims and Christians in Spain came to an end, replaced by intolerance, prejudice and mutual suspicion.[42]

The accounts of a religious nirvana in Spain are "historically unfounded, a myth,"[43] writes scholar Dario Fernández-Morera, because, in fact, many Christians and Jews were killed and brutalized by the Muslims in Spain. The Muslim ruler Al-Mansur, for example, inspired fear in people of other faiths and sacked the cities of Zaragoza, Osma, Zamora, León, Astorga, Coimbra, and Santiago de Compostela. In 985 he burned down Barcelona and enslaved the survivors he did not kill. In 1066 Muslims rioted and destroyed the entire Jewish community in Granada, killing thousands—more, in fact, than the numbers killed by Christians in the Rhineland at the beginning of the first Crusade. In the twelfth century, the Muslims expelled the entire population of Christians living in the cities of Málaga and Granada and sent them to Morocco.[44]

The Christians found a rallying cry when they discovered what they believed to be the burial place of Saint James (in Spanish, Santiago), the apostle who had reportedly set off for Spain, in the kingdom's far northwest. They built a church, a humble structure with mud walls, to house the body. Soon the site, known as Santiago de Compostela, became the great pilgrimage destination for Christians throughout western Europe, and a more ornate structure was built there. In 997, the Muslims attacked and seized the town of Santiago. They preserved the tomb of Saint James but destroyed all the public buildings and razed many churches.[45] Actions such as these had the effect of turning the Christian effort to recover land and territory into a crusade.

Even when Muslim rulers were tolerant, they viewed non-Muslims with contempt. "A Muslim must not act as a masseur to a Jew or Christian; he must not clear their rubbish nor clean their latrines," wrote the Muslim jurist Ibn Abdun.

In fact, the Jew and the Christian are more suited for such work. . . . It is forbidden to sell a coat that has once belonged to a leper, a Jew or a Christian, unless the buyer is informed of its origin; likewise if this garment once belonged to a debauched person. . . . No Jew or Christian may be allowed to wear the dress of an aristocrat, nor of a jurist, nor of a wealthy individual. . . . A distinctive sign must be imposed upon them so they may be recognized and this will be for them a form of disgrace. . . . It is forbidden to sell to Jews and Christians scientific books.[46]

Issues that affected women were always of particular interest to Isabella, and gender relations also colored the perceptions of people living in Spain. All three great faiths—Judaism, Christianity, and Islam—honored women in certain ways but were also patriarchal and made women second-class citizens in other significant ways. And while conditions for women in Christian Castile were far from ideal, conditions were arguably worse in the Muslim-occupied lands. Women's activities there were legally restricted: They were not allowed to take boat trips with men; they were forbidden to wash clothes outside; they were banned from sitting on the river shore in the summer, when men were there. Moreover, they were required to wear voluminous clothing, such as the hijab, despite the sweltering heat of southern Spain; they were separated physically from men; they were generally confined to the household.[47] These conditions of confinement would have been unimaginably awful for Isabella, who grew to be a strong, energetic, and physically active woman who traveled for miles on horseback, sometimes with only a handful of companions.

Another disturbing element for an independent-minded woman like Isabella was that tens of thousands of women were held in sexual servitude under the Moors. These lives are seldom depicted in art or literature, and male historians seldom mentioned them except in passing, so it is difficult to gauge what the lives of these women might have been like. One rare set of pictures of concubines appears in a set of illustrated manuscripts at El Escorial, capturing the mournful faces of women wearing diaphanous, see-through gowns while they serve food and drink to men playing chess and other board games.[48]

Polygamy was another divisive issue. It had been practiced in the early phases of all three religions, but it never faded away in the Islamic culture as it had in the other two. Muslim culture permitted men to have up to four wives but did not permit women to have multiple husbands. Muhammad had eleven recognized wives of various ages. Wealthy Muslim men could emulate the prophet by similarly maintaining stables of women, stocked in harems, with war providing a steady stream of females for this purpose. Men aspired to such a lifestyle. The Muslim ruler Abd Al-Rahman, the one often mentioned as the guiding light of the golden era of Granada, left two hundred children, 150 of them male and the rest female.[49] He was reported to have 6,300 women in his harem.

It must have been disturbing to Isabella to imagine all the dejected first wives throughout the empire, lying in bed at night and overhearing their husbands making love with younger women, new wives who had been introduced to the family home.

It was difficult for Muslim rulers to obtain enough women on this scale by wooing them, so a brisk business developed in the trafficking of kidnapped Christian and Jewish women. They would be renamed once they were enslaved, and renamed again when impregnated, often with the prefix Umm, which means "mother of." Thus, Egilona, wife of the unfortunate Visigoth king Roderic, wed to one of the Muslim soldiers, became known as Umm-Asim, or "The Mother of Asim."

Many women did not find harem life appealing, so they had to be guarded. A vast caste of castrated slaves served as their captors. White slaves from eastern Europe, or "Slavs," had their testicles removed but the customary practice for black slaves from Africa was to remove both their testicles and their penises. That way the captors and the captives could not engage in sexual relations with each other.

* * *

A major historical event occurred in Isabella's childhood that made the Moorish invasion of 711 seem just a moment away in time. In 1453, when she was two years old, and about the time her father died, Constantinople fell to Muslim Turks. Its conquest had been foreseen for decades, but still, when it finally happened, it was as though the tectonic plates of the earth had shifted. For a thousand years this exotic city, far to the east, had been the great metropolis of Christendom. Hagia Sophia had been the largest cathedral in the world when Justinian completed its construction, and it was still the largest in the world more than nine hundred years later. Through all these years the city was a living relic of the classical world. The residents there still called themselves "Romans"; they regularly read the Greek classics, including Homer; they saw themselves as the continuation of the eastern half of the Roman Empire. For most of those thousand years, Constantinople had also been the military bastion of Europe. It guarded the crucial crossing of the Bosporus and kept the nomadic armies of Asia out of Europe. The city had withstood a multi-year siege by Arab armies in 674–78, and a second, still more determined siege in 717–18, aided by its massive defensive walls and the technological wizardry of "Greek fire," a substance like napalm, whose formula was a closely guarded secret.

But the city was fatally weakened when it was sacked in 1204, by its fellow Christians of the Fourth Crusade, as the result of a pay dispute. Thereafter it entered a long decline. Its territory shrank each year until it finally encompassed little more than the city itself. Pleas for aid from western Europe went unheeded by western Europeans who were too busy fighting each other to consider the plight of a distant city, and who were still angry at the great schism between Western and Eastern Christianity, which made them unsympathetic to the Orthodox Christians in Constantinople. When the Turkish sultan Mehmed II made his final move in 1453, Constantinople could marshal only 7,000 defenders, including 700 Genoese, to oppose an attacking force of 80,000. The city fell on May 29 after a seven-week siege. The fate of the last Byzantine emperor, Constantine XI, is not known for certain. Most accounts say that he personally waded into the fighting and was killed; his body was later identified only by the purple shoes he wore. Fighting alongside him as he went to his death was a nobleman from Spain who was one of the very few western Europeans who had come to help defend the city.

The final assault and destruction of Constantinople was a horrifying spectacle. Eyewitnesses such as the Genoese archbishop of Mytilene, Leonard of Chios, and Niccolò Barbaro of Venice describe the sack in violent terms, of mass slaughter, rape, and enslavement. Churches were burned down, precious relics discarded, and approximately 120,000 books and manuscripts, some from earliest antiquity, were lost, burned, or destroyed: "From only three days of plunder and careless destruction of books, which held little value for the foot soldiers who sacked the city, the Turks became known by Western scholars as one of the worst threats to high culture and learning Europe had ever faced."[50]

Alarmed observers throughout western Europe thought that all civilization could be at risk. To Isabella, the fall of Constantinople was an omen of the possibility of many bad things that could come to pass. When her court chronicler Alonso de Palencia, a man she paid to tell her story, wrote his account of the times, Isabella's birth was given about one page. But the account of the fall of Constantinople went on for three pages, with Palencia describing it as a "catastrophe" and a "disaster" that could mean "the extermination of Christianity."[51]

In the following years, survivors wandered around Europe, dazed and bereft. Many had been personally devastated by the conquest of the city. The Muslims disposed of women and children in the same way they had in 711 in Spain. George Sphrantzes, a diplomat employed by the Byzantine emperor Constantine, wrote that his wife and children were taken after the fall of the city and ended up in the possession of the sultan's *mir ahor,* master of the horse, "who amassed a great fortune by selling many other beautiful noble ladies."[52]

Western Europeans, particularly those in Spain, were terrified about where the Muslims would strike next. Mehmed swore his horse would eat its oats from the great altar at St. Peter's in Rome. And, Spain, of course, was considerably closer to Muslim population centers than Rome, just eight miles from North Africa. "Islam twice posed a universal military challenge to Christianity," writes the historian John McManners. "First during the rapid conquests of the mid-seventh to mid-eighth centuries when, for a time, all Christendom seemed in danger of invasion and defeat. And second, in the fifteenth to seventeenth centuries, when the Ottomans made their bid for world supremacy."[53]

It was at that second point in time that Princess Isabella was born. And though little is known of those earliest years of her life, neither her birthdate or her baptism, one item seemed notable enough that it was memorialized. It marked the first official action Isabella took, of her own accord, when she was a young girl. It was a donation of money—some 200 maravedis—to be used to help pay the costs of reconquering Granada, the remaining bastion of Muslim control on the Iberian peninsula.

TWO

A CHILDHOOD IN
THE SHADOWS

I sabella's mother never really regained her mental health, and so the child's older half brother, King Enrique IV, a man who has been called "possibly the single most controversial personality in the history of Medieval Spain,"[1] became the dominating figure of Isabella's childhood, a man whose mercurial whims and moods influenced every aspect of her life. Exactly how and when Isabella first came into close contact with Enrique isn't clear because so many of the details of her childhood have been lost to time.

In her earliest years, they saw each other only sporadically. Isabella's father died when she was three years old and her brother Alfonso was an infant. Sometime after the king's death in 1454, Queen Isabel took the two children and retreated to a remote rural town, Arévalo, some fifteen miles from Isabella's birthplace of Madrigal de las Altas Torres, and far from the glitter of court life. Arévalo was another heavily fortified town, located at the confluence of the Adaja and Arevalillo Rivers and site of a powerful fortress that had once housed the imprisoned wife of a former king. Isabella's new home was a castle with thick stone walls with tiny windows high off the ground and blank exterior walls, a residence never modified for comfort, light, or airiness, surrounded by a dry moat. It was far off the beaten track: Rodrigo Sánchez de Arévalo, a noted scholar associated with the court, called it forlorn, "*esta desierta villa de Arévalo*."[2] Enrique had wanted the queen to remain at court with the children, and when she refused, the king sent two hundred men to act as guards over them, which protected them from marauding gangs of robbers and kidnappers but also kept them closely sequestered.[3] Even the physical environment was fierce and brutal, alternating between bitter cold in the winter and blistering heat in the summer. The snow-capped Guadarrama Mountains were visible in the distance, many miles away, across the flat, dry countryside.

The instability of Isabella's family life mirrored conditions in the kingdom as a whole. The vacuum of leadership under the feckless King Enrique had permitted the kingdom to descend into chaos. The kingdom's nobles, who could have helped rule in their regions, instead became brutal and bickering warlords, terrorizing the peasantry, cornering the resources of an increasingly impoverished land. Rape, theft, and murder were rampant.

This social breakdown occurred because the Iberian peninsula of Isabella's youth was splintered into feuding fiefdoms: the combined kingdoms of Isabella's homeland, known as Castile and León, encompassed the north and central parts of what would become Spain; the Portuguese held the lands along the western edge, facing directly onto the Atlantic Ocean. The kingdoms of Valencia, Aragon, and Catalonia, in eastern Iberia, were joined together in an uneasy and unstable confederation, yoked through marriage to Navarre, a separate kingdom on the peninsula's far north perimeter; they were oriented toward the east, to the Mediterranean Sea. The Moorish Kingdom of Granada, which stretched across the southern part of Spain from the Rock of Gibraltar to the port of Almería, the area known as Andalusia, controlled the Mediterranean coastline across from Africa.

With no central authority on the peninsula, chaos reigned, and most of the residents of Spain lived, as Isabella did, near or inside heavily armed compounds. The landscape was so dotted with these stone or wood fortifications, many planted atop steep precipices, that the central kingdom was named Castile, or Land of Castles. The Spanish people lived indoors, crouched behind thick walls made of stone, peering out through tiny windows that served as arrow slits, scanning the horizon for signs of danger, existing in a state of perpetual readiness for conflict. Isabella grew up in a land that was almost perpetually at war.

* * *

Despite all these problems, Isabella had a particular advantage. During her childhood, a coterie of competent adults stepped in to fill the parental void in the lives of Isabella and Alfonso, during the years in which they learned to walk and talk. Only one of their grandparents was still alive, Queen Isabel's mother, Isabel of Barcelos, a Portuguese widow in her fifties who came from the wealthy and powerful Braganza clan. Grandmother Isabel came to live with her daughter's family in Arévalo when the young Princess Isabella was still a toddler. She kept a watchful eye over the household. Isabel of Barcelos was an intelligent and competent woman, with life experience that allowed her to help shape Isabella's worldview and prepare her for governance. "A notable woman of great counsel," she was also a "great help and consolation to her daughter," said chronicler Diego de Valera.[4]

Grandmother Isabel was part of what the Portuguese call "the Illustrious Generation," the children of King João I of Portugal, who lived from 1358 to 1433. His oldest son, Duarte, was known as a philosopher; the next son, Pedro, was a patron of the arts; another son was Henrique, the famous Henry the Navigator; the youngest son, Fernando, martyred in Morocco during a failed invasion attempt, was named a saint. Isabel's own husband had been João, the son best known for his sage advice and wisdom, who had held the influential position of constable of Portugal. Grandmother Isabel also had royal blood, as she was herself a granddaughter of King João I. The Portuguese ruling family believed the key to the future was maritime seafaring and international trade, and they aggressively pursued it. Such overseas expansions were enriching Portugal and giving it an outsize role in world affairs. These were lessons taught to Princess Isabella and that she took to heart.

A husband-and-wife team attached to the family would also play a significant continuing role in Isabella's life. The wife was Clara Alvarnáez, Isabella's governess, who had come to Castile from Portugal with Isabella's mother and grandmother. Clara's husband, Gonzalo Chacón, had been a courtier to Isabella's father, King Juan II, and he was one of the people to whom the king had entrusted the education of his children. Chacón was also administrator of Queen Isabel's household—a role he had also played for Álvaro de Luna, which meant that he, like Isabella's mother and grandmother, had previously participated in the governing of the kingdom. They were out of the limelight now, but they had all lived in the bright, hot center where politics, family, and governance intersected. Moreover, they were ambitious to return to the focal point of power.

The governor of the castle in Arévalo was a man named Mosén Pedro de Bobadilla, married with three children who became Isabella's playmates.[5] The two families grew close. The Bobadilla family had a long history of service to the crown, with an ancestor who had served as chief of the treasury to Alfonso XI, and who had been sent as an ambassador to the pope at Avignon. Pedro's daughter Beatriz, who was about a decade older than Isabella, assumed a sisterly role with the princess. Comely, persuasive, and piercingly intelligent, she became Isabella's most loyal friend and confidante. From these unlikely beginnings, the two women rose together to dominate Spain. Beatriz was more than a friend. She was a brilliant ally and strategist, with a magic touch for bringing new allies to their side.

During these years, there was hardly any mention of Isabella's existence in court documents or chronicles. A scrap or two of a phrase would suggest the princess had been moved from place to place or had been taken to visit a historic site—once she visited the historic Visigothic capital city of Toledo—but nobody was paying much attention to her. She grew up to be pretty, demure, and devout, third in line for the throne but valued mainly for her potential value as a pawn in a political marriage at some future point. Her birth had gone almost unnoticed in Spain and foreign capitals, and her childhood passed unremarked as well. Why would she, in any case, have attracted much attention? Girl children at the time were viewed as scarcely worth mentioning, not just in Christian culture but also in the Hebrew and Arab worlds as well. It was almost inconceivable that a woman would exert any real power, much less change the world.

In Arévalo the princess was taught her letters and became an avid reader. She was curious about the world, intrigued by accounts of odd and strange animals and plants found in distant lands. She favored stories about King Arthur's court, and heroic accounts—mythological, biblical, and legendary—of people behaving nobly in the face of adversity. A Hispanicized book about Joan of Arc's life, called *La Poncella de Francia,* was presented as a model for Isabella's life, and Joan's militant religiosity was explicitly described as a "better example" for Isabella to follow than the lives of "any of the other ladies."[6] Isabella also liked Aesop's fables, collections of stories about animal characters that teach moral lessons.

Her formal education was solid but perfunctory. She was taught protocol and domestic skills and was introduced to grammar, philosophy, and history. She was multilingual, reading French and Italian and speaking not just Castilian Spanish but also Portuguese, the language of her mother and grandmother. She was musically gifted, as was her mother, and she played several instruments well and also sang sweetly. She was a good dancer.

She was not, however, given the education that a man would have received, particularly to a man being prepared to govern. For example, she received no childhood instruction in Latin, the language of international diplomacy. This clear and embarrassing deficiency in her education was one of which she soon became acutely aware.

Instead she was trained in needlepoint and embroidery, then essential ingredients in the rearing of female children, and was tutored in the other skills expected of the wife of a ruler. She also developed the requisite social skills. She was strong and active, physically fearless, a good horsewoman at home in the saddle. She loved to hunt; she enjoyed parties, games, art, and architecture. Her behavior was viewed as appropriate for her age and station, attracting little additional comment.

Most important for her future, during these years she developed an iron-willed self-control, which allowed her to conceal her emotions while she pondered how to respond to the situations that presented themselves to her. This came to be an important part of her character because she learned to keep her own counsel. Soon she would realize that this skill was the key to her survival.

She became devoutly religious. Christianity was the bedrock of life in medieval Europe, and religious instruction formed a large part of Isabella's education. There was an active Franciscan monastery in Arévalo, so religious scholars were always present, and Isabella became particularly fond of that religious order, and of Saint Francis, its founder, who had dedicated himself to a life of poverty and simplicity. She considered her own patron saints to be Saint John the Baptist and Saint John the Evangelist, the only one of the twelve apostles who was not martyred in the early days of Christianity, and who had cared for Jesus's mother in Ephesus in her old age. It was this second patron saint, John the Evangelist, who had written the Gospel according to John, one of the four canonical accounts of the life of Christ.

Many of her mother's friends were also deeply religious. Beatriz de Silva, the Portuguese noblewoman who had attracted the king's eye and been locked in a closet before embracing a religious vocation as a nun, participated in Isabella's education, as did an attendant of her mother's named Teresa Enríquez. Beatriz founded a new female religious order, Concepcionistas, which celebrated the special spiritual role played by Jesus's mother. Enríquez was given the sobriquet *loca de sacramento* because of her zeal for taking communion. These one-on-one lessons in faith were supplemented in her teenage years by what was viewed as appropriate reading material, such as Friar Martín de Córdoba's *Garden of Noblewomen,* which was a guidebook for character development in women, written specifically with Isabella in mind. It stressed extreme piety, even providing a specific list of acceptable activities, which included attending mass each day, reciting prayers, hearing sermons, and conversing with church elders about religious teachings. Female purity was also essential, according to Martín: "Even if a woman's virtues might have mounted to the heavens, without chastity they are nothing but dross and ashes in the wind; because the woman who is not chaste, even if she is lovely, makes herself foul, and the more beautiful she is, the greater the filth and corruption."[7]

* * *

Isabella's childhood was not altogether austere, however. Although Arévalo and Madrigal were comparative backwaters, one nearby town became a favorite destination for the princess. Medina del Campo, twenty miles from Arévalo, a long day's ride by horse or mule, was one of Europe's preeminent shopping destinations. It was a market town that drew merchants from all over the known world who bought and sold rich fabrics, jewelry, foodstuffs, leather goods, tools, toys, cosmetics, medicines, rare spices, and exotic fruits. It was a beautiful town, with forty church and convent spires rising in the sky, and streets lined with splendid homes inhabited by wealthy merchants, financiers, and noblemen.[8] Its international ambiance made it one of Castile's most cosmopolitan cities. "There was no other luxury market in all Europe, not even in the courts of the Italian princes, that could compare with the one of Castile," writes the historian Jaime Vicens Vives.[9]

The source of all this prosperity was the wool trade. Wool, the product of the kingdom's great flocks of sheep and the primary source of wealth for the nation's nobility, was the core commodity in Medina del Campo. The town's affluence made wool seem a secure staple of life to Isabella and the nation's nobles, and so they did not appear to pay much attention to the industrial and mercantile development that was under way elsewhere on the continent, new trends that were reshaping the economy of the rest of Europe.

Certainly Isabella must have looked on the bright array of merchandise for sale in Medina del Campo with a great deal of longing, for her family's finances were frequently straitened. That should not have been the case. King Juan's will had provided comfortably for the widowed queen and her children. The queen was to retain custody of the children "as long as she remained chaste."[10] She was also to receive the tax revenue from the towns of Arévalo, Madrigal, Soria, and the suburbs of Madrid. Isabella was to receive the taxes from the town of Cuéllar, and on her twelfth birthday, she was slated to receive one million maravedis from the town of Madrigal. When her mother died, the tax proceeds from that town were destined to go to her, which would ensure a comfortable inheritance. Alfonso, the next heir to the throne, was provided for even more generously. He was to become the grand master of Santiago, the rich post that Álvaro de Luna had once held, and on his fourteenth birthday, he was to step into the job as constable of Castile. He was given the tax revenues from four towns and was slated to inherit the taxes from all his mother's holdings, except Madrigal, when she died.

But King Enrique "did not respect his father's wishes," chroniclers noted, and instead gave away the territories and properties that Juan had intended to provide for his second family's support.[11] He gave the mastership of Santiago to one of his favorite friends, and he made another the constable. And he later stripped from Isabella the revenue generated by Cuéllar, and gave it away. Enrique "worked actively to deny" Isabella her inheritance, a course that caused the princess "financial hardship," writes the scholar María Isabel del Val Valdivieso.[12]

This left the family in a more precarious financial situation than they should have been in. In fact, one court chronicler, Hernando del Pulgar, wrote that Isabella had faced "an extreme lack of necessary things" in her childhood—something that must have been painful to a young girl who longed for fine clothes and jewelry, and who later dressed in such splendor that foreign diplomats found her appearance startling in its grandeur.[13]

There were other signs as well that King Enrique did not have the best interests of Isabella and her family foremost in his mind. Shortly after Juan's death, Enrique went to Arévalo to see Queen Isabel, his stepmother. He was accompanied by a courtier, Pedro Girón, who was ostensibly master of the order of Calatrava, a celibate religious and military order sworn to defend the faith. Girón, however, was not in fact a holy man but a degenerate roué who considered his vocation something of a joke, a tedious trade-off for the financial benefits the position conveyed. Enrique allowed Pedro, clearly the queen's social inferior, to make some sort of a distasteful sexual advance to the pious twenty-six-year-old widow, which chronicler Alonso de Palencia said offended her deeply. The incident humiliated Queen Isabel and underscored the powerlessness of the onetime queen. She found it menacing. After that time, Palencia noted, she "closed herself into a dark room, self-condemned to silence, and dominated by such depression that it degenerated into a form of madness."[14]

What were the men thinking? Pedro Girón may have just been a lout, or he may have been genuinely interested in an amorous encounter with the queen, who was still attractive. And what about King Enrique? It's possible that the new king thought it was funny to take his young and pretty stepmother down a peg. He might have thought it was comical.

Or he might have had a more ominous motive. The sexual proposition, if it had been welcomed by the lonely young widow, could have also created an incident that would have allowed Enrique to claim that the queen had failed to remain chaste, as specified in her husband's will. And if the queen were deemed to be unchaste, she would consequently lose custody of her children.

The incident therefore raised the troubling possibility that Enrique and his allies intended to try to gain control of the children at some point. This event was one more reason that the queen and her mother kept the children out of the limelight, sequestered in Arévalo, where they stayed for at least seven years.

The ugly scene was a good example of the contradictions at play within King Enrique's character. For while he was in some ways a sensitive soul, he could also be a clumsy oaf. Even his physical appearance was an odd dichotomy. He was tall and blond, with large fingers and hands and "a fierce aspect, almost like a lion," that struck fear in those who saw him.[15] But his mannerisms were much at odds with his appearance, because he liked to sing, in a voice that was "sweet and well-modulated," preferring sad and melancholy songs. Gruff and unpolished in demeanor, he was softhearted and malleable to those who had learned how to manipulate him. One of his few surviving portraits depicts him wearing a flowery hat, riding sidesaddle on the back of a horse festooned with ribbons and bells.

At the beginning of his reign, Enrique initially basked in popularity in Castile and was known by the sobriquet Enrique El Generoso. He built many buildings and was a great benefactor to churches and monasteries. He was known to be contemplative and thoughtful and enjoyed long and uplifting conversations with clerics in beautiful and serene settings.[16]

His favorite home was the majestic city of Segovia, the site of the towering Roman aqueduct and many beautiful churches, a place where he had found peace and happiness ever since his childhood. Although he moved around the kingdom a good deal because the Spanish royal court was essentially itinerant, Segovia was always his preferred destination. He fondly called it "mi Segovia," something he did with no other place in Castile. He favored the city in many ways and financed public works and construction projects that provided many jobs, spreading affluence through the population. Residents of the city felt privileged and grateful for the royal association and the prosperity it created, and warmly welcomed him each time he arrived.

A home had been built specifically for him in Segovia when he was a boy, and it was a place he always loved. It was known as the Royal Monastery of St. Anthony, or San Antonio El Real, located on the outskirts of the city, which allowed him easy access to city life, the Alcázar fortress, and also the great outdoors, as he spent many hours riding in the countryside and communing with nature. He probably intended to be buried there one day, because a large room adjacent to the nave seemed to offer suitable space for a burial chamber or memorial. He felt secure and safe in Segovia.

Enrique was also a gentle animal-lover who kept his own menagerie, including lions, deer, bear cubs, leopards, and his personal favorite, a large mountain goat. He spent long hours hunting in the forests surrounding Segovia and Madrid. But he employed such pursuits to avoid dealing with the unpleasant tasks of governing. Deferring troublesome decisions did not resolve them, however, and his indolence and aversion to hard work often caused small problems to worsen.

Enrique was, in short, a man of placid good will, conciliatory, who sought to make friends rather than create enemies, and in another era he might have remained a well-loved figure. He and his father had been in fierce opposition to each other for much of Enrique's young adulthood, but when his father died, the prince had been at his side. One of his first steps upon becoming king was to permit 159 of his father's political appointees to keep their jobs, rather than putting his own appointees in the positions. "I don't doubt that the death of the king, my father, who has gone to glory, has left you with great pain and sadness," he told them.[17] He also pardoned political adversaries who had been exiled, shunned, or imprisoned, returning their properties and titles to them, which allowed them to begin circulating around the kingdom once again.

These were the actions of a kind and tolerant man—but they had unfortunate political ramifications. Soon Enrique was surrounded by people who had no particular sense of allegiance to him and who came to view their posts as sinecures they held as a matter of right. Moreover, it gave the enemies of his family, notably his Aragonese cousins, envious of his Castilian domains, free rein to engage in treasonous activities designed to undermine his administration. Released to do mischief, they were not grateful but worked constantly to undermine him. It was a ruthless era, and Enrique had made a fatal error.

* * *

Another aspect of Enrique's life made him particularly vulnerable to attack. He enjoyed frequent and lengthy getaways with handsome young men, often meeting with them at his hunting lodges on the outskirts of town. He was almost certainly a homosexual. This would not have been a political problem as long as he managed to produce enough heirs to the throne to assure a smooth succession. But this he failed to do, and it happened at a time when attitudes toward homosexuality were hardening in Europe. Through much of the Middle Ages, there was tolerance and even romanticizing of same-sex relationships, but as economic times grew tougher and financial conditions more competitive, cultural attitudes began changing. The hedonism and cultural flowering of the early Renaissance was also causing a conservative backlash. Religious fanatics urged church faithful to renounce worldly ways and the pleasures of the flesh and vigorously chastised those who failed to do so. Born within one year of Isabella, for example, were two Florentine men, the painter and scientist Leonardo da Vinci, who was vividly and flamboyantly gay, and Girolamo Savonarola, a fiery, ascetic priest who preached against art as a contributing factor in the spread of vice and spiritual decay. The era's clash of cultural values wasn't limited to Spain.

The overt homosexual behavior in Segovia was criticized by many Spaniards and noticed even by some foreigners. The Czech pilgrim Schaseck, traveling with a nobleman who was entertained by King Enrique at the Alcázar in Segovia, was shocked by the activities he witnessed at Enrique's court. "Indeed they live such an impure and sodomitical life that one would be reluctant and ashamed to speak of their crimes," Schaseck wrote in a memoir of his trip that was widely circulated upon his return home.[18]

And sadly, as his father had done before him, Enrique developed attachments to certain men that allowed him to be easily manipulated, in ways that frequently damaged his own interests or hurt his family. The initial object of his affections was one Juan Pacheco, the brother of Pedro Girón, who had made the sexual advance to Queen Isabel.

Pacheco in turn had been a protégé of Enrique's father's friend Álvaro de Luna and, in fact, had been introduced to the royal household by Álvaro, who was then acting as guardian to young Enrique, with his father's acquiescence. Soon after he assumed the throne, Enrique named Pacheco to be the Marquess of Villena, a post that brought him great riches and that allowed him to advance the interests of his brother, the distasteful Pedro Girón, including having him named master of the prestigious and lucrative order of Calatrava.

Enrique was mesmerized by Juan Pacheco and greatly influenced by him, even dominated by him, often in ways that would prove detrimental, for Pacheco did not possess the redeeming qualities or loyalty that Álvaro de Luna had displayed toward King Juan. Pacheco was cunning, duplicitous, and self-serving, willing to cause grave injury to others to obtain even a small advantage for himself. The normally mild-mannered chronicler Enríquez del Castillo described him as a "mirror of ingratitude, tyranny, insatiable disordered greed."[19]

Pacheco was not the only one who took advantage of Enrique. The king was generous to a fault and frittered away his treasury on gifts and grants to boyfriends who simply became greedy for more, making them impossible to satisfy. It was in this manner, rather than through spite on Enrique's part, that the rents and properties that should have been given to Isabella's family migrated elsewhere.

Castillo, Enrique's chronicler, reported that Diego Arias, Enrique's chief accountant and treasurer, warned him that he was becoming over-extended: "Certainly Your Highness has too many expenses, and without any benefit, because you are giving much to eat to many people who aren't serving you, and who don't deserve it, and it would be better if you changed course and paid only those who served you and not those who provide you with no benefit." Enrique replied mournfully that he had no choice—that a spirit of magnanimity was expected of a king who wished to maintain the support of his subjects.[20]

King Enrique temporarily moved his court to Arévalo in 1454 and 1455, when Isabella was about four years old, which is about the time most children begin to have an awareness of the broader world around them. Intense excitement followed in his wake, because he soon declared war on the Muslims in Granada. As was family custom, Enrique raised the standard of his ancestor, the Visigothic leader Pelayo. "As faithful Christians . . . we must destroy the enemies who persecute our faith," he told his countrymen, winning cheers and applause.[21] Many were eager for a new war. Some of course were eager to embark for religious reasons, but there was also the promise of booty. Even making the announcement of an impending military campaign got money flowing: additional taxes were levied against nobles, the towns, and the clergy to pay for the expense, and the Spanish-born pope, Calixtus III, who was from Aragon, gave Enrique the power to raise additional money by granting him the right to sell indulgences to soldiers, who could use them to wash away their sins. The pope later allowed Enrique to sell indulgences for posthumously removing sins of dead people, thus allowing relatives to ensure that their deceased loved ones made it to heaven, regardless of the extent of the transgressions during their lifetimes.[22]

Moreover, a royal wedding was on the horizon, normally a festive and celebratory event that everyone would enjoy. Enrique was engaged in marriage negotiations with a beautiful Portuguese princess named Juana, who was much admired for her fine dancing skills. There was much excited chatter over the impending nuptials, which could affect the succession to the crown if Enrique produced an heir. And then Enrique and his courtiers were again on their way, this time to the wedding site in Córdoba, leaving Arévalo behind. His young siblings were not included in the wedding party.

Princess Juana, buxom and flirtatious, arrived for the wedding in May 1455, with a train of pretty Portuguese ladies-in-waiting dressed in gowns "cut to reveal rather than to cover."[23] Enrique, however, appeared less than enthusiastic about the wedding and maintained a dour demeanor, seemingly not in the mood for a "fiesta."[24]

The courtiers soon found that extravagant gifts and costly entertainments were the most effective way to make the young queen happy. At a lavish banquet in Córdoba, a bishop who wanted to curry favor with her passed around a bowl containing jeweled rings, allowing Juana and her attendants to each pick one out as a party favor.

King Enrique was free to marry Juana because he had just succeeded in obtaining a divorce from his previous wife, his cousin Blanca, a "virtuous and beautiful" princess from Aragon.[25] He had been married to Blanca for thirteen years. The union had started out on the wrong foot from the beginning when the prince, then a shy and awkward fifteen-year-old, failed to consummate the marriage on the wedding night. The nuptial night had been admittedly stressful—Blanca's father, Juan, the ruler of Aragon, who was feuding with Enrique's father, strode around in the hallway outside the bridal chamber, so it was not too surprising that the young couple failed to reach their goal. But thirteen more years passed, and they still failed to have a child. Finally Enrique elected to seek a divorce on the grounds of nonconsummation of the marriage, saying that he had been "bewitched" and unable to achieve an erection with the princess, most probably because of sorcery.[26] He blamed all this on the unfortunate princess, arranging for two prostitutes to testify that he had performed admirably in their company. A three-priest panel approved the divorce, and Blanca was sent packing back home to Aragon.

But in a grim reminder of Enrique's previous wedding night, the marriage with his new bride, Juana, was not consummated on this occasion either. Again, a crowd of court officials gathered in anticipation of viewing the bloodstained bedsheets, and again, they left disappointed. The wedding night "pleased nobody," a court observer said.[27]

Soon after the public nuptial ceremonies, Enrique and his new bride went to the king's home in Segovia, where the bridal couple were feted at a seemingly endless round of balls, hunting expeditions, and entertainments. They split their time between two palaces—the Alcázar and another nearby residence called the San Martín palace, both in Segovia, where Enrique embarked on a round of architectural remodeling. The Alcázar was "completely renovated," with the addition of much rich ornamentation, under the direct supervision of the king. The court's reputation for "magnificent opulence and splendor grew moment to moment," writes the historian Don Eduardo de Oliver-Copóns.[28]

But as admiration grew in some circles, many other people came to view the king's diversions as distracting him from the kingdom's most pressing business. Criticism of his administration mounted. Leaders who see their power eroding frequently launch a military campaign to draw popular jingoistic support, but even this time-honored political tool backfired on King Enrique when he at last set off to reconquer Granada.

The campaign had been financed with money contributed by the church faithful. It became common knowledge that a large share of the campaign money went to Beltrán de la Cueva, a charming and handsome courtier who had found favor with both the king and the new queen, while soldiers were left unpaid.[29] Once on the road with his court entourage, Enrique treated the expedition as more of a burlesque than a campaign. The giddy young queen and her attendants trailed along. At one point the ladies rode out to the battlefield, and Juana laughingly shot arrows into the air in comic participation. The king seemed to take it all as a great joke, and in fact, he accepted gifts from North African leaders while purportedly assailing their allies. The king of Fez sent him melons, lotus fruit, and specialized horse fittings and, for his wife, musk, frankincense, and vanilla-scented balsam.[30] Seasoned soldiers and those deeply concerned about Islamic intentions in southern Spain were "shamed and angry" and shared their concerns with the archbishop of Toledo, Alfonso Carrillo, for whom it became one more piece of evidence that conditions in Castile were deteriorating by the day. Coming just a few years after the fall of Constantinople, Enrique's cavalier or benign attitude toward Muslims attracted much critical comment in Castile. Some came to see it as a betrayal of Castile's culture and religion.

Given the tenor of the times, Enrique's methods of war-making also made him a laughingstock. Much of the practice of war in those days entailed one side doing economic damage to the other—setting fire to their crops and killing their livestock—opening the prospect that the weaker side would pay bribes to make the marauding soldiers go away. Part of the pleasure of the enterprise was permitting people to undertake activities that would never be tolerated in peaceful times. Young men in particular relished the chance to display their machismo through daring acts of vandalism that took them into contact with the enemy. But Enrique commanded that they were not to burn down olive groves, because they took too long to grow and bear fruit. He lectured his troops on the preciousness of both human and natural life, leaving his soldiers "incredulous."[31]

* * *

During those years, Enrique's younger half siblings Isabella and Alfonso remained in Arévalo with their mother, grandmother, and family friends. Alfonso had a special role as heir to the throne, but the close-knit group continued to live apart, in their own little world, hearing only distant reports from the front. The same core group of adults—grandmother Isabel, the Bobadilla family, and Gonzalo Chacón and his wife—shielded and sheltered them and gave them a sense of security and stability.

As Isabella left behind her early childhood years, she became interested in hearing stories about other girls and their lives, as girls her age often are. Fascinating news came from France when Isabella was about five. Europe was engaged in an intense reevaluation of the role of Joan of Arc, the French teenager who had organized her countrymen around a religious banner to eject a foreign invader. Joan, born in a small village, believed she had been told by visions of saints to rally the French people against the English, in defense of the heir to the French throne, the Dauphin Charles. Joan had shamed her countrymen into seeing war not as an economic enterprise or as a demonstration of valor but as a spiritual quest. Joan was caught by the English and burned at the stake for the heresy, in 1431, two decades before Isabella was born.[32] The specific charge was that at war and in prison, Joan had worn men's clothes, something that is prohibited in the book of Deuteronomy. The French government convened a second trial in 1456 that reevaluated all the evidence, cleared Joan's name, and paved the way for her eventual elevation to sainthood. Joan's experience and sacrifice was a story that many men and women of a spiritual bent found mesmerizing in these last days of the medieval era. People everywhere debated what role God had played in helping Joan achieve her signal victories.

This conversation had particular resonance at the palace in Arévalo. Some of the people who were educating Isabella had been much taken with Joan and her military successes. Rodrigo Sánchez de Arévalo, one of the clerics associated with the Castilian court, had been living in France during Joan's meteoric career and was a fervent admirer of hers. Gonzalo Chacón, head of their household staff and the husband of Isabella's governess, shared his recollections of how Isabella's father had welcomed Joan's envoys with great respect. He carried about with him a letter purportedly from Joan herself and displayed it like a holy relic. He is believed to have been the author who wrote about a character like Joan in an anonymous chronicle, saying that God alone had inspired her.[33] Some versions of that chronicle, the book known as *La Poncella de Francia,* were explicitly dedicated to Princess Isabella. In this version of the tale, the young woman called La Poncella did not die but rode off happily into the sunset.[34]

Some of the people around Isabella may have been presenting Joan of Arc's life as an ideal that Isabella could emulate, as a "heaven-sent" woman who could "save the realm" from an outside invader.[35] Joan's life was being reconceived, reengineered, as an acceptable role a woman could play in warfare. The goal of those circulating these stories may have been to influence Isabella and bring her to see herself as a second Joan of Arc. In any case, whether the idea was impressed upon her or she came up with it herself, it found fertile ground in Isabella's imagination, because she already had a tendency to view herself as something of a martyr for a cause and she had the kind of romantic temperament that appreciated people who made great sacrifices in pursuit of a common good. Moreover, she had a deep and fervent belief in miracles and signs from God. Soon she would seek out people to work with her who viewed the world in the same way.

In this phase of her life, however, Isabella's primary importance was still as a political pawn in the royal marriage market. In 1457, when she was six years old, Enrique negotiated a double marriage for Isabella and Alfonso. Isabella was to marry Ferdinand, the younger son of King Juan II, their Aragonese cousin, and Alfonso would marry Juana, King Juan's youngest daughter.[36] This was a solid but second-choice marriage proposition for Isabella because the boy, Ferdinand, was not the heir to a throne. He had an older brother, Carlos, who was heir to the thrones of Aragon and Navarre, two kingdoms that abutted Castile. And a marriage to Juana was good enough for Alfonso because Enrique assumed he would at some point have an heir of his own, who would someday be the king and would marry a woman of highest rank. For Isabella, marriage to Ferdinand seemed a pleasant prospect. He was about her age and was reported to be athletic, personable, and quick-witted. He was also her second cousin. The close interactions and fierce rivalries within the family would have guaranteed that reports about the boy frequently reached her ears. She came to believe Ferdinand was her intended mate and Aragon her likely destination.

Then, when Isabella was about ten years old, Enrique announced a new alliance with Ferdinand's older half brother Carlos—and offered Isabella as wife to him instead. Carlos, eager to solidify ties to Castile, quickly agreed. Now, instead of a fiancé of her own age, Isabella learned she was pledged in marriage to a forty-year-old man. This development would certainly have been disconcerting to the princess, particularly after years of being told she would marry an attractive boy her age. But no trace of her reaction remains. In fact, she would not have been expected to have much of an opinion. It was not an issue in which she had any control. Her brother the king had complete authority over her person, to give in marriage as he saw best. For the next year, Isabella adjusted herself to this new development.

* * *

Around the same time, Isabella's life suddenly changed in an even more immediate way. In about 1461 or early 1462, when she was ten years old and her brother was eight, King Enrique ordered the two children to join him immediately. Isabella and Alfonso were abruptly yanked from the sheltered home they shared with their mother and were moved to court permanently, under armed guard. Their relocation from a stable rural base to a series of sophisticated metropolitan hubs came at a time of rising international tensions. The marriage negotiations had been part of a shifting political strategy that was reaching a sour conclusion. King Juan II of the neighboring Kingdom of Aragon, the father of Carlos, Ferdinand, and Juana, was stirring up trouble for King Enrique with his Castilian nobles; King Enrique in return was encouraging the Aragonese to rebel against King Juan. Enrique wanted to be sure he had control of the two children, the promised marriage partners and current heirs to the throne, but other issues were also coming into play. Even Castillo, Enrique's most sympathetic chronicler, acknowledged that some among the court had "sinister motives" for gaining possession of the children.[37] As long as Enrique remained childless, they were potential competitors to the throne. And as step-siblings to the king, the two children were vulnerable to his whims.

The two semi-orphaned children were being sent off to a court that was growing increasingly licentious and undisciplined. There was little apparent plan for caring for the children. Queen Juana was young and callow, a teenager operating in a court with minimal adult supervision. She and her ladies-in-waiting engaged in exuberant flirtations with male courtiers. Their sexual escapades offended older, more conservative, and religious court observers. "Generous damsels" is how they were described by one wit, who was not referring to their purses.[38]

Enrique was also a less-than-stellar parental figure. His court was dominated by his corps of all-male friends—"peasants, jugglers, entertainers, muleteers, sharp-eyed peddlers," people at whom noble families were likely to look askance in such a class-conscious society, and with whom Enrique liked to socialize in private settings.[39] He enjoyed holding forth in the Moorish style, sitting on cushions and rugs instead of upon a throne, often dressed in a turban or hooded cape, an affectation that would have seemed harmless or romantic except for the fact that Castile was at war with Granada. The charming young courtier Beltrán de la Cueva attracted considerable attention as well, particularly after he won the affections of both monarchs. "He could please the king as well as the queen," scholar Teofilo Ruiz notes tartly.[40]

Isabella, aged about ten, began to act as a lady-in-waiting to Juana and observed the goings-on as part of the queen's entourage, which kept her in constant proximity to Juana, almost around the clock. She became aware at a young age of the sexual escapades that were engulfing the court. She did not get drawn into them, however, maintaining a detachment and unusual seriousness of purpose and piety, behavior that must have made her seem oddly old for her years and certainly out of step with the crowd. During the next few years, she remained part of the queen's household, living principally in Segovia, in its majestic Alcázar.[41] Alfonso's education was handed over to a well-trained gentleman of the court; Isabella was to be educated by the feckless young queen.

Isabella later recalled this period of her life as a frightening, isolating, and forlorn time. "When my brother Alfonso and I were children," she would write, "we were forcibly and intentionally taken from the arms of our mother and raised under the authority of the Queen Doña Juana. . . . It was a dangerous guardianship for us and . . . had infamous influences."[42] She told her older brother Enrique, in a letter also written in later years, that she sought to keep herself as much in seclusion as possible for self-protection: "I remained in my palace in order to avoid your immorality, taking care for my honor and fearing for my life . . . [persevering] through the grace of God."[43]

She learned to take consolation, as she did throughout her life, in religion. One of Spain's most respected clerics happened to live in a monastery just down the hill from Segovia's Alcázar, and his important family connections made him venerated. He was a Dominican friar who dressed in simple monk garb, lived abstemiously, and retreated from time to time into a cave for quiet contemplation. His uncle was a famous cardinal living in Rome, but this nephew had not gone to live with his well-heeled uncle but instead stayed home to play a vital role in the community's spiritual life. His name was Tomás de Torquemada, and he became, at least from time to time, confessor to both Isabella and Alfonso during these childhood years.

It was not surprising that Isabella would place her trust in a sober local prelate. Both children needed powerful allies wherever they could find them.

* * *

And now there was more news at the court. Queen Juana had at last become pregnant, surprising everyone, and in February 1462 she produced the long-desired heir. Isabella was there at the childbirth, as part of the queen's entourage. Following specific rules of court ritual, the queen gave birth squatting, with a platoon of observers flanking her. One nobleman supported her body as the queen writhed in pain. On one side stood Juan Pacheco, the king's favorite, observing the proceedings. On the other side stood Alfonso Carrillo, archbishop of Toledo, with two other dignitaries. It was a difficult labor, after which she gave birth to a daughter, who was named Juana, in the family pattern of naming the child after the parent. Soon afterward the baby was baptized by Carrillo. Princess Isabella served as godmother to the child.[44]

Given King Enrique's previous problems with sexual performance, some whispered at the time about whether the king was truly the baby's father. The thirteen years of impotence during his first marriage raised questions, but he may have found a medical solution to his infertility. Jerónimo Münzer, a German physician who visited Spain in those years, said he was told that Enrique's "member was thin and weak at the base but large at the head," making it difficult for him to sustain an erection, but that the queen had undergone artificial insemination by having a golden tube filled with Enrique's semen inserted into her vagina.[45] Some Jewish physicians who were consulted about the problem, however, believed Enrique to be hopelessly infertile.

Enrique added some grist to the rumor mill on his own. Within a week of Juana's birth, Enrique named Beltrán de la Cueva to be the Count of Ledesma, a major new honor for a nobleman of fairly humble birth. This fact became another item of salacious gossip at the court.

Many festivities were held to celebrate the birth, including a joust. In May, Enrique brought the nobles together in Madrid to swear an oath of support to the newborn princess. In July in Toledo the Cortes, the kingdom's governing assembly, repeated the pledge.

The Castilian nobility took the oath of loyalty to the baby girl as the heir apparent. But given his previous testimony about impotence in his divorce proceedings with Blanca, Enrique's opponents soon raised questions about Juana's legitimacy and right to the throne. They dubbed the child Juana la Beltraneja—or Juana the daughter of Beltrán, the bisexual courtier. On the very day that Enrique's close friend Juan Pacheco swore the oath of obedience to the infant princess, he drafted and signed a document disputing the child's right to the throne. In that statement, Pacheco said he swore the oath out of "fear" of the king but "did not intend ... to harm nor cause prejudice in the succession of the said kingdom."[46]

Certainly there was some reason for questioning the child's parentage. Queen Juana's flirtatious interactions had fueled speculation about her morals. People began recalling a particular incident, one that had been witnessed by foreign diplomats, in which De la Cueva fought a joust in which he ostentatiously bore the letter *J*, the initial of the woman in whose honor he was competing. Many inferred that his love object was the queen herself.[47]

Against this backdrop of sexual intrigue and gossipy chatter, Isabella as a person virtually disappeared into the woodwork. Her name would pop into conversations as an available bargaining chip in potential foreign alliances, and she became a pawn in one political scheme after another, particularly after 1461, when Prince Carlos of Aragon, her intended, suddenly died. Carlos's death opened up new possibilities for Enrique because of King Juan's unpopularity at home. A group of Catalans proposed, after Carlos's death, that Enrique should become the next king of Aragon—an idea that Enrique found agreeable. The dispute threatened to become murderous, as Carlos's father, King Juan of Aragon, who was still living, did not think it was a good idea at all.

In his typical double-dealing manner, Juan Pacheco suggested that King Louis XI of France, a man who was living up to his new nickname "The Universal Spider," be permitted to mediate the succession dispute, giving the French king a valuable commission for which Pacheco would be generously rewarded. At Pacheco's urging, Enrique foolishly agreed. Then King Louis accepted a generous bribe from Aragon as well and threw his weight to Carlos's father rather than to Enrique, making Enrique feel both stupid and angry. That added to the strains between Pacheco and Enrique and also put Castile at loggerheads with both Aragon and France.

Now Enrique needed a new alliance, another kingdom that could give him military support. He reached out to negotiate with England, starting in 1463. Suddenly a marriage offer from that distant land opened up a new world of possibility for the young princess. Ambassadors from England came to Spain to negotiate for her possible marriage to "Europe's most eligible bachelor," the dashing and handsome occupant of the English throne, Edward IV.[48]

Soon, it appeared, Isabella of Castile, the younger sister of the king, would become queen of England.

THREE

FRIGHTENING
YEARS

In February 1464, when Isabella was not quite thirteen years old, her brother Enrique accepted the English offer and agreed to give her in marriage to King Edward IV, in a gesture of political alignment between the two countries.[1] This would at once make Isabella a queen.

It might have been a generous act on Enrique's part, to help ensure an illustrious future for his half sister. Certainly Isabella and Enrique showed visible signs of affection from time to time. They both loved music, and sometimes he would sing while she would dance. They shared some of the same interests—riding, hunting, deep and thoughtful discussions—and they held the same religious convictions. However, it is just as likely that the marital alliance was Enrique's attempt to remove Isabella from the direct line of succession in Castile and relocate her to a distant land, particularly at a time when rumors were brewing about Juana's legitimacy.

Regardless of Enrique's motives, however, the proposition of marriage to the English king would have been appealing to most young women. The twenty-two-year-old Edward of York had recently assumed the throne of England. Charming, blond, strong, and six feet four inches tall, he was intelligent, excellent at the courtly games of hunting and jousting, dressed elegantly in furs and rich jewelry, and was fond of chivalric romances. This combination of traits made him irresistible to women, upon whom the lusty young king was eager to lavish his own attentions.

Even discounting for the customary fawning by courtiers, Edward drew accolades that were seemingly genuine. "He was a goodly person-age, and very princely to behold ... of visage lovely, of body mighty, strong and clean made," wrote Sir Thomas More. "Remarkable beyond all others," said a German traveler, Gabriel Tetzel, in 1466. Even his critics acknowledged his physical beauty. "I don't remember having seen a more handsome prince," wrote the French courtier Philippe de Commynes.[2]

Marriage to Edward would of course have been an intriguing, even dazzling, prospect for Isabella, who loved hunting and stories of courtly love. It would give her a splendid husband, make her the envy of other women, and install her as queen of a kingdom with which she had long ancestral links. Isabella believed that Spain and England had a natural dynastic affinity. Her great-grandmother was Catherine of Lancaster, the daughter of the famous English nobleman John of Gaunt, son of King Edward III, whose marriage to Constance of Castile had made him a contender for the throne of Castile. Edward IV was also descended from Edward III, making him a distant cousin of Isabella's. If the alliance pro-ceeded, an old family tie would be reconnected.

The marriage presented some strategic opportunities for England as well. Edward's descent from King Pedro, through Pedro's daughter, already made Edward a potential claimant to the Castilian throne, and this claim would be strengthened if he were to marry Isabella. English poets were already writing doggerel extolling Edward as not just king of England and deserving of France but also the future inheritor of Spain: "Re Angliae et Franciae, I say, It is thine own, why sayest thou nay? And so is Spain, that fair country."[3]

Once the match was proposed, Isabella waited at home for the deci-sion. Given the difficulties in communication at the time, messages from one court to another sometimes took months because courtiers needed to physically travel from one place to another. Finally she some-how learned, to her great disappointment, that another woman had been selected, in a most unusual way.

Unbeknown to the king's councilors, who were negotiating Edward's marriage prospects in both France and Spain, King Edward had already impulsively married a comely widow, Elizabeth Woodville. She was one of the few women who had successfully resisted his blandishments, and in a fever, he chose marriage to obtain lawfully what he could not obtain by courtship. They wed in a furtive ceremony on April 30, 1464, at the home of friends of her family, with only a handful of people in attendance.[4]

Edward must have regretted the elopement almost instantly because he sought to conceal the match for the next six months. Even his friends were not informed.

The circumstances were even more awkward for his officials who were abroad discussing terms of potential marriages with foreign princesses. The French king, Louis XI, wasn't officially informed of the secret marriage until October 10, 1464, after six months of deliberations and negotiations over a possible marriage of Edward to Louis's sister-in-law Bona. The Earl of Warwick, an important ally of Edward working on his behalf in France, was humiliated and chagrined to realize he had been left uninformed while "pressing actively" for the French alliance.[5] An English chronicler described his reaction: "And when the Erle of Warwyke come home and herde hereof, thenne was he gretely displesyd."[6]

The course of European history could have been shifted in many ways if Isabella had managed to marry, win over, and provide assistance in governing to the high-spirited but short-sighted and pleasure-loving king of England. Both countries might have evolved in better directions. Edward's marriage turned out to be disastrously bad for him, as the woman he wed was "grasping and ambitious for her family's interests, quick to take offense and reluctant to forgive."[7] She was also a member of the Lancaster clan, enemies to the Yorks, and to please his wife, Edward was forced to find posts at court for her two children from her first marriage, five brothers, and seven unmarried sisters. Like King Enrique, Edward ended up surrounding himself with people who did not have his best interests at heart. The king's irritated emissary to France and former ally, the Earl of Warwick, turned against him. Edward's dynastic aspirations collapsed even though he had ten children with Elizabeth, and after his death, his two oldest boys, aged ten and thirteen, were spirited away and rumored to have been killed in the Tower of London by persons unknown.

In faraway Castile, Isabella, still a young teenager, brooded over her rejection, much later telling ambassadors that she had been passed over for a mere "widow of England," making it clear she had harbored resentment at her rejection for the next twenty years. Like Elizabeth Woodville, she was not a woman to suffer a slight lightly or forgive easily.[8] In addition to Isabella's good qualities, a certain hardness of character was developing in her. It made her able to survive the difficulties of her childhood and adolescence, but it also made her rigid and unforgiving.

While Enrique awaited word from England, at some point suspecting that the match with Edward would evaporate, he began to consider instead marrying Isabella to King Afonso V of Portugal, a war hero whose support would bolster Castile's defenses. Such a match would be equally effective in getting Isabella out of the kingdom and out of the path of little Juana's claims, and it would also improve relations with Portugal. And Portugal already had an heir apparent, Afonso's son João. In this scenario, João's children would rule Portugal; Juana's children would rule Castile. Isabella's children would be safely out of any line of succession.

In April 1463 Enrique took Isabella, just turning thirteen, and Queen Juana to El Puente de Arzobispo, in central-western Castile, closer to the Portuguese border, to meet King Afonso. The thirty-one-year-old Portuguese king—paunchy, middle-aged, and pompous—was "much taken" with his young cousin. Isabella, for her part, under pressure from the queen and her own mother, who was Portuguese, and undoubtedly playing for time while she awaited word on the English alliance, tactfully or innocently led the Portuguese king to believe he was her choice as well.[9] This was an error on her part.

King Enrique's popularity in Castile was plummeting, however, and the proposed Portuguese marriage was not well received. Two men in particular took it as an affront. Alfonso Carrillo, the rich and powerful archbishop of Toledo, had grown weary of Enrique's vacillating leadership. He was also a partisan of the envious Aragonese cousins and had long hoped to steer public policy in Castile toward Aragon rather than toward Portugal. Juan Pacheco, meanwhile, was angry and out of sorts because he was being supplanted in the king's affections by other men. Carrillo and Pacheco began to foment a rebellion against Enrique. As a first step, they wanted to get control of young Prince Alfonso and Princess Isabella and insisted they be given custody of the children, ostensibly to ensure their continued security. They warned that people of "damnable intent" had planned to kill Alfonso and marry off Isabella, to give "succession in these realms to [one] to whom by right it does not belong," by which they meant the child Juana.[10]

They announced their split from the king in an open letter to the kingdom that was widely circulated. The document, called the Representation of Burgos, oozed contempt and derision and made a series of demands. Enrique was ordered to get rid of his Moorish bodyguard, whom they accused of sexually assaulting both men and women; to discard his new favorite, Beltrán de la Cueva; and to drop the charade about Juana's legitimacy. "It is quite manifest that she is not the daughter of your highness," the statement read.[11]

Enrique, always eager to mollify his critics, deferred to Pacheco and Carrillo and agreed to their demands, even to the extent of repudiating his daughter's claim to the throne and giving it to his young half brother Alfonso: "Know ye, that to avoid any kind of scandal . . . I declare that the legitimate succession of this kingdom belongs to my brother the Infante don Alfonso and to no other person whatsoever." Beltrán was sent away. At a ceremony in Cabezón, the nobility took oaths in support of Alfonso as the successor, and the mastership of Santiago was transferred to him. Young Alfonso was handed over to the custody of Juan Pacheco, the Marquess of Villena, who had played such a pivotal role in Enrique's own youth.[12]

* * *

This was an unfortunate period in Alfonso's life, for there were reports that he was badly treated, and perhaps sexually molested, while he was in Pacheco's care. The chronicler Palencia said that Pacheco attempted a pedophilic seduction of the boy, in hopes of making him more malleable, something that was widely believed to have been done to Enrique in his youth. In fact, by this time, similar allegations had been raised regarding three generations of Trastámara men—their father Juan, Enrique, and now Alfonso.

This is a distinct possibility. There is a long tradition of sex being used to manipulate politicians and other powerful people. In this case, an unusual set of facts seems to suggest a possibility of adolescent sexual abuse. Sexual predators generally seek out their victims when they are young, often almost under the noses of their parents or guardians, woo them in a pattern known as "grooming," and after having sexual relations with them, assert dominance over them in other ways. Certainly patterns characteristic of molestation were visible among the men in Isabella's family. In all three cases, the parents were absent or preoccupied by serious problems, leaving a void in the child's life. Sexual predators thrive in those conditions.

King Juan, Isabella's father, had been just six years old when he fell under the spell of eighteen-year-old Álvaro de Luna, who was soon sleeping in the child's bed. Juan's father had died, and his mother was trying to administer the nation at a time of terrible civil strife; she was initially appreciative when Álvaro took such a kindly interest in the boy. "The king did not want to be without Don Álvaro de Luna either by night or by day," wrote a chronicler of the time.[13] At some point, however, the queen mother became concerned that the relationship had become so "intimate," writes historian Teofilo Ruiz. She ordered "Don Álvaro removed from the court, only to bring him back at the pleading and insistence of her son."[14]

Álvaro, for his part, had been the illegitimate son of a nobleman who took no interest in him. He had been separated from his mother and raised in the household of the Catholic pope who was his uncle, surrounded by priests whose religious vows kept them from marriage. Álvaro de Luna was handsome, charming, and amiable; he eventually married and had children. In his twenties, however, though many women were attracted to him, he was never associated publicly with any of them, which he encouraged people to believe was evidence of his unusual gallantry toward the ladies of the court. But it could also have meant that his sexual interests were primarily elsewhere. In Álvaro's own household, for example, an unusual boy, Juan Pacheco, served as a teenage page, and Pacheco repeated the pattern established by Álvaro de Luna.

After King Juan grew up, married, and had a son, Enrique, Álvaro de Luna similarly introduced Juan Pacheco, six years older than Enrique, to the young prince and placed him in the prince's household. Soon Juan Pacheco held Enrique in thrall as Álvaro had done with his father.

Both Álvaro de Luna and Juan Pacheco had exhibited a remarkable degree of personal power over Juan and Enrique—in both cases, it was so noteworthy that it was likened to witchcraft. This pattern is common among sexual predators and their victims. The sexual involvement is not a romance but an abuse. The molester often takes satisfaction from humiliating the object of his or her attentions, sometimes in a public place, with the goal of demonstrating dominance. The victim often feels some combination of anger and shame, because at times the interactions are sexually pleasurable. Adults who were molested as children frequently have difficulty maintaining relationships and are either easily sexually aroused or become incapable of having sex. Moreover, the victims frequently become very religious out of a sense of guilt, in seeking redemption for what they believe to be their own culpability for what occurred.

A chronicler of Juan who lived at the court said: "Juan II ... lived his life under the influence of Don Álvaro de Luna, up until the time when, under pressure from nobles, the King, crying, ordered him decapitated."[15] Another added: Juan was "weak of character and suggestible to the point of shameful submission" to the tutelage of Don Álvaro de Luna.[16] This relationship, of course, had been the insuperable obstacle for Isabella's mother, who had struggled to get her husband to break from Álvaro's spell, then watched as her husband descended into black melancholy at Álvaro's death.

Similar things were said about Enrique and Juan Pacheco a generation later. A chronicler of Enrique, an eyewitness, reported that "abuses and delights became his habit" under the influence of Juan Pacheco. He became a "passive instrument of Don Juan Pacheco, intentionally placed at his side by Álvaro de Luna . . . Not a single thing was done unless he had ordered it."[17] One contemporary historian went so far as to call Pacheco a "monster of nature."[18] Another, Fernando del Pulgar, said Enrique was introduced at age fourteen to "unseemly pleasures" he was unable to resist because of his sexual inexperience.[19]

For both King Juan and King Enrique, the relationships between king and favorite had sparked criticism and ridicule, undermined their authority, and led to open hostilities in their kingdoms. To gain even a small advantage, Juan Pacheco had been willing to shed blood, and in some cases innocent bystanders were killed as a result of his machinations.

* * *

At this point, however, angry over the long chain of insults and humiliations by Juan Pacheco, King Enrique unexpectedly began to resist his control. That, sadly, was his undoing. Enrique called his new favorite, Don Beltrán, back to court and elevated him further, by making him not just a count but also the Duke of Alburquerque. This was a final straw to many people around Castile. A large faction of the nobles exploded in anger. Burgos, Seville, Córdoba, and even the ancient capital city of Toledo rose against Enrique. The king retreated, barricading himself in Segovia. His most implacable enemy turned out to be the chief Christian prelate, the warlike archbishop of Toledo, Alfonso Carrillo. Enrique wrote to the clergyman, asking for his support. Carrillo responded curtly to the messenger bearing the request: "Go tell your King that I am sick of him and his affairs, and that we shall now see who is the real king of Castile."[20]

On June 5, 1465, in a fateful act of revolution, nobles gathered in the walled city of Ávila to enact an unusual ceremony. They essentially staged a coup against Enrique by dethroning him in effigy. A life-size mannequin representing the king was placed in a chair on a stage. One noble approached and knocked the crown off its head. Another removed the scepter. It was a ritual designed to be a public spectacle, just as the execution of Álvaro de Luna had been a real decapitation but also a symbolic event. The effigy puppet was kicked to the ground. As the final act, the twelve-year-old Prince Alfonso was brought into the plaza, carried on the shoulders of other officials, and the crown was placed on his head. The rebels now had control of a boy pretender to the throne. It became obvious why the courtiers around Enrique had insisted so strenuously on obtaining physical control of the king's brother.

King Enrique was horrified, feeling stricken and defenseless against the assault, which seemed not just a parody of Castilian succession tradition but also something close to sacrilege. He was blindsided and desperate for allies because many of the kingdom's leading noblemen had participated in the events at Ávila. This played precisely into the hands of Juan Pacheco, who promised Enrique he would return Alfonso to him and bring troops to the king's defense and support, but only if Enrique would permit his brother, Pedro Girón, master of the Calatrava religious order, to marry Princess Isabella. This extraordinary proposition would have placed Pacheco's family in the direct line of succession and possibly even permit them to rule Castile, if Alfonso were to die and if Juana's legitimacy continued to be questioned.

The fact that this proposal became a matter of such high-level deliberations makes it clear that Isabella was being pulled out of the shadows. The symbolic dethroning of King Enrique meant she too had become a contender for supremacy in the nation. From this point on, Isabella's existence became a topic of interest to court chroniclers, and her comings and goings were noted with some regularity. After the king had deferred once to the nobility on the question of Juana's legitimacy, that child's right to succession was forever diminished, and now Enrique's own right to rule had been challenged.

King Enrique caved in once more. The weak-willed king, always pitifully eager to find a peaceful resolution to a problem, agreed to Juan Pacheco's proposition, promising his fifteen-year-old sister to a religious leader who had pledged to remain chaste but was in fact notoriously debauched. Enrique dispatched an emissary to the pope, asking for a dispensation releasing Girón from his purported vow of celibacy.[21]

Now it was Isabella's turn to be horrified. Just a year or two before, she had believed she was being affianced to one of the most admired young kings in Europe; now she was being thrust into the arms of a degenerate man who regularly betrayed his obligation of celibacy, who was far beneath her in lineage, and who was considerably older than she. There was even the embarrassing family memory of the vulgar sexual advance Pedro Girón had once made to Isabella's mother.

Pedro Girón set out on horseback for Madrid, where Isabella was staying, eager to make her his bride. This is the first event in Isabella's life that is fully described in court records. Chroniclers wrote that she turned to God for help and guidance, begging to be spared the marriage and spending almost two days on her knees in prayer.[22] Despairing, she asked God to preserve her from the marriage by death if necessary—either hers or that of Pedro Girón.

The members of her household circle were similarly disgusted and appalled by this new development. According to some stories, Isabella's loyal friend, Beatriz de Bobadilla, grabbed a knife and vowed to kill Pedro Girón. But fortuitously, at least in the view of Isabella's supporters and chroniclers, Girón suddenly dropped dead. He had been making haste to marry Isabella when he fell ill from an acute infection of the tonsils that blocked his breathing, and he died on the road. Girón's abrupt and unexpected death was a huge relief to Isabella and her friends. Later, after many other events occurred, some people even began to say it had been a miracle.

* * *

Princess Isabella was transferred to Enrique's most secure base, the beautiful city of Segovia, whose solid walls, stout fortress, and perch on a rocky precipice created an air of impregnability. Girón's death had freed her from her immediate fear, but it had also dealt a blow to the peace negotiations between Enrique and the nobles of Castile. Alfonso remained in the nobles' custody and continued his claim to the throne, while animosities turned into hostility once again. Isabella sheltered in Segovia, accompanied by Queen Juana, Enrique's wife, who by now was more her captor than her companion. Isabella's existence had long been beside the point for the young queen, but now Isabella was an actual threat to her, her husband, and her daughter. It placed Isabella in a most precarious situation, and some courtiers feared the queen would have her killed to get rid of the problem.

The tensions in Segovia spread all over the kingdom. Everyone was forced to pick sides between Enrique and the young claimant Alfonso, and sporadic violence turned to civil war. "All the realm was arms and blood: no nobleman or city remained neutral," wrote chronicler Diego de Colmenares.[23]

Chaos broke out everywhere, and criminals took advantage of the situation. A group of noblemen visiting Spain from Central Europe that year on pilgrimage had a safe-conduct from a Portuguese princess who had married the Holy Roman emperor but found it provided almost no protection. They reported being attacked by a polyglot gang of Christians, Jews, and Muslims in the far north, on the banks of the Cadagua River, and escaped only by bribing them; in Valmaseda, near Bilbao, they were threatened with murder and again had to pay in order to escape with their lives; and in Olmedo, armed robbers tried three times to force their way into the house where they were staying, pelting them with stones when they ventured outside, in hopes of provoking a response that would permit a more open assault. One member of their group disappeared and was believed to have been sold into slavery in Muslim lands; and in Molins de Rei, near Barcelona, they narrowly escaped execution at the hands of a local vigilante group that was hunting for a stranger who had committed a murder. The pilgrim group found life considerably more peaceful in Italy, where they went after they left the Iberian peninsula.

The troops of Alfonso and Enrique met in an inconclusive clash of arms near Olmedo, in August 1467. Prince Alfonso, now thirteen and styling himself King Alfonso, fought alongside Alfonso Carrillo, the archbishop of Toledo, who wore his priestly robes over a coat of armor. King Enrique humiliated himself by fleeing the battlefield, hiding out in a nearby village until the fighting was over, but Alfonso fought valiantly. In the following days, some of Enrique's supporters defected, and most shockingly for Enrique, the city of Segovia, his hometown and the place on which he had lavished his largesse and support, willingly opened its gates to Alfonso and his troops. Even Segovia had repudiated Enrique.

As Alfonso came to the city, accompanied by the malevolent Juan Pacheco, who had helped foment the rebellion, the boy stopped to take revenge on his older half brother in a particularly unsettling way. Normally a good-natured child, Alfonso ordered the beasts in Enrique's menagerie slaughtered. Only one animal was left alive—Enrique's beloved mountain goat, because Juan Pacheco intervened to ask Alfonso to spare that one animal. Alfonso's strange and disturbing brutality is so unusual that it provides another piece of evidence that Alfonso might indeed have endured some sort of humiliating mistreatment. Cruelty to animals is another common indicator of child sexual abuse; sociologists have found that there is a high correlation between domestic abuse and animal abuse.

Alfonso's arrival put Isabella on the spot. The young princess, who had been sequestered in Segovia with the queen, her hostile sister-in-law, faced a stark choice. She could continue to ally herself with her older brother, King Enrique, which would be a precarious position with the city now about to fall; or she could take her chances with the young upstart, her brother Alfonso. She made her decision. She cast her lot with Alfonso and switched her allegiance to him. Her teenage brother made a triumphant entry into the city, and Isabella rushed to join him. In the next months, she frequently traveled by his side, an enthusiastic supporter of his claim to the throne. They rode together to their first destination: home, to their mother's side, and to safe refuge once again, in Arévalo.

* * *

As Isabella and her entourage became part of Alfonso's court, and as the prince engaged in an intense civil war against their half brother, another important figure in Isabella's life made his first appearance. Most of the rebels surrounding the young people, of course, were adults, some of them very mature, even elderly. But this young man was only about fourteen years old, which made him a year older than Alfonso and a year younger than Isabella. His name was Gonzalo Fernández de Córdoba. When the rebellion against Enrique started, Gonzalo's family had promptly joined the rebels. His older brother was slated to inherit the family's prosperous estate in Andalusia, and Gonzalo was being groomed for a life as a soldier. In 1467 Gonzalo was sent to Castile, under the care of a tutor, to become a page to Alfonso, with the idea that he would establish ties to the court that could secure his future life. Soon he grew close to both Alfonso and Isabella, who were similarly trying to find their footing in the adult world.

Traveling from place to place, coping with the uncertainties of the campaign trail, Gonzalo and Isabella developed a deep friendship. The relationship appeared to be platonic—she was going to be a queen, at least through an eventual marriage, and he would always be the second son of a nobleman—but it was an era that romanticized courtly love, where a nobleman of sterling character would pledge undying affection for a noble gentlewoman. Early on, Gonzalo pledged himself to defend Isabella's interests, and she soon began to do the same for him.

In many ways, they were mirror images of each other. Gonzalo was idealistic, articulate, and poised, even as a teenager. An avid reader with a gift for language, he was a keen student of military history and viewed military prowess as a manifestation of religious devotion. He chose as his personal motto these words: "For your honor, give your life. For your God, give both honor and life."[24]

He spent hours each day perfecting his soldiering skills, preparing himself for battle, if and when it came. "I used to take a rapier and spend hours fencing in a room all alone where no one would see me," he later recalled. "For not only did swordsmanship come as naturally to me as walking or running, but it seemed to me an activity perfectly suited to the natural movement of the body."[25]

Gonzalo was attractive and stylish. He was greatly loved by his older brother, who gave him the money to live an elegant life at court. He dressed beautifully, once described as wearing a "carmoisine velvet cloak, lined with sables, which cost 2,000 ducats," on a day that was "not a major festival either."[26] He had been short as a boy but grew up strong and tall, an excellent horseman, skilled at games of martial arts. He was particularly gifted at a popular medieval game called canes: "He would come . . . now entering at a gallop, now turning in flight, still riding at top speed, bending over and snatching canes from the ground as he flashed past. . . . Again he could be seen, wheeling suddenly and galloping, shield up, so that though the others threw a thousand canes at him nothing or no one could harm him."[27]

Isabella came to look on Gonzalo with considerable favor, calling him the Prince of the Caballeros.[28] Soon, as a result of his military victories, he became known to others as the Great Captain. Indeed, he was confident of a glorious future.

His brother, who held the family purse strings, pleaded with him to restrain his extravagance, lest he be "ruined before a year." But Gonzalo brushed him aside. "Surely you do not wish to abandon the great aspirations God has given me with such vain threats of future poverty," he wrote to his brother. "But I am as certain that you will never fail to provide for your much-loved brother as I am that God, whose unfailing Providence always seems to favor those who have no goal but honor, will not see me go short of the confidence to achieve that which my stars foretell."[29]

* * *

It was a time of soaring great expectations in the court of King Alfonso, and an exuberant time for the young people who were preparing themselves to govern, imagining themselves as rulers of a better world. Isabella was confident that Alfonso was intended for glory. She organized a great party for his fourteenth birthday, performing in a masque at the celebration, predicting in verse his greatness: that he would go forward in dispensing justice, prove victorious, and be generous to his subjects; that God would find him praiseworthy; and "that his dominions would extend as far as the eye could reach."[30] She said his riches would equal those of King Midas, and his military triumphs would rival those of Alexander the Great. And she foretold eternal fame for him, that his actions would win him both "earthly and celestial glory."[31]

Prince Alfonso returned Isabella's love and affection and responded warmly to it. In Arévalo, while they were at their mother's home, he made her a generous gift. He presented to her the jurisdictions and rents of Medina del Campo, one of the cities that had early pledged its support to him. This was a tribute to her and a highly satisfying grant because she had always loved going to the fair there and had enjoyed many happy childhood hours in its abundant and overflowing market stalls and shops.

That was the high point for Alfonso and his allies, for afterward the political tide began to run against the prince-turned-king. When Gonzalo Chacón, the long-time family friend who now served as Isabella's chief of staff, went to Medina del Campo to take possession of the city on her behalf, he encountered resistance to the transfer. Medina del Campo's residents were shifting sides and returning to their support of King Enrique.

Then bad tidings arrived from Toledo, which had been one of Alfonso's strongest bases and where his ally, Carrillo, served as archbishop. An explosive set of events had erupted into warfare in the streets, in such a way that Alfonso's good character would become a political handicap to him. The facts were murky and complicated, but they went to the heart of the religious dissensions that were pulling Castilians in different directions. Toledo had early declared its allegiance to Alfonso, but as the civil war wore on, the absence of an effective central government invited social disruptions.

The most thorough account of the key events comes from the Israeli historian Benzion Netanyahu, who traced their origin to the summer of 1467, when church officials in Toledo hired a Jewish tax collector to seek payment of some debts owed to the church. A pro-Alfonso judge who was a converso, a man of Jewish descent who had converted to Christianity, opposed the appointment of this individual, saying he had not authorized it. Church officials responded by excommunicating the judge. Enraged and indignant, he gathered a band of heavily armed conversos and attacked a church during worship services, killing two of the officials who were involved in the dispute. Some longtime Christians began preparing for war against the conversos, fearing a broader assault by people who were only posing as Christians.

The conversos, for their part, began to fear another anti-Semitic massacre like the one that had happened in 1391; they mobilized four thousand recruits, using the cathedral as a base, placing artillery at its gates and firing upon passersby and people they suspected might be preparing an attack. They maintained this position for almost a day, causing many injuries. But then Christian mobs organized a response, and they greatly outnumbered the converso group. Pitched battles broke out between roving bands of longtime Christians and conversos. Entire blocks of streets were put to the torch. More than 150 conversos were killed in the ensuing battles, and many more had their homes and possessions stolen. Others were protected from injury by their neighbors who were longtime Christians and believed they were being unfairly attacked.

Tensions were so high that many people believed peace between the religions was no longer possible in Toledo. In the aftermath of the riots, a great many conversos left Toledo and moved elsewhere. Greedy Christian officials took advantage of the situation and passed regulations that stripped all conversos of government positions and allowed their assailants to keep stolen goods.

Christian officials in Toledo wrote to Alfonso and asked him to confirm the new rules and pardon them for any wrongdoing done to the conversos. They reasoned that Alfonso was so weak and young that he would simply agree. Instead, however, he told them that the actions in

Toledo had been "dishonorable and shameful" and that he would rather risk losing Toledo from his camp than condone what they had done. King Enrique struggled with the issue as well but ultimately agreed to the demands set by the Christians and authorized them to keep the goods taken from the converso families. Consequently, Toledo moved back to Enrique's side in the civil war. This was a major blow to Alfonso, because of the strategic and historic importance of the city.

Alfonso and Isabella had been enjoying a day at the fair at Medina del Campo when they learned what had happened in Toledo and how city officials had repudiated him. Alfonso decided to hurry to Toledo to lay siege to the city and reclaim it. Isabella rode with him southward toward the great walled city of Ávila, a way station on their path to Toledo.

Then in Cardeñosa, a small village almost within sight of Ávila, Alfonso fell ill. A chronicler recounted the events:

With the king, Don Alfonso[,] . . . was Her Most Serene Highness, the Princess, Doña Isabella, his sister. And as they sat at dinner, among the other viands was brought a trout pastry, which he partook of willingly, though he ate only a little of it. And afterward he fell in a heavy sleep, most unusual for him, and went off to bed without speaking to anyone, and slept until the hour of terce [nine a.m.], a thing he never did.

And those of his bedchamber came and felt him with their hands and there was no heat in him. As he did not waken they began to call loudly and yet he did not respond. And their shouts made such a din that the archbishop of Toledo and the Master of Santiago [Juan Pacheco, the Marquess of Villena] and My Lady the Princess came, but he answered them not. And they felt all his members but found no swellings.

The physician, coming in haste, ordered him to be bled, but no blood came; his tongue was swollen, and the mouth seemed black, yet no sign of plague appeared. So, despairing of the life of the King, those who so greatly loved him, their wits forsaking them, began shouting out, begging Our Lord for his life. Some made vows to enter religion, some to go on distant pilgrimages. Others made different promises. And, no remedy availing, the innocent King gave his soul to Him who created it on July 5, 1468. . . . His death was believed to have been brought about by poisonous herbs because, though young in years, he seemed to his followers more likely to become a more vigorous governor than his brother.[32]

It was unclear whether Alfonso had plague—in which case no one knew where it might strike next—or even worse, that he had been poisoned. Suddenly Isabella was alone and exposed, after having defied Enrique in the most dramatic way. Her grandmother by now was dead; her mother could provide no assistance. And Isabella was now dangerously high in the line of succession in a kingdom where the heirs to the throne frequently suffered untimely deaths. Certainly many were hoping she would soon be gone as well.

FOUR

ISABELLA FACES THE
FUTURE ALONE

Human life in the Middle Ages could end abruptly at any time—something Isabella had already repeatedly experienced. Her father's death at forty-nine had left her nearly an orphan; her would-be husband Pedro Girón had contracted a throat ailment and was dead within hours.

But the death of the young, robust, and healthy Alfonso, in the midst of galloping across the plain on a cross-country journey, left many people pondering dark questions of how and why it had happened. One day he had been in the prime of his life; just a few days later his companions had to decide how to transport his corpse. Alfonso's body was taken to his hometown of Arévalo, for burial in the convent of San Francisco, whose priests had played a steadying role in the children's lives during their youngest years.

The details of his last hours were seared in the memory of those around him: Had he somehow caught the plague, while others in the party were miraculously untouched? Had he eaten something unhealthy? And most alarming of all: Was there a chance he had been poisoned?

The idea was not far-fetched. For thousands of years, toxic substances had been tools of succession in treacherous times; one early poison recipe was written on an Egyptian papyrus. The ancient Greeks, ancestors of the Spaniards, had long used poison to execute criminals or for suicide.

Hercules was believed to have been killed by poison spread on the inside of his tunic, and one of the most famous accounts of self-inflicted death was that of Socrates, carried out by hemlock in 402 B.C. During Isabella's time, people talking about death by poisoning often referred to the use of "herbs," such as hemlock, but also including wolfsbane, foxglove, or wormwood. Chroniclers quickly speculated that Alfonso had died from the administration of what they called "hierbas."

It would have been easy enough to arrange. Poisons are portable and easy to disguise, simple to mix and match to cause strange and mystifying symptoms. Most are administered through food and drink, with surprising ease. Some poisons are so toxic that even a taste—less than seven drops—can induce death.[1] Many others require less than one ounce. Arsenic can be ground into a powder; toxic mushrooms can be dried and whipped into a tasty meat sauce; and some poisons can be absorbed through the skin, perhaps as the victim takes a stroll wearing a handsome but doctored set of gloves presented as a gift.

A successful poisoning can mimic natural ailments, making it hard to detect. Arsenic, for example, causes severe gastrointestinal distress and low blood pressure, symptoms that might also accompany acute food poisoning. Poisonous mushrooms, sliced into a salad or sautéed with meat, can cause violet spots to appear on the victim's skin, making it a popular method of murder at the time, because some kinds of infectious pestilence caused similar discoloration.[2] Indeed, Queen María, King Juan's first wife, and Leonor, Juan's sister-in-law, queen of Portugal—the Aragonese sisters who died within days of each other—were reported to have been covered with just such spots. If just one of them had died, it would have looked like plague, but because two relatives suddenly perished in cities distant from each other, with notably similar symptoms, it was widely believed that they had fallen victim to foul play.

Crafty methods of application are the key to success for the poisoner. The Persian queen Parysatis applied poison to one side of a knife and sliced a portion of meat with it, giving the poisoned side to her daughter-in-law while eating the other portion herself without apparent consequence. Antimony, another poison, is soluble in water, and its taste is easily masked with other flavors, making it a favorite with cooks eager to accelerate someone's journey to the afterlife.

Poison attained a new level of popularity as the late Middle Ages faded and the Renaissance began, about the same time that Isabella was growing to adulthood. Schools of poison began operating in Venice and Rome. One murder academy was so bold as to distribute a price list, with costs that varied depending on the status of the customer and the identity of the target. Indeed, poisoning became so common on the Italian peninsula that a new word was coined—*Italianated*—to refer to murder by poison. One prominent Spanish family from Valencia, the Borjas—or Borgias as they were known in Italy—became noted experts in the field after they moved to Rome.

But others observed that Alfonso's symptoms didn't fit neatly into any known category of poisons. Wasn't it possible that Alfonso had died of plague after all? Certainly it was an omnipresent threat at the time. Virulent and contagious diseases were sweeping through Europe with regularity. The Black Death of the 1350s, brought to Europe via the Silk Road from China, was estimated to have killed one-quarter of the continent's population. The city of Ávila had reportedly been struck by such an epidemic that very summer.

But poisoning remained a definite possibility, and almost immediately rumors began circulating that Alfonso had indeed been murdered. King Enrique had ample reason to hate his younger half brother. Seizing his beloved city of Segovia and killing his menagerie of pets certainly would have been enough to turn Enrique into Alfonso's mortal enemy, even if his younger half brother was not also trying to unseat him from the throne. But who might have actually carried out the deed?

One possibility, of course, was an anonymous professional answering directly to Enrique. Or the murder could have been performed by Juan Pacheco, Enrique's paramour and nemesis. He had a long history of double-dealing, of feigning friendship and shifting to treachery. Perhaps he believed that Alfonso's prospects were dimming, and he decided to throw his support back to Enrique. Removing Alfonso from the situation would make this shift easier to explain. And indeed it soon became evident that Pacheco was communicating and collaborating not just with the rebels opposed to Enrique but also with Enrique himself.

Other motives may have been at work as well. Alfonso's support for the conversos of Toledo had suggested that the boy prince would be less malleable than his supporters had hoped; that might have persuaded them to cut their losses. The Spanish historian María Dolores Carmen Morales Muñiz, a biographer of Alfonso who spent years sifting through the evidence, concludes that he was killed.[3]

But if someone murdered Alfonso, how had he accomplished it? The episode of the trout pastry at Cardeñosa rose to people's minds almost immediately. Alfonso alone of the party had eaten it; no one else had gotten ill. But scraps of the meal had been fed to the village dogs, and none of them had been visibly sickened. Still, dogs often have a stronger stomach for spoiled food than humans do, and perhaps they ate a poisoned pastry but did not suffer from it.

Grappling with this new disaster, and far from friends and family members, the grief-stricken young princess turned these questions over in her mind because she had to decide how to tell the kingdom what had happened. And as she reflected on it, she was forced to make a decision about her own future as well. With Alfonso dead, Isabella was now next in line to the throne. And if Alfonso had been viewed as a mortal threat by someone and had been put to death, then Isabella too was in danger. Making an accusation that her brother had been murdered would make her even more of a target. If she made such an accusation, the killer or killers would almost certainly strike again. She declared Alfonso's death to have been caused by plague. It was at least a way to buy time. She sent out letters informing officials that Alfonso had "died at three o'clock of the pestilence."[4]

* * *

Alfonso's supporters, meanwhile, suddenly became less than protective of Isabella. They moved her quickly to Ávila, where they argued intensely about what to do with her. This was an odd decision: if Alfonso had not been poisoned, then he had died of plague. Now Isabella was being sent to the city that was the epicenter of a new outbreak. The deliberations underscored their chilling lack of concern for her well-being.

Two men wanted Isabella to declare herself queen. Juan Pacheco wanted to remove her from Ávila, presumably to a place of his own choosing—something that would certainly have rung alarm bells for the young princess. Carrillo wanted to keep her there, despite the epidemic, but where he controlled the garrison. Pacheco said he wanted her to marry King Afonso of Portugal. Carrillo said he wanted her to marry Ferdinand of Aragon.[5] Each man intended to make her a puppet who would dance to his will. Isabella found herself a bystander as the men battled it out.

She had good reason to try to claim the throne for herself. She had joined the rebellion, allying herself with the group who believed Enrique had to be deposed, so it would be consistent for her to take the crown in her own name now. This might also be the safest course. A king, once crossed, cannot be relied upon to be forgiving. Her claim also seemed to have political support: the city of Seville, one of the kingdom's largest commercial hubs, had quickly proclaimed her queen in Alfonso's place.[6] She was waiting to hear from other cities as well. Officials in Murcia, for example, had been informed of Alfonso's death and promised to respond promptly.[7]

At this point, Isabella made one of the first of many life decisions that demonstrated her steely self-discipline. Throughout history, those who have tasted power, as Alfonso and Isabella had done, have shown enormous reluctance to surrender it. Pretenders to a throne persist in their efforts, often unto their deaths. The nobles urged her to take the throne. Isabella came under intense pressure from them to continue the rebellion, because that would delay their own day of reckoning with the king, and of course, she might possibly win.

Retreating to the Convent of Santa Ana in Ávila, praying and living among the nuns, Isabella pondered what to do next. Her decision to join Alfonso had turned out to be terribly wrong. She weighed her loyalty to her brother Enrique against her own political ambitions. This time she charted a safer course. Sensibly recognizing that her claim to the throne was weaker than Alfonso's because she was a woman, and also realizing that the nation had been undecided even about Alfonso's right to rule, Isabella made her announcement. "Return the kingdom to Don Enrique my brother, and thus you will restore peace to Castile," she wrote in a letter sent across the kingdom. "But if you hold me daughter of the King Don Juan, my lord and father, and worthy of the name, have the King my brother, and the nobles and prelates, after his life—and may that be long—declare me to be the successor to the realm. . . . This I will take as the greatest service you can render me."[8]

Enrique was the true king, she told her countrymen, and she should not be seen as the monarch at this time, but she would be his successor. She underscored her support for his reign, but added a note suggesting she hoped he would govern more wisely. "Now that it has pleased God to take from this life Alfonso my brother," she wrote to Juan Pacheco and Archbishop Carrillo, "so long as King Enrique may live I shall not take over the government, nor call myself Queen, but will make every effort to the end that King Enrique while he lives, may govern this realm better than he has done."[9]

Enrique responded gratefully and positively, glad to have an opening to put the unpleasant episode behind him. After a flurry of negotiations in Ávila and elsewhere in August 1468, Isabel and her brother reached agreement on many things. She was recognized as his heir, and she was given as her own property the city of Ávila; prosperous Medina del Campo, home of the fairs that drew tradesmen and shoppers from across the continent; and the towns of Huete, Molina, Escalona, and Ubeda, which gave her possessions scattered around the kingdom. She was also assured she would never have to marry against her wishes—but in return, she promised not to marry without Enrique's consent. Enrique promised to divorce his wife, who had caused him such embarrassment, and send her home.[10]

Soon a preliminary deal was struck. Within two weeks, she signed a letter to her old tutor Gonzalo Chacón: "Isabel, by Grace of God Princess and legitimate hereditary successor to these kingdoms of Castile and León."[11]

This was one of the first examples of what observers would come to call the "extraordinary prudence" with which she governed her life.[12] A number of cities soon turned tail and swore obedience to the king. The officials in Murcia never responded to Isabella's letter about Alfonso's death. If she had allowed her head to be turned by the importuning nobles, she would have ended up without substantial support and in direct personal confrontation with the king, who was soon working to solidify his position.

Instead, her demonstration of fidelity to the king gave Enrique the priceless gift of saving face, and the two sides formalized the terms of their reconciliation. The king based himself in Cadalso, and Isabella moved to nearby Cebreros, both towns in central Spain, while they hammered out the details. Envoys sped from one camp to the other. Finally, on September 18, 1468, about two months after Alfonso's death, the two siblings met in person about fifty miles from Ávila, on the fields of Toros de Guisando, a place freighted with ancient significance. The site was known for its life-size, weather-beaten statues of bulls placed at the foot of a mountain pass in some long-ago time, their specific purpose lost to memory. It was a spooky place, from another age of the world, suggestive of Greek mythology's reverence for bulls and for the sport and festivals related to their life and death.

Isabella and Enrique were publicly reconciled in this windswept open field. Isabella arrived on a mule with Archbishop Carrillo walking beside her, symbolically representing herself as both royal and humble. In the ceremony that followed, she was officially named the king's successor, and she, in turn, pledged to marry only with Enrique's approval. The king granted her all the towns he had promised, and even more symbolically, he also gave her the principality of Asturias, the hereditary title of the heir to the throne.[13] The papal nuncio endorsed the arrangement, which gave the event a spiritual veneer.

The ever-treacherous Juan Pacheco, for his part, emerged at the meeting—this time at the king's side. He had switched allegiances once more and was almost seamlessly back in the king's good graces, again his closest councilor and confidant. King Enrique appeared to have forgiven Pacheco all that he had done. The person who stood by Isabella at that perilous moment, both figuratively and literally, was Carrillo, the archbishop of Toledo, making himself the likely target of the mercurial king's wrath.

In the coming weeks, the king recognized Isabella publicly as his heir, even to the humiliating point of admitting that the child Juana was not his own. "I married and procreated in such a manner in these kingdoms that I do not have a legitimate successor to my lineage," he told town officials throughout the kingdom in a letter.[14]

Queen Juana, for her part, was further disgraced, having borne another child while living separately from Enrique during the civil war. While Alfonso and Enrique had been off on campaign against each other, Juana had been lodged for safekeeping with Bishop Fonseca and had become, embarrassingly enough, pregnant by the prelate's nephew. Even so, when she learned about the negotiations between the king and Isabella, she was furious. She had not given up hope that her daughter would become queen. In advanced pregnancy, she sought to depart from Bishop Fonseca's home by night: she arranged for her servants to help her out of an open window and into a basket to be lowered to the ground. The ropes broke, however, and the queen tumbled to the ground, suffering bruises and scrapes. A widely circulated story had it that the disheveled queen had then rushed to the house of her onetime suitor Beltrán de la Cueva seeking sanctuary—and found him disporting himself with a band of male friends. He was reported to have rudely sent her on her way, returning to tell his snickering friends that he had never much cared for her "skinny legs." Queen Juana was forced to travel on in search of friends and allies, finally reaching the home of the powerful Mendoza family. The Mendozas were traditionalists who supported royal prerogatives, and they sheltered the queen.

The king and Isabella, meanwhile, had departed from Toros de Guisando and rode off together to Cadalso, where Enrique had been staying, to dine together and mend fences. Isabella reunited with Enrique wholeheartedly, presenting to him a "very happy face" and full "obedience," a chronicler reported, and soon afterward, when Enrique left for the town of Ocaña, Isabella traveled with him.[15]

Isabella spent the next nine months in Ocaña, a municipality controlled by Pacheco located some distance from the cities she knew best— Segovia and Madrigal—and a place where she was a stranger. But this new location had its advantages: She was able to stay in the home of Gutierre de Cárdenas, the nephew of Gonzalo Chacón, her childhood mentor from Arévalo. This put her among friends. Both Cárdenas and Chacón had supported Alfonso, so her living arrangement also showed that Enrique trusted her once again and was allowing her to select her own entourage. Isabella's financial situation improved as well, as Enrique finally turned over to her the jurisdiction and revenues from Medina del Campo. Isabella began to prepare herself for her future role as queen, writing to nobles and presiding over events. She was now princess of Asturias.[16]

But within weeks, once the rebel army disbanded, Enrique's promises again proved fleeting and unreliable. It became clear that he did not intend to do all the things he had said he would. He didn't transfer the other properties he had pledged to Isabella, and at Juan Pacheco's urging, he began to undercut her position in many small ways. Archbishop Carrillo became worried enough for her that he established himself in a fortress seven miles from Ocaña, where he could keep an eye on the comings and goings of her court, and he bribed servants there to keep him apprised of developments.[17]

There were soon many reasons for concern. As time went on, Queen Juana's adamant insistence that little Juana was the king's own daughter convinced more people, and the king became ashamed that he had disinherited the child, whom he truly loved, and ashamed also of reports about his impotence and his "weakness of heart." Soon he came to blame Isabella for everything that had hurt him and damaged the realm. "And the king . . . not only lost the love he had borne for the princess, but also came to view her with hatred," an eyewitness recalled later.[18]

Then, contrary to the promises Enrique had made, he began pressing once again for a foreign marriage that would dispose of Isabella by sending her abroad. Her new strategic importance and position guaranteed that many potential husbands now came courting. Her good looks and social graces added to her allure as marriage material. She had reached full physical maturity by this point and many people found her lovely. A chronicler described her as being "of middle height, well made in her person and in the proportion of her limbs, very white and fair; her eyes between gray and blue, her glance graceful and modest, the features of her face well set, her face very beautiful and gay."[19]

Four suitors, at least, would receive serious consideration from Enrique in the year ahead.

One was another intriguing English candidate, a man about the same age as Isabella. He was Richard, the soon-to-be-famous younger brother of King Edward IV.[20] He was described as being of middle height, darker in hair and skin tone than his fair-haired and taller Plantagenet brothers, and he had the misfortune to have been born with one shoulder higher than the other. But he had a number of good qualities. He had won acclaim by leading part of the army in defense of Edward and had become the second most powerful man in England, after the king. At this point he was considered a suitable match for the princess. But Richard did not remain long in the marriage contention. He was the first candidate rejected, because Castile was already moving toward a break in diplomatic relations with England that would happen in July 1469, for an ephemeral combination of political, economic, and military reasons.[21]

That was a lucky turn of events for Isabella, for although Richard eventually became king of England as Richard III, he lost power and was killed in the brutal civil war that brought the usurping Tudor family to power in the person of King Henry VII. "Entirely loyal himself, he was unable to recognize treachery in others or to deal with it with sufficient ruthlessness when it became obvious," writes the historian V. B. Lamb. "His leniency towards traitors was both remarkable and fatal; it cost him his crown, his life, and his reputation."[22]

Richard's reputation was later to be sullied by none other than William Shakespeare, who curried favor with the Tudor dynasty by painting a grotesque portrait of Richard III as a dark and hunchbacked villain who had murdered his brother's two young sons. "It was quite remarkable how the views of men of letters changed almost overnight after Henry's usurpation," one historian said acidly.[23] Isabella had thus avoided association with that dismal page of history.

The second bachelor candidate was Charles of Valois, Duke of Berry, the younger brother of the French king, Louis XI. The historic animosity between Spain and France made that match less than likely. Isabella made discreet inquiries about him just the same: she sent a chaplain secretly to France to get a look at the duke. He reported back to her that Charles was "soft and effeminate, with spindly legs and weepy half-blind eyes."[24] It was an assessment unlikely to win a young woman's heart.

Pushing for that candidate nonetheless, Louis's envoys visited Isabella in Madrigal de las Altas Torres, where she was staying with her mother. Isabella was careful not to show her hand. "She merely indicated she would obey the laws of the realm, and do what was best for the honor, esteem and glory of Castile and the Castilian crown": that ambiguous answer allowed her to maintain her countenance while still appearing compliant with the men's negotiations over her future.[25] Soon Charles too was put on the sidelines.

That left two plausible prospects for Isabella's life partner, both men from the Iberian peninsula, and both closely related to her. The first was King Afonso V of Portugal, her mother's thirty-seven-year-old cousin. He was the candidate favored by the powerful Mendoza clan, by Juan Pacheco, and by the king, even though he was not a particularly attractive choice for a seventeen-year-old woman.

Even the way Afonso publicly presented himself would likely have made him unappealing to a teenage girl. Tapestries from the period commissioned by the Portuguese king depict him wearing overly elaborate and out-of-fashion, old-school armor rather than the newer styles preferred by younger warriors and their ladies.

Afonso was the marriage partner whom Enrique preferred for personal reasons. Enrique continued to be tormented by mixed feelings about little Juana. Her parentage was tarnished, but he clung to the idea that she was his daughter and that he should protect her prospects if only he could find a way to do so. Under this plan, Isabella would marry King Afonso, and Juana would marry his son, the heir to the Portuguese throne, Prince João. That would mean that Juana's children would most likely reign over both countries, and Isabella would be consigned to the sidelines of history, married fruitlessly to a man she considered "odious."[26]

But the cards were stacked in King Afonso's favor, as King Enrique sought to take revenge on his young sister by forcing her into a marriage she dreaded. Afonso, for his part, was most favorably impressed by the pretty princess he believed favored his suit, and in his mind, his amorous and dynastic ambitions merged. He began seeing the marriage as a transaction completed. On April 30, 1469, Enrique and Afonso reached a final agreement on the terms of the marriage. The nuptials were to take place two months after Afonso's arrival in Castile, and if Isabella did not agree to it, she and her supporters were to be declared outlaws. This agreement expressly gave Afonso the right to wage war on Castile if the marriage did not occur. The terms of the agreement allowed Afonso to begin calling himself Prince of Asturias, giving him the title traditionally borne by the heir to the Castilian throne. There was also a backup plan: if the marriage did not take place, Afonso would have the right to marry young Juana and, in alliance with Enrique, to wage war upon Isabella and her allies.[27]

But Isabella had another marital possibility as well, and this was the choice closest to her heart, the young man she had believed was her intended in her childhood. He was Ferdinand, an attractive sixteen-year-old, a second cousin who was destined to rule in neighboring Aragon and Catalonia. The death of his older brother Carlos had made Ferdinand an even more attractive match than he had been as a child. Moreover, he was already a crowned head of state: his father had recently named him king of Sicily, and marrying him would at once make Isabella a queen. Ferdinand was also the preferred choice of Alfonso Carrillo, archbishop of Toledo, who for years had been working stealthily and steadily to advance his cause, in tandem with Ferdinand's father, King Juan of Aragon.

King Enrique flatly forbade Isabella to marry Ferdinand.

Despite her brother's adamant opposition, the princess, who was soon to turn eighteen, believed that Ferdinand would make the best husband for her. Unbeknown to her brother, she was already secretly negotiating a marriage contract with Ferdinand.

"It has to be he and no other," Isabella privately told her allies.[28]

FIVE

MARRIAGE

I sabella had privately decided that the young and athletic Ferdinand of Aragon was her choice. Ferdinand felt the same way. But as in any good romance, their union would face formidable obstacles. Thus began a story that Spaniards, ever the romantics, would weave into legend.

The marriage negotiations between Isabella and Ferdinand had to be conducted clandestinely, through secret messages and undercover communications. Enrique might have broken many of his promises to Isabella, but she still had committed herself not to marry without his permission. So the young couple corresponded at first by letter. One early exchange already conveys the discreet flirtatiousness and clever manipulation of male psychology that would be Isabella's hallmark. Having received a letter from Ferdinand, she wrote back, in a letter that any seventeen-year-old boy would have found pleasing in its feminine submissiveness and its promise of sexual pleasure ahead: "Now you should inform me what you wish to be done, for that I must do. . . . From the hand that will do as you may order, La Princesa."[1]

A marriage compact between the pair was finalized on March 5, 1469. Ferdinand promised to respect the rights of the Castilian cities and acknowledged that Isabella would be the true monarch of that land. He also pledged to reside permanently in Castile.[2]

The couple had a religious hurdle to surmount as well. The Catholic

Council of Agde, a conference of bishops held in A.D. 506 to integrate Roman and Germanic laws as the Roman Empire collapsed, had prohibited marriages of first or second cousins, unless the church gave special permission. Ferdinand and Isabella were second cousins, sharing the same great-grandfather, King Juan I of Castile, so they needed a permit from the pope, known as a papal dispensation, for their marriage to be legal. Such paperwork could be costly and difficult to obtain, because the pope had to be convinced to approve the union. King Juan of Aragon solved the problem by obtaining the dispensation from the bishop of Segovia, Juan Arias, who based his decision on a marriage dispensation that King Juan told him he had gotten from the pope in the past.

Isabella's allies, including Archbishop Carrillo and Gonzalo Chacón, arranged for a relatively safe proxy wedding ceremony between her and Ferdinand, which soon occurred. She was supposed to receive a wedding gift of 40,000 gold florins.[3] The promised cash did not arrive in full, but part of it did, as well as a gift of jewels, which Isabella soon began to flaunt.

Then the teenagers decided to stage an in-person marriage. This would be far more difficult to arrange, as there were several obstacles. The powerful king of Portugal, who was self-confidently building a global empire for the maritime nation he had inherited, believed he was Isabella's destined bridegroom. King Enrique, sensing that something was in the wind, threatened Isabella with imprisonment in Madrid if she tried to leave the city. King Juan feared for his son's life if he were captured in Castile. Consequently, the initial rendezvous between Ferdinand, seventeen, and Isabella, now eighteen, was cloaked in secrecy and high drama. The teenagers and their allies concocted an elaborate subterfuge and bided their time.

First they waited until King Enrique left Ocaña, in central Castile, to deal with some pressing administrative problems in Andalusia. The king made the princess promise specifically not to marry while he was gone. But he was scarcely out of town when Princess Isabella announced her plan to visit her brother's tomb in Arévalo, which was also her mother's home and her own childhood residence. This was a logical excuse—her beloved brother had been dead for only a year and his memorial rites were overdue. She left Ocaña at night, on horseback, accompanied by two attendants.

The trip did not begin well. King Enrique had given Arévalo to his ally, the Count of Plasencia, and the count, fearing that Isabella intended to reclaim the city for her mother, stopped her at the gate and blocked her from entering. Isabella had to be content with honoring Alfonso's body in the Franciscan convent where he was buried. She then traveled to see her mother, who had been moved to Madrigal de las Altas Torres.

In these few weeks, Isabella was more alone than she had ever been. She was putting herself directly and openly at odds with her brother the king, and with the Portuguese king as well, who was threatening to bring war on her head if necessary to stop her from marrying another man. Her mother was no help; her mental health problems made her dependent on Isabella rather than a source of strength. Isabella's beloved grandmother had died by this time, and now faint-hearted friends dropped away as well. Even some of Isabella's closest friends turned against her. Juan Pacheco had convinced Beatriz de Bobadilla and Mencía de la Torre, Isabella's ladies-in-waiting, that a marriage to Ferdinand would be a bad idea and to block it. The women participated in a plan to track Isabella and watch her whereabouts.

In Madrigal, Isabella learned how closely she was being watched. King Enrique knew where she was staying, and at his suggestion the French envoys went there to present their proposed betrothal of Isabella with the French king's brother, the Duke of Berry. When they arrived, she temporized with them coolly, despite the fact that she was already secretly married by proxy to Ferdinand at the time. She handled it so glibly that the arrogant French diplomats left thinking they had successfully wooed the princess and that she would soon become the duke's bride. They rushed off to France with the good tidings.

But King Enrique, aware that Isabella had disobeyed him by leaving Ocaña, grew suspicious and warned officials in Madrigal that they would be punished if she succeeded in marrying Ferdinand. The princess fled with a few companions to a nearby town, then to a convent, and then to Ávila, where frantic watchmen waved her party away from the city's high medieval walls—it had been struck once again with plague. After a journey that lasted almost a full day, the princess finally staggered into the city of Valladolid, where town officials promised to give her haven. The archbishop of Toledo's niece, María, wife of a nobleman named Juan de Vivero, welcomed the princess to her home near the city's central square. Isabella arrived on the night of August 30, 1469.

Meanwhile, Ferdinand was facing a harrowing journey as well. Two envoys from Isabella—Gonzalo Chacón's nephew, Gutierre de Cárdenas, and the courtier Alonso de Palencia—were sent to Aragon to escort him to Castile. They learned that they would face almost universal opposition on the return journey and that the castles along the frontier were on the watch for the young lovers. Cárdenas thought Ferdinand would not come; Palencia thought he would because when he had gone to collect the jewels that were the wedding gift, Ferdinand had been eager to ride to Isabella's rescue and free her from her overbearing older brother.[4]

Palencia and Cárdenas arrived in Zaragoza and met the young prince amid great secrecy in a cell of a Franciscan monastery.[5] They found him eager to rush to Isabella's side.

But Ferdinand had to find a way to sneak across the heavily guarded border from Aragon into Castile without attracting attention. The trip was more than 225 miles, over a steep mountain range. Ferdinand decided to travel by night, incognito, with only five close friends as his guard. This was a brave move: conditions in both Castile and Aragon were so perilous that most people traveled in large groups for self-defense.

The young prince, attractive, slim, and strong, donned ragged clothes and disguised himself as a mule driver, even acting as servant to his companions at an inn, to keep his identity a secret. They moved smoothly and surreptitiously, usually traveling by night to avoid Enrique's spies. They took refuge on one occasion in a fortress near El Burgo de Osma, at about the halfway point. They arrived earlier than expected and startled a night sentry who was not expecting them. The sentinel raised an alarm, shouting, and threw a large rock down at the strangers attempting to enter the castle's gates, narrowly missing the prince. But Ferdinand was eventually recognized and welcomed by nobles in the castle who supported his cause, and he traveled the rest of the way to Valladolid, where Isabella was waiting, with a two-hundred-man military escort.

Princess Isabella wrote her brother on October 12, 1469, telling him of her plans and asking him to accept her decision. She had informed him but not gained his consent. Now the die was cast.

* * *

Finally, on the evening of October 14, Isabella and Ferdinand met at midnight at the home of Juan de Vivero, the Castilian nobleman who was related to the archbishop of Toledo, who was helping orchestrate the match. Ferdinand and his entourage arrived by horseback at the fortified palace, located in the heart of Valladolid, and was brought inside by the back entrance. As he entered the room, Gutierre de Cárdenas excitedly shouted, *"Ese es, ese es,"* exuberantly pointing him out to Isabella.

But they had spotted each other right away. When they saw each other for the first time, they both gazed in admiration. Some nobles had insisted Isabella require Ferdinand to kiss her hand as a sign of obeisance; she said it was not necessary, that they were equals, and that he was perhaps even her superior as a reigning king.

Isabella saw before her a well-made young man, slightly shorter than she, with his hair cut in the fashionable long and underturned style that was very much the rage in Europe. His travel clothes had been set aside, and he arrived "richly dressed," for Ferdinand always made an elegant appearance.[6] While not exactly handsome, he was fit and athletic, darker-complexioned than Isabella and swarthy in a rakish way. He appeared to her as a fine specimen of manhood.

Young Ferdinand "was a man of middle height, well proportioned in his limbs, his features well-composed, his eyes merry, his hair dark and straight, and of good complexion," wrote the chronicler Hernando del Pulgar.[7] "He rode very well; he jousted with ease. . . . He was a keen sportsman and a man of good endeavor and much activity at war. . . . He had a singular grace, to wit, that all who spoke to him at once loved him and wished to serve him, for he had a friendly intercourse."

The youth had a passionate nature, something that no doubt quickly communicated itself to the pretty young princess. They liked each other so well and so instantaneously that they might have begun to embrace almost immediately, Palencia recalled, noting that the "amorous impulses" of the two were evident, restrained only by the presence of the fifty-nine-year-old archbishop of Toledo, who chaperoned the meeting, which lasted two hours.

They exchanged formal promises to marry, which were recorded as a legal matter by a notary. The archbishop read aloud the marriage agreement as well as the papal dispensation because of close blood kinship of the bride and groom. With the legal formalities out of the way, Archbishop Carrillo thought it best that they marry as soon as possible in case Enrique unexpectedly returned from Andalusia.

Five days later, on October 19, 1469, Isabella and Ferdinand were formally wed, in the great hall, or *sala rica,* of the Vivero home. The marriage ceremony was followed by a nuptial mass. The couple were so poor that they were compelled to borrow to meet the wedding expenses.[8] The official witnesses were the Admiral and María de Acuña, Ferdinand's grandfather and aunt; a large crowd of local dignitaries were present as well.

The marriage was consummated that night, to the satisfaction of all parties. Witnesses entered the bridal chamber playing trumpets, flutes, and kettledrums, and the bloodstained bedsheet was displayed to the expectant crowd outside.[9] Seven days of great celebrations followed in Valladolid; the townspeople cheered the couple's passage through the streets.

This first meeting and their nuptials became the stuff of legend. Isabella had fallen deeply in love with the gallant young prince; he proved an ardent suitor. Her brother's opposition provided ample reason for concern, but surely he would soon see the appropriateness of the match and bless their union.

Even one possible cause of trouble might also have been, properly considered, a blessing in disguise. Ferdinand was intelligent, charming, and passionate, yes, but even at his young age he came into her world encumbered with two illegitimate children. They would need to be provided for in some way. Given the fertility problems in Isabel's family, however, Ferdinand's proven virility probably seemed an asset.

Only one truly disquieting note hung in the air. It would probably have escaped the attention of an enamored young woman, but it was no doubt on the minds of many of the wedding guests. Ferdinand was a prestigious marriage partner because he was the heir to a rich and important set of kingdoms. He was already king of Sicily and would one day inherit Aragon, Valencia, and Catalonia, with its crown jewel being the splendid city of Barcelona. But he had become the heir only as a result of the sudden, unexpected deaths of his older brother and sister. Just what, exactly, had happened to Carlos and Blanca?

SIX

FERDINAND AND
HIS FAMILY

From nearby Aragon, King Juan, Ferdinand's seventy-one-year-old father, watched avidly as events unfolded in Valladolid. This successful marriage represented the culmination of his lifelong plan to gain control of neighboring Castile, which he had enviously coveted ever since his boyhood years.

King Juan was sending his beloved son Ferdinand off to gamble his life—for the family's enemies would willingly have killed the young man—for the goal his father had sought for decades, mastery of Castile. So Juan kept a close eye on news from Valladolid, using a network of correspondents and spies to watch and report back everything that happened.

The fact that King Juan could see anything at all was testament to his steely resolve to overcome obstacles in his path. As he entered his sixties, he had developed cataracts in both eyes and had become blind, in an era without antibiotics, anesthesia, or modern surgical skills. In the summer of 1466, when he was sixty-eight, he had decided to put himself into the hands of a skilled Jewish physician trained in the ancient Hindu and Roman techniques of removing cataracts by inserting a sharp, red-hot needle into the eyeball. Juan's family tried to dissuade him from the operation, warning that the surgery was too dangerous, particularly for a man of his age. Even the doctor hesitated. But Juan had been willing to jeopardize his health in order to regain his sight, and the operation was a complete success. It was a hallmark of a life of tenacious determination and of a willingness to risk everything for what he wanted.

King Juan had been born to a Castilian royal family that was adept at making the best of opportunities. His father had been the uncle of King Juan II, Isabella's father, and became king of the combined neighboring kingdoms of Aragon, Valencia, and Catalonia through a political deal. Juan, in turn, had been the third of seven children, but he, too, wanted to be a king. At age twenty-one, in 1419, he married a thirty-two-year-old childless widow who was queen of the Kingdom of Navarre, and through this marriage, he became king of Navarre. But he was only the king-consort, not the real monarch, and he spent most of his time in Aragon. Together they had three children, Carlos, the heir to the throne of Navarre, and two daughters, Blanca and Eleanor. But instead of focusing on what he had—his growing family and the administration of Navarre—Juan tended to obsess about what he did not have.

When the queen of Navarre died in 1441 at age fifty-four, King Juan kept the title of king, though by right it belonged to his son Carlos, who was twenty. Then King Juan remarried, this time to a nineteen-year-old Castilian noblewoman named Juana Enríquez, and together they had two more children, Ferdinand and Juana. This second family was twenty years younger than the first, and from early on, King Juan showed his preference for them in countless ways. He was especially close to his son Ferdinand, who was to become Princess Isabella's husband, with whom he always shared a natural affinity.

Juan of Aragon's obsession with Castile had started when he was very young because two generations of his family had dreamed of ruling the kingdom. Juan's father—another Ferdinand—was a younger son of the Spanish royal family. He got a taste for power while serving as regent for Isabella's father, King Juan II of Castile, who had inherited the throne of Castile and León at age six, when he was too young to rule. Serving merely as regent was a bitter pill for Ferdinand, and he longed to rule in his own right, so when the king of the adjacent Kingdom of Aragon died without an heir, and his subjects offered Ferdinand the opportunity to become their ruler, he eagerly accepted and moved his family from Castile to Aragon. He became Ferdinand I of Aragon. But Aragon was hardly the paradise he had hoped. It was an unwieldy amalgam of three separate realms—Aragon, Catalonia, and Valencia—and had a daunting set of problems, making it difficult and stressful to govern.

Ferdinand I served only briefly as king of Aragon before he died, leaving the kingdom to his son Alfonso, Juan's oldest brother, who used it as a base to conquer Naples, a large and prosperous city on the shores of the Italian peninsula. Captivated by the cultural and intellectual delights of Italy, its food and its congenial climate, King Alfonso found one excuse after another to delay his return home, leaving his wife and his younger brothers, including Juan, to administer Aragon in his name. For these brothers, as it had been for their father Ferdinand, the pleasure of regency proved decidedly second rate, given the grinding governmental problems of the kingdom.

Juan and his brothers in Aragon began to reminisce about the fine life they had left behind in Castile and began conspiring how best they could retake power there. They cast covetous eyes on the Castilian kingdom of Isabella's father, who by now had grown to adulthood, and imagined themselves replacing him. King Juan's poor management of Castile convinced them that they could do better, given the chance.

Consequently, throughout his entire life, Isabella's father had had to watch over his shoulder for incursions by these men, his cousins. This was one reason he had come to rely so thoroughly on Álvaro de Luna, because Álvaro had effectively defended his interests. Matters had come to a violent head in 1445, six years before Isabella's birth, when the Aragonese cousins invaded Castile and tried to seize control. Álvaro de Luna had bravely defended Castile and defeated them. One of Juan's brothers died of wounds he suffered in the battle, important allies were taken prisoner, and Juan retreated alone to Aragon, returning to his life as regent and brooding darkly over the public humiliation.

For the next two decades, as Isabella grew to adulthood, Juan had been plotting his revenge. He intended to obtain through duplicity what he had been unable to seize by force. Now his plan was to reclaim Castile through his descendants, by marrying his favorite son to Isabella.

* * *

Juan's first attempt at dynastic control had involved marrying his daughter Blanca to Enrique, back in 1440. But Blanca's failure to produce children had dashed that dream.

Moreover, King Enrique's unhappy experience with King Juan of Aragon as a father-in-law had made him wary of any further entanglements with him. Enrique's thirteen-year marriage to Blanca had not been consummated, and in all likelihood, he suffered continuing scorn from Blanca's father. It was King Juan of Aragon who had stalked the halls outside Enrique's first bridal chamber on his nuptial night thirty years earlier, when he had been unable to perform.

Now Ferdinand's marriage to Isabella gave King Juan a second chance at achieving his goal. Getting control of the princess who was heiress to the throne would be another path to controlling Castile, now finally within reach. This was one reason Enrique had so strenuously opposed the marriage between Isabella and Juan's son Ferdinand. Even Isabella's loyal friend Beatriz de Bobadilla had sought to impede the match by reporting on Isabella's whereabouts, possibly motivated by concern that Isabella could be jumping from the frying pan into the fire.

In other words, through her marriage Isabella had expanded her family and asserted her independence from her brother, but in the process she had taken on some risk to herself. Her new father-in-law was a vicious, vengeful, and selfish man who would do anything to attain control of her lands—and whose nickname in Aragon was "Juan the Faithless."

Juan's faithless qualities were evident even in his family dynamics. He had a strained relationship with his oldest son, Carlos, who was a very different type of man from his father. Carlos was courteous, cultivated, and intellectual, a Renaissance prototype, which made him enormously popular in an era of changing tastes, while his father Juan seemed much more a product of the Middle Ages, a fearless warrior who preferred life in the saddle to reading a poem or attending a play. Carlos's preferences made him enormously popular in Aragon and in his uncle Alfonso's Italian dominions. In fact, Carlos had traveled to Naples to live with Alfonso, where the two men shared a gentlemanly passion for art, literature, poetry, and music, irritating Juan to his very core. "Whereas Juan had little taste or time for the arts in any form, Carlos's avowed interest in them struck a welcome chord with his cultured uncle," writes the historian Alan Ryder.[1]

King Juan had found a kindred spirit in his second wife, Juana Enríquez, whom he married in 1447, three years after his first wife died, and seven years after Enrique and Blanca were married. Juana Enríquez shared his vision for reclaiming Castile, and in the words of an Aragonese historian, her "intrepid spirit and unprincipled ambition" matched his own.[2] Their first child together, Ferdinand, was born in 1452, and their daughter, Juana, a few years later.

Jealousy was a hallmark of this new family, and Queen Juana looked upon Carlos with the malevolent resentment of a stepmother who saw the children of a first marriage receiving the advantages of placement and position. She wanted the kingship of Navarre for her own son, not for the child of Juan's first wife. King Juan also came to resent his popular eldest son, who seemed to win friends with amazing ease, and he began to plot ways to advance Ferdinand, whom he preferred. The family was a smoldering cauldron of hurt feelings and insults, with the older children recognizing that they had been displaced in their father's heart by the new family.

King Juan's daughter Blanca, from his first family, complained plaintively of her father's treatment of her after Enrique set her aside for nonconsummation of the marriage. Instead of helping the unfortunate princess mend her wounded spirit when she came home, Juan saw her as an embarrassing failure, although she had done nothing wrong. In a mournful document issued near her death, Blanca wrote that the "aforesaid King, Don Juan had forgotten the love and paternal affection" he should have had for his children from the first marriage.[3]

Matters in Aragon came to a head in 1458, when King Alfonso, still enjoying life in Italy, finally died. His brother Juan was his heir and assumed the rule of his dominions in Iberia and Sicily, while Alfonso's children retained control of Naples. Juan should have publicly named his oldest son Carlos the next heir, both of Aragon and Navarre, but he declined to do so.

Meanwhile the family's Aragonese subjects had become increasingly restive over all the foreign adventuring and interfamily squabbling, which was taking place amid a disturbing economic decline. Barcelona, the hub of the principality of Catalonia, its largest city and historically its most prosperous, had seen its foreign trade decline, and Catalans had come to believe they were the victims of neglectful, shortsighted, and absentee administration. The city's two hundred richest families, who lived primarily on their investments, had seen their incomes erode over the last century, and they had been waiting eagerly for Carlos to assume control of the realm. Instead they faced the dawning realization that King Juan had no intention of transferring leadership to Carlos.

* * *

This recognition raised real concerns for the citizens. At the beginning of the fifteenth century, when the Trastámara family moved to their new kingdom, Catalonia had been prosperous and solid, carrying on a brisk trade in cloth, coral, spices, silks, and cottons. But King Alfonso had sailed off for Italy, claiming Naples and Sicily and shifting his interests to that peninsula. No one seemed to be looking out for Aragon's best interests anymore.

By the time of Ferdinand's birth in 1452, the Aragonese, particularly the Catalans, felt their nation was disintegrating. "This is Catalonia, the once fortunate, glorious and most faithful nation which in the past was feared by land and sea," the despairing bishop of Elna, Joan Margarit, told legislators in Barcelona in 1454. "Now it is seen totally ruined and lost through the absence of its glorious prince and lord, the lord king. Behold it bereft of all strength, honor and ecclesiastical jurisdiction; powerful barons and knights are ruined; cities and towns, corrupting the common weal, are torn apart; knights' steeds have become mules; widows, orphans and children seek vainly for consolation; corsairs and pirates plunder the ports and roam through all the seas."[4]

The principality also suffered under a particularly cruel set of government policies, known as the *mal usos,* that made life miserable for the bulk of the population. It was an enforced serfdom that dominated economic life in Aragon, Catalonia, and Valencia. This system had been common elsewhere in Europe but not in Castile, where peasants were not serfs. There, they were free to move around, marry whom they chose, and pursue the occupation they preferred, although most in reality had very limited options, given the overwhelming and disproportionate power of the nobility, who controlled 97 percent of the realm's wealth.

In Catalonia, however, conditions for peasants were far bleaker, having deteriorated over about five centuries. In the ninth and tenth centuries, Catalonia had been settled by free peasants who established their own small farms, dispersed widely over the countryside. Women at that time had inherited equally with men. Married women had maintained control of the property they brought into a marriage and possessed a right to 10 percent of their husband's holdings at his death, which gave most women some financial security in old age.[5]

But as Europe came under assault from invaders, many castles were built so that residents could better defend themselves. By the late eleventh century, there were more than eight hundred castles in Catalonia, many spaced only three to five miles apart. Residents clustered their homes in the shadows of these fortifications for protection, or around churches, because they believed that people who lived within thirty paces of a church would be immune to violence, enjoying the same sanctuary as within the religious edifice itself. This arrangement made the peasants increasingly dependent on their protectors, either the secular leaders or the church elders. These local chieftains came in turn to see themselves as holding rights over the residents who became their subjects.

Aristocratic power grew, and the position of women deteriorated. The dowry, a payment made by a bride's family to the groom's family, grew in importance, which had the effect of making female children less economically valuable than males. Then it became increasingly common for inheritance systems to favor one child over the others, which was good for maintaining a strong family estate but bad for the family's younger children.

Consequently, ever fewer people held ever greater power over others. Peasants were compelled to place themselves under the power of a lay or ecclesiastical lord, acknowledging they were subject to his authority. Peasants were commonly required to live on their land. Property transactions included the right to control not just the real estate but also the lives of the people living on the land. To move away, peasants had to pay money to purchase their freedom, called redemption. Some peasants were required to name the person, specifically which of their children, would succeed them as serf on the land. They were fined if their wives committed adultery or if a building on their property burned down.

Disease had a more disastrous impact in Aragon than elsewhere in Europe, according to Aragonese historians. In the mid-1300s, when the Black Death that swept through Europe killed off at least 25 percent of the population, Catalonia, a trans-Mediterranean shipping center that was a hub of world trade, was even harder hit, losing up to 50 percent of its population in the decades following the first outbreak.[6] But while the reduction in the labor force gave workers increased power in many places, it had the opposite effect in Aragon because it came at a time when the underlying economy was crumbling as well. The aristocrats responded to losses of income with increasingly oppressive treatment of the surviving peasants.

Many farms were depopulated, because of either death or desertion by the peasants who lived there, and nobles began to pursue serfs who had abandoned the fields. Peasants who wanted to leave had to pay increasingly high prices for their freedom. Taxes were also raised on women who wanted to marry men from other lords' territories. Some lords refused to accept these payments and thus barred people from leaving. In addition, new laws made it illegal for peasants to bring law-suits against their lords if they disagreed with the oppressive conditions. They were required to comply with the lords' demands whether they felt they were fair or not.

In other words, the nobles in Catalonia responded to the epidemic of plague by finding new ways to make money off the declining number of serfs. In 1402 Queen María of Aragon had written to Pope Benedict XIII of the desperation among the peasantry, calling the situation "pestifer-ous" and noting that the church itself was the largest holder of peasants.[7] But conditions only worsened.

The system grew increasingly harsh and exploitative, developing the name *mal usos* or "bad customs." According to a report prepared in 1462, nursing mothers in Aragon were commonly required to serve as wet nurses for their lords' children, which had the effect of leaving less milk for their own offspring. The peasants reported that lords were in the habit of requiring newly married women to lie with them the first night of their marriage, a charge that the lords said was untrue, but that they agreed to outlaw.[8]

The Aragonese branch of the Trastámara family, Kings Ferdinand, Alfonso, and Juan, recognized the problems inherent in the system, but they were reluctant to take measures to solve the problems. On the contrary, they took advantage of the situation to blackmail both lords and serfs into payoffs that supported their foreign adventures. "Alfonso also frequently promised to come back from southern Italy to attend to matters in his increasingly desperate capital," writes the historian Alan Ryder, "but from the time of his expedition to Sicily in 1435 until his death 23 years later he never returned, ruling Catalonia in absentia and in an increasingly tenuous fashion."[9]

The Trastámara rulers in Aragon instead shifted back and forth on this issue. They banned the *mal usos* in 1455 but repealed the ban a year later to win favor with the nobles. The policy changed again in 1458. Simi-larly, in December 1461, Queen Juana, King Juan's second wife, ordered the nobles to cease their oppression of the peasants, but the next month she reversed herself. She praised the nobles for their efforts to restrain the peasants even as she took advantage of her peasant support to rally an army to defend herself against nobles who were growing increasingly disgusted by their vacillating ruling family.[10] Soon the Trastámara family had to deal with both restive peasants and restive nobles.

* * *

As King Juan attempted to cope with these issues, his popular and amiable son Carlos was always a thorn in his side. In October 1459, after his brother Alfonso died in Italy, Juan attempted to have himself and his wife crowned rulers of Aragon in the capital city of Zaragoza, but the Catalans protested that it could not occur unless Carlos, the Prince of Viana, was present. The prince came back to Barcelona from Italy in 1460.

That was the time Prince Carlos decided to try to strengthen his claim to the crown of Aragon by marrying Princess Isabella of Castile. He was enthusiastic about the match, referring to Isabella as a *"muy excelente princesa."*[11] King Enrique of Castile had for a while energetically promoted the marriage of Isabella and Carlos, partially to avenge himself on his former father-in-law King Juan, who had been hoping that Isabella would marry his favored son Ferdinand.

But King Juan's wife became hysterical at the news of this prospective match, which would thwart her plans for her son Ferdinand. The Aragonese chronicler Jerónimo Zurita said the queen was reported to have been "crying and cursing."[12] King Juan decided to steer Carlos toward a marriage with the Portuguese princess Catalina instead, and Carlos allowed himself to be lured back to his father's side with what a historian subsequently called "specious assurances of paternal goodwill."[13] Instead Juan seized Carlos and held him as his prisoner. This act dismayed the Catalans, who considered Carlos the rightful heir and believed King Juan was upending the law. "Sympathy for Carlos, a seemingly penitent son harshly used by a vengeful father," was "universal."[14]

The crisis came to a head on February 6, 1461, in Lleida, in Catalonia. Catalan emissaries insisted that King Juan release Carlos and acknowledge him as his heir. Juan refused to allow them even to present their case, saying he was too busy. He tried to leave the town but found the gates closed against him.

Juan then faced the emissaries and coldly insisted that Ferdinand would be his heir. "Ambassadors, you shall have no prince other than my son, don Ferdinand," he said, in a statement that was followed by a fanfare of trumpets and a listing of Ferdinand's titles, among them Prince of Aragon. The Catalans angrily responded in shouts: "Don Carlos, by the grace of God!"[15]

King Juan was eventually forced to accept Carlos as his heir, but he accepted this bitter pill with ill-concealed rage: "Publicly Juan ordered celebrations and illuminations in Zaragoza to make the accord; privately he nursed a yet deeper hatred of Carlos and the Catalans who had brought him to this humiliating pass. Age had not dimmed his fiery energy nor his thirst for revenge against those who had thwarted him."[16]

The Catalans almost certainly thought Juan, a blind and ailing sixty-three-year-old, would die soon, and that by maintaining their opposition, they could eventually outwait him. But Juan surprised them, by tenaciously hanging on to life and undergoing surgery to restore his eyesight.

Instead it was Carlos who died, in Barcelona on September 23, 1461, after a brief illness. Many people believed he had been poisoned, possibly by his stepmother Queen Juana, who had openly lobbied for her son Ferdinand's elevation as king. The circumstances were not entirely clear. Carlos had suffered a bout of pneumonia; the historian Alan Ryder blames Carlos's death on "pulmonary infection aggravated by stress."

But the timing certainly looked bad. Even if Juan had not ordered his son's murder, Carlos's death certainly seemed a fortunate development for him, as it paved the way for his and his wife's favored child, nine-year-old Ferdinand, to become his rightful heir.

But Ferdinand's path to the throne was still not easy. The Catalan public, convulsed with grief over Carlos's death, was slow to embrace the new heir. Instead, amid huge public demonstrations of sorrow in Barcelona, some began calling the recently deceased Carlos a saint and venerating his remains. Contact with his coffin was said to cure tumors, heal skin diseases, and restore sight to the blind. Vast crowds gathered to witness these miraculous recoveries, and word spread widely that "the lord primogenit" continued to do great deeds through the "divine power" contained in his remains.[17]

King Juan tried to dispel these stories, saying that poor people were being bribed to report miraculous cures, but it was hard for him to maintain moral authority when he simultaneously announced that Ferdinand's mother Juana, the woman believed to be the poisoner of Carlos, would now act as regent for Ferdinand as the heir apparent because of the boy's youth. Carlos's death in some ways served to heighten tensions in Aragon rather than diminish them.

The young Ferdinand could therefore travel the kingdom only when

accompanied by a large entourage to ensure his safety from his own subjects. His mother traveled to Barcelona but departed abruptly, fearful of
attack. After Ferdinand and his mother left, their opponents claimed
that the queen had been involved in a plot to kill people who "revered
blessed Saint Carlos"; the rebel groups publicly executed several officials
who they claimed had participated in the queen's scheme.

With the population showing so little respect for the ruling family,
confrontations between nobles and bands of armed peasants broke out
across the countryside, leading to violence. To gain support for suppress-
ing his rebellious subjects, Juan embarked on a serpentine set of secret
treaties and arrangements that would have long-lasting and complicated
consequences.

The next person to fall victim to these intrigues was his eldest daughter Blanca, who was back home after the end of her marriage to Enrique.
She had loved and supported her brother Carlos, and now, as a result
of Carlos's death, she was the heir to the Navarrese throne, although
unmarried women were not allowed to govern alone in that kingdom.
But that made her an obstacle in King Juan's path. Juan conveyed his
unfortunate daughter into the custody of the Countess of Foix, Blanca's
younger sister. Blanca was "carried off by force into France [and] died in
captivity," widely believed to have been killed by poison.[18]

Blanca's death was another extremely fortunate event for King Juan
and his second family. But before she died, Blanca had reasserted her
own claim to Navarre and bequeathed her claim to the kingdom to her
former husband, King Enrique of Castile. In other words, she had preferred that her former husband, who had rejected her in such a humiliating fashion, inherit her realm rather than her duplicitous father and
younger half brother.

Sending his daughter to France was only the first step in King Juan's
new scheme. He entered into a secret treaty with King Louis XI of France
to get his help in putting down his rebellious subjects. Louis was to send
an army to aid Juan in defeating the rebellion in Catalonia. In exchange,
Juan promised to permit French garrisons to occupy the Aragonese castles of Perpignan and Collioure. By this extraordinary action, King Juan
ceded land to Aragon's ancestral enemy, France. "With this reckless, ill-
judged agreement," Ryder writes, "which was to haunt the rest of his life,
Juan had thrown away any remaining hope of a peaceful solution to the
troubles of Catalonia."[19]

King Juan was determined to bring his subjects to heel at any cost. He launched a raid on Lleida and destroyed the harvest, threatening the town with starvation. Astonished and horrified by the ferocity with which their king undertook to subdue them, the Catalans became even more determined to unseat Juan and his family. Catalonian officials told Juana that they were stripping her of her position as queen and asked her to leave, taking Ferdinand with her if she chose. The queen decided to fight. She took up her position in the fortress at Girona and, with the king's encouragement, prepared for war. The assault on the fortress began on June 6, 1463. On June 26 a large party of soldiers briefly broke through the walls, panicking the defenders. Juana reportedly ran through the streets looking for her son; when she found the twelve-year-old playing outside the cathedral, she fell into an exhausted faint. The attackers finally faded away, demoralized and out of money, by July 22, but it had been a long seven weeks for the besieged mother and son. King Juan's hard line had succeeded.

Hatred and contempt for King Juan grew among his subjects, however. Word of Juan's secret treaty with France disgusted the Catalans, who considered the French their longtime mortal enemy, and they viewed Juan as a traitor for opening the doors of the kingdom to them. As one historian writes, "The triumphant royalist cause was now identified with foreign oppression and atrocity."[20]

To fight Juan, the Catalans needed a powerful ally, and much as Juan had turned to the French, the Catalan nobles now turned to Castile and its king Enrique, who had been a friend to Carlos. They stripped the right to succession from Ferdinand and offered it instead to Enrique, whose first impulse was not to seize the opportunity but to hesitate. Before he accepted their offer, he said, he needed to seek advice from his council, which caused a delay of some weeks; but in the meantime, he took under his control a few scattered towns in King Juan's kingdoms. This development, of course, infuriated King Juan. Instead of King Juan seizing Castile from a weak ruler, that weak ruler was now claiming soil that Juan considered his own. Juan now faced the prospect of war not just within his own kingdom but also against the Castilians.

Just as risk of hostilities between Castile and Aragon was opening, the French king Louis cunningly offered to arbitrate between the two nations. He took a bribe from King Juan for handling the task, and he gave a bribe to Juan Pacheco for enabling it to happen. King Enrique arrived at the meeting place to discuss the judgment. Typically awkward and insecure, Enrique showed up in splendid array, surrounded by a three-hundred-member Moorish bodyguard, but King Louis induced him to cross the River Bidassoa to reach the parley location. Compelling Enrique to ford the river in his party clothes put him on the defensive, making him appear both bedraggled and overdressed. Then Louis, ostentatiously underdressed, delivered the coup de grâce: he announced that Enrique should yield Catalonia to Juan and also disgorge territories that the Castilians had seized in Navarre, Valencia, and Aragon. Catalonia was told it had to submit to this judgment, though the Catalans had not been party to the deliberations.

The Castilians and Catalans were aghast. King Enrique, humbled once again, slunk away, with the dawning realization that he had been played for a fool by his best friend, Juan Pacheco, and by his former father-in-law, King Juan of Aragon. This was another reason King Enrique opposed Isabella's marriage to Ferdinand.

The Catalans, meanwhile, saw in this still another reason to despise their sovereign, King Juan of Aragon, who had betrayed their interests once again. In June 1463 the Catalan council made it a crime punishable by death to utter even a good word about him.

But King Juan's ambitions for himself and his son remained undimmed. Ferdinand was named heir to the throne of Aragon and Sicily on September 21, 1464. Even his opponents recognized that he was strong, sturdy, and competent, and youth always stirs optimism, so there was a prospect that his ascension would improve conditions in Aragon.

By July 1465, when Princess Isabella was fourteen and Ferdinand was thirteen, King Juan was back to his old trick of trying to destabilize Castile, even as he struggled to maintain his own rickety footing on the throne of Aragon. This time he lent his support to the nobles led by Carrillo who were rebelling against Enrique, playing a role in forcing Enrique to name his younger brother Alfonso his heir, rubbing salt in the wound for the Castilian king once again. King Juan remained, according to the historian Henry John Chaytor, "more anxious to stir up intrigues in Castile with the hope of interfering in her politics to his own advantage than to secure the peace and prosperity of his own dominions."[21]

But Prince Alfonso's untimely death meant that political conditions in Castile had changed once again, and King Juan began pressing anew for a marriage between Isabella and his son Ferdinand. He reached out to his old friend Alfonso Carrillo, the archbishop of Toledo, and together Carrillo and King Juan again worked the levers of power to marry the young Castilian princess, Isabella, and the young Aragonese prince, Ferdinand.

It was this Ferdinand, the product of this process and the son of this father, who now stood beside Isabella on her wedding day. Isabella had just married King Juan's favorite child. Behind his smiling eyes and easy laughter, young Ferdinand was his father's son.

SEVEN

THE NEWLYWEDS

Their family histories were tangled, but one aspect of the young couple's early life together was simple and self-evident: their sexual chemistry. They had seen each other for the first time on October 14, 1469, and married within the week; Isabella was pregnant within three months. King Enrique's infertility had been a source of shame and worry for the nation, but Isabella had proven her own fruitfulness in a remarkably short time. Observers who had helped to bring about the alliance noted with satisfaction that the relationship appeared to be warm and passionate.

Both were strong and physically fit, energetic and decisive. Isabella was the more intellectual of the two, enjoying the company of scholars and people of a romantic temperament; Ferdinand was a man of action with great personal charm. Isabella was eager to have a child, and Ferdinand was happy to do his part to make it happen.

In addition to their physical bond, the two teenagers had much else in common. They were both Spaniards, inculcated from birth with the same beliefs about their nation's history, destiny, and challenges. When Ferdinand first stepped into the Great Hall in the Alcázar of Segovia and gazed upward at the frieze of statues showing the long line of Spanish Christian monarchs, he was looking at his own ancestors as well as Isabella's.

As they established themselves as a couple, Isabella and Ferdinand observed the symbolic practices that were customary in the late Middle Ages. For example, royal couples adopted a symbol or drawing of some kind to represent their union and make the nuptials common knowledge at a time when many people were illiterate. Isabella's symbol was the *flecha,* or arrow, for the *F* of Ferdinand; Ferdinand's symbol was the *yugo,* or yoke, for the *Y* of Ysabel, the common spelling of her name in Castile at the time. These two symbols were artistically interwoven and bound with a chain to link them together, a pictorial manifestation of their marriage. This device would eventually appear on government buildings and churches all across Spain.

This same reverence for ritual was reflected in the couple's religious observances, although Isabella was the more devout of the two. Both were Catholics who had grown up surrounded by clerics. Both now employed confessors and regularly consulted with priests to examine the state of their souls.

Ferdinand was easily popular with many people. He was a gifted horseman and a good jouster and falconer, and he excelled at ball games like pelota. He liked playing chess and cards and gambling. He was not much of a reader. Isabella had interests in embroidery and sewing that allowed them to pursue their interests in parallel, both enjoying themselves while chatting and laughing, often surrounded by courtiers eager to curry their favor. Entertaining and witty banter in the court added to the amusement by day; at night they enjoyed music and dancing.

Ferdinand and Isabella had psychological and emotional similarities as well. They had both been raised in the shadow of older siblings who were expected to rule. Both had grown up surrounded by the war and civil unrest that follows a leadership vacuum, making them feel exposed and vulnerable to danger, even as children. Both were determined to bring to the job of governing the kind of determination that had previously been lacking.

And they both were the product of unconventional childhoods. Isabella had never known her father and tried to launch married life out of her imagination as she thought it should be. Trained by nuns to spin, weave, and embroider, she made all of Ferdinand's shirts by hand.[1] They worried about money almost constantly, but at least their sense of shared sacrifice provided some excitement. Ferdinand "had gone to Castile without any money, and the Princess didn't have any either," an Aragonese chronicler noted.[2] Ferdinand frequently begged his father for funds but often came away empty-handed because the king of Aragon, enmeshed in civil war, had so little left for his son.

It was an exciting and optimistic time for the young couple: if their child were to be a boy, Isabella's claim to the succession would be considerably bolstered, as the mother of the next male heir. Their child would reign over both Castile and Aragon, joining the crowns in a reunited Spain, a vision held for Spain ever since Pelayo climbed down from the cave to begin recovering the peninsula.

And finally, through her marriage, Isabella had established an indisputable royal identity for herself. Ferdinand was king of Sicily, and Isabella was his queen. The princess who had struggled to find a legitimate role for herself was now consort of a head of state. She adopted his titles with pride, intensely proud of their shared noble lineage. And so she became not only his lover but his fierce defender, eager to preserve their splendid isolation, even against blood relatives, the cousins who were the male heirs to Ferdinand's grandfather, the admiral of Castile. "One day the Admiral spoke quite sharply to him during a game of cards," an observer recalled, "and when a courtier observed that [the Admiral] was, after all, the King's cousin, Isabella replied instantly that Ferdinand had no relatives, only vassals."[3]

* * *

But the marriage exacerbated problems in her own family. Isabella was worried about the rift with her brother King Enrique and hoped to mend fences quickly. After the wedding, she and Ferdinand sent three separate envoys to him, asking him to accept what they had done and promising in return their respect and loyalty. They pleaded for the king's forgiveness, calling themselves "obedient children" who hoped "to help him and bring harmony and peace to his realms."[4]

Enrique's response was slow in coming and chilly when it arrived. He said he would comment after consulting with his advisers, but no further missive arrived. He was clearly furious over the match and was not interested in forgiving Isabella. He no doubt felt that his old enemy King Juan II of Aragon, his former father-in-law, had bested him once again, and that Juan's son Ferdinand would eventually reign in place of little Juana.

Isabella and Ferdinand wrote to Enrique again in March 1470. They again begged the king to forgive them and asked whether an ecclesiastical court could help resolve their differences. This time Enrique declined to respond at all.

The people around Enrique encouraged this rift between brother and sister. Each had his or her own reasons. Queen Juana of Castile wanted to protect the rights of her daughter to the throne. Juan Pacheco, whose proudest possession was his title as Marquess of Villena, was worried about the new marriage because his title had previously belonged to King Juan II of Aragon, back before the Battle of Olmedo, when Álvaro de Luna had defeated Juan; he suspected the family might want back what they believed rightfully belonged to them. Others in the king's entourage were no doubt eager to point out that his younger sister had publicly defied her brother by marrying Ferdinand, an affront that most kings of that era took very seriously. In that day and age, it was almost unthinkable for a young woman to arrange a marriage on her own without deferring to the authority of the head of the family.

To sway public opinion, Isabella issued a public statement explaining why she had married Ferdinand. To establish their credibility and underscore their seriousness of purpose, they held their first formal meeting of a council of state on October 22, just a few days after the wedding.

Isabella reached out to people she thought might help restore peace in the family. King Enrique had given the rights to the town of Arévalo, Isabella's mother's property, to the Count of Plasencia, an act that had irritated Isabella enormously. Nevertheless, Isabella wrote the countess a friendly letter discussing the situation and emphasizing her loyalty to the king; she asked her to intervene with Enrique on her behalf. "Dear countess," she wrote, "by now you will have seen a copy of the letter I sent to the king my brother giving him the reasons why I left the town of Madrigal and went to the noble city of Valladolid."[5] She told her she was begging Enrique to approve the marriage, which she said she had chosen "in the service of God, and his, and for the serenity of the realm, proffering my will and strong heart with which to serve him and follow him." She ended with what she called "an affectionate request," that the countess forward the message to Enrique.

This effort bore no fruit; again Enrique did not respond. His silence became ominous. The young couple now realized they had made lasting enemies of King Enrique and Queen Juana and their ruthless ally Juan Pacheco. They became increasingly worried about their personal security and asked Ferdinand's father to send troops to protect them. But King

Juan, cash-strapped and beleaguered by the civil war in Aragon, had no forces to spare. Instead he urged them to seek advice from Ferdinand's Castilian grandfather and from the archbishop of Toledo, Alfonso Carrillo, who remained their most steadfast friend.[6]

Almost immediately Isabella's political support began to evaporate. Even Valladolid, the city that had hosted her nuptials with Ferdinand, abandoned her cause and allied itself again with the king. Enrique cut off Isabella's sources of income, forcing the couple to live hand to mouth. Soon Isabella and Ferdinand possessed only Medina del Campo, which was held for them by the ever-present Gonzalo Chacón, and Ávila, held by Chacón's son, Juan.[7] They retreated to the nearby town of Duenas, about twenty miles from Valladolid, looking for safe harbor for their new marriage, in an area controlled by Archbishop Carrillo.

King Enrique's animosity toward Isabella and Ferdinand became common knowledge in Castile, and soon many Spaniards began avoiding them. "Few grandees wanted it to be known that they supported the young sovereigns," an Aragonese ambassador wrote to King Juan.[8]

Ferdinand made matters worse by clashing with the couple's single most important ally, Archbishop Carrillo, who by this time was essentially supporting them. King Juan had given his son specific instructions to listen to Carrillo and follow his advice, but Ferdinand found the archbishop bossy and overbearing. Carrillo in turn thought Ferdinand willful and obstinate. Ferdinand told Carrillo "that he would not be put in leading-strings like so many of the sovereigns of Castile."[9] Carrillo soon complained to King Juan, in a steady stream of letters and messages, that the teenagers were ignoring his advice.

The dissension put Isabella in an awkward position. Ferdinand was her husband and she owed him her loyalty, but Carrillo had been a steadfast friend who had stayed by her side when others had abandoned her. King Juan also thought Ferdinand was being foolhardy and wrote him repeatedly telling him to do as Carrillo told them.

Then a new problem cast a further shadow on the young couple. The dispensation for their marriage that Ferdinand had provided turned out to have been hastily forged and was now exposed as fraudulent. Archbishop Carrillo and King Juan's envoy, Mosén Pierres de Peralta, had arranged the ecclesiastical document.[10] The two men had been eager to expedite the match and so had tried to pass off a dispensation granted at another time for another wedding as the necessary authorization. The failure to get the proper document from the pope meant that the marriage was now characterized as incestuous. Ferdinand put much pressure on his father to try to get a proper dispensation and make things right.

These developments were unsettling for Isabella. It was essential to obtain the proper dispensation so that her soon-to-be-born infant's birth would be legitimate. But obtaining the document might be difficult if the pope was reluctant to risk angering King Enrique by providing it. This proved to be the case. Pope Paul II threw his support to Enrique and declined to provide the necessary papers.

Long months passed while they waited. Pope Paul II, who was fifty-three years old, refused to relent, and it eventually became apparent that only the arrival of a new pope might resolve the problem. This delay was a scarring experience for Isabella. Ever afterward she would go to great lengths to ensure that proper approvals from the Vatican regarding marriages of relatives were secured well ahead of time, so that questions could be laid to rest before they even arose. Such dispensations from the pope would be needed frequently because the royal families of Europe commonly intermarried. Isabella's later preoccupation with papal dispensations would have long-lasting and cataclysmic consequences.

But for now the uncertainty was simply adding to the stress of the first-time mother. Isabella, not legally married in the eyes of church or state, was waiting with bated breath for the birth of her child. The arrival of a boy would secure her position because it would make her the mother of the undisputed heir to Aragon, and a male child would be able to assert his primacy over two other candidates for the throne of Castile—Isabella and Princess Juana.

Isabella went into labor on October 1, and the long and difficult childbirth lasted through the night: "the caballeros and Ferdinand spent many anxious hours worrying about Isabella's dangerous condition."[11] The baby was born in the late morning on October 2, 1470. Isabella's life may indeed have been at risk: At that time, childbirth was generally dangerous, and many women died as a result of complications, infection, or blood loss.

Five witnesses attended the birth to ensure that the child presented to the world was indeed borne by the mother. No one wanted rumors of switched babies to complicate the succession picture even more. Isabella was probably attended by a midwife, not by a doctor, according to fifteenth-century custom. She asked to have a silken veil placed over her face during labor so the witnesses would not see the pain etched there. The child, when she arrived, proved to be a girl. Archbishop Carrillo christened her Isabel, the same name as her mother, grandmother, and great-grandmother.

Princess Isabella shared the disappointing discovery with the kingdom that afternoon. "Our Lord has given us a princess," she announced in a letter.[12] It was terrible news, particularly in Aragon, where females could not inherit the throne. King Juan received the news with "open dismay," for it threatened to unravel his carefully set plans for his descendants to rule over Castile.[13]

But the news was heartening for King Enrique. A girl child was less of a threat to little Juana than a male would have been. As soon as he learned of the birth, he moved to strip Isabella of her remaining possessions and titles. He took her beloved town of Medina del Campo in his own name. And in what can only have been an act of spite, he announced that Juana, now age nine, would marry a French nobleman, Charles, Duke of Berry, the one with the spindly legs who had previously negotiated to marry Isabella. Charles was no longer heir to the French throne, because his older brother's wife had given birth to a son, but Juana's marriage to a French lord would likely result in French pretensions to the throne of Castile. Soon the French made those intentions clear: They insisted that little Juana, to be worthy to wed a man third in line for the French throne, be named heir to the Castilian throne. Enrique agreed. With that thoughtless act, King Enrique demonstrated the full extent of his rage against his half sister. He was willing to cede his kingdom to its archrival, France, rather than see it go to Isabella and Ferdinand.

On October 26, 1470, in a public ceremony in the Valley of Lozoya, near the Aragonese border, Enrique made the formal declaration that he was disinheriting Isabella and that Castilians should "neither consider the princess the legitimate heir nor obey her as such."[14] It was no idle gesture. Enrique underscored his intention of dispossessing Isabella and Ferdinand by issuing a proclamation that as soon as Juana and the French duke married, the Duke of Berry would be named Prince of Asturias and primary inheritor of the Castilian throne.[15]

* * *

It was a very bad month for the young couple. Isabella was still recovering from childbirth. Ferdinand had suffered a bad fall while on horseback and developed a frighteningly high fever, in an age without antibiotics. In this already-bad situation, the new French alliance was an alarming development. King Juan worried that the young couple and their baby daughter were at personal risk and told his councilors that he believed they faced "great danger."[16] He was already at war with the French himself over the towns he had ceded to them during the Aragonese civil war, and he believed that French soldiers might seize Ferdinand with King Enrique's encouragement, thereby removing them as contenders for the succession. He was not wrong. On December 8, King Enrique secretly wrote to Charles, Duke of Berry, Isabella's former suitor, urging him to send his "most powerful soldiers" to capture Isabella and Ferdinand.[17]

Suspecting the truth and realizing that Enrique's spies were watching their movements, Isabella and Ferdinand moved from place to place, seeking refuge. They moved to an estate owned by the Enríquez family, relatives of Ferdinand's mother, and then into Carrillo's home. Living with the archbishop was tense, as he and Ferdinand continued to feud with each other.

The next three years—from the end of 1470 to late 1473—were frequently dismal for Isabella. King Juan II of Aragon was still enmeshed in war against the French and called for Ferdinand to join him in the campaign. It was a foolish war, caused by his father's mismanagement of his own realm, but the stakes were not imaginary. King Juan, now in his eighties, needed Ferdinand's youthful energy and intensity to defeat the French. Ferdinand left for Aragon in February 1472.[18] For most of the next two years, he was gone; Isabella and her little daughter, left behind in Castile, were impoverished and nearly friendless.

To make matters worse, Ferdinand, once he arrived back home in Aragon, was not alone. He took up company with other women. Very early in their relationship, Isabella had had to learn to live with Ferdinand's nearly constant sexual infidelity. He had come into the marriage with two illegitimate children, after all, and in the beginning Isabella accepted easily and generously what had happened before their union.

But episodes of unfaithfulness, some of long and humiliating duration, started very soon after the wedding. When Ferdinand left for the battlefield, he was accompanied by his mistress Aldonza Roig de Ibarra, later made Viscountess of Ebol, a pretty young Catalan woman from the town of Cervera. Aldonza dressed up in men's clothes while on military campaigns with Ferdinand, but she wasn't fooling anyone about her gender. Together they had already produced two offspring, Alonso and Juana, both of whom Ferdinand recognized as his children.

Soon another woman came into his field of vision, and he passed time with her in the winter of 1472–73, also near the battlefields of Perpignan, on the French-Catalan border. She was Joana Nicolau, daughter of a low-level official. Together they produced a child who was also named Juana. A few years later, when he was visiting Bilbao, he spied a young woman called Toda de Larrea, and a torrid encounter produced yet another child, a girl who was named María. The baby's mother was proud of her royal liaison and flaunted the child's existence. Lacking an official title, the child was popularly styled La Excelenta. And there were others. "Although he loved the Queen his wife greatly, he gave himself to other women," the court chronicler Pulgar said with a sigh.[19]

Ferdinand's infidelities made Isabella jealous and hurt her deeply even though she presented a stoic face to the world. The two of them came to blows about it on one occasion in Segovia, in a room in the Alcázar. Courtiers heard shouts and blows, then the plaintive sound of muffled sobs.

Isabella's desolation was visible to those who cared to look. The Castilian poet and nobleman Gómez Manrique, for example, wrote a piece of poetry about Isabella that referred to her "sad, beautiful" face, adding that the "lady herself is as lonely as the empty city where no one dwells."[20]

In April 1473 Ferdinand made preparations to set off to Perpignan once again, once more to fight the French. Isabella was unhappy about it. It had now been more than three years since her daughter Isabella was born, and she worried she wouldn't become pregnant again. She was also very vulnerable, living alone in Castile with King Enrique's heart turned against her. She crafted a letter to her father-in-law that subtly conveyed her irritation: "I felt such great anxiety on hearing the news of the invasion of the French into your kingdom, that if matters here had permitted, I would not have been able to endure not to go with the prince my lord to rescue Your Majesty, because certainly it would have been less onerous for me to travel with him than to remain behind."[21]

In fact, by the time Ferdinand arrived, the battle was already won. Nevertheless, he stayed there for the next seven months, helping his father rebuild his defenses and undoubtedly renewing old friendships. He didn't return until December 1473.

In November of that year, Isabella wrote to Ferdinand begging him to return. She told him that King Enrique, who was ailing, might die at any moment, or become incapacitated, and she needed her husband's support. Ferdinand turned her down, stressing the urgent crush of business, but he was evidently using his absences to pressure Isabella into persuading King Enrique to make him his heir and to administer the oath of succession to him instead of Isabella. Ferdinand's letter, one of only a few surviving pieces of correspondence between the husband and wife, is a masterpiece of artful duplicity, threat, and menace, masked as romantic yearning:

> I do not know why Our Lord has given me so much good with so little pleasure in it, since in three years I have not been with you seven months. Now I must tell you that I have to go to induce these people to do their duty. But all this cannot happen before Christmas, and if in this time you can arrange it so that the King calls me for the oath, within the hour I could be on my way [to you], but otherwise I would have no excuse for my lord the King. Although I do my best, this unfortunate predicament puts me in such a mood that I do not know whether I am coming or going. I beg you to work at this, or at least to write to the Archbishop and Cardinal. I do not mean to imply that this is your task, or that I do not think that for me there is no higher duty than fulfilling your wishes. . . . I beg, my lady, that you would pardon me the annoyance and trouble I do not know how to describe, with all the delay in my coming. Awaiting your answer, I ask to be now and to the end, your slave.[22]

In fact, despite Ferdinand's honeyed words, his mind was often elsewhere. In letters to his father during these years, Ferdinand frequently discussed his illegitimate children, particularly Alonso, but he seldom mentioned little Isabel, his child with his wife. In the summer of 1474 he publicly acknowledged the boy as his son and began looking for a regular source of income for him. Despite the distress she felt, Isabella was eager to make sure that Ferdinand's children received proper educations. "He is a son of my august husband, and consequently must be educated in conformance with his noble birth," she once said in talking about Alonso.[23]

Ferdinand's misplaced fertility was another sore point in the marriage. Isabella needed to produce more heirs to the throne to solidify her position, but Ferdinand's extended absences made that impossible. She had conceived a child in the first days of the marriage; now long years passed without another successful pregnancy. Little Isabel was growing up as an only child. As the years ticked by, it became apparent that while Ferdinand loved Isabella, he also resented her and was choosing to stay away more than was absolutely necessary. Perhaps he thought that he could make himself heir to the Castilian throne if Isabella were to fail to produce a male child. He would certainly have had a strong claim based on his own ancestry. He may have been hedging his bets, preparing for various outcomes and giving himself as much maneuvering room as possible.

Another man at court, however, stood in a notable contrast to Isabella's faithless husband. This was her longtime friend Gonzalo Fernández de Córdoba, still in his early twenties. He had been part of her younger brother Alfonso's entourage, and he had been with Isabella when Alfonso died. He was deeply fond of Isabella and completely loyal to her from those teenage years. Soon after Alfonso died and Enrique resumed power, Gonzalo had traveled back with his tutor to the town where Isabella was living, taking up residence nearby. When he was asked why he had come, he replied, "Not for any self-interest, but in the hopes of being able to serve Her Highness, the Princess, in some way."[24]

Gonzalo joined Isabella's court and in the next few years frequently traveled as one of her escorts, always maintaining a discreet distance from her. In the months when Isabella was preparing to marry Ferdinand, Gonzalo had traveled with her guard from Enrique's court in Ocaña to Madrigal, and later, when Enrique's troops were riding to take her prisoner, he accompanied her from Madrigal to Valladolid.[25] He had been present at Isabella's marriage to Ferdinand, serving as her page.

Gonzalo remained with the court during the early months of Isabella's marriage but left around the time her first child was born. He went to a monastery near his hometown of Córdoba, seeking admission to the order. The prior turned him away, saying that God had other plans in mind for him;[26] Gonzalo then began staying at the chapter house of the Knights of Calatrava, the religious military order, when he visited Córdoba. There he lived under Benedictine rule, bound to a life of chastity, keeping the required silence in the dormitory, eating meat only three times per week, and fasting regularly. Even so, he kept his sword girded at night, to be always ready for action, in defense of the faith or the weak.[27]

His chivalrous behavior toward women made him the subject of local legend. A story was told of a wealthy bachelor, an "audacious libertine," who had become enamored of a beautiful and impoverished orphan girl. She rebuffed his advances, so he decided to kidnap her and forcibly take her to his home. Gonzalo was walking nearby when he heard gasping cries from the young woman as three armed men dragged her down the street. Gonzalo dashed to the scene, his sword drawn, wounded the nobleman, and killed one of his henchmen. He then escorted the young woman safely home, winning the affection and respect of the neighborhood.[28]

Gonzalo eventually returned to court and stayed in attendance on Princess Isabella until Ferdinand finally came home from the French campaign, at the end of 1473. At that point, Gonzalo left once more, in an abrupt manner that attracted some comment. He briefly married, but his wife died soon thereafter in childbirth. Gonzalo was not in a hurry to remarry, remaining a bachelor for more than a decade. His continued attentiveness to Isabella's needs made some people suspect he loved the princess or that she loved him. There was never any record of misconduct between the two, however, except for a single cryptic remark later made by Ferdinand "when Isabella taxed him with infidelity, . . . implying that she too had a favorite, Gonzalo Fernández de Córdoba," writes his biographer Mary Purcell. "There is no foundation for this conjecture. . . . It is possible that Ferdinand, jealous of a young man who was his equal in bravery and sporting prowess, his superior in appearance and address, had him sent away. More likely Isabella, who to an exceedingly sensitive conscience joined a determination to be her subjects' exemplar in all things, discharged Gonzalo from the court rather than have her name coupled with his, in however innocent a connection."[29]

Isabella, indeed, was extremely careful to protect her reputation for virtue. Having seen Queen Juana's life unravel as a result of her sexual escapades, she took extreme measures to ensure that no one would ever question the paternity of her children. Her caution doubled whenever her husband was away. Then her ladies-in-waiting all slept in her room, witnesses to one another's conduct. At a party in Alcalá, when the king was away and the queen wanted to dance, she pointedly offered her arm to one of her ladies-in-waiting rather than dance publicly with a man who was not her husband.

Most important of all, Isabella was a profoundly devoted Catholic, to whom marriage was a lifetime commitment and to whom divorce was unthinkable. She had joined her life to Ferdinand's, and the two were a couple. But at some point, Isabella realized Ferdinand's political interests were different from hers, and that she would need to manage her own life and chart her own course. If she were to get back into King Enrique's good graces, win the support of the Castilian nobility, and be restored as heir to the crown, she would need to find a way to do it herself.

EIGHT

THE BORGIA CONNECTION

In these years of Isabella's isolation and abandonment, when her future was anything but assured, an ally and counselor appeared from the east who had, one might say, celestial credentials.

Powerful in body, overtly sensual, elegant, and magnetically attractive to women, Cardinal Rodrigo Borgia was a Spaniard by birth. He was the nephew of Pope Calixtus III, whose papacy had resembled the founding years of a dynasty more than a spiritual mission. Calixtus had elevated Rodrigo to a cardinalship when he was only twenty-five years old, even before he had become a priest, and soon thereafter conferred a great many other ecclesiastical honors on him as well. After his uncle's death, Rodrigo had adroitly managed to retain these elevated posts, which required particular cunning. The Italian cardinals who dominated the halls of the Vatican tended to hate and scorn foreigners, particularly those who threatened their stranglehold on power in Christendom, and they could call out Roman gangsters to attack people identified as outsiders. These gangs would have been glad to dispatch Rodrigo to accompany his uncle into the next life.

In the face of this formidable opposition, Rodrigo had managed to maintain his position as one of the highest churchmen in Roman Catholicism. In the summer of 1471, when Isabella was a twenty-year-old newlywed in a precarious spot, Rodrigo was a man with considerable power. This was important to Isabella, because Pope Paul II refused to give the couple the marriage dispensation that would legitimize their baby's birth. In July 1471 they learned that Pope Paul had died, and that a new pope, the Italian Francesco della Rovere, had been elected to replace him, taking the name Sixtus IV. Rodrigo was in a position to be helpful in obtaining the correct paperwork, for it was Rodrigo who had placed the crown on the pope's head at the ceremony at the Vatican.

Then, in 1472, when Isabella's little girl was still a toddler, Rodrigo announced he was coming home to Spain for a visit. Pope Sixtus had decided he too would raise an army to help beat back the Muslim advance, and he dispatched envoys to the courts of Europe to solicit support for the cause. Borgia was sent to smooth tensions in Castile and win King Enrique's backing for the new campaign. Ferdinand and Isabella quickly realized that Borgia's visit presented them with a unique opportunity to make an ally who could help them in many and profound ways.

Rodrigo had now lived in Italy for more than two decades, but his loyalty and affection for Spain remained paramount to him. He still spoke Catalan as his first language. "For Rodrigo," writes the historian Marion Johnson, "the return to Spain was also something of a sentimental journey, a chance to refresh himself at the family source and to remind himself that his roots lay in the province of Valencia."[1]

Ferdinand and Isabella saw that Borgia's affinity for his native land gave them an entrée to him. They realized that he needed allies as well. He was an ambitious man, and he must have already realized that the papacy was within his reach, if he managed his career properly and reached out for support as needed. Immigrants like the Borgias were on particularly shaky ground in Rome because of the prejudice against non-Italians. Rodrigo knew he needed firm backing from his native Spain.

Rodrigo de Borja had been born in 1431 in Xàtiva, a craggy hilltop town with a medieval castle crowning its highest point, located near Valencia. Borja retained a great sense of affiliation with the crown of Aragon, as he believed himself a descendant of an old and venerable line that had fought valiantly in the reconquest of the land from the Muslims. The Borjas were a numerous clan—proud, fearless, and, as it turned out, unscrupulous—and young Rodrigo early took his mother's last name to more closely align himself with his uncle, his mother's brother. They were not a wealthy family, and the Borjas were good at making the best of any advantage that came their way.

The Borja clan first moved into high-level church politics through their connections with a Spanish cardinal named Pedro de Luna, the uncle of Álvaro de Luna. Spaniards were rare among the elite order of cardinals at the Vatican. When Pope Gregory XI died in 1378, Pedro de Luna was the only Spaniard among them, all the rest being French or Italian. To be effective in these councils, Pedro de Luna had needed Spanish allies at home, as was soon made abundantly clear. Within days of the pope's death—Gregory XI had been born in France—a fiercely ethnocentric confrontation erupted. The cardinals, including Pedro de Luna, gathered in conclave with great ceremony to choose the next pope, following custom and tradition. This time, however, the building was surrounded by a seething Roman mob who demanded that the new pope should be an Italian from Rome. The terrified cardinals, fearing they would be torn limb from limb, looked about the room and spotted an elderly cleric who they thought had been born in the city. Despite his energetic protests, they draped him in the papal mantle, pressed the mitre on his head, and shoved him up to the altar, thus naming the next Vicar of Christ. Then they quickly fled the building.

Once seated, this unlikely candidate, Pope Urban VI, decided to take his selection seriously. He set out to reform the church, condemning luxuries and vices. This attitude was as alarming to the cardinals as the street mob had been, so they once more fled Rome. Soon they named a replacement pope, another Frenchman, Clement VII. But Urban vociferously refused to step down, and Christianity found itself with two rival pontiffs, one based in Rome and the other in Avignon. Italy and northern Europe sided with the Roman pope, Urban VI; France and Spain aligned themselves with the Avignon alternative, Clement VII. Church hierarchies everywhere had to choose sides, forcing kings, bishops, monasteries, charitable institutions, and universities to align themselves with one or another of the camps. Even after Urban and Clement both died and replacements moved into their posts, the schism continued until 1418. The moral authority of the church diminished as the faithful witnessed leading prelates behaving like grasping and squabbling children. Spaniards such as Pedro de Luna found themselves navigating these uncharted waters in relative isolation.

Meanwhile back in Aragon, amid this dispiriting scene, a pious young man from Xàtiva named Alfonso de Borja (Borgia in Italian) was growing to maturity. Devout, determined, and diligent, he soon came to the attention of church elders, including a wandering Valencian preacher named

Vincent Ferrer who was drawing crowds from all over southern Europe with his fire-and-brimstone sermons. Ferrer was having great success convincing Jews to convert to Christianity, either out of fear for their lives or because of his powers of persuasion. His converts soon filled top government posts in Spain. Spotting Alfonso de Borja's face in the crowd at one of his sermons, Vincent Ferrer prophesied that Alfonso would one day be pope. This kind of recommendation was helpful to Alfonso and also inspirational, and he began to believe that he might have a special role to play in healing the divide within the church.

Alfonso de Borja eventually became a religious adviser to King Alfonso of Aragon. When King Alfonso moved to Naples and never came home, his conscientious and hardworking adviser, Alfonso de Borja, went with him, soon adopting the name Alonso Borgia, as the Italians spelled it. Borgia proved his mettle by helping bridge the schism, just as he had hoped, and with a reputation as a peacemaker, he began climbing the pontifical ladder. As a reward for his faithful service to the king and to the pope, Alonso was named a cardinal in 1444. He, in turn, relied on the support of another helpful Spanish ally, Cardinal Juan de Torquemada. Soon the Spaniards formed a tight little fraternity at the Vatican.

By 1451, when Princess Isabella was born, Pope Nicholas V, an Italian, was reigning in the Vatican. The Renaissance was dawning, and Nicholas V became a patron of literature and the arts and amassed a great personal collection of books and manuscripts, which would become the core of the Vatican Library. He arranged for the translation of many ancient texts into Latin, and rebuilt a great many classical monuments, as well as palaces, bridges, and roads. All these cultural enterprises and public works projects meant his friends in the Vatican had multiple ways to prosper.

By this time Cardinal Alonso Borgia's high rank and improved financial standing allowed him to help his own relatives, including his able and ambitious young nephew Rodrigo, who was growing up within the crown of Aragon. Alonso secured for his promising nephew his first ecclesiastical post in Valencia when he was only fourteen years old. A few years later Alonso brought Rodrigo to Rome, where the young man soon made himself useful at the Vatican.

When Pope Nicholas V died in 1455, the College of Cardinals selected Alonso as the next pope, and he took the name Calixtus III. Some observers said he had been chosen in spite of his Spanish heritage because he was crippled with gout and looked old. The other cardinals thought he would die soon, giving them more time to prepare their own candidacies. But Calixtus turned out to be stronger than he looked. And in Spain, his ascension was a subject of intense nationalistic pride, viewed as a fitting recognition of the peninsula's role as a bulwark of Christianity. Through Isabella's early years, this Spanish pope was Christ's vicar on earth and the leader of Christendom, the final arbiter of all things spiritual, and congregants prayed for him and for his continued good health.

To bolster his position, Calixtus quickly elevated friends and relatives from Spain. One of his first official acts was to name the deceased Vincent Ferrer a saint. Ferrer, of course, had had the great good luck to have foretold the coming—and unlikely—greatness of Alonso Borgia.

Three weeks after Calixtus's investiture, Rodrigo, at twenty-four, was named apostolic notary and given a number of lucrative benefices in Valencia, which ensured him a rich income. At twenty-five, though he was not yet a priest, his doting uncle made him a cardinal, and the next year, he was promoted to the most prestigious post in the Vatican after the pope, that of vice-chancellor of the church, as administrator of the "government of Christendom," a position that provided an annual income of 20,000 ducats.[2] Next he was made bishop of Valencia, which added another 20,000 ducats and made him caretaker of the souls of the second-largest kingdom within Aragon.

Pope Calixtus placed other relatives in positions of power throughout the Vatican. "They kept on appearing—relations, and relations of relations—and for every one of them there was a corner in the sun," writes the papal historian Clemente Fusero, "for each applicant one of those countless sinecures or odd positions which the hypertrophied development of the Papal bureaucracy had created over the centuries."[3] The Italians disdainfully called them "the Catalans."

As a native of Spain, Pope Calixtus carried with him the ancestral Iberian obsession with the Muslim threat, something that had been part of the peninsula's culture since 711. He had been deeply disturbed by the fall of Constantinople in 1453, two years before his election, and he avidly listened to reports of subsequent events in eastern Europe. "He ascended the Papal throne," Fusero writes, "with one great and all-devouring project in mind—to free Christian Europe from the Turkish scimitar which, more especially since the occupation of Constantinople, had been pointed at her throat. All his efforts, all his thoughts, all his political activities converged on this one end."[4]

Very few European Christian rulers shared his intense concern. Preoccupied with their own territorial rivalries, the Europeans had done little to prevent the conquest of Constantinople, and their subsequent efforts against the Muslims were halfhearted and ineffectual. This state of affairs made the cities of Europe seem easy pickings to the Turks; their wealth and women seemed available to anyone with the pluck and determination to take them. In the 1450s, in the wake of his victory, Mehmed II began calling himself Caesar and styling himself the emperor of Rome, leading an army three hundred thousand strong and preparing once more for attack. Pope Calixtus issued a clarion call for funds and troops to fight the Turks, but the response was tepid. The threat seemed too distant, too ephemeral, particularly for northern Europeans and for the warring northern Italian city-states.

Pope Calixtus resolved to defend Christianity on his own. To raise money, he introduced an austerity program at the Vatican, a reversal of course after the free-spending ways of Pope Nicholas. Calixtus ordered gold and silver plate from the papal treasury to be melted to raise money for armaments. When a marble tomb was unearthed and found to contain two mummified corpses dressed in robes of gold-woven silk, he delightedly ordered these items to be brought to the Vatican, not to preserve or study them, but to sell them for the value of the gold they contained.

Calixtus also drummed up support by encouraging public admiration for religious warriors. He was the prelate who had pressed for the reexamination of Joan of Arc's life, which recast her as a God-fearing soldier of liberation against an invading force. Her legend grew as that taint of heresy dropped away. As a result of this review of her case, which happened when Isabella was six, Joan of Arc was declared innocent, rehabilitated, and placed on the path toward sainthood. "Only on the battlefield does the palm of glory grow," Pope Calixtus once said.[5]

His preoccupation with Christian self-defense intensified as reports from eastern Europe grew more alarming. Turkish troops were headed for Hungary and up the Danube River. In 1456 Turkish troops engulfed Athens; recognizing that no assistance was at hand, its residents opted to surrender. Having shown no resistance, the Athenians survived and were allowed to follow their own religious traditions. But the people who had coined the term *democracy* were labeled *rayah* or slaves by the Ottomans. The Parthenon was converted into a mosque; the Erechtheum, with its statues of the female caryatid statues, was used as a harem. Strong young boys were sent away to be trained as Ottoman soldiers; good-looking girls were shipped off to serve as concubines to wealthy Muslim men. According to the historian T. C. F. Hopkins, "The fall of Athens in 1456 to the Ottomans was a shocking blow for Europeans and Christians, for it had been assumed that Athens would hold out against any and all attacks as a bastion of Western thought and moral superiority. . . . Many Europeans feared that the Ottoman conquest was coming and they would be helpless against it."[6]

During Calixtus's pontificate, and using the funds he had stockpiled, the pope engaged in the strongest counterattack organized by the Christian world to that time. He outfitted and sent out a fleet to oppose the Turks, and they had some initial success. The Turks were defeated in a sea battle in the Greek Isles. Elsewhere the city of Belgrade, besieged by the Ottomans, succeeded in holding them off.

But Calixtus was eighty years old, and he had been selected for the papacy because of his declining health. In the summer of 1458, when Isabella was seven, he grew ill and was reported to be dying. Churches throughout the Christian world were placed on alert; vigils were held; fervent prayers were raised for his recovery. Rodrigo was vacationing in Tivoli when he got word of his uncle's illness. He rushed home to Rome, but by the time he arrived, the news had spread everywhere. Disorderly throngs of Italians were converging to attack the Spaniards who had profited and prospered during the reign of the Aragonese pope. Rodrigo's servants disappeared, and his home was looted. Most Spaniards fled the city. Rodrigo stayed to tend his uncle, who died on August 6. Only one steadfast friend, the Venetian cardinal Pietro Barbo, remained behind with Borgia at this frightening time, and his loyalty earned Borgia's lasting gratitude.

As Pope Calixtus breathed his last, and despite the seething anti-Spanish sentiment, the younger Borgia held his ground. When the conclave of cardinals convened to elect the next pope, Rodrigo Borgia and Pietro Barbo were still in Rome. They threw their combined support to an Italian who took the name of Pius II, earning the prelate's appreciation.

* * *

Rodrigo prospered mightily in the next years. Thanks to his skillful management of the politics of papal succession, he had maintained all his holdings, even his title of vice-chancellor of the Vatican, and in the subsequent years, he continued to expand his domains, in some cases inheriting the fortunes that other family members had been granted under Calixtus's papacy.

Rodrigo used this capital to organize his own path toward the papacy. He spent his money to richly reward his friends and allies, and on lavish entertainments that made his sumptuous home a center of attention in a city that appreciated earthly splendor. Rodrigo was a consummate Renaissance man who enjoyed the pleasures of both the flesh and the intellect. Poets, artists, and musicians profited from his patronage; he was an early patron of the printing presses that were beginning to churn out works from both ancient and modern writers. Italian visitors described his home in Rome in tones of awe, referring rapturously to its "storied tapestries," a massive bed furnished with "crimson hangings," and a sideboard "crowded with fine-wrought gold and silver vessels."[7]

He was, nevertheless, a study in contrasts. He was a religious man, moderate in his consumption of food and drink, abstemious toward liquor, and undeniably pious. But he was also handsome, and his spiritual role gave him the allure of forbidden fruit in the eyes of many women. Rodrigo found it hard to resist temptation. It was difficult to shock a Roman in the Renaissance era, but even by the intemperate standards of the day, Rodrigo's sexual vices soon stirred scandal. An infant's baptismal feast in May 1460 somehow sparked a two-week sexual bacchanalia. Many lovely ladies were invited to attend; their husbands were pointedly excluded. Soon Rodrigo's sexual exploits became so notorious that it was necessary, even in this libidinous time, for successive popes to urge him to restrain himself to protect the church's dignity.

This kind of notoriety was not what the church needed when it was still struggling to shake off the stigma of the schism. Even as church leaders, notably popes Calixtus and Pius, sought to highlight the threat from abroad—the menace from the Ottoman Turks—it became impossible to overlook the threat from within. Vice and corruption were undermining the Christian church, and making it hard for it to assert the moral authority needed to mobilize the faithful against the invading Muslim forces.

A growing list of ecclesiastical and secular misdeeds drew the attention of church critics. These practices included simony, or the buying and selling of spiritual goods and church offices; nepotism, conspicuously practiced by Pope Calixtus; and widespread violations of oaths of clerical celibacy. Another festering problem was the selling of indulgences, which allowed the wealthy to pay for sins and buy off church leaders regardless of the extent of their wrongdoings. Secular rulers, meanwhile, interfered in the appointment and installation of bishops and abbots, a practice called lay investiture. This had the effect of allowing rulers to place their own unworthy and unqualified candidates, often their illegitimate children, in religious posts.

Many of these weaknesses were manifestly observable in Rodrigo, who encapsulated the best and worst of the Renaissance. He was cultured and tolerant, but also a libertine whose cynicism left him without moral guideposts. The hypocrisy was proving problematic for both Borgia and the church.

Still, Rodrigo's wealth and power continued to grow. Borgia's friend Pietro Barbo became the next pope, reigning as Pope Paul II, and when Pietro Barbo died, Rodrigo was in an excellent position to help Francesco della Rovere take the papal throne, with the title of Pope Sixtus IV. Sixtus began a remarkable Renaissance reign, building the Sistine Chapel, establishing the Vatican Archives, and rebuilding Rome.

It was thanks to Borgia's intervention, under Pope Sixtus IV, that Isabella and Ferdinand finally legitimized their marriage by obtaining the long-withheld marital dispensation from the pope.

And now the fates of Borgia, Ferdinand, and Isabella grew closely intertwined. As Sixtus mounted the throne, further Turkish incursions were reported, and the new pope decided to send emissaries throughout western Europe to ensure domestic tranquillity in the lands under his spiritual dominion and to secure financial support to fight off the Turks. It made perfect sense to send Borgia home to Spain as his ambassador there.

Rodrigo voyaged in opulence in early 1472, arriving in Aragon in May, returning in triumph as a prince of the church. Three bishops accompanied him, and he brought along two Italian painters, whom he set to embellishing the cathedral in Valencia that was Rodrigo's home bishopric.

Borgia met with King Juan of Aragon and Ferdinand in Valencia, having entered the city in a procession, riding under a silken canopy, to the accompaniment of blaring trumpets. Borgia hosted the throng with an elaborate banquet, featuring many delicacies and fine food. Over the next fifteen months, he met with Ferdinand and his father in a series of talks that had far-reaching consequences. The three men found they had much in common.

Rodrigo was, quite literally, their subject, an Aragonese man who happened to be living in Rome. Courtiers said that Juan and Ferdinand were acutely aware of this status. The upheavals in Italy had made it quite apparent to Rodrigo that his fortunes there could never be guaranteed, that a non-Italian pope would always inspire popular resentment. Being a far-sighted and cautious man, albeit one of great ambition, he wanted to give himself an alternative plan if he should ever need to make a hasty exit from Rome. He was therefore inclined to be helpful to his king. And once he and Ferdinand met, each recognized in the other a compatible individual who could prove very useful.

Ferdinand was careful to keep his father informed on all these developments. In August 1472, for example, he wrote him about the progress of his meetings with Borgia.[8] In March 1473, in a letter to his father, he referred casually to Borgia as his "compadre."[9]

Another important meeting occurred in Valencia in mid-September 1472. This time Borgia was joined by Pedro González de Mendoza, a scion of the rich and influential Mendoza family and the bishop of Sigüenza. Borgia made a grand entry into his native city—and Mendoza an even grander one.[10] Borgia was ambitious, but so was Mendoza

Borgia then traveled to Alcalá de Henares at the end of February, where he spent three weeks with Isabella at the home of Alfonso Carrillo, the archbishop of Toledo, the man who had been Isabella's most constant supporter. Carrillo expended huge sums of money on food and entertainments for Borgia, as he hoped that the Vatican would name him a cardinal of Spain, a position he believed he deserved.[11] Borgia seemed impressed with Isabella; Isabella was less impressed by him. But the sign of papal support implicit in this visit strengthened her case as successor to Enrique.

Rodrigo was undoubtedly looking to advance his own career, but he also came, in time, to see the young couple as Spain's hopeful future, and he gave them his good wishes and practical support. A master at building strategic alliances, he had soon identified the single individual that Isabella needed to complete her team. He was Pedro González de Mendoza, bishop of Sigüenza and Enrique's most stalwart supporter among the nobility. King Enrique had inadvertently made that alliance easier by sending Mendoza himself to meet with Borgia, hopeful that he could win the Vatican to his side in his conflict with his sister. Instead Mendoza ended up shifting his allegiance to Isabella.

Soon a number of deals were struck. Borgia was promised future lands and titles in Aragon, and King Juan negotiated for Mendoza to be given the cardinal's hat and to be named archbishop of Seville. In exchange for these grand titles coming from the Vatican, Isabella and Ferdinand eventually received the support of the powerful Mendoza clan, which included not only the bishop of Sigüenza but also the Count of Tendilla, Diego Hurtado de Mendoza, and their vast network of vassals and allies.[12]

This assistance was crucial for Isabella and Ferdinand. "In the last years of Enrique's reign," writes William Phillips, biographer of Enrique IV, "the Mendoza family agreed that while they would not oppose the king, they would do nothing to help his daughter Juana after his death."[13] By promising one member of the family a cardinal's hat, Rodrigo had drawn the Mendozas to Isabella's side, giving her crucial future support. Mendoza would be loyal to King Enrique during his lifetime, but his investiture symbolized a future commitment between the new cardinal, who would be the Vatican's foremost prelate in Castile, its spiritual leader, and the princess who wished to reign as its secular leader.

How did Isabella view Rodrigo after these negotiations? It is difficult to know what she thought of him. She was an avid advocate of church reform, of purifying religious practice and rooting out corruption. Her own religious advisers were devoutly spiritual men who emulated the simplicity and poverty of Jesus and Saint Francis of Assisi. But Isabella was able to overlook the earthly sins that plagued some chief prelates. Borgia was not the only libertine among the clerics. Mendoza also had a famously roving eye and was the father of several children, whom Isabella once referred to as the archbishop's "pretty little sins."

On some level Isabella must have accepted human nature as it was, particularly when it was to her advantage to do so. And certainly she would have enjoyed some aspects of Rodrigo's personality, notably his interest in culture and learning. He was more intellectual than her husband, and certainly well versed on the latest developments in art and culture in Rome, topics that she found fascinating and inspirational. Perhaps they discussed the new styles in art while he was in Spain—she would come to know much about this topic in a short time. By the time he sailed back to Rome, he was firmly in her sphere of influence, as she was in his. He had agreed to legitimize the little princess Isabel, her daughter, and he had even promised to serve as the child's godfather.

Borgia's promise may have reflected his belief in Isabella's aptitude to rule. Or it may have reflected his expectation that Ferdinand would soon come to rule through her. But the deal was almost certainly negotiated for his own future benefit as well. Rodrigo was forty-two years old, and though he was a priest, he was looking to posterity. The scheming prelate, well on his way to becoming a future pope, was starting a family despite his required vows of chastity. He already had one illegitimate son, Pedro Luis, and when he returned to Rome, he would establish a long-term liaison with a young Roman matron named Vanozza dei Catanei, with whom he proceeded to have four more illegitimate children: Cesare, Juan, Lucrezia, and Geofredo. He was an indulgent father and must have known he would need sinecures, properties, and titles to bestow on his progeny. He had a vision of his children returning one day to Spain as landed noblemen. King Juan had promised him lands and titles for his family. Isabella and Ferdinand, if they became the next rulers of Castile and Aragon, would have the ability to guarantee that future.

Rodrigo, who would go down in history as the infamous and spectacularly corrupt Pope Alexander VI, had been converted into yet another invaluable ally.[14] The full benefit of the association between Isabella and Borgia would have world-changing implications. But for now in Castile, trouble was brewing.

Archbishop Carrillo realized he had been betrayed and passed over for the cardinal's job that he most assuredly thought he deserved. His lavish entertainments of Borgia had not produced their intended result. Moreover, the deal had been struck by Isabella and Ferdinand, young people whom he had gone to considerable trouble to back and support, even though he had cast his lot with Isabella and supported and sheltered her in those turbulent years when it was uncertain she would ever reign. Instead the princess and her husband had joined a cabal to grant the highest ecclesiastical honor in the land to a man who had been Enrique's ally.

How could this have happened? One possibility is that princes—and princesses—are not always notable for their gratitude. Carrillo had been helpful to Isabella and Ferdinand in the past, but Mendoza was essential for their future, and that consideration may have ultimately prevailed. Another possibility is that Ferdinand remembered and resented the years of his teenage frictions with Carrillo. And there was one other possible consideration as well. Mendoza was widely respected and as a human being was simply superior to Carrillo. His judgment would soon prove invaluable to the young couple in myriad ways.

In any case, the decision was made. Pedro Mendoza got his cardinal's hat in the spring of 1472. The event was celebrated by a procession through the streets of Segovia, with the hat carried by Andrés de Cabrera, Enrique's *mayordomo mayor,* or chief of staff, who supervised both the fortress of Segovia and the royal treasury; he was also the mayor of Segovia. He was a leader of Segovia's conversos and an examplar of the shifting allegiances of the day. Cabrera had been with Juan Pacheco at the farce of Ávila when King Enrique was ritually dethroned, but then had repented and returned to Enrique's good graces. Now married to Isabella's childhood friend Beatriz de Bobadilla, Andrés de Cabrera was moving into Isabella's camp.

By March 1473, power had shifted perceptibly in Isabella's direction. "All the work that had been done to assure the succession of the most serene princess, my Ladyship wife, and everything that surrounds it has been completed,"[15] Ferdinand wrote to his father. All the pieces were now in place—Rodrigo Borgia, Andrés de Cabrera, and Cardinal Mendoza. Isabella had arranged the chessboard. She was ready for her next big move.

NINE

PREPARING TO RULE

T he alliance with Rodrigo Borgia was just one prong of a concerted campaign Isabella had undertaken to restore her right to the throne. She conducted this campaign largely on her own, taking advantage of help offered by Ferdinand and his father but also relying on her own resources. From 1471 to 1474, Ferdinand was usually far away on the French-Aragonese border. In his absence, she sought to restore old friendships with members of the nobility, to shore up support in the kingdom's cities, and ideally to find a way to mend fences with her brother Enrique. She did all these things to make herself ready for a new role as queen of Castile, even as conditions in the kingdom rapidly deteriorated and the magnitude of the task became ever more daunting.

Operating from Alfonso Carrillo's stronghold in Alcalá de Henares, Isabella moved simultaneously on many fronts. To some individuals, she simply offered new titles and land grants if they would swing their support in her direction. She also astutely courted officials from cities that had supported King Enrique but who had been angered by the way he dispensed urban benefices, suggesting that she would be more amenable to their interests than Enrique had been. Some of them privately shifted their allegiance to her.

She recruited foreign allies as well. In the summer of 1472, for example, she hosted diplomats from Burgundy at a lavish entertainment. Soon they began pressing Enrique to restore Isabella as his successor.

She initiated her own foreign policy by forging links with France, which was at war with her husband's Kingdom of Aragon, by offering her daughter's hand in marriage to Charles, the son of Louis XI. "She cultivated the friendship of France," writes the scholar María Isabel del Val Valdivieso, "so that, when the latter invaded Roussillon in June 1474, she not only did not confront Louis XI, but informed him that she still agreed to the marriage of her daughter to Charles of France."[1] In other words, she was not deferring to her husband's family's interests—she was looking to her own.

Isabella's efforts to establish herself as an independent source of power were both complicated and aided by the civil strife that had erupted all over Castile. The kingdom was in crisis, and although this made it hard for her, or for anyone, to function there, it allowed her to define herself as the savior who would bring a solution to the chaos.

King Enrique's indecisiveness and weakness were allowing criminals to steal, rob, murder, and rape with little fear of punishment. Counterfeit money was circulating everywhere, making people fearful that coins no longer had value. Inflation soared, making it hard to buy the necessities of life. Famine struck, and people began to starve. In Galicia more than fifty castles had been turned into fortified robbers' dens, and petty warlords would make forays out into the countryside to steal what little food and money could be had from pilgrims, peasants, and travelers.

Much of the dissension was religious. In cities across Castile, hostilities were breaking out between longtime Christians and the conversos, people of Jewish descent whose families had converted to Christianity within the previous hundred years. Many converso families had prospered after this change of faith, stirring jealousy and envy, amid allegations that the conversions had been insincere. In truth, some people had sincerely converted while others had only pretended to convert, and it was often difficult to ascertain the real facts in any individual case.

In March 1473 anticonverso riots broke out in the city of Córdoba. A religious procession was passing through a converso neighborhood when a child tossed some sort of liquid, possibly urine, out the top-floor window of a house, splashing a statue of the Virgin Mary. A blacksmith took offense at this act, which he claimed was intentional, shouting for longtime Christians to avenge the sacrilege by attacking converso families. People took to the streets. A number of longtime Christians, including nobleman Alonso de Aguilar, the brother of Isabella's young soldier friend Gonzalo Fernández de Córdoba, tried to intervene to prevent the rioting mob from harming the conversos, but the crowd turned on them just as viciously. Pitched battles erupted all over the city. The day ended with a massacre of conversos, with men killed, women raped, and homes pillaged and burned.

News of the confrontation spread across the south of the peninsula. Criminals and miscreants took advantage of the leadership vacuum to duplicate what had happened in Córdoba, but now with no provocation at all and no goal other than murder and theft. Atrocities occurred in a number of cities, according to the Israeli historian Benzion Netanyahu, including Montoro, La Rambla, and Santaella.[2] In Almodóvar, Jerez, and Écija, it took stern measures by local officials to prevent similar violence.

In Seville, thousands of conversos mobilized to defend themselves, raising fears among longtime Christians there that they would engage in revenge killing for what conversos elsewhere had suffered. Then a converso stabbed a longtime Christian, and a mob began sacking a converso neighborhood. But this time a coalition of longtime Christians, armed conversos, and city authorities held back the rioters and restored peace.

This religious violence further destabilized a kingdom already riven by war and civic breakdown. It erupted just as conditions were rapidly worsening overseas. The Muslim Turks continued their aggressive march into Europe. Building on their victories in Constantinople and Greece, Muslim troops invaded Serbian lands, the lands later known as Albania and Yugoslavia. A letter from the Count of Brotardi to the Spanish court in February 1474 warned that a "formidable" army was advancing toward Italy, "preparing for the ruin of Europe . . . and Christianity."[3]

Later that year the Albanian fortress city of Scutari, just across the Adriatic Sea from Italy and part of the Venetian Empire, was besieged by the Turks and narrowly avoided being taken in September, though three thousand residents died of starvation or thirst before the Turks departed. Italian humanist George Merula, an eyewitness, warned that the Turks had retreated to Constantinople only temporarily, where they were "constructing a great fleet" to make another assault. Their ultimate goal, he wrote, was western Europe.[4]

In October 1474 word came from Italy that the Turks were indeed preparing additional attacks on Christian cities in the Balkans, and ambassadors advised Spanish officials that Serbians and Italians were living in great fear that another invasion was looming.[5] These reports frightened people living all along the Mediterranean coast, particularly in Sicily, where Ferdinand's domains were likely to feel the first attack if the Turks decided to move against the Italian peninsula.

Isabella became increasingly convinced that Castile's future was at stake, that it was her destiny to rule, and that only she could provide the strong hand that would protect her kingdom. King Enrique seemed too passive to mount an effective defense if one were needed. It became even more imperative to Isabella that she win his blessing and persuade him to name her once again his heir. She turned for help to her childhood playmate, Beatriz de Bobadilla, now an influential young matron living in Segovia.

Isabella had been a good friend to Beatriz when she had been in the position to help her. With Isabella's assistance, Beatriz had married Andrés de Cabrera, the man who had custody of the royal treasury at the Alcázar and who was the mayor of Segovia. It was an affectionate match; the couple already had several children. Beatriz had developed into an attractive and intelligent woman who was respected by other men of the court, including the amorous Cardinal Mendoza and King Enrique himself. During a time when Andrés de Cabrera had fallen ill, Beatriz had served in her husband's place, ruling the city and guarding the Alcázar. Now Beatriz was ideally placed to return the favor and help Isabella in her time of need.

Beatriz was a highly admirable woman. A contemporary described her as the very picture of "noble lineage in her conduct, in which prudence, virtue and bravery were combined."[6] A woodcut depiction of her suggests she was slim, with a straight nose and full lips; she was also physically strong, like Isabella, bearing up well under a constant string of pregnancies, producing nine children in all, including seven sons and two daughters. She brought to Isabella's sphere not just a friendship but a friendly dynasty.

Her husband, Andrés de Cabrera, was also described as handsome in body and spirit. He was a charming courtier, a bit taller than average, with blue eyes, regular features, and straight chestnut hair. He was one of Enrique's most trusted officials, having started his career with Enrique as chief chamberlain, managing the king's household from the time Enrique took the throne. Later he became responsible for the king's primary base in Segovia, managing his treasury. In a court that was widely criticized for corruption, Cabrera, a converso, stood out for his moral rectitude, his dedication to work, and his effectiveness.

Beatriz convinced her husband that they needed to look to the future, and that aligning themselves with Isabella was a wise move. Her husband, meanwhile, had had an unpleasant run-in with Juan Pacheco and was prepared to make a shift of allegiance. On June 15, 1473, Isabella signed an agreement with Andrés de Cabrera, promising him that if she became queen, he would be named Marquess de Moya, a town near Cuenca and near his birthplace.[7]

Isabella's chief negotiator in this agreement was Alfonso de Quintanilla, her chief accountant, who shuttled back and forth between the court at Segovia and Alcalá de Henares, where Isabella was living with Archbishop Carrillo. In addition to his strategizing with Beatriz and Andrés de Cabrera, Isabella instructed Quintanilla to do everything he could to restore peace between herself and her older brother. This meant that Isabella had constant and close links to the court. Beatriz and Cabrera whispered privately to the king that it was time to reconcile with his sister.

Eventually Beatriz decided to bring the issue to a head. She took Enrique aside in a quiet room in the Alcázar palace in Segovia and spoke frankly, even harshly, to him about conditions in the kingdom, according to a chronicler who wrote about the exchange decades later. Beatriz reminded him of the treachery he had experienced at the hands of Juan Pacheco and pointed out that Isabella had been both loyal and loving to him over her lifetime. She urged him to break his emotional chains to Juan Pacheco and reach out to Isabella, to make her his heir, and to restore the nation's strength. If he made peace with Isabella and allowed her to come home, she told him, the kingdom would turn from being "a dead tree" and instead "bloom green buds."[8]

The melancholy king acknowledged that much of what she said was true, and said he felt he was to blame for it all, his answer reflecting his deep depression and sadness. Betrayed by so many people he had loved, he had little faith in the ones remaining in his life. "The great destruction . . . of my realms and my people," he told her, "are, as you have said, the result of my sins; my great errors have brought me disgrace before God."[9] He had felt so beleaguered and beaten down by the disappointments and psychological assaults that he sometimes had ignored "good advice" and persisted in a path of self-destruction.

The situation, he said, was hopeless: "Not even if I embrace the prince and the princess, as you ask, will there be any remedy for these realms, as lost as they are. The confusion and disorder in the kingdom have reached such a point that no living person could repair it. Although I know that reconciling with my sister would be the best road I could follow for the best outcome, there is nothing that can repair the damage."

But Enrique at last agreed to meet with Isabella, whom he had not seen in person for four years, and a rendezvous was arranged for the Christmas holidays, in Segovia. Beatriz de Bobadilla and Archbishop Carrillo rode together to Alcalá de Henares to give Isabella the invitation. Ferdinand was already there, having recently arrived from Aragon. The princess was advised to leave quickly for Segovia but to travel with only a few attendants to avoid alarming anyone.[10] She chose to take one in particular—Gonzalo Fernández de Córdoba—and prepared for a speedy departure. She told Ferdinand to follow them at a short distance, to keep an eye on events, and to prevent both of them from being captured. She decided to leave her daughter behind in case the mood soured completely.

Isabella and her companions rode through the night on horseback, galloping across the arid plains along the crumbling road system built by the Romans a thousand years earlier, and arrived in Segovia at daybreak on December 29, 1473. Isabella was fearless in the face of danger, with Gonzalo riding at her side. It was entirely possible that the mercurial King Enrique would have changed his mind by the time Isabella arrived, and with prodding from Juan Pacheco, he would have been capable of doing her harm. Ferdinand kept close at hand, lodging in the town of Sepúlveda, some thirty-five miles from Segovia, and awaited further word. Everyone watched anxiously to see what would happen. Four long years had passed since brother and sister had been together, and many unresolved grievances had accumulated.

But when at last the reunion between Enrique and Isabella occurred, the angry feelings dissipated in moments. Despite all the animosity of the previous years, the brother and sister were genuinely pleased to see each other. Enrique was in a happy mood, having just returned from a hunting trip, and she was waiting for him at the Alcázar, where she welcomed him "with grave humility." He greeted her with delight and "embraced her lovingly."[11] The two wandered off to a nearby room, where they sat down together. She swore her loyalty, apologized for having offended him, and asked him to please consider the "good consequences" for Castile of her marriage to Ferdinand.[12]

His initial reaction was pleasant but noncommittal. That night they dined together at the Alcázar, and he even gave her a choice of any bauble she might want from the treasury. Then they turned to music, as had been their custom in earlier years, with Enrique singing and Isabella dancing. In the following days they strolled through the city together and rode out side by side, and Segovians noticed the harmony in their interactions.

Things went so well, in fact, and Enrique and Isabella were so happy in each other's company, that soon Ferdinand was invited to join them. He arrived on New Year's Day, and the two men—Isabella's brother and her husband—met in person for the first time. It was friendly and cordial. Over the next week, they enjoyed holiday festivities together.

Then on January 9 the three of them joined Beatriz de Bobadilla and Andrés de Cabrera for dinner.[13] Before the evening was out, Enrique suddenly doubled over, stricken by a stomach complaint. He was rushed home to the Alcázar, as Isabella and Ferdinand waited anxiously outside his bedchamber for reports on his health. Soon Juan Pacheco appeared and voiced the suspicion that by now was in everyone's mind: had King Enrique been poisoned? Nobody knew for sure. Pacheco urged the king to arrest Isabella, something he declined to do, but relations between Isabella and her brother cooled very quickly. The debilitated king soon left Segovia for the perceived safety of Madrid. Isabella and Ferdinand remained, determined not to flee again. Whatever happened, Isabella had decided she would stay in Segovia. She even had her daughter brought to her side. She was staking her claim as the king's successor.

Over the next year, Enrique's health deteriorated, and Isabella's power grew. But these months were unsettling for the realm, as is always the case in a kingdom as power changes hands. Courtiers were forced once again to pick sides. Those who chose wrongly could become victims. They had reason to have faith in the young couple: Isabella and Ferdinand offered freshness, strength, and hope for the future. On the other hand, King Enrique was only forty-eight and was likely to recover. He had made mistakes, but he was not a bad person and had tried to rule well.

Even Andrés de Cabrera and Beatriz de Bobadilla were caught up in the conflicting loyalties in the court. Two longtime allies of the king, the Count of Benavente and Cardinal Mendoza, asked them to persuade Isabella to give the custody of her daughter to them as insurance they would be treated well if Isabella became queen. Isabella initially resisted but in the end reluctantly agreed.[14]

Notwithstanding her agreement, however, Count Benavente then became part of a plot to kidnap Isabella, according to court chronicler Alonso de Palencia, who reported that he overheard a group of conspirators, including Benavente, discussing their plans. When Isabella heard about it, she urged Ferdinand to flee, reasoning that he was in danger but that she was relatively safe because of her blood ties to Enrique. Ferdinand left, ostensibly to go hunting, and young Isabel was indeed moved, but to a safer location in Sepúlveda, in the care of Ferdinand's Castilian grandfather.[15] And in August, Ferdinand left Castile for Aragon, to once more help his father on the border with France. During the following months, Isabella was again alone, in a perilous place.

Living in Segovia, Isabella grew closer to Cardinal Mendoza, which proved to be a new irritation to his longtime rival Carrillo, the jealous archbishop of Toledo. Isabella and the cardinal did much to placate Archbishop Carrillo, arranging an advantageous marriage for one of his nieces and a bishopric in Pamplona for his nephew, but the archbishop continued to brood on the slight he had received in being passed over for the cardinalship. The simmering animosity flared into outright hostility over a relatively minor provocation. Archbishop Carrillo was interested in the field of alchemy and employed a charlatan and necromancer who had told him he could manufacture gold. Isabella's religious confessor, Friar Alonso de Burgos, argued with the alchemist, and the dispute turned to fisticuffs. Isabella thought alchemy was nonsense and threw the alchemist out of the palace in Segovia.[16] Carrillo, insulted, stormed out of the city.

For Archbishop Carrillo, it was the last straw. In a dramatic shift of allegiance, he broke with Ferdinand and Isabella and rushed to King Enrique's side, urging him to name little Juana his heir. The rift between brother and sister reopened. Soon violence erupted, as the rival partisans of Enrique and Isabella squared off in towns around the kingdom.[17]

Then King Enrique was dealt a serious psychological and emotional blow. On October 4, 1474, Juan Pacheco suddenly and unexpectedly died, falling victim to a throat ailment, in circumstances oddly similar to the malady that had taken the life of his brother, Pedro Girón. His servants promptly stole his possessions and hid his body among some wine vats.[18] It was a major setback for Enrique, for though Juan Pacheco had been treacherous and grasping, he had nevertheless been Enrique's most important sounding board, lifelong colleague, and the most powerful man in Castile after himself. Enrique had known little love in his life. His relationship with his father had been combative; his mother had died suddenly, probably from poison administered by an enemy; and his relationships with his two wives had been tragic and lonely. Juan Pacheco had been the single most constant figure in his life, and his death seemed to strip from the king even the will to live. As hard as it is to understand, Enrique seemed to have loved Pacheco.

King Enrique forlornly lamented that Pacheco had been as a father to him. As a favor to Pacheco's son, he promptly named him master of Santiago, giving him the coveted position controlling the powerful religious order and its extensive landholdings. Isabella had wanted the mastership conveyed back to the crown, as a possession of the royal family, as her father had intended, but with this action, Enrique created another important rival for power in Castile in Pacheco's son, the new Marquess of Villena.[19]

Emotional blows often lead to physical deterioration. Enrique became even more dispirited and his health continued to erode. Isabella's strength and power, however, were still growing. As support swung increasingly in her favor, she changed her tone, becoming even more conciliatory. She reassured Enrique's allies that she would not take revenge on them for opposing her. She wrote to the Count of Haro, for example, asking him to meet and confer with her. She took pains to stress that he need have no fear of her, or Ferdinand, or the archbishop of Toledo, and that she swore that oath "to God, to Holy Mary, making the sign of the cross with my right hand."[20]

Enrique continued on a downward health spiral, now vomiting blood. He traveled to Madrid, "where he hoped rest would allow him to recover,"[21] but he grew light-headed soon after his arrival when he was taking a stroll in the autumn air. Then he collapsed in his bedchamber. By December he was too weak to ride a horse to his hunting lodge outside the city. A week into that month, King Enrique's condition deteriorated so sharply that he realized he was dying. Over ten hours on his last day, he lapsed in and out of consciousness. A friar was called to hear his confession, and the two men spoke together for a long hour. The king told him that he was leaving his affairs in the hands of Cardinal Mendoza, the youthful new Marquess of Villena, and a handful of other officials. He asked that his jewels and possessions be used to pay off his debts, and that he be buried next to his mother at the church of Santa María de

Guadalupe, the scene of a famous miracle where a statue of the Virgin Mary had been found, in a rocky, mountainous area in Extremadura.

He breathed his last at about two a.m. on December 11, 1474, at the age of forty-nine. At his deathbed were Cardinal Mendoza, the Count of Benavente, the new Marquess of Villena, and other council members.[22] A swift horseman delivered the news to Isabella, who had taken Enrique's place in the Alcázar in Segovia from the time he had fallen ill at Christmas a year earlier.

Reports about what actually happened at Enrique's bedside as he died were mixed.[23] Chronicler Palencia said that Enrique declared his daughter to be his heir, but he left no will, or at least no will was found. Some witnesses and other historians claimed there had been a will but that it had been stolen, hidden, or destroyed. Indeed it was hard to believe that King Enrique had made no specific provision for little Juana, for he was fond of the child, who was only thirteen, and although she was not living with him, he had written notes to friends inquiring solicitously about her health.[24] It was also hard to believe that after all that had happened, the king had neglected to make plans for the succession.

Still, on his deathbed Enrique apparently rejected much of what he had loved in his lifetime. He had endowed several fine churches in Segovia, his beloved city, but now he asked to be buried next to his mother, María of Aragon, who had also been the sister of King Juan II of Aragon. Enrique's cruel father-in-law Juan had also been his uncle, in other words, and these family strains had contributed to the rift between Enrique and Isabella. Enrique's choice to be buried next to his mother was another example of how twisted, convoluted, and ultimately pathetic the ties of family and power had become in the Trastámara family.

The religious services were conducted with dispatch, and as the nobles were eager to make their way rapidly to the side of the new queen, his body was quickly interred at the shrine of Santa María de Guadalupe. Enrique had even lost Segovia to his younger half sister. His friends Beatriz de Bobadilla and Andrés de Cabrera were already in the process of transferring the treasury and its contents to Queen Isabella.

TEN

ISABELLA TAKES
THE THRONE

In Segovia, when Isabella got the word of Enrique's death, she cried, describing herself as feeling "profound sadness."[1] Her emotions must have been mixed, for while Enrique had done many things to her that were cruel, she and he had also had moments of real affection. He had been the last surviving and active member of her immediate family. Her father and her brother Alfonso were both dead, and although her mother was still alive, the dowager queen's mental health problems meant that she played no role in public life. Ferdinand was far away in Aragon, and Isabella faced Enrique's death alone. His passing was an important turning point in her life.

Whatever level of grief Isabella felt, however, she seems to have been prepared for the news, because she swung into action quickly. Her friends—Beatriz de Bobadilla and her husband, Andrés de Cabrera; Gonzalo Chacón, her childhood mentor, and his nephew Gutierre de Cárdenas—quickly gathered at her side. Nobody else in Segovia knew that the king had died. Isabella's group wanted to use the element of surprise to decisively assert her right to rule, and to push young Juana out of contention by promptly confronting her with a fait accompli. Within hours Isabella and her allies set their plan in motion. Then, when the preparations were finalized, Isabella donned mourning garb and sent out letters across the kingdom informing Castilians that King Enrique was dead, calling for funeral services throughout the city.

The day following Enrique's death was momentous from morning until night, and residents of Segovia would remember the events for decades to come. At ten in the morning the bells of the Church of San Miguel, the main church in Segovia, about a quarter mile from the Alcázar, started ringing; soon the other churches in the city chimed their bells as well, in a cacophony that echoed through the streets. Beginning at eleven a.m., priests celebrated the funeral mass at the Church of San Miguel. Composed of psalms, readings from Scripture, and specific prayers, with responses from the congregation, the mass would have conformed to a familiar and well-established ritual known as the Office of the Dead. Conducted in Latin, it was accompanied by the sound of bells and song, and candles were lit for the repose of the soul.

At eleven thirty, when the service was over, the officials and townsfolk filed out onto the street and gathered in the central plaza. An official called out to the crowd that King Enrique was dead, and that as he had died without a legitimate heir, his sister Isabella would assume the throne. Two people who had attended Enrique at his death publicly confirmed that the king was dead.

Princess Isabella had attended the mass. Within hours after it ended, she took off the dark dress of mourning and reemerged wearing resplendent garb, decked in gold jewelry and precious stones. She headed back toward the same church, to have herself proclaimed queen. She had orchestrated a splendid symbolic transition in a surprisingly short time. It became obvious she had been planning it for months.

Soon a procession entered the plaza. First came men-at-arms bearing Isabella's coat of arms and those of the Trastámara family, whose members included both Isabella and Ferdinand. They were followed by Gutierre de Cárdenas, nephew of Isabella's mentor, the loyal Gonzalo Chacón. Then came the glittering princess, astride a milky-white horse rather than the modest mule she had ridden at Toros de Guisando. She made her way to the Plaza Mayor, accompanied by musicians playing kettledrums, trumpets, and clarinets. At the door of the Church of San Miguel, she climbed up onto a platform covered with brocade.[2]

Following close behind and flanking her were Andrés de Cabrera, Enrique's trusted treasurer and the mayor of the city, with his wife, Beatriz de Bobadilla. The bishop of Segovia, the converso Juan Arias Dávila, and a number of other city officials and clerics, all on foot, followed the royal entourage. So did members of the Jewish community, including

Rabbi Abraham Senior and his followers, visibly lending their support for the princess's elevation to queen. Others in the crowd, according to a notary, included the papal legate, some knights and nobles, a group of Franciscan and Dominican friars, Segovia's merchant elite, and a large group of ordinary townspeople, most of whom made their livings as employees of the wool-making firms that were the city's major industry.

Isabella addressed the crowd loudly and clearly. Standing on the platform, raised above the heads of the crowd, the twenty-three-year-old princess pledged to defend the church and the people of Castile and León. She placed her right hand on the Bible and swore by God that she would obey the commandments of the church. She swore to look to the common good of the people, improve their fortunes, do justice, and protect the privileges of the nobility. The crowd swore its allegiance as well, in traditional words that conveyed acceptance of her as ruler.

The officials then knelt before her and took an oath to her as their queen, and to Ferdinand, her husband. Cabrera handed Isabella the keys to the Alcázar and the treasury, which were now her possessions, and she returned them to his safekeeping. He swore allegiance to her, promising to care for the "castles and fortresses" in the region. Isabella very quickly rewarded her closest friends, Cabrera and Chacón. Cabrera and Beatriz would soon become the Marquess and Marquessa of Moya, as Isabella had promised; Chacón would be elevated to the position of chief of staff to the queen. The point was clear: those who had shown her loyalty in the past would receive visible signs of Queen Isabella's favor.

Isabella's four-year-old daughter was lifted up and presented to the crowd as the next heiress to the throne, underscoring the right of female succession in Castile, at present and in the future. No queen had ruled alone in Castile and León since Urraca, from 1109 to 1126, and Queen Berenguela in 1217. More than two centuries had passed with the crown transferred from man to man to man. Now Isabella was the monarch and her daughter was her heiress.

Queen Isabella had made her announcement as a "proclamation" rather than through acclamation, as was traditional in Castile; in effect, she engaged in a form of self-coronation.[3] Then the men-at-arms shouted: "Castilla, Castilla, Castilla, for the very high and powerful Princess, Queen and Lady, our Queen Doña Isabel, and for the very high and very powerful king, Don Fernando, as her legitimate husband!" Applause and fanfare burst from the crowd, with everyone trying to make as much noise as possible, townspeople later recalled.

Then the queen and her procession passed back into the church, entering the arched gateway at Saint Fructus, as the crowd followed behind. She fell to her knees in front of the main altar, then prostrated herself in subjugation to God. Afterward she rose and took in her hands the royal pendant and placed it on the altar like an offering. Although she was behaving as though her authority were ordained by God, she was actually engineering a coup. King Enrique had vacillated about who would succeed him, but for the last five years of his life, he had been clear that little Juana would follow him as ruler. Now Juana's name was not mentioned.

The question of whether Isabella or Juana was the legitimate ruler of Castile and León has perplexed historians ever since that day. Perhaps Juana was indeed the king's daughter, in which case Isabella usurped her throne. But probably Juana was not the king's child. In any case, on that day in Segovia, where Enrique and his successive wives had spent many of their married years, the local population was inclined to believe that Isabella was indeed the true and rightful ruler of Castile and León.

A procession formed around Queen Isabella again as she exited the church. This time Gutierre de Cárdenas rode in the vanguard, holding a sword aloft, point up, symbolizing the advance of justice. The crowd murmured, Palencia wrote, in a hum of shocked reaction, because this was the first time that a woman had asserted the right to be the bearer of justice and punishment. Isabella consciously adopted masculine symbolism, something she would do in ceremonial occasions thereafter. She even commissioned a tapestry that showed a queen holding a sword, entitled "Fame."[4]

It was a carefully planned display. Carrying the sword in that manner, point up, created a visual image of a "militant cross." From her first moments in office, Queen Isabella began crafting an image for herself—serene, calm, resplendent, holy, and ordained by God through her birth.

She passed through the city, back along the edge of the Jewish quarter to the Moorish-decorated palace that was her home. She rode surrounded by nobles on foot, with city officials following behind. She traveled majestically through the winding streets of the medieval city, heading toward her ancestral home, the fortress on the cliff, taking her place as a living queen among the statues of her ancestors.

She had taken the throne alone. Now she stepped inside the fortress, the Alcázar, claiming it, and the riches stored within its towers, as her rightful possessions. "And that night she slept in the palace," a Segovian scholar later noted.[5]

* * *

In the next few days, Isabella began to get word of how her coronation had been received by her subjects elsewhere in the country. Archbishop Alfonso Carrillo promptly declared for her, giving her the support of the spiritual head of the kingdom's primary see, Toledo, and he traveled to Segovia to pledge his allegiance to her. Cardinal Pedro González de Mendoza, after accompanying Enrique's body to his final resting place, rushed to Queen Isabella's side. Rodrigo Borgia's intervention in making Mendoza a cardinal had borne fruit almost immediately upon Enrique's death: Mendoza had thrown his support to Isabella, not to Juana.

Reaction poured in from all over the kingdom. Isabella's self-coronation was applauded in the northern half, particularly in Old Castile, including Ávila, Sepúlveda, Valladolid, Tordesillas, Toledo, and Murcia. Some doubts were raised in the Christian-controlled portions of Andalusia and in Extremadura, where Isabella was not so well known. Clearly she would need to go there soon to make her presence felt. Galicia seemed on the verge of rebellion,[6] but its problems also went deeper than those in the other parts of the kingdom.

More personal reactions, however, caused the first two crises in the new reign. One was a marital spat that threatened the stability of the kingdom; the other came from a jilted suitor. These problems erupted amid a general and continuing breakdown in social order and the economy in Castile, which left Isabella furiously juggling many issues simultaneously.

The marital crisis came first. Isabella had not rushed to inform Ferdinand of Enrique's death. He was at home in Zaragoza, the capital of his Kingdom of Aragon, about 175 miles from Segovia. "She did not appear particularly anxious that her husband should join her," notes the historian John Edwards.[7] She had sent a slow messenger to Ferdinand, telling him about Enrique's death and advising him to do what he thought best in the circumstances, given conditions in Aragon. And she had not urged the messenger to make any particular haste. By not telling him in time for him to participate in the ceremony, she had cut him out of any chance to make a claim to the succession.

So Ferdinand first learned of the tumultuous chain of events—that the king had died and that Isabella had assumed the throne in his place—several days after the coronation. His father's old friend Archbishop Carrillo had sent a swift messenger, stressing that Ferdinand's presence was required immediately in Castile. And Cardinal Mendoza had sent word when Enrique was dying, also suggesting Ferdinand should hasten to Segovia.

Others in Queen Isabella's entourage were also eager to tell the king what had happened. Gutierre de Cárdenas, for example, wrote to Ferdinand, telling him with innocent pride about his unique role in the ceremony, holding the sword of justice. Ferdinand received this letter on December 21, a week after the ceremony in Segovia. He flew into a rage when he learned that his wife had asserted this authority on her own.[8] He promptly jumped on a horse and sped toward Segovia.

"I never heard of a queen who usurped this male privilege," he told the chronicler Palencia, who was traveling with him from Aragon.[9] Palencia tried to calm the king, saying that she was "after all, a woman," and would doubtless reconsider her actions once she realized she needed his manly presence for her protection. Others in Ferdinand's entourage were more unsettled; one male chronicler suggested there was "something sinister" in what Isabella had done.[10]

Ferdinand shook off his anger, persuading himself that Isabella surely had had a momentary lapse of judgment. Once he arrived in Segovia, he told himself, she would realize that she had overstepped and would defer to his authority. He had enormous faith in his sexual power to sway her opinions. "In conquering with patience," a chronicler recalled, he "felt certain he would triumph through satisfying assiduously the demands of conjugal love, with which he could easily soften the intransigence that bad advisers had planted in his wife's mind."[11]

By the time Ferdinand arrived, Isabella had been ruling on her own for more than two weeks, and she had had time to consider what sort of tone she wanted to set. By then Ferdinand was playing for time as well. When he drew near Segovia on December 30, he didn't go directly to the city. Instead he waited in the nearby fortress of Turégano, while Isabella and her officials arranged the terms of his ceremonial arrival. Messages flew back and forth as preparations were made.

On January 2 Ferdinand entered Segovia through the city's great gates, dressed magnificently in furs and cloth-of-gold. Queen Isabella did not go out to greet him; instead, a large throng of officials and clerics, including Mendoza and Carrillo, met him and escorted him with panoply to the portico of the Church of San Miguel, the same place where Isabella had taken the throne two weeks earlier. He was formally asked whether he would reign as the husband of the queen, and he gave his assent. The councilmen of Segovia then pledged their support for him, vowing that "they would obey and receive His Highness as legitimate husband of Our Lady the Queen."[12]

Then Ferdinand traveled in procession to the Alcázar, where he found Isabella awaiting him inside the gates. Suddenly their roles were reversed. She was in control. Now he would come to her, not she to him. She was proceeding according to legal precedents established by previous queens of Castile and León, but those women had reigned hundreds of years earlier, and their memory was preserved mainly in old chronicles. Isabella's accession had seemed something of a theoretical possibility—it was viewed as plausible that a woman would rule in her own right—but it was quite shocking as a reality, particularly for the men in court circles. Male dominance was so customary that even Isabella's supporters were perplexed and confused about the situation. Scholars turned to the history books to establish the precedent for female sovereignty. What Isabella had done was not unprecedented, but it was highly irregular.

Isabella, therefore, was flying in the face of tradition in Spain and, more dramatically, elsewhere on the continent. "The panorama was similar across Europe, where queens were generally able to rule in their husband's name only when the king himself had appointed them and was in a position to impose this choice on his subjects," wrote scholar Nuria Silleras-Fernández.[13]

Queen Berenguela, however, had ruled for only a few months before turning the reins of government over to her son. Only Urraca, who ruled from 1109 to 1126, had held the throne for an extended period. She had taken a husband, but the marriage splintered and Urraca had ruled on her own.

"Urraca defied the notion that a man who married a ruling queen should automatically share in the governance of his wife's realms," writes scholar Theresa Earenfight.[14]

Ferdinand's counselors were especially dismayed and struggled to make sense of what had happened. Palencia blamed the situation on "womanly . . . petulance" that had been urged upon Isabella by people who had "ceaselessly fomented" such behavior in her.[15] This, however, does not seem to have been the case. For reasons of her own, Isabella had decided that she was better off taking the crown alone than risking the complications that might be raised by Ferdinand's participation. Possibly she no longer trusted him. His long absences from Castile, his refusal to return home when Isabella needed him, and his sexual infidelities certainly made him appear unreliable. There was also the chance that he would try to maneuver her out of the line of succession.

When at last the royal couple met in person, tempers flared, and a "disagreeable discussion" took place.[16] As she had feared, Ferdinand and his relatives thought he should be the undisputed ruler, as the closest living male relative to Isabella's father. Some of his supporters believed that women did not have the capacity to govern. Isabella and her partisans, however, maintained that Castile and León had a long history of women sovereigns who ruled in their own right, most notably Queen Urraca. They said that Isabella was the direct descendant of King Juan II of Castile, and that whatever authority Ferdinand might hold in that kingdom would be derived through his marital association with Isabella. Both Isabella and Ferdinand, in other words, saw themselves as the legitimate ruler, and the other as consort.

Ferdinand was deeply offended, his virility undercut by what he viewed as a public humiliation. He announced he was leaving for Aragon. Isabella begged him to stay, "protesting that she would never for any reason have wanted to cause the least humiliation to her most beloved consort, for whose happiness and honor she would sacrifice willingly not only the crown but her own health." She said she "would not or could not live separated from him."

Isabella had a true marital crisis on her hands, a breach that could have destroyed her marriage and her kingdom. At this point, she might easily have folded under the pressure and given him control of the kingdom, simply to maintain marital harmony.

She needed a man by her side to help her overcome the gender stigma she was facing. "Women, even those with a clear right of succession, were rarely accepted as monarchs unless they were married," writes historian Janna Bianchini about Queen Berenguela.[17]

And the marriage also needed to be fruitful to establish Isabella's authority, which also required Ferdinand's presence. "Medieval queenship might be achieved because a woman was the wife or daughter of a king, but almost inevitably, a successful queen was a mother,"[18] writes scholar Miriam Shadis.

It was essential that Isabella should find a way to keep Ferdinand in

tow. So, while she continued to hold her ground, she did it with such sua-
vity and in such soothing terms that Ferdinand's resistance eventually
dissipated. She convinced him that the division of power would be more
superficial than real, and that as her husband, he would enjoy personal
power and autonomy. She suggested that if he were to oppose her right
to reign, he would also undermine the rights of their only child, their
daughter, who was also a female. He also had to acknowledge the validity
of the prenuptial agreement he had signed with Isabella, in which he had
agreed to serve as prince consort rather than as king.[19] He had signed in
the rush of excitement over the wedding and had not perhaps at the time
appreciated its significance.

Isabella found ways to placate him with a power-sharing agreement
he found acceptable. The archbishops of Toledo and Seville helped draft
a new contract, called the Concordat of Segovia, that gave Ferdinand
little real power but much symbolic importance. Isabella remained "pro-
prietary queen" of Castile, and her children, but not Ferdinand's children
by other women, would inherit the throne. They agreed, however, that
Ferdinand's name would be joined to Isabella's in documents, in proc-
lamations, and on coins, and that his name would always go first. But
sovereignty in Castile and León, as well as the right to appoint officials
and decide how to spend money from the treasury, would belong solely
to Isabella.

A motto was crafted to present a unified front to the world: *Monta
tanto, tanto monta,* meaning "as one is, so is the other," Isabella is as Ferdinand, Ferdinand is as Isabella. This saved face for Ferdinand and allowed
him to claim responsibility for much that Isabella did in the rest of their
marriage. But it was merely a facade of mutuality, because in fact, as Isabella's associates noted, Ferdinand's letters were edited and ripped up if
she did not approve of what he said, and his limited proficiency in Latin
meant that he could not read letters sent between the Castilian court and
other heads of state. Isabella, on the other hand, soon embarked on an
intensive program of Latin instruction to make herself more competent
in the language of international diplomacy, requiring her daughter and
ladies-in-waiting to take the same courses.

When Ferdinand and Isabella were not together, however, he would
enjoy equal power with the queen and the power to act in her place.
The negotiations for the concordat were conducted over the Christmas
holidays, and he remained in Castile for the next five months.[20] It was

Ferdinand's longest stay at Isabella's side since the first year of their marriage.

Isabella had held her ground—Castile would be hers to govern—but she had damaged her standing in the eyes of history. During her lifetime, she would hold precedence over Ferdinand, and in fact she ruled in Castile, which was much larger and more important than Aragon. But the nomenclature issue—the fact that his name came first—had long-term effects, for they commonly came to be known as "Ferdinand and Isabella," which seemed to imply his dominance. The happenstance of the Spanish language exacerbated this situation: in English, husband-and-wife monarchs are known as the king and the queen, but in Spanish they take the male forms in the plural, so Ferdinand and Isabella were known as the Reyes, rather than as Rey and Reyna. English speakers would gain the impression that it was the king in Castile who acted, when actually it was the queen. Isabella's role in Castile as reigning queen was so rare in world history that observers and commentators seemed unable to comprehend that a woman could be sovereign, and they persisted in identifying Ferdinand as the ruler regardless of the facts. And so it happened that Ferdinand's name has always been cited first, in documents, then in diplomatic circles far from the Iberian peninsula where news accounts arrived secondhand, and finally in history books. In time he began to receive the credit for her accomplishments.

This was a concession Isabella had been willing to make to try to keep her husband happy. And in some ways, it did. He was still young, only about twenty-two, but he was already cynical, and he may have realized that the perception of power can be almost as valuable as the reality.

The extended marital renegotiation and reconciliation between Isabella and Ferdinand eventually led to another odd turn of fate. A local churchman, Tomás de Torquemada, the Dominican friar whose uncle had been a powerful cardinal in Rome, played an important role in bringing the couple back together and helping them reach agreement on the thorny issues of joint administration. Isabella had met Torquemada during her childhood, though it is difficult to say to what extent they interacted. Certainly she knew him, for he was a cleric of considerable standing in Segovia as prior of the Convento de Santa Cruz la Real, or the Royal Holy Cross Monastery, which was an ancient Dominican establishment. Torquemada and Ferdinand soon discovered they had a natural affinity for each other; Torquemada became Ferdinand's favored confessor and a personal confidant. The Dominican friar soon began accompanying the king as he traveled from place to place in Castile, keeping close at hand, to such an extent that his presence came to be noted by other officials. In June 1475, for example, when Ferdinand traveled to Valladolid and Burgos, leaving Isabella behind in Ávila, he was accompanied by Torquemada. Two months later Torquemada was in Valladolid with the king; he is also recorded as traveling with Ferdinand in November of that year. He was in the king's entourage again in January and February 1476, and he traveled with the king on extended trips at least two more times that year.

Given the fragility of the marriage at that time, it was not surprising that the couple chose to highlight their unity by showing special favor to Torquemada, who had helped bind their spiritual, marital, and political lives. They ordered an expansion of his monastery, crowning the work with a spectacular new door to celebrate their union. Elaborately decorated with symbols representing them both, and with the inscription TANTO MONTA, MONTA TANTO as a recurring architectural motif, the building was one of the first major construction projects undertaken by the couple. The portal commemorated their accession to the Castilian throne, and in an extraordinary display of royal favor, they gave their closest friends, Andrés de Cabrera and Beatriz de Bobadilla, a conspicuous place in its sculptures. Directly over the great entry doors was a crucified Christ, with the Valencian proselytizing friar Vincent Ferrer, now a saint, at his feet. Below the figure of Christ was a tableau that contained depictions of people closely associated with Christ in his lifetime. But Queen Isabella and her friend Beatriz were carved in stone on the right side of the Holy Family, and Ferdinand and Andrés de Cabrera were placed on the left. In that way, Isabella and Ferdinand told posterity of the central role that Beatriz de Bobadilla, Andrés de Cabrera, and Tomás de Torquemada had played in the creation of their reign.

Queen Isabella certainly needed Torquemada's help in keeping her marriage on a steady course, for at times the power-sharing arrangement seemed more a facade than a reality. Isabella attempted to perpetuate the perception of Ferdinand's significance because it helped ease marital tensions, and because her position was more secure if a man appeared to be playing the dominant role. Once she established herself as the sole wielder of power in the kingdom, she began pretending that she was acting in partnership with her husband. Hernán de Talavera, confessor to the queen, recalled that when she was dictating a royal order for him to draft, she told him to sign it in the form of a joint effort. *Pongase rey y reyna*, she told him, or "Sign it king and queen."[21]

Isabella promoted an impression that theirs was a happy, unified marriage—two people working together in harness for the betterment of the nation. But we have many indications that the marital bliss may have been illusory, what would later be called a "nuptial fiction."[22] When they were living separately, he had more authority than when they were living together. He frequently took to the road, often heading off in a different direction from her.

Isabella and Ferdinand jointly appointed officials for their household and administrative staffs. Isabella's longtime friend Gonzalo Chacón was named primary financial officer, and Gutierre de Cárdenas was secondary financial officer. Gabriel Sánchez, of Aragon, was appointed to handle household finances. Many of the leading official posts were given to highly educated conversos of proven ability—people who received their jobs through their own merits and not through inherited position. The Castilian Alonso de Burgos, for example, grandson of the former rabbi of Burgos, served as a political and spiritual adviser to the court and as confessor to Isabella. Just as close to Isabella was Andrés de Cabrera, also of converso background, who was married to her friend Beatriz de Bobadilla.

But even as Isabella eased tensions with one man in her family, problems erupted with another.

* * *

King Afonso V of Portugal, who was her cousin and the brother of Enrique's second wife, Queen Juana, still felt that Isabella's elopement with Ferdinand had shorn him of his prize—Isabella and the crown of Castile. In the four years since Ferdinand and Isabella were wed, Afonso's reputation had grown. He had won an important set of victories in 1471, with the invasion and conquest of Asilah and Tangiers, both in North Africa, giving him control of rich gold mines there. Afonso had become wealthy. A vain and proud man, he memorialized his victories in triumphant tapestries, woven from wool and silk, that depicted his troops swarming over the walls of the cities, seizing them, and setting the women and children to flight from their homes.

Afonso depicted himself heroically in these tapestries, showing him-self and his son João on horseback at the center of the battle, bedecked in fine suits of armor, jostling among the crush of soldiers who marched alongside them on foot. His actual performance was considerably less glorious than presented. The Muslims at Asilah had wanted to surrender, but while Afonso was negotiating the terms of the truce with them, his adrenaline-fueled soldiers had decided to attack the walls of the city on their own rather than accept an orchestrated victory. Afonso was quickly swept up in the melee, storming the ramparts with his men. The Muslims were unprepared for hand-to-hand combat, and Afonso and his soldiers slaughtered some two thousand of them and took five thousand captive, engaging in a particularly brutal assault on a mosque where some resi-dents had taken refuge.[23] Afonso could keep the captives as slaves, because he had gotten a special ruling from Pope Nicholas V that exempted him from the Christian ban on slavery, as long as the people who were being enslaved were "Saracens, pagans and other non-believers."

The actual conquest was the capstone to a day that had begun badly. Afonso had set a particular day for his landing from the sea, and when that morning dawned cloudy, windy, and stormy, he insisted on head-ing for the beach anyway. His men followed him, boarding unseaworthy boats. Many of the vessels were soon swamped by the waves or crashed on the rocks. Some two hundred knights and infantrymen drowned that morning, their heavy equipment dragging them underwater. The terrible incident was recorded in a section of one of the tapestries; it told viewers that Afonso was willing to pay a high price in human lives to secure a footnote in history for himself.

Because he was accustomed to getting his own way, Afonso still felt "personal rancor" toward Isabella for what he perceived as a rejection, and he was not the sort of man who could easily forget a slight.[24] Now Isabella's enemies saw a way to stir up his old resentment to their own advantage, by offering to make him king of Castile, long a rival to Por-tugal. Castile would have been a valuable plum to him: it encompassed about two-thirds of the Iberian peninsula and population; Portugal held only about one-quarter.[25] Gaining control of Castile and León would have turned Afonso, already heady with his recent victory in North Africa, into one of the leading rulers of Europe.

They could even hold out the promise of a replacement bride, because little Juana, the daughter of the late Enrique IV and the Portuguese queen, who had a claim to the Castilian throne, was available to be married. Juan Pacheco, the son and namesake of King Enrique's old ally, had taken control of Princess Juana when his father died. The princess, now thirteen years old, was offered in marriage to King Afonso of Portugal. Isabella and Ferdinand tried to counter the offer by proposing that Afonso instead marry Ferdinand's younger sister, who was at home in Aragon.

King Afonso rebuffed that offer and demanded that Isabella and Ferdinand step down, asserting that his niece and bride-to-be, little Juana, was the true queen. Isabella responded that the people who were now asserting Juana's right to rule were the same people who had previously insisted that the child was illegitimate.

The dispute with Portugal was clearly a ground for concern. But at this early point in her reign—still only a few months after the coronation—Queen Isabella had different priorities. Needing to assert her authority over her own kingdom, she launched her reign with pageantry designed to boost the status of the monarchy and her right to rule. She was finally free, and had the resources, to dress splendidly, as did Ferdinand. Golden threads were woven into their garments, and they wore jewels and furs. They had the gratifying opportunity to circulate in places they had known in their earlier lives, receiving adulation and admiration from the crowd. They traveled to Valladolid, where they had been married so hastily to evade Enrique's guards and soldiers, but this time they were feted with parties of all kinds, jousts and bullfights, great banquets and musical entertainments, where the young people could perform the latest popular dances.

But the celebration ended on a jarring note when the two monarchs learned that King Afonso's troops were massing on the border with the intention of invading Castile. Juana had accused Isabella of poisoning her father and illegally seizing the throne. King Afonso of Portugal had decided this wrong needed to be avenged and that the Castilian crown was his to take.

In late May the war commenced. Afonso surged into Castile with more than ten thousand warriors on foot and horseback, supplied with two hundred cartloads of provisions, heavy artillery, and other baggage. His wealth was conspicuously on display, as he hauled a vast cache of golden crosses, coins, and engraved silverplate, intending to demonstrate his superior strength and resources. "He spent a great sum of gold" to win the support of Castilian nobles who would accept his proposed marriage to his niece Juana and have him as their king.[26] Their close familial relationship required a papal dispensation, but the king pressed on with his plans nonetheless. King Afonso celebrated his engagement to Juana and then their wedding with lavish festivities in Extremadura, near the Portuguese border, then returned to the work of preparing for war.

Isabella and Ferdinand readied themselves for battle as well. As would soon become their pattern, she handled logistics while he led the troops in the field. She urged him on ferociously; he set out almost immediately.

Isabella commanded her subjects to carry the war to Portugal and to attack its cities and towns, not just to wait until the Portuguese troops surged into view. "You are aware that Don Afonso, King of Portugal," and his troops have invaded Castile, with the goal of provoking "outrages" against the kingdom, she wrote in a letter circulated around the kingdom. And so, she announced, she had ordered Don Alfonso de Cárdenas "to make war, by fire and by blood, against that King of Portugal," to enter his kingdom, and to destroy towns and places there. She expected her subjects to pick up arms in defense of Castile, she added, to demonstrate their "ancient and accustomed loyalty" to the throne.[27]

Nine months of intense border raids ensued, with battle lines shifting from place to place. Isabella and Ferdinand mobilized fairly quickly but still seemed at a disadvantage because of King Afonso's reputation as a wily and experienced soldier. The odds seemed stacked against them. The grandees of Castile were compelled to take sides once again, this time in what became known as the War of 1475 to 1479. Many remained loyal to Isabella, while others were more equivocal, and one important former ally defected altogether—Alfonso Carrillo, the mercurial archbishop of Toledo. The powerful prelate had grown angry at both Ferdinand and Isabella. He was annoyed by Ferdinand's lack of deference to him; he was insulted by their growing collaboration with his rival Mendoza, who had been given the cardinal's hat; and he had had that embarrassing public clash with Isabella over the alchemist. Now when Isabella most needed Carrillo's help and support, he turned against her.

Isabella rode to Carrillo's stronghold, hoping he would join in her defense. Instead the archbishop rudely informed her, through a messenger, that he had switched sides. "If the queen comes in one gate, I will go out another," he told his servant.[28] She was stunned by this abrupt reversal, as Archbishop Carrillo had been her ally for almost a decade. Observers said she fell to her knees, praying to God for help, feeling abandoned. Archbishop Carrillo had been at her side ever since they had traveled together in support of her brother Prince Alfonso, and his defection wounded her deeply.

But she had had a great many disappointments in her life by this point, and as she usually did, she soon rallied and went forward. Within a year, her outreach to nobles, offering them clemency and rewards if they laid down arms, proved effective and the tide shifted in her direction. King Afonso was forced to pull troops out of Castile to defend his cities in Portugal that Isabella had placed under assault.

The two sides finally and climactically clashed, in the major confrontation known as the Battle of Toro, on March 1, 1476. The Portuguese army, led by King Afonso, his twenty-one-year-old son Prince João, and the rebellious Archbishop Carrillo of Toledo opposed Ferdinand, the Duke of Alba, Cardinal Mendoza, and other Castilian nobles leading the Isabelline forces. Foggy and rainy, it was bloody chaos on the battlefield, where fierce hand-to-hand fighting erupted. Hundreds of people—perhaps as many as one thousand—died that day. Some of the Portuguese who died were not killed in battle but drowned in the Douro River in the darkness and confusion.

It was difficult to re-create later exactly what had happened because the Portuguese and Castilian accounts differed. Troops led by Prince João won in their part of the battle; some troops led by King Ferdinand won in another part. But the most telling fact was that King Afonso had fled the battlefield with his troops in disarray; the Castilians seized his battle flag, the royal standard of Portugal, despite the valiant efforts of a Portuguese soldier, Duarte de Almeida, to retain it. Almeida had been holding the flag aloft in his right arm, which was slashed from his body, and so he transferred the pendant to his other arm and kept fighting. Then his other arm was cut off, and he held the flag in his teeth until he finally succumbed to death. The Portuguese, however, later managed to recover the banner.

The battle ended in an inconclusive outcome, but Isabella employed a masterstroke of political theater by recasting events as a stupendous victory for Castile. Each side had won some skirmishes and lost others, but Ferdinand was presented in Castile as the winner and Afonso as a craven failure and laughingstock. In medieval terms, the possession of the flag also signified a triumph. Isabella announced it as a sign of God's will and support for their reign. She walked barefoot in the winter cold to give thanks at the Monastery of San Pablo in Tordesillas, and she vowed to found a monastery and church in Toledo for perpetual remembrance of the triumph.

Management of the perception of the battle rather than the event itself ended up influencing people's opinions, and ultimately their belief about what had occurred. "Not a military victory, but a political victory, the battle of Toro is in itself, a decisive event, because it [resolved] the civil war in favour of the Catholic Monarchs," wrote a group of Spanish historians who studied the battle and its aftermath.[29]

Peace did not come quickly, however, only by fits and starts over the next four years, with continuing loss of life on both sides. The war did not officially end until 1479, when Isabella reached a peace agreement by negotiating it directly with her Portuguese aunt, Beatriz, her mother's sister. These were high-level talks because of the family ties they represented. Beatriz was King Afonso's cousin and Prince João's mother-in-law and therefore was related by blood and marriage to all the disputants. She was an unusually wise woman, as her mother, Isabella's grandmother, had been, and everyone ultimately agreed to abide by the terms she devised to settle the grievances.

King Afonso himself had dropped out of the war after the first year. But given his military renown and stature, the drawn Battle of Toro was still a humiliating defeat for him. Unnerved, he turned to France in search of reinforcements and assistance and spent a fruitless year there begging for help, until gradually he realized that the faithless King Louis was considering handing him over to Ferdinand. When he began formulating plans to escape from France wearing a disguise, Louis shamefacedly ordered ships to send the humiliated sovereign home.[30] Afonso returned to Portugal, where he shared power with his son João, who took the title King João II, until the father finally died in a monastery in 1481. He had been utterly vanquished by the young man and woman whom he had once dismissively viewed as mere willful teenagers. Young King João accepted the truce but stewed with resentment over this turn of events, continuing to view Queen Isabella with enmity. She watched him warily from Castile.

Little Juana's life also disintegrated. Her father, King Enrique, if he was her father, had not effectively secured her future. Her mother, the former Queen Juana, Enrique's wife, who had gone on to give birth to two illegitimate children, died in 1475 in Madrid. She was young at her death—only thirty-six—and the cause was never determined. She had disgraced her once-proud brother, King Afonso of Portugal, whose efforts to support her daughter's cause and uphold the family honor had led to such abject humiliation. "Some say she was poisoned by her brother . . . and others that she died attempting to abort another child," writes the scholar Nancy F. Marino. "No one mourned at the time of her death."[31]

Little Juana, after her mother's death and her husband Afonso's abandonment of her while he wandered off to France, was left adrift. The truce arrangement between Isabella and Beatriz offered Juana the option of joining a nunnery, and she agreed, either willingly or because she believed she had no choice. Four years after the war started, Juana entered the Convent of Santa Clara in Coimbra, Portugal, later moving to the Castle of Saint George. She never gave up her belief that she was the rightful queen and signed her letters Yo, La Reina, for the rest of her life. Living quietly, however, and causing no trouble for anyone, she appears to have had a fairly normal life until her death in 1530.

Did Isabella usurp Juana's throne and take her place as queen? It is possible that little Juana was indeed the king's daughter and should have been declared queen. But her mother's sexual behavior certainly raised questions about the child's legitimacy.

Enrique's own sexual behavior raised further questions. The king failed to produce any other children, either legitimate or illegitimate, during his thirty-four years of physical maturity, which included two decades of marriage, first to Blanca and then to Juana. The other rulers who were his peers produced far more offspring. King Edward IV of England had ten legitimate children and possibly five more out of wedlock; Maximilian I had two legitimate children and twelve more who were illegitimate; as a cardinal, Rodrigo Borgia had between four and eight children, despite his vow of chastity; King Louis XI of France had at least eight; King Afonso had at least five. Many women would have been honored to bear a royal child. King Enrique almost certainly had a serious reproductive problem of some sort, and his physicians thought he was infertile. If he was homosexual, he probably had a low level of sexual interest in women as well.

How much of this did Isabella know? Probably a lot. She had lived at court as a lady-in-waiting to Queen Juana, which put her into close, direct, around-the-clock contact with the young queen. She may have witnessed things that persuaded her that Juana was illegitimate.

It is also possible that Isabella wasn't entirely sure about Juana's legitimacy but had come to believe that she herself was destined to rule and that her kingdom needed what she had to offer. She certainly took the kingdom's problems enormously to heart and began, as soon as she took the throne, to confront unaddressed conditions that had deteriorated over the past decades. There is no sign that Juana, in contrast, had any sense of obligation to the citizens at large.

* * *

Regardless of the legalities or the ultimate justice of the situation, as the Portugese threat began to fade, Queen Isabella turned her full attention to the core problems facing Castile. She convened her first administrative council, or Cortes, in April 1476. The challenges were staggering. The kingdom's currency had been debased, its finances were in chaos, consumers were being defrauded, and criminals prowled without fear of apprehension. She began to work at setting things to rights and quickly achieved some notable successes.

She reinvigorated an old system of armed local militias known as the Santa Hermandad, or the "Sacred Brotherhood," law-enforcement brigades empowered by towns and cities to capture criminals. These Hermandad units, paid for by the municipalities, soon became organized as a kind of independent royal militia, trained to maintain order and accountable to Isabella as queen of Castile. Isabella conducted many trials herself. Some critics might have questioned whether accused people were receiving due process before they faced summary judgment, up to and including execution, but most people were grateful that civil order was being restored after the rampant lawlessness of previous decades.

Isabella also changed the composition of the royal council, which had been dominated by the aristocracy during her brother's reign. To her new council she appointed three nobles and nine lawyers. The head of the council was a cleric; one of her early choices for this post was the converso Alfonso de Burgos. Through this means she began to administer the government more professionally, creating a bureaucracy comprised of an educated elite chosen by merit, not just by noble birth. Her frequent choice of conversos to hold key positions underscored this shift from medieval to modern management principles, and it encouraged more Jews to see advantages in converting to Christianity.

She also applied new scrutiny to the church. She promoted scholarship, valued education for clerics, and sought to clean out corruption, which was a growing concern throughout the Christian world.

Queen Isabella's allies watched sympathetically as she juggled the demands of the job. She is "so young" to take on governing "so hard" a nation, wrote the converso courtier Hernando del Pulgar to the Spanish ambassador to Rome, "listening every hour to so much advice, so much information, one thing contrary to another, and ... words of trickery that challenge the simple ears."[32] But crime was so widespread that she was obliged to take up those burdens, he added, noting that "the land is in threat of eternal damnation because of the lack of justice."

But all the while, Isabella was pondering the single most important item on her agenda: creating and financing an army to field against the Islamic emirate in Granada, which she believed could become a beachhead once again for a Muslim attack on the Iberian peninsula. Looking ahead, she feared that a confrontation was looming with Mehmet the Conqueror, ruler of the expanding Ottoman Empire, and she was worried about protecting her family, which was at last starting to grow.

ELEVEN

THE TRIBE OF ISABEL

L ittle Isabel, the namesake of her mother and grandmother, was almost eight when at last she became a big sister.

Her mother the queen had experienced seven long years of infertility, of waiting and hoping, as the conception and delivery of healthy infants was the single most important responsibility of royalty. Queen Isabella anxiously consulted doctors; she prayed at sanctuaries where she sought intervention by saints known to aid with childbirth; she starved herself and engaged in self-mortification. She had at least one miscarriage during those years, and the fact that the child had been a male made the disappointment all the more acute.

Then Ferdinand came home for a few months in the fall of 1477, and matters resolved themselves. Isabella became pregnant once again, to the relief of all. The pressure had been palpable. "It is good, Your Excellency, for here is the most grave and grand matter of Spain, and nothing is more necessary or desired," a courtier wrote to Ferdinand in March 1478.[1] While awaiting the baby, Ferdinand fervently prayed for a son and pledged that he would show his appreciation to God if his wish were fulfilled. Isabella, meanwhile, had an idea in mind for how to show their thankfulness.

This baby was born in Seville on June 30, 1478, when Isabella was twenty-seven years old. The birth followed royal custom: Isabel was attended by a midwife, and the room was packed with noblemen and city officials, who would all be able to swear the infant was indeed the child of the queen. When Isabel finally *da a luz,* or "gave light" and life to the infant, the entire city erupted in paroxysms of joy—a wild and boisterous celebration that lasted three days and nights.

The child was a boy, the long-desired male heir, and the disappointment of little Isabel's birth was quickly forgotten. They named the baby Juan, the name shared by both his maternal and his paternal grandfathers. That was also the name of Isabella's patron saint, John the Evangelist, and of Ferdinand's, Saint John the Baptist. But Isabella's joy was such that when she referred to her son, she most often called him her "angel." He even looked like a cherub, with his pale blond hair and delicate features. Spaniards all over the kingdom rejoiced, seeing the boy's arrival as proof of God's favor. This child would reign over both Castile and Aragon, making a lasting political union of the two kingdoms that were now linked only by marriage.

Unlike the birth of Queen Isabella or her daughter Isabel, this child's arrival was greeted with ostentatious ceremony. On July 9, about a week after Prince Juan was born, a stately procession wound its way through the streets of Seville from the palace to the cathedral, as throngs of onlookers and well-wishers crammed into the narrow streets to add their shouts of welcome to the baby heir to the throne. The child's nurse, riding a mule, carried the infant swaddled in brocade cloth, under a brocade canopy, flanked by eight city officials decked in black velvet cloaks. Three young court pages followed behind, bearing gifts of gold and coins. Elegantly attired courtiers vied for spots in the line; clerics held aloft silver crosses. The archbishop of Seville, Pedro González de Mendoza, whose support had been won with the gift of the cardinal's hat, officiated at the baptismal service.

"All the crosses from all the churches in the city" were hauled into the open to greet the procession as it passed through the streets. "Infinite numbers of musicians playing all sorts of instruments, of trumpets," and drums and flutes welcomed the infant prince.[2]

A month later a second ceremony, even more elaborate than the first, took place. This time, Queen Isabella, having recovered from childbirth, marched in the procession, dressed in a bejeweled gown shimmering with pearls, surrounded again by Castile's highest courtiers. She attended high mass at a service conducted at the main altar of the church.

"The queen went to mass to present the prince to the temple, and to offer him to God according to the custom of Holy Mother Church, very triumphantly," wrote the chronicler Andrés Bernáldez, in an obvious analogy to the New Testament stories of the presentation of the baby Jesus.[3] According to the Gospel of Luke, Mary and Joseph took Jesus to the temple in Jerusalem forty days after his birth, following Jewish custom. It was a popular ceremony in the Middle Ages and included prayers of thanksgiving for the mother's survival and the baby's continued good health.

Indeed, Juan's birth seemed nothing short of sacred and miraculous to loyal Spaniards. Isabella and Ferdinand were increasingly identified with the Holy Family—and Isabella, especially, as the abundant and fertile mother, the Mary figure to the Catholic way of thinking, the woman who bore the sacred male child, the queen not just of the earthly plane but also of heaven. To the conversos in the court, Catholics of Jewish descent, such as Diego de Valera, Hernando del Pulgar, and Isabel's new confessor Hernán de Talavera, the child's birth was the kind of event predicted in Holy Scripture. "Clearly we see ourselves given a very special gift by God, for at the end of such a long wait He has desired to give him to us," wrote Pulgar in a letter to a colleague.

> The Queen had paid to this kingdom the debt of male succession that she was obligated to give it. As for me, I have faith that he has to be the most welcome prince in the world, because all those who are born desired are friends of God, as were Isaac, Samuel and Saint John. . . . And not without cause, then were they conceived and born by virtue of many prayers and sacrifices. . . . Because God rejected the temple of Enrique and did not choose the tribe of Alfonso; but chose the tribe of Isabel whom he preferred.[4]

The happiness of the birth offset some of the bitterness of the previous years. It wasn't surprising that Isabella had failed to become pregnant for such a long time, because Ferdinand had almost never been home in the initial years after she became queen. At first the war against the Portuguese provided a plausible explanation: Ferdinand's presence was frequently needed on the front lines. But the periods of separation were often lengthy. In the early months of her reign, Isabella and her husband had been together, but for much of the rest of 1475 they had lived separately. In 1476 the couple spent only about eleven weeks together and forty-one weeks apart. In 1477, 1478, and 1479, they were together about only half of each year. It's hard to imagine that people who were deeply in love would willingly spend that much time apart.

One letter from Ferdinand, written in May 1475, suggests that the periods of separation were now more Isabella's choice than his, perhaps because she was generally working so feverishly and galloping from place to place to deal with problems on the ground:

> My ladyship, now at last it is clear which of us two loves best . . . I can see that you can be happy while I lose my sleep, because messenger comes after messenger and brings me no letter from you. The reason why you do not write is not because there is no paper to be had, or that you do not know how to write, but because you do not love me and because you are proud. . . . Well! One day you will return to your old affection. If you do not, I shall die and the guilt will be yours.[5]

Is it possible that Isabella sometimes treated Ferdinand badly? At least one observer said she treated him cavalierly, ordering him about. "The queen is king, and the king is her servant," a foreign visitor wrote. "He immediately does whatever it is that she decides."[6]

Certainly they had their tiffs. In July 1475 in Tordesillas, they exchanged sharp words in other people's presence. Ferdinand had left Tordesillas and set out against the Portuguese, who appeared, ready to do battle, just as his supplies were running low. Outnumbered, Ferdinand decided to withdraw back to the town to gather supplies and more troops. Isabella lashed out at him for what she saw as his timidity and failure, her words laced with sarcasm: "Although we women lack the intelligence to know, the courage to do, and the tongue to speak, I have discovered that we have eyes to see," she said to him scornfully. "The truth is that I saw a great army departing from the fields at Tordesillas and it seems to me, as the woman that I am, that I could have conquered the world with it, as it included such good knights, horses and soldiers."[7] He needed to have shown more grit, she told him. "The one who begins nothing ends nothing."

Ferdinand, for his part, defended his action, saying that he had been outnumbered ten to one, and that to have joined the battle would likely have meant many deaths. She seemed disappointed that they had returned alive but without a victory, he said, instead of offering more appropriate "words of consolation."[8] "There has never been a man born who can satisfy you," he told his wife bitterly. Soon thereafter the Battle of Toro was joined, and at least for practical purposes, it was won.

The occasion at Tordesillas wasn't their only point of disagreement. They also quarreled over women, and Ferdinand's inability to remain faithful to the queen. Most of his known philandering occurred far from the court, when he was at home in Barcelona or traveling elsewhere in his kingdom, but sometimes he engaged in affairs closer to home as well.

A young woman who became a particularly notorious seductress had entered court through her connections with Isabella's closest friend and confidante, Beatriz de Bobadilla. Beatriz's proximity to the queen was advantageous to her own extended family, who also moved into the inner circle of the court. Through this means Beatriz's alluring niece, also known as Beatriz de Bobadilla, attracted Ferdinand's eye. She and Ferdinand soon began a passionate affair. The young woman's father had been the royal master of the hunt, a fact that inspired much ribald humor around court, where people tittered about amorous individuals stalking and capturing their prey. Someone drew charcoal pictures of what the Italian courtier Baldassare Castiglione termed "lascivious animals" on the door to the young woman's home, and it happened that the queen passing by spotted the drawings. One court wit was so bold as to point them out to her, saying, "Behold, Madam, the heads of the beasts that [Señorita] Bobadilla slays every day in the hunt."[9] The jest was clever but must also have shamed and embarrassed the queen.

The queen finally ordered the young woman to marry a nobleman visiting the court, then dispatched the newlyweds to the distant Canary Islands to subdue the rebellious native population. Beatriz was not the only young woman to be married off and sent away in this manner. There is no record of Ferdinand ever protesting this method of handling relationships that had become tedious or awkward. Perhaps he grew tired of the young women himself and didn't mind being relieved of a potentially acrimonious ending.

The king and queen also differed over the administration of the church. Isabella was preoccupied with reforming the church, easing out people who saw their posts as sinecures and replacing them with priests and nuns who had a real commitment to preaching and leading the flock. It must have been supremely irritating to her that Ferdinand was pursuing a church position for his illegitimate son—exactly the kind of conduct that church reformers were singling out for criticism.

In late 1475 Ferdinand's illegitimate brother Juan of Aragon died. Their father had arranged for Juan to be named archbishop of Zaragoza, the highest church official in the Kingdom of Aragon, who had responsibility for the souls of many parishioners and also controlled vast wealth and a large number of vassals on church-owned estates. Now, with the position open, Ferdinand asked his father if the job could be given to his own illegitimate son, Don Alonso of Aragon, who was six years old.[10] This request was problematic: how could a six-year-old provide spiritual guidance to a congregation? And it was on its face corrupt because the obvious goal was to gain control of church funds that would be administered and used by the archbishop—or his father. To make matters worse, the job had already been promised to a well-qualified, mature prelate, Ausiàs de Puggio, who was well along in his preparations for taking over the post.

In March 1476, Ferdinand asked again. The Vatican's preferred candidate, Ausiàs, refused to step aside. Ferdinand and his father warned the man that if he persisted in seeking the spot, his family's lands in Aragon would be seized. At this point Ausiàs prudently decided to drop his claim. Falling quickly into line, Pope Sixtus IV named Ferdinand's child, now seven years old, as archbishop of Zaragoza.

For Isabella, who was sincerely interested in cleansing the church of simony, or the corrupt awarding of church offices, these negotiations must have been touchy on several levels. She disapproved of just the kind of thing Ferdinand had accomplished for his illegitimate son. Unlike her husband, she always sought the strongest and best candidates for these church offices. Vatican officials generally didn't like being pressed by kings and queens to appoint particular people of their own choosing to church posts, something they called "lay investiture," but in Isabella's case, the people she chose exemplified altruistic church ideals. "Isabella, however, it must be said, used her privilege in favour of really excellent men," wrote the Vatican historian Ludwig Pastor, noting that most church appointments at the time went to the wealthy and well connected, not to those most deserving or worthy of their clerical posts.[11]

* * *

But if Isabella and Ferdinand differed on some fronts, in other ways their religious convictions, dynastic ambitions, and sense of divine mission welded them together. To celebrate Ferdinand's purported victory against the Portuguese in the Battle of Toro, Isabella initiated the construction of a new church at Toledo. She named it San Juan de los Reyes, to honor her deceased father, King Juan II of Castile, and Ferdinand's still-living father, King Juan II of Aragon. That name also allowed her to simultaneously give homage to their two patron saints, Saint John the Evangelist and Saint John the Baptist.

Isabella was growing very interested in architecture, and in this building she began to develop her own style and taste, melding the style that came to be known as Isabelline with the style known as Plateresque. This style featured traditional Iberian elements, with simple but soaring and cavernous Gothic-inspired interiors, and rich sculptural treatments for the exteriors, all carved in golden stone. Soon churches, colleges, and hospitals built in this style were erected in Salamanca, Segovia, Valladolid, Aranda de Duero, Burgos, and Seville, all bearing her personal marks— her coats of arms and the yoke and *flechas,* the epigraphic symbols for her marriage to Ferdinand. Ropes signifying the Gordian knot tie these elements together. That is a reference to the riddle of the Gordian knot that Alexander the Great famously confronted, and a problem he solved by slashing the rope in two with his sword. And that, in itself, represents an idea: that the end justifies the means.

The first Isabelline-style building, and the one that most clearly bore her personal mark, was San Juan de los Reyes. Construction was started in 1477, and within a year, the church and attached monastery were already housing a contingent of Franciscan monks. But when the queen and king came back in 1479 to inspect the work under way, she was scathing in her evaluation. "Have you built such a trifle for me here?" she was said to have asked.[12]

More complex and ornate plans were quickly drawn up under the queen's supervision by architect Juan Guas. Isabella's tastes evolved, in keeping with the development of Renaissance styles coming into vogue, and later she would sponsor something entirely different in Rome. But for Castile, this style came to be her hallmark, a mixture of classical, Iberian, and Muslim motifs. These buildings became the enduring visual record of the places she came, saw, conquered.

The structure Ferdinand and Isabella jointly undertook to build in Rome, to honor the birth of their son Juan, became the world architectural masterpiece known as the Tempietto. It is located on the site where

Isabella and Ferdinand believed that Saint Peter—the apostle whom Jesus called the "rock" on which he would build his church—was crucified about A.D. 64. Peter is believed to have died during a persecution initiated by the emperor Nero, who blamed Christians in Rome for a fire that destroyed the city. The actual location of Peter's martyrdom is unknown, but this particular site had a legendary association with the event and also with an earlier monument, the Roman Temple of Vesta, the goddess of hearth, home, and family.

Consequently, an ancient monastery had been located on the site, known as San Pietro in Montorio, for hundreds of years. By the 1470s, the institution had become neglected and been abandoned, and in 1472 Pope Sixtus IV decided to revitalize it. He asked his personal confessor, Amadeo Menezes da Silva, to undertake restoration of the site.[13] And this led to the connection to Queen Isabella—for the monk Menes da Silva had been born a Portuguese nobleman and happened to be the brother of Beatriz da Silva, the saintly noblewoman who founded the Conceptionist religious order.

Beatriz's brother Amadeo took to this new responsibility to restore the sacred spot with particular gusto, reporting that he had experienced mystical visions at a grotto on the property, which attracted additional support for the work at hand. In 1480, when little Prince Juan was two, King Ferdinand announced that he intended to pay for the construction work at the site because of a vow he had made to build a church to Saint Peter.[14] It was the family's way of thanking God for the gift of a son.

Amadeo Menezes da Silva died in 1482, and within a few years, Ferdinand and Isabella had shifted responsibility for the work to Bernardino López de Carvajal, whom they sent as their ambassador to Rome. He assigned the task of building the special commemorative structure to a little-known, middle-aged architect from Milan who was beginning to make a name for himself by combining ancient and modern styles of construction and building ornamentation. His name was Donato Bramante, and what he built on the site is considered the first example of High Renaissance architecture in Italy. It would delight, fascinate, and amaze generations of art historians. Domed, with Doric columns, the "circular plan symbolizes divine perfection," according to the *World Atlas of Architecture*. "Inspired by ancient temples, the Tempietto is both a homage to antiquity and a Christian memorial."[15]

* * *

Juan's birth, when it came in 1478, had seemed to have eased the tensions between his parents and provided the means by which they could project themselves as an ascendant Christian monarchy with a long history and a great future. After 1479 Ferdinand and Isabella were together more than they were apart. The babies started coming like clockwork, one after the other.

In November 1479, in Toledo, Isabella again gave birth, this time to another daughter, whom they named Juana. She too was named in memory of all the great men named John. "And they gave her the name of that glorious Juan, he whom God had chosen among men," sang a minstrel about the child's birth.[16]

This time, however, the name had special poignancy because in January of that year, Ferdinand's pugnacious and resolute father had finally died, at age eighty-one. Ferdinand had succeeded him and was now finally and fully ruler of Aragon, Valencia, and Catalonia as well as Sicily. His new daughter was a living memorial to her grandfather Juan's fierce determination that his bloodline would rule Iberia. She was an unusually beautiful child, more impulsive and willful than her dutiful older sister, Princess Isabel, and her agreeable and charming brother Juan.

Then Isabella became pregnant again, growing unusually large and uncomfortable in comparison with previous pregnancies, making it difficult for her to travel. The thirty-one-year-old queen went into labor in June 1482, in Córdoba, and it soon became apparent that something was unusual with the delivery. She quickly gave birth to a baby, but the labor went on for another day and a half, and then a second child, a twin to the first, was delivered stillborn. The surviving twin, a blond-haired girl, was named María. After that dramatic birth, however, María's childhood drew little notice. With three older siblings, she somehow got lost in the crowd and did as she was told.

Three years later Queen Isabella delivered still another little girl and named her Catalina, or Catherine, after their ancestor, Catherine of Lancaster. This baby was ushered into an increasingly majestic world on December 16, 1485, a setting of wealth and opulence in a beautifully tapestried bedchamber in a palace in Alcalá de Henares. Strong, intelligent, and determined, she looked much like her sisters, fair-skinned with strawberry blond hair that darkened to light auburn as she left early childhood. She later received an identifying sobriquet that would tie her to her father's hereditary kingdom in the memory of future generations: she became known as Catherine of Aragon and soon thereafter as the Princess of Wales, the future queen of England. Of all Isabella's children, she was the one who was most like her mother.

Queen Isabella delivered all her children with her typical stoicism and extraordinary fortitude. "I have been informed by the ladies who serve her in her chamber that, neither when in pain through illness nor during the pains of childbirth . . . did they ever see her complain, and that, rather, she suffered them with marvelous fortitude," a court observer commented.[17]

At thirty-three, with five children, Isabella's family was complete. The independent queen, once easily able to jump astride a horse and travel effortlessly from town to town, now traveled with a vast entourage. The court remained itinerant, and so the queen needed to move not just her own things but the accoutrements required by a large brood of children at various stages of development.

They traveled constantly, as the demands of administering the kingdom never slackened. Queen Isabella started the year 1481, for example, in Medina del Campo and moved to Valladolid in February, staying there until April, when she moved to Calatayud in Aragon. In June she went to La Muela and then to Zaragoza. From August to November she was in Barcelona. In the last month of the year, she and Ferdinand moved almost daily, traveling from Molins de Rey, to Tarragona, to Cambrila, to Perello, to Tortosa, to San Mateo, to Almenara, to Murviedro, to Valencia, and on the last days of the year, back to Murviedro.

Traveling was no simple affair. In 1489 Queen Isabella employed about four hundred courtiers and household staff workers, all of whom traveled with her.[18] Her highest-paid ladies-in-waiting, representing the highest-ranking noblewomen in the kingdom, included not only Beatriz de Bobadilla, now known as the Marquesa de Moya, but also Teresa Enríquez, Inés Manrique, María de Luna, Leonor de Sotomayor, and Ana and Beatriz de Mendoza. Guards, pages, cupbearers, cooks, laundresses, musicians, and court physicians rounded out the staff. Isabella's obligations included feeding them, housing them, and frequently clothing them as well.

Her children had their own assigned households. Prince Juan employed eighty-two people in 1493, when he was fifteen years old. Catherine's household staff numbered fifteen when she was thirteen.[19]

These peregrinations resulted in lengthy processions. Tetzel, a pilgrim who visited Castile around that time, described watching a nobleman's itinerant court on the move. The man would ride a mule, he said, while his servants would run alongside him on foot, sometimes foraging for food along the way, then hurry ahead in time to prepare meals and arrange lodging or campsites. He saw household servants who were so tired "they can hardly walk." He came away impressed with their fortitude. "The Spaniards," he said, "are a people who can endure hunger and work."[20]

Traveling by horseback or on mules, accompanied by heavy-laden carts, must have been not just exhausting but a testament to careful planning, for Isabella and Ferdinand were required to move from place to place with imperial good grace and polish. The dress and appearance of the children, for example, was not just a source of pride but also an imperative of governing, conveying the family's social status and importance. They dressed in jeweled gowns, in velvets and brocades. All this clothing had to be cleaned, mended, transported. Regal settings had to be composed at every location as well, which meant that paintings, illuminated manuscripts, tapestries, and rugs were hauled from place to place to accompany the royal family. Court documents, legal decrees, and correspondence were transported in great leather and metal chests.

Isabella, acutely aware of the gaps in her own education, placed extreme importance on how the children were raised and educated. She had not been taught Latin in childhood, which meant she had to undertake the more difficult task of learning it as an adult, and she had had to hire a tutor for herself, the female scholar Beatriz Galindo. Isabella and all the ladies in her court, including her daughters, participated in these lessons.

Humiliated when she made errors in Latin, Isabella was careful not to repeat the mistake of giving her children a second-rate education when they would be expected to operate in the most elevated intellectual levels of society. Isabella's emphasis on girls' education helped spawn an academic revolution for women across Europe, as her court set a new standard of expectations for females who would rule either on their own or in partnership with their husbands. Under Queen Isabella's watchful and demanding eye, the children of the court received an extraordinary education.

Isabella's children were taught not only the Bible and the works of

Saints Augustine, Jerome, and Gregory, but also the classics, including Seneca, Prudentius, and the Roman historians. Isabella saw humanism not as the antithesis to religion but as a complement to it. Descendants of the Greeks, she and other Spanish nobles were creatures of the classical world as well as the biblical one.

Isabella retained as tutor to the boys the brilliant Italian humanist author and scholar Peter Martyr d'Anghiera, also known as Pedro Mártir de Anglería, whose place in their household gave him a unique window into Spanish history and international affairs. And he, in return, made the children objects of marvel throughout Europe. The Dutch scholar Erasmus would later describe Catherine as "miraculously learned for a woman" and a better scholar than her eventual husband, the erudite King Henry VIII.[21] Princess Juana could converse easily and casually in Latin with courtiers from other countries, and by the time she was a teenager, she was reciting and composing verse in that language.

Instruction at court operated as a kind of academy, as famous scholars led groups of children in Aristotelian discussion and debate. Artists and scholars mingled with noblemen, sharing thoughts and perspectives, writing poetry, songs, epigrams, and soon, the first of the early novels. "A key feature of Isabella's court was her patronage of artists and her love of culture, and she was the driving force behind artistic policy," writes a scholar of Renaissance art. "A number of painters made their living almost exclusively from court patronage, such as Juan de Flandes, . . . and Michael Sittow. . . . Isabella's conspicuous patronage of the arts established a fashion that was followed by the noble families in Spain."[22]

In addition to crafting artworks and literature, these artists were also required to teach the royal children and their pages and attendants. Prince Juan, for one, was tutored in these early years by a Dominican who was a professor at the University of Salamanca. As the children grew, the curriculum expanded to include catechism, Latin, and Castilian grammar, religious and secular history, philosophy, heraldry, drawing, music, and singing. A German scholar described a Latin class taught by Peter Martyr, with the students clustered around him: "His students were the duke of Villahermosa, the duke of Cardona, don Juan Carrillo, don Pedro de Mendoza, and many others from noble families, whom I saw reciting Juvenal and Horace," he wrote. "All these are awakening in Spain the taste for letters."[23]

Soon to join the youngsters were two new arrivals, the sons of a Geno-ese explorer who called himself Cristóbal Colón, or in English, Christo-pher Columbus. These two boys, Diego, sixteen, and Ferdinand, six, who was named after the king, came to Isabella's court as pages to her son Juan. They became fixtures. Diego was described by the historian Bar-tolomé de Las Casas as "tall, like his father, of gentle manners, well pro-portioned with an oval face and high forehead," well liked but lacking his father's intense intelligence. The younger brother, Ferdinand Columbus, was charming and popular, "of great affability and sweet conversation," and he took to the stimulating environment with great enthusiasm.[24] His father frequently traveled, and so Diego and Ferdinand Columbus were essentially raised to adulthood at Isabella's hands, first as pages in the court of her son and then as pages to the queen herself.

The two boys took advantage of the opportunities around them. Books were a rare and precious commodity, but young Ferdinand Colum-bus owned 238 of them by the time he was sixteen.[25] He was such an able pupil that he came to serve as an unofficial assistant and protégé of Peter Martyr, which exposed him directly to developments in Renaissance Italy. "In the Court of the Catholic Sovereigns, patrons of Italianate Renais-sance culture, . . . Ferdinand formed the taste for books [and] for schol-arship that grew into a ruling passion," wrote scholar Benjamin Keen, in his introduction to Ferdinand's fascinating biography, *The Life of the Admiral Christopher Columbus,* which Columbus's son wrote in defense of his famous father's achievements.[26]

In time, and as wealth came his way in adulthood, Ferdinand Colum-bus developed into one of the most notable scholars of the Renaissance in his own right, amassing what is believed to have been the largest pri-vate collection of books in Europe, some 15,400 volumes that he acquired in his travels on behalf of the Spanish monarchs, whom he served for more than fifty years. His carefully catalogued personal library included valuable ancient manuscripts, works from the classics, mathematical and scientific treatises, religious works, and the first books produced on printing presses. His collection of 3,200 prints included many works by the painter Albrecht Dürer.

In this environment, intellectual competition flourished, and soon many of the court's children began attracting attention from scholars in other parts of Europe. Peter Martyr took enormous pride in what he had helped to bring about. "I was the literary foster father of almost all the princes, and of all the princesses of Spain,"[27] he later said, when his charges' accomplishments drew compliments across the continent.

Many of the scholars and artists drawn to Isabella's court, who subsisted on her patronage, formed friendships that lasted for decades, enjoying a common bond that reached from court to court all over Europe. These ties extended to the young nobles they had tutored, who were soon in positions of becoming artistic and literary patrons themselves.

The girls received an education similar to that of the boys of the court, but they were also trained in the domestic arts, as though they were being groomed not just to be consorts to kings but to be practical and dutiful wives as well. They learned to sew, weave, embroider, and bake. Catherine famously sewed her husband's shirts in marriage, as her mother had in hers.

The royal daughters were urged to emulate their mother, who was developing a larger-than-life persona, and to similarly see themselves as warriors for Christianity. One militant melody from a *cancionero,* or book of songs, for example, urged Princess Juana to "follow the shining great Queen of Castile who is the fountain of virtues" and to go forward to "carry the cross" in conquest.[28]

The royal children were raised with acute awareness of their future stations and duties. In addition to receiving the general education offered to all the court's children, the prince and princesses were also instructed in court ritual and the arts of self-presentation. They were expected to make a decorous, dignified, and impressive appearance. Specific rules were attached to their clothing, to keep them in bandbox perfection.

To look his best, Prince Juan was expected to order two new pairs of shoes each month, and two new pairs of slippers or Moorish boots each week. He was allowed to wear his hats, caps, and other clothing only three times before giving them up. He was expected to wear a new belt every day. He was required to give away these garments to his household staff, for their use or resale, on a particular schedule. The queen became very angry when she learned that Prince Juan and Princess Juana hoarded their favorite items rather than passing them along to their attendants. She also required the children to distribute uneaten or excess food to the household staff so that nothing would go to waste. This could sometimes amount to a vast quantity of food because there were so many rituals surrounding mealtimes in the court.[29] These gifts constituted part of the compensation received by courtiers for working in the royal household, so Isabella's wrath reflected a profound sense of noblesse oblige, a core belief that those of superior rank had to be both generous and just.

The fact that Isabella and Ferdinand had only one son was a cause for concern. Having more boys would have given the monarchy a more solid base for the future. Juan's delicate health made the situation seem all the more fragile. But the births of the girls also offered advantages because each of them could secure a unique diplomatic alliance with another kingdom. Each could serve as a sort of living treaty, an ambassador in another capital.

This advantage was predicted very soon after Juan's birth secured the succession. "If your highness gives us two or three more daughters," Hernando del Pulgar wrote to Isabella in 1478, "in 20 years time you will have the pleasure of seeing your children and grandchildren on all the thrones of Europe."[30] And indeed, Isabella and Ferdinand would seek to use their daughters' marriages to firm up their alliances and shore up their defenses in western Europe.

The memory of the recent war with Portugal was much on their minds, and though they toyed with a number of possible marriage prospects for their oldest daughter Isabel, they ultimately negotiated an engagement and gave her in marriage to the Portuguese heir, which was suggested to them at the time of the truce with Portugal. The little Princess Isabel soon came to be known as the future queen of Portugal and was treated as a monarch-in-training. She was slated to marry the grandson of King Afonso V, the son of his son King João, a boy named Afonso. (The Portuguese royal family had the same habit as the Castilians and Aragonese in naming children after their fathers, mothers, and grandparents.)

Isabella and Ferdinand sought to encircle their French rivals by establishing a double alliance with the Hapsburg family. The future Holy Roman emperor, Maximilian of Austria, who ruled Germany, had married Mary of Burgundy, and they had two children roughly the same age as two of Isabella's children, Juan and Juana. Juana was engaged to Archduke Philip of Austria, known as Philip the Handsome, and Juan was to be married to Philip's sister, Margaret of Austria. The double marriage would bind Castile tightly to the court of Burgundy and to the Hapsburg family.

Little Margaret of Austria, even though she was only a child, had already had a turbulent marital history. At age three she had been betrothed to the French dauphin, the future king Charles VIII, and was raised in the French court as his consort and the future queen of France.

But Charles jilted her to marry Anne of Brittany, the heiress to that king-dom and the wealthiest woman in Europe. The unfortunate Margaret lingered in France for two more years, until she could be shipped back home. This humiliating treatment made the young princess all the more eager to cast her lot with a rival of France, and she welcomed, and eagerly awaited, the proposed marriage with Prince Juan of Castile.

Isabella's two younger daughters, María and Catherine, were consid-ered for a number of matches. Ultimately the youngest, Catherine, was affianced to the English court in marriage to Prince Arthur, the oldest son and probable heir of King Henry VII. The English court was consid-erably less powerful than those of France and Castile and more fitting for a younger daughter. King Henry, eager to claim a Spanish bride for his son and heir, made the first overtures to Castile about Catherine in 1487, when she was still a two-year-old and Arthur was just an infant.[31]

As the children grew up, foreign diplomats described Isabella and Ferdinand's family in glowing terms, both for their splendor and for the affectionate nature of their relationships with one another. Roger Machado, an envoy from France, attended a bullfight where the king and queen were present with their children; he noted with interest that Queen Isabella held baby Catherine on her lap during the event, lovingly interacting with her.[32]

Not everyone, however, received the news of the expanding family with such jubilation. In 1478, according to Pulgar, the emir of Granada, Abu al-Hasan Ali, sent ambassadors who noted the birth of Prince Juan—but they took the occasion to tell Isabella and Ferdinand that they would no longer send the customary tribute money to maintain the truce between the kingdoms, and they immediately stopped doing so. Abu al-Hasan Ali may have gone even further. He reportedly added that the kings of Granada who had given such tribute were now dead, and that he himself planned to turn the mints that made the coins into factories for forging lances to attack the Christians.

These menacing remarks came at the same time that the Castilians received word that a large Ottoman army was massing to attack the island of Rhodes in the eastern Mediterranean or perhaps, even more frightening, some other southern European objective. The young queen, a new mother with the heightened protective instincts of most women toward their vulnerable young, was troubled by these reports, which car-ried the most dire threats for her kingdom as well.

Her state of mind in these years, from the 1470s to the early 1480s, was captured in an unusual painting housed in the Monastery of Las Huelgas in Burgos, near the mausoleum and shrine to her parents in that city. It depicts Isabel and Ferdinand, kneeling in prayer next to each other, with three of their children—likely Isabel, Juan, and Juana—grouped behind them. Perhaps the painting was completed before María and Catherine had been born, which would date it to the early 1480s. Isabella's face appears sad and anxious. A cluster of nuns stand nearby, their faces likewise drawn with worry.

In the center of the painting, a giant figure of the Virgin Mary rises up into the sky, stretching her arms out to protect the family and the nuns, who are sheltered under her embroidered cloak. Mary is holding clusters of arrows in her hands. Across the top of the canvas, two demonic figures with horns and clawed feet prance across the sky, menacing the family beneath. One devil carries arrows, longer and sharper than those held by Mary, and the second is heavy-laden with books. It is unclear if he is bringing the books or taking them away.

Isabella's home life may have been all that she could have asked for, but, in the broader world, the queen saw herself painted into a terrifying scene.

TWELVE

THE WHOLE WORLD TREMBLED

Queen Isabella's reign was shadowed by the existence of a man she never met but who terrorized eastern and southern Europe for most of her life: the wealthy and powerful Sultan Mehmed II, known as Mehmed the Conquerer.

He was an enigmatic character—beloved and revered by Muslims as a great and powerful warrior, admired by many Jews for the benign tolerance in which he permitted them to live in his realm, but feared as a relentless aggressor who was determined to expand the Ottoman Empire by swallowing Europe. He was willing to pay a high price for this success: he was directly responsible for the deaths of an estimated 873,000 people, or some 29,000 per year.[1] His conquest of Constantinople, accomplished soon after he assumed the throne, was the first of his major victories, completed in 1453 when Isabella was two years old.

Through Isabella's childhood and early adulthood, Mehmed repeatedly said he intended to destroy Christianity. When he was twenty-one, he began styling himself as Caesar and set out to make good on his pledge to seize Rome. He planned to capture it by moving in from the east, through eastern Europe, Austria, and Greece; from the south, which could mean using Sicily as the entry point; or from the West, using North Africa as a base to invade Europe through Spain. The last idea was all the more menacing because it had proven effective in the past. Threats to either Sicily or Spain, of course, represented aggression directed specifically at Queen Isabella and her family.

Mehmed was the youngest son of Sultan Murad II, a fierce warrior who had already extended the dominions of the Ottoman Empire. Murad presided over a multiethnic and multilingual culture, in which most people were Muslim but some were Christians, some Jews, some Christians and Jews who had wholeheartedly converted to Islam, and some who had pretended to convert to Islam to get better treatment and avoid the taxes levied on nonbelievers. It was also advantageous to convert to Islam because slaves and soldiers were usually non-Muslims. The Ottoman Empire had built up a highly effective war machine that fed on invasions of foreign countries.

Mehmed's father Murad laid the groundwork for the planned assault on western Europe by pressing deep into present-day Romania, Albania, and Greece. He attacked the ruler of Wallachia, a principality north of the Danube River, and seized his two sons as hostages. The boys were indoctrinated in Ottoman ways so they could return to their homeland and be installed as puppet governors.

Murad also conquered the Albanian principalities and took as hostage the son of an Albanian prince, John Castrioti. That boy nominally converted to Islam. He took the name Skanderbeg and initially acted as a loyal ally to Murad, even becoming something of a favorite with the sultan.

One of Murad's signal victories was the conquest of Salonika (today's Thessaloniki), formerly the second-largest city in the Christian Byzantine Empire and a major stopping point on the road between Rome and Constantinople. He trounced the city's Venetian defenders in 1430, then urged his men to the slaughter with promises of what they could take from the ruined city. "I will give you whatever the city possesses," he is recorded to have said. "Men, women, children, silver and gold—only the city itself you will leave to me." With screams of enthusiasm, his men climbed over the city's parapets "like wild animals."[2]

The city's defenses collapsed, and the Venetian garrison fought its way to the port to escape on waiting galleys. The Turks rampaged through the city, murdering many people and carting away some seven thousand into slavery. According to a survivor, Ioannis Anagostes:

> They gathered up men, women, children, people of all ages,
> bound like animals, and marched them all to the camp outside
> the city. Nor do I speak of those who fell and were not counted

in the fortress and in the alleyways and did not merit a burial. Every soldier, with the mass of captives he had taken, hurried to get them outside quickly to hand them over to his comrades, lest someone stronger seize them from him, so that any slave who as he saw from old age or some illness perhaps could not keep up with the others, he cut off the head on the spot and reckoned it a loss. Then for the first time they separated parents from their children, wives from their husbands, friends and relatives from each other. . . . And the city was filled with wailing and despair.[3]

Murad's successes made Christians question why God was allowing this to happen. "He seized cities and regions of the West during his lifetime," wrote Manuel Malaxos; "he subdued countless regions in Serbia and Bulgaria, since God had allowed it, on account of our sins, and because no one prevented him."[4]

Mehmed, Murad's son, was intelligent and learned but even more ruthless than his father. Born in 1432, two years after the conquest of Salonika, Mehmed was the sultan's third son, the child of a slave girl who was one of Murad's concubines. It was not legal to enslave Muslims, so she is believed to have been of Christian or Jewish origin. Her name is unknown, as many of the women in the harem were not identified by name. Mehmed grew up with his mother in the harem at Edirne Sarayi, southwest of Constantinople, where he developed a reputation, despite his academic interests, for "insolence, savagery and violence."[5]

In 1437 Mehmed's oldest brother died. In 1443 his second brother was murdered by an adviser, who also killed that prince's two sons. The adviser was quickly executed "without revealing the motive for his crime,"[6] which led to suspicions that the assassination had been designed to clear the way for the succession of Mehmed, now age eleven. Sultan Murad began preparing this son to rule in his place. Together Murad and Mehmed worked on extending their dominions throughout western Greece.

In 1450, the year before Isabella was born, the Turkish sultan and his son were forced to deal with a tenacious insurrection by the Albanians, led by their former ally, the Albanian captive Skanderbeg. He had converted back to Christianity and renounced Islam. Then he successfully fended off the Turkish attack, becoming a hero in western Europe. Murad and Mehmed were forced to retreat, returning home to their palace at Edirne Sarayi.

The Spaniards in particular rallied to Skanderbeg's assistance, recognizing his effort as the first successful opposition in eastern Europe to the growing dominance of the Turks. King Alfonso of Aragon and Naples, uncle to Ferdinand and the cousin of Isabella's father, gave Skanderbeg both financial and military support, as did Pope Calixtus III, Rodrigo Borgia's uncle, which allowed Skanderbeg to hold the line against the Ottoman expansion for more than a decade.

The disappointing reversal in Albania set Sultan Murad back on his heels, and in February 1451 he suddenly died of apoplexy. Mehmed, who was then eighteen, was acclaimed as sultan. He went straight to his father's harem, where the women consoled him on his father's death. While Mehmed stood speaking with his father's highest-ranking wife, Halima Hatun, one of his men strangled her infant son in his bath, thus eliminating a potential future rival for the throne. Mehmed felt no shame about that act—soon, in fact, he made it a specific legal requirement for a sultan to kill his brothers. "It is fitting for the order of the world that he shall kill his brothers," Mehmed stated in an imperial edict.[7]

He was even more brutal to his enemies, becoming a practitioner of many barbaric cruelties, which contributed to his infamy. The Genoese merchant Jacopo de Campi, for example, described the hideous tortures Mehmed devised. One means of death was to place the victim on the ground and insert a sharp pole into his rectum, then pound it into the victim's interior with a mallet. He ordered people's hands cut off, or their nose, or their feet. Often he ordered their eyes gouged from their heads. "In short," Jacopo wrote, "if ever a ruler has been feared and dreaded, ruthless and cruel, this one is a second Nero and far worse."[8]

Certainly Mehmed was no ordinary man; even his appearance was singular. He had bright, piercing eyes and a long hooked nose. His face was heavily bearded and his head habitually crowned with a voluminous turban. He was "well-formed" and slightly above average in height, wrote a Venetian envoy who saw him. "He is skilled in the use of weapons. His appearance inspires fear rather than respect. He laughs rarely. . . . There is nothing he studies with greater pleasure and eagerness than the geography of the world, and the art of warfare; he burns with the desire to rule."[9]

As soon as Mehmed became sultan, he set himself an ambitious goal—the conquest of Constantinople, the heart of the Byzantine Empire, the inheritor of the mantle of Rome. For decades Ottoman sultans had chipped away at the surrounding countryside, so that by 1452, Constantinople was an island in a sea of Turkish dominion. But its defenses had been constructed for the ages—it had stood as a bastion against attacks from the east for a thousand years. It was securely located on a triangular peninsula bounded on the south by the Sea of Marmara and on the north by a body of water known as the Golden Horn. A triple defense wall protected the third side and enclosed its seven hills. It was viewed as virtually impregnable.

Mehmed began by building a fortress eight miles north of Constantinople. At first he seemed to be doing it in a friendly way, and local residents even provided him with construction materials to speed the work along. But soon he attacked villagers and dragged them into slavery. Next he assembled a fleet of more than one hundred assault vessels and mobilized more than eighty thousand troops for the attack.

Constantinople had been under intense military and economic pressure for decades, and by 1452, its population was only about 45,000. Emperor Constantine XI, the city's ruler, sent envoys to the courts of western Europe begging for aid, but most rulers were too enmeshed in their own troubles to send assistance. A group of Genoese arrived to help, as did a group of Spaniards, including some Catalans from Barcelona and a Castilian nobleman named Don Francisco de Toledo. Ultimately, however, only about seven thousand able-bodied defenders, most of them Greek, manned the walls. They were greatly outnumbered at sea as well, having only about one-fifth the number of fighting ships as the Turks.

Mehmed told Constantine and the local officials that if they delivered the city to him peaceably, they could continue to live there. But they believed that reinforcements from Venice were on the way and refused to surrender. Mehmed launched an intense bombardment of the city on April 6, 1453. He promised his men that when they conquered Constantinople, they would be given three days to sack it, which was the established Muslim practice. "Religious law required him to grant three days of pillage," wrote Turkish historian Halil İnalcık. "The city had been taken by force and therefore . . . movable property was the lawful booty of the soldiers and the population could be legally enslaved."[10]

A problem for the Ottomans, however, was that a great many people in their ranks were not Muslim and had mixed allegiances. There were many Christians among the Turkish soldiers, and they frequently betrayed

Ottoman interests by slipping the Christian forces inside information on Mehmed's plans, which allowed them to shore up their defenses at vulnerable attack points. "They communicated to our side through letters (or epistles) projected by artillery or bows, fastened to arrows; and with such cunning they secretly dispatched them to our side," wrote a Florentine merchant, Giacomo Tetaldi, who fought in defense of Constantinople and managed to escape by swimming to safety.[11]

Constantinople's defenders fought stoutly, but over the next six weeks, the city's defenses were slowly and surely worn down. The inhabitants, despairing of deliverance, marched in religious processions, singing hymns and praying to Christ and the Virgin to protect them from the Turks.

On the last day, a crowd of men, women, children, nuns, and monks "sought refuge" in Hagia Sophia, "encouraged by superstitious belief that when the Turks reached the Column of Constantine, an angel would come down from heaven, hand a sword to a poor man sitting by the column and say, 'Take this sword and avenge the people of God.'" Instead, however, the Turks broke down the doors of the church with axes and dragged the congregants off to slavery. The statues of the saints were smashed; church vessels were seized. "Scenes of unimaginable horror ensued," historian Franz Babinger writes.[12]

The final Muslim assault was led by Janissary warriors, young Christian men who had been taken captive in early childhood, converted to Islam, and trained for battle. Emperor Constantine, with Don Francisco of Toledo close beside him, were fighting valiantly together when they were last seen alive. Soon a crucifix topped with a Janissary cap "was paraded around in mockery."[13]

The Turkish soldiers killed four thousand in the siege and enslaved almost the entire population of the city. They plundered the churches, the imperial palace, and the homes of the rich, and they did considerable damage to much of the city's fabled architecture. Within days the majestic Hagia Sophia basilica was converted into a mosque. Its storied mosaics were plastered over because Islamic law prohibited representational images. Its holy relics, highly venerated and viewed as sacred objects by the faithful, were discarded, desecrated, or ridiculed; unique and rare classical manuscripts were torn apart for the value of their bindings and thrown into the garbage.

Mehmed entered Constantinople in glory on May 29, 1453, and was said to have cried when he saw the damage to the buildings. "What a city have we given over to plunder and destruction," he reportedly said.[14]

But his self-recrimination, if it actually happened, was short-lived. In a ceremony held inside Hagia Sophia during the noon prayer that Friday, a special turban was placed on Mehmed's head, and he held aloft a naked sword. He shouted, "Praise be to God, the Lord of all the World," and then, according to a chronicler, the "victorious Muslims lifted up their hands and uttered a shout of joy."[15]

Soon stories circulated around western Europe of what had happened to the women of Constantinople. Many of them, including very young girls and nuns, were indisputably raped, sometimes gang-raped, and sexually tortured.

Other stories may have been apocryphal but had particular implications for European queens and princesses. According to one story making the rounds, the daughter of the Byzantine emperor was taken by Sultan Mehmed for his personal use. In some versions of the tale, she resisted his sexual advances and was murdered; in other versions, she was raped on the altar of Hagia Sophia. In another variant, Mehmed tried to forcibly convert her to Islam, and when she refused, she was stripped naked and decapitated.[16] It was widely believed in western Europe that royal princesses could expect this kind of treatment if their countries were ever to fall to the Muslims.

It is certainly true that from among the captives, royal or not, Mehmed selected some for his personal pleasure. Two nephews of Emperor Constantine went into Mehmed's service, and at least one of them was believed to have become his lover. Constantine's chief of staff, George Sphrantzes, survived and was released after eighteen months of captivity, but his son was killed and his daughter placed in Mehmed's harem. In September 1455, Sphrantzes wrote, "my beautiful daughter Thamar died of an infectious disease in the sultan's seraglio."[17] Some rulers of nearby realms voluntarily sent their daughters to Mehmed as wives or concubines, hoping to win his favor and avoid his wrath. He accepted more than a few, and they too went to live in his harem, under the watchful eyes of eunuchs, and disappeared from recorded history.

Mehmed renamed the city Istanbul and departed on the night of June 24, 1453, with a long train of Greek girls and women trailing behind him as his plunder. Jewish families were transported to the city from the conquered city of Salonika to repopulate the empty homes in Istanbul.

The victory filled Mehmed with enthusiasm for additional adventuring. He became "so insolent after the capture of Constantinople," wrote the Genoese official Angelo Lomellino, after meeting with Mehmed in person, "that he sees himself soon becoming master of the whole world, and swears publicly that before two years have passed he intends to reach Rome."[18]

Indeed, according to Turkish historian Halil İnalcık. Mehmed began styling himself "Sovereign of the Two Seas," which referred to the Black Sea and the Mediterranean Sea, making his intentions crystal clear.[19]

* * *

Western Europeans were horrified at the news of what had happened in Constantinople. Pope Nicholas V called Mehmed the "son of Satan" and tried to organize a coordinated response to reclaim the city, but he died before he could get the effort under way. He was replaced by the Spaniard Afonso Borgia, who became Pope Calixtus III in 1455. Calixtus, uncle of Rodrigo, also took the Islamic threat seriously and wrote to the young King Ladislaus Posthumos of Bohemia and Hungary pledging his support and calling for the Turks to be expelled not just from Constantinople but also from all Europe.

Mehmed allowed himself time for carnal pleasures in these years of his reign; his Jewish and Christian captives were the particular object of his attentions. He had four hundred women in his harem. "Mehmed spent many nights in debauchery," wrote Mustafa Ali, "with lovely-eyed, fairylike slave girls, and his days drinking with pages who looked like angels."[20]

In 1454 and 1455 he launched assaults into Serbia and Hungary, pincer moves designed to expand his realm and to advance his campaign into western Europe. He soon took the town of Novo Brdo, where he ordered the officials decapitated. He shared the seventy-four girls in the town with his men, and took 320 boys as Janissary recruits. At the major city of Belgrade, however, the Turks were repulsed, thanks to military support and reinforcements sent by Pope Calixtus. Mehmed was wounded but undaunted.

The next year, 1456, when Isabella was five, Mehmed's forces attacked Athens and Corinth and captured both cities. These conquests resonated painfully on the Iberian peninsula because the Spaniards believed themselves to be the inheritors of Greek culture.

Isabella seated at the foot of the Madonna and child, believed to have been painted in 1520 by one of Isabella's favorite court painters, Michael Sittow. Colegiata de Santa María la Mayor, Toro, Spain. *(Album / Art Resource, NY)*

TOP: The castle of Arévalo. Isabella and her brother Alfonso spent much of their childhood here, away from the corrupt Segovian court, where their older half brother, King Enrique IV, known as Enrique El Impotente, presided.
(Guillermo Pis Gonzalez / Shutterstock.com)

MIDDLE: The austere and foreboding castle at La Mota, in Medina del Campo, where Isabella still managed to spend many happy hours as a child, and where she would later hold Cesare Borgia prisoner while he was awaiting trial for murder.
(Marques / Shutterstock.com)

BOTTOM: The walled city of Ávila, where nobles staged a coup against Enrique by dethroning him in effigy and replacing him with his younger half brother.
(Lukasz Janyst / Shutterstock.com)

TOP: Engraved portrait of Beatriz de Bobadilla, Isabella's best friend, at Museo de Historia, Madrid. *(Album / Art Resource, NY)*

BOTTOM, LEFT: King Enrique IV, Isabella's older half brother, on a stained-glass window at the Alcázar of Segovia. *(Roberaten / Shutterstock.com)*

BOTTOM, RIGHT: Gonzalo Fernández de Córdoba, Isabella's lifelong ally and protector, sculpted by Salvador Amaya. Parque histórico de Navalcarnero, Madrid. *(Salvador Amaya)*

TOP: The Alcázar, Enrique's palace-fortress home in Segovia, where Isabella prepared herself for taking the throne in a carefully conceived coup d'état. *(matthi / Shutterstock.com)*

BOTTOM: The throne room within the Alcázar, with statues depicting Isabella's ancestors as far back as Pelayo, the Visigoth credited with beginning the Christian reconquest of the Iberian peninsula in the eighth century. *(Anton_Ivanov / Shutterstock.com)*

TOP: Marriage portrait of Ferdinand and Isabella. Madrigal de las Altas Torres, Augustinian convent, Ávila.
(Album / Art Resource, NY)

MIDDLE: Portrait of Catherine of Aragon, Isabella's daughter, by Juan de Flandes. Thyssen-Bornemisza Museum, Madrid.
(Museo Thyssen-Bornemisza / Scala / Art Resource, NY)

BOTTOM: Juana of Castile, Isabella's daughter, and her husband, Philip the Fair. Royal Chapel, Granada.
(Album / Art Resource, NY)

TOP: One of forty-seven devotional paintings commissioned by Isabella depicting scenes from the life of Christ. In *Miracle of the Loaves and Fishes* Isabella appears as a bystander in the crowd. Palacio Real, Madrid.
(Album / Art Resource, NY)

BOTTOM: Another devotional painting commissioned by Isabella, depicting the marriage at Cana. Isabella's son Prince Juan appears here as the groom, and Margaret of Austria, his wife, as the bride. Metropolitan Museum of Art, New York.
(Copyright © The Metropolitan Museum of Art. Image source: Art Resource, NY)

TOP: Mehmed the Conquerer, ruler of the expanding Ottoman Empire during Isabella's formative years. Topkapı Museum, Istanbul.
(Gianni Dagli Orti / The Art Archive at Art Resource, NY)

BOTTOM: A sixteenth-century depiction of a battle between Turks and Christians, by Venetian painter Jacopo Tintoretto. Prado Museum, Madrid.
(Album / Art Resource, NY)

A fifteenth-century painting showing the Virgin Mary standing in protection over Isabella and Ferdinand, their three oldest children, and a group of nuns, as demons dance across the landscape above them, by Diego de la Cruz. Monasterio de las Huelgas, Burgos. *(Album / Art Resource, NY)*

TOP: Seville's famous Giralda tower. *(Ethan Pilla)*

MIDDLE: The Great Mosque of Córdoba, which had been converted into a cathedral during an earlier phase of the Reconquest, and remained so during Isabella's time. *(Francesco R. Iacomino / Shutterstock.com)*

BOTTOM: The Alcazaba of Córdoba, the fortress that served as Isabella's military headquarters during the Reconquest, a war that lasted ten years, with terrible casualties and losses on both sides. *(Anibal Trejo / Shutterstock.com)*

TOP: The Castilian siege of Ronda, which sits on a hilltop surrounded by sheer cliffs, was a major victory for Isabella, particularly because it freed some four hundred Christian slaves who were being held there.
(*Cornfield / Shutterstock.com*)

MIDDLE: A depiction of the attempted suicide attack on Beatriz de Bobadilla, one of fifty-four woodcarvings that Isabella commissioned for the choir stall of the great Cathedral of Toledo.
(*Album / Art Resource, NY*)

BOTTOM: Queen Isabella's first major architectural commission, San Juan de los Reyes in Toledo, where the queen ordered the manacles on freed Christian slaves to be mounted on the exterior walls so the ordeal would not be forgotten.
(*Tony Page / Travelsignposts.com*)

TOP: The Alhambra of Granada, the Moorish-built palace of the Nasrid dynasty whose walls were inscribed with Arabic poetry and holy writ.
(Madrugada Verde / Shutterstock.com)

BOTTOM: A painted wood-carving depicting the coerced baptism of the Muslim women of Granada after the Reconquest.
(bpk, Berlin / Capilla Real de Granada / Alfredo Dagli Orti / Art Resource, NY)

TOP: A nineteenth-century painting depicting Isabella, Ferdinand, and Boabdil at the surrender of Granada, Europe's first significant triumph against Islam in hundreds of years. *(Album / Art Resource, NY)*

BOTTOM: Francisco Jiménez de Cisneros, archbishop of Toledo, confessor to Isabella and later cardinal and regent of Spain, sculpted by Salvador Amaya. Parque histórico de Navalcarnero, Madrid. *(Salvador Amaya)*

TOP: A nineteenth-century painting depicting the expulsion of the Jews from Spain in 1492, with Tomás de Torquemada, the chief inquisitor, angrily rebuffing a Jew seeking permission to remain in his homeland. Prado Museum, Madrid.
(Copyright of the image Museo Nacional del Prado / Art Resource, NY)

BOTTOM: Friar Hernán de Talavera, Isabella's long-time confessor and archbishop of Granada, a converso who fell victim to the Inquisition after being accused of using his home as a secret temple. San Lorenzo de El Escorial, Spain.
(Album / Art Resource, NY)

TOP: Rodrigo Borgia, the notorious Pope Alexander VI, who enjoyed the pleasures of both the flesh and the intellect, and who bitterly clashed with Queen Isabella. Museo Diocesano D'Arte Sacro, Orte. *(Gianni Dagli Orti / The Art Archive at Art Resource, NY)*

BOTTOM, LEFT: Cesare Borgia, the son of Pope Alexander VI, whom Isabella came to view as a public menace. Palazzo Venezia, Rome. *(Scala / Art Resource, NY)*

BOTTOM, RIGHT: The Tempietto by architevct Donato Bramante, a masterpiece of High Renaissance art that was commissioned by Ferdinand and Isabella to commemorate their son, Juan. Vatican Hill, Rome. *(Daniele Silva / Shutterstock.com)*

TOP: Explorer Christopher Columbus, who considered Isabella his most significant patron, sculpted by Salvador Amaya. Parque histórico de Navalcarnero, Madrid. *(Salvador Amaya)*

BOTTOM: A statue commemorating Isabella at the front entrance to the Washington, D.C., headquarters of the Organization of American States. The thirty-five member nations include Argentina, the Bahamas, Barbados, Bolivia, Brazil, Canada, Chile, Colombia, Costa Rica, Cuba, Dominican Republic, Ecuador, El Salvador, Guatemala, Haiti, Honduras, Jamaica, Mexico, Nicaragua, Panama, Paraguay, Peru, the United States, Uruguay, and Venezuela. *(René and Peter van der Krogt, http://statues.vanderkrogt.net)*

One of some 370 spectacular tapestries owned by Queen Isabella,
The Triumph of Fame depicts the Petrarch poem on glory and memory.
Metropolitan Museum of Art, New York.

(Copyright © The Metropolitan Museum of Art. Image source: Art Resource, NY)

Pope Calixtus, the Borgia from Valencia, died in 1458. The next pope, Pius II, tried to stop Mehmed's advance but proved ineffectual. By the end of 1459, when Isabella was eight, all of Serbia had fallen under Mehmed's control. About 200,000 Serbs were enslaved by the Turks. Soon he attacked the city of Gardiki, in Thessaly, killing all six thousand inhabitants, including women and children. He had accepted the surrender without struggle of the Genoese colony of Amasra, on the Black Sea coast, where he enslaved two-thirds of the population.

By 1461, around the time Isabella was moved to her brother Enrique's court, only one Byzantine leader was still holding out against Mehmed: David Comnenus, ruler of the city of Trebizond, also on the Black Sea coast. Mehmed warned David that if he did not surrender, he would be annihilated. David accepted Mehmed's terms and went into exile in Thrace, the area northwest of Constantinople. But two years later, Mehmed ordered him executed, along with six of his seven sons and a nephew. His youngest son, George, age three, was spared, as was his daughter Anna. George was given to a Turkish family and raised as a Muslim. When he grew up, he ran away and reverted to Christianity, dropping from sight. His disappearance marked the end of the fabled Comnenian dynasty. His sister Anna ended her days in Mehmed's harem.[21]

Mehmed had now added the entire Black Sea coast of Anatolia to his realm. In the spring of 1462, he set off against Wallachia. His father's former hostage, Vlad, raised in the Turkish court, beaten and abused, had been sent back to rule, but he turned against the Ottomans and formed an alliance with the Christian ruler of Hungary. Vlad fought Mehmed ferociously, earning himself the name Vlad the Impaler, the prototype for the character that came to be known as Count Dracula. He is estimated to have killed tens of thousands of people, partly in efforts to repel the Turks. He was finally assassinated.

Mehmed rested for a while in Istanbul in 1465, when Isabella was fourteen. But in 1466 he was back on the road, this time attacking Albania once more. The Albanian leader Skanderbeg, the forced convert who had reverted to Christianity and gone on to attack the Turks, was growing old and tired. He traveled to Rome to beg for financial support and arms to fight the Turks, but the only help he got was from Ferdinand's cousin, the king of Naples. Support was dwindling even more: western Europeans had become numbed to news of defeats by the Turks.

In January 1469, when Isabella was almost eighteen and preparing to marry Ferdinand, a terrifying report came from the east: tens of thousands of Turks had struck into the center of Austria, near Vienna, killing more than twenty thousand people. The Sultan Mehmed was at that time preparing a naval assault, but no one knew his intended destination. Word went out that he had outfitted 250 sailing vessels, including 120 galleys, and at least eighty thousand soldiers. He repeated the preparations he had undertaken in his attack on Constantinople: meticulous planning and a fearsome concentration of military might. He was said to be planning a "campaign against Europe" and intended to attack by sea. That meant that every kingdom with a southern Mediterranean coastline was a potential target.[22]

In June 1470 his vast armada set sail and headed for Negroponte, the second-largest Greek island, located off the peninsula's eastern coast. It was the place known in earlier centuries as Euboea or Euripus. Mehmed crushingly defeated the defenders of the city of Chalcis, which allowed him to seize the entire island. The day after its capture, he gave orders that all prisoners with beards should be brought to him. They were told to kneel in a circle, with their hands bound. Hundreds were beheaded. Women and girls were parceled out to the victors. Then the Turks renamed the island Egriboz. They controlled it for the next four hundred years.

In July the Ottoman army moved westward onto the Greek mainland, passing through Thebes on July 28, Athens on July 29, and many other cities thereafter. Many Greeks were taken into slavery; the entire town of Havsa was depopulated. The sultan ordered settlers from other places to be relocated there.

In 1471, when Isabella was twenty, Mehmed gave himself a year of rest and recuperation before returning to the warpath. That Christmas Pope Sixtus IV sent out five cardinals to raise the alarm about the oncoming Turks, and to encourage western Europe's defense. It was as part of this mission that Rodrigo Borgia went to Spain, to make sure residents there knew the magnitude of the threat Christians were facing. In Princess Isabella he found a willing listener.

By 1474, when Isabella was twenty-three and preparing to take the throne, Mehmed was forty-two and suffering from gout. He had grown obese and was riddled with disease. But he continued plotting conquests from his palace. By now Skanderbeg had died, and in his absence the Albanian principalities were visibly weakening. In May 1474 more than 80,000 Ottoman troops surrounded the town of Scutari, also known as

Shkodra, on the Adriatic coast, across from the Italian peninsula's boot heel. Mehmed's troops battered the 6,000 inhabitants, only about 2,000 of whom were active defenders. Eyewitnesses said that as the Ottomans attacked the walls of Scutari, they shouted, "Rome! Rome!," making it clear that they saw the town as just one more step toward that goal.[23]

At Scutari, the Albanians managed to hold back the Ottomans once more, narrowly surviving drought and starvation behind the castle walls. But in 1479 their luck ran out. The Turks came back one more time, and this time the Venetian rulers negotiated a truce with the Ottomans and departed, making it clear that the Albanian population had no choice but to surrender. Many dispossessed Albanians fled, making homes in exile for themselves in Italy and Spain.

All this destruction was caused by one man, Mehmed, "who introduced all the gloom and devastation; he wrecked and ruined everything—he was a true plague," wrote Marin Barleti, an eyewitness at the siege of Scutari. "Who knows how many regions, cities, states, kingdoms and empires he subdued! The whole world trembled because of him."[24]

The Frenchman Pierre d'Aubusson, the grand master of the Order of St. John of Jerusalem, compared Mehmed to Satan, to Lucifer. He called him

> the unspeakable tyrant who has destroyed the souls of so many children whom he compelled to abjure their faith, and thus blinded they have descended into hell. [He] caused virgins and maidens to be defiled, slaughtered young men and old, profaned sacred relics, polluted churches and monasteries, destroyed, oppressed and seized kingdoms, principalities and cities, including Constantinople, which he took for himself and made the scene of unbelievable crimes.[25]

By 1480, when Isabella was twenty-nine and the mother of three children, two of them daughters, another great assault by Mehmed was looming. He was preparing the long-awaited attack on Italy. A fleet—including some 140 vessels and a seaborne expeditionary army of 18,000—landed on the heel of the Italian peninsula.[26] The original plan was to attack Brindisi, but the force shifted to Otranto. The town was small and only weakly defended and fell quickly to the Turks. Of its 22,000 inhabitants, only 10,000 survived. As in Constantinople, the residents flocked to the local cathedral, which only made them easier to slaughter. About eight hundred people were led to a nearby hill and told they could live only if they converted to Islam on the spot. They refused and were beheaded; their abandoned corpses were devoured by animals. Some eight thousand people were loaded onto ships and carted off to Albania as slaves.[27]

Isabella was specifically aware of this development and watching the situation anxiously. She wrote to the Neapolitans that help was on its way from Castile—and indeed, reinforcements and armaments were soon delivered.[28]

Meanwhile, Mehmed was preparing for his final invasion of western Europe. Many people thought the fate of the Christian nations was sealed. In 1481, for example, the classical scholar Peter Schott, canon of Strasbourg, traveled from Bologna to Rome to take a final look at the city. He went there, he wrote, to see it one last time, "before the Eternal City was taken by the Turks."[29]

By early 1481 Mehmed, now forty-nine, had mobilized. He set out with a great fleet, heading west. No one knew what his destination might be. It could be Ferdinand's Kingdom of Sicily. Ominously for Isabella, he was also rumored to be heading for an attack on the Mamluk sultanate of Egypt. That course would fill the hearts of Spaniards with deep terror—for it had been with an invasion from North Africa that Spain had been taken in 711, in another period of aggressive Muslim expansion. "Every day news came to the King and Queen that the Turks had a great armada on the sea, and that they were sending it to conquer the kingdom of Sicily," wrote Isabella's court chronicler Hernando del Pulgar. "And everywhere they went on the land, they were taking Christians and cruelly murdering them."[30]

Isabella and Ferdinand began preparing for the assault they expected to come any day. They ordered every church in the land to organize daily prayer sessions to explain to the people what was happening and to encourage them to prepare for the attack. They reached an agreement with the king of Naples, Ferdinand's cousin, that they would help defend Naples if he would help defend Sicily. They sent a trusted official, Alonso de Quintanilla, to crisscross their kingdoms and make an inventory of their weapons, ships, and fortresses. They sent other officials to inspect the ports to determine how vulnerable they might be to a naval assault. They looked to the English and Portuguese for guidance on strategies for repulsing attacks by sea.

Isabella was making it her mission to shore up her forces against the impending onslaught, using religious faith to mobilize troops for her kingdom's self-defense. Everyone was told of the "great plans being made by the Turks for the spilling of blood, and what they were doing each day to the Christians, and the great necessity that all Christianity would resist that enemy," Pulgar wrote. "And like good Christians they should give thanks to God that something had appeared that was so great that they would be reminded of the great zeal they should show for the honor of King and homeland, and to sing the praises of the Christian religion."[31]

In the end Isabella's efforts would be successful. But the methods she used would blacken her name forever.

THIRTEEN

THE QUEEN'S WAR

As soon as she put the problems with Portugal behind her, Queen Isabella directed her attention to southern Spain. This region was a priority for two reasons. In the short term, she had to deal with a new aggressiveness from the neighboring Muslim Emirate of Granada, at a time when border defenses were weak, splintered, and unreliable. And in the longer term, she needed a strong position on the Mediterranean Coast in order to protect Castile and Aragon against the growing threat from the Ottoman Turks.

The first step was to secure Castile's border with the Islamic world. Queen Isabella had to find ways to make peace among the squabbling nobles living in the Christian-controlled portion of Andalusia, which had been wracked for years with civil unrest because of King Enrique's lax administration of lands that were distant from his home in Segovia. It was particularly important to quell domestic disturbances in Seville, the biggest city and most important river port in the south, because new hostilities were breaking out on the frontier.

Just across the border was the last surviving Muslim realm in Iberia, the Kingdom of Granada, now controlled by the warlike Nasrid dynasty. This heavily armed emirate stretched about 250 miles along the Mediterranean coast, reaching about 93 miles inland; formidable castles defended its perimeter. The kingdom's biggest city and crown jewel was Granada, located in the mountainous heartland, but the Nasrids also controlled the important Mediterranean seaports of Málaga, Marbella, and Almería, which gave them ready access to reinforcements from overseas and a continuing source of supplies.

From these secure bases, the Granadans were able to send lightning-strike raids out into the Castilian lands to capture Christians to enslave them, to sell them for ransom, or to use them as laborers or in sex trafficking. "Taking advantage of the disturbance and revolts sweeping through Castile at this time, [they] sent yearly expeditions there during the reign of Enrique IV, until his death in 1474," wrote the historian Ahmad ibn Muhammad Al-Maqqari.[1]

In 1474, the year King Enrique died, a new leader came to power in Granada. Abu al-Hasan Ali was more belligerent than his recent predecessors. He built up the Muslim army and its capacity for offensive action, with the help and support of his equally strong-willed primary wife, Fatima, who was also his cousin. The sultan's militancy worried even his own countrymen. One Arab chronicler called Abu al-Hasan "magnanimous and valiant, a lover of wars, and the dangers and horrors of them."[2] It was a time of glorious Islamic expansion, and no doubt he wanted to emulate the successes being achieved by the Ottoman Turks in the east, confident that God was on his side as well as theirs.

Abu al-Hasan grew steadily bolder and more determined. "He put great dread into the Christians, who had never been so harried by the Muslims," according to Arab historians. He did not seize land but instead concentrated on raids that brought "rich spoils of booty and captives."[3] In April 1478 he staged a huge military parade to put his troops and armaments on display. This new aggressiveness, coming as it did at a time when the Ottoman Empire was expanding in the Balkans, was worrisome to the Castilians, who feared that the Nasrids would ally themselves with the Turks and allow them to use their Mediterranean ports for an invasion of Spain. It could be a repeat of 711, of 1086, and of 1195, when Muslim rulers in Andalusia had gained reinforcements from other Muslim lands.

The Christians, however, were not just innocent victims. They, too, led raiding parties into Muslim areas and had engaged, in fits and starts, in aggressive advances that had allowed them to conquer vast tracts of land that had been home to Muslim families for hundreds of years. The Christians saw each victory as reclaiming what had been theirs; the Muslims saw each defeat as theft of their own homeland. Isabella was as convinced as Abu al-Hasan that her viewpoint was correct and that the entire south of Spain belonged by right to her, allowing her to rationalize and justify the need for a military response to any provocation.

Abu al-Hasan now saw Isabella's rise to power as a welcome sign of Castilian vulnerability. Soon after the princess became queen and just around the time the Portuguese invaders surged into Castile, he made his ominous vow that he would no longer make the vassalage payments that Granada had been giving Castile to maintain their uneasy truce. Arab sources reported that he delivered this message in specifically threatening words. He said the days of Granadan tribute to Castile were over: "The sovereigns who paid tribute to the Christians are dead, and in Granada the only thing we are minting is ... iron and lances to use against our enemies."[4] The Italian scholar Peter Martyr, who lived at Isabella's court, said he was told that Abu al-Hasan made that threat while menacingly fingering the point of a sharp metal lance.

The result was satisfying to Granada. The Christians made no immediate response and appeared to be accepting peace on those terms. Inside the Castilian court, however, the signal had been received. "The King and Queen were disturbed by this message," Peter Martyr wrote.[5] But there was little Isabella could do about it, engaged as she was in wars on two of her other borders and trying to establish peace within the kingdom. But she realized that she was working against the clock, that she faced not just a newly militant Granada but also the likelihood that the emirate would be bolstered by Muslim allies from North Africa, Egypt, or Turkey. And in fact, as Isabella feared, the Muslims of Andalusia soon approached the Muslims of North Africa for assistance and reinforcement. And then they turned to the Turks as well.

In the middle of 1477, to closely evaluate the situation, Queen Isabella traveled to Seville for the first time and stayed there for more than a year. She found the city in bad shape. The royal palace, the Alcázar, was in crumbling disrepair. Street crime was rampant; it was too dangerous to venture outside at night. Two of Andalusia's leading noble families, those of the Duke of Medina-Sidonia and the Marquess of Cádiz, were literally at swordpoint with each other. Disagreements of all kinds simmered under the surface of public discourse, ready to boil over into violence. But she did her usual things to bring justice to the region—presiding for hours on end over judicial procedures to resolve disputes, allowing people to air their grievances, and trying to bring adversaries into a semblance of harmony. Her customary brand of stern justice brought wrongdoers to heel. She even had some success in beginning a rapprochement between the families of the duke and the marquess. She spent about three more months in the second most important city of Andalusia, Córdoba, before heading back to Castile, where a number of other issues were awaiting her attention. Trying to buy time, she signed a three-year truce with Abu al-Hasan in 1478, and she did not press her demand for tribute money.[6]

Back in Castile in 1480, after finalizing the peace treaty with Portugal, Isabella barely had time to catch her breath before receiving what Isabella's Spanish chronicler Palencia called the "terrifying news" of the successful Ottoman attack on Otranto. The Spaniards learned with horror that the Turks had conducted a successful surprise raid on the town, and that although the people of Otranto had not put up the "least resistance to the enemy," many had nevertheless been slaughtered. The long-dreaded attack had given the Turks a foothold on the Italian peninsula, from which they could ravage the interior and prepare to seize Rome. The seriousness of the attack could not be underestimated. Its goal was "extinguishing the Catholic religion," Palencia wrote.[7]

The speed of Otranto's fall made it painfully obvious how easily the Turks could do the same thing on the Iberian peninsula, particularly if they used a beachhead like Málaga, Almería, or Marbella and found allies among the Muslims of Andalusia. It was becoming clear that if the Turks came in this way, it would be impossible to fend them off. And since war was inevitable, the threatening beachhead had to be eliminated before it began. From this point on, Isabella and Ferdinand seemed to be looking for an excuse to fight. Soon an opportunity presented itself, in the form of another surprise attack, this time from Granada.

During Christmas week of 1481, the Muslims of Granada invaded and attacked the mountain enclave of Zahara, located well within Castilian territory, on what Arab sources called a "stormy, rainy dark night."[8] Under the cover of these conditions, they audaciously clambered up the walls of the poorly guarded and ill-prepared fortress. "The Christians were terrorized and without any hope of rescue," the chronicler Palencia wrote. They couldn't resist the Muslim assault, and "a great number of them were killed by being slashed with swords, and the rest were captured and were marched to Granada."[9] Abu al-Hasan took possession of the town and left a garrison there to secure it. "He returned to Granada very satisfied and content with the good outcome of his venture," Arab historians would write.[10]

But some older, wiser people in Granada, worried that the move had been rash, expressed concern about how Abu al-Hasan was governing the realm. Overtly provoking the Christians might lead to a bad outcome. Some in Granada began to see omens and portents of doom, troubling signs in nature that unsettled the superstitious.

Isabella and Ferdinand were in Medina del Campo when they heard about the fall of Zahara. They received this news with special dismay. Not only did the attack represent another in a long line of border skirmishes—it was also a blow to Spanish pride. Zahara had been conquered from Granada after a grief-filled siege by Ferdinand's grandfather, Ferdinand of Antequera, in 1410. Now, in addition to these most recent deaths, some 150 people of Zahara had been marched into captivity and were being held in the impregnable town of Ronda. And, troublingly for Isabella and Ferdinand, Zahara was now permanently occupied.

From this new base, the Muslims made further incursions in the direction of Jaén, Córdoba, Sevilla, and Murcia, and nobody could stop them. Ferdinand and Isabella were too far away to intervene. Now the region was, in the words of the Countess of Yebes, "practically at the mercy of the infidel."[11] Nobody was safe.

A problem that had existed as a dull ache in the Spanish psyche had suddenly become a ringing migraine. Isabella and Ferdinand had launched their marriage with the vague intention of someday reclaiming Granada as part of Christendom, but now the situation had taken on an intense immediacy.

But what should they do? Achieving victory over the Muslim forces of Granada would require a herculean commitment by all the Spanish kingdoms, because Granada was formidably protected by hilltop fortresses everywhere, each almost impossible to successfully besiege. The Nasrids' close proximity to their coreligionists in North Africa, meanwhile, made it likely that they would receive, in short order, succor and assistance. Reinforcements and relief were "so apparent, so certain and so close," wrote the Aragonese chronicler Jerónimo Zurita, that the monarchs realized it would take "all the power and the force and the pushing" they could muster to "free that part of Spain and of the world of the subjugation and servitude from such enemies."[12]

Not yet prepared to mount such an all-out effort, the Spanish sovereigns at first relied on defensive tactics to protect themselves while they organized for what they saw would be a battle to the death. Isabella and Ferdinand ordered the Castilian fortress cities ringing the Granadan kingdom to strengthen their own defenses and prepare for war. They also initiated a naval blockade that began to interfere with the shipment of goods and soldiers between North Africa and Granada's port cities.

But before the sovereigns could complete their preparations for war, the Sevillian nobleman Rodrigo Ponce de León, the red-haired and hot-headed Marquess of Cádiz, the man who had been feuding with the Duke of Medina-Sidonia, decided to take matters into his own hands. An informant, a former slave who had been held in the dungeon there, told Ponce de León that the heavily walled town of Alhama, located in the rich agricultural heartland of the Kingdom of Granada, was poorly defended and might be a good target for a counterattack. On his own initiative, the Marquess of Cádiz decided to capture the town. He and his allies chose the date of February 27, 1482, and launched their attack at night, as the Muslims had done in Zahara. They rushed the town and took it, killing eight hundred Muslims and capturing three thousand, and planting a cross on the battlements of a high tower. And so the long-expected war began in a chaotic and unplanned fashion.

Now it was the Muslims who reacted with shock and horror, for they viewed Alhama as a critical link in the wall of defense ringing Granada. The city had been known as the "eyes" of Granada, because its watch-towers had alerted the citizens to Castilian forays into their lands. From their perspective, this too was a surprise attack. Moreover, the methods employed by the Castilians, who had been looking for revenge, inspired rage in the Muslims. "[The city's] walls, streets and temples were left filled with corpses and bathed in blood," Arab historians wrote.[13] The Castil-ians threw the bodies of the dead over the town walls.

This was the first big victory in Isabella's chapter of the Reconquest. Almost immediately she recognized its significance. But its methods had been brutal, and they paved the way for all-out war.

* * *

The Muslims quickly assembled an army to recover the town, and upon their arrival outside its walls, they were enraged and repulsed to discover wild dogs gnawing the decaying corpses of their countrymen. This was a double affront to Muslim sensibilities because they believe dogs to be unclean animals. The soldiers from Granada, determined to eject the Castilians from the fortress, besieged it for weeks. The Castilians were trapped inside, with limited water supplies, and began slowly dying of thirst. They managed to send out messengers first announcing their victory, then revealing their plight.

Isabella and Ferdinand were again in Medina del Campo for the winter, four hundred miles away, and Isabella was once again pregnant. But nevertheless they quickly prepared to lead a force to rescue the besieged Spaniards. The king left almost immediately, and the queen made plans to follow him to Córdoba within a few weeks. The wife of the Marquess of Cádiz, meanwhile, turned to her husband's longtime rival, the Duke of Medina-Sidonia, begging him to rush to the fray as well. The duke responded readily, setting aside his longtime enmity, and he was the first on the scene in defense of the Christians. The two men embraced when they saw each other on the field, and an important new alliance was formed, with long-lasting consequences.

As the Spanish reinforcements arrived, the Muslims besieging Alhama realized that they would soon be outnumbered and decided to withdraw. But they made it clear they intended to one day return and retake the town. In the meantime, they went on the attack throughout the south of Castile, taking whatever transient opportunities presented themselves to kill Castilians, claim land, and seize captives.

Isabella and Ferdinand convened in Córdoba, establishing the austere and foreboding fortress of the Alcazaba there as their military headquarters, and together they deliberated with the Andalusian nobility about how best to proceed. The queen was adamant that no retreat would be acceptable. She and the others took courage from the successful reconquest of Otranto, where circumstances had permitted Christian forces to eventually drive out the Turks, the chronicler Palencia recalled.[14] The Spanish had sent seventy ships to the aid of the Neapolitans,[15] who had combined with troops sent from Portugal and Hungary and rallied to expel the Turks. They were aided in their efforts by internal turmoil within the Ottoman Empire—Mehmed had unexpectedly died, setting off a succession battle, which induced the Ottoman forces to withdraw from southern Italy. Although Otranto was now largely depopulated, its recovery was an important symbol of Christians' ability to rally in self-defense. Queen Isabella referred to Otranto pointedly as she urged her troops into battle.

The queen's resolution and involvement were so great that she was engaged in a war council when she went into labor with her fourth child. She excused herself and gave birth to a daughter, the one they named

María. Little María, named for the mother of Christ, was actually one of twins—as we have seen, the other infant died stillborn. The Castilians took that death as an omen—being as superstitious as the Muslims—and as a bad signal from the heavens. The court traveled in procession to Córdoba's main cathedral, convening for a ceremony that mixed celebration, sorrow, and anguished spiritual reflection.[16]

The service was held in the glorious former mosque of Córdoba, with its lofty ceilings and an interior forest of stately columns; it had been converted to use as a cathedral after the city was taken in 1236, in an earlier phase of the Reconquest. The Muslim mosque had been built on the site of the former Visigothic church of St. Vincent, which in turn had displaced a Roman temple that once stood on the site. The mosque's lovely columns had been constructed from structural elements stripped from the church and the temple.

The death of the second twin baby was indeed a bad omen, for much death and bloodshed was on its way. The success at Otranto turned out to have been a rare speedy victory for Christian forces. The reconquest of Granada would last ten long years, with terrible casualties and losses on both sides. The Castilians would require intense concentration to win, for the Granadans were great warriors and resolute in opposition to the Christians. For both sides, it was unrelenting agony. "The war was so wild and so cruel that there was no place in the realm that was not bloodied from it, from the deaths of the victors and the vanquished," wrote the chronicler Zurita.[17]

The terrain was as difficult a challenge as the adversary's military skill. Just to march from the north of the peninsula to the south, to reach the field of battle, was an extraordinary venture, requiring the Castilians to cross parched and arid plains, and to drag men, matériel, and cannons up and over steep mountains. The war would require painstaking mobilization and much financial sacrifice, for the kingdom's entire resources would have to be focused on this one vast enterprise. The outcome was "in doubt until quite late in the 1480s," writes the historian L. P. Harvey.[18]

Not until 1489 did Isabella become confident of success. In that year she commissioned the first of a series of artworks to memorialize each victory of the Reconquest. Initially choosing twenty events to be immortalized, she placed an order with the wood sculptor Rodrigo Alemán for twenty relief carvings, designed to serve as the seat backs in the choir stall of the great Cathedral of Toledo, the most important church in Spain since Visigothic times. As the years wore on, she ordered twenty more seats because there had been twenty more significant battles or individual surrenders. The number of events deemed worthy of remembrance eventually totaled fifty-four. The relief carvings, a form of early military photojournalism, provide eyewitness records of tumultuous events that have otherwise slipped from historical memory. They are, writes the Spanish historian Juan de Mata Carriazo y Arroquia, "a work of immense historic and archaeological value."[19] Dying soldiers, grieving Muslims, devastated castles, and daring feats of heroism on both sides are depicted over and over in this remarkable series of tableaux.

The sovereigns spent much of the next ten years in their two Andalusian bases of Seville and Córdoba, orchestrating the campaign. Isabella was preoccupied with the war, Ferdinand less so, being frequently distracted by events in his own Kingdom of Aragon and by his continuing disputes with the French over the northern provinces. But each time his energy flagged, Isabella would exhort him to greater efforts. It became, as historian Peggy Liss describes it, "The Queen's War."[20]

The sovereigns were not initially ready for a war of this kind, however, and the first few years brought them nothing but disappointment. In the summer of 1482, King Ferdinand and the Marquess of Cádiz impulsively decided to attack Loja, a fortress redoubt on the mountainous western edge of the Kingdom of Granada. The Muslims sent a large army against them, both sides fought fiercely, and the Castilians were thrown back. One of the king's key lieutenants, moreover, Don Rodrigo Téllez Girón, master of one of the three knightly orders, Calatrava, died when he was shot with a poisoned arrow. The Count of Haro and the Count of Tendilla were both badly wounded. "The Castilians withdrew in confusion, leaving behind, on the field of battle, artillery and siege equipment," writes Harvey. "This was a disaster for King Ferdinand, who was forced to take the long road back to Córdoba to begin to build up his forces anew."[21] Queen Isabella, awaiting his arrival in Córdoba, was mortified by the loss and by the casualties inflicted on her troops. To both sovereigns, the defeat underscored the need for better strategic planning.

A second defeat then drove home the need to respect the strength, resilience, and ingenuity of their opponents. The king had been called away to Galicia to deal with problems of civil unrest there, and in his absence, and seeking to avenge their losses at Loja, the Castilians of Andalusia pulled together their own major foray against Granada. The cream of the Andalusian nobility convened for the venture, wearing resplendent coats of armor. Merchants leading packhorses trailed along in anticipation of a rich haul of booty. This force set off toward the seaport of Málaga, traveling through an area known as the Axarquía, a rich agricultural valley lined with steep mountains, confident in the strength of their numbers and in their fine and elegant armaments. They dreamed that their conquest of Málaga, Granada's most important seaport, would be a quick and decisive blow against the Muslims. The Marquess of Cádiz, chastened by his prior wartime experiences, urged caution but was overruled.

But an army on the march, strung out so that the different parts can't support one another, is always vulnerable to attack. The men rode through the countryside of Granada, burning crops and pillaging, then moved into the mountain passes north of Málaga. The people of Málaga could see the plumes of smoke rising from the places the Castilians had set on fire. Abu al-Hasan sent out two of his top commanders, who coordinated a very effective ambush. As the long, fragile column of Castilian soldiers entered the last valley leading to the coast, the Muslims were waiting on the high ground on each side of a place where the valley narrowed. From those positions, they attacked the Christian line of march.

Loaded down as they were, and ill prepared for the ferocity of the Muslim attack, the Castilians were trapped and slaughtered. Thousands were killed. Some soldiers stumbled into a rocky ravine in the dark, where they were picked off one by one by skilled marksmen. The Marquess of Cádiz, who had opposed the expedition, narrowly survived, but many of his relatives died. His brothers Diego and Beltrán were killed, as were two of his nephews. More than eight hundred horsemen were killed, and fifteen hundred were taken prisoner. The Count of Cifuentes was captured. Castilian soldiers were found stumbling around, dazed. Some were reportedly so demoralized that they allowed Muslim women to lead them into captivity.

It was a total victory for the Muslims. This successful enterprise "put much dread into the Christians and much spirit into the Muslims," Arab sources exulted.[22] For the Christians, it was another complete and humiliating rout. The queen was in Madrid when the bad news arrived. If the loss at Loja had taught the need for good planning, the crushing defeat at Axarquía showed the risk of hubris. The Muslims were proving to be valiant and resourceful soldiers who knew the local terrain and used all their advantages in what they were coming to view as a struggle to preserve their homes and way of life.

From this point on, the king and queen began to work more and more effectively as a team. Ferdinand led the troops into battle, while Isabella handled the provisioning and supplies and made sure camp hospitals were ready to receive the injured, tend them, and return them to battle. For both, raising money for expenses was a constant challenge. Ferdinand was more frequently the person at hand for each victory; Isabella was waiting and watching nearby, noting with meticulous attention to detail episodes in which the troops had not achieved all she had hoped or maximized each opportunity that presented itself.

And in consequence, they conquered Granada in a bit over a decade, "partly through force, partly through surrender, partly through prudence, and partly through gold and silver." With the latter they bribed local government administrators, who accepted the payments and immigrated to North Africa or the Ottoman Empire, leaving the residents in the citadels to fend for themselves.[23] The Castilians also used a process of slow starvation, as they cut off supply ships from arriving and destroyed crops and harvests.

For the Muslims, the two important early victories should have taught the lessons that they could defeat the Castilians as long as they used their resources wisely, bided their time, seized opportunities that arose, and presented a unified front. Both Ferdinand and Isabella had weaknesses that could be exploited. Ferdinand sometimes rushed headlong into danger; Isabella hated to see people on either side die unnecessarily, a characteristic at odds with the imperative ruthlessness of war. Moreover, the long supply lines left the Castilians at a marked disadvantage. Having to carry food and munitions made them vulnerable every time they moved from one place to another.

* * *

But the Muslim victories did not have the beneficial effects that they should have had. Instead, the Granadans began fighting among themselves, for they had their own problems at home.

Abu al-Hasan, the fierce sultan who had provoked the war with his threats, now found his personal life interfering with his own effectiveness. His regime had been well ordered and militarily successful as long as he stayed focused on the work at hand. His primary wife, Fatima, had been his lover, friend, supporter, and adviser. But polygamy presents a number of thorny logistical and romantic challenges, and such complexities brought Abu al-Hasan low when he began showing preference for a pretty young Christian woman in his harem. The "two very beautiful women in his harem that he loved more than the others," according to Arab sources, became embroiled in a deadly competition. The more powerful of the two wives was Fatima, who was Abu al-Hasan's cousin and mother of the prince Abu Abd Allah, known to Spaniards as Boabdil. The other was Isabel de Solís, the daughter of the mayor of Martos, a town near Jaén, who had been captured in a Muslim raid some years before; she had converted to Islam and went under the name Zoraya. The king had become badly smitten with Zoraya, and together they had two children whom he favored over the others. But the sultana, mother of the prince Boabdil, "not only hated to death the mother of the children, but also tried to kill her and kill them."[24]

This nasty family spat soon spread. Fatima was the daughter of a former sultan and had many influential friends, and she urged her son Boabdil to try to unseat his father. Abu al-Hasan's reputation suffered. Where he had formerly been viewed as a mighty warrior in defense of Islam, he now came to be seen as "hard and cruel," according to the Arab sources, and his son Boabdil came to be perceived as the courtly one, "affable and graciously mannered."[25]

So instead of being free to crush the Spanish forces in these years while they were still getting organized, Abu al-Hasan had to return to Granada to try to put down what Arab historians called "a terrible rebellion that split open the souls of the Granadans."[26] According to the Arab chronicler Nubdhat Al-Asr, the family strife broke into the open on the very day of the Muslim victory at Loja. Fatima soon led her sons, including Boabdil, to the town of Guadix, "where they were hailed by the people as rulers, and then they were acclaimed in Granada itself."[27]

The internal dissensions broke into physical fighting. The people of Granada took sides against each other. Some supported Abu al-Hasan, who was backed by his competent brother Abdalah El Zagal, a respected military veteran. Others supported Abu al-Hasan's son Boabdil. The young man was eager to prove his mettle on the battlefield to show up his father and uncle, a poor decision that would eventually spell his ruin.

In 1483 King Ferdinand took to the battlefield again. Up until now the tides of war had run against the Castilians. But a simple twist of fate changed the balance of power. Seeking a victory that would inspire universal admiration, Boabdil decided to lead an attack on the town of Lucena, well inside Castile. The battle quickly devolved into fierce hand-to-hand combat. Queen Isabella's commissioned carving of this scene depicts a crush of horses and human beings struggling for survival in the fields outside a fortress, brandishing medieval weaponry—swords, crossbows, and pikes. Several of Granada's most celebrated military leaders were killed in the battle, including Boabdil's father-in-law, the bold mayor who had led the defense of Loja. In the tableau, he crashes to the ground, nobly and with dignity, in a posture reminiscent of the famous Dying Gaul of Greek art. During the battle, the prince's exhausted horse fell into a river, and Boabdil, fearful that he would be killed, surrendered and was taken prisoner by the Castilians.

This was a major turn of events. With Boabdil's fortuitous capture, the most valuable of all possible war prizes had fallen into the hands of the dumbfounded Castilians. But what was the most strategic way to take advantage of this extraordinary opportunity?

King Ferdinand urgently consulted his advisers, who were divided about what to do. Some wanted the young prince to be kept captive, others to release him so he could return home to continue to foment rebellion. Queen Isabella cast the deciding vote. "The advice, which was most astute and fatal for the Muslims," was followed by the king of Castile, Arab sources wrote. They noted with amazement that Ferdinand subsequently treated Boabdil with elaborate respect, speaking to him "very honorably and with much love, and would not allow him to kiss his hand, but instead embraced him and called him his friend."[28]

Here King Ferdinand and Queen Isabella again demonstrated their unique ability to bend or win other people to their will. Boabdil had been treated badly by his father, but Ferdinand treated the spoiled young prince with exquisite politeness. To secure his release, Boabdil's mother Fatima sent "a great treasure" in ransom money to Ferdinand, which he accepted. For himself, Boabdil pledged his vassalage to Isabella and Ferdinand and promised to make large tribute payments to them yearly. He also agreed to return three hundred captive Christians.[29]

News of the prince's capture and ransoming was received in Granada with both joy and misgivings. The charming young prince returned home, but his people now wondered about his loyalty to them and their cause. His father, meanwhile, was contemptuous that his son had accepted vassalage to save his life. Internal warfare again broke out on all sides.

But Abu al-Hasan was ailing and soon became ill enough to have to step aside as ruler, passing the throne to his brother, the respected

El Zagal. Abu al-Hasan left Granada and went into retirement, taking with him his young wife and their children, and he died soon thereafter. Zoraya soon took back her childhood name, Isabel, converted back to Christianity, and changed her sons' names to Ferdinand of Granada, to honor King Ferdinand, and Juan of Granada, to honor the prince. Within a few years, the three of them were living in comfort at Queen Isabella's court, participating in Christian religious services.

Abu al-Hasan's death, however, left El Zagal and his nephew Boabdil in unmediated competition with each other in Granada. This succession crisis weakened the emirate. With its leadership in continuing disarray, new developments from then on favored the Christians rather than the Muslims. Isabella achieved a steady string of successes, although many of the advances came at a steep cost, both in money and in lives.

In June 1484 the Castilians conquered the town of Alora. Alemán's woodcarving of that event shows that the Spanish were growing more adept at the art of war. The walls of the fortress are depicted as having been badly damaged by cannon bombardment. Heavy artillery was becoming a more important part of their offensive tactics. Once the walls collapsed, all the defenders could do was surrender. The carving commemorates the moment when the commander of the fortress kneels in submission to Ferdinand, presenting him with the key to the town. The Muslims appear dazed, while the Spaniards look somber.

Ferdinand and Isabella spent that winter in Seville, planning their next steps. The following summer they struck and took the towns of Coín and Cártama, and then turned to one of Granada's most difficult targets, Ronda, which sits on a mesa surrounded by sheer cliffs on all sides. Here a clever trick led to victory. Ferdinand made a feint toward the port city of Málaga, which caused the Granadans to rush their available soldiers in that direction to protect that vital link to the outside world. Meanwhile, however, the Marquess of Cádiz doubled back to Ronda and put the town under siege before the garrison could be reinforced. The Castilians besieged and bombarded Ronda and cut off its water supply.

The battle of attrition lasted two weeks. Ronda "was defended by many of the most valiant Muslims in the kingdom, and all the Moors were brave warriors," wrote Zurita. The fighting went on night and day, but finally "moved by the begging and crying of the women and the little children who wanted to surrender," the Muslims asked for peace terms.[30] The Castilians took the town on May 22, 1485.

This victory was particularly significant to Isabella, because capturing Ronda freed some four hundred Christian slaves who were being held there. Among them were some of the people who had been seized at Zahara. They were weak and starving and needed to be nursed back to health. Queen Isabella ordered the heavy chains they had worn to be placed in carts and hauled to Toledo, to hang on the exterior walls of her Monastery of San Juan de los Reyes, as a reminder to worshipers of the hardships Christians had suffered.

The residents of Ronda were allowed to remain in their homes. Municipal leaders were required to take an oath of loyalty to Castile, to pay the same taxes they had paid to the Nasrid dynasty, and to fight on behalf of Castile if asked to do so. King Ferdinand promised not to interfere with their practice of Islam and allowed them to settle disagreements under sharia law.

From there the Castilians marched to the port city of Marbella, which promptly surrendered. In fact, the city's top officials contacted King Ferdinand before he arrived, asking to be given the choice of becoming vassals of the Spanish sovereigns or departing to "any place they wish," on ships to be provided by Ferdinand.[31] Alemán's woodcarving of the surrender of Marbella shows a Muslim soldier who has changed sides and is providing assistance and advice to the Castilians as they approach the city gates.

With Ronda and Marbella both secured, the sovereigns decided they could at last head home for a while. Isabella and Ferdinand spent the winter in Castile, in Alcalá de Henares, near Madrid. Princess Catherine, the future Catherine of Aragon, was born there on January 16, 1486. Queen Isabella remained off the campaign trail for a while, suffering from a postpartum infection, but Ferdinand set out on an expedition to Granada on his own on May 13, leaving at dawn. He apparently had no particular plan of attack, instead advancing as quickly as possible and intending to look for promising targets of opportunity. Isabella wasn't sure where he was at times, once writing to him "at the siege wherever you have gone."[32]

Ferdinand marched down toward Andalusia. He crossed the Las Yeguas River near Córdoba, where he paused to receive the supplies that were being shipped to him from all over the peninsula. The Marquess of Cádiz arrived as well, bringing additional reinforcements. Here Ferdinand was informed that Boabdil had reconciled with El Zagal, despite his pledge of loyalty and fealty to Isabella and Ferdinand, and was now planning how best to make war on the Christians. El Zagal and Boabdil had resolved their differences by dividing up the cities of Granada between themselves.

At night Ferdinand gathered his nobles to consult about where to direct their effort. On the advice of the Marquess of Cádiz, they decided to make another attempt against Loja, the town they had failed to capture four years earlier and that now was being defended by Boabdil himself. In preparation, the Spaniards besieged and took the nearby towns of Íllora, Moclín, Montefrío, and Colomera. The Spanish nobility participated in this effort in force, as well as some newcomers from England and France. A man they called Lord Scales made a particularly jaunty appearance on his arrival with a contingent of English troops.

While Ferdinand was away from her, Queen Isabella wrote to him with painstaking care for his pride, with exaggerated courtesy and respect. She suggested at one point that Boabdil could have possession of the citadels of Baza and Guadix, properties that were held by El Zagal, in exchange for his surrender of Loja, but then ostentatiously appeared to catch and excuse herself: "Pardon me, your wife, because I speak about things I do not know."[33]

The artillery attack on Loja began on Sunday, May 28. Ferdinand was ferocious in his assault, wrote Peter Martyr, who was there. The bombardment was fierce but did not last long. The chronicler Hernando del Pulgar said the bombardment lasted one day and two nights before Boabdil surrendered the fortress.

Isabella's public role during the battle at Loja had been ostentatiously religious. She had spent her days and nights in prayer and fasting, asking God for victory and fretting about the fate of her husband and the other soldiers. She rejoined the army soon after the Castilians gained control of the city.

Boabdil was back in their hands once again. Again he asked to be freed, and again Isabella and Ferdinand agreed, even though he had earlier pledged vassalage to them and then reneged. By this point it was clear that Boabdil was more valuable to the sovereigns when he was in Granada fomenting trouble than when he was in their custody. And now, in exchange for his freedom, Boabdil reached a secret agreement with Queen Isabella, very similar to the one she had proposed to King Ferdinand. She promised to support him in a plan for a coup against his uncle.

The shifts in fortune so evident in Loja put Isabella in a reflective mood, and she wrote to Ferdinand on May 30: "May it please the Lord to continue the victory that Our Lady has given" in delivering that town to them, she wrote, calling it "a marvelous thing." Nevertheless, the loss of life disturbed her. "The Moors died defending [Loja], and our people also did so," she wrote. " . . . The deaths weigh heavily on me."[34]

But there could be no hesitation. The sovereigns pushed ahead toward Íllora, Moclín, and Montefrío, which all surrendered. The queen herself entered Moclín with six-year-old Princess Juana to accept its surrender, according to Alemán's choir stall woodcarving. Isabella and her daughter are shown, accompanied by Cardinal Mendoza and what appear to be several young pages. The woman and child, riding on horseback, enter a chaotic and frightening scene. The carving shows the tower ablaze as a result of mortar fire that caused an explosion. The mortar fire had ignited the Muslims' gunpowder depot, according to the chronicler Hernando del Pulgar.[35]

Returning to Córdoba, the queen prepared a grand victory reception for King Ferdinand, who arrived four days later. With this event, the campaign of 1486 ended.

* * *

Isabella and Ferdinand spent that winter in Salamanca and then, when winter ended and the new campaign season began, went back to their military headquarters in Córdoba. With the spring came Boabdil's promised coup. On April 7, 1487, Ferdinand left to besiege Vélez-Málaga, a town near the crucial port of Málaga. After a pitched battle there, the Muslims surrendered on April 27. El Zagal had set out with troops from Granada to defend the town, but soon after he left, Boabdil took control of the capital. This was a huge blow to El Zagal, and, seeing no point either in trying to defend Vélez-Málaga or in returning to Granada, he and his followers headed instead for the town of Guadix. Now Granada's troops were permanently divided into two separate contingents that would no longer be working together.

Boabdil had been able to oust his uncle because of the secret pact with Queen Isabella. He had written to her explaining that he had an opportunity to unseat El Zagal, but needed troops, arms, and provisions to do it. Isabella had sent her childhood friend, Gonzalo Fernández de Córdoba, to render that support. Together they locked El Zagal out of

Granada, and Boabdil was declared king. On April 29, Boabdil wrote to Queen Isabella announcing his triumph against his uncle and reaffirming the obedience he had sworn to her in Loja. He had also reached an agreement with her, as she had suggested, that "he would turn over Granada, when he could, in exchange for places in the eastern part of the kingdom, which was then loyal to El Zagal."[36] At this point, according to the historian L. P. Harvey, he was almost certainly a "secret ally" of Isabella and Ferdinand. [37]

Ferdinand and Isabella next proceeded to a rich target, the seaport city and fortress of Málaga. They understood that it would be the most important battle of the war, because the seaport was the vital link between the Muslims of Granada and Muslims elsewhere in the Mediterranean. It was also probably the most difficult single target, as it consisted of three separate fortresses. If they were to win it, then victory over the inland city of Granada would be a virtual certainty. Ferdinand had arrived on May 6, while Isabella got there two weeks later. Her arrival, coming as it did among reports of a plague epidemic, demonstrated her personal resolve to take the port city. The sovereigns established a tent encampment outside its gates.

First they tried to negotiate for Málaga's surrender, something that they had managed to achieve with a number of other Moorish towns. They warned that if the Muslims did not submit, they would be enslaved. Given that El Zagal had moved away from the front, Ferdinand and Isabella were able to argue that the garrison was unlikely to get much support from other Muslims in Granada. But the defenders adamantly rejected the offer of a negotiated settlement. So Ferdinand and Isabella began a tight blockade and siege to starve the inhabitants into submission.

The bombardment began; the city was besieged for three long months. Food ran low, and the residents began to starve. Morale also flagged among the Castilian troops, and some deserted. Málaga's Muslim commander threatened to kill the six hundred Christian prisoners inside the city if the Castilians did not withdraw. Ferdinand responded that he "would kill every Muslim in Spain" if the Christian slaves were injured.[38] At last the city surrendered, but the ferocity of the battle had hardened the sovereigns' hearts, and they were punitive toward the inhabitants.

All the surviving residents of Málaga became the property of the king and queen. Women slaves were given to Christian noblewomen. The pope was given one hundred slaves; Cardinal Mendoza received seventy. The Jews of Málaga were allowed to keep their property but were forcibly relocated until their ransom, some 10,000 gold castellanos, could be paid. Chief judge and rabbi Abraham Senior, Isabella's childhood friend from Segovia, raised the money for the ransom of the Jews and paid it. No one stepped forward to pay the ransoms of the Muslims. Of about 5,000 people captured, about 4,400 ended up sold into slavery.[39] The mosques were turned into churches. The six hundred Christian captives, as sick and wizened in appearance as the slaves in Ronda, were freed, fed, and nursed back to health.

With the collapse of Málaga, western Granada now belonged entirely to the Castilians, and only a handful of major Granadan towns remained under Nasrid control. Guadix, Baza, and the capital, Granada, were important towns and cities in the interior of the kingdom; Almería was Granada's last major seaport.

In 1488, after spending some time in Ferdinand's realms, Isabella and Ferdinand captured the towns of Vera, Vélez-Blanco, and Vélez-Rubio. That year the urgency of their cause increased, because word came that the Turks were on the move once again, this time with a land army of some 100,000 soldiers and a fleet of 505 galleys.

Baza was the next major siege. The Castilian troops arrived in June 1489. It became a long, hard slog. They made little progress and considered departing. King Ferdinand sent messengers to the queen, who was in Jaén, asking her advice, and she insisted that the Castilians stand their ground, saying that she would find a way to provide whatever was needed to win the victory. She urged her troops to take courage from the Castilians' growing record of success, and to have confidence that they were doing God's bidding. "It is the same enemies and now they are weaker," she told her husband and his troops. She promised, moreover, to keep God on their side by offering perpetual prayers for their support. This message cheered and roused the troops. "Therefore we fix our foot," Peter Martyr concluded, meaning that they would not back down and would not withdraw from the siege.[40]

By 1489 the Castilian troops encamped around Baza had become a cohesive fighting force, and the comity and high morale among them were evident to everyone. The soldiers came from all different parts of Spain—from Asturias, from Galicia, from the Basque country, and from Extremadura—and joined with the Castilians and Aragonese. All spoke different dialects but nevertheless got along surprisingly well, united in a sense of combined public purpose. They were becoming a nation, organized under a religious banner. "It is incredible to believe that among so many idioms of various nations, different manners, various disciplines of eighty thousand foot and fifteen thousand horse there should be the greatest concord" in the camp, Martyr told Milanese Cardinal Ascanio Sforza. "So great is the reverence of the Royal Majesty that to this day, no tumult has arisen to disturb anything; there are no thefts, no highwaymen on the roads; no private quarrels. But if by chance any arise, the rest are deterred by severe reprimands to the authors."[41]

The military discipline reminded the humanist scholar of the ancient Greeks. "Yet all anonymous, shut up in one camp, so practice warfare, so obey the orders of the chiefs and prefects, that you would suppose them all brought up in one house with one language and the same discipline," he wrote. "You would believe our camp to be a city founded on Plato's Republic."[42]

In the fall of 1489, Queen Isabella moved from Jaén to the nearby town of Ubeda, close enough to keep an eye on events in Baza. In November, she decided to go to Baza itself, as she had in Málaga, to boost morale. Her presence caused the Moors' resistance to crumble. She arrived in a stately procession, accompanied by her eldest child, nineteen-year-old Princess Isabel. With Queen Isabella present, the town leaders and residents felt confident that the terms of surrender would be merciful and would be observed. Soon they reached an agreement with her that allowed the elite to take their possessions and depart, while the townspeople were left to live according to their customs.

The agreement they reached gave the Muslim soldiers of Baza money in exchange for helping the Castilians attack El Zagal's remaining strongholds. Sidi Yahya, the principal leader in Baza, left for Guadix, where El Zagal was living, and convinced him that resistance was futile. By December 22, El Zagal had surrendered the port city of Almería, and he gave up Guadix on December 30. He sold all his personal property in Andalusia for 20,000 castellanos and departed to a new home in North Africa. Arab sources said he did it to spite his nephew Boabdil. According to Nubdhat Al-Asr:

Many people assert that [El Zagal] and his commanders sold these villages and districts ruled by them to the ruler of Castile, and that they received a price for them. All this was with a view to taking revenge on the son of his brother . . . and on his commanders who stayed in Granada, with just the city under their government and with benefit of a truce from the enemy. By his action, he wanted to cut Granada off, so as to destroy it in the way that the rest of the country had been destroyed.[43]

The surrender of Almería had great strategic importance: it meant that the entire southern coastline was closed off from Granada and that the Nasrid dynasty had lost its last outlet to the sea and the possibility of reinforcement. King Ferdinand, Queen Isabella, and Princess Isabel all participated in the official surrender of the city. Alemán's woodcarving shows a bearded man with a turban, probably El Zagal, approaching King Ferdinand, almost on his knees, to kiss the king's feet. Meanwhile, over the door, a Muslim raises his hands in either greeting or lamentation.[44]

This series of episodes in 1489, and specifically the siege at Baza and Isabella's role in its surrender, left a lasting mark, among other things, on the games we play today. Chess was enormously popular in Spain at the time, and soon after this battle the Queen became the single most powerful piece on the chessboard, able to move great distances in all directions; her mission is to protect and defend the key piece on the board, the King. Some versions of chess had had a Queen figure before Isabella's birth, but it was at this time that the game, originally invented in India, underwent a complete metamorphosis and the Queen became a dominant figure. The changes in the game were chronicled in a popular book on the new rules of chess, published in Salamanca about 1496, written by Ramírez de Lucena. He described the game now as "queen's chess," and her new powers allowed her to "advance as far as she liked, as long as her path was clear."[45] Queen Isabella had memorialized herself as a powerful player in the game of war.

Isabella and Ferdinand's most recent victories had been crucial to completing the Reconquest. By 1490 the Nasrid dynasty was finished, but the war was not yet over. In 1490 and 1491 the sovereigns began their siege of Granada's capital. The Muslims hoped that when winter came, the Spaniards would depart to escape the harsh cold, but these hopes were dashed when the Granadans saw them building a permanent garrison town outside Granada, which they named Santa Fe, or Holy Faith. But the Granadans hung on, hoping against hope. Starvation set in, and conditions inside the city became desperate.

The final year of the campaign, 1491, was a year of perpetual skirmishes as the Muslims found ways to strike at their attackers. The exact role played by Boabdil, now the emir of Granada, is unclear. He had promised to give Granada to Isabella and Ferdinand, but now that the end was near, he seemed immobilized. A group of leading Granadan noblemen, clerics, and dignitaries met with him and pointed out the emirate's dismal situation, its food shortages, and the deaths of its strongest warriors, leaving no one else to fight. And there was no help on the horizon. "Our brethren the Muslims who live across the sea in the Magrib have already been approached, and none of them has come to help or risen to our assistance," this delegation said.[46]

Boabdil told them to discuss the problem among themselves and to suggest what should be done. The city elders decided to send an emissary to the Spanish sovereigns to ask for a negotiated settlement, and Boabdil agreed. Many scholars now believe that Boabdil had already reached a secret agreement with the Castilians but feared he would be killed if his subjects knew. By pushing the problem onto others' shoulders, they shared responsibility for the opening of peace talks.

By this time, too, Boabdil appears to have been primarily looking out for his own interests. In his negotiations with the Castilians, who were represented by Gonzalo Fernández de Córdoba, a fluent speaker of Arabic, Boabdil asked for personal reassurances: "Tell me what certainty can [I] have that the king and the queen will let my lord the king have the Alpujarras, which is the first clause in our negotiations, and that they will treat him as a relative as promised?"[47]

"The obligation, and the [grant of] lands will last, Mr. Governor, sir, for so long as His Excellency remains in the services of their highnesses," Gonzalo was said to have answered.[48] In other words, Boabdil was required to accept a permanent state of vassalage to Isabella and Ferdinand.

The final settlement, according to Harvey, was really dependent "on a private and secret understanding" between Boabdil and the Spanish sovereigns. And so the surrender of Granada was secured.

The public agreement, which was widely circulated, gave the Muslims of Andalusia the right to stay in their homes, keep their possessions, operate under their own sharia system of law, and leave for North Africa at the expense of Castile, as long as they left within three years. Muslims were to be allowed to keep their own faith without being compelled to convert to Christianity. The Muslims had to free their Christian slaves at the time of surrender. Christians were forbidden to enter mosques.

Two specific provisions applied to the Jews living in the Nasrid empire. They were not permitted to collect any taxes or hold any power over Muslims. And the rights that had been granted to the Muslims would apply to Jews residing in Granada for the next three years only, after which, if they did not become Christian, they would have to move to North Africa.

Under the agreement, the Alhambra was to be handed over on January 6, the Christian holiday known as Epiphany, to commemorate the day the Magi arrived bearing gifts for the infant Christ. But Boabdil suggested they speed up the transfer because the residents of Granada were becoming agitated about losing their homeland. They advanced the date, and Boabdil got a "suitable written receipt," in Harvey's words, confirming the deal had been concluded.[49]

And so, at the beginning of 1492, Isabella and Ferdinand at long last took the capital of Granada. On January 2, Boabdil ceremonially handed over the keys to the city, and the two sovereigns, accompanied by fourteen-year-old Prince Juan, passed through the gates. Zurita recalled it as a day of "incredible fiesta and happiness."[50] They entered with surprising serenity, considering the circumstances. Boabdil had sent his son to them as a hostage to ensure a peaceful transfer of the city into Castilian hands. When the city was secured, the boy was returned to his family.[51] Crosses and Castilian flags were planted at the highest points of the fortresses, while priests sang hymns and celebrated mass.

Boabdil, who had just traded away his birthright, departed over a bridge that came to be known as the Bridge of Sighs, with his once-proud mother at his heels, reportedly carping at him for his failure to hold it for his descendants. El Zagal had already left for North Africa; Boabdil followed soon thereafter. The Spanish sovereigns clearly wanted him to leave, regardless of the assurances they had given him at the time of the surrender, and he was unhappy living under Spanish domination. He is believed to have died in Fez. What happened to these men's harems is unknown.

Taking possession of the city was a momentous experience for Ferdinand and Isabella and their children. The beautiful Alhambra of Granada, the Moorish-built palace of the Nasrid dynasty, struck the sovereigns as lovely, and they wandered its byways and gardens with awe and appreciation, wondering about the flowing designs of Arabic script. Its walls were inscribed with Arabic poetry and holy writ. One inscription, which Isabella noted, was repeated over and over: ONLY GOD IS THE VICTOR, or ONLY GOD IS ALL POWERFUL.[52]

Inside the palace, whose immense size awed the visitors, were visible signs of the Muslim domination of the peninsula. At the entrance, an eyewitness said, they discovered seventeen Castilian standards, each representing a specific victory against Christian forces, including one that was more than 150 years old.[53] And this fairytale palace, they learned, had been built with Christian slave labor.

Another discovery also jarred the sensibilities of the Castilians. A group of nearby caves had been used as prisons, and many of the captives had been allowed to starve to death during the siege. The German traveler Jerónimo (Hieronymus) Münzer, who went there a few years later, said he was told that only 1,500 of the 7,000 Christian slaves were found alive when Isabella and Ferdinand arrived. They emerged, emaciated and filthy.

About 750 of these captives were at death's door. As they left the dungeons, they sang songs about Jesus as their savior, and they threw themselves on the ground before the feet of Isabella and Ferdinand, crying and shouting prayers of thanksgiving. It took two large carts to haul away the chains with which they had been bound.

Most had managed to retain their Christian faith despite the difficult circumstances. Isabella asked one wizened captive who had been held for forty-four years whether his faith had sustained him: "What would you have thought in the first year of your captivity if you had been told that Jesus Christ had not been born to be your redeemer?" The man answered, "I would have died of the pain."[54]

Nine Christian captives—two Lombards and seven Castilians—had turned away from Christianity and become Muslim. That was heresy and apostasy and could not be permitted, so the king ordered them killed. They were beaten and then burned at the stake, the common penalty for heresy.

The victory over Granada won acclaim for Isabella and Ferdinand throughout Europe, because it was the first significant triumph against Islam in hundreds of years, and to many Europeans, it was partial payback for the loss of Constantinople. "Perpetual peace resulted from the conquest of Granada," wrote Zurita. "It was famed and celebrated through all the realms of Christendom, and it extended to the farthest and most remote lands of the Turk and Sultan. . . . It was an end to a war so continuous and cruel, that had lasted for centuries, with a nation so barbaric and fierce, such an enemy and an infidel."[55]

Ferdinand moved quickly to make sure he was given full credit for the achievement. "We desire you to know that it has pleased our Lord to give complete victory to the King and destruction to the Kingdom of Granada and to the foes of Our Catholic faith and after many labours, costs, deaths and much shedding of our subjects' blood, on second January of this year of Grace 1492," he wrote exultantly that very day in a letter to the rulers of Venice. " . . . Henceforth you have here a Catholic land."[56]

In addition to Alemán's fifty-four choir stall carvings commemorating the war, another set of artworks memorialized it as well. They are part of the altarpiece of the Royal Chapel of Granada. They consisted of painted wood carvings of the surrender, fashioned within living memory of that early day in January 1492. One carving shows Isabella and Ferdinand entering Granada on horseback.

In a second carving, Boabdil approaches the king and queen to hand them the keys of Granada. A long line of Christian captives straggle out of the fortress behind him. A third panel shows Muslim men submitting to baptism in a fountain. A fourth shows heavily draped Muslim women being baptized, their mournful eyes visible under the heavy veils.

Clearly, assimilation of this new province into Spain was not going to be painless. But a new institution of religious supervision and control had already been established by the Spanish sovereigns, and it was ready to be deployed against the Muslims as well.

FOURTEEN

ARCHITECTS OF THE
INQUISITION

D uring these years when religious hatreds were on the forefront of everyone's mind, when Muslims and Christians were
at war in Spain and in eastern Europe, and when both sides
in both places justified their actions by calling it devotion to God, Queen
Isabella authorized the creation of a joint church and state initiative
called the Inquisition.

The Inquisition applied only to people who had formally identified
themselves as Christians but whose behavior caused others to doubt the
sincerity of their beliefs. In Isabella's lifetime, the Inquisition focused
primarily on conversos, people of Jewish descent who had publicly converted to Christianity and were calling themselves Christians. It did not
initially apply to Muslims or Jews. Its goal was to ferret out insincere
Christians and, if they were found guilty, to correct them, and if they
were deemed unrepentant, to kill them by burning them at the stake, the
traditional penalty for heresy. But when Isabella and Ferdinand decided
that the presence of practicing Jews in the kingdom was leading conversos astray, they decided to try to force all the Jews in Spain to convert
to Christianity. Those who did not accept baptism were compelled to
leave. Later the same thing happened to the Muslims, despite the specific
promise made to them at the surrender of Granada that they could keep
their faith. Both policies increased the number of reluctant Christians
who would become subject to the Inquisition.

The queen is known to have begun pondering the idea of an inquisitorial panel when she was in Seville for the first time in 1477. She formally launched it in 1480, the year the Turks seized Otranto and as the war with Granada was on the verge of breaking out. She did it, though reluctantly, as a result of intense lobbying by clerics in Seville and elsewhere who told her that heresy among conversos in Andalusia was epidemic, was jeopardizing souls, and was undermining security. The Spanish Inquisition therefore owed its origins in part to the strains of wartime, when suspect loyalties were less tolerated than usual and suspicions were running high. But it turned out to be such an effective tool for government repression and control that it survived as an institution for three hundred years, giving successive rulers a convenient way to suppress enemies and punish various kinds of social nonconformity that the majority of the population found irritating.

Its first victims were Christians of Jewish descent who had continued to follow some Jewish customs, a practice called "Judaizing," which made it difficult to tell if they had sincerely converted to Christianity. But as time wore on, homosexuals, people of Muslim descent, Protestants, and divorced people all came under the same type of scrutiny. So did political enemies of the government, or people accused of various kinds of unconventional thinking.

Nonetheless the Spanish Inquisition, also known as the Holy Office, was a popular institution with the wider population, because they believed it was needed. After years of civil unrest, many people welcomed evidence that a strong authoritarian central government was eliminating social discord. The Spaniards had come to value religious orthodoxy. Bigots, or even the ordinary narrow-minded and pedantic, were the Inquisition's most enthusiastic proponents; its victims or prospective victims hated and feared it. It became, in the historian Henry Kamen's words, "a standard feature of the Spanish landscape."[1]

Nobody knows for sure what Isabella had in mind when she started the Inquisition. And nobody knows for sure how many people it affected. The scholars who have studied it have often brought their own personal biases to their work. It has been depicted so frequently in fiction that truth and perception have become confused and intermingled. Propagandists from England cited the existence of the Inquisition as evidence of their kingdom's moral superiority to Spain, even while English authorities were cruelly oppressing their own religious minorities at home. Sultan Bayezid II is said to have roundly criticized the Inquisition shortly before the Ottoman Empire killed tens of thousands of its own heretics—those following a mystical Sufi variant of Shia Islam, instead of the government-authorized Sunni teachings. In other words, religious oppression is nothing new and is not uniquely Spanish.

In more recent decades, hundreds of scholars have pored over the surviving fragments of documentary evidence of what the Inquisition was and did. Historians once believed that immense numbers of people were burned at the stake, but more recent scholarship has cast doubt on those assertions, and the estimates of actual deaths have been substantially reduced. Claims that hundreds of thousands of people were killed have been proved to be erroneous.

But there is no question that during Isabella's reign, hundreds of people were put to the flame, probably at least 1,000 and perhaps as many as 2,000. In the religious capital, Toledo, for example, the inquisitors killed 168 people during Isabella's lifetime.[2] About 85 in that same district were tried and found innocent. Another 120 were tried in absentia, having fled elsewhere or having already died. One reason the numbers are hard to determine is that inquisitors often tried people who were already dead, using the inquisitorial mechanism of documents as testimony, then burning their bones. People who ran away were tried in absentia and burned in effigy, much as a puppetlike figure of King Enrique had been constructed and then symbolically dethroned in Ávila when Isabella's brothers were fighting over the throne. In those days, wax, wood, or cloth representations of people were viewed as having ritual significance.

The Spanish Inquisition was not a new idea conceived by Ferdinand and Isabella. Through most of recorded history, and before the concept of a separation of church and state was invented, government and religion were inextricably linked. In most cultures, opposing religious doctrine has been tantamount to defying political authority. Therefore the Inquisition was an institution with very old roots and a prescribed set of rules, although the Spaniards introduced many new twists.

The governing principle of an Inquisition is that failing to conform to religious and political norms is treason. In Isabella's age, church and state were one—religious authority and secular power were intermingled. Threats to religious orthodoxy were seen as threats to the political establishment. Kings and queens assumed their thrones, they believed, by the will of God, and questioning God was tantamount to questioning royals' political legitimacy. Moreover, kings and queens were viewed as spiritually responsible for the guardianship of their subjects' lives and souls. A failure to root out heresy put the souls of the king and queen at risk as well.

The word *Inquisition* comes from the Latin noun *inquisitio,* or "investigation," and the Spanish Inquisition followed specific Roman codes of law. The Romans had authorized the use of torture to gain confessions, for example, believing that most wrongdoers would not voluntarily share information that would place them at risk of punishment. But they knew that confessions obtained under torture were often unreliable, and they required officials to obtain statements afterward from the suspect confirming what he or she had said under intense duress. The Roman emperors found torture effective in achieving the desired goals. In later centuries, writes the historian Lu Ann Homza, "the use of torture for the purpose of interrogation also became more widespread . . . especially in cases of treason."[3] Torture became a customary tool of law enforcement in Spain, too: victims were forced to experience the sensation of drowning by having water poured into their mouths, or were dangled from overhead beams to dislocate their shoulders.

Over the years, a number of kings and popes had called for Inquisitions against various kinds of heresies, and burning heretics at the stake was the traditional punishment. Joan of Arc, for example, had been convicted of breaking church rules by wearing men's clothing and was burned at the stake. The nine former Christians found in Granada at the Reconquest who had converted to Islam were deemed apostates and were sentenced to death.

The biggest single previous Inquisition had involved the Cathars, a Christian religious splinter group that spread in western Europe between the 1100s and 1300s. They deviated from church orthodoxy by permitting women to be religious leaders, criticizing the moral corruption of Rome and clerical hierarchy, and following a special diet that made them very thin. They said their beliefs made them special; they called themselves "Perfects." In 1234 Pope Innocent III authorized an Inquisition to suppress them and kill those who would not renounce their beliefs. On a single day in March 1244, about two hundred Cathars were burned on a funeral pyre in France. Those who were not willing to die for their unorthodox beliefs pretended to have seen the errors of their ways and went underground.

In those days, there was no presumption of innocence for people accused of crimes; they were simply assumed to be guilty. Under the Inquisition, people who were accused of practicing unorthodox customs but who admitted their sins and confessed were forgiven but were still punished in some way: they were made to wear a pointed hat or a special shirt, or were forced to walk barefoot or naked, or were made to do some other kind of penance. Those who returned to their previous errors received the death penalty.

Under the inquisitorial system, informants were encouraged to come forward and anonymously identify people whose seemingly innocent habits might reflect an insincere commitment to Christianity—things such as avoiding pork, wearing clean clothes on the Jewish Sabbath, or lighting candles on Jewish holidays. Large numbers of people, it turned out, were willing to anonymously finger their friends, employers, and associates. The ability to denounce people without incurring personal risk brought out the worst in the human character.

On the basis of such testimony, people were hauled into jail and sometimes tortured until they confessed. If they confessed wholeheartedly, they might escape death and be given limited punishment. But if they relapsed or if their heresies were viewed as persistent, church officials would "relax," or turn them over, to government officials, who would perform the executions.

How did a ferocious outbreak of such injustice erupt in Spain? Answers to this complex and paradoxical question go back to the origins of Christianity. Jesus, the preacher whose teachings are the foundation of Christianity, was born a Jew. He was killed by Roman officials in Judea with the acquiescence of Jewish leaders, who may have feared that his unconventional proselytizing would cause them political problems with the Roman overlords, and who may have seen it as a challenge to their own authority as well. There is only limited secular history on these events, but they are a core article of faith for Christians.

Jews of the first century had had good reason to be concerned about the Romans and their methods for maintaining order, for within a few decades of Jesus's death, they were forced from their homes in Judea as a result of another rebellion. Some moved to Hispania, an important part of the Roman Empire, where other Jews had already made their homes. By Isabella's day, some Jewish families had been living on the Iberian peninsula for more than fifteen hundred years.

The Hebrew historian and financier Isaac Abravanel, one of Iberia's most influential Jews at the time of the Inquisition, wrote that his family had lived in Seville during the time of the Second Temple in Israel.[4] More Jews came after the destruction of the Second Temple in A.D. 70. In the period after the "flames had reduced the beautiful Jerusalem to ashes," writes one scholar, some Jews went to Babylon, and some to Egypt, but "the families of greatest consideration were brought to Spain, among whom were the remnants of Benjamin and Judah, descendants of the house of David."[5] In fact, the word *don* as an honorific may have originated in the Hebrew word *adon,* meaning "lord or master," although others say the word originated from the Latin *dominus.*

Displaced Jews prospered in Spain under the Roman Empire, and some became great scholars across many fields of inquiry—philosophy, medicine, literature, astronomy, and science. When the Roman Empire disintegrated, they experienced a period of oppression during the Visigothic era but were not forced from their centuries-old home. Their alliance with the Muslims allowed them to maintain comfortable lives, and they experienced a cultural zenith in sophisticated Córdoba about A.D. 1000. Many became Arabic speakers and grew comfortable with Arab customs. The close association of Jews with Arabs, however, made them suspect in Christian eyes, because there was still a cultural memory among Spanish Catholics that Jews had aided the Muslims in the conquest of the Iberian peninsula.

During the centuries of Islamic dominance, Jews were forced to essentially buy tolerance from the Muslims by paying special taxes and by submitting to regulations directed against them. Their lives were not entirely serene because of periodic surges in Islamic fanaticism. In December 1066, for example, a Muslim mob killed some fifteen hundred Jewish families in Granada.[6] They also suffered periodic persecutions at the hands of Christians, who were gradually recovering the peninsula from the Muslims. Jews frequently found themselves caught between warring bands from these two faiths and survived by adapting themselves as best they could.

During these centuries, the Spanish royal family generally saw itself as holding a legal and moral obligation to act as protectors of the Jews. It was difficult to do this consistently in the face of ancient hatreds. In 1391, about sixty years before Isabella was born, a rising tide of Christian fanaticism directed itself against Jews. Anti-Semitic preachers roamed the kingdom, delivering fiery speeches about the death of Jesus, warning of the dangers of Judaism, and urging the rabble to attack Jews and destroy synagogues. Many people were killed, many thousands of Jews were forcibly converted to Christianity, and Jewish houses of worship were converted into churches. The epicenter of this violence was Seville; thereafter Seville became the home of many Jews who had embraced Christianity for survival. Other Jewish families, like the Abravanels, moved to Portugal to escape the oppression.[7] Others migrated to Granada or North Africa. Many families splintered: some accepted baptism, while others courageously clung to their Jewish faith. Another spasm of intense proselytizing led to mass conversions of Jews to Christianity in 1411.

These episodes of anti-Jewish fanaticism usually occurred at times when the central government was weak. The persecutions of 1391, for example, broke out the year after eleven-year-old Henry III, known as Henry the Sick or Henry the Feeble, became king. He attempted to punish people who had abused Jews, but he also bent to political pressure and permitted new restrictions to be imposed on Jews. By the time Isabella took the throne, the total number of Jews in Spain had fallen to about eighty thousand, in a population of about six million Christians.

People who had been forced to convert to Christianity, both in 1391 and 1411, were given the right to renounce vows taken under duress, and once the danger was past, they could have reverted to Judaism without further persecution. But for a variety of reasons, some chose to retain their new affiliation with Christianity. Some had wholeheartedly converted. Others saw that converting opened up jobs and opportunities that had been closed to them as non-Christians. This latter group converted as a matter of convenience. The end result was that during Isabella's lifetime, there were many elderly people who had practiced Judaism in their own childhoods but had changed religions. These people, and their children, were known as conversos. There were tens of thousands of them, and many lived between two worlds.

After 1390 many conversos moved into lucrative and influential jobs in the government. Their success, both financially and professionally, stirred jealousy among longtime Christians, who faced new competition for positions that had once been granted almost as a matter of inheritance, from Christian father to Christian son.

Conversos also entered the religious hierarchy of the church, becoming priests and bishops. It was understandably an issue of concern if people who did not hold sincere Christian beliefs were placed in positions of providing pastoral care to Christians. In Castile during Isabella's lifetime, at least four bishops were conversos, and according to the Inquisition historian Henry Kamen, so was Cardinal Juan de Torquemada, who represented Spaniards at the Vatican.[8]

Certainly anti-Semitism was at work among some proponents of the Inquisition. However, the situation in Spain was more subtle and complicated than the blatant bigotry found in northern and eastern Europe. Relations between Christians and Jews had usually been better in Castile than elsewhere on the continent. Jews had been expelled from England in 1296 and from France in 1394, but this had not happened in Iberia, and many of the refugees from those countries had settled there. Jews and Christians in Iberia had been tied together with bonds of affinity and proximity for centuries.

There does not appear to be any evidence that Isabella was anti-Semitic. She had close and friendly relationships with a number of practicing Jews. One was Castile's most prominent rabbi, Abraham Senior, from Segovia, a longtime supporter of the queen. In addition, Isaac Abravanel, whose family had been in Iberia for more than one thousand years, served as financial adviser to the queen and to her Portuguese cousins. Their families had worked together for years. Abravanel had been forced to flee Portugal when King João began persecuting Isabella's relatives there after the war over the Castilian succession, so Abravanel relocated back to Castile with trusted references. For the same reasons, Isabella's own cousins fled to Castile at the same time. By 1491, Abravanel was the queen's personal financial representative.[9]

The queen also relied personally on a number of people of Jewish descent. She surrounded herself with conversos. Her confessor, Hernán de Talavera, was a converso. The man she hired to write the history of her reign, the chronicler Hernando del Pulgar, was a converso. And she immortalized Andrés de Cabrera, the treasurer of Segovia, with a stone carving celebrating his help in securing her kingdom.

And there was likely Jewish blood closer to home as well. Spanish Jews believed that Isabella's husband, Ferdinand, was a converso through his mother. According to Rabbi Eliyahu Capsali, who spoke to a number of Sephardic Jews who fled Spain, they believed that Ferdinand's Castilian great-grandfather, Fadrique Enríquez, had fallen in love with a beautiful young Jewish matron named Paloma, with whom he had an affair and who became pregnant. The son they produced together was so admirable that he was taken into Enríquez's home from his boyhood and raised among the other Enríquez children. This boy became the admiral of Castile, one of the highest-ranking nobles, and the father of Juana Enríquez, who married King Juan of Aragon.[10]

But by the time Isabella became queen, conversos had become unpopular, and simmering animosities were erupting between them and longtime Christians. There had been pressure for decades for some sort of ecclesiastical investigation into whether some conversos were actually Christians or were practicing a subterfuge that allowed them to hold lucrative positions historically restricted to Christians. Isabella's brother Enrique at one point had requested permission from the pope for his own Inquisition but did not pursue the matter. Later, as Isabella was doing all she could to mobilize a united front against Granada, the issue reached the boiling point.

The man who most scholars believe instigated the Inquisition was a priest known as Alonso de Hojeda, the prior of the Dominicans in Seville and a man with a public reputation for holiness. He had come to believe that many people who had converted had done so dishonestly. When Isabella settled in Seville in 1477–78, Alonso de Hojeda pressed her hard with reports of insincere conversions in the local community. She was not from Seville, so she might have been inclined to listen to him as someone who knew the local community better than she did.

Not everyone agreed with the need for the Inquisition. In fact, Isabella's confessor and closest religious adviser, Hernán de Talavera, was "opposed to the founding of the Inquisition."[11] Her converso chronicler, Pulgar, also objected to it, saying it would unfairly penalize people in Andalusia whose only error was that they had not been properly schooled in Christian theology. "I believe my lord," Pulgar wrote in 1481 in an open letter of protest to Cardinal Mendoza,

> that there are some there who sin because they are bad, but the others, who are the majority, sin because they follow the example of those who are bad, whereas they would follow the example of the good Christians if there were any of them there. But since the Old Christians there are such bad Christians, so the New Christians are such good Jews. I am certain, my lord, that there are ten thousand young girls between ten and twenty years of age in Andalusia, who from the time they were born have never left their

homes or heard of or learned any [religious] doctrines save that which they have observed of their parents indoors. To burn all these people would be a very cruel thing.[12]

But soon anonymous reports began questioning Pulgar's own religious sentiments and loyalty to the crown, causing him to retreat from public discussions of the issue. He believed, however, that Isabella's intentions had been understandable when she established the Inquisition—or at least that was what he said at the time.[13]

Without question, Isabella was feverently religious herself and spent many hours in prayer at her private altar seeking to divine God's purpose for her life, obsessively attending mass, even living inside a suite of rooms positioned above the choir at the Cathedral in Toledo when she was visiting Castile's spiritual center. When she wasn't at worship, another favorite pastime was embroidering altarcloths to be used in churches in her kingdom and in Jerusalem. When she sought a break from the rigors of court life, she retreated to the monastery at Guadalupe, which she called her "paradise."

Her religiosity had a dark side. She feared unknown and dangerous things in the spiritual realm. It's no coincidence that she commissioned the large family portrait that showed her sheltering under the arms of the Virgin Mary while menacing demons danced above their heads.

At the time the converso question erupted, the queen was especially vulnerable to the arguments of churchmen. Her daughter Isabel was seven years old, and Queen Isabella had been unable to produce another child. She was under intense social and political pressure to conceive and give birth to a male heir who could inherit the thrones of both Castile and Aragon and permanently unite the two realms. She had become concerned that her infertility might be a sign of God's disfavor, and she was open to suggestions on what she might do to restore herself in the eyes of heaven.

In addition, news accounts of invasions by the Ottoman Turks frequently contained credible and factual reports that the Turks had been assisted by insincere converts to Christianity who gave them material assistance—maps, advice, and inside information—that allowed them to conquer Christian communities. Certainly a number of such incidents occurred during the reconquest of Granada. Moreover, some Jews in Christian Europe were secretly cheering the successes of the Ottoman

Empire, as part of a messianic belief that the fall of Christendom "was preliminary to the deliverance of the Jews" and was spurring the "advent of the messiah."[14] Rabbi Capsali, in Crete, clearly articulated such a belief in his Seder Eliyahu Zuta, which portrayed Mehmed the Conquerer as a hero who was cruel only to the wicked.[15]

An obsessive concern with religious treachery was developing across Europe.

* * *

The controversy over conversos came to a head in the late 1470s, just as Isabella was engaged in an aggressive law-and-order campaign. She was headed toward Seville, arguably the kingdom's most important city and a hub of international commerce, for her first visit. It was in disarray and disunited, and she was trying to prove that central government authority could reduce anarchy. On her way south, in the medieval town of Cáceres, for example, she paused long enough to make a personal effort to reestablish justice and peace, punishing criminals and setting things right. The rule of law was reestablished and everyone in the town was left "very content," Pulgar wrote. She did this while she simultaneously engaged in an inspection tour of the kingdom's frontier defenses, making a side trip to Badajoz on the Portuguese border.

When Isabella got to Seville, she found it in a state of chaos, with "scandals and dissensions and wars," in Pulgar's words, that had left many dead or injured.[16] She immediately initiated a replay of the pattern that had won her the support and adoration of her people elsewhere—she set out to restore justice.

Each Friday she held a public audience in the Alcázar for people to bring their grievances and complaints about events that had occurred. She sat in a great room in a high chair covered with cloth of gold, her courtiers and legal advisers surrounding her and helping her ascertain the facts in each case. Then she would issue a judgment. Criminals were sentenced, many receiving the death penalty; victims received prompt recompense. Within two months she had accomplished much; street crimes and robberies had largely disappeared. Seeing her seriousness of purpose, many criminals and those accused of wrongdoing fled Seville. "And because of the justice she had brought forth," Pulgar wrote, "she was very loved by the good people, and feared by the bad."[17]

But her methods, while effective and perhaps necessary, were also harsh and arbitrary. Eventually the residents of Seville began to feel terrorized. Don Alonso de Solís, bishop of Cádiz, pleaded with her to show more mercy to miscreants, urging that God valued those with "humility of heart" who showed mercy.[18]

The queen relented. "Seeing the multitudes of those men and women tribulated by the fear of justice, moved to compassion by their tears and moans," she decided she would issue a general pardon for ordinary crimes.[19] The word spread, and soon more than four thousand people came home to the Seville area. Isabella's fierce justice had been roundly applauded.

It wasn't a great step to expand this kind of inquiry to the religious realm. Soon Hojeda had more supporters for his quest to start an Inquisition. One enthusiast was Friar Filippo de' Barberi, the Sicilian inquisitor, who had recently arrived in Castile. He was seeking to confirm an ancient decree, from 1223, that permitted an Inquisition in Sicily to drive out heresy; it also permitted one-third of the possessions of any heretics to become property of the Inquisition. The papal legate Niccolò Franco, bishop of Treviso, shared these views, and soon all three were importuning Isabella for action.[20]

Then they found another ready ear in King Ferdinand. An Inquisition, once established, promised to be a useful mechanism for rooting out all kinds of dissent and also for collecting money from people accused of heresy—money that could be diverted for other purposes. The king soon joined the chorus. He already had picked out just the right man for the job of running the Inquisition—his longtime confessor, the rigid and ascetic Tomás de Torquemada, Cardinal Juan de Torquemada's nephew.

"To Ferdinand it is probable that the suggestion was not without allurement," writes the historian Rafael Sabatini,

> since it must have offered him a way at once to gratify the piety that was his, and—out of the confiscations that must ensue from the prosecution of so very wealthy a section of the community—to replenish the almost exhausted coffers of the treasury. When the way of conscience is also the way of profit, there is little difficulty in following it. But after all, though joint sovereign of Spain and paramount in Aragon, Ferdinand had not in Castile the power of Isabella. It was her kingdom when all was said, and although his position there was by no means that of a simple prince-consort,

yet he was bound by law and by policy to remain submissive to her will. In view of her attitude, he could do little more than add his own to the persuasions of the three priestly advocates, and amongst them they so pressed Isabella that she gave way to the extent of a compromise.[21]

Isabella reluctantly agreed that a preliminary investigation should be done to determine the extent of Judaizing among the new Christians, and in 1477 she asked Cardinal Pedro Mendoza to begin alerting the populace to the issues. Cardinal Mendoza ordered the preparation of an instruction manual explaining the rules and rituals of Christianity for those who were unfamiliar with them or had forgotten them. It has been described as a sort of catechism, with explanations of baptism, confession, and the basic beliefs of the faith. Mendoza ordered this instruction to be preached in every church in Spain, in pulpits and in schools. Others advocated more strenuous means of purifying the church of nonbelievers, but initially Isabella and Cardinal Mendoza were not inclined to use aggressive methods.

But something happened that started a downward spiral of events. During Holy Week of 1478, a young Castilian, of the famous Guzmán family, was courting a young converso woman. He claimed that while he was at her house, he overheard her father blaspheming the name of Jesus and disparaging Christianity. He went to a Dominican priest to inform him of what he had heard. Hojeda heard of the incident and quickly called an inquiry into the home of the accused man. He and five friends confessed and they were forgiven. But the fanatical prelate said this was not adequate recompense for the sins the men had committed, and he redoubled his efforts to call the queen's attention to what he considered dangerous religious lapses. According to the church historian Sabatini, the queen again resisted, at least for a while.[22]

But the advocates of an Inquisition had by now gained a powerful ally. Tomás de Torquemada had been the prior of the Dominican convent in Segovia and a respected cleric for decades. He had known Isabella since childhood and had traveled from place to place with Ferdinand as his spiritual counselor and confessor. Moreover, as the nephew of a former cardinal, his word carried great weight, and now he brought it to bear against the conversos.

Queen Isabella reluctantly agreed to seek a papal bull, or official legal document, authorizing an Inquisition in Spain. Pope Sixtus IV granted permission to establish an Inquisition on November 7, 1478. It gave the sovereigns the right to select three bishops, archbishops, or priests to serve as inquisitors throughout their kingdoms. But Isabella remained hesitant to initiate the kind of fierce inquiry that some were demanding of her. Instead she redoubled her educational efforts to ensure that people were instructed about possible religious lapses rather than punished for them. Meanwhile she and Ferdinand traveled to Toledo, where the Cortes of Castile assembled to swear an oath of fealty to their infant son and heir, Juan; there Isabella gave birth to another child, Juana. Two years passed, and nothing more was done to follow through on an Inquisition.

* * *

But the discussions about a prospective inquisitorial panel naturally incited fear among conversos. One New Christian wrote a pamphlet criticizing the sovereigns for even considering it.[23] Attacking the throne is always a perilous affair, and some took this critical pamphlet as confirmation that a serious and dangerous affront to royal power was brewing. It began circulating at a bad time, right after the Ottoman conquest of Otranto.

In September 1480 the sovereigns decided to put the papal bull into effect and named two senior inquisitors to head it, Mendoza and Torquemada. The two men appointed others to initiate the work, establishing a base in Seville, where people had complained the problem was worst. Soon a group of white-robed, black-hooded inquisitors were marching in procession from northern Castile to Seville. People were told to either confess their offenses and receive absolution, or face the consequences.

Some converso families panicked and abruptly fled Seville. Their hasty departures made them appear suspicious to the inquisitors, and soon the crown sent out notices seeking to identify all the people who had moved and where they had gone across the land. The Inquisition's tentacles reached out geographically. The inquisitors announced that they would arrest anyone who had fled Seville in that way. Nobles around the kingdom assisted in rounding up the suspects. Conversos began to be tried, and some were found guilty.

The first public execution, an auto-da-fé, took place in Seville on February 6, 1481, only months after the Inquisition was begun. Six people were burned at the stake. The priest Alonso de Hojeda triumphantly preached the sermon that day, but within weeks he was dead of a plague himself. In other times, the disappearance of the most vocal advocate of the Inquisition might have put an end to the enterprise. But Hojeda had unleashed something very big and very ugly. The fact that scores had fled meant that they had to be tracked down and investigated. Hundreds of people came forward in Seville to confess past offenses, filling the prisons to overflowing while they awaited fuller investigations of their deeds or misconduct. More clerics were needed to handle the workload. Seven more were hired, according to a papal brief of February 1482. This happened as religious fervor was mounting and in the same month when Isabella issued a call to all knights in Spain to lend support for the war on Granada.[24]

Reports of more widespread problems with conversos led to the creation of similar inquisitorial tribunals in Córdoba and Jaén, the two other military bases of the Reconquest. In 1485 a panel was established in Toledo. Soon active Inquisitions were operating across the kingdom in Ávila, Medina del Campo, Segovia, Sigüenza, and Valladolid. Ferdinand opened similar operations in Barcelona, Zaragoza, and Valencia.

The Inquisition in Ferdinand's domains almost immediately acquired an even more unsavory reputation than that in Castile. In a papal bull of 1482, Pope Sixtus IV protested strenuously about what was reportedly happening there. He charged that the Inquisition in Ferdinand's realm was

> moved not by zeal for the faith and the salvation of souls, but by
> lust for wealth, and that many true and faithful Christians, on the
> testimony of enemies, rivals, slaves and other lower and even less
> proper persons, have without any legitimate proof been thrust
> into secular prisons, tortured and condemned as relapsed heretics,
> deprived of their goods and property and handed over to the secu-
> lar arm to be executed, to the peril of souls, setting a pernicious
> example and causing disgust to many.[25]

Ferdinand responded quickly, expressing his "astonishment" that the pontiff had been taken in by the "persistent and cunning persuasion of the said conversos" and warned him to "take care therefore not to let the matter go further."[26]

Within weeks, the pope backed down. But opposition continued among the citizens in Ferdinand's kingdom, many of whom thought the process was unfair and contrary to traditional laws. There was an uprising against the Inquisition in Teruel, near Zaragoza, but troops put it down. Then on the night of September 15, 1485, the inquisitor Pedro Arbués was stabbed to death while praying at the altar at the cathedral in Zaragoza, by assassins who were either conversos or paid by conversos. The assassination ended up making things worse for the conversos because Arbués, killed while kneeling in prayer, quickly came to be viewed as a saint. The conspirators were executed, and the public mood in Aragon shifted to support the Inquisition.

At the opening of each new tribunal, an "edict of grace" would be issued that called upon the faithful to come forward to confess their sins and be forgiven. They were told that if they came forward with sincere repentance, they would be forgiven, but if they did not, their sins would be exposed later, with judgment all the harsher for the lapse. The Vatican historian Sabatini believed that Queen Isabella and Cardinal Mendoza intended to use this process to get people back into the good graces of the church without bloodshed.

But the implementation of the edict resulted in more people being accused. Many came forward to seek amnesty and confess their heretical misdeeds. But to prove their sincerity, the people who confessed were required to denounce others who were still engaged in Judaizing. If they denounced anyone, they subjected that person to terror and possible death; if they did not, their confession would be deemed incomplete and insincere. "The wretched apostates," wrote Sabatini, "found themselves between the sword and the wall. Either they must perpetrate the infamy of betraying those of their race whom they knew to be Judaizers, or they must submit not only to the cruel death by fire, but to the destitution of their children as a consequence of the confiscation of their property."[27]

Many possible misdeeds were identified as marking the insincere Christian: saying that the Messiah had not yet come; saying that the law of Moses was as good as that of Jesus Christ; keeping the Jewish Sabbath by wearing clean shirts or refraining from work on Friday evening; following Hebraic dietary codes; eating meat during Lent; keeping the Fast of Esther or other fasts required by Judaism; reciting the Psalms of David without adding the words "Gloria patri et Filio et Spiritui Sancto"; refraining from going to church for forty days after childbirth; circumcising one's children or giving them Hebrew names; marrying in the Jewish manner; holding a valedictory supper before setting out on a long journey; carrying Jewish religious items; turning one's face to the wall to die; washing a corpse with warm water; mourning in the Jewish manner; burying the dead in a Jewish cemetery.[28]

Of course, many of these practices could have been carried out by conversos as a matter of family custom without intentional religious significance. Some were common in traditional Christian households as well, which meant that even people who engaged in no heresy at all, even the most adamant of Catholic believers, could be found guilty. The Spanish historian Juan Antonio Llorente, reviewing the record, believed the rules had been established "with deliberate malice," to cast as wide a net and catch as many people as possible.[29] Some inquisitors did their work with maniacal zeal.

Patently ridiculous allegations were made in some cases to justify executions. A long-standing medieval folk legend had it that Jews would kidnap a Christian infant and kill it, in a twisted reprise of the death of Jesus Christ. Now a story surfaced about a child, known as the Holy Child of La Guardia, who was allegedly murdered in just such a sacrificial ceremony in Spain. As a result of an investigation into this purported sacrificial murder, six conversos and five Jews were sentenced to death in Ávila in 1491. Some had confessed after being tortured; but no child was reported missing, and no child's body was ever found.[30]

The financial aspect of the Inquisition gave further impetus to its escalation because it was generating money for the government. As the historian José Martínez Millán has shown, the Inquisition was designed to be financially self-supporting: inquisitors and incarceration costs were paid from the estates of people accused of heresy.[31] This was long-standing tradition. In 1477 Pope Sixtus IV had given Isabella permission to collect any goods or money confiscated by the Inquisition, with the money going to the royal treasury. This rule was incorporated into the Instructions of Seville in 1484.

The specified procedures followed three steps: sequestration, confiscation, and sale. Sequestration occurred when someone was first arrested for heresy. The prisoner was called for a hearing and told to declare all his or her possessions. An inventory was prepared and completed and read aloud to the prisoner for signature. Records were prepared in triplicate, and court officials noted whether the prisoner had attempted to hide anything. The prisoner was kept in jail to await hearing; his or her goods were confiscated and held by the state. Any outstanding debts were paid to creditors; the Inquisition office then maintained the goods and property in the name of the prisoner. If the prisoner was not convicted, his or her goods and property were returned. But if the person was convicted, the property was given to the Inquisition treasury. The goods were appraised, and then the crown put them up for auction. Relatives of the convicted person were not allowed to purchase them.

Obviously this created a financial incentive to find people guilty. Sometimes rich and powerful people were able to pay off the Inquisition to spare some portion of their goods from confiscation, but many victims of the Inquisition were poor and had little to seize. Consequently, many impoverished families lost even their meager belongings.

But because many of those prosecuted were poor, revenues were often insufficient to cover the costs of feeding and housing all these prisoners, and so the crown sometimes had to subsidize its work. Ferdinand tried to find ways to cover the financial shortfalls, but Inquisition officials often went without being paid in a timely manner. Church officials were often selected for these jobs because their ecclesiastical salaries could be expected to cover their cost of living.

As a result of the Inquisition, many formerly Jewish families faced impossible choices. Some had become devout Christians. But as Pulgar had warned, religious instruction typically begins during a person's early youth, and so a great many people who had changed faiths were poorly instructed in the basic sacraments and rituals of Christian life. Others had converted in name only and maintained their internal allegiance to Judaism. Some mixture of these attitudes existed in almost every converso home, each with its own set of tensions.

For example, if a converso family's Jewish cousins came to visit, how would their food be prepared? Regardless of how the host family ate, they would naturally cook according to Jewish custom for their guests; but in so doing, the converso woman would put herself at risk of heresy, charged with maintaining Jewish customs. If a disgruntled servant were to report the incident, the housewife could be prosecuted.

Similarly, if the converso family accepted hospitality from the Jewish cousins, and was served a meal prepared according to Jewish guidelines, the converso family was open to prosecution. If a baby was born and the family—even one that was regularly attending mass—turned to traditional customs to celebrate the birth, they could be prosecuted.

There were so many ways to go wrong. Giving charity to Jewish beggars was a sin. Visiting a synagogue on a Jewish holy day was a sin. Not eating pork was suspicious.

Jealousy and spite quickly came into play, along with the belief that Jews had obtained riches improperly. Riots in Córdoba in 1473, for example, erupted because of anger that "the great wealth of the Cordovan conversos . . . enabled them to buy public offices," wrote the chronicler Diego de Valera. The new officials used their positions in an "arrogant" way, which aggravated Old Christians.[32] Sometimes Jews gave testimony against their former coreligionists who they believed had converted only to obtain financial advantage.

Another problem for conversos was that many were employed in professions that by their nature made them unpopular. Moneylending, a risky endeavor that often involved charging high interest rates that left debtors in financial distress, was viewed as a sinful occupation for Christians but one that was permissible for Jews. Tax collectors are seldom loved by their fellow citizens, but many conversos had concentrated in that field of work, placing themselves in the position of seeking to maximize tax collections at a time of growing financial strain among the lower classes. In 1480, Seville, for example, had twenty-one tax farmers and two treasurers, and all of them were conversos.[33]

Jews and conversos similarly dominated the top jobs in the royal treasury and tax-collecting enterprises of the Castilian monarchy. The converso Diego Arias Dávila, for example, was the kingdom's foremost treasurer under King Enrique; the converso Andrés de Cabrera performed this function in Segovia, first for Enrique and then for Isabella.

Inquisition records in the city of Toledo suggest that the people who were actually prosecuted there, certainly in the early days, were middle-class people, not the elite. Among the people marked for death were shoemakers, butchers, weavers, and merchants and their wives. But wealthier people were ensnared in the net as well.

Much about the Inquisition, unfortunately, remains unknown. Were the people who were burned at the stake for heresy actual heretics to Catholicism, or had they truly converted to Christianity and merely retained some Jewish customs? Scholars who have reviewed the plentiful trial testimony and surviving chronicles disagree. The Israeli scholar Benzion Netanyahu came to believe most were actually Christians, because of the disdain and hatred heaped upon them by practicing Jews who saw them as opportunistic turncoats. Contemporary Jewish writers, he notes, initially expressed "open manifestations of glee" as they watched the travails of the New Christians. The Hebrew scholar Jabez called the conversos "enemies of God," and Ibn Shuaib said "the wickedness" of the conversos "is greater in our eyes than that of the gentiles."[34]

But other historians believe the convicted people were "crypto-Jews," secretly Jewish and maintaining that faith underground in the face of intense pressure. Renée Levine Melammed, who has reviewed many of the court transcripts, believes that many women of Jewish descent were trying valiantly to maintain a core Jewishness within their families, even as they outwardly conformed to Christian requirements:

> All of these women, the mothers, aunts, sisters and wives, who had
> Judaized and had taught or been taught, were identifying with
> their Jewish heritage. All of them were taught to consider them-
> selves as daughters of Israel, knowing fully well that they were
> taking the risk of their lives. All were willing to silently subvert
> the teaching of the Catholic Church and to ignore the threat of a
> fate in the inquisitorial prisons or on the scaffold. All had a clear
> consciousness of what they were doing.[35]

If Melammed is correct that large numbers of Jews were merely pre-tending to be Christians, then it is not surprising that many Christians at the time were suspicious of them. A number of priests and nuns were conversos, and some had risen to top positions within the church. Did that mean they were preaching what they did not believe? The trials found some reason to think they were. In Toledo, in the first ten years of the Inquisition, two priests and a nun were accused of Judaic heresy; the men were absolved and the woman was condemned to death.[36]

A prominent case was that of Juan Arias Dávila, the bishop of Segovia and head of one of the most important churches in Spain. His family had converted from Judaism to Christianity as a result of the persuasive preaching of Saint Vincent Ferrer in that city in 1411.[37]

Juan's father, Diego Arias Dávila, and his mother, Elvira, had con-sequently prospered: Diego became treasurer under King Enrique. But rumors circulated that the family had only pretended to convert, in order to gain financial advantage, and that they privately practiced Judaism and ridiculed Christianity. The whispering about the family grew louder when Diego and Elvira's son Juan joined the priesthood and then became bishop of Segovia at twenty-four.

Years after the deaths of Juan's parents, the inquisitors came, and the questions became more pointed. The bishop of Segovia protested about the Inquisition, then took his complaints directly to the pope at the Vatican; he first took the precaution of digging up the bones of his relatives, including his parents, and transporting them with him to Rome. Some people thought he was appropriately protesting the Inquisition's heavy-handed techniques, and others thought his actions were proof of his own family's deceitfulness. The bishop of Segovia never came home to Spain and ended up dying in Rome in 1497.

Back in Castile, a prolonged investigation was under way into his family's activities. According to the historian David Martin Gitlitz, "scores of witnesses testified about the family from 1486 to 1490," reporting that during the years when the Diego Arias Dávila family had been pretending to be Christian, they had in fact kept the Jewish Sabbath, observed major festivals, set a kosher table, supported the synagogue, and avoided going to church. Moreover, Juan's father had "frequently disparaged the trappings of Christianity, particularly the saints."[38] This testimony, naturally enough, raised questions about the religious sincerity of his son, the bishop of Segovia.

One particular scandal at the heart of Catholicism in Spain likely contributed to the growing sense that the church itself was being undermined by nonbelievers. The single most important pilgrimage location in Spain, after Santiago de Compostela, was the shrine of Guadalupe, the site that was also the most sacred to Queen Isabella, who visited it almost annually.

The spiritual focus was a dark-complected statue of the Virgin Mary, which legend said had been carved by Saint Luke, and that was buried to keep it out of the hands of the Muslims after the invasion of 711. Once Christians succeeded in winning back the territory, the statue was rediscovered as a result of a vision by a local peasant, who told priests where to go to dig it up. A popular shrine sprang up at the site.

The statue was an object of veneration to the faithful, who associated it with a number of miracles, including helping Christian slaves escape Muslim captors. Spanish Catholics from all over the peninsula made the difficult journey to Guadalupe to pray or seek penance, confess their sins, and receive absolution from a small clerical community of about 130 friars who lived there.

Guadalupe was the holiest shrine in the holiest diocese of Spain, under the ecclesiastical control of Toledo. That was the spiritual seat of the most powerful prelate in Spain, the archbishop of Toledo, Cardinal Pedro Mendoza, Isabella's close friend and adviser.

All these valuable associations brought wealth to the shrine, and allowed the friars living there to reside in comfortable affluence and devote themselves to scholarly works and artistic endeavors such as illuminating manuscripts. They ate well, and there was hot and cold running water at the priory.

The town also feasted on spiritual tourism, with restaurants, hotels, and merchants prospering by selling goods and services to the hordes of pilgrims who arrived each year. About 10 percent of the local population was converso, according to scholar Gretchen Starr-LeBeau.[39]

Once the Inquisition got rolling, reports began circulating that converso priests at Guadalupe were favoring converso businessmen in town, dispensing advice about how to retain Jewish customs, encouraging them to maintain the kosher dietary laws, and finding ways to trick Christians into thinking they shared their beliefs. King Ferdinand visited Guadalupe in September 1483, according to Starr-LeBeau, and soon both community residents and the shrine's friars were under investigation.

Some converso families fled from Guadalupe. One large, extended family moved to Muslim-controlled Málaga, which was at war with Castile, and began living openly as Jews.

In 1485, seventy-one of the townsfolk of Guadalupe were found guilty of Judaizing and burned at the stake in autos-de-fé, and another forty-five were found guilty posthumously or in absentia, writes Starr-LeBeau. Other conversos were exiled from the town.[40]

A super-secret council of the Inquisition then met to probe claims that the priests at Guadalupe were also heretics, Starr-LeBeau reports, and soon credible evidence emerged that the allegations were true. One converso, Friar Diego de Marchena, for example, a confessor, was reported by several witnesses to have given specific guidance on how to avoid Christian rituals, such as eliminating meat from the diet during Lent. He told his fellow friars that they could avoid detection by eating boiled rather than roasted chicken on Good Friday, so that no one would know. He also publicly questioned whether the Virgin Mary was in fact a virgin, something that was an article of faith to Spain's pious Catholics, and told people he had never been baptized.

Witnesses said another converso cleric, Prior Gonzalo de Madrid, pretended to be vomiting on his deathbed so he did not have to take a communion wafer when he received extreme unction at his death. Friar

Luis de Madrid, a converso, had talked openly in the priory saying that he knew of two converso friars who were refusing to consecrate the host during holy communion, but he refused to say who they were. Three friars were found to be circumcised. Several more were reported to have feigned illness to avoid attending mass or singing in the choir.

Ultimately, 21 friars of 130 employed at the holiest site in the center of Spain were censured for their purported Jewish activities. One was jailed for life, and Diego de Marchena was burned at the stake, according to Starr-LeBeau.[41]

The Catholic Church in Spain attempted to keep the scandal under wraps by concealing the documentation they had gathered about the activities of the converso friars inside the monastery. But some of the documents were never destroyed and were analyzed at length by Starr-LeBeau for her 2003 book, *In the Shadow of the Virgin*.

What had happened was widely known in Spain, however, and fueled speculation about which other religious orders might be similar magnets for nonbelievers.

Queen Isabella, meanwhile, was most assuredly aware of the situation in Guadalupe, for she ordered that 1 million maravedis seized from conversos in that town should be used to build a hospital for pilgrims. She then contributed the same amount herself to pay the remainder of the costs of construction.

Even those Spanish conversos who were devout Christians sometimes aggravated the tensions within the community by holding themselves apart or viewing themselves as superior. The concept of lineage loomed large in their minds, as it did in the minds of the longtime Christians. In Barcelona and Valencia, they worshiped as a group within former synagogues that had been converted to churches. Some claimed direct lineage from Jesus's family. Alonso de Cartagena, the bishop of Burgos and son of Rabbi Selomah ha Levi, who became Paul of Burgos after he converted, was said to have recited the Hail Mary in this manner: "Holy Mary, Mother of God and my blood-relative, pray for us." In Aragon, they called themselves "Christians of Israel."[42]

"These converso attitudes were probably created by self-defensiveness rather than arrogance," writes Henry Kamen, a noted historian of the Inquisition. "But they contributed to the wall of distrust between Old and New Christians. In particular, the idea of a converso *nation,* which rooted itself irrevocably in the mind of Jewish Christians, made them appear as a separate, alien and enemy entity. This had fateful consequences."[43]

In the end the conversos found themselves without sincere friends in either the Jewish or the Christian community, at a time when Castile and Aragon were plunging into war. By now, suspicion had been aroused almost everywhere. In the 1440s, writes Netanyahu, only "a minority" of conversos had been viewed as possibly heretical, but in the next few decades public opinion among Old Christians shifted to the point where they viewed their suspicions as "certainties about the overwhelming majority."[44]

* * *

Whatever the underlying reality, the conduct of the Spanish Inquisition was extraordinarily un-Christian, fierce, and hateful. It was at odds with another strong principle in Spanish thought, once articulated by Isabella's older brother Enrique, that forgiveness was an essential hallmark of Christianity. Once pressed to punish a nobleman who had repeatedly betrayed him, Enrique had the man brought into his presence and released him, saying that forgiveness was a key tenet of his faith. "I pardon you," Enrique said, "so that God may pardon my soul when my time comes to part with this life."[45]

In that case, King Enrique showed forgiveness to someone who had actually done wrong. But now Isabella unleashed cruelty on people who had done little or no harm. She must have been conflicted about it herself, for she permitted people close to her to raise far-reaching questions about the justice and morality of the Inquisition, though she expressed no doubts herself. She permitted her chronicler Pulgar to write, in a court-financed publication, that the "ecclesiastical Inquisitors and the secular executors behaved cruelly and showed great enmity, not only toward those they punished and tormented, but also toward all [New Christians]."[46]

It is unlikely that the unprincipled Ferdinand would have found in any of this much of a moral dilemma. In fact, the historian Benzion Netanyahu believed that Ferdinand was "the real architect of the Inquisition."[47] Ferdinand, he wrote,

> sought to appear ethical and religious; for he accurately assessed the crucial part played by ethics and religion in human affairs. Instead of openly defying morality, he sought to employ it for his own ends. He knew how to evaluate mass feelings as a factor in

social life, and used the force of popular passions ... as steam to move his ship of state. Thus he harnessed the hatred of the conversos and the laws of the Church concerning heresy to advance his political interests, all the while trying to appear as Holy Mother Church's true son, whose eagerness to guard religious law even exceeded his desire to guard the civil one.... Accordingly he refrained from formally inquiring into the Inquisition's judicial proceedings, so as to avoid responsibility for its verdicts and prevent anyone from disputing his claim that he had full confidence in the Inquisitors' judgments. But he often intervened in the gathering and division of the Inquisition's spoils.[48]

What then about Queen Isabella, who in many other aspects of her life was described as humane and a student of the life and teachings of Christ? How could she justify this cruelty, these murders?

The short answer is that Isabella was a complex personality, in which diverging elements were all present. While she was beneficent in many ways, she also seems to have had an unforgiving streak that made her harsh, punitive, and unbending in punishing people she saw as evildoers and in seeking to accomplish her goals. Perhaps she rationalized that the Inquisition was a means to a worthy and justifying end, that she needed wholehearted support from the Old Christians of Andalusia, particularly those of Seville and Córdoba, to win the war with Granada, and that these people were deeply antagonistic to the conversos. Perhaps she believed that her whole way of life was at risk and that only the most ruthless tactics would permit survival for Christian Spain against the Turks. Or she might have been motivated by a sincere, if misguided, concern for the spiritual well-being of her subjects. For the zealous of each faith, only their own specific practice holds the keys to the universe. In any case, Isabella was entirely able to rationalize establishing and supporting the Inquisition. Successful rulers are usually willing to sacrifice others in pursuit of something they see as a greater good. For Isabella, wrote Netanyahu, "safe control of Andalusia obviously depended on finding a way to reduce the unrest."[49]

After the war against Granada was over, however, her attitude did not change. If anything, the targets of her rigor expanded. In March 1492, after secret deliberations, she and Ferdinand ordered the Jews—who had previously been spared the brunt of the Inquisition—to convert to Christianity immediately or be expelled. They had decided that the presence of Jews in Spain was tempting conversos to abandon their Christian faith, thereby risking their salvation. When Jews came to her to plead their case, she told them that the decision had come to Ferdinand in a dream and was God's will. "Do you believe that this comes upon you from us?" she told the Jewish representatives begging her to change her mind. "The Lord hath put this thing into the heart of the King." Pressed further, she refused to make a protest to her husband. "The king's heart is in the hands of the Lord, as the rivers of water," she told them. "He turns it whithersoever He will."[50] And from this point, Isabella's Jewish subjects knew that the matter was set in stone.

This new, hardened position had been foreshadowed by a provision in the surrender treaty between Castile and the Muslims. It said that Jews in the conquered lands who did not convert to Christianity within three years would have to move to North Africa. But amid the excitement of ending the long war, this provision had gone unnoticed.

So the majority of Jews were shocked, even dumbfounded, when the order was announced. Queen Isabella and King Ferdinand had not signaled in any way that they were angry at Jews. They had shown them respect and friendship. Ferdinand was believed to be of Jewish descent himself. Isaac Abravanel, a trusted counselor and financial adviser to Isabella and her family for much of his adult life, later said he could hardly believe his ears. "I was at court when the royal decree was announced," he recalled. "I wearied myself to distraction in imploring compassion. Thrice on my knees I besought the king: 'Regard us, O king, use not thy subjects so cruelly. Why do thus to thy servants? Rather exact from us our gold and silver, even all the house of Israel possess, if he may remain in his country.'"

The offer of a large bribe, not surprisingly, intrigued Ferdinand and he visibly hesitated, pondering it. But his confessor, Tomás de Torquemada, physically recoiled and, gesticulating angrily, he accused Ferdinand of being tempted into betrayal of his faith for thirty pieces of silver, the reward Judas was believed to have received for delivering his friend Jesus into the hands of the Romans for execution. Ferdinand decided not to relent. Abravanel then begged his friends to intervene to block the edict,

> but as the adder closes its ears with dust against the voice of the
> charmer, so the king hardened his heart against the entreaties
> of his suppliants, and declared he would not revoke the edict for

all the wealth of the Jews. The queen at his right hand opposed
it, and urged him to continue what he had begun. We exhausted
all our power for the repeal of the king's sentence; but there was
neither wisdom nor help remaining. Wherever the evil decree was
proclaimed, or the report of it had spread, our nation bewailed
their condition with great lamentations; for there had never been
such a banishment since Judah had been driven from his land.[51]

Some, like Isabella's childhood ally Rabbi Abraham Senior, reluctantly
decided to convert. He was baptized at the monastery of Guadalupe with
the queen beaming at his elbow. "Thousands and tens of thousands" also
regretfully accepted baptism.[52]

Others departed, knowing that the risks of the road were so great that
some of their family members would not survive. Don Isaac Abravanel
exhorted and encouraged people to keep firm to Jewish law, even at the
risk of life and property. His faith was paramount to him. He and his
family fled to Naples and later to Venice. Others went to Portugal, the
Ottoman Empire, North Africa, or elsewhere in Europe.

Chroniclers said the Jewish exodus from Spain was a pitiable sight.
"Within the term fixed by the edict the Jews sold and disposed of their
property for a mere nothing; they went about begging Christians to buy,
but found no purchasers; fine houses and estates were sold for trifles; a
house was exchanged for an ass; and a vineyard given for a little cloth or
linen," the Castilian chronicler Andrés Bernáldez wrote.

Although prohibited carrying away gold and silver, they secretly
took large quantities in their saddles, and in the halters and harness of their loaded beasts. Some swallowed as many as thirty
ducats to avoid the rigorous search made at the frontier towns
and seaports, by the officers appointed for the purpose. The rich
Jews defrayed the expenses of the departure of the poor, practicing toward each other the greatest charity, so that except very few
of the most necessitous, they would not become converts. In the
first week of July they took the route for quitting their native land,
great and small, old and young; on foot, on horses, asses, and
in carts; each continuing his journey to his destined port. They
experienced great trouble and suffered indescribable misfortunes
on the roads and country they traveled; some falling, others rising;
some dying, others coming into the world; some fainting, oth-

ers being attacked with illness; that there was not a Christian but what felt for them and persuaded them to be baptized. Some from misery were converted; but they were very few. The rabbis encouraged them, and made the young people and women sing, and play on pipes and tabors to enliven them, and keep up their spirits.[53]

The Jews of Segovia spent their last three days in the cemetery "watering with their tears the ashes of their fathers; their lamentations excited the pity of all who heard them."[54] Many left carrying little more than precious Hebrew manuscripts they removed from the synagogues before departing.

The first to leave were a large group of Jewish families who had been living in Granada, and others followed soon after. They made their way to ports, where Ferdinand had arranged for ships to transport them. Some drowned at sea or narrowly survived shipwrecks. Some died of exposure to cold. Many fell ill. They were attacked by robbers, who stole their possessions, even their clothing, and sold them into slavery. Some were dumped on distant shores. One group traveled to Fez, which was suffering a drought, and they were turned away. They were forced to pitch camp in an arid plain and soon began starving to death themselves. Reports that they had swallowed gold to smuggle it out of Spain circulated widely; Muslims in Africa "murdered a number, and then ripped them open to search for it."[55]

The exiled Jews found a mixed reception in Christian lands. Many went to Portugal, where they were given admission for a limited time, as long as they paid a hefty entry tax. In Genoa, they were greeted by priests carrying bread in one hand and crucifixes in the other; conversion was the price to be paid for the relief of their hunger.[56] The notorious Pope Alexander VI, reviled by so many other people, was kinder and granted them asylum and protection in the Papal States.

The Spanish Inquisition was vicious and tragic. But from Isabella's perspective, it unified Spain and allowed it to quell internal religious dissension and look outward. It was one of the largest and, from Isabella's point of view, one of the most successful forced conversions in Spanish history. Eliminating outsiders has had its advantages; religious tolerance is not a universal concept. Spain was now on the verge, ready and sufficiently ruthless, of becoming the greatest world power ever known.

FIFTEEN

LANDING IN PARADISE

I t was almost inevitable that Queen Isabella, once she had secured the boundaries of her kingdom and dealt with tensions within it, would begin to turn her attention outward—even beyond the confines of Europe. A new age of global exploration was dawning. Spain and Portugal had been rivals within the narrow confines of the Iberian peninsula, but they were now also becoming rivals on a world stage as well, engaging in a fierce competition to secure overseas lands and trade routes. Discovery of new territories was becoming the great new entrepreneurial enterprise, and only a few countries, most notably Portugal and Castile, had recognized the magnitude of what was coming. Those that seized these opportunities would reap the profits and gain the glory. Those that didn't would be left behind.

The Portuguese had pioneered this activity under Henrique, or Henry the Navigator, the prince most responsible for Portugal's outward expansion southward and around the perimeter of Africa. What has been called the Illustrious Generation of Portugal's royal family had introduced a whole new way of looking at the world—seeing the potential for acquiring distant lands by finding them, charting them, settling them, and taking possession of them. Portugal, consequently, was swelling with arrogance and newfound wealth.

The drive toward mercantile adventuring was a family interest for Queen Isabella. Her beloved grandmother, the Portuguese noblewoman

Isabel of Barcelos, had been cousin and sister-in-law to Prince Henry the Navigator; Prince Henry was therefore Isabella's great-uncle. In Isabella's youth, between 1462 and 1487, while Castile had been engaged in debilitating civil wars, Portugal had commissioned eight separate maritime expeditions into the Atlantic Ocean, claiming more and more territory and outstripping Castile year by year.[1]

Isabella had come to the throne very conscious of these new developments at sea, for they had been at play in the peace negotiations with the Portuguese following the war of 1475 to 1479. The Treaty of Alcáçovas in 1479 had given her control of the Canary Islands but had forced her to concede to the Portuguese exclusive rights to any newly discovered lands on Africa's West Coast, as well as the Cape Verde Islands. King João of Portugal had immediately set about increasing and consolidating power in those areas, strengthening the Portuguese trade routes and mercantile empire. He was intensely competitive with Castile and kept his explorers' discoveries state secrets, but they were pushing further and further toward the Orient: first they went south by sea, discovering the Congo River in 1484 and rounding the Cape of Good Hope in 1488; then they made forays into the interiors of India and Ethiopia by land.

Isabella, meanwhile, had asserted and consolidated Castilian control in the Canary Islands, making the island of Grand Canary a colony in 1480. These subtropical islands, located off the west coast of Africa, were inhabited by a native tribe known as the Guanches. Western Europeans had made their way there in ancient times, but regular visits by Spanish and Portuguese explorers started only in the early 1400s. Castile and Portugal had fought for possession of them, but after the Treaty of Alcáçovas, Castile was able to begin a more systematic settlement process. The Gaunches resisted Castilian domination but were subdued, partially due to the brutal and remorseless efforts of Beatriz de Bobadilla's sultry exiled niece and her new husband, and the islands were incorporated into the Kingdom of Castile. The islands became prosperous colonies and provided a base for further exploration.

So when a charismatic and opportunistic seafarer from Portugal with an intriguing exploration proposal showed up at Isabella's court in the mid-1480s, claiming he had links to her Portuguese grandparents, the queen was disposed to listen. This mariner, an Italian who had been living in Lisbon, was named Christopher Columbus. He had been married to Felipa Moniz, whose father had served in the household of

Isabella's grandfather, the Infante Don Juan of Portugal.[2] The family of Felipa Moniz had also been associated with Prince Henry the Navigator and had participated in some of the early Portuguese explorations. When Columbus married into this family, his mother-in-law gave him some navigational instruments and maps that her husband had owned, which Columbus reportedly received with joy.[3] Columbus's wife Felipa had since died, and now the widowed explorer had formulated a plan for an audacious sea exploration that he avidly wished to pursue. Columbus, a single father with his young son Diego in tow, moved to Castile and began to propose his idea to the queen.

Christopher Columbus, or, as he was known in Spain, Cristóbal Colón, believed it was possible to sail westward around the globe to arrive at the Indies, bypassing the Turkish monopoly on silks and spices from the East. It was common knowledge then that the world was round, but nobody had yet been able to circumnavigate it because of the great distance across the open ocean with no stopping points along the way. Efforts to make such trips had been rumored, but none had been substantiated. Columbus believed he had the grit and sailing skills for the test. The expedition, he told the queen with passionate conviction, would allow the sovereigns to replenish their dwindling treasury, depleted by the war with Granada, and could perhaps even fund a new crusade to reconquer Jerusalem from the Muslims. This, of course, was music to the queen's ears.

Columbus's pitch to the monarchs was more romantic than pragmatic. From the beginning he wooed them with a siren's song, addressing them in letters as "King and Queen of the Islands of the Ocean."[4] Given Isabella's background and knowledge, she was inclined to listen. Nevertheless, she was preoccupied with the war against Granada, she was raising five children, and much of the court regarded Columbus's proposal with skepticism. It took some seven years of persistent persuasion before he was able to set off from Castile with his small squadron of three ships. Twice Isabella had referred the proposal to commissions for further study, a time-tested administrative technique for delaying a difficult decision, and twice the learned scholars had reported back that the trip was too risky, too unlikely to succeed.

Isabella nevertheless decided at some point that she would commission the trip and that Columbus would be a good choice to lead it. He seemed more than competent for the undertaking, for he had a kind of genius as a seafarer and navigator, and he had demonstrated his skills more prosaically to a land-bound court through the production of careful and detailed maps. But he was a bit vague, even oddly secretive, about the journey's exact route. From his perspective, he was trying to preserve his good idea and keep others from poaching it, but some observers thought his ideas lacked specificity. Moreover, in an era when classical learning was viewed as the source of all wisdom, heated debates over the merits of his concept revolved around what the ancients had said about the topic thousands of years earlier.

Columbus had first made his proposition to the Portuguese King João during the civil war following King Enrique's death. Columbus had tried to persuade the Portuguese to fund his trip and fruitlessly negotiated with João over the terms. Columbus had entertained outlandishly inflated expectations for the rewards he should receive if the trip were successful. Bartolomé de Las Casas, the author of *Historia de las Indias*, recounted that Columbus had asked to be knighted, to be given the title "Don," and to receive one-tenth of the king's income from gold and other salable items found in the areas he discovered. King João, who by this time was experienced at managing these kinds of expeditions, laughed him off as an overreaching "fantasticist" whose claims would prove unfounded.[5]

Unwilling to make the financial pledges Columbus asked, the crafty king nonetheless used the information Columbus had provided him to dispatch an expedition in the direction described. But the sailors sent to sea failed to find land and came back complaining bitterly that Columbus was a mistaken fool. Columbus was enraged over this betrayal, suspecting that the Portuguese king had stolen his confidential material. In high dudgeon, he left Portugal and went to Castile to plead the same case. He sent his loyal brother, Bartholomew, on a similar mission to England, but according to fellow explorer and historian Gonzalo Fernández de Oviedo y Valdés, King Henry VII "made fun of what Columbus said, and took his words to be in vain."[6]

Columbus presented his idea personally in Castile, weaving a tale that mixed astronomy and navigation with mythological history and essays by the ancients. He had not come from a wealthy family, however; he was self-taught, and his incomplete and faulty grasp of classical learning quickly became apparent to the scholars at court. Two panels of experts, asked to analyze his proposal, rejected his premise, saying—correctly— that the globe was much larger than Columbus claimed and concluding that his trip was likely to be a costly and embarrassing failure that would lead to nothing but loss of life for the sailors.

But the intense and mystical foreigner mesmerized many others, including the queen, who decided to back the enterprise. They embarked on a kind of minuet. Columbus danced attendance at court for years, trying to show his enthusiasm for Castile's interests, even volunteering as a soldier in the war against Granada. He had personal conferences with the queen, sometimes with both the king and queen, at least four times over these years, including meetings in the audience chamber at the Alcázar in Córdoba, at the sovereigns' battlefield encampments at Baza and Málaga, and at Santa Fe, where they were conducting the siege of Granada. Some of these meetings became the stuff of legend—several times Columbus stalked away from court, only to be drawn back by someone who took his parting message to the queen, and she would call him back to tell her more. When he wasn't at court, he was living at the monastery of La Rabida in Huelva, in the south, so a royal command meant that he appeared to be leaving monastic life to return to the world to discuss the business venture at hand. Of course, this was just the kind of approach tailored to attract the queen's attention and respect. It does not mean, however, that Columbus was practicing priestly celibacy, for within a few years he acquired a second son, whom he named Ferdinand, through an extended out-of-wedlock love affair with a woman from Seville. He now had two children who depended on him for their sustenance.

Isabella strung Columbus along, giving him encouragement and just enough money, small though it was, to make him hope that she would endorse his project. She essentially had him on call for whenever she would be ready to send him off. Columbus was paid 3,000 maravedis from the Castilian treasury on May 5, 1487; the same amount again on July 3; 4,000 on August 27, when he was asked to go to the royal encampment in Málaga; the same amount on October 15; and then another 3,000 on June 16, 1488. In other words, he was given a retainer of about 12,000 maravedis a year, the approximate wage of "an able seaman" of the day, according to the naval historian Samuel Eliot Morison.[7]

The amount was too meager for him to support himself at the peripatetic court, so he appears to have depended on charity at different times as well. He became increasingly threadbare in appearance, which would have undermined his credibility among the haughty and ostentatious Spanish courtiers.

The next year Isabella pushed off his expenses onto her other subjects, requiring tavern owners and innkeepers to help with his upkeep. On May 12, 1489, the sovereigns furnished him with an open letter to all municipal and local officials, ordering them to give food and lodging to "Cristóbal Colomo," "who has come to our court."[8]

Columbus's hopes rose and fell with each new development. The queen was keeping him dangling, even as he received offers of funding from other sources. Two well-connected Spanish officials, the Duke of Medinaceli and the Aragonese financier Luis de Santángel, both said later that they had been willing to finance Columbus's expedition. The Duke of Medinaceli said he had supported and housed Columbus for two years while the mariner was waiting for the Castilian commission, and that he had had three or four ships at the ready at his own facilities and could have sent Columbus on his voyage without delay. But he had informed the queen of his intention, and the queen had opted to keep the mission and its possible gains exclusive to Castile, something that irritated the duke, who later believed he had been one of the first to recognize the trip's potential but had been waved off.

"But since I felt that this was a job for the Queen, our Lady, I wrote to her Highness about it from Rota, and she answered that I should send Columbus to her," the duke later wrote to Cardinal Mendoza.

> So I sent him to her, and besought her Highness, since I did not care to try it and was getting things set up for her [behalf], that she let me be given a piece of it, and that the ships be loaded, and [on their return] unloaded, at the Port. Her Highness received him and turned him over to Alonso de Quintanilla, who wrote to me on her behalf that she did not hold this business likely to come off; but that if it firmed up, she would graciously grant me a piece of it. But, after she had quizzed him, she decided to send him to the Indies [herself].[9]

From fairly early on, observers saw that Isabella and Columbus had a certain affinity; their conversations were such that people referred to them as "chatting." They were almost the same age—they even resembled each other, with their reddish hair and pale skin, standing out in a realm where most residents were dark-haired and dark-eyed—and they shared a romantic fascination with exotic places, animals, plants, and people. They were curious about the world around them. A little less apparent, but clear to the intuition, both possessed a messianic sense of destiny, intermingled with intense religiosity. Both wanted to spread the Christian faith, and both thought earthly rewards would come their way for doing so. Without question, their motives were simultaneously material and spiritual. They sought worldly riches but did not want to be perceived as doing so.

Columbus possessed the same tangled view of world history as Isabella, mingling classical learning and mythology with recorded events in the recent past. He based his proposed trip on Ptolemy's *Geography,* a book written in the second century that had been rediscovered in the 1400s. He anticipated finding certain people and places when he reached the Orient, based on the accounts of the Venetian Marco Polo, who had gone to Asia in the thirteenth century. Like the queen, he believed in the legend of Prester John, the mythical Christian king marooned among the Muslims or Mongols somewhere in East Asia. He promised to deliver to Isabella the kind of world that she had already commissioned Diego de Valera to write about in his *Crónica.*

But Columbus also had a streak of madness, which is perhaps why he was willing to undertake a trip that almost everyone thought would lead to his death. He had a wild imagination. He signed his name with a secret signature he had devised himself, an indecipherable combination of letters and images. Some people believe that it was his coded way of sharing his Jewish ancestry with his children. But writing in some kind of cipher was a popular fad at the time among intellectuals—a fellow Italian, Leonardo da Vinci, who was roughly the same age as Columbus, famously wrote in script that was readable only in a mirror. Columbus, like Leonardo, spent many hours developing his theories, writing feverishly in notebooks, journals, and in the margins of books he owned. In his copy of *Plutarch's Lives,* he made special notations on ninety-nine pages where "auguries, portents and . . . forms of divination . . . [including] the conjuration of demons" were mentioned. He was particularly fascinated by accounts in which individuals, such as Marcus Caecius, heard "voices in the air."[10]

Later he would claim that he heard such "voices in the air" himself. But this medieval preoccupation with angels and demons, and fears of them, haunted Isabella as well.

Columbus was a fascinating, contradictory, and inscrutable character. He was evasive about his origins, though Italians were confident that he was born in Genoa. He may have had Jewish blood. Some thought he was a spy for Portugal. He was probably born poor. He was undoubtedly motivated by a need for money and by a desire to transform himself, and his descendants, into members of the titled nobility. That may have been why he was vague about his considerably more humble lineage, and perhaps why he never married the mother of his son Ferdinand, who most likely also came from a lower social class.

At the same time, however, he was most certainly a devout Christian. His son Ferdinand later said his father was "so strict in matters of religion that for fasting and saying prayers he might have been taken for a member of a religious order."[11] Columbus seemed that way to others as well: when his pilot and sometime rival, Juan de la Cosa, depicted Columbus in an illustration, he depicted him as Saint Christopher, delivering Christianity to the masses in the New World.

Unraveling fact from fiction has been a challenge for Columbus's biographers ever since, because he created so many fables about himself. After his fortunes faltered, for example, he began to view himself as a martyr, describing himself as having been alone and friendless in the Castilian court. In fact, however, as a result of his great personal charm and intriguing ideas, from a fairly early point he drew many and varied supporters to his side. He came to be admired by Cardinal Mendoza, whose counsels were greatly respected by Queen Isabella. The Castilian treasurer Alonso de Quintanilla backed Columbus financially, as did a group of Genoese merchants, and so did the two would-be patrons of the endeavor, the Duke of Medinaceli and the Aragonese financier Luis de Santángel. Several priests, including one of Isabella's confessors and one of Prince Juan's tutors, endorsed his effort. And Beatriz de Bobadilla, Isabella's best friend, is known to have considered the expedition a risk worth taking.

The biggest and most influential cluster of Columbus's supporters was the circle that comprised the court of Prince Juan, who was fourteen years old in the summer of 1492. These members of the sovereigns' entourage were carefully selected, having been charged with the development, education, and moral guidance of the future king. Queen Isabella carefully monitored the upbringing that her beloved son was receiving. His confidants had her ear. Chief of the prince's household, for example, was Gutierre de Cárdenas, the man who had carried the sword aloft during the ceremony when Isabella proclaimed herself queen. By this time, he had been a trusted adviser to the queen for more than twenty years, holding a variety of posts of increasing responsibility.

Another close associate of the queen was the humanist tutor to the young men at the court, including the prince. Peter Martyr grew friendly with Columbus and would become an early and prolific historian of the discoveries of the New World. Another influential supporter of Columbus was the prince's governess, Juana de Torres y Ávila, who was close to the queen. Columbus wrote Juana a letter that suggested that he was a close and trusted friend of hers. Juana's brother Antonio traveled with Columbus in his second voyage to the New World. When Columbus later needed to deliver a message to the Castilian court, and wanted to make sure it reached the queen, he put the missive into Antonio's hands.

Foremost among Columbus's supporters, however, was the queen herself, according to observers. She alone saw the big picture of what he was offering to Castile—an opportunity that might change its fortunes for years to come. Her husband showed barely any interest at all, always being more preoccupied with the Mediterranean world than with the Atlantic Ocean. "She always aided and favored him," Columbus's son wrote later, "while the King he always found somewhat reserved and unsympathetic to his projects."[12]

By the summer of 1491, with the war against Granada still under way, Columbus was discouraged and had lost faith that he would ever get the go-ahead from the queen. He went to La Rabida to collect his son, Diego, intending to head to France to seek the backing of King Charles VIII. Juan Pérez, chief friar of the monastery and formerly a confessor to the queen, offered to intercede with her. Pérez sent her a letter and two weeks later got a response. Isabella told Pérez to come to court himself, and the friar set off for Granada on a mule that Columbus had rented for him. When he arrived, Pérez reminded Isabella of Columbus's proposal and informed her of his penury, and she sent for Columbus once more, this time including a sum of 20,000 maravedis so that he should arrive appropriately garbed.[13]

So Columbus, at Isabella's expense, was at Granada when the city finally fell to the Christians. He thought the final hurdle had been surmounted. But the court scholars once again rejected Columbus's proposal as unsound. Downcast, he saddled his mule and packed up, setting off with Pérez for Córdoba and points north. That had been the final straw. "Columbus resented this treatment all his life long," writes Morison.[14]

But Columbus now found himself with a new advocate, one who was finally able to bring good fortune. The converso Luis de Santángel, keeper of the privy purse for the king, decided to intervene. Santángel

> went to find the queen, and with words which his keen desire to persuade her suggested, told her that he was astonished to see that her Highness, who had always shown a resolute spirit in matters of great pith and consequence, should lack it now for an enterprise of so little risk, yet which could prove of so great service to God and to the exaltation of his church, not to speak of very great increase and glory for her realms and crown; an enterprise of such nature that if any other prince should undertake what the Admiral offered to her, it would be a very great damage to the crown, and a grave reproach to her.[15]

Santángel said, moreover, that he would pay for the fleet himself. Isabella said she would reconsider and perhaps pledge her jewels for the expense, which Santángel quickly assured her would not be necessary. The queen sent a messenger after Columbus, and the servant caught up with him at the village of Pinos Puente, about ten miles from Granada. At last the trip was approved.

* * *

The long series of delays and disappointments for Columbus may have been partly caused by the audacity of his personal requests—that if he succeeded, he be named "Admiral of the Ocean Sea," which would be a very high rank in Castilian nobility; that he be named viceroy and governor over all the islands and mainland; that he have absolute authority to appoint and remove officials; and that he appoint the judges to oversee the affairs in each port. He also demanded a tenth of all the value of the goods bought, bartered, or produced in the lands to be discovered.[16] His requests were extraordinary—but so was the risk he was undertaking. Sailing west from Europe into uncharted seas was likely to prove fatal, it was thought. The Portuguese, in their own explorations, were hugging the coast of Africa.

The complexity of his demands made for extensive paperwork, and the terms would become matters of intensive scrutiny in later years. Columbus and Isabella worked up a set of contracts to confirm the terms of the arrangement, and documents to ease his way. Columbus was given official royal permission to make the journey, an agreement as to the titles and compensation he would receive if the trip succeeded, and a passport and official letters of introduction to give to the foreign potentates he would no doubt meet when he got to Asia.

Isabella agreed to pay for the expenses of his trip. They were not, all in all, particularly great, just three ships, and salaries and provisions for a crew of about ninety men. The total cost was about 2 million maravedis,[17] or about approximately "the annual income of a middling provincial aristocrat," writes the historian Felipe Fernández-Armesto, "but the enterprise was risky, the pundits were derisive and in time of war cash was short."[18]

From the beginning, Isabella stressed that the expedition was a purely Castilian endeavor. Among the promises Columbus made to her, according to explorers Bartolomé de Las Casas and Gonzalo Fernández de Oviedo y Valdés, was that the crew would be Castilian. Of the ninety men and boys who signed on, eighty-five were Castilians from Huelva and Andalusia, one was Portuguese, and four, including Columbus, were Italian.[19] None were from Aragon.

Though the queen claimed the entire venture was a royal prerogative, she did not advance the money for the trip. Perennially cash-strapped, she ordered the town of Palos to provide two ships for Columbus as repayment for a fine that the crown had previously levied against it. Town officials were ordered to provide the fully equipped ships "within ten days of receiving Our letter, without further notice from us, without deliberation or delay," and were warned that if they failed to comply, they would risk "forfeiting Our favor" and would be fined 10,000 maravedis each.[20] They jumped into action and soon provided two sailing ships, the *Niña* and the *Pinta*.

Luis de Santángel and a Genoese named Francesco Pinelli advanced the additional funds needed, reportedly by borrowing money from the treasury of the Santa Hermandad. They were later reimbursed "from the sale of indulgences," writes Fernández-Armesto, who adds that the money was "all recovered in due course from the proceeds of the sales in a poor diocese of Extremadura," a dry and dusty province where most residents eked out a marginal existence.[21] It was ironic that such a poor district financed the expedition. And it was also ironic, and perhaps not at all coincidental, that many of the explorers who would risk their lives by following in Columbus's footsteps in the centuries ahead would hail from Extremadura.

Even with the queen's specific support, however, organizing the trip wasn't easy. Many sailors thought it a pointless and potentially lethal journey, heading west into the boundless and pitiless ocean. "It was difficult to find sailors willing to sail more than a day without sighting land," wrote Las Casas later, "because, in those days, losing sight of the coast was considered a frightening and horrible experience no sailor would undertake."[22]

Anticipating that problem and hoping to encourage volunteers to sign on, the queen ordered that any criminals who joined the expedition would be released from punishment. Four men joined the crew to take advantage of that get-out-of-jail-free card.[23]

Columbus had a stroke of luck when the three Pinzón brothers, excellent mariners who were well known in maritime circles in Castile, signed on in leadership positions. Martín Alonso Pinzón, the eldest, served as captain of the *Pinta,* while Francisco signed on as master; Vicente Yáñez, the youngest, served as captain of the *Niña.* Other sailors then signed on for the trip out of respect for the Pinzóns and in recognition of their talents and competence. Another prominent maritime family, the Niños, from the town of Niebla, also came along and persuaded still more to join as well.

A key volunteer was ship captain Juan de la Cosa, who brought to the venture his own ship, the *Santa María,* the largest vessel of the three, and served as master of it. Columbus, leading the expedition, sailed with him aboard the *Santa María.*

The recruitment effort was assisted by rumors swirling in the seafaring community that ancient accounts or secret documents substantiated Columbus's theory. A story made the rounds that among the "tools and maps" that Columbus had received from his mother-in-law were a set of documents known as a "rutter," a maritime handbook containing written sailing directions. These documents were considered so valuable that in Portugal they were kept as state secrets and divulging them was a criminal offense. Nevertheless, despite the core of competent officers, the group that assembled for duty in early August 1492 seems to have been a bit ragtag.

Every man on board was required to confess his sins and receive communion before departing from Palos. They set sail on August 3, 1492, a half hour before sunrise. They passed the monastery at La Rabida, where Columbus had spent many hours among friends, and from the vessels they heard the friars chanting the ancient liturgy for the hour of Prime.[24] Then they headed out in the direction of the newly colonized Canary Islands, west of Africa.

The trio of tiny sailing ships, none longer than sixty feet, dropped anchor briefly in the Canaries, and then set sail again on September 6. By nightfall, all trace of land had been left behind, and Columbus and his crew were sailing into an uncharted sea. A month passed, day after day. At some point Columbus began doctoring the logbook so he could minimize to the crew the great distance they were sailing away from known land.

Mariners who traveled on that first voyage later said that as they traveled "across the great ocean sea," their terror mounted, and that "each hour the fear in them grew as their hope of seeing the land they were seeking waned." The crews grew restive, and some began "murmuring" questions about Columbus's competence at navigation. They feared they had been tricked into joining the trip and that they would be lost at sea; they wondered whether the king and queen were cruelly risking their lives for an uncertain outcome. And "they discussed among themselves whether to throw Columbus in the sea." Columbus comforted the mutinous crew with "sweet words," telling them they would win glory and good fortune by persevering. "He promised that within a few days there would be an end to the fatigue and travel, with much and undoubtable prosperity."[25]

Then the ships' officers too began questioning Columbus's leadership. Sometime in the first week of October, Columbus and Martín Alonso Pinzón had an "acrimonious interview," where they fought over the direction they should be heading. Columbus thought Pinzón was rebelling against his authority and resented it, but the men agreed to continue on the course Columbus was plotting.[26]

Some of the stress lifted in early October, when the sailors spotted bits of drifting vegetation that suggested they were near a coastline. Then very early on the morning of October 12, after they had been sailing in the open sea for five weeks, a shout rang out: "Land!"

The sailor who made the first sighting was Rodrigo de Triana, aboard the fastest of the ships, the *Pinta*. This was a great coup for him, because the first to spot land was to receive a silk jacket and a reward of 10,000 maravedis from the queen.

"When the Admiral saw the land, he fell to his knees, and it brought tears to his eyes with the extreme pleasure he felt," and he began to sing *Te Deum Laudamus*.[27] The men embraced one another with joy. But Rodrigo de Triana did not receive the promised gifts. Columbus soon claimed that he had been the first to spot land because he had noticed lights on the horizon the night before and pointed them out to a ship's officer. Saying the reward belonged to him was not the most effective way to build good morale among people who were being asked to risk their lives, and it was an omen of what would come later.

The three ships landed on an island somewhere in the Caribbean, probably in the Bahamas, although no one knows which one precisely. Columbus's changes in his logbook during the trip complicated the task for later scholars who tried to replicate his voyage. In addition, copies of his original seaboard diary mysteriously disappeared. They were perhaps stolen because the information had become valuable, a kind of treasure map to the Americas. Or they may have been discarded in a careless purge of family books and papers in Seville after Columbus's sons died, or been dumped by Castilian courtiers eager to lighten the load while the king and queen moved from palace to palace. But Bartolomé de Las Casas, through friendship with Columbus's children, obtained access to an early version and transcribed large sections of it, and his account remains the single most important source of information about this world-changing voyage.

The men saw before them a beautiful tropical isle, with palm trees and flowering bushes waving in the wind. At home the weather was growing cold and blustery, but here in this new place, the balmy breezes made it feel like an eternal spring. They saw strange and exotic plants and animals they had never encountered before, including delightful, brightly colored parrots. They groped to describe what they saw, and as many travelers to the Caribbean do, they likened it to paradise.

They were dazzled by the colors—all brighter and somehow lighter than the hues of Europe. The sands of the beaches, made up of particles of coral, were glistening white, quite unlike the dark stones of Spain. The waters near the shore took on this same coloration from the sandy bottom and showed up as an impossibly light blue, almost turquoise, scarcely blue at all. Even the sky seemed to be a lighter, brighter shade of blue than elsewhere.

This world looked gentle and welcoming. The jagged reefs of coral might have been dangerous, but once the sailors were safely ashore, the islands seemed to hold few threats. The waters at the beach, inside the sheltering reef, were serene and calm. The winds, so often filled in Europe with clouds and rain and cold, blew here only as a warm, steady breeze that caressed and soothed the skin.

Pelicans circled steadily along the shore, plummeting into the waters at intervals in search of their next meal and soon finding it. Colorful fish swarmed in the shallows. Fruit could be had from the trees for the taking. And the most pleasing of these trees—the palm—grew everywhere along the shoreline, sometimes in groves, sometimes as single trees leaning out over the water, giving a picturesque quality to the view and the welcome prospects of shade and building materials.

Columbus was most struck by the first thing he saw: naked people. On the beach were a group of islanders, almost all of them men, wearing almost nothing. Within a few days, the sailors had seen women, too, beautiful women also nude, physically agile and casually proud of their strong and shapely bodies.

The lack of clothing made sense for people living in a place with constant moderate temperatures. October's weather averaged in the eighties Fahrenheit by day and in the seventies at night, making clothing essentially unnecessary. This was a revelation for Europeans, who were bound most of their lives in heavy woolen garments that protected them from the elements but that also confined them to the social caste and class within which they had been born.

When people in cold, windy Europe read the seamen's descriptions of this place, it sounded like heaven. That people walked around nude was a titillating detail. It also carried connotations that echoed across Europe: the simplicity recalled an easier, less complicated, and less materialistic time; the purity resembled that of Saint Francis, who had spurned rich clothing and renounced material possessions; and the suggestion of unbridled and unrestricted sexuality stood at odds with conventional European morality. But Columbus was not alone in highlighting the nudity—it was the one single thing emphasized in every report from the first European men who landed in the New World.

Columbus added to the sensation by describing the islanders as a "gentle and peaceful people and of great simplicity," to whom he gave trinkets of little red caps and glass beads that they hung around their necks.[28] In exchange, he said, they gave him gold.

The first interactions with the Indians were amiable. They were friendly and seemed eager to cooperate with their surprising new visitors. No doubt they were repulsed by the men's body odors and fascinated by their bearded hairiness, for the islanders kept themselves very clean and removed their body hair, but they were too polite to share those thoughts. They were curious about the newcomers, and some seemed to wonder whether they came from earth or from the sky.

Columbus immediately began thinking about how best to enslave them, according to entries in his logbook, which he intended to share with Isabella and Ferdinand upon his return to Castile. On the first day, October 12, 1492, he noted that they learned quickly and "ought to make good servants." On October 13 he began to press them to look for gold, though they were not much inclined to do so. On the third day, he noted that they were so unskilled in arms that "with 50 men they could all be subjected and made to do all that one wished." Soon the Spaniards picked up some Indians and took them along in the ships, without noting whether the Indians had protested.[29]

Columbus and his men sailed on through what is believed to have been the Bahamas, observing the flora and fauna. Columbus, who believed he had landed among islands on the coast of Asia or India, took careful note of the characteristics of the islands. He waxed more and more poetical about the beauties of the landscape because he was not finding anything that looked like an advanced mercantile civilization and he was collecting only small amounts of gold, mostly by bartering trinkets for jewelry that the natives were wearing on their bodies or attached to their noses.

He gave each island a name as he reached it. To thank God, he named the first island San Salvador, or Holy Savior, the second he named Santa María de Concepción, the third he named for the king, calling it Fernandina, and the fourth he reserved for the queen, calling it La Isabela.

Disconcertingly, on November 20 Martín Alonso Pinzón, master of the *Pinta*, sailed off with his ship without warning. He may have been fighting with Columbus, or perhaps he decided to hunt for gold, but it was frightening for the officers and crews of the two other ships to be alone thousands of miles from home. They were irritated at their departed comrades but also worried about them. All they could do was continue without them.

In early December, Columbus arrived at the island of Hispaniola, or as the inhabitants called it, Haiti, and took possession of it for Ferdinand and Isabella. He was told that there were gold-bearing regions in the interior, and that more gold was to be had in neighboring islands.

On December 20, Columbus received an invitation to visit from a tribal chief, or cacique, who held sway over a large part of the island. As a welcoming gift, the cacique, whose name was Guacanagari, sent a beautiful garment of woven cotton and multicolored fishbones with an ornamental mask in the middle made of a large, stiff piece of hammered gold. Baskets of food and presents were delivered next. The timing for the meeting seemed propitious—Christmas Eve 1492.

That night, however, Columbus must have let his guard down. In the early morning hours, everyone was fast asleep on the *Santa María*, and the watchman on duty had dozed off. The ship, their largest vessel and the one carrying most of their provisions, slid onto a sandbar and became stranded. The tides pushed it onto coral reefs at the edge of the island, the ship's bottom began to shred, and the hull took on water. Some of the crew panicked, jumped into a rowboat, and paddled to the *Niña*, abandoning ship.

The men quickly realized that the ship could not be saved, but they also realized they must do all they could to remove its cargo and equipment, so essential to their survival in an alien land. The cacique Guacanagari appeared just at this point, when the Castilians were at their most vulnerable. He mobilized all his people to help the Europeans transport their goods to shore, commiserating with them over the loss and ensuring that the items were safely removed and stored. Gaucanagari told them not to worry, that he would give them two large houses in which to live now that they had no place to stay. More Indians soon came bearing additional gifts of gold, and that night the cacique treated the Christians to an elaborate feast with many delicacies, including yams and lobsters and bread made from the cassava plant.

Columbus believed that he had a real friendship with this man, and he made a momentous decision. The *Pinta* had not reappeared—perhaps it was gone forever. The remaining men were too many to fit on the *Niña*, the smallest of the three. So he told himself it was God's will that the *Santa María* had gone aground, because he was destined to build a fortress there and make the place a European colony. He would leave a contingent of men behind on the island, and because it was Christmas, he named the new settlement La Navidad.

A small fort was built securely with the planks and timbers from the *Santa María*. There was bread and biscuit for a year, and wine and ammunition, in addition to the abundant food sources available on the island. Columbus told himself the men would be fine. He picked thirty-nine people to stay behind, including a ship carpenter, a man with medical skills, a gunner who was also an engineer, a tailor, and a number of sailors. No accounts as to how this was decided survive. Some of the men may have wanted to stay. A few of the colonists were upper-class, including one who had served on the king's staff and another who was nephew to a prominent cleric, so this duty may not have been seen as a punishment. Perhaps some wanted the opportunity to be first to collect the available gold on the island. Others may have been charmed by the area's beautiful and generous-spirited women. But it also seems safe to say that some members of Columbus's team were not thrilled to learn they had been chosen to remain behind.

On January 2, 1493, exactly one year after the surrender at Granada, the explorers held a farewell party. Columbus was anxious to be on his way for fear that Martín Alonso Pinzón would get to back Spain ahead of him and perhaps tell false tales that would put Columbus in a bad light. Leaving the colonists behind seemed like a reasonable decision, as relations between the Indians and the new colonists were splendid. "The cacique showed the Admiral much love, and great grief at his parting, especially when he saw him embark," according to Columbus.[30]

Columbus started to make his way back home, winding his way back through the Caribbean islands. On January 6 Martín Alonso Pinzón and the *Niña* suddenly reappeared, and Pinzón told Columbus that his departure had been unintentional. Columbus had an angry confrontation with him, saying that Pinzón was lying and had left the other ships out of "insolence and greed." He accused Pinzón of disloyalty and bitterly called his actions "the evil works of Satan, who wished to hinder that voyage, as he had done up to that time."[31]

Columbus had some justification for making these charges. Pinzón reportedly gathered up a good quantity of gold for himself and his crew. But Pinzón, for his part, was disturbed that Columbus had left thirty-nine people behind. The clash widened, and now Columbus seemed to be at odds with all the Pinzón brothers.

Another jarring event occurred on January 13. As the two remaining ships were continuing home, the winds died down, and they ended up in an exposed harbor. Columbus sent some men ashore to collect yams for eating, and they encountered some Indian warriors unlike any they had seen to date. They were very fierce in appearance, and their charcoal-painted faces gave them a ghoulish appearance. Columbus and his men conjectured that they might be the fearsome cannibals that the more peaceful Indians had mentioned with dread. They engaged in some barter, but these Indians suddenly turned and attacked them with bows and arrows. The Spanish defended themselves, wounding two of the Indians, and the rest of the group quickly fled, disappearing into the forest. It was the first violent clash between Europeans and Indians in the New World.

It made Columbus and his men even more eager to get home. They made some repairs to the ships, then set sail to the east. They took samples of the foodstuffs they had found, parrots, gold objects, and a small group of natives they had captured. The return journey took about two months. They hit bad weather, and Pinzón was driven toward Galicia, in northern Spain, and then had to turn back south.

Oddly, however, Columbus did not sail directly to Spain. Instead, providing grist for those who suspected he was secretly a spy for Portugal, he landed first on islands near Portugal, in late February 1493. He claimed he had later been blown into the port of Lisbon by a powerful storm that he had been unable to resist. It was from Lisbon that he wrote to Queen Isabella about his discovery. While there, however, he had at least three separate private conversations with King João. Columbus almost certainly gloated, given that he had once sought financial support from Portugal and been rejected.

King João, who had frequently been outmaneuvered by Queen Isabella already, was seriously out of sorts when he got the news of Columbus's discovery. According to his courtiers, he considered killing Columbus as a traitor who had probably stolen navigational secrets from the state. But he decided instead to turn to diplomacy to protect his interests.

Columbus was greeted with great fanfare in Lisbon. People mobbed the streets to see the marvelous objects he had brought back and the Indians in his entourage. Many in the crowd that day remembered it for years to come, fueling a groundswell of desire on the Iberian peninsula to set out on maritime adventures. Among the people employed at the Portuguese court at that time, for example, was a fourteen-year-old page named Ferdinand Magellan.

King João opted to let Columbus go, with a stern warning that the Treaty of Alcáçovas had given the Portuguese the rights to the lands

Columbus was claiming. He vowed to take up the question with the queen in Castile.

So Columbus was permitted to depart. In Palos he caught up with the rebellious captain Pinzón, but only briefly. Pinzón had contracted a mysterious ailment and died within days of his arrival home. This removed a potential rival and a man who had been a thorn in Columbus's side. But reports soon began to circulate that the Pinzón brothers had been most responsible for the successful voyage, while Columbus had wanted to turn around. Later on, after everyone realized the immense value of the lands they had reached, the matter would become the subject of a protracted legal dispute.

* * *

The queen immediately understood the importance of Columbus's discovery. She urged him to hurry to see her in Barcelona, where the sovereigns were living while tending to domestic issues that had been put off for years during the war with Granada. On April 7, Columbus received a letter from the sovereigns addressed to Don Cristóbal Colón, underscoring his new honorific title.[32] Isabella clearly wanted to move immediately to follow up with further expeditions:

> We have seen your letters and we have taken much pleasure in learning whereof you write and that God gave so good a result to your labors, and well guided you in what you commenced, whereof He will be well served and we also, and our realms receive so much advantage. It will please God that, beyond that wherein you serve him, you should receive from us many favors. . . . Inasmuch that which you have commenced with the aid of God be continued and furthered, and we desire that you come here forthwith, therefore for our service make the best haste you can in your coming, so that you may be timely provided with everything you need; and because as you see the summer has begun, and you must not delay in going back there, see if something cannot be prepared in Seville or in other districts for your returning to the land which you have discovered. And write to us at once in this mail which departs presently, so that things may be provided as well as may be, while you are coming and returning, in such manner that when you return hence, all will be ready.[33]

As Columbus was passing triumphantly through Seville, an excited young boy, standing near the ancient Church of St. Nicholas, watched his arrival. He was Bartolomé de Las Casas, who would become an explorer in the Indies, a colonist, a priest, and an activist for Indian rights in the decades ahead. Columbus was creating paroxysms of enthusiasm for overseas exploration, parading through the streets with beautiful green parrots, Indians in exotic regalia, chunks of gold, and face masks made of precious stones and fishbones. "The news spread over Castile like fire," Las Casas later recalled, "that a land called the Indies had been discovered, that it was full of people and things so diverse and new, and that the discoverer himself was to take such and such a route accompanied by some of the Indians. They flocked from all directions to see him; the roads swelled with throngs come to welcome him in the towns through which he passed."[34]

In Barcelona his reception was even more splendid, and the sovereigns listened to his story with rapt attention. Columbus's son recalled:

This news caused them great joy and happiness; and they ordered a solemn reception be held for him as befitted one who had rendered them so great a service. All the Court and the city came out to meet him; and the Catholic Sovereigns received him in public, seated with all majesty and grandeur on rich thrones under a canopy of cloth of gold. When he came forward to kiss their hands, they rose from their thrones as if he were a great lord, and would not let him kiss their hands but made him sit down beside them.[35]

In Barcelona, another excited boy was in the crowd, the future explorer Gonzalo Fernández de Oviedo y Valdés, who was employed as a court page. He remembered the excitement, the presents of gold, the odd foods and new spices, the jewel-toned birds, and the fascinating and strangely garbed people: "And then came the Admiral, don Cristóbal Colón, with the first Indians from those parts that arrived on the first voyage of discovery,"[36] Oviedo wrote.

The king and queen treated Columbus as a grand gentleman: "He was very benevolently and graciously received by the King and by the Queen." Then he gave a long account of all that had transpired and of the riches that were there. They also talked of the millions of lives that were at risk of damnation if they were not evangelized and saved, for troublingly, the expedition had found signs of "idolatry, and diabolical sacrifices, and rites that gave reverence to Satan."[37]

The sovereigns listened "with profound attention and, raising their hands in prayer, sank to their knees in deep gratitude to God," Las Casas wrote.

> The singers of the royal chapel sang Te Deum Laudamus while the wind instruments gave the response and indeed, it seemed a moment of communion with all the celestial joys. Who could describe the tears shed by the King, Queen and noblemen? What jubilation, what joy, what happiness in all hearts! How everybody began to encourage each other with plans of settling in the new land and converting people! They could tell how the Sovereigns, especially Queen Isabella, valued the propagation of the Faith by showing such words and actions that their principal source of pleasure was having found such favor in the eyes of God as to have been allowed to support and finance (though with mighty few funds) the discovery of so many infidels ready for conversion.[38]

Meanwhile Cardinal Mendoza, a nobleman of such high stature, and so admired by Isabella, that he was known as the third king of Spain, hosted Columbus at a great dinner, another extraordinary mark of favor. The mariner was seated at the "most eminent place next" to the churchman, and "for the first time, Columbus was served a full course dinner with covered dishes and a food taster," amid an atmosphere of pomp and festivity. "The rulers showered honor upon honor on the Admiral."[39]

The greatest honor of all was that the queen ordered the mariner's two sons, Diego and Ferdinand, to come live at court among the prince's entourage, as pages to the prince. There they would receive the same education given to the young aristocrats at court. Columbus's sons, in effect, were raised among the children of the queen and became particular friends of Prince Juan, serving him as pages. The two young men were "favored, and stayed in [the] house" of the prince even after the prince grew to adulthood.[40]

And so for the next voyage, Columbus was sent to sea in style. He was ordered to return to these new lands, lavishly equipped, with seventeen ships and a horde of passengers. Many people of wealth and position elbowed each other for the chance to journey to this wonderful land, this paradise, where gold nuggets could be found on the ground. There was an air of great expectation, of wealth just readily at hand. Within six months, Columbus set off once again.

In the years ahead, as a result of his second, third, and fourth trips, Columbus's fortunes would wax and wane. He would steadfastly cling to his belief, against a growing mountain of proof, that he had found a path to India, even as the evidence increasingly suggested he had discovered a land previously unknown to the European world.

Columbus would always believe that his single most stalwart supporter, his most reliable defender, was the queen. Their relationship at that point was at its zenith. He spoke to her in the terms of courtly love permitted to her top-ranked courtiers. "The keys of my desires I gave to you in Barcelona," he told her in a letter. "If you try a taste of my good will, you will find its scent and savour have only increased since then. . . . I dedicated myself to your Highness in Barcelona without holding back any part of me, and as it was with my spirit, so it was with my honour and estate."[41]

Even as Columbus was acknowledging the importance of Isabella's sponsorship, however, the memory of her role was being erased elsewhere in Europe. On February 15, after he had landed in Portugal, Columbus had composed a letter about his journey to Luis de Santángel, the Aragonese financier who had helped back the expedition, wrapping it within a letter meant for the crown. He described the beauty of the islands, their rich natural resources, the attractive naked people he had seen, "men and women, as their mothers bore them," the easy availability of gold, and the presence of "ferocious" cannibals.[42] All this was given in triumph to the "most illustrious King and Queen," he wrote, "and to their renowned realms, for this all Christendom ought to feel joyful and make celebrations and give solemn thanks to the Holy Trinity with many solemn prayers for the great exaltation that it will have, in the turning of so many peoples to our holy faith, and afterwards for material benefits."[43]

The letter to Luis de Santángel, bearing these new and sensational tidings, was soon widely circulated and became a publishing phenomenon, reproduced all over Europe, thanks to the new printing press. Sixteen separate editions, published in Latin, German, Spanish, and Italian, were produced in Antwerp, Basel, Paris, Rome, Florence, Strasbourg, and Valladolid. A strange thing happened, though. Columbus's text mentioned the queen as well as the king, and the trip had been an entirely Castilian undertaking sponsored by Isabella, yet almost all the printed versions named or depicted Ferdinand as the trip's patron and sponsor. Some versions even included woodcuts of Ferdinand dressed in armor. None gave any credit to the queen, observes Columbus biographer Morison, finding the omissions "curious."[44] And when they mentioned the islands that Columbus had named, they specified Fernandina and the others; but the island he had named for the queen, La Isabela, was unaccountably renamed La Ysla Bella, or the Beautiful Island.

If Isabella reacted to these embarrassing slights, or if Ferdinand sought to set the record straight, it is unrecorded. Perhaps the new discoveries were more comfortable for everyone if they believed a man had been author of them. That perception allowed Isabella to focus on the work at hand. The task ahead was immense: she had to find a way to ensure that the benefits of the expedition would accrue to her kingdom and her people. She had to make sure the lands would belong to Castile, and she had to be able to appeal for final judgment to the highest kind of arbiter.

And so once again, she reached out to Rome, to the Vatican, where her ally, the Spaniard Rodrigo Borgia, had just been enthroned as pope and had taken the name Alexander VI.

SIXTEEN

BORGIA GIVES HER
THE WORLD

As luck would have it, Rodrigo Borgia had been elected pope in August 1492, the same month that Columbus set off on his voyage of discovery. It was only the second time in history that a Spaniard had been named to the church's highest office, and his tenure was to be memorable in many ways.

It started with the most sumptuous pontifical ceremony that veteran Vatican-watchers had ever seen. Thirteen contingents of men in armor marched in procession, commanded by the mercenary soldiers known as condottieri. Next came the households of the cardinals in brightly colored uniforms. The cardinals themselves promenaded on horseback, wearing their miters and silken robes. Twelve white horses, conducted at the bridle by twelve handsome youths, preceded the pope. Shops and homes along the parade route were decked in colorful banners; cannons were fired in thundering celebration; frenzied crowds roared "Borgia, Borgia" to welcome the new pontiff.

Borgia made his way by horse or mule from the Vatican Palace to St. Peter's Basilica, taking a seat in a gilded chair while court officials came forward to kiss his feet. Then he climbed to the Chapel of St. Andrew and positioned himself on St. Peter's golden throne. The triple crown of the pope was placed on his head.

Borgia had the highest expectations for his pontificate. He had taken the name of the great Greek conquerer, styling himself Alexander VI. And he was ecstatic. "It was said he put on the papal vestments with an almost childish enthusiasm," writes one historian.[1]

Not everyone in Europe shared this enthusiasm. Already rumors were circulating that the process of selecting the pope had been more secular than spiritual—that Borgia's election had been the result of blatant bribery of the other cardinals, with gifts and church benefices changing hands in exchange for secure votes. Four stout mules had reportedly been needed to move treasure from Borgia's home to that of a key swing vote, Cardinal Ascanio Sforza, who was promptly named to the prestigious post of vice-chancellor of the church.

Buying the papal tiara, if that was what he had done, was not unique to Borgia, however. The purchase of high ecclesiastical office was frowned upon but nevertheless endemic in the Vatican of the Renaissance. It was a world where earthly rewards paid for spectacular pomp and display, and where clerics racked up benefices to enable themselves to indulge in ostentatious shows of wealth.

Some of this wealth was poured into the creation of great artworks to glorify God. On a commission from Pope Sixtus IV, Sandro Botticelli and Domenico Ghirlandaio had created frescoed panels depicting the life of Moses for the walls of the Sistine Chapel. Cardinal Jean de Bilhères de Lagraulas paid Michaelangelo to chisel Jesus and Mary in marble, the poignant *Pietà*. The family of Cardinal Sforza paid for Leonardo da Vinci's rendition of Christ's Last Supper. But the more elevated the physical manifestations of spirituality on Vatican Hill became, it sometimes seemed, the lower the moral quality of its inhabitants.

Church corruption was not new. Decades earlier, in 1458, after Calixtus III, Rodrigo's uncle Afonso de Borgia, died, politicking had been rife as well. Cardinal Enea Silvio Piccolomini met with then-young Cardinal Rodrigo Borgia in the Vatican latrines at dawn, and Borgia told him he had pledged to give his vote to the French cardinal Guillaume d'Estouteville in exchange for a written promise that he could keep his lucrative post as vice-chancellor of the Vatican. Piccolomini told Rodrigo that he was a "young fool," and that Guillaume's promise was worth less than the paper it was written on. Guillaume's loyalties would be to his fellow Frenchmen in the College of Cardinals, he told Borgia; by voting for him, Borgia would end up losing the vice-chancellorship and damaging the church to boot. The next day Borgia shifted his vote to Piccolomini, who had gathered the other necessary votes. Piccolomini assumed the papal tiara as Pope Pius II, and Rodrigo retained his vice-chancellorship and became the elder cleric's favored protégé.

In the next thirty-four years, as three more popes wore the Ring of the Fisherman, Rodrigo prospered. When Pius II died, Rodrigo was again fortunate: his friend Pietro Barbo, who had stayed with him during the anti-Spanish rioting when Calixtus died, became Pope Paul II. Rodrigo had been ill during the conclave in which Pietro Barbo was chosen, but his longtime alliance with the future pope left him in good stead nonetheless.

Two more popes had followed—Sixtus IV, the one who sent Rodrigo to Spain as a papal legate when he had proved so helpful to Isabella and Ferdinand; and then Innocent VIII, who had served as the Holy Father from 1484 to 1492. As Innocent VIII lay dying, he bemoaned the woeful state of the church and told the cardinals gathered around his deathbed that he bitterly regretted that he had himself been such a disappointment. His pious views were noted, but his change of heart came too late to correct the ruinous course of events he had set in motion by urging investigations into witchcraft in northern Europe, selling ecclesiastical posts to the highest bidders, and inviting King Charles VIII, with the assurance of papal support, to invade Italy and take possession of the Kingdom of Naples.

During those years when he was a high-ranking functionary, Cardinal Rodrigo Borgia had continued to perform as a trusted official of the Catholic Church, known for his intelligence, perceptiveness, and diligence in performing his assigned tasks. He was also notable for his adroit maneuvering within the Vatican, and his steady accumulation of lucrative church benefices and posts. Rodrigo was given the bishoprics of Albano, Porto–Santa Rufina, Valencia, Cartagena, and Majorca. He had possessions in Italy, too, including Nepi, Civita Castellana, and Soriano, strongholds controlling the Via Cassia and Via Flaminia, main arteries to the north of Rome. In 1482, he received the rights to the revenues generated by the Abbey of Subiaco, which controlled twenty-two villages. He similarly received the revenues from the Abbey of Fossanova, on the route to Naples. This meant that he controlled key properties on the entry and exit roads to the north and south of Rome.

Some of his expanding empire of benefices came to him with the blessing of King Ferdinand of Aragon. Valencia, Cartagena, and Majorca were all parts of Ferdinand's dominions. Then with Ferdinand's acquiescence, Rodrigo became the first archbishop of Valencia, when the city was elevated to a higher ecclesiastic status.

Rodrigo's rise at the Vatican occurred in parallel with that of his countrymen back home in Spain, whose prestige was growing almost daily. The conquest of Granada was viewed throughout Europe as the most significant military achievement of Christian forces in centuries. It was even viewed as partial compensation for the loss of the great Christian capital of Constantinople. Rodrigo Borgia had played up those associations to the hilt, staging an elaborate celebration in the streets of Rome when Isabella and Ferdinand completed the seven-hundred-year-long Reconquest in January 1492: "The event was celebrated in Rome by illuminations and bonfires and diversions of every kind, including a bull fight, in which five bulls were slain, the first entertainment of its kind that had ever been seen in Rome, and which was the special contribution of Cardinal Rodrigo Borgia."[2]

* * *

The resounding victory in Granada was no small thing for Cardinal Borgia, because the Italians who predominated in the church hierarchy were disposed to look upon foreigners with contempt. Rodrigo's high position left him vulnerable to criticism as an outsider, and he valued his ties and support from home. Spain's increased prestige increased his own as well.

But the relationship between Rodrigo Borgia and the Spanish sovereigns had encountered some stumbling blocks. When Isabella heard about Rodrigo's rise to the papal tiara in the early fall of 1492, she was conflicted. Borgia was a subject of theirs, which was of course advantageous to Ferdinand and Isabella, and she knew him personally. He had helped her obtain the throne, and she had reason to be grateful to him. He started off on a good note, promising to reform the church and cleanse Rome of its rampant street crime. Taking a leaf from Isabella's playbook, he initiated a thorough search for gang leaders and murderers, and when wrongdoers were apprehended, they were promptly hanged until dead, their bodies left rotting on the gallows along the Tiber River.[3] He also proposed some important reconstruction work in the now-faded capital of the Roman Empire. He built a roadway, the Via Alexandrina (later called the Borgo Nuovo), to make a grand approach from Castel Sant'Angelo to St. Peter's and the Vatican.[4] He also initiated some beautification projects at the holiest of Rome's shrines, something Isabella warmly applauded.

But Isabella also had some serious concerns about Pope Alexander VI's morality and fitness for a post of such importance. Publicly she and Ferdinand expressed pleasure at the news of his elevation, but privately they indicated their reservations. According to the Italian humanist Peter Martyr, who had worked at the Vatican before moving to Castile to join Isabella's court, the sovereigns feared that although Rodrigo was brilliant and had great potential for good, he also demonstrated troubling character flaws and possessed ferocious ambition in seeking to advance the fortunes of his many illegitimate children. To Martyr, the parentage of the children, who were becoming young adults, was undisputed. He referred specifically to Borgia's sons in numerous letters over more than a decade, and his opinion was shared by others in the pope's inner circle in the Vatican.

"There is no movement of the mind in my Sovereigns for joy on account of this thing, no serenity of brow," Peter Martyr wrote soon after Borgia had been named pope. "They seem to foretell rather a tempest in the Christian world than tranquil ports and they are more grieved because he basely boasts that he has sacrilegious children than [glad] because he is a subject of theirs. They suspect that there will be a disruption of Peter's tiara." But they would hope for the best, he wrote: "If perchance Christian charity should overcome the paternal power of nature he will establish a bridge to heaven for all Christians stronger than a pillar of stone. . . . God grant that we may hear that he has turned his ability, in which he very much abounds, to the better part."[5]

To his friends in Rome, Peter Martyr expressed concern about the rumors circulating that Rodrigo had paid bribes to secure the papacy, something Martyr feared would injure the Christian faith if it were to be exposed. "Someone has whispered in my ear . . . base, sacrilegious and criminal things, as that your patron had built the steps to that height of affairs not by letters or continence or fervor of charity, but that he has made himself a ladder of gold and silver and great promises," he wrote to Franciscus, a Valencian, a friend of the pope. "If that is so, this ladder is placed against the walls of Paradise, so that Christ may be thrown down, not worshipped, for the acquiring of glory." Moreover, the balance of power in Italy and Europe could be upset if Rodrigo persisted in his "insane desire to raise his sons to the highest."[6]

Peter Martyr took the extraordinary step of expressing his concerns to one of the men alleged to have benefited most directly from Borgia's bounty, Cardinal Ascanio Sforza, a childhood friend of Martyr's from Milan who had supported Borgia's campaign for the papacy and was raised by him to the position of vice-chancellor.

> But take this, Most Illustrious Prince, that my Sovereigns are
> neither pleased at the death of Pope Innocent [n]or that the Ponti-
> ficate should have come to Alexander, although their subject.
> For they fear lest his greed, his ambition, and what is worse his
> softness toward his children should drag the Christian church
> headlong. Nor are you free from a mark because you are said to
> have helped the man to be raised. . . . May God turn it well and
> grant that he may keep a grateful mind toward you and your
> family.[7]

Similar concerns were being raised by idealistic and pious Christians across Europe, who believed that the church was becoming dangerously corrupt and that the secular power of the papacy was growing. Many deeply devout Spaniards, including Isabella, were disturbed by this state of affairs. She was doing much to try to elevate the morals and standards of the Catholic Church in Spain, so it was particularly disheartening to see serious misconduct at the apex of the church hierarchy in Rome.

Isabella's ambassador to the Vatican, the Castilian Bernardino López de Carvajal, had been invited to address the assembled cardinals for Holy Mass on August 6, 1492, as the men entered the conclave to choose the new pope. He used the opportunity to deliver a fiery sermon on what he saw as a spiritual crisis in the church and the need to select an upstanding man to replace Pope Innocent VIII:

> It is fallen, it is fallen, that glorious majesty of the Church of
> Rome, which used to stand so high! . . . At the present time, we
> are suffering from even deeper wounds. These vices expose us to
> the disobedience of our inferiors, to the contempt of peoples and
> princes, to the mockeries and plunder of the Turks; for while we
> are engaged in our pleasures, our ambitions and our cupidities,
> the majesty of the ecclesiastical throne vanishes, and all vigilance
> of pastoral care is thrust aside.

He called for the election of a pontiff who would lead and inspire, holy enough to perform what he said would be "little short of a miracle to lift the Church from so deep a ruin, almost from a dunghill."[8]

One particular concern was that cardinalships and other high church positions were being filled by relatives of powerful prelates, nobles, and kings, not by learned people with a true religious vocation. These coveted posts generated substantial amounts of revenue, without a specific requirement that the holder perform any work on behalf of parishioners. Many people who held high ecclesiastical offices therefore never even bothered to set foot in the dioceses given to their care. Previous efforts had been made to stop this plague of nepotism. In 1458, for example, the cardinals gathered in the conclave had attempted to use the passing of Pope Pius II as an occasion for improving and cleansing church administration. They gave almost unanimous support to a petition that called for structural changes at the Vatican. Every cardinal promised that, if he were elected, he would institute specific reforms. The pledge called for the Sacred College of Cardinals to be limited to twenty-four members, so as to give each of them a greater voice. It called for a ban on appointing cardinals younger than thirty and those who were uneducated. It limited each pope to naming only one nephew as cardinal. It called for the pope to govern more democratically, requiring him to seek approval from the College of Cardinals before entering into political alliances or disposing of church property. It required a promise to make war on the Turks. It was agreed that soon after the election, the new pope would announce this pledge and all that it entailed.

But these pledged reforms were never enacted. When Rodrigo's friend Pietro Barbo was elected pope, taking the name Paul II, his first act was to quietly repudiate the pledge. In exchange for retaining the power held by the pope, however, he upgraded the cardinals in status. He ordered them to wear silken robes that were red, the most costly color of dye. He ordered them to travel with corps of retainers, and he made sure that those who had limited funds received payments from the church to boost their incomes. He in essence transformed them into princes of the church. This new emolument made the repudiation of the pledge more palatable to the Sacred College, but it also accentuated the perception of unseemly clerical worldliness and avarice. Then Paul II named three of his nephews as cardinals.

The role of nephews in the Vatican was particularly vexing. Being pope was a difficult job, typically undertaken by a man in advanced years, and new pontiffs naturally would want some people standing at their side who had only their best interests at heart. Aging people typically turn to their adult children to perform that role. In the presumptive absence of children, nephews were the next best thing. But many of the nephews who got appointed were simple loyalists that the church supported in luxury, having little apparent religious calling.

Several popes in fact had children of their own, but usually they had been born before the men joined the priesthood, or they had died before the cleric assumed a high-visibility position. Innocent VIII had two illegitimate children, conceived before he entered the clergy. Others may have had children but discreetly concealed their parentage by calling them nephews or cousins.

Concealing the existence of children was considered necessary because one of the key tenets of advancement in Christian leadership was the vow of celibacy. In the early church, almost all clerics had been married men. Christ is believed to have been unmarried, but most of his apostles had wives. As the Roman Catholic Church grew wealthier, however, celibacy was required in the belief that it represented an institutionalized disdain for earthly pleasures and made it easier for clerics to concentrate on the work at hand. It also ensured that the church could maintain better control of its financial resources, without fear that funds would be siphoned off for the children of church officials.

Once Rodrigo Borgia became pope, however, a group of about a half dozen young people emerged in close association with him. These young adults have attracted avid attention among generations of historians. Rodrigo himself was mysterious on the subject of their parentage. Some scholars have chosen to believe that they were his nieces and nephews. To the Spanish, however, their parentage was no secret and unquestionable. Rodrigo's growing brood of illegitimate children were not concealed to them because he was busy seeking positions of wealth and power for them in Spain. No one is sure exactly how many there were, or how old they were, or who their mothers were, but certainly there was a crew of young people over whom he kept a careful eye, and whose advancement he seemed to value as his own.

They were remarkably attractive children, beautiful and intelligent, and perhaps it proved impossible for Rodrigo to forgo taking credit for their existence. They began making their appearance in society while Rodrigo was still a cardinal.

The one believed to be the eldest was named Pedro Luis, and Rodrigo was particularly eager to make a place for him. In May 1483 he provided him with 50,000 ducats to buy a fiefdom in Spain; that November Pope Sixtus IV issued a bull declaring that, in the eyes of the church, despite any possible questions about his parentage, Pedro's birth was legitimate. His property and name secured, Pedro traveled to Spain when he was about twenty and joined the Spanish in the war against Granada. He served bravely at the siege of Ronda. At the end of 1485, Ferdinand gave the young man the prestigious title of Duke of Gandía, which included the right of hereditary transmission. A dukedom is the highest level of nobility, inferior only to kings and princes, and it was a valuable grant. The town of Gandía was delightful, beautifully laid out and located near the sea. Soon Pedro Luis built two imposing homes in Aragon, including one in Gandía and a city home in Valencia.

Moreover, King Ferdinand welcomed the young Borgia into his family, giving his approval for Pedro Luis to marry his young cousin, María Enríquez de Luna. The marriage couldn't occur right away because María Enríquez was not yet of age, but this betrothal gave the Borgias a direct marital tie to the Spanish royal family.

Unfortunately the promising young man died on a vacation in 1488 while visiting his family in Italy. But there were heirs to spare back in Rome. The child next in line to assume Pedro's estate and title was called Giovanni in Italy and Juan in Spain; Pedro Luis had named him as his beneficiary in his will. That meant that Juan would become the next Duke of Gandía.

There were at least three other youngsters. Cesare, handsome and sharp-witted, was destined for the priesthood, as was the custom for younger sons of noble families. By age six he was an apostolic protonotary; three months later he was named a canon of Valencia Cathedral, archdeacon of Játiva, and rector of Gandía. He was legitimized by Pope Sixtus in 1480. When his father became pope, young Cesare, then about sixteen, became archbishop of Valencia, which made him, theologically speaking, responsible for the pastoral care of everyone who lived in the province of Valencia and the Balearic islands of the Mediterranean.

A daughter Lucrezia, meanwhile, was noted for her sweet disposition and extraordinary beauty, with long, flowing golden hair and a graceful step to her walk. And there was at least one other son, a boy named Jofre.

But even the appearance of sexual immorality by clerics was anathema to Isabella. She was relentless in cleaning up corruption and nepotism within the Spanish Catholic Church, and she selected for her own religious advisers men of impeccable moral authority, chaste living, and asceticism. She had chosen as her personal confessor Hernán de Talavera, on the basis of his strict adherence to Christ-like simplicity and compassion, and when she completed her conquest of Granada, she elevated Talavera, who was from a converso family, to the important new post of archbishop of Granada, charging him with the religious shepherding of a greatly expanded flock in Andalusia, and sent him to Granada to supervise the church's progress there.

To replace him as her confessor, she chose a hermitic former monk named Cisneros, who traveled from place to place by foot, begging for bread to eat, a practice dating from the earliest mendicant traditions. The prelate wore a coarse undergarment designed to chafe his skin, known as a hair shirt, to remind himself of the sufferings of the church martyrs, slept at night on a wooden board, and was rumored to flagellate himself as punishment for his perceived sins and shortcomings. She asked Cisneros, who joined her court with the greatest reluctance, to govern her soul with the same diligence he did his own.

Not unsurprisingly, friction emerged between Isabella and Pope Alexander VI. Early on, she complained to his ambassador to her court, Francisco des Prats, that the pope was behaving immorally by ostentatiously flaunting his out-of-wedlock children. Franciscus told her that Alexander's activities were not really out of the ordinary for recent popes. He reported their conversation back to the pope and told him that he had essentially told the queen that she was being naïve. "And I revealed to her some things about Pope Sixtus and Pope Innocent, demonstrating how much more worthily Your Holiness behaved than the aforesaid [pontiffs]," he wrote to Alexander.[9]

The marriage arrangements for the Borgia adolescents soon caused international complications. Lucrezia had been promised to first one and then another of two Catalan gentlemen. That second engagement was terminated in November 1492.[10] With her father having won the papacy, bigger things were in store for Lucrezia now.

Another, more prestigious marriage was being arranged for her, this time with Giovanni Sforza, a minor prince of the important Sforza family of Milan. He was the lord of the pretty town of Pesaro, on the Adriatic Coast. The marriage negotiations were conducted with some secrecy because of the earlier nuptials that had been planned. Marriages of ranking nobility in Spain needed approval by the sovereigns, and King Ferdinand had given his official blessing to the previous match. Then the cast-off bridegroom inconveniently showed up in Rome, requiring the pope and the Duke of Milan to pay him off to go away.

Once that matter was tended to, however, wedding plans for the new match could proceed. The ceremony was held within the Vatican. The lovely bride, Lucrezia, arrived wearing a sumptuous gown, bedecked with shining jewels. She was accompanied into the hall by nineteen-year-old Giulia Farnese, the spectacularly beautiful woman who many observers believed to be the pope's mistress. The groom wore a long robe made of golden cloth; Lucrezia's brothers Cesare and Juan looked on. The pope and an Italian nobleman officiated at the wedding ceremony. The pair were feted at a banquet attended by church officials and Roman nobles. Isabella was not pleased with news that the elaborate wedding party had been held in the hallowed and sacred halls of the Vatican, and she again communicated her concerns to the pope.

The queen and the pope also differed on the question of heresy and the Jews. The pope thought Ferdinand and Isabella were being unreasonably harsh in their conduct of the Inquisition and in forcing Jews to convert or leave Spain. In Rome, Jews were allowed to settle freely and to maintain their faith if they did not practice it in public. A group of Jews who left Spain took up residence in a camp near the Roman mausoleum of Cecilia Martella, under the protection of the pope.

The Spanish ambassador to the Vatican, Diego López de Haro, was irate when he learned the pope had decided to welcome the Spanish Jews: he insisted that as head of the church, Alexander should be the first to expel them. The pope disregarded him. Ferdinand did not believe this was a matter of kindness or humanity on the pope's part. He said Alexander allowed them to stay only because he could make money out of them by charging them extra taxes. "His Holiness makes money out of everything he can sell!" Ferdinand snorted.[11]

* * *

Despite these differences, Isabella was not looking for a showdown. She had some important business to conduct with the pope, and for now, points of contention were set aside. As soon as she received word from Columbus about his discoveries, she set out to make certain that she would have sole right to whatever had been found. She forwarded Columbus's letter to the pope, asking for a determination on the ownership of these islands, even before the Genoese arrived in her court. Isabella must have sent her request to the pope by swift messengers as soon as she got word of Columbus's discoveries.

The astute pope immediately understood, as Isabella had, the significance of the discoveries and the need for prompt action. He also understood that he owed much to the Spaniards, and particularly to Ferdinand. In addition to the political cover and support they afforded him, Ferdinand had allowed Cardinal Borgia, before becoming pope, to hold three lucrative Aragonese bishoprics at the same time, had provided a document that legitimized the pope's son Cesare, and had nominated young Cesare to the bishoprics of Pamplona and Valencia. Ferdinand then agreed to permit the teenager to further rise to the rank of archbishop in Valencia.

In 1493, early in his tenure, Pope Alexander was eager to similarly accommodate Isabella and promptly issued four bulls on the New World. (Bulls were legal documents stamped with a seal of lead, or *bulla,* giving them special authenticity and significance.) All four gave Isabella exactly what she had asked. According to the twentieth-century historian Samuel Eliot Morison:

> Eager to square himself with his royal patrons, he practically let
> them dictate a series of papal bulls on the new discoveries, with-
> out considering the just claims of Portugal. These four bulls were
> not arbitrary decisions. They were acts of papal sovereignty in
> favor of Castile based on the Holy Father's presumed right to dis-
> pose of newly discovered lands and heathen peoples not hitherto
> possessed or governed by any Christian princes.[12]

Three papal bulls concerning the discovery were issued on May 3 and 4, 1493, amazingly prompt for such formal documents, given that Christopher Columbus had arrived in Lisbon only two months earlier. Multiple copies of the bulls were made so that future explorers could display them to anyone who might be inclined to dispute the claims.

In the formal introductions of all four documents, the pope greeted both Ferdinand and Isabella, but interestingly, the bulls gave the discovered lands specifically to the rulers of "Castile and León," meaning that the lands belonged to Isabella alone. Ferdinand, always quick to angle for personal advantage, must have thought that the new lands would prove to be relatively valueless; otherwise he would certainly have made sure that the documents gave him specific rights as well.

The bull dated May 4, 1493, known as *Inter Caetera*, neatly gave half the globe to Queen Isabella. This grant of papal sovereignty did

> give, concede and assign . . . all islands and mainlands found and to be found, discovered and to be discovered towards west and south, [by] establishing and constituting one line from the Arctic pole, that is the north, to the Antarctic pole, that is the south, whether the mainlands and islands found and to be found are towards Indian or [toward] any other part whatever; which line shall be distant from any of the islands, which are commonly called the Azores and Cape Verde, one hundred leagues towards west and south,[13]

as long as the new lands were not possessed by any other Christian king.

Pope Alexander stressed, however, that these rights were granted in the expectation that religious evangelization was the primary object of the enterprise of discovery. He expected Ferdinand and Isabella to build upon their record of success in expanding Catholicism in Spain. *Inter Caetera* emphasized proselytizing as the justification for the territorial grant:

> Among other works agreeable to the Divine Majesty and desirable to our heart this is truly the most important, that the Catholic Faith and the Christian religion, particularly in our times, shall be exalted and everywhere amplified and spread, [and] that the salvation of souls may be provided for and barbarous nations subjugated and brought to the very true faith. And whereas we are called to this Holy Seat of Saint Peter by the favour of Divine clemency, though not with like merits, and recognizing that you as true Catholic Kings and Princes, such as know that you have ever been, and as your famous deeds already well known to almost the entire world prove, not merely desired this, but with every possible effort study and diligence, sparing no labours, no expenses, no dangers, shedding even your own blood, are accomplishing it and have devoted to this aim already for a long time your entire mind

and all your efforts, such as attests the recovery of the kingdom
of Granada from the tyranny of the Saracens, achieved in these
very times with such great glory to the Divine name. Justly we are
induced and not undeservedly, and we ought even spontaneously
and graciously to concede to you the means whereby you may be
enabled to prosecute a purpose so sacred and praiseworthy and
so agreeable to the immortal God with daily increasing fervor to
the glory of God himself and the propagation of the Christian
Empire.[14]

The pope wrote, in the same bull, that the colony that his "beloved
son Christopher Columbus" had established in the New World, with
"one sufficiently well fortified tower, in which he has placed certain
Christians who had gone with him," had begun the process of establishing the new empire.[15] He was referring, of course, to the little community
that Columbus had left behind when the *Santa María* ran aground.

The Portuguese, naturally, were not happy with the pope's ruling on
who had which rights to undiscovered lands. Isabella and King João of
Portugal therefore negotiated their own division of the globe, in talks
held in Castile, at the town of Tordesillas. The agreement they reached in
June 1494, known as the Treaty of Tordesillas, pushed the north-to-south
dividing line west to 370 leagues from the islands of Cape Verde, instead
of the pope's 100 leagues to the west, thereby allowing Portugal to retain
all rights to the coast of Africa that Castile had already conceded. The
Portuguese were pleased: they may have sent exploratory ships west as
soon as Columbus came back in 1493 and found a large bulge of land
in the east of the South American continent, present-day Brazil, which
would now fall within their sphere. The resolution of the dispute, at least
at this time, and from the perspective of Isabella and João, was that Spain
now owned the western side of the new lands, and Portugal owned the
southern section, which included both Brazil and the African coast. The
two cousins had divided the cookie in half.

* * *

Now other parts of the world had to be apportioned as well. Ferdinand,
for his part, wanted the pope to favor his Neapolitan relations to govern
the Kingdom of Naples. At the time Rodrigo became pope, Ferdinand's
younger sister, Juana, was queen of Naples, married to their cousin, Fer-

rante, who was king. Rodrigo, in fact, had performed the wedding ceremony and coronation for them.[16] The ruling families of Aragon and Naples, therefore, were closely linked and generally allies.

Naples was a very rich kingdom, heavily populated, with a spectacular physical setting; the kingdom's holdings comprised the entire southern half of the Italian peninsula. Naples consequently played a huge role in Mediterranean commerce and was eyed with envy by a number of other European powers, including, most notably, France. The French believed they had a legitimate claim to the Kingdom of Naples because they had held the throne before it was taken by conquest by Alfonso the Magnanimous, Ferdinand's uncle. The pope was being asked for a final determination on who the rightful king or queen should be. The previous pope, Innocent VIII, had feuded with Ferrante and decided he preferred King Charles VIII of France, which obviously created potential problems.

In addition, the ruling family of Milan, the Sforza clan, was also feuding with the family of King Ferrante of Naples. Ludovico Sforza added his encouragement to Charles VIII, telling him that if he invaded Italy and seized Naples, the Sforzas would help him. All this meant that pressures were mounting on the Neapolitan rulers, even as the new pope, Rodrigo Borgia, took office. King Ferrante of Naples and King Ferdinand of Aragon wanted to make sure the pope endorsed Ferrante's continuing control of the realm.

To aid his cousins, Ferdinand made an offer that Alexander VI couldn't refuse. In mid-year 1493, Diego López de Haro, the Spanish envoy to the Vatican, went to the papal court to offer his homage. In exchange for the pope's support for the Aragonese claims to the throne of Naples, he was authorized to offer to permit Borgia's son Juan to marry Ferdinand's cousin María Enríquez de Luna. This was a great opportunity for the social-climbing Borgia clan. Alexander told his son Juan that he wanted this royal connection but was also hoping to obtain former Moorish estates in Granada from Queen Isabella, now or in the near future.[17]

There was another alliance-building nuptial proposition as well. The Neapolitan ruling family offered King Ferrante's illegitimate granddaughter, Sancia, in marriage to the pope's son Jofre, along with a generous dowry. It gave the pope yet another royal nuptial for his offspring, and the two teenagers were married in 1494.

In exchange, the pope gave Kings Ferdinand and Ferrante what they requested, which was continuing control of Naples in Trastámara family hands. When Ferrante died in early 1494, the pope announced that the crown would go to Ferrante's son Alfonso, not to King Charles VIII of France. That decision, of course, angered both the French and the Milanese, who began to plot together to upend the pope's decision and undermine his alliance with the House of Aragon.

The marriage between Juan Borgia and Ferdinand's cousin María Enríquez was an extravagant and memorable affair, representing as it did the triumph of the Aragonese Borgia clan, who had now made good. Juan was sent with an entourage and presents worthy of a royal wedding. His father loaded him up with valuable merchandise to take to Spain, including "boxes and boxes of rich velvet, damask, brocade, cloth of silver, satin and furs . . . cushions, bedcovers studded with gold, bed hangings in white damask brocade with gold fringes and crimson satin lining, tapestries woven with the history of Alexander the Great, and of Moses, huge quantities of table silver." And there were jewels: a pendant with a huge emerald and a huge diamond for Juan to wear attached to his cap, and for the duchess, a golden cross studded with pearls and diamonds, encapsulating a piece of the True Cross, which had been placed there by the Holy Father himself.[18]

The ostentatiousness of the enterprise attracted much critical comment. "This Duke leaves very rich and loaded with jewels, money and other valuable portable goods and silver," the Mantuan envoy reported. "It is said he will return within a year but leave all his goods in Spain and come back to reap another harvest."[19]

When Juan married María Enríquez in September 1493, he became a cousin to King Ferdinand and a relation by marriage to the most elite families in Spain. But the young man behaved badly from the moment of his arrival. He drank prodigiously, gambled heavily, spent many hours in brothels, and entertained himself by such reprehensible pastimes as shooting dogs and cats for sport. His father even heard a disturbing report—which soon proved untrue—that his son had failed to consummate the marriage. In fact, his wife became pregnant twice in short order, giving him a son and a daughter.

Juan did not earn high marks among the Spaniards. "A very mean young man, full of false ideas of grandeur and bad thoughts, haughty, cruel and unreasonable," one observer remarked.[20] His conduct did not endear him to Ferdinand and Isabella either, and they did not protest when he was called home to Rome for a visit of undetermined duration. His wife, María Enríquez, stayed behind, raising the children on her own.

Meanwhile, the pope's administration of the Vatican was making people angry. Alexander VI was facing outright rebellion from the College of Cardinals. In an effort to bolster his control over the group, he proposed an unprecedented thirteen new candidates for membership. Three were his secretaries, a fourth was Alessandro Farnese, brother of the beguiling Giulia, and a fifth was his own son Cesare. The existing cardinals objected strenuously, but the pope said he intended to make the change whether they liked it or not, and so he did. At a meeting of the consistory on September 20, eleven cardinals appeared; seven voted for the pope's plan and four abstained. Ten other cardinals, however, boycotted the meeting.[21]

Thus it was with limited support that Cesare Borgia was invested as cardinal in a ceremony on September 23, 1493. It was obvious to everyone that he had no religious vocation whatsoever, and very soon he began to make it clear he wanted to be released from his clerical vows.

The Borgia controversies at the Vatican came at a time when tensions were bubbling over on the Italian peninsula. The region had never established any sort of central administration, leaving civil governance dangerously unstable because of the ferocious competition and constant bickering among its largest city-states, which included Venice, Milan, Rome, Florence, and Naples. Milan, Naples, and Rome were at odds over the throne of Naples. Venice was facing a losing war against the Turks over its Balkan possessions. And there was a power vacuum in Florence. The statesman Lorenzo de' Medici had died in 1492, leaving his maladroit son Piero in his stead.

Milanese humanist Peter Martyr believed Italy was on the verge of war. "The Italian princes I think are turning the times to their own ruin," he wrote in September 1492, describing the hatred and jealousy brewing in Milan and Naples, which seemed likely to provoke a violent intervention by France: " . . . Thus Italy forges by degrees the sword by which to kill herself."[22]

Indeed, the French were preparing their invasion. To make sure that the Spanish would not intervene when they marched south, King Charles reached out to King Ferdinand to offer to return Roussillon and Perpignan—the lands mortgaged away by Ferdinand's father, Juan, when he was putting down the civil uprising in Aragon. Spain and France began negotiations. Observers noted that Spain would in effect be stepping away from any oversight role in Italy as a result of the treaty, and it seemed like one more piece of proof that a war between the Italians and the French was on its way.

For it was becoming increasingly clear that Pope Alexander VI did not have the moral authority to act as a stabilizing force in the land where the Catholic Church made its home. At a church consistory on June 12, 1493, Spanish envoy López de Haro denounced the pope's foreign policy, saying it was keeping Italy "in a constant state of war," and he also criticized "the venality of his curia, the scandalous auction of benefices."[23]

But these differences were muted—at least for now—by the shared religiosity of Pope Alexander VI and his patrons in Spain. Unquestionably, they were all deeply committed to their practice of Catholicism, if not to its underlying values, and they sought to communicate their faith in ways that would increase the church's prestige.

This was the period when Ferdinand, Isabella, and Pope Alexander VI pushed ahead with architect Donato Bramante to design and construct the commemorative tomb called the Tempietto in Rome. A masterpiece of High Renaissance art with precise echoes of the classical world, the building was commissioned by Isabella and Ferdinand, and decorated with the scallop-shell motif that represents Santiago de Compostela and pilgrimage in Spain. Its foundation stone, planted in the wall in 1502, bore the names of Ferdinand and Isabella, written in faux medieval script. Isabella and Cardinal Bernardino López de Carvajal collaborated to collect more than five dozen holy relics for the site, including pieces of the True Cross and fragments from the crib of the infant Jesus. The building struck observers in Rome as something completely new and innovative; it was also a visual representation of the ways in which the joint reign of Isabella and Ferdinand marked the transition between the Middle Ages and the modern era.

Another shared Spanish endeavor was the splendid redecoration of the Basilica of Santa Maria Maggiore, a large church in Rome, dedicated to Christ's mother. The pope paid for construction of the building's magnificent gilded ceiling; the actual gold used was said to be among the first of the precious metal to be brought back from the New World, and was a gift to the church from Isabella.[24]

The queen and the pope shared a belief in the importance of the discoveries in the New World and a sense that the church was destined to make great progress there. In his private apartments at the Vatican,

Alexander VI commissioned a monumental painting by Pinturicchio, done sometime between 1492 and 1494, that showed the pope kneeling in prayer before the Risen Christ. This work, called *The Resurrection,* contains in the background, just above Christ's empty tomb, a depiction of native Americans. They are shown as naked, strong, and muscular, wearing feathered headdresses. It is the first known representation of Indians in European art, and the decision to include them in this masterpiece underscores the pope's early interest and awareness of the pivotal significance of bringing Christianity to a new land.

The pope's quick appreciation of the issue paved the way for Isabella to impose her own religious values, in ways both good and bad, on an entire new hemisphere. She brought in Castilian-style education, health care, political systems, and spiritual values to millions of people. She also introduced the Inquisition to the New World, soon after it had taken root in Spain. It meant that the uniquely Spanish combination of intellectual inclinations—broad-mindedness in secular matters combined with intolerance of religious differences—made the leap across the ocean, where it would affect cultural and political life in Latin America for more than five hundred years.

But the pope's most valuable gift to Isabella and to Spain's future was the fact that he had carved the world in half and given such an important part to Isabella. All in all, it was an extraordinary transaction—first that an individual would have the audacity to divide up the planet, and second that the Catholic Church was so powerful that many people in generations to come never even considered defying the ruling.

The gift was immediately questioned by native Americans in the New World, however, when they were later informed that the pope had taken land occupied by millions of them and ceded it to the Europeans with a wave of a pen and a dollop of sealing wax. They struggled to grasp the concept that one man—the pope—would be believed to have that much power over heaven and earth.

When it was described to two Indian Cenu chiefs in Colombia in 1512, they shook their heads in wonder. "The Pope must have been drunk," one said to the other.[25]

SEVENTEEN

LANDS OF VANITY
AND ILLUSION

I n the centuries since 1492, generations of scholars have heatedly
debated who actually were the first non-Americans to step on the
shores of the New World. Some say the credit should go to Norse-
men, or Welsh, or Africans, or Polynesians, or, most recently, Chinese.
Some or all of these people may in fact have gotten a glimpse or more
of the Americas before Columbus did. They looked, they left. But one
thing is certain: only one person in history immediately recognized the
importance of the discovery, claimed it for herself, and turned the venture promptly into a keenly pursued enterprise that resulted in one of the
most dramatic population shifts in history. And that person was Queen
Isabella.

She alone of all the rulers of those various lands appreciated from the
start the significance of what had been found and took effective steps to
institutionalize future expeditions and colonize the Americas. The English and French lagged behind by a century, finally claiming the leftover
lands in North America that the Spaniards had found unappealing. The
Portuguese at first focused their efforts on mercantile exchange, creating
only a network of trading posts that supported their trade routes. The
Spanish, however, resettled themselves in great numbers almost immediately, intermingling the blood of Castilians and native Americans to
forge a new people.

Soon after Columbus's return in 1493, Queen Isabella came to the conclusion that what he had found was too momentous for any one man, even her friend, to have sole right to exploit. As soon as she secured the pope's blessing, she began to throw resources and effort into forming new expeditions, with proper financial controls, that would primarily benefit her subjects, the Castilians. Within months she sent Columbus back with more men and ships, but she sponsored other explorers as well. Soon ship after ship, with different Castilian captains and crews, was heading west from Seville on her mission.

Columbus was dispatched on three further voyages with varying degrees of success. But in the next decade she sent out at least six other expedition parties as well. Alonso de Hojeda led a group accompanied by the pilot from the first trip: Juan de la Cosa went with Amerigo Vespucci, a Florentine who wheedled his way on board, and after whom the Americas were accidently (and unaccountably) named. Other expeditions were led by Vicente Yáñez Pinzón, the youngest of the three Pinzón brothers; Diego de Lepe, a capable seaman who was a cousin to the Pinzón family; Pedro Alonso Niño, from the Niño maritime family; and Rodrigo de Bastidas, a wealthy merchant from Seville, who was joined by a young man named Vasco Núñez de Balboa.

With her express permission, within the next ten years these expeditions reached and charted thousands of miles of coastline in the Americas. Columbus visited most of the major islands of the Caribbean as well as the coast of Central America. Alonso de Hojeda reached what are now Colombia and Venezuela. Juan de la Cosa explored a cluster of islands off the coasts of Colombia and Panama. Vicente Yáñez Pinzón visited Brazil and was the first European to see the Amazon River. Bastidas, accompanied by Balboa, was the discoverer of mainland Panama. The expedition to Panama was particularly significant because the narrowness of the isthmus at the point soon made it possible to traverse from the Atlantic Ocean to the Pacific. Balboa was the first European to spot the Pacific Ocean from American shores.

Each expedition spawned others, in a cascading effect that continued for decades. Hernán Cortés, who arrived in the Caribbean in 1504, became the conqueror of Mexico and later explored Baja California. Juan Ponce de León, who first went to the New World in 1493, charted the coasts of Florida, in what would become the future United States of America. Francisco Pizarro traveled to the Americas with Alonso de Hojeda in 1509 and conquered Peru in 1533. And the explorations were multigenerational. Pedro de Vera Mendoza helped conquer the island of Gran Canaria in the 1480s; his grandson Álvar Núñez Cabeza de Vaca set out for the coast of Florida, got marooned and enslaved there, and ended up walking for nine years across the south of Texas and the American Southwest before making his way to safety in Mexico.[1]

Isabella's decision to allow others to go exploring was painful to Columbus, who believed he had negotiated the exclusive right to exploration and mercantile exchange in the lands he had discovered. But his original supposition that he had landed in India was soon proved inaccurate, and although Columbus showed himself to be an excellent mariner, he was also exposed as a terrible administrator and a man of poor judgment, something that would soon become obvious to almost everyone.

At first, however, Isabella placed complete confidence in the Italian seafarer. Within a month of Columbus's arrival in Barcelona, she had prepared sixteen royal orders making preparations for his next departure. Using the customary royal boilerplate heading that joined her name with Ferdinand's, Isabella gave him specific instructions for the trip. The first and most important point—and the one that she most fully elaborated—called for the religious instruction of the Indians, whom she said Columbus should "by all ways and means . . . strive and endeavor to win over," to convert them to "our Holy Catholic faith," teaching them Spanish so that they would understand the religious instruction they would receive. To that end, she sent a contingent of twelve priests to begin the missionary work.

Queen Isabella was explicit about how Columbus and his men should interact with the native Americans. She ordered them to "treat the said Indians very well and lovingly and abstain from doing them any injury, arranging that both peoples should hold much conversation and intimacy, each serving the other to the best of their ability." The queen said that if any person were to "maltreat" the Indians "in any manner," Columbus should "punish them severely," under the authority she had granted him as admiral, viceroy, and governor.

She wanted to make sure that the expedition's finances were solidly managed, both as to its initial expenses and as to the income she expected to eventually derive. For better oversight, she put the acquisition of the ships and supplies under the joint control of Columbus and Don Juan de Fonseca, a bureaucrat from an aristocratic family based in Coca, not far from Isabella's family headquarters in Segovia, and whose family had long been faithful servants to the crown. Fonseca was not a mariner, but he was an expert logistician whom Isabella had employed on other complicated tasks. He shared responsibility with Columbus for hiring and expenditures.

New rules and regulations were imposed that determined how the lands would be colonized. Everyone who went on the new explorations was required to register and take an oath of loyalty to the crown of Castile. A customshouse was established in Seville so that the kingdom could track the arrival of shipments from the New World. The right to barter for goods was restricted to the Castilian crown.

* * *

On September 25, 1493, just six months after his triumphant return from the Indies, Columbus set sail on his second voyage. This time he led a much larger enterprise. His effusive description of the wonders of the lands he had found—a paradise where gold was available to be plucked from the ground like the luscious fruits hanging in the trees, free for the taking—had inspired a groundswell of enthusiasm, and people clamored to join the voyagers. This time seventeen ships set out, with some fifteen hundred men participating. There is no complete list of the voyagers, but a number of well-connected courtiers took part this time, including many who would go on to play important roles in future trips of exploration, such as Juan Ponce de León and Alonso de Hojeda, both of whom had already made names for themselves by serving bravely during the war with Granada. A few Aragonese noblemen also joined up, including a man named Mosén Pedro Margarit, who had close and long-standing ties to King Ferdinand.

There was a larger contingent directly linked to the queen and her household, including Diego Álvarez Chanca, the queen's physician; Antonio de Torres, the brother of the crown prince's governess; Melchior Maldonado, a former envoy to the Vatican; and Francisco de Penalos, a courtier of the queen, and his brother, Bartolomé de Las Casas. These last two men told their stories firsthand to Bartolomé's son, who shared his father's name and became one of the first historians of the Indies. Columbus was permitted to take along a few Italian friends, including his brother Diego and a Genoese named Michele de Cuneo.

We have many more sources of information for this second expedition than for the first one. Columbus kept a journal on this trip, and

although his account has not survived, it was accessible to the first generation of historians of the New World. At least three other participants—
the younger Bartolomé de Las Casas, Diego Álvarez Chanca, and Michele
de Cuneo—all wrote letters or books about the second voyage based on
what they saw or heard on good authority. In addition, contemporary
accounts were circulated by historians Gonzalo Fernández de Oviedo y
Valdés and Peter Martyr, who also had inside knowledge of the events.

Columbus had been given everything he asked. He was granted the
fine title of "Viceroy and Admiral of the Ocean Sea and the Indies," which
would be inherited by his children. He had been instructed by the sovereigns to "treat the Indians well and lovingly" but was also given the
specific right to judge civil and criminal cases and punish wrongdoers.
He was authorized to claim new lands for Castile.

Not surprisingly, tension arose between Columbus and Fonseca very
early in the preparations. Columbus saw himself as the unquestioned
commander of the expedition, but Don Juan de Fonseca saw his role as
ensuring that the sovereigns' interests were protected and advanced. The
conflict erupted over a number of small matters: the size of the guard
that would defend Columbus, and the quality of the horses chosen for
the trip. Fonseca was not a sailor or a discoverer, which irritated Columbus, but he was nevertheless a master of planning and managing elaborate enterprises. His function was essentially to serve as the crown's
"chief minister for colonial affairs,"[2] and his role would grow increasingly
powerful over the next few years.

With Fonseca's oversight, Columbus's fleet was generously equipped
for a six-month voyage, with plentiful food, equipment, tools, domesti-
cated animals, seeds to plant, and a substantial quantity of arms. It was a
unique and costly enterprise. "No European nation had ever undertaken
an overseas colonizing expedition on anything approaching this scale,"
writes the naval historian Samuel Eliot Morison.[3]

It was just the first of many follow-up voyages. Soon the crown would
establish a semiregular shuttle service of ships between Europe and the
New World, carrying mail, food, and supplies to the explorers and colonists, and in return hauling back whatever riches could be gleaned from
the territories the crown now claimed as its own.

Columbus and his massive fleet set out from Spain to the Canary
Islands, as they had done before. But this time the Italian explorer was
an important celebrity, and he was feted and squired about the island by
none other than King Ferdinand's former paramour, Beatriz de Boba-

dilla, the still-young niece of Isabella's best friend, whose reputation and behavior had not improved in the intervening years. Amid festivities, island promenades, and blazing cannon salvos, Columbus engaged in an intense amorous fling with Beatriz that lasted three long days, leaving more than a thousand soldiers dawdling, rolling their eyes, and laughing behind Columbus's back at his romantic hijinks.[4] It was not an auspicious beginning for the trip, and word of the dalliance with Ferdinand's former flame almost certainly made its way to the queen.

Once Columbus left the Canary Islands on October 13, however, he made good time. Despite some stormy weather, they arrived in the Indies after a three-week voyage. The first sight of land was a joyous experience, as it had been on the initial trip. "At sunrise on Sunday, November 3, they could see land from all the ships and were as happy as if Heaven had suddenly opened up before them," Las Casas wrote. " . . . They sang the Salve Regina as sailors do at sunrise and marveled at the scent of flowers blowing from the coast; they saw green parrots flying together like thrushes and screeching all the while."[5]

But then things started to go downhill. Soon after their arrival at a string of islands to the east of present-day Puerto Rico, the Castilians encountered a fierce tribe of Indians known as the Caribe, who ran away into the mountains when they saw them. Meanwhile some of the Spaniards were so eager to start searching for treasure that they took off on their own, according to Cuneo. A band of about a dozen set off into the wilderness "for purposes of robbery" and to search for gold.[6] They promptly got lost, forcing Columbus to assign several hundred men in four squadrons to go looking for them.

The Caribe Indians whom the Spaniards had encountered, it turned out, were cannibals, and the horrified Castilians who entered their encampment discovered them cooking up what looked to the Castilians like a dinner of human flesh. They "found salted human legs, hanging from beams as we are accustomed to do with pigs, and the head of a young man recently killed, still wet with blood, and parts of his body mixed in with goose and boiled parrot meat, ready to be in pots, as well as other parts near the fire ready to be roasted on the spits," wrote Peter Martyr to a friend in Italy, having heard the account firsthand from a survivor of the expedition. They also found some captives held by the Caribes, including very plump young women and young men who had been castrated, presumably to make their meat more tender.[7]

Versions of this story were told in all the surviving accounts. Interpretations of their meaning have varied. Some scholars now describe these activities as ceremonial rituals honoring brave enemies or deceased family members. But the explorers' accounts called it cannibalism, and they were united in their belief that the Caribes were using human meat as a source of protein.

This sight, of course, terrified the expeditioners, who concluded that their lost shipmates were probably on the menu elsewhere on the island. But in fact the Spanish brigands had made it to a mountaintop and lit a fire that allowed them to be located. The main party found them and brought them back to the ships with the assistance of a helpful old Indian woman, who showed them the way. The Spaniards left the island, taking with them thirty Indians who had been captured by the Caribes and held under conditions suggesting that they were being enslaved and cannibalized. These now-freed native Americans were eager, at least at first, to leave with the Spaniards.

The Castilians had a series of clashes with Caribes soon afterward, in which a few people on each side were killed. Oviedo, who arrived a few years later and wrote his own history of the first contact between Europeans and Indians, said that the warlike Indians, called *bravos* or braves, were armed with arrows tipped with a toxic substance that attacked the nervous system. There was no available medical treatment—people shot by the arrows "died raving ... and biting their own hands and flesh, regardless of the great pain they were feeling."[8] Some Spaniards who had received poisoned arrow wounds survived, although it wasn't clear why— perhaps good diet or better treatment. Others died, and no one knew what to do for them because different tribes used different kinds of poison. The randomness of it was unnerving and made the others all the more anxious about the unknown dangers they were facing.

By now Columbus was growing increasingly worried about the fate of the thirty-nine colonists he had been forced to leave behind when the *Santa María* was wrecked on the first voyage. He had entrusted them to the care of a seemingly friendly cacique, but now he had reason to feel concerned. The Spanish fleet made its way through the islands toward the place where the colonists had been left, stopping to establish a settlement they called La Isabela, after the queen. It was located on the island variously known as Hispaniola or Santo Domingo, which now comprises Haiti and the Dominican Republic. This island became Castile's primary base of operations and staging area for subsequent expeditions.

Columbus's fellow travelers quickly discovered that he had oversold the pleasures of this new place. The foliage was lush and exotic and the weather was warm and balmy, all true, but insects multiplied quickly in the tropical humidity, leaving the men crazed with mosquito bites. Painful boils erupted on their legs, causing them to sprout infections that sapped their strength; many got sick and died. The provisions from home ran short, and the food available locally was hard to find and difficult for them to digest. "Everyone [was] demoralized by the number of sick, dying and hungry, which, to the healthy among them, was a sad and tearful spectacle," Las Casas wrote.

> The Christians' misery grew stronger every day as the possibilities of relieving it diminished.... And what made it worse was the idea that they were going to die of starvation so far away, without any of the usual consolations afforded a dying man, not even someone to give them a glass of water.... So, then, many noblemen raised in comfort who had never known a day of hardship in their lives found their misery intolerable and some died in a state of great turmoil; even, it is feared, of utter despair.[9]

To survive, the Spaniards were forced to eat dogs and reptiles, but for many even this was not enough. About half the Spaniards were dying of hunger, but the number of Indians who were dying was even greater. They fell ill from exposure to infectious diseases from Europe—smallpox, measles, cholera, typhoid, and bubonic plague among them—that were being introduced to the Americas for the first time. Corpses were everywhere. "The stench grew very great and pestiferous," Oviedo was told.[10]

Riches, meanwhile, were not as easily found as Columbus had said. They could be obtained only through grueling work—mining ore from the ground or in riverbeds, or planting crops, all under a blazing sun.

Worse news soon followed. When Columbus finally reached La Navidad, the place on Hispaniola where he had left the thirty-nine settlers, he found that they had all been killed, probably within the previous month. About a dozen corpses had been left to rot in the sun. Michele de Cuneo said their eyes had been removed; he believed that the Indians had gouged them out to eat them.[11] The village had been burned to the ground.

The cacique, or chief, who Columbus had thought was a friendly ally was vague about what had happened and tried to avoid their questions by pretending to have suffered a leg injury. The Spaniards easily saw through this deception and bickered among themselves about how the cacique should be punished for his role in the deaths. Columbus argued that they could not punish the man without knowing all the facts, and that punishing him could expose them to further attacks by even less friendly natives.

The full story gradually came to light under questioning, as the Indians and the Spaniards became increasingly able to understand each other. The thirty-nine settlers had provoked ill will by stealing food and women from the Indians living nearby. Columbus's son Ferdinand said that the members of the marooned colony had begun fighting among themselves almost as soon as their shipmates departed. The men had claimed "four or five wives apiece"—women they took from Indian men—and they also went in search of gold, quarreling over it. An Indian tribe attacked and killed some of them; others died of sickness.

Without question, however, a large number had been murdered. Some members of the second expedition concluded that Columbus was allowing natives to murder Spaniards with impunity, which they saw as proof of the mariner's weakness or disloyalty to his crewmen. Even some of the missionaries wanted Columbus to take a hard line against the Indians and execute possible perpetrators. Columbus saw that he could be criticized for leniency as well as for harshness.

* * *

On both sides of the Atlantic, Columbus was blamed for the deaths of the men who had been left behind. Spaniards back home had no recognition or understanding of the environment in which the newcomers were trying to operate. No words could describe the extreme culture shock that Spaniards experienced in the New World. People living in this alien environment developed strange fancies and fears. The town of La Isabela, which was soon abandoned, became known as a haunted place where the ghosts of the dead noblemen walked the streets at night, howling and crying.

The reports of the murders, the deaths, and the signs of cannibalism were disturbing to the Spaniards, and some came to view Indians as not fully human. And this, of course, allowed generations of explorers to justify all kinds of barbarities.

Columbus himself permitted many cruelties to occur. In one skirmish the Castilians had captured a Caribe woman, and Columbus's friend Michele de Cuneo asked for her to be given to him. Cuneo took the woman into his cabin on the ship and "conceived desire to take pleasure" from her.[12] She fought him, screaming loudly for help. He whipped her harshly with a rope. Nobody on the ship came to her aid, and finally she submitted. This was the first recorded rape of an Indian woman among many that would occur in the Americas. Columbus did nothing to stop it or interfere, raising the question of what else he might have allowed to happen or done himself.

It was on this second voyage that the massacres of the Indians began as well. Bartolomé de Las Casas described the first serious incident as a violent overreaction by Columbus and the Castilians to a minor provocation. Five Indians who had been instructed to help three colonists ford a river had instead left them stranded and taken some bundles of clothing the Spaniards owned. The cacique of that tribe was believed to have taken the clothing for himself. One of Columbus's attendants, Alonso de Hojeda, was outraged at the theft and imprisoned some of the Indians who had been involved and ordered that one of them should have his ears cut off, a common European penalty for theft at the time. Columbus, however, ordered that three other Indians should be executed for their involvement in the crime. He later relented, but then word came that the cacique's men had attacked some other Christians, as revenge for the threatened executions. The Spanish response to a simple theft of goods had been prompt and brutal, and it established a terrible cycle of action and revenge on both sides. "This was the first injustice committed against the Indians," wrote Las Casas, " . . . and the beginning of the flow of blood which was to flow so copiously from then on all over the island."[13]

Las Casas thought Columbus's ferocity in dealing with the Indians was a direct contradiction of his orders from Queen Isabella about how to interact with them. The sovereigns had given specific instructions that the Spaniards treat the Indians respectfully, sending messengers to arrange parlays, bringing gifts when they did so. Instead, the writer said, Columbus had trespassed on their lands and had not acted in the spirit of "Christian benignity, gentleness and peace."[14]

Columbus also quickly proved himself to be a poor administrator who had difficulty getting the men to follow his orders. He faced an almost constant sequence of mutinies among his crews. This was not entirely his fault. It was proving difficult to get people to accept the chain of command, given the unprecedented problems that were emerging thousands of miles from established authority figures. Fear, disorientation, and resentment created a combustible mix.

Columbus was also viewed with a measure of contempt. Many of the Castilians in the crews were proud of their nationality and looked down upon him because he was a foreigner. His lack of an authentic aristocratic pedigree also devalued him in their eyes, living as they did in a culture that gave prime importance to blood lineage and descent. Many of the people who had joined the expedition, like the Aragonese Mosén Pedro Margarit, were of noble blood, which gave them a sense of entitlement that was hard to overcome. Many did not want to work at all and thought it inappropriate that they were being asked to do so, especially by someone they perceived as belonging to a lower caste.

King Ferdinand's friend Margarit eventually decided he had had enough. Gathering up some other dissidents, he seized three ships and sailed to Spain, rushing to court to tell the king and queen that the expedition was a disaster and that Columbus was committing abuses there. The handful of Aragonese who came along on the trip found that complaints about Columbus could be taken to Ferdinand, who gave them a ready ear.

Without question, Columbus was using a heavy-handed approach in managing his men. "The admiral had to use violence, threats, and constraint to have the work done at all," Las Casas wrote. "As might be expected, the outcome was hatred for the admiral, and this is the source of his reputation in Spain as a cruel man hateful to all Spaniards, a man unfit to rule."[15]

The Spaniards, including Columbus, had grown strangely inured to the pain and suffering of others, particularly the Indians. To them it seemed simply odd that Indian women were willing to jump from the Spanish ships and swim miles to shore through choppy waves to escape and return home. By the time Columbus and some of his men returned to Spain in February 1495, leaving a large contingent behind as colonists, the Indians were deservedly mistrustful of Europeans. On this second trip, the Castilians had captured sixteen hundred native Americans. They couldn't fit them all aboard the ships, so they chose the best of the lot to transport, and some four hundred were released.

The natives' reaction to their own release showed that relations between the Castilians and native Americans had certainly soured. Those who were permitted to go were frantic to get away from the Spaniards, Cuneo noted with some bemusement. Many of the women among the captives had been nursing infants, and they simply abandoned the children in their desperate haste to get away: "They, in order to better escape us, since they were afraid we would turn to catch them again, left their infants on the ground and started to flee like desperate people" into the mountains, running for days to put as much distance as possible between themselves and the Castilians.[16]

Columbus had viewed these slaves as booty that could be sold to make money while the Spaniards figured out how to collect gold and other conventional riches. But Queen Isabella was furious when she learned that the explorer had returned home with ships heavy laden with hundreds of slaves. She had insisted that the Indians be treated kindly. Columbus had disregarded her express order. She ordered that all the slaves be returned to the New World as soon as possible, which was done for some, although by this point many of the Indians had died of cold or exposure to new diseases.

Young Bartolomé de Las Casas saw this firsthand, for his father and uncle had brought him a young male Indian as a slave, and Bartolomé and the boy became friends. When Isabella ordered all the surviving slaves returned to the New World, Bartolomé's friend was sent back as well. That friendship, however, affected the Castilian deeply and began shaping his view toward the Indians, causing him to later become the period's most vocal Indian rights advocate.

The capture of slaves had not been the only way Columbus defied the queen. When she was negotiating with the Portuguese in Tordesillas over the territorial rights to the new lands, she had asked him to return to Spain to help, but he had been preoccupied with his problems in the Caribbean and did not go. She had had to make the case for her rights without his participation, even though he knew more about the lands in question than anyone else.

When Columbus finally returned to Spain from this second voyage, he sought other methods to convince the queen of the importance of his discoveries. He began wearing the garb of a Franciscan priest, perhaps to display his piety to Queen Isabella. But in addition to bringing the slaves, he also came bearing gifts and amazing objects even more splendid than those from the first voyage.

These marvels included, according to people who saw the items, "a collar of gold ... that weighed 600 castellanos," wrote the chronicler Andrés Bernáldez, and also

> crowns, masks, girdles, collars and many woven items made of
> cotton, and in all of them the devil appeared in the shape of a
> cat, or the face of an owl, or other worse shapes made of wood ...
> he carried some crowns with wings, and they had golden eyes on
> their sides ... and especially a crown that they said belonged to the
> cacique Caonabo, which was very big and tall, with wings on its
> eyes like a shield and golden eyes as large as silver cups weighing
> half a mark, each one placed there as if enameled in a very strange
> and ingenious manner, and the devil too was represented on that
> crown; and I believed that so he appeared to them, and that they
> were idolators and regarded the devil as their lord.[17]

To Castilian eyes, these items underscored the mortal peril to the souls of the people living in the islands and made new evangelization efforts more urgent.

By now, however, some of the novelty of the discovery was wearing off, and criticism of Columbus and his administration of Hispaniola was fully setting in. "There were great rumblings against him, that he had not found gold," Bernáldez wrote, and people heard stories that the earlier colonists were starving to death: "There were reports that the people there were in great want of necessities."[18]

Isabella continued to view Columbus with friendliness, but now she and others harbored growing doubts about the Genoese explorer's administrative talents and aptitude. From this time on, his power declined, and Isabella began to shift responsibility for Castile's overseas expansion into other hands. Columbus's star had risen and fallen.

But she still appreciated the bravery he had demonstrated, and she remained his most important patron. Now he stayed around the court, making himself useful. In early 1497, for example, the queen was living in Burgos, awaiting a fleet from Flanders that was bringing her son's bride to Spain, but bad weather had delayed the ships' arrival. While waiting, she was scheduled to make a side trip to the town of Soria and made ready to go, but the night before her departure, Columbus wrote her a note to let her know that the winds were changing, and that the fleet would soon arrive in northern Castile. The next day the first of the ships came into port, and Isabella was there to greet the full convoy soon after it arrived.

She was grateful for Columbus's expertise and was reminded once again of his maritime knowledge, writing him later:

> It is very good [to have] a learned man who has much experience of the matters of the sea. I am grateful to you and hold it a special obligation and service, both for your timeliness in sending it (as your warning and advice was most useful to us), as for having tendered it with the true goodwill and affection which have always been known in you; and so believe that all is received as coming from a special and faithful servant of mine.[19]

In February 1498, she drew Columbus's family even closer to hers by appointing his two sons as pages in her personal service, a mark of particular favor.[20]

But Columbus had become very unpopular elsewhere at court, and it was getting more difficult for others to stand up for him. He compounded his own problems by denying what was patently obvious. He had promised the sovereigns that he would find a path to the Orient. He had stumbled on something large and important, but it was not the Indies. China and India had sophisticated and well-developed cultures, and their rulers lived in palaces in large cities. So far, the Indians Columbus had encountered lived on little islands in grass huts. His refusal to accept this reality—that they were not in China or in India, no matter how much he wished otherwise—made him seem disingenuous at best, a liar at worst.

Some people blamed all the woes they found in the New World on Columbus. His great promises now seemed false. Many—perhaps as many as half—of the people who had traveled with him to the Americas had died, and large numbers had been financially ruined. Others had come back ill, suffering from syphilis, a painful and sometimes fatal disease they had contracted there. The disease came in stages, and in a far more virulent form in these first years of European exposure when people had much less resistance to it. Within two to four weeks of sexual contact with an infected person, a sore or lesion, or a "bubo," would appear on the body, although the sufferer might otherwise remain in good health at first. Grotesque ulcers would erupt on their lower limbs. A second stage would strike in about three months, when the patient began to suffer malaise, weakness, nausea, fever, and body pains. Then those symptoms might disappear. The final stages included blindness, sterility, and death. It was therefore possible for men to have become infected in December but to suffer no serious symptoms until they arrived back home in March, contaminated with an infectious disease they then spread to others.

Gonzalo Fernández de Oviedo y Valdés, Ferdinand Columbus, and Bartolomé de Las Casas were all emphatic that syphilis had migrated from the Americas to Europe, and several other contemporary medical treatises from these years echo this opinion. "Some Christians who accompanied Columbus on the voyage of discovery and some who were on the second voyage brought this plague to Spain," Oviedo wrote. "From them other people were contaminated."[21]

Las Casas had the same opinion. "It is abundantly verified that all the incontinent Spaniards who in this Island did not hold to the virtue of chastity, were contaminated by it, and out of a hundred hardly one escaped, except when the other party had never had it," he wrote. "The Indians, men or women, who had it were very little affected by it, scarcely more than if they had smallpox; but for the Spaniards, the pains thereof were a great and continual torture, especially so long as the buboes did not appear."[22]

The Indians were familiar with syphilis and called it by different names in different languages, depending on the tribe, according to Friar Ramón Pane, a missionary who went with Columbus on his second voyage and who collected folklore of the Taino tribe. A Taino legend described a mythological hero who had traveled to a distant land and contracted the disease from a foreign woman. It's possible the disease originated elsewhere, perhaps in a different form, from another part of the planet, maybe from Europe, or Asia, or Africa, and mutated in various ways over time. Indeed, the concept that the disease came from a foreign land, from outsiders, resonated throughout Europe too, where the Spanish called it the French disease, and the French called it the Neapolitan disease. The papal court's Spanish physician, Caspare Torrella, wrote: "This malignant pestilence began, it is reported, in the year 1493 in France, and thus by way of contagion it reached Spain, the Islands and Italy, and finally spread till it covered the whole of Europe."[23]

A Spanish surgeon named Ruy Díaz de Isla, however, said the disease was first observed in Spain in "1493, in the city of Barcelona, which city was infected and in consequence all Europe and the universe,"[24] adding that it came specifically from Hispaniola. Columbus and his men had certainly been given a warm welcome in Barcelona when they came back to Spain.

Who were among the first to contract it? According to Ruy Díaz de Isla, the mariner Martín Alonso Pinzón, who had died so quickly upon arriving back in Spain from the first voyage, was one of the earliest; another was Mosén Pedro Margarit, described by Oviedo as "in such suffering and complaining so much that I also think he had the agonies which those who are afflicted with this painful disorder usually have."[25] Cesare Borgia soon contracted it as well, according to his physician Caspare Torrella. Several of the women in the Neapolitan ruling family were also infected at an early point, according to recent archaeological evidence.[26] Christopher Columbus himself may have contracted it, for he fell ill for five months at about the same time that half of the group under the command of Mosén Pedro Margarit were known to have been sick with syphilis.

Soon the disease had spread throughout Europe, according to Oviedo:

> In the above mentioned year 1496, these pains began to be felt by some courtiers, but in the beginning it was the disease of the humble people and those of low quality, and so it is believed that they picked it up in the company of public women and by this evil and lecherous behavior, but afterwards it caught on among better and more important people. . . . Great was the wonder that it caused in all who saw it, both because the pestilence was so contagious and frightful and because many died of this infirmity. And since the disease was something new, the physicians did not understand it and did not know how to cure it, nor could others give counsel from experience.

But in Hispaniola, he wrote, it is a "very common thing and they know how to cure it."[27]

This was yet another unfortunate turn of events for Columbus's sons, who were verbally abused by the families of the people who were sick or had died. When Ferdinand and Diego went out in Granada, crowds of angry people would hound them, despite their close association with the queen, shouting, "There go the sons of the Admiral of the Mosquitos, of him who discovered lands of vanity and illusion, the grave and ruin of Castilian gentlemen!"[28]

Columbus's reputation suffered, and now Isabella showed reluctance to give him another chance. But he pleaded with her, and after more than two years, she finally relented and authorized a third expedition.

* * *

On May 30, 1498, Columbus departed with a fleet of six ships, a significant reduction from the large fleet of the second voyage. This time Don Juan de Fonseca managed the planning for the trip with an iron hand. Again the queen sent Columbus with specific instructions. At the top of the list was a requirement that he handle the Indians calmly and gracefully, leading them to "peace and quiet," and that they be converted to the Catholic faith.[29]

But Columbus confronted bad news upon his arrival in Santo Domingo, finding "the island in great tumult and sedition, because a great part of the people whom he had left there were already dead, and of the others more than 160 were ill with syphilis."[30]

Despite the chaos he encountered on his arrival, Columbus soon sailed away, always more interested in finding new lands than in governing those he had already discovered. He followed this pattern again now, making new discoveries off the coast of South America. When he got back to Hispaniola, however, things were completely out of hand. His men had often been on the verge of mutiny before; now on the third trip they went over the edge. Columbus went to extreme lengths to reestablish control. Word of this flew back to the Castilian court, and people there solidly turned against Columbus. They had come to view the Italian mariner and his brothers, Peter Martyr wrote, as "unjust men, cruel enemies and shedders of Spanish blood," who "took pleasure" in killing people who opposed them.[31]

Columbus was on the way to getting replaced. Back in Castile, three new expeditions were being planned, backed by the queen and organized by Fonseca. None would be commanded by Columbus.

The first was led by Alonso de Hojeda, who had served in the war with Granada and traveled with Columbus on his second voyage. He was given permission to go adventuring to the south. He departed in May 1499 and soon reached the shores of South America, discovering a place he called Little Venice, or Venezuela.

The pilot Alonso Niño set sail a bit later in 1499, also exploring South America, and came back loaded with treasure. In the autumn of that year, Vicente Yáñez Pinzón reached the coast of Brazil. Another explorer, Diego de Lepe, went still farther south along the Brazilian coast later that year.

An even bigger step, one that would have significant future consequences for Spain and the world, came in 1500, when an affluent notary from Seville, Rodrigo de Bastidas, explored the coast of Panama, returning to Spain in 1502, not knowing that he was only a few dozen miles away from the vast Pacific Ocean. That discovery remained in the future for Bastidas's shipmate, Vasco Núñez de Balboa.

Of course, all these trips came and went without the consent of Columbus, in direct contradiction to the legal promises the explorer had obtained from the crown when he had undertaken his risky mission in 1492. Seeing his franchise being eroded, he increasingly viewed himself as an underappreciated martyr, identifying himself with others who had been made to suffer from malevolent interlopers. His religiosity grew more intense, and so did his paranoia.

But sometimes even a paranoid is actually correct. Isabella was indeed in the process of replacing Columbus, not just as an explorer but also as an administrator. In spring 1499, responding to reports of problems in the Indies, she sent Francisco de Bobadilla, a man of good reputation and connections, to investigate, giving him the power to arrest rebels and take over the forts from Columbus. He was also a relative, and perhaps the brother, of Isabella's friend Beatriz de Bobadilla, which would have placed him within Isabella's inner circle. When Bobadilla arrived in Hispaniola in August 1500, he was greeted by the grim sight of seven Spanish corpses hanging from the gallows as he entered the port, and he was told that five more were to be hanged the next day. Columbus and his brothers, who were helping him manage the enterprise, were carrying out increasingly harsh punishments against those they thought were undermining their efforts.

Columbus was away adventuring once again when Bobadilla arrived, so he was not there to state his case during the investigation undertaken by Bobadilla. But a Pandora's box of cruelties erupted into view as a result of the inquiry. Columbus had ordered one woman's tongue cut out because she had defamed him and his brothers. He had ordered a man's throat cut for engaging in homosexual behavior. He had ordered people who stole bread when they were hungry to be hanged. He had ordered harsh and potentially fatal lashings for other such crimes.

Hearing these hair-raising stories, Bobadilla promptly seized control of the city, moved into Columbus's house, and impounded his possessions. Columbus's administration of lands in the New World was over.

When Columbus arrived back in Hispaniola, Bobadilla's contempt for him was so great that he would not even give him the opportunity to defend himself. He clapped him in irons and sent him home. After they cleared the port, the captain offered to remove Columbus's chains, but the mariner proudly refused. He said he would wear them until the queen ordered them removed.

But Queen Isabella was not terribly eager to see him when he returned. At this point he had repeatedly defied her specific instructions. He languished in jail in Spain for six long weeks before she summoned him to an audience in the Alhambra in Granada. She spoke to him kindly, in words he found heartening, but for him, the die was cast.

In 1501 the queen recalled Bobadilla to Spain but did not invite Columbus to return to his old post as governor of Hispaniola. Instead, she assigned another bureaucrat, this time Friar Nicolás de Ovando, to administer justice in the New World. Ovando was another Castilian, from Extremadura, with long family ties to Isabella. His mother had been a lady-in-waiting to Isabella's mother, and Ovando himself had served in the household of Prince Juan, Isabella's son. He was named governor on September 3, 1501. Both Bobadilla and Ovando proved to be competent administrators. Their colonists continued to die at the same alarming rate as they had under Columbus, but by now this had become a standard and expected part of the colonization process, and they were not blamed for it as Columbus had been.

On his departure for the New World, Ovando was given some specific new rules to enforce. Only Castilians would be permitted to stay in the Americas; he was expected to send back to Spain people of any other nationality that he found there. No expedition could be permitted without express permission from the Castilian crown. And, again, he was to treat the Indians kindly and to convert them "with much love and without using force."[32]

To add insult to injury, from Columbus's perspective, the queen sent Ovando with a fleet of twenty-seven well-provisioned ships—"far the largest fleet that had yet set out for the New World"—with some 2,500 settlers, including men and women, farmers and artisans.[33] This was the expedition in which the young Bartolomé de Las Casas made his first arrival.

But this was not yet the end for Columbus. Isabella sent him on one final trip of discovery, his fourth, in 1502, with a fleet of four ships. He had been told to stay away from Hispaniola, but he decided to go there first just the same. Bobadilla's fleet of almost two dozen ships was preparing to return home, and Ovando was just assuming command. Columbus tried to warn Ovando that a big storm was brewing at sea and that Bobadilla's fleet should delay in port a bit longer before starting. But Columbus had so little credibility that Ovando insulted him and ridiculed his warning. Bobadilla's fleet set out, loaded down with 200,000 pesos of gold that the Spaniards had extracted from the Caribbean islands. The hurricane that Columbus had predicted struck with all its fury; Bobadilla and almost his entire fleet were lost at sea. Only three ships crept back to Santo Domingo. Columbus's ships, meanwhile, had stayed close to shore and remained undamaged.

And so began Columbus's most treacherous but also most successful trip, for on this fourth voyage to the New World he sailed along the Caribbean mainland of Latin America, reaching Panama and a harbor so lovely he called it Portobelo, with a sheltered, narrow mouth surrounded by hills, protected from heavy wind, and lined with thick jungle foliage, with birds chattering in the trees.

It could be an ideal place of embarkation for goods to be shipped to and from the New World, Columbus thought. Perhaps it would be a good location for a customshouse. In time, just such a building was constructed there.

In Panama, Columbus heard, there was much gold buried underground—it was a funerary custom for the Indians to bury treasure with the corpses of their loved ones. He predicted that one day many precious objects would be dug from the earth there. And that too came to pass.

In Panama he also learned that there was a large body of water not far away. In fact, the Pacific Ocean was a mere fifty miles distant, across an isthmus that contained a large river, the Chagres, suitable for navigation partway to the other side. This would become, in time, the famous Path Between the Seas, the Panama Canal, the waterway that would link Europe to Asia. That revelation would come to Vasco Núñez de Balboa, who within a few years would cross the isthmus of Panama and catch the first European glimpse of the Pacific Ocean, which provided the second half of the water route to India and China, bypassing the Ottoman Turk chokehold. The route had been there all along.

By now reports were circulating that the gold Columbus had promised did indeed exist, though it was located on the mainland of the Americas, not on the islands. It would soon be made available for transport back home to Castile, huge ships full of riches that Castile could use for its own purposes. The Casa de Contratación, the central national customshouse, was established in Seville, and no one could travel to the Indies without permission of the Castilian officials who ran it. Its sister institution would be established in Portobelo, and from there huge shipments of gold and silver would pass from the New World to the Old. Portobelo became the most important port on the Isthmus of Panama, and site of a large annual market, where huge Spanish galleons could gather in safety to transport the wealth of the Americas to Spain. Sugar, tobacco, quinine, glass, and wine passed through this port. And in exchange, about one-third of the gold in existence in the world was said to have passed through Portobelo on its way to the royal treasury, providing a steady flow of funds for Isabella's children and grandchildren to use in their continuing defense of Europe and the Catholic faith.

* * *

Whether ultimately positive or negative, Isabella's influence on the New World cannot be underestimated. The discoveries and the colonization would make Spain the wealthiest and most powerful nation in the world for the next two centuries, though at great cost to many. About half the colonists and explorers who went to the New World died young; the death toll for the indigenous population, mostly as a result of exposure to new diseases, was far higher. The entire native American population was decimated in the original islands Columbus discovered. The microbes that killed them cannot be blamed on European malice, nor can the microbes that migrated from the Americas to Europe, but millions of people were inevitably affected.

Most of the indigenous survivors in the New World were those who intermarried with the Spaniards and formed a new race. Under Queen Isabella, this new race was an Hispanic people. She established Spanish as the official language; its grammatical rules were regularized by a grammar published by a professor at the University of Salamanca and widely disseminated. Isabella had exported Castilian culture across the globe.

She also established Christianity as the formal religion. Human sacrifice and cannibalism would be prohibited, and by 1542, so too would slavery. The strengths of Catholicism would spread across the continent—with its support for family, respect for education, access to charity through church-affiliated organizations, and a tradition of self-reflection that can lead people of conscience, such as Bartolomé de Las Casas, to work in defense of the weak and powerless.

But if she imported the strengths of Castile to the New World, Isabella also imported its weaknesses, including the institution of the Inquisition. Wrong thinking would not be tolerated in the New World, either. Moreover, political and economic mistakes made in Castile would be replicated in Latin America as well.

All this happened because of the joint enterprise between a brave and bold explorer, Christopher Columbus, and his far-sighted sponsor, Queen Isabella. Because of her willingness to explore, because she recognized the possibility that the world was a bigger place than people had believed at her birth, she has been called the single most important person in Spanish history.

And no single person was more responsible for Spain's expanded dominions than Columbus. "He planted the Christian faith in places so foreign and far," Oviedo wrote, and because of him, "so many treasures of gold, and silver, and pearls and other riches and trade goods went to Spain. No other Spaniard ever brought such wealth to the kingdom."[34]

EIGHTEEN

FAITH AND FAMILY

Isabella's life was changing as her children moved into their teenage years. There were five of them—Juan, her heir, and his four sisters—and she had much to do in monitoring their educations and training them to rule. She was orchestrating their marriages with royal houses throughout Europe, and each negotiation was separate and complex, requiring consummate political and diplomatic skills. Meanwhile each child needed to be tutored and prepared to step into his or her future role as king or queen.

Queen Isabella was an affectionate but demanding mother. Stern, doggedly determined, and devoutly religious, she expected the same qualities in her family. No one was allowed to shirk responsibility or question obligations. The children's behavior was expected to be impeccable, not only when they were on display at state events but also privately as they interacted with people inside the court circle. Isabella had a strong view of right and wrong. Her world was almost entirely black-and-white. Self-control was required, not optional.

Her standards for proper dress and demeanor were correspondingly high. She was torn between her need to operate successfully in the public sphere, which called for opulent external display as a demonstration of the kingdom's wealth and power, and an internal tug in the direction of the traditional Christian values of simplicity and humility in garb and appearance. Ostentatious apparel was an essential tool for mesmerizing the public, intimidating rivals, and impressing foreign envoys. Such magnificence paid dividends—ambassadors went home speaking in awed tones about the continent's new emerging superpower. The conquest of Granada, moreover, had made Ferdinand and Isabella into celebrities, imposing on them, even more than before, the obligation that appearances be maintained.

Consequently, in public, Isabella dressed herself and her family with splendor that became the talk of Europe, but she also made sure her children were warned about the moral hazards and superficiality that this kind of dress represented. Her choice of clothing was politically and socially savvy, but she also knew that it represented, at its core, false values.

But if court clothes were just vanity, they were vanity on an extraordinary scale. A soldier accompanying the English envoy on a trip to negotiate the marriage between Princess Catherine and Prince Arthur was astonished by the clothing and jewelry displayed by the Spanish royal family. Ferdinand "wore cloth of gold lined with fine sables," while Isabella wore a black velvet cape lined with gold and set with precious gems.[1] The next day Ferdinand appeared in crimson velvet, and Isabella wore cloth of gold. The oldest children, Juan and Isabel, joined the adults briefly; Juan made his appearance in crimson velvet, like his father, and Isabel dressed in cloth of gold, like her mother, with a great train of green velvet and a cap of "net in gold and black, garnished with pearls and precious stones."[2] Day after day, the family entertained the envoys with banquets, balls, bullfights, and jousting tournaments. And at each event, the members of the family appeared in new, different, and dazzling ensembles.

* * *

But all the time, Isabella's confessor, Hernán de Talavera, was exhorting the faithful not to succumb to the snares of conspicuous consumption and to avoid "sumptuous dress." He wrote a treatise on the ways good Christians should dress themselves and eat so that they would not fall into bad habits that led to sin and gluttony. Excessively revealing clothing, for example, was against the laws of nature because people were intended to cover their bodies to protect them from cold or the burning rays of the sun. Nudity was absolutely forbidden, he added, and had been ever since Adam and Eve. He also recommended that women cover their hair to promote modesty. And he urged people to dress and eat in "necessary and reasonable," not "costly or extravagant," ways.[3] Each was to dress appropriately for his or her station in life.

Not surprisingly, Isabella's choice of garb for herself and her family raised some eyebrows in church circles. Talavera several times questioned her about her apparel and behavior, and she squirmed with discomfort. Once he told her that her vanity would "offend God."[4] She replied that she had to dress as she did on state occasions and to help shape the image of Spain as rich and influential. But these kinds of issues caused her many hours of anxious reflection about whether she was living up to her own spiritual ideals.

Her inner conflicts were revealed in a set of small but exquisite paintings she commissioned. These were a set of depictions of scenes from the life of Christ, mostly following biblical text, designed for Isabella's personal devotional use. They were probably intended as components of an altarpiece. Of the forty-seven oil paintings produced for the series, about two dozen are known to have survived. In their totality, they provide a remarkable window into Isabella's thinking and religious philosophy and the ideas that she communicated to her children. They reveal her life as what the art historian Chiyo Ishikawa calls a "pointedly conservative enterprise" and show her deep desire for a court designed with "simplicity and austere understatement."[5]

Believed to have been executed by two court painters whom Queen Isabella maintained on her staff, Juan de Flandes and Michael Sittow, both trained in Flanders, the paintings depict characters from the stories of the New Testament. The figures are dressed in the garb that was current at the time they were produced, making the images more directly relevant to the observer than scenes that more accurately portray the distant past. Many of the accessories shown—a convex mirror, a cuckoo clock, a classical entablature, a Gothic arch, a small hunting dog known as a whippet—were trendy objects that would have been found in the homes of the wealthy in the 1480s. It is believed that Archbishop Talavera helped in the conception of the project.

Isabella and her children became integral parts of this series. Members of her family were painted as spectators and participants in scenes from Christ's life. Placing family members in a painting was not particularly unusual at the time; many noble families commissioned pictures of themselves dressed in splendid robes, kneeling in prayer before an idealized Holy Family. But Isabella's artworks did not portray herself and her family in the glorious foreground. Instead, they appear as bit-part actors, dressed as ordinary citizens, in the unfolding dramas. In one painting that depicts Christ's miraculous feeding of the multitude with just a few loaves and fishes, Isabella appears as a humble and pious onlooker dressed in a simple robe and cloak, sitting as part of the crowd.[6]

Her son Juan and his bride-to-be may have been similarly worked into the scene as the wedding couple at the Marriage at Cana. Juan, blond-haired with delicate features, gestures with his hand as he speaks to a blond young woman, her hands held in prayer. Christ, dark-haired and pensive, sits next to his mother at the table, near the young couple. A convex mirror, a popular home accessory at the time, hangs from the wall. The table is set with a white cloth, looking something like an altar, with bread and wine visible, suggesting Holy Communion. In this picture, a wedding is turned into a religious service, a kind of mass.[7]

In other paintings, stylish and revealing garments are equated with sin. In one scene a blindfolded man, who is probably Jesus, is mocked. His tormentors appear as affected and haughty young Castilian courtiers dressed in high fashion. The men's tights reveal the slender, shapely, and wiry muscles of their lower limbs; one sneering fellow wearing bright-red leggings has a particularly bulging codpiece.[8]

Simple, unaffected clothing that conceals sexuality, therefore, was viewed as the ideal in Isabella's mind, even as her own court clothing grew more and more ornate in keeping with the new spirit of the Renaissance. The problem of properly balancing the secular and the spiritual would manifest itself in different ways for her and her children in the years ahead. All the children internalized the religious obsession that drove Isabella and came to share it, even while they struggled with the worldly power they wielded.

The way she saw the religious conflicts among Europe's three faiths is also apparent in these paintings. In the depiction showing the mocking of the blindfolded man, for example, a Jewish high priest in a broad-rimmed hat hurries away, aware of the cruelty of the action but doing nothing to stop it. In a scene depicting the moment where Jesus is ridiculed by having a crown of thorns pressed onto his head, a turbaned man who looks like a Turk watches but does not intervene. Both, however, look troubled and pained by the events. The Jew and the Turk, as individuals, are not presented as intrinsically evil but are depicted as enabling painful events to unfold.

The paintings Isabella commissioned also illustrate the ways she viewed herself and her family as the defenders of Christ and his interests. In the depiction of a humbly garbed Christ calming the waves in the Sea of Galilee, for example, Jesus's boat is flying a flag with the coat of arms of Castile and León. In another scene that is supposed to have occurred after the crucifixion, when Jesus appears to his mother, the Castilian escutcheon is painted on the roof of Mary's home.

Interestingly, however, in the New Testament, Christ does not appear to his mother at all after his death, although he reportedly made appearances to over five hundred other people on at least a half dozen occasions. The fact that Queen Isabella added this noncanonical image to the mix suggests that she was interested in giving the mother of Jesus a more important role in the Christian story, either for her own reasons or because she felt Mary's role was being undervalued by the church. At the same time she was actively advocating the growth of the female religious order called the Conceptionists, which promoted the Virgin Mary as holy in her own right, not just through her son.[9] Of course, it is a law of nature that mothers feel underappreciated for their efforts on behalf of their offspring, and perhaps Isabella thought Mary deserved more credit than she was getting.

As the children grew from childhood into adolescence, Queen Isabella kept them close at hand. They joined her at war during the turbulent 1480s and 1490s. These were not children who spent their early years frolicking in the countryside. Isabella's children spent their childhoods at war against the people they commonly called the "infidel." They lived in heavily fortified castles on the frontier of enemy activity and in encampments while on campaign. The travels were grueling, over steep mountain passes and arid plains, in blazing heat and freezing cold. They sometimes lived in tents, sweltering in the summer and huddled next to coal braziers for warmth when the winter set in. A portable altar allowed them to worship on the road; a contingent of priests, including confessors to the king and queen, and chaplains to the family, accompanied them, holding large crosses aloft as they marched. They lived a kind of perpetual and militarized pilgrimage.

This level of direct family involvement in a war is unusual. Most rulers don't want to put their own families at risk, certainly not their wives and small children. Most wars entail rulers sending people they barely know off to distant lands to risk being killed. The core of the Ottoman army at the time, for example, was made up of slave soldiers. Similarly, the Italian rulers of the same period relied on mercenary soldiers hired to fight their battles for them. When noblemen in the recent Middle Ages had gone to war, they had tended to treat their trips as sporting expeditions to be limited to the pleasant summer months. Their ritualized play at battle, the jousting tournaments, survived into Isabella's day as a popular amusement at festivals and holidays.

But for Isabella, Ferdinand, and their children, war was real, immediate, and personal. The campaign against Granada lasted ten years. Isabella's oldest child, Isabel, named for her mother, spent almost her entire childhood with her parents on campaign, first against the Portuguese and then against Granada. She was twenty-one when the Muslims' capital city surrendered in 1492. The youngest, Catherine, was seven. Isabella was in a war council when she went into labor with her daughter María.

The family was totally absorbed in the effort to reconquer Spain. They spent their daily lives surrounded by soldiers who were members of their own extended family or else friends and relations of their friends. When a contingent went off to battle, frequently with King Ferdinand leading the troops, they watched and waited to see who would come back and in what condition. Often the warriors killed in combat were just a few years older than Isabella's children and may have been their playmates just a few years earlier. Queen Isabella knew personally the noblemen who commanded the units and their parents and had visited the cities where they lived. When one of them died, she often knew firsthand the people who would be most affected by the loss.

Isabella and her family lived with constant wartime risks. One night at their camp outside Granada, for example, after Ferdinand had fallen asleep, she was up praying through the night in her tent. She accidently dropped a torch, setting her bed linens on fire. The fire spread quickly in her temporary quarters. Amid cries of alarm, everyone was rousted from bed. The men scrambled to grab their swords in the belief they were under enemy attack. As the flames leaped higher, the queen quickly gathered up her maps and battle plans and went out in search of her husband and thirteen-year-old son, finding them both safe. But the camp was destroyed. All their possessions were lost. The family donned borrowed clothing when they returned to the work of fighting the enemy.

The children had occasional intense, frightening, or sad interactions with their opponents. When the troops were besieging a city, they could sometimes hear the cries and lamentations of the inhabitants inside the city walls. They saw the enemy, and they also saw the innocent victims of war.

Even the act of accepting the surrender from the town could be hazardous duty if tempers suddenly flared. When the Spaniards accepted a town's surrender, it was King Ferdinand who typically marched in to receive the oath of fealty from its leading citizens. Often the decision to surrender had been controversial. The residents wondered if they had been betrayed, and their suspicions were not infrequently grounded in truth.

Ferdinand wasn't the only one who directly placed himself in harm's way. Isabella entered at least four cities herself to accept their surrenders, including Almería and Baza. In Baza, she was accompanied by the teenaged Princess Isabel. Princess Juana joined Queen Isabella at the surrender of Moclín. Prince Juan was part of the contingent at Jaén. When Boabdil surrendered in Granada, the keys to the city were given first to King Ferdinand, then passed to Queen Isabella, and then to thirteen-year-old Prince Juan. All five children spent considerable time at the forward command post, the Alcazaba in Córdoba.

Princess Isabel was drawn into specifically perilous situations on at least two separate occasions. When her parents were at war with the Portuguese, she had been left behind in Segovia under the care of Beatriz de Bobadilla's father, Pedro. Isabella had granted control of the city to Beatriz and her husband, Andrés de Cabrera, and many residents of Segovia were unhappy about the transfer of power and wealth. The residents of the city rose up against the new administrators and seized the city and the citadel where the princess was staying. Princess Isabel, who was about seven years old, was trapped for some days in a tower of the Alcázar while milling crowds inside the fortress shouted and demonstrated their rage. When she got the news, Queen Isabella rushed to her daughter's aid, galloping to Segovia with only a handful of companions. The citizens of Segovia tried to block the queen's entry, complaining that they were unhappy with the governance by Andrés de Cabrera, who was also unpopular because he was a converso. The queen haughtily demanded that the residents permit her to enter, and she promised to investigate the situation. On her own, the queen entered the city and took back her daughter. As she had promised, she looked into the matters at issue but remained adamant in her decision about who would rule the city. For her daughter, however, it must have been a terrifying experience.

Similarly, it must have been upsetting to Princess Isabel when she was traded as a hostage to the Portuguese, as a guarantee that her parents would abide by the terms of the treaty. That had happened when she was eight. She had been sent away from her family to live in Portugal for three years. But no matter what happened, Princess Isabel was expected to go forward, without showing weakness or hesitation.

The threat of a suicide attack, meanwhile, was a constant source of fear. When the Spaniards were besieging Málaga, for instance, a Muslim who entered the camp presenting himself as a helpful informant was allowed to wander around while he waited to speak with the queen. When he spied an elegantly attired couple, a man and woman playing chess in a tent, he assumed they were Ferdinand and Isabella and viciously attacked them with a knife. The woman was Beatriz de Bobadilla, and the man was Isabella's cousin, a Portuguese nobleman. Through good luck both survived the attack. The assailant was caught and killed. But this attack inside their own camp underscored a troubling fact: that people who presented themselves as allies in wartime could actually be threats, and dangers were lurking everywhere.

It is indeed rather surprising that no one in the family was killed. In addition to being at war with the Muslims, they were also angering a great many other people. Jews, wavering conversos, critics of the Inquisition, and Muslims, in Granada and elsewhere, all had ample reason to want to injure the royal family. Some people in Aragon and Catalonia, meanwhile, had never forgiven Ferdinand's family for the brutal civil war his father had waged in the 1460s.

Knowing themselves to be at risk, the king and queen lived in a constant state of alert. For that reason, when King Ferdinand was attacked in Barcelona by a knife-wielding madman in December 1493, their first assumption was that it was a premeditated attack. The king was stabbed in the back of the neck and survived only because the heavy gold chain he customarily wore blocked the blade from plunging deeper. Queen Isabella's first thought was that the attack on Ferdinand was the beginning of an uprising by the Catalan nobles. So she first made sure to protect young Juan, the heir to the kingdoms, ordering him rushed away to safety in a ship offshore before heading to her husband.

When they learned that the attack did not appear to have been fatal, Isabella sent out messages reassuring their allies in France, Spain, and Italy. Then she and the girls took up positions at Ferdinand's side. For about fifty days, burning with fever, he clung to life, his condition now improving and now declining. They called for the best medical advice. "A crowd of physicians and surgeons is sent for," Peter Martyr anxiously told the Count of Tendilla and archbishop of Granada. " . . . We labor between fear and hope."[10]

Queen Isabella and her daughters used every religious tool at their disposal to plead for the king's survival. She prayed the stations of the cross every day for his recovery, a process that involves imagining oneself walking in Christ's footsteps from the time he was sentenced to death until he was laid in the tomb. Each of the steps requires special prayers and a time of quiet contemplation before proceeding to the next. The children made their own sacrifice by going on a barefoot pilgrimage over a nearby mountain; some of them climbed on their bare knees, "having so vowed to God for the safety of the King," as Peter Martyr wrote a few weeks later.[11]

In addition, the queen swore that neither she, nor her ladies-in-waiting, nor her daughters, would wear hoop skirts "made of brocade or silk," one of the queen's favorite styles but one that was disapproved by the clergy as a troublesome, flamboyant new invention, and *deshonesto*.[12]

As a result of all these ministrations, spiritual and medical—and thanks also to Ferdinand's strong constitution—the king gradually recovered. Queen Isabella must have soon decided that with the war behind them and God's favor amply secured, her pledge to scorn brocades and silks was no longer necessary, for soon she was busily engaged in making plans for wedding celebrations, and elaborate clothing seemed to be in everyone's future.

For as the five children approached adulthood in the 1490s, marriages were being arranged for them that would increase the role of Spain on the world stage and secure its borders as well as the religious practices of Spanish society. After all, the Spanish needed help: they ruled over Sicily and Spain, which were open to attack by the Ottomans, and their cousins were ruling the Kingdom of Naples, which had already been hit hard once by the Turks at Otranto. Ferdinand's sister, Joanna, the queen of Naples, kept them informed about worrisome developments in southern Italy and the eastern Mediterranean.

It was only a matter of time until combined forces would be necessary to protect southern Italy from Ottoman assault. The strait of Otranto, the narrow waterway between Christian Italy and Muslim-occupied Albania connecting the Adriatic and Mediterranean Seas, is only forty-five miles wide, or a day or less under sail or in a ship rowed by galley slaves. Every alliance would help reduce the chances of another Muslim invasion.

To stabilize her kingdom, Isabella used her family as she had her people, her armaments, and her castles—she employed them to make Spain an impregnable fortress, bolstering its defenses by forging ties around Europe that would reinforce the connections and alliances among the Christian nations of western Europe.

Every match was strategic. The oldest daughter, the dependable and trustworthy Isabel, would protect their backs and promote Spanish interests by marrying the heir to the Portuguese throne. Catherine, their youngest, would marry the heir to the throne of England, which would make that island nation more closely attuned to the needs of the Spaniards and the Christian-controlled parts of the Mediterranean. It seemed a fitting match, as young Prince Arthur, born in 1486, was just one year younger than Catherine. María, the fourth child, was still the subject of consideration and negotiation. For her, Isabella was eyeing James, the promising young heir to the throne of Scotland. Isabella believed that if her two daughters were married to the kings of England and Scotland, they could bring peace to the British Isles, and the two countries could be converted into more reliable supporters of Christendom.

The pièce de résistance, however, involved her second and third children, the male heir Juan and his younger sister Juana. A double marriage was arranged, between Juan and Juana and two grandchildren of the Holy Roman emperor, Philip and Margaret, designed to forge iron bonds of codefense and cooperation between Spain and the German and Austrian confederation of states. These matches would mean that the largest single state in central Europe would act with Spain as a bulwark against the inroads of the Ottoman Turks. The Holy Roman Empire, moreover, had a historic role as protector of the Catholic Church, an aspiration shared by Isabella. As an added bonus, Philip and Margaret were also the heirs to the rich Duchy of Burgundy and the Low Countries.

Isabella wasn't just coldly pragmatic, however. She sought to find her children marriages that had a better-than-average chance of happiness. This was a time when older men with money in their pockets cast covetous eyes on fair young maidens, and families who offered their most beautiful daughters to aging kings often got advantageous benefits from them in terms of cash, lands, or paid court positions for relatives. Isabella was certainly looking for beneficial marriages for her girls; there would be no love matches in this family. But still she hoped to find suitors for all of them who were attractive, approximately the right age, and had attributes that would promote marital happiness, or at least a measure of contentment. No doubt she remembered her own maiden years when one man after another was proposed as a potential bridegroom. There were no weepy eyes or spindly legs among the suitors considered for Isabella's brood.

Still, these transactions had much in common with buying a piece of livestock. A surviving account in the British Archives details the negotiations that served as the backdrop for the marriage of Catherine to Arthur, the Prince of Wales. Ambassadors from Spain and England met to hammer out the terms of the deal, which involved determining how much dowry should be paid by Catherine's parents and how much by the Tudor king Henry VII of England, the father of the prospective bridegroom. Henry VII wanted the marriage to happen quickly so that Catherine's blue blood would bolster his family's wobbly claim to the English throne, but he was also notoriously penurious. This account of the meeting was sent back to Spain:

> The English commissioners declared that with regard to the alliance there was not much to confer about, and began directly to speak of the marriage. They were exceedingly civil, and said a great many things in praise of Ferdinand and Isabella. That being done, they asked the Spaniards to name the sum for the marriage portion.
>
> The Spanish Ambassadors replied that it would be more becoming for the English to name the marriage portion, because they had first solicited this [marriage] and their party is a [son].
>
> The English Commissioners asked five times as much as they had asked in Spain.
>
> The Spanish Ambassadors proposed to refer this matter to [Ferdinand] and [Isabella], who would act liberally in proportion to the confidence shown them.
>
> The English Commissioners said that such a proceeding would be inconvenient for both parties, and that Ferdinand and Isabella would not agree to it.
>
> The Spanish Ambassadors complained that the English were unreasonable in their demands. Bearing in mind what happens

every day to the King of England, it is surprising that Ferdinand and Isabella should dare to give their [daughter] at all. This was said with great courtesy, in order that they might not feel displeasure or be enraged.

The English Commissioners abated one third.

The Spaniards proposed that, as there was sufficient time for it, two or four persons should be selected as umpires.

The English Commissioners declined it, and gave their reasons.

The Spaniards desired the English to name the lowest price.

The English abated one half.

The Spaniards said this marriage would be so advantageous to the King of England that he ought to content himself with what is generally given with Princesses of Spain.

The English desired to have everything defined in order to avoid disputes after the conclusion of the marriage. They asked twice as much as they had asked in Spain.

The Spanish Ambassadors offered one fourth.

The English asked why, as the money was not to come out of the strong boxes of the King and the Queen, but out of the pockets of their subjects, they should not be more liberal? They referred to old treaties with France, Burgundy, and Scotland, proving by them that even higher marriage portions were given.

They also urged that England is a very dear place, the smallest coin being worth eight Spanish maravedis, and that the great men spend large sums. The English aristocracy is rich and prosperous in the Dukedoms of Clarence, Lancaster, Buckingham, Somerset, Norfolk, York, the counties of Warwick, Salisbury and Lincoln, and the Marquisate of Dorset. Such being the case, and there not being a "drop of blood" in existence from which any danger might arise, the English saw no reason to lessen their demands.[13]

And so it went. For the next twenty years. For while both families wanted the match, both were ferociously angling for advantage. Henry VII was always watching his pennies, which eventually made his son and heir a very rich man, and Isabella had four daughters to dower. The families dickered over the prices each should pay and the terms of the arrangement from 1488 to 1509, from the time Catherine was three years old until she was twenty-four.

Isabella dictated many terms of the dowry negotiations, specifying the details of the dowry and deciding which Castilian officials would accompany Catherine to England, according to correspondence and documents in the British Archives.

This set of records demonstrates that Isabella was the driving force in handling international affairs, including organizing military alliances, negotiating trade pacts, and arranging marriages. In the 1850s a German scholar living in England, Gustav Bergenroth, would spend years investigating correspondence between Spain and England. To do so, he had to break the ciphers and code language that Isabella had used to communicate with her envoys in England. Her hand is visible in many places, while Ferdinand's is seldom to be found, except on the boilerplate introductions to the letters. These introductions typically presented the correspondence as coming from both the king and queen, but inside some of the lengthy letters, Isabella forgot the fiction she was creating and referred to herself in the singular as *"Yo, la Reyna,"* or "I, the Queen." These references slipped through in letters ostensibly from both regents at least twice, once in January 1497 and again in December 1502.[14]

Isabella used the same mixture of flattery and manipulation in her international negotiations as she did in domestic affairs. In September 1496, for example, in a letter to her ambassador in England, she referred to King Henry as a "prince of great virtue, firmness and constancy," praise that she clearly assumed would be repeated to the English king, who was insecurely perched upon a throne he had usurped.[15] She promised in the letter that she expected the relationship between England and Spain to become much closer once their children married—knowing that Henry was eager to form an alliance with an old and respected blue bloodline.

She was simultaneously angling to improve relations between England and Scotland, something that would have thrown France off balance and bolstered northern European support for the problems of southern Europe, particularly the threat posed by the Turks. Dangling the prospect of the marriage between Arthur and Catherine, Queen Isabella pressured Henry to improve his own relations with King James. "Henry must marry one of his daughters to the King of Scots," she told González de Puebla after all Isabella's own daughters were wed, and indeed, Princess Margaret of England was married to King James in 1503.[16]

Despite the complexities of the negotiations, however, all the marriages seemed very promising, both from the standpoint of Spain's position in Europe and for the young people being betrothed. All, however, also ended up presenting challenges, as marriages, even the happiest, always do.

Isabel, the oldest, was the first to marry, in 1490. At twenty, she married Prince Afonso, King João's son, who was fifteen. She knew him well. For the three years when Portugal and Castile had exchanged children as a peace guarantee, the two youngsters had lived in Moura under the care of Isabella's Portuguese aunt Beatriz, her mother's sister. The children, Afonso and Isabel, had spent time together during those years beginning when she was eight and he was three, and became fond of each other. To ensure Doña Beatriz's commitment to caring properly for the children, Don Manuel, who was Beatriz's son, had gone to live in Castile, where he had met Queen Isabella and come to trust her.[17] He was a pleasant and affable boy, something that Isabella probably saw as an insurance policy for the future. It was always good to have an ally in a foreign court. And if anything happened to Prince Afonso of Portugal, the king's heir, Manuel, could one day become king.

The two Iberian families had had their differences. They had even gone to war. But King João had come to the conclusion that a marriage between Portugal and Castile would be ideal. Afonso was more than amenable, and soon so was young Isabel. Portugal's new possessions were bringing the kingdom unprecedented wealth, and the reports about Afonso, though no doubt exaggerated by slavish courtiers, described the young prince as "the handsomest and best looking known to the world."[18]

In August 1488 the Portuguese nobleman and chronicler Ruy de Sande traveled to Castile bearing a letter discussing the marriage of Afonso and Isabel. Isabella and Ferdinand received him warmly, despite the fact that the queen had grave reservations about the character of the boy's father. The plans led to happy celebration. There was revelry in Seville. The court stayed up late dancing; Isabella and her daughters were known for their graceful movements on the floor. At last Isabel said, "It is now late," to the Portuguese ambassador to signal the party was over. "Not late, but very early, Lady!" he responded, for the first daylight was coming through the windows.[19]

According to the French courtier Philippe de Commynes, Isabella and Ferdinand agreed to the match to improve the security of the Iberian peninsula: "They had married their eldest daughter to the King of Portugal, that all Spain might be in peace, for they were entirely possessed of all the provinces, except the kingdom of Navarre."[20] It was the first royal wedding of a generation for both families. An exciting schedule of festivities was planned and coordinated in both kingdoms. First there were several weeks of celebrations in Seville, which were attended by young Isabel's parents and sisters. Then a procession of Spanish and Portuguese grandees conducted the bride from Castile to the city of Évora in Portugal. Princess Isabel's entourage was led by the archbishop of Toledo, Cardinal Pedro Mendoza, who had been an important ally of her mother's ever since King Enrique died and Isabella had taken the throne of Castile.

To meet her new family, Princess Isabel was accompanied by her Portuguese cousin Don Manuel, who had lived in Castile during the hostage swap. He was now Duke of Viseu and also Duke of Beja, having been granted the titles by João II after the king had killed Manuel's older brother Diego, who had originally been the heir. Manuel was the same age as Isabel, and in the course of traveling across the two kingdoms, he came to particularly admire her.

The young Isabel was greeted with immense enthusiasm when she arrived in Portugal. As she passed through the streets, such a happy clamor of trumpeting and cheers greeted her that, according to a Portuguese chronicler, "truly it seemed the earth trembled."[21] The living accommodations for the young couple were prepared with "rich brocades and fine tapestries," and the princess was given many gifts.[22]

Isabel and Afonso were married on November 25, 1490, in the town of Évora. Many "great festivals," banquets, balls, and other celebrations were scheduled for the weeks ahead.[23] At one event, called a mummery, King João initiated a joust, "ornamented artfully as the Knight of the Swan, with a great deal of wealth, charm and graciousness," the chronicler recalled.

> He entered through the doors of the hall with a large fleet of great ships, set on bolts of cloth painted as stormy and natural waves of the ocean, with great thunder of ordnance being fired, and trumpets and horns and minstrels playing instruments, with wild shouts and the turmoil of whistles by make-believe masters, pilots and mariners who were dressed in brocades and silks. . . . The king sallied forth in his very luxurious masquerade dress and

danced with the Princess, and in like manner the others with their ladies .... And they danced that night, and there were many farces and festivities.[24]

It was a spectacular send-off for these two beloved children of increasingly wealthy nations. Afonso was only fifteen years old and Isabel was twenty, but despite the difference in their ages, their childhood friendship kindled into intense love. Things got off to a very promising start, and when the events were concluded, the chronicler noted, "all left very happy and content."[25]

This was a vital marriage for Spain because the war with Portugal was still a recent memory and the peace treaty between Portugal and Castile had left lingering resentments. João's father had done in Portugal what King Enrique had carelessly done in Castile: given lands, properties, and benefices to top-ranking noblemen to win their support and loyalty, weakening himself in the process. During his grandfather's reign, there had been only two dukes and six counts; but at the death of King Afonso V, this tally had grown to four dukes, three marquesses, twenty-five counts, one viscount, and one baron, according to the historian Antonio Henrique de Oliveira Marques, who notes that all had been given valuable lands and revenues. By the time King João II finally inherited the throne, he noted with disgust that the only property his father had left him by right was the land under the roads.[26]

When his father died and João became king in 1481, he embarked on the same program of centralized royal administration that other successful European countries, including Spain, France, and England, were employing to stabilize themselves and place a check on nobles who had grown arrogant and lawless during times of disorganized governments and civil chaos. He set out to bring the nobles to heel—but in this respect he clashed again with his relative Queen Isabella. Isabella's mother's family included the Dukes of Braganza and Viseu, and they were Portugal's wealthiest and most powerful family—similar to the Mendoza clan of Castile. King João learned that they had been corresponding with Isabella in ways that he believed to be traitorous. After finding some suspicious documents, he imprisoned the Duke of Braganza, put him on trial and, after he was convicted, ordered him to be executed. Later, in a fit of anger, he killed Don Manuel's older brother, who may have involved himself in a plot against the king. Nobody was clear on the details of

how the duke was stabbed to death—some said the king had done it himself, others that he had had the help of courtiers—but the action horrified people across western Europe. The French courtier Commynes, for
example, called João "barbarous"—he was one of many who believed João
had murdered his cousin with his own hand.[27]

Queen Isabella had been greatly disturbed by the killings and had
offered refuge in Castile, giving land and property to many of the grandees whom João had persecuted. She did not utter João's name much
after that. From then on she called him, in tones of withering contempt,
El Hombre, or "The Man."

Young Isabel, although greatly beloved by her parents, had clearly
pulled the short straw in taking on the challenge of restoring international harmony. This, obviously, was going to be no easy task for a young
woman. Isabel had some things working for her, however. Her childhood
years in Portugal meant that she already spoke Portuguese and was familiar with the kingdom's customs; she performed its dances so elegantly
that her movements were a source of pride to her family and she was
asked to perform at court events and diplomatic banquets. But she bore
her mother's stamp and made her marriage a splendid success. She even
managed to win the affection of her father-in-law, the tough and cold-
blooded King João.

* * *

The first few months of the young people's marriage was idyllic. On one
lovely day, the couple sailed on a river in a flag-festooned barge, picnicking
joyfully in the countryside. Then one day in July 1491, King João proposed
a late-afternoon horseback ride, and the prince decided at the last minute
to gallop off to join his father. Sometime on the ride, his horse stumbled
and fell, and the prince landed on the ground, crushed by the horse's
weight. His mother got word that the prince had been injured, and she
and Isabel rushed to his side. They begged and pleaded with God to save
him, but he never spoke again, and within three hours he was dead.[28]

Prince Afonso had been greatly loved by the Portuguese people, and
the whole kingdom grieved at his death. Men tore out the hair from their
heads and beards; the women ripped at their faces, leaving large bloody
gashes from their nails. "Very sorrowful cries and exceedingly loud lamentations" were heard everywhere.[29]

Afonso's parents were bereft. But no one suffered more overtly than his wife, Isabel. She grieved so ferociously that it attracted favorable comment in the family for generations. Sobbing, she cut off her golden hair, put a veil over her head so no one could see her face, changed into mourning clothes, and refused to change her outfit for forty days to chasten her body. She stopped eating almost entirely and grew very thin, finally consenting to sip a small amount of broth. She took ill with fevers. She spent her days in a darkened room with only a single candle for illumination, reading religious and devotional texts. She attended mass daily and received communion over and over. She became preoccupied with dark imaginings about what had caused this disaster to befall her and Portugal. She engaged in intense self-examination about ways she might have displeased God.

This level of grieving was not unusual at the time. It was customary for people in Portugal to cut off their hair, neglect their hygiene, wear dirty clothes for extended periods, and do other things to express their sorrow. During this period King João and his wife, for example, stopped sitting at a table to eat and instead ate "seated on the ground and off of vessels of pottery, deprived in every respect of all magnificence."[30]

The grief that his widow demonstrated helped to distract the young man's parents. Worried about her well-being, even her survival, they moved her bed into their own bedchamber, where she consented to accept only minimal comforts, including merely a very thin Indian bedspread for warmth.

Isabella and Ferdinand were both saddened by the news of Afonso's death as well. Isabella wrote her daughter letters of tender, heartfelt consolation, as did Archbishop Talavera, according to an account of the events that was preserved in a book about proper conduct for Christian women that was commissioned by Queen Isabella's granddaughter fifty years later. The letters, according to the account, were themselves heartrending: "There is no one who, unless they had a heart of stone, could hear it without shedding many tears!"[31]

As Princess Isabel mourned Afonso's death, she became preoccupied with what sins they may have committed to cause God to take the young man from them. She became convinced that Afonso had died because Portugal had allowed heresy to fester.[32] No one knows who came up with this idea, but the growing suspicion that God was punishing Portugal for harboring nonbelievers would have far-reaching consequences in the years to come.

Isabel's parents sent for the princess to come home, eager to have her back and to help her recover. She returned devoutly religious and continued to starve and scourge herself. She said she would never again marry. Instead she stepped back into her comfortable role as companion and assistant to her mother, Queen Isabella, who was forty by now and juggling problems both at home and abroad.

Afonso's death had led to political turmoil in Portugal. The succession was thrown into dispute—João hoped to name his illegitimate son Jorge his heir, but many would clearly view Jorge's succession as invalid. In Portugal, where Juana la Beltraneja, the child that King Enrique had believed to be his daughter, was still living in a convent, even the suspicion of illegitimacy was enough to destroy a monarchy. But this was no longer Princess Isabel's problem, and she left her life in Portugal behind.

In late 1495, however, King João II died. He had reluctantly decided to leave the throne to his cousin, Manuel, who had received the title Duke of Viseu after his older brother had been killed. It was a stroke of almost unbelievable good luck. Manuel had been the eighth of nine children and, for most of his life, a most unlikely inheritor of the throne. But his older brothers had all died, one by one. Manuel's placid disposition and tact had helped him survive the king's tumultuous reign. Portugal's new prosperity, moreover, meant that the nation, even though small, was developing a valuable global trading empire. Soon the young man was being called, appropriately enough, Manuel the Fortunate.

Manuel had one particular further stroke of luck in mind. He wanted to marry Afonso's widow Princess Isabel. He had first been attracted to her when he escorted her to Portugal. Maybe it was her charm, or maybe it was her enchanting way of dancing. It probably didn't hurt that she was second in line for the crown of Castile and Aragon, after her brother Juan. Some were whispering that Prince Juan did not seem altogether healthy. There was a chance that Manuel could end up as king of Portugal, Spain, and all their combined dominions.

Queen Isabella and King Ferdinand offered King Manuel the younger daughter, María, but he could not be swayed. It would be Isabel, or he would look outside Iberia for a bride. So Isabella and Ferdinand began pressuring the young widow to renounce mourning and her exaggerated religious rituals and marry Manuel. Isabel refused, with complete resolution. A determined young woman, she adamantly insisted that she would never again "know another man," Peter Martyr wrote, and "up to this day she can by no means be conquered."[33]

There the matter rested. A lot was going on in Castile already—wars and voyages of discovery were under way—and the issue was temporarily set aside as less pressing than other matters.

* * *

The family spotlight shifted to Juan, his mother's beloved "angel," who continued to receive the favored treatment enjoyed by the firstborn male of all families at that time. By 1496, when he was eighteen, he had a large household of his own, with a minutely structured schedule of activities each day. Dozens of attendants waited on him, making sure that each garment he placed on his body, with the assistance of the proper official assigned to that role, was perfectly prepared so that his appearance was impeccable. His wardrobe was extraordinary, consisting of numerous garments made of brocaded satin, cloth of gold, and velvet. One man's primary task was to keep the prince's silver chamber pot close at hand for convenient use.

Juan kept his own court of advisers and associates as well. They were primarily the sons of wealthy and noble families, but a few others, such as the two sons of Christopher Columbus, were also fit into the mix.

The boys of the court continued to be tutored in the latest humanistic learning by the Italian scholar Peter Martyr, who took enormous pride in preparing the future king of Spain. He playfully described himself as operating a *palaestra*, the ancient Greek term for a wrestling school for youths. "I have a house crowded all day with the petulant youths of the Nobles," he wrote with a boastful swagger to the archbishop of Braga, a top Portuguese cleric.

> They are now beginning by degrees to turn themselves from the empty loves, to which as you know very well they have been badly accustomed from tender years, to letters. They now begin to learn that letters are not a hindrance to warfare as they had falsely imbibed from their ancestors, may they also confess that they are a great help. I strive to persuade them that no one can otherwise become famous in peace or war. This our palaestra so pleases the Queen, a living example of all the virtues in the royal scepter, that she has ordered . . . her cousin to frequent my house, and has also ordered the Duke of Villahermosa, nephew of the king by his brother, [to do the same] and that they are never to leave it unless as urgent cause presses. All the young heirs of potentates, as many

as either Spain possesses, follow there. They bring with them two tutors to listen that they may go over with them at home the rules of grammar according to my plan, and what they hear they repeat together.[34]

Martyr and others described the prince as a sensitive and scholarly young man, who had great potential but was not terribly strong. Martyr commented on the young man's "tender palate," noting that the prince's diet was carefully monitored to help him maintain his strength. There was a bit of foreboding in one letter: if only the young man should live, "you will see the world happy with Spain."[35]

Many good things seemed to be in store with Prince Juan, and also for his younger sister Juana. As a result of the family's dynastic planning, Juan was to marry the lovely Margaret, the granddaughter of the Holy Roman emperor and the heiress, with her brother Philip, to the vastly wealthy realms of Burgundy and Flanders. Juan's younger sister Juana was to marry Philip.

It would be a truly thrilling match, particularly for aficionados of early Renaissance art and culture such as Isabella and her children. Margaret and Philip came from a world that was socially and artistically avant-garde and sophisticated. The land over which they reigned was the most affluent in Europe and the home of many masterpieces of the early northern European Renaissance. The Ghent Altarpiece, with its haunting pictures of Adam and Eve, painted by the master Jan van Eyck, had created an international sensation and helped launch a new era in painting. It had been commissioned for Philip the Good, the great-grandfather of the two young prospective spouses. This kind of art was greatly admired in Spain as well, for Isabella's father had commissioned the Miraflores Altarpiece from a contemporary of Jan van Eyck's named Rogier van der Weyden.

The brother and sister, Philip and Margaret, were attractive and highly eligible marriage prospects in their own right. Numerous portraits of them were painted for the family, for public purposes, or for delivery to prospective spouses around Europe. A set of double panels called a diptych, dating from about 1495, contained portraits of both, with their coats of arms hovering around their heads to advertise the vast territories they were slated to inherit. Both teenagers—Philip was about sixteen and Margaret about fourteen—had seventeen separate shields and a separate coat of arms ringing their torsos.

Both appear in their portraits to have been fair-skinned and russet-haired, with delicate features and full red lips, physical characteristics that were much admired at the time. The portraits also communicated their extreme wealth: Philip is shown with a wide gold necklace, more precisely a golden collar, and an ermine-trimmed robe; Margaret wears a longer gold chain and a pendant with a large red stone at her throat; her dress is made of richly embroidered cloth. Their heads are covered—Philip with what appears to be a black velvet hat and Margaret with a red cap covering her hair and black veil cascading down the back onto her shoulders.[36]

Margaret was universally praised, but it was Philip who drew the deepest admiration. In fact, he was so good-looking that he had become commonly known as "Philip the Fair" or "Philip the Handsome." But the praise lavished on him didn't seem to go to his head, as he was uniformly described as having courtly good manners and great personal charm.

Despite their wealth and position, their childhoods had been tragic and difficult. Their mother, Mary, heiress to the rich Duchy of Burgundy and the grandchild of Philip the Good, had been married to Maximilian, the son of the Holy Roman emperor, and they produced the two children in quick succession. In 1482 Mary and Maximilian went hunting in the meadows near Bruges, and while jumping a waterway, Mary's horse swerved, the twenty-five-year-old woman fell off, and the horse fell on top of her. She suffered internal injuries, and three weeks later she was dead. Her death raised the usual succession complications, and while their grieving father tried to deal with them, Philip and Margaret were placed in the care of their step-grandmother. They spent the next years with her in the northern European territory of Flanders. Philip was four years old; Margaret was only a toddler.

Margaret was soon betrothed to the future king of France, Charles VIII, and at age three was transferred for proper instruction to the French court at the palace of Amboise. But Charles VIII jilted her when a richer heiress, Anne of Brittany, became available on the marriage market, and Margaret, at the vulnerable age of eleven, was sent home to await a different future. This was a double humiliation for Margaret and her father, because the widower Maximilian had intended to marry Anne of Brittany himself. Philip, meanwhile, the child heir to the Duchy of Burgundy, passed into the hands of a variety of self-serving courtiers, not unlike what had happened to Isabella's father and brothers. When they were betrothed to Juan and Juana, this history should have set off some alarm bells for Queen Isabella.

The marriage processions took a good bit of logistical planning. Juana, seventeen in 1496, would wed Philip first. A fleet would accompany her north to Flanders and would then return, bringing Margaret to Castile for her own marriage to Juan.

As the day approached for Juana's departure, the queen indicated that she had misgivings about the trip and perhaps also about Juana's ability to handle her new responsibilities. A long and risky sea route was necessary because hostilities had erupted across Europe as a result of France's invasion of Italy to seize Naples. But the journey from Castile to Flanders would take them along the coast of France. Isabella worried about what might happen to Juana if she were captured by the French and became a prisoner of war. The queen organized a fleet of 110 ships, with about ten thousand sailors and soldiers, to accompany her daughter. If bad weather hit, they would be unable to seek shelter in France and would be forced to sail west, farther out into the Atlantic Ocean, to try to reach England. Fearing the worst, Isabella accompanied Juana to her place of departure, the port city of Laredo, on the northern coast, and spent two nights aboard the ship with her daughter. She was very sad to see her go. When Juana finally left, Isabella remained behind watching from land and "bewailed her daughter a little,"[37] Peter Martyr wrote, before returning home to Burgos.

Queen Isabella sent at least four letters to the English court and King Henry VII, begging them to take care of Juana if by chance her ship should be driven onto English shores. In one letter she asked her ambassador to ensure that Juana would be given a "cordial reception" if she landed there. In another she asked King Henry VII to treat Juana as lovingly as he would treat his own daughter if she arrived in his lands.

Queen Isabella was "greatly distressed about her daughter," wrote Peter Martyr,

> because it was uncertain what mad winds, what the huge rocks of the stormy sea, what in fine the various dangers of the sea may have brought to her child, a weak girl . . . She turned over in her mind not only those things which are wont to happen to those sailing through this Spanish sea, but agitated with sighs she feared whatever might happen. She had with her day and night sailors skilled in this immense ocean and constantly inquired what winds blew, what they thought was the cause of the delay, lamenting her

lot that she had been forced to send her daughter to the farthest
Beglee [Belgium] at this season when the sea is almost impassable
on account of the approaching winter and the land on account
of the French enmity is precluded from having plenty of messengers.[38]

Juana was Isabella's first child to go so far away, but her mother's level
of concern seemed out of the ordinary for her. Juana seemed ready to
make the transition from home and was described as eager and happy
to go. She wasn't going to be a king or ruler herself, and so she hadn't
received quite the same education as her brother, but she was prepared
well enough. Juana and her sisters and their mother had studied Latin
with a young woman who had been a scholar at the University of Salamanca, Beatriz Galindo. Beatriz had an excellent command of Latin, and
people were impressed with Juana's adept facility with the language of
diplomacy. Juana was even able to compose verse in Latin, which drew
some favorable comment.

Nor had Juana received quite the same coaching in statecraft as her
brother Juan and older sister Isabel. For while the older children frequently accompanied their parents at state events, learning from early
ages how to handle the necessary protocol and court etiquette, Juana,
Catherine, and María were frequently left behind. Now, however, Queen
Isabella seemed reluctant to let Juana out of her sight. She seemed to
detect some sort of vulnerability in this girl, her middle child.

Queen Isabella was also off her stride because of other sad news she
had received. Her mother, who had been living all these years in Arévalo,
had finally died, in mid-August. This news hit the queen hard. Her
mother had lived in seclusion, "worn out and enfeebled by age,"[39] in Martyr's words; but Isabella had visited her once or twice a year, traveling on
horseback across the kingdom to do so, and spending time with her. She
had customarily waited on her mother personally during these visits. The
death was a shock to her, for her mother was the last remaining member
of Isabella's own original family. When Isabella at last left the coast for
Burgos, she was also going to take charge of her mother's interment.

Just days after Juana departed, and while Isabella was still dealing
with the melancholy of watching her daughter leave, she turned to the
duties of arranging for her mother's funeral procession and burial. She
wanted to make sure that her mother, so long forgotten in public life,

was nevertheless "carried honorably as became a Queen," wrote Martyr. Queen Isabella ordered her mother's body transported to a Carthusian monastery near Burgos, "where she laid her to rest near her father King Juan and her brother Alfonso, who had died so young himself."[40]

They were placed together in death in a Gothic monastery at Miraflores, located on the Santiago de Compostela pilgrimage trail, close to the burial places of several other kings and queens of Castile. The abbey had been founded by her father, and it was there that he had placed his prized altarpiece painted by Rogier van der Weyden. A Flemish-born sculptor, Gil de Siloé, designed their alabaster sepulchre. Its base is an eight-pointed star, a sacred symbol to Christians, Jews, and Muslims. It is extremely elaborate, densely textured and exuberantly three-dimensional, with a plethora of free-standing figures of saints and apostles guarding them in death. Isabella had wanted to make sure her parents were laid to rest together in a place they loved, near art objects they admired.

* * *

Meanwhile Juana arrived safely in Flanders on September 8, 1496, after a terrible seventeen-day voyage. As her mother had suspected, the ship had briefly landed in England before continuing on its way. Juana had lost many attendants and the bulk of her wedding presents when one of the ships accompanying her sank in a storm. And in the end, Philip was not there to greet her; he was in Austria's Tyrol with his father. He did not arrive to meet Juana for more than a month. Instead his sister Margaret, age sixteen, greeted Juana as the representative of the family.

Juana was temporarily lodging at a monastery, where "sixteen noble ladies and a matron clothed in cloth of gold" formed her entourage.[41] She and Margaret traveled together to Lille, to await Philip's arrival. Philip finally reached her on October 12. The long and embarrassing delay no doubt filled Juana with dismay. She had had five weeks to wonder whether she was being left at the altar, something that had in fact happened to her new sister-in-law Margaret.

But once in Philip's presence, all doubt disappeared. Juana and Philip had an immediate attraction to each other. All the reports about his looks and charm turned out to be accurate, and she was soon deeply smitten by her new husband. Six days later they received the blessing of Juana's chaplain for their marriage, and they consummated it immediately. They had their official wedding ceremony on October 20. Together they made a splendid appearance. "God turned out to be a good matchmaker when he gave that wife to that husband, and that husband to that wife," said Philip's father, Maximilian, basking in paternal pride.[42]

With the nuptial ceremonies concluded, Juana became a ruler of Burgundy through her marriage to Philip, who governed Burgundy. He ruled the land essentially as king, but his titles variously called him duke or archduke because of an historical anomaly in how the confederation of states it represented had come together—as a duchy designated by a French king for rule by his son, a duke. This realm was composed of a crescent-shaped set of provinces that included Holland, Belgium, and areas of northern France, particularly the Burgundy region. To the east was the Holy Roman Empire, which was ruled by Philip's father and grandfather, but to the west and south was France, which was a powerful and dangerous ally. France cast envious eyes at Burgundy's wealth and its cultural flowering, which actually preceded similar Renaissance developments in Italy.

Together Philip and Juana toured their domains with a large entourage, in what became a sort of grand tour of Burgundy and its important cities of Brussels, Ghent, Lille, Antwerp, and Bruges. They were enthusiastically greeted along the way as the duchy's new ruling family. Not a lot of news came back from Flanders, but of course it was a long trip, and the weather had been stormy. But eventually word arrived in Castile that Juana had been warmly received by her subjects, and Queen Isabella's concerns were laid to rest.

One chronicler was giddy with enthusiasm, describing Juana's triumphal entry into Antwerp, with trumpeters and other musicians celebrating her arrival:

> This very illustrious and virtuous lady ... of handsome bearing and gracious manner, the most richly adorned ever seen before in the lands of monsignor the archduke, rode a mule in the Spanish fashion with her head uncovered, accompanied by sixteen young noble ladies and one matron who followed her, dressed in golden cloth and mounted in the same manner, having pages with rich adornments.[43]

The archduchess was feted with great pageantry, in city after city, in an event known as a "joyous entry." Local officials would present the keys to the city. Feasts, balls, and tournaments were held everyplace, and each city sought to outdo the other with innovative and entertaining new kinds of revelries.

In the Great Square of Brussels, for example, a series of living tableaux, with actors representing fictitious, mythological, and historical figures, were presented for Juana's education and entertainment. One tableau depicted Juana in the guise of the biblical Judith, killing Holofernes to free her people. Similar scenes also showed women as heroines defying male authority. The exploits of Queen Isabella, Juana's mother, seemed to have attracted attention everywhere as representing a new model of woman as warrior, and clearly Juana's new subjects expected her to do more of the same in Flanders.

These scenes, tableaux, and amusements were considered so remarkable that an effort was made to preserve their memory. They were re-created in a special illuminated manuscript, called *The Joyous Entry of Joanna of Aragon-Castile,* which became a model for artworks of its kind. The extravagance of the court is unmistakable.

The illuminated manuscript makes it clear that the naïve and reserved young princess, who had been raised in a modest and chaste atmosphere, was seriously over her head in a sensuous and pleasure-loving court, where regular bribes from the French king had made the Flemish courtiers more loyal to the flamboyant French royal family than to Philip and Juana. Some of the living tableau scenes, for example, were subtly or overtly hostile to Juana and to her family.

In one scene, a richly dressed princess, portrayed as a dark-skinned Ethiopian, is depicted astride a horse, surrounded by strangely garbed companions, who are wearing hairy body suits and carrying clubs.[44] Racist northern Europeans commonly described Spaniards as being closely related to Africans, and this outlandish scene was insulting. In another tableau, Juana's mother Isabella is depicted taking the crown of Boabdil of Granada, who kneels before her. This presentation has a double edge: it acknowledges Isabella as having led the battle of reconquest against Granada, but a woman with a man kneeling before her, not in courtship but in subjugation, raises uncomfortable questions about gender dynamics.

Other scenes added a risqué twist. In a scene labeled "The Judgment of Paris," the three goddesses are depicted dancing nude, something that was not commonly portrayed in conservative Spanish art. A picture of the Flemish court, meanwhile, shows what appear to be many open displays of sexual activity between men and women while a male figure, perhaps the archduke, appears to be passed out in a drunken stupor on the edge of the revelry.

Meanwhile, in Castile, there seemed to be some trouble getting correspondence back and forth from Flanders. Juana didn't write home much and gave excuses for not responding to letters. Isabella and Ferdinand learned she was expecting a child, which was happy news for the grandparents-to-be. In August 1498 a Spanish cleric sent as an envoy said he had seen her in July and gave an encouraging account. "She is very handsome and stout," the cleric wrote. "Her pregnancy is much advanced."[45]

A few months after Juana's arrival, Margaret, Juan's bride, was sent on her way to Spain. The weather was again stormy, and the loss of the ship from Juana's fleet had made everyone a bit fearful about stepping on board, but eventually Margaret set out for Spain. She experienced the same kind of harrowing journey Juana had had; at one point, conditions aboard the ship seemed so perilous that the spunky princess put pen to paper and composed a poem in French about her plight: *Cy gist Margot la gentil Damoiselle, Qu' ha deuz marys et encore pucelle.* (Here lies Margaret, a gentle mademoiselle, two times married and a virgin still.)

But the fleet made it safely to the port of Santander, and Prince Juan and his father dashed out to meet her. She tried to kiss their hands to show respect in the traditional manner, but they instead welcomed her warmly and lovingly and conducted her to Burgos. There she met the queen, who was splendidly attired and embraced the girl upon meeting her.

Margaret charmed everyone and gathered crowds everywhere she went: "If you were to see her you would think that you beheld Venus herself," Peter Martyr gushed to a Spanish cardinal in Rome."[46] The apparent future queen of Spain and its possessions was welcomed with joy; the wedding ceremony took place on Palm Sunday, April 3, 1497. She was given a huge array of valuable gifts.

The marriage turned out to be one of those fortuitous situations where everyone in the family was instantly compatible. Even if they had not been related by marriage, it seemed they all would have been friends. Ferdinand praised the girl's "genteel, happy," and "benign" temperament.[47] Margaret turned out to share many of Isabella's interests. She was devout, like Isabella, and spent much time doing spiritual exercises from her Book of Hours, but she was also very active intellectually and was fascinated by art, as Isabella was.

Both women loved fine tapestries, which were expensive luxury items at the time. Particularly valuable ones, woven from silk or wool, sometimes with golden or silver thread, could cost as much as a warship and took teams of weavers up to a year to complete. Isabella had one of the finest tapestry collections in Europe, eventually numbering some 370; Margaret showed up in Spain with seventeen in her possession, and soon Isabella gave her more.[48]

They also liked paintings that featured women as the focal points. Scenes of women from the Bible were favorite subjects of Isabella's, and in time they proved to be a key part of Margaret's collection practices as well. One such painting, owned by Isabella and commissioned around the time Margaret arrived, somewhere between 1496 and 1499, shows Salome coolly displaying the severed head of John the Baptist to King Herod and her mother, Herodias. It was painted by one of Isabella's favorite artists, Juan de Flandes, or John of Flanders, whom Margaret also admired.[49] Isabella had wooed him to Castile from Flanders, and he was one of her court painters, paid a regular salary.

In these years, Isabella was also putting together the set of paintings illustrating Christ's life, which were painted by Juan de Flandes while Margaret was at court. One scene is believed to depict Margaret as the bride in the Wedding at Cana. As it turned out, Margaret particularly appreciated these paintings and recognized their merit.

Isabella took joy in giving Margaret presents. The young woman loved flowers and was given many pieces of jewelry that featured botanical designs. Some included daisies, a play on the French version of her name, Marguerite, or Daisy. Isabella kept to this theme in a gift of a piece of jewelry for Margaret designed to look like a white rose. It was made of gold covered with white enamel.[50]

The only problem was that there was a little awkwardness between the Flemings and the Spaniards. The Flemings were put off by the stiff formality of the Spanish and their elaborate and courtly rituals and customs. They thought the Spanish were priggish and inhibited. The Spanish felt the Flemings were lax, sloppy, and undisciplined. But the happy couple seemed to get along just fine.

* * *

Prince Juan frankly adored and idolized his wife. In fact, court doctors became concerned that he was so in love that he was wearing himself out and cutting into his sleep with his ardent lovemaking. According to Peter Martyr, physicians urged the queen to separate Juan and Margaret to give the prince some rest from his apparent new obsession with "frequent copulation," but Isabella was happy to see her son in love and chose not to intervene, adding that she believed that "it does not become men to separate those whom God has joined in the nuptial marriage bond."[51]

Juan and his bride took up residence in the university city of Salamanca, where the professors and students rejoiced at the prospect of increased patronage for their intellectual and artistic endeavors. The University of Salamanca was one of the greatest and oldest universities in Europe, and Queen Isabella supported scholarship there. She was encouraging higher education by employing scores of the school's students, or *letrados,* as bureaucrats to staff the growing governmental apparatus. She was also commissioning other new buildings similar to her parents' tomb that featured her signature architecture style, called Isabelline, which was ornately Gothic but with Flemish and Islamic influences and a great deal of surface decoration. The facade of the main building of the University of Salamanca was soon constructed in such a style, garnished with floral designs, fantastic creatures, and heraldic devices, all emphasizing the grandeur of the empire that Spain was becoming. The fact that the crown prince was establishing his home in Salamanca further burnished the civic luster. Adding to everyone's joy, Margaret learned she was pregnant.

This period—the spring and summer of 1497—was the high point of Isabella's personal life. She had defeated the Muslims at Granada and restored peace in Castile. Columbus had brought back exciting news of the lands he had reached on the other side of the Atlantic Ocean, and future prosperity for Spain seemed increasingly assured. Juan was happily, even blissfully, married; the reports from Flanders were more mixed, but Juana had unquestionably made a very good match. Princess Isabel was back at home, which was a comfort to the queen, and María and Catherine were growing into lovely and respected young ladies who were a pleasure to their parents. Catherine was preparing for her eventual departure to England.

Everything was going so well. Now all that remained was securing the Castilian border with Portugal with another marriage between the Cas-

tilian and Portuguese royal families. Queen Isabella continued to negotiate with King Manuel of Portugal, urging him again to accept María,
but he remained insistent that Princess Isabel, and only Princess Isabel,
would do. He rejected María again. Princess Isabel continued to say no.
Manuel persisted in asking for Isabel's hand. It became a test of wills
between Isabel and her mother.

Of course the outcome was predetermined. There was no test of wills
that Queen Isabella did not win. Finally Princess Isabel agreed, to King
Manuel's delight. Queen Isabella and King Ferdinand spent the summer together in Medina del Campo and visited Juan and Margaret in
Salamanca, then headed west to Valencia de Alcántara, where the marriage between Princess Isabel and King Manuel was going to occur. The
reluctant bride had asked that the wedding be celebrated with as little
festivity as possible, so the events that had been planned were subdued
in nature.

As the wedding day of Manuel and Princess Isabel approached, however, word came by fast horsemen that Prince Juan had suddenly fallen
seriously ill. Friar Diego de Deza, bishop of Salamanca, wrote that Juan,
who had been so happy just days before, was weakening and had lost his
appetite. "All of us here are begging Your Highnesses to come here, that
there can be an improvement in his health; it is of such a necessity that
we did not wait for your command to call the queen's doctor and other
physicians," he wrote to Ferdinand and Isabella.[52]

Ferdinand rushed to Juan's side; Isabella could not come because she
was deep into the preparations for Princess Isabel's wedding. In the next
few days, the king sent his wife conflicting messages designed to hide the
fatal prognosis. Crazy with grief, he even sent a vague report implying
that he himself had died, thinking that it would lessen the queen's pain
if she eventually discovered her husband had been spared even as her son
was taken.

King Manuel also wanted to fend off the news. When he heard that
Juan was dying, he asked that the information be withheld until he and
Princess Isabel were wed, to prevent her from experiencing that pain at
her wedding. He probably also feared the princess would attempt to delay
their nuptials during the period of mourning.

Prince Juan, for his part, meanwhile, had accepted his fate with serenity, trying to comfort his father, who pleaded with him to make a greater
effort to live. He said he was content with going to God. His placid accep-

tance of his precipitous death suggests he had been ill or weak in the past. He was known to be sickly, with a weak stomach, and he may have finally succumbed to tuberculosis.

Juan's final act, besides asking his parents to care for his young wife, who was now pregnant with their child, was to request that money from his estate be used to buy freedom for Christian slaves held captive in Muslim hands. That bequest dwarfed all the other bequests in his will, even that of providing for his unborn child. He died on October 4, 1497. When Queen Isabella received the terrible news, she accepted it with sorrowful resignation: "God gave him to me and He has taken him away."[53]

Prince Juan was buried in Salamanca and later transferred to Ávila, where he had wished to be buried. Margaret, grief-stricken, fell desperately ill herself. Isabella rushed to her side and nursed her back to health lovingly. Margaret later told her father that she thought Isabella's ministrations had saved her life. Her baby, however, was born prematurely and died. Margaret's father Maximilian privately harbored suspicions about what had caused the healthy young woman to lose the baby. He speculated that the French might have found a way to place abortion-inducing herbs into Margaret's food so that she would miscarry. It's not impossible: certainly the French would have viewed the infant—who would have been heir to Castile and Aragon and linked to Burgundy and the German confederation, but under Spanish domination—as an enormous geopolitical threat.

Regardless of what caused the miscarriage, however, the fact of the matter was that Juan's child was gone as well. "This new loss" dashed the hopes of Isabella and Ferdinand, Zurita wrote, and "their woes deepened."[54]

This tragic news—the death first of Juan and then of his heir—spread across Europe. The kingdom descended into a pit of mourning. "The only light of all Spain is extinguished," Peter Martyr wrote to Hernán de Talavera, now archbishop of Granada. " . . . The sovereigns endeavor to dissemble [their] so great grief, but we discern their mind prostrate within them. They often cast eyes at the face of each other sitting in the open when what is hid comes out."[55]

Even their enemies felt compassion for the family. The French ambassador Philippe de Commynes said that Juan's death caused "unspeakable grief of the king and queen, but especially the queen, who was more like to die than to live, and certainly I never heard of so solemn and universal a mourning for any prince in Europe."[56] Commynes said he was told that all the tradesmen donned coarse black garments and shut up their shops for forty days. Even the animals were dressed in mourning. The nobility and the gentry covered their mules with black cloth down to their very knees, and all over their body and heads, so that there was nothing to be seen but their ears. Black banners were hung on all the gates of the cities.[57]

> What a terrible blow must this be to a family, which had known nothing before but felicity and renown, and had a larger territory (I mean by succession) than any other family in Christendom! . . . What a sad and surprising turn must this accident be, at a time when they had reduced their kingdom to obedience, regulated the laws, settled the administration of justice, were so well and happy in their own persons, as if God and man had conspired to advance their power and honor above all the rest of the princes in Europe.[58]

But this turn of events, tragic for Castile and his family, was another piece of extraordinary good fortune for King Manuel the Fortunate of Portugal. In one fell swoop, he had attained the wife he wanted and also became heir to a truly huge empire. He and the young Princess Isabel, now the heir apparent in Castile and Aragon, would dominate the entire Iberian peninsula, as well as all overseas holdings of Portugal and Spain. By 1497, it had become apparent that those overseas territories might be immense.

Conceivably Queen Isabella had anticipated this series of events when she negotiated the division of the New World with Portugal at the Treaty of Tordesillas. Is it possible that when she gave half the world to King João, she had known then that the other half would likely devolve to her daughter Isabel as queen and heiress to Castile? Had she sat at the table knowing that Manuel would likely inherit the throne, that he would cast his eyes on Isabel, and that Isabel would likely become the queen's heiress as well? When she split the world in half, in other words, did she know she was keeping half of it for herself and giving half to her beloved daughter as the queen of Portugal, and that the two halves were likely to come together in the next generation?

All that is of course unknowable, but given Isabella's keen perception about politics and family dynamics in Portugal and Spain, it seems more than probable. When the Treaty of Tordesillas was signed in June 1494,

King João had no legitimate male heir to his throne, and he was attempting to have his out-of-wedlock son, Jorge, legitimized by Pope Alexander VI so that he could inherit the throne. But the pope refused, and so in that last year of João's life, it had become obvious that Manuel would one day be king of Portugal.

Prince Juan's death meant that Isabel and Manuel had to return to Spain to be sworn in as the heirs to the kingdom. The succession was complicated by the fact that Princess Isabel was a woman. That was not an issue in Castile, where Queen Isabella's success in governing had made the issue a moot point, but the Cortes of Aragon balked at the idea of a female succession. For that reason, there was great excitement when it was discovered that Princess Isabel was pregnant. If she had a son, the boy would inherit everything. In this matter, Princess Isabel had once more done everything expected of her. She became pregnant within months of her marriage to Manuel, and she produced a male child on August 23, 1498, in Zaragoza.

But Princess Isabel's fasting and self-denial at last took its toll. She was very thin when she gave birth, and she died within an hour of the baby's arrival. She had asked to be buried dressed as a nun and to be interred at the Convent of Santa Isabel in Toledo, in Castile. In death she wanted to remain at home. Queen Isabella held her daughter in her arms as she expired.[59]

This new and terrible tragedy befell Isabella and Ferdinand just one year after Prince Juan's death, when they were still grieving the loss of their son. This time, however, they were able to take consolation in the birth of a son, the new heir to the thrones of Portugal, Castile, and Aragon, as well as all the overseas dominions held by both countries. Aragon quickly granted him the right of succession. They named the infant boy Miguel de la Paz, but it soon became apparent he was weakly and would need careful tending to survive. King Manuel, now a widower, was needed back in Portugal, and so he went home, trustingly leaving the child in his mother-in-law's care. Queen Isabella gave the child her full attention, but observers saw that the boy had only a small chance of growing to adulthood.

* * *

As these sad events unfolded, Princess Margaret had been staying with her in-laws, lovingly and supportively. She was close to her mother-in-law and had learned much from her about governing. But now she needed to decide what to do with her own life. Her Flemish attendants had never really taken to Spain, and it seemed to her that it was time to go home. Her departure was painful for Queen Isabella, because she had had such high hopes for Margaret's marriage with Juan and had hoped that her intelligent and thoughtful daughter-in-law would be the mother of her grandchild and heir. Juan's death made that dream go up in smoke, or so it seemed at the time.

Margaret returned to Flanders and took up residence at her brother Philip's court, where she had friendly relations with Juana, whom she had met three years earlier when Juana arrived as a bride-to-be. Margaret remained loyal to Spain, wearing Spanish costume to underscore her allegiance. Almost immediately, however, the men in her family began pondering other marriage alliances for her, and soon she was shipped away to the Duke of Savoy, who ruled an area of southeastern France adjoining Italy and Switzerland. She made the best of it, as she always did, and within a few years her new husband died, and she was home again for good.

But she was in Ghent for a very happy event in early 1500. It was the birth of Charles, the firstborn male child of Philip and Juana. He was born on February 24, which was, under the Roman Catholic calendar, the Day of Saint Matthias, a point that Isabella considered particularly significant. It was a day freighted with fortune and obligation, because according to Christian belief, after Jesus died and ascended to heaven, the eleven remaining apostles discussed among themselves how to replace the turncoat Judas, who had killed himself, as the twelfth member of their group. Two men were considered, and after praying, the apostles cast lots to decide who would be named. Matthias won the honor but also the obligation, as many of the disciples knew they faced the possibility of martyrdom. "Believe me, Sire," Isabella told the king when she learned of Charles's birth, "that as the lot fell on Matthias, so the lot has fallen on this one to be the heir to these our realms."[60]

Again Queen Isabella had been prescient. In the summer of 1500, just a few months after Charles was born, little Miguel de la Paz, Manuel and Isabel's son, died in his grandmother's arms. Charles, living in faraway Flanders, was now the heir to the kingdom but was being raised far from the land that Isabella had spent her life so fiercely defending. This final blow, the death of Miguel, was like a wound to Isabella's chest, and from this time, she began a downhill slide in energy, health, and drive.

The widowed Margaret was there for the baptism of little Charles, however. She was named the godmother and was selected to hold the infant over the baptismal font before the Ghent Altarpiece, also known as *The Adoration of the Mystic Lamb*. Again loyally wearing Spanish clothing and still grieving over her husband's death, Margaret cradled Juan's little nephew in her arms. She had asked that the boy be named Juan, both for herself and as something his mother, Juana, might have appreciated as well, because of the name's long history in their family. But Archduke Philip, Juana's husband, insisted on naming the boy Charles after his own grandfather.[61]

Just the same, Margaret was there now to watch over things, just as she would have done with her own child.

NINETEEN

TURKS AT THE DOOR

s Isabella fully entered middle age, when she was in her forties, she realized that the problem that had haunted her since her youth—the aggressive expansion of the Ottoman Turks—was not going away and in fact seemed on the verge of accelerating. That was a terrifying prospect for the Christians of southern Europe, who could see the Turks were heading their way.

It meant that Queen Isabella, even after twenty years on the throne, would get no rest. She had spent the first four years of her reign at war with Portugal to bring peace to Castile's western flank; she had spent the next three years crisscrossing Castile to bring order to a kingdom that had been torn by civil war and rampant criminality; she had spent the next twelve years fighting the Nasrid dynasty to secure Granada and hence the Iberian peninsula. The next nine years of her life—from 1494 to 1503—would be absorbed by efforts to protect and strengthen southern Europe from assault by the Ottoman Turks, who seemed invincible.

The Ottoman Empire was a kind of perpetual war machine. Military operations were at the core of its existence. Circulating the booty won in war was the cornerstone of its economy. Extensive slaving operations gave the empire a constant supply of human fodder to send off to battle. "The ideal of *gazâ*, holy war, was an important factor in the foundation and development of the Ottoman state," wrote Turkish historian Halil İnalcık. "Society in the frontier principalities conformed to a particular cultural pattern, inbued with the ideal of continuous Holy War and continuous expansion of the . . . realms of Islam until they covered the whole world. Gazâ was a religious duty, inspiring every kind of enterprise and sacrifice."[1]

It was also a system of "endless predation."[2] According to the historian Jason Goodwin, "The Ottoman Empire lived for war. Every governor in this empire was a general; every policeman was a janissary; every mountain pass had its guards, and every road a military destination. . . . Even madmen had a regiment, the *deli,* or loons, Riskers of their Souls, who were used, since they did not object, as human battering rams, or human bridges."[3]

The Turkish empire presented Christians with a daunting ideological challenge as well as a military threat. The Turks were admirable in many ways: at home they were well ordered, philanthropic, personally clean, and often devoutly religious, something that can make people kindly, patient, and at peace with themselves. For those under their domination, the Turks were remarkably tolerant for the age: many of the Jews who left Spain found safe haven in Turkish lands; homosexuality, which was a crime in western Europe at the time, was accepted without criticism. A number of Catholic clerics who had been opposed to Isabella's insistence that they live simply and honor their vows of chastity found that life in the Muslim world was more pleasant. They took their concubines with them and settled into happy married life. Islam itself is an attractive religion, and most people under Ottoman rule eventually converted to that faith, either out of sincere belief or because it made life easier. For many men it would have been a fairly easy transition, assuming they were not deeply committed Christians or Jews. People who wished to retain their own religious beliefs could do so by paying extra taxes and accepting the embarrassment of being treated as a despised infidel, but it was more advantageous to convert. For all those reasons, people who lived in Muslim lands generally converted to Islam.

But people in other lands who resisted Turkish domination for religious reasons, or because they preferred self-rule or feared life under the Turks, found themselves facing an entirely different prospect: enslavement, pedophilia, theft of children, robbery, death, and annihilation. For women, there were the additional threats of rape, sexual abuse, and submission to increasingly conservative rules governing female behavior. For Queen Isabella, there was no option but resistance.

The Turkish challenge was growing. Long feared for their powerful land armies, the Turks were beginning to move into the maritime arena as well. They were amassing a huge fleet of ships to make new rounds of attacks on western Europe and were becoming masters of the Mediterranean Sea. Turkish-supported piracy, meanwhile, was becoming a plague along the coasts of southern Europe, causing people to abandon the coastal regions.

Meanwhile childish squabbles among Christian rulers in western Europe were destabilizing the balance of power and making the Italian peninsula, in particular, appear weak and ripe for the plucking. In 1494 the French king Charles VIII had proceeded with his crazy scheme to seize Naples, and amazingly enough, he had been able to march through Italy almost unimpeded, looting and pillaging all the way down the peninsula. The callow and corrupt tyrants who ran Italy's city-states simply surrendered, one after the other, as he arrived and offered him free passage through their lands. When Charles VIII arrived in Naples, his men descended into an orgy of drinking and licentiousness, just as syphilis from the New World was making its unhappy appearance in Europe. Fewer than one-tenth of his army ultimately staggered back home; the rest had died through battle, starvation, or disease. Italy had been exposed as completely vulnerable to assault, and Ferdinand's Aragonese cousins who ruled Naples had proven themselves so incompetent and unpopular among their subjects that they had ended up fleeing for their lives rather than remaining to defend their people.

But the Ottoman Empire had undergone some changes since 1480, when the Turks had captured Otranto, and it had a new leader. The Neapolitans, with help from Spain, Portugal, and Hungary, had managed to recover Otranto during a moment of Ottoman weakness. In May 1481, Sultan Mehmed the Conqueror suddenly died. Many people suspected he had been poisoned. His death set the stage for a bitter succession battle. Mehmed had preferred his son Djem as his successor, but another son, Bayezid, wanted the throne as well. This was ordinarily the circumstance that led to the murder by one brother of the others, as Mehmed had specified by law.

The two brothers gathered their supporters and clashed in battle, and Bayezid emerged as the victor. But then Djem did a surprising thing: he fled to refuge in Christian Europe, surrendering at Bodrum, a strongly fortified castle on the Turkish coast that served as one of Christianity's few surviving outposts in the region. The commanders at Bodrum, the ancient home of the Mausoleum of Halicarnassus, accepted Djem and transferred him to the even more heavily fortified base of Rhodes, operated by the Knights Hospitaller, or the Order of St. John, originally a mission to the poor in Jerusalem that was a remnant from the First Crusade. From Rhodes, Djem was sent to mainland Europe and finally to Rome, where he became a guest and hostage of Pope Innocent VIII.

Sultan Bayezid was glad to have Djem out of his realm, which allowed him to establish and secure his own reign, and he began paying the pope 400 golden ducats a year for keeping Djem as a guest and prisoner in the Vatican. Over the next decade, Djem became a valuable asset for rival European powers because he remained a potential contender for the Ottoman throne and thus a potent threat to Bayezid that made the Turkish sultan reluctant to engage the Europeans in direct combat. Djem lived in Rome until the French king Charles VIII invaded Italy. Then when Charles left Rome, he took Djem with him as a political bargaining chip, and the Turkish prince died mysteriously on the way to Naples in 1495. He had perhaps been poisoned on Bayezid's orders, or he may have fallen victim to his own overindulgence in women, food, and drink. Whatever the cause, his death lifted the check on Ottoman aggression.

These events filled the twelve-year period when Isabella was completing the conquest of Granada. The Ottoman army at the time was by far the most powerful land force in Europe, able to muster hundreds of thousands of soldiers when it decided to launch an attack. If it had chosen to intercede on behalf of the Muslims of Granada, it could have landed troops through Granada's Mediterranean ports and prevented completion of the Reconquest. It could even have gone on to invade northward into Spain itself, in a repeat of the events of 711.

In fact, the Muslims in Granada had sought help from the Turks, but according to a Turkish-Greek pirate named Khair ad-Din, known in the West as Barbarrosa, or Red Beard, the Turks had decided the Muslims of Andalusia were a lost cause and chose not to intervene.

But they were planning to get to western Europe eventually. First they needed to deal with the Mamluks of Egypt, many of whom were embracing a mystical sect called Sufism, which was a subset of the Shiite branch of Islam; the Sunni Muslims of the Ottoman Empire considered it a doubly dangerous heresy. Once Egypt and adjacent North Africa were secured, southern Europe would be a short jump across the Mediterranean Sea.

But Bayezid was chafing at the inaction against western Europe because the war establishment that he commanded was constantly pressuring him to make immediate advances on the Christian West. Year by year more and more threatening reports came to Spain—delivered by envoys in letters, and in person by desperate refugees from eastern Europe who had migrated to the West—warning that Bayezid was assembling a fleet to target Mediterranean islands that were held by Christian rulers. Popes Innocent VIII and then Alexander VI sent a steady stream of warnings as well. Bayezid's movements were a constant source of concern for Isabella and Ferdinand, whose islands, Sicily and Majorca, might be particular targets for attack.

In 1488 the Venetians were told that a "huge fleet" that included "warships of every kind" was being assembled by Bayezid to attack Venetian possessions in the Aegean Sea, and that the sultan "had set his heart on Cyprus," a Venetian outpost near the coast of Turkey.[4] The Venetians sent out a fleet to meet him, and Bayezid retreated home. In 1490 the Turks were on the advance again, and Venetians hastily prepared for battle once more, but the clash that followed was inconclusive.

The Ottomans finally found an overland opening into Europe after the death of the doughty warrior Matthias Corvinus, king of Hungary, prompting them to engage in massive raids into the leaderless kingdom in 1492. "The great incursions of 1492 brought swift and terrible ruin to the Christians," writes the Ottoman historian V. J. Parry. They hit again the next year: "The incursions were renewed in 1493 with increased ferocity, Croatia and lower Styria being ravaged once more and the Croat nobility almost annihilated at Udbina on 9 September."[5]

* * *

The terrible losses on the Christian side that year came at what became known as the Battle of Krbava Field, near the small inland town of Udbina, just across the Adriatic Sea from Italy, in southern Croatia. Some seven thousand Croatian soldiers lost their lives in a single day, and most of the kingdom's nobility was killed or enslaved. It caused another vast movement of population, as waves of Croatian refugees fled toward Austria and the Italian coast to escape from the Turks.

In western Europe, there was a macabre guessing game each year of wondering where the Turks would strike next. Would it be Sicily? Cyprus? Rhodes? Rome? Naples? The reports from the places the Turks had successfully conquered fueled additional terror.

Refugees fleeing the Ottoman advances were traumatized. Marin Becikemi, an Albanian survivor of the Scutari attack, who had been an eleven-year-old eyewitness to the slaughter of twenty-six of his thirty family members, told the Venetian Senate that he believed Bayezid II was the "bloodiest person the world has ever seen." Years later he recalled:

> With my own eyes I have seen Venetian blood flow like fountains. I have observed that countless citizens from the most noble stock have been made to roam. How many noble captains have I seen slain! How many harbors and shores have I seen littered with the corpses of highborn men of renown! How many ships have been sunk! How many vanquished cities have I seen disappear! To recall the terrible dangers of our day causes the hearts of all to tremble.[6]

The surviving accounts from Ottoman and Arab sources suggest that Christian fears were not unfounded. The Persian scholar Idris-i Bitlisi, speaking about the raids on the castles of Zabljak, in Montenegro, and Drisht, in Albania, said Muslim warriors at one point caught the Christians as they were trying to flee in boats loaded with their possessions.

> The heroic men of valor had never seen such vessels, filled to the brim with precious plunder beyond description, not to mention the handsome boys and the women as beautiful as the houris of paradise. Enflamed with lust for loot and remuneration, the men swarmed the riverbank. A host of trained swimmers disrobed and dove into the water, clenching their swords between their jaws. They swam furiously to unleash their swords of courage. In a moment they cut down the infidels with their sharp sabers and took all the families and the beautiful women captive. They also took booty, money, and countless possessions.[7]

The Ottoman Turks were callous about the deaths of people they called "infidels." An Ottoman account of the siege of Scutari (or Shkodra), near Kosovo in Albania, where many of the inhabitants holding out against the Turkish assault starved to death, described the inhabitants with contempt. "Those squalid pigs ate whatever they could find, swallowing anything, regardless of whether it was pure or foul," wrote Ottoman chronicler Kemal Pasha-zade.[8]

This was all bad enough. But in addition, the Ottoman Empire was

growing increasingly oppressive to women of all walks of life, as a fun-
damentalist orthodoxy clamped tighter and tighter controls on women's
behavior. Reports of life under the Turks would have been unimaginably
distasteful to a woman like the strong-willed and independent-minded
Queen Isabella, who was physically active and regularly rode cross-
country across her domains governing and dispensing justice in public
forums. And as a mother of four daughters, the accounts would have
been particularly chilling.

The rape of captured Christian women was not only condoned but
advocated by Ottoman rulers. When the pirate Barbarossa and his chronicler wrote his memoirs, called in Turkish *Gazavat-I Hayreddin Pasa,* or
Holy War of Hayreddin Pasha, Barbarossa described how his father had
taken possession of his mother after the Turks conquered Mytilene, a city
on the Greek island of Lesbos, in 1462:

> When Sultan Mehmet took Mytilene from the Christians, he left
> behind to guard them a military encampment of soldiers. They
> were men and had arrived without women, and there were no
> Moorish women they could marry because all the women on the
> island were Christian—and they asked for some to be provided so
> they could continue in his service. The Great Sultan, seeing their
> just petition, ordered that they should ask for wives among the
> daughters of the Christians. And, because [the Christians] did not
> wish to give them to them, they took the women by force and mar-
> ried them. And in this way there was good communication and
> employment of them and the land was guarded. The soldiers, with
> this provided, remained content.[9]

And so Barbarossa's mother, a widow, subsequently produced four sons
and two daughters with her new husband. The boys became pirates who
attacked Christian vessels and made their living capturing Christians
and Jews to enslave them.

Bayezid II, the new sultan, was more conservative, more orthodox
than his father Mehmed had been. In the fourteenth century, western European merchants had described Ottoman streets teeming with
women; by the sixteenth century, merchants reported that there were
few women to be seen outside at all. As the years went by, women were
required to conceal their bodies in voluminous robes, some eventually

covering not just their heads but also their faces and their eyes, leaving them stumbling along the streets when they were allowed to venture out of their homes.

Conditions for women deteriorated over the years, according to reports issued much later by the Turkish Ministry of the Interior, describing what had become invisible to Western visitors. Women were increasingly sequestered inside their homes, living within high walls, seeing sunlight only through latticed windows, often guarded by eunuchs. They were forbidden to go to public places in the company of men, even with their husbands. Educating them was seen as problematic, even verging on being what the Turkish government called a "sin." Women had to be concealed from the world. "Even the tips of her fingers were not to be seen," one government report said.[10]

The Ottomans were contemptuous of the Christians for allowing their women to talk to men and walk about unaccompanied. The Ottoman Evliya Celebi, the scion of a wealthy family with ties to the court, wrote an account of his travels, *Seyahatname,* in the early 1600s. He visited a resort town near Vienna:

All the infidel notables and sophisticates of the walled town of Vienna take their pleasure for weeks and months in this city and its gardens and orchards.... Because the climate is delightful, the lovely boys and girls of this city are renowned. Indeed, the men and women do not flee from one another. The women sit together with us Ottomans, drinking and chatting, and their husbands do not say a word but rather step outside. And this is not considered shameful. The reason is that throughout Christendom women are in charge, and they have behaved in this disreputable fashion ever since the time of the Virgin Mary.[11]

Being captured by the Turks was a social death sentence for Christian or Jewish women, because they would be viewed in negative terms in their own cultures if they ever managed to get home. Female slaves in the Ottoman Empire were required to provide sexual services to their masters. The demeaning and degrading practice of polygamy, meanwhile, which gave men the right to have multiple wives and was forbidden by Christian and Jewish practice, was universally accepted in Ottoman lands. This meant that a woman who married while under Turkish domination and who then managed to escape would have committed a sin, and broken the law, by participating in a bigamous union.

Of course, slavery was not unique to the Ottoman Empire. It was widespread all over the world in 1500; in Castile and Aragon, most prisoners taken in war, particularly Canary Islanders and black Africans, were kept captive in homes. Some Muslims captured in the war against Granada, such as following the siege of Málaga, were also enslaved. Isabella's daughters each had two or three in their royal entourages when they married and moved from Spain.

But in Ottoman Turkey, the enslavement of Christians was one of the empire's leading and most lucrative industries, fueled by raids and constant military expansion. Nobles and serfs were equally at risk. Tens of thousands of Christians were enslaved each year; Barbarossa himself seized at least forty thousand in his career, according to his own accounts. In the 1500s about 17,500 slaves were taken each year from Russia and Poland.[12] The eastern European slave trade was so great that the words *slave* and *Slav* are related.

Expert slave merchants accompanied Turkish raiding parties, gathering up the captives and calculating their worth. The slaves were collected in groups of ten, bound in chains, and forced to march with their captors; younger captives, including children and infants, were placed in baskets and bags and carried in carts or on mules. Sometimes the children were seen as valuable because they could be adopted and trained for work or put to sexual use. But sometimes the littlest children were left behind as unnecessary nuisances when their parents and older siblings were led away. In June 1499, following an Ottoman attack near Zadar in Dalmatia, the Venetians found about fifty abandoned infants in a field.[13]

Islamic law permitted slavery for people born as slaves or captured in war. Free Muslims were not permitted to be enslaved, but it was permissible to enslave Christians, Jews, and pagans. The entire economy "rested upon slavery," according to the Turkish historian Halil Inalcik. "Endless wars provided a continuous supply of slaves," writes the historian Pal Fodor.[14]

The going price of slaves rose and fell according to supply and demand. Inalcik, who analyzed estate records in the Ottoman Empire, has written that they were the third most important part of estates left when people died, after cash and real estate. Silk weavers, for example, depended on slaves as trained laborers who produced the merchandise they sold. But sometimes an excess of slaves made them less valuable: at one point, slaves sold for "as little as a fur cap."[15] Selling the labor of slaves was another industry, according to Inalcik: "Many people made a livelihood of hiring out their slaves for 7 or 12 akçes a day."[16] (Akçes were a small copper coin of minimal value.)

Once people were enslaved by the Turks, they were typically never heard from again. Mass deportation to a distant land was the system the Turks used to break the bonds between a captive and his or her home. Sometimes for a brief period after a raiding party struck, survivors, if any, could ransom their family members; but few families had the ready cash to pay the kind of ransoms that were demanded. Slaves who attempted to escape were cruelly punished by being beaten, starved, or forced to wear heavy chains. Once a slave was moved thousands of miles away from home, the chances of escape became remote. Escape was viewed as so unlikely that it could only occur through supernatural forces. Shrines in Hungary contain accounts of miraculous escapes from Turkish captors, usually through the intercession of angels. Those who escaped with their shackles on their bodies deposited them in churches, a custom that Queen Isabella repeated when she placed the chains of liberated Christian slaves on the walls of the church she built in Toledo, San Juan de los Reyes.

Not many people in those times were literate, so first-person accounts of life in captivity were rare, compelling, and widely circulated. One Christian, a student at the time of his capture, spent twenty years as an Ottoman slave and was bought and sold seven times before he escaped. Georgius de Hungaria's memoir of his experiences became a best seller across the continent, printed and reprinted between 1480 and about 1550. He became a cleric in Rome and described how the slave industry operated in the Ottoman Empire:

In all the provinces, just as for other sorts of trafficking, a particular public place is held for buying and selling human beings, and places legally assigned for this purpose. To this location and public selling ground, the poor captives are brought, bound with ropes and chains, as if sheep for slaughter. There, they are examined and stripped naked. There, a rational creature made in the image of God is compared and sold for the cheapest price like a dumb animal. There (and this is a shameful thing to say)

the genitals of both men and women are handled publicly by all
and shown in the open. They are forced to walk naked in front of
everyone, to run, walk, leap, so that it becomes plainly evident,
whether each is weak or strong, male or female, old or young (and,
for women,) virgin or corrupted. If they see someone blush with
shame, they stand around to urge those on even more, beating
them with staves, punching them, so that they do by force that
which of their own free will they would be ashamed to do in front
of everyone.

There a son is sold with his mother watching and grieving.
There, a mother is bought in the presence and to the dismay of her
son. In that place, a wife is made sport of, like a prostitute, as her
husband grows ashamed, and she is given to another man. There
a small boy is seized from the bosom of his mother, and . . . his
mother is separated from him. . . . There no dignity is granted, nor
is any social class spared. There a holy man and a commoner are
sold at the same price. There a soldier and a country bumpkin are
weighed in the same balance. Furthermore, this is just the beginning of their evils. . . .

. . . Oh how many, unwilling to bear the crisis of such an experience, fell to the depth of desperation! Oh how many, exposing
themselves to die in various ways, fled into the hills and woods
and perished because of starvation or thirst, and there's also this
final evil: taking their own hands against themselves, they either
wrung out their own lives with a noose, or hurling themselves
into the river, they lost the life of their body and spirit at the same
time.[17]

Slaves who attempted to escape and were caught, Georgius wrote, were
"whipped, tortured and beaten," crippled by having their limbs burned
or had their ears or noses cut off.[18]

He also confirmed the accounts of how women lived within the Ottoman Empire. Women were not allowed to buy or sell anything, he wrote.
They were not allowed to ride horses. They went veiled even in their own
homes. In one house where he had lived, the daughter-in-law had never
eaten, spoken a word, or uncovered her face in the presence of her father-
in-law, despite having lived in the same house with him for twenty years.
And "a conversation between a man and a woman is so rare in public that

if you were among them for a year, you would scarcely be able to experience this once."[19]

There was more. A government-imposed program of child slavery, called the *devsirme* system, operated within lands that were already securely under Turkish domination. The system had been initiated in about 1432 but was expanded under the regimes of Mehmed II and Bayezid II, during the time that Isabella's children were being born and growing to adulthood. Each year between 1451 and 1481, some fifteen to twenty thousand Christian children were collected through this system.[20]

It had specific rules. Every three or five years, a group of Turkish officials would travel from town to town in Christian regions. Children between the ages of eight and eighteen would be brought into public squares for their inspection, and Turkish officials would select the most intelligent and attractive and take them away. The children of nobles and clerics were preferred. Only Christian children were taken; Jewish children were viewed as better suited to commerce. Particularly good-looking children would be sent to the palace; strong and healthy ones would become workers or soldiers. All were removed from their families, circumcised, and taken to Turkish homes to be raised before they entered service of some kind.[21] Many were trained as Janissary warriors and spent their lives killing people. They were forbidden from marrying, which had the effect of maximizing their ferocity.

Some scholars of Ottoman history claim that being selected for the child tribute was actually a favor to rural children, to whom it represented a chance at upward mobility within the military or government bureaucracy. But most families preferred not to have their most promising children taken from them, never to be seen again. Some parents were known to have maimed their children to make them less desirable as slaves.

Meanwhile, back in western Europe, as they had been before and after the fall of Constantinople in 1453, a series of popes were begging the Christian princes to take note, resolve their differences, and come together for a common defense of Christendom against the Turks.

Rulers of the lands in the path of the Turkish advance—Hungary, Venice, and those adjoining the Mediterranean and Spain—were acutely aware of the situation and dealt with it to the best of their ability. Rulers in England and Scotland, however, felt it was not their problem and repeatedly pleaded poverty when asked for help. King James IV of Scotland, for example, rebuffed Pope Innocent VIII when he was asked for funds in 1490 to help fend off the Turkish advances that were threatening Italy. "My kingdom, situated to the west and north, at a very great distance from Rome, does not overflow with silver and gold, although it abounds in other proper commodities," the king told the pope.[22]

Similarly, in late 1493, Pope Alexander VI wrote to the English king Henry VII about the threat from the Turks, describing the massacres that had occurred in Dalmatia and Croatia. Henry responded, as most northern European rulers did, with fervent expressions of sympathy about the "immense slaughter" but nothing of substance. Writing from Windsor Castle on January 12, Henry told the pope that though he found the news "very distressing," the "great distance and embarrassment by a variety of cares" impeded him from offering anything more concrete.[23]

This was one reason Queen Isabella was so insistent about the marriages of her daughters to the kings of England and Scotland. She was trying to get those rulers to take a greater interest in joining efforts against the Ottomans.

But Isabella wasn't the only ruler in Christendom who wanted to fend off the Turks. Ironically, the subterfuge under which King Charles VIII had launched his attack on Italy had involved claiming that he was a Christian warrior preparing to fight back against the Turks. He may have believed this himself, at least on some level. But according to his ambassador, Philippe de Commynes, King Charles never had any intention of doing anything that difficult: the king "talked much at his first entrance into Italy" of his "designs against the Turks, . . . declaring he undertook that enterprise for no other end but to be nearer and more ready to invade him; but it was an ill invention, a mere fraud."[24]

Some people had hoped that what Charles was saying was true. As the most powerful ruler in western Europe, the French king was best equipped to make a stand. Pope Alexander VI wrote to Ferdinand and Isabella in March 1494 asking them to urge Charles VIII to set aside his interest in Naples and focus on the threat from the east.[25] The next month, on April 6, 1494, the pope wrote to Charles himself, praising him for his intention to make war on the Turks.[26]

Inside France, however, the king's plan seemed like madness. "For to all persons of experience and wisdom it was looked upon as a very dangerous undertaking," Commynes wrote. Moreover, the expedition, though gaily adorned, was poorly equipped and outfitted: "The king was young, foolish, and obstinate, without either money, officers or soldiers."

He had borrowed the money for the expedition from the bank of Genoa at a high interest rate, marching off without "tents or pavilions, though it was winter when the army entered into Lombardy."[27]

The Italians didn't take the French king very seriously, viewing him as foolish and gullible; moreover, his head appeared overly large and misproportioned to his body, causing him to be called Charles the Fathead. Most rulers across Europe seemed to view his proposed military expedition as a "holiday excursion by a hare-brained youth," according to the historian John Addington Symonds.[28] But Charles's naïveté and desire to somehow win glory for himself made him vulnerable to the scheming of others. The ruling family of Naples was unpopular in Italy; Charles was told that he would be welcomed as a liberator by the Neapolitans.

That was in fact true: King Ferrante of Naples, who was Ferdinand's cousin and also his brother-in-law, was not well liked. He was illegitimate, which raised succession issues, and he used a variety of brutal tactics to establish and maintain power, including imprisoning and killing many members of the ancient Neapolitan nobility. He kept some nobles imprisoned for years; he had ordered others killed, and then had their corpses stuffed and mounted like trophies and arranged them around a banquet table. He found it particularly amusing to kill people who had just enjoyed his hospitality. This had the understandable effect of silencing much dissent in Naples, but it did not win him many friends.

Consequently, when Charles first set out toward Italy, no one acted to oppose him. Venice, for example, waited to see what would happen next. The city did not want "to arouse the king's ill-feeling," recalled Venetian chronicler Pietro Bembo,

> especially since it was possible that Charles would abandon the undertaking of his own accord, as the generality of men change their minds almost at a whim; or young and ignorant of the military arts as he was, he might be put off by the difficulty and scale of the war to be waged; or again, if some other delay arose, or other rulers put difficulties in his path, he might be unable to extricate himself.[29]

In Florence, meanwhile, the government was foundering. The brilliant leader Lorenzo de' Medici died in early 1492, leaving his son Piero as ruler, but the young man turned out to be a disappointment to the

Florentines. They were, in any event, engaged in deep introspection about their place in the world, mesmerized by the prophetic fire-and-brimstone preaching of Friar Girolamo Savonarola, who was exhorting the multitude to reject the secular materialism and corruption of the modern world and of the church itself. Rodrigo Borgia's ascension to the papacy only made Savonarola's criticism of the church in Rome even sharper and isolated Florence even more than before.

Many Christians, moreover, hoped on some level, as did Pope Alexander VI, that King Charles would succeed in using Italy as a base to fight the Turks. Ever since the fall of Constantinople in 1453, Christians had suffered an almost unending string of disappointments, defeats, and setbacks at the hands of Muslims. The word spread through eastern Europe that Charles was coming with a mighty army to set things right. The Turks heard of his advance and warned their allies in the conquered lands of Albania, Croatia, and Macedonia to retreat to positions in the hills; the Christians in those countries watched the coastline and prayed for deliverance.

Isabella and Ferdinand were apparently taken in as well, at least to some extent. In a memorandum they sent from the royal court in Burgos to the English court in July 1495, they said they had offered to assist Charles, promising to allow French forces to use a base that they had occupied in North Africa to launch his invasion of the Holy Land. They had told him that it was a good time to strike, "for the glory of God and the oppression of the infidels," because the Moors were "much debilitated by hunger and pestilence." But Charles, they said, had been cool to their suggestion.[30]

The sovereigns were also trying to turn the situation to their own advantage. Charles offered to give back to Ferdinand, for free, Perpignan and Roussillon, which Ferdinand's father, King Juan, had lost during the Catalan civil war. That offer was too good to pass up, and Ferdinand and Isabella quickly signed a peace treaty with France to that effect. That agreement put Spain on the sidelines, and in no position to oppose French initiatives elsewhere, at least for a while.

Soon Charles's true intentions became clear. Ferdinand and Isabella decided that the French king's real goal was unseating King Ferrante, who was, of course, their blood relation. They sent Antonio de Fonseca, another member of the influential Fonseca family, as their ambassador, instructed to intercept Charles and head him off, warning that the right to succession of the Neapolitan crown should be decided through legal processes. The Spanish sovereigns told Fonseca that if Charles did not agree to halt, he was authorized to "tear up the draft of the old treaty before his eyes and declare hostilities."[31] That was exactly what Fonseca did. Ferdinand and Isabella gave substance to this gesture by gathering an army and dispatching a fleet to Naples, under the command of Isabella's childhood friend, Gonzalo Fernández de Córdoba. The fleet soon departed from the Castilian port of Málaga.

But Charles was undeterred and continued on his way. Within weeks, he and his invading army reached Rome, entered it without a trace of resistance, humiliated the pope, and laid waste to the countryside everywhere they passed. It was on that occasion that they took the Turkish prince Djem into their custody, then continued on their march south to Naples. Charles said he planned to topple Bayezid from power and replace him with Djem as a puppet sultan under Christian control. But that idea, if it was ever anything more than a pipedream, evaporated with Djem's death.

Coincidentally, around that same time, the tyrannical King Ferrante of Naples suddenly died. His son Alfonso replaced him on the throne. But when Alfonso realized that Charles was on his way south with an army, the kingship ceased to have the same appeal as previously. Alfonso timorously fled from his own kingdom, leaving his twenty-four-year-old son Ferrandino to rule in his place. Alfonso crossed to Sicily, which was ruled by his Spanish cousin, King Ferdinand, and meekly declared himself a private citizen. Young Ferrandino attempted to rally a defense but blanched in the face of the ferocity of the French and urged his citizens to surrender to avoid being killed. His subjects agreed with alacrity and blocked Ferrandino from reentering Naples; he departed the city with his relatives and moved his remaining forces offshore.

King Charles was consequently invited to enter Naples. This welcome, on February 22, 1495, was soon bitterly regretted by the city's inhabitants. His troops began pillaging the city; they seized valuable properties for themselves from ancient families.

As if that weren't bad enough, a strange, mystifying, and disturbing new disease erupted catastrophically in the city. It was that virulent strain of syphilis, the ailment so new to Europe that it lacked a name. Depending on where it first came to public attention, it became known as the "French disease" or the "Spanish disease." It soon spread from the south of Italy to the north, and then to the Ottoman Empire, where

Turkish statesman Idris-i Bitlisi, who contracted it, called it a previously unknown disease.[32] The Venetian chronicler Pietro Bembo was one of the earliest to describe it in Europe:

> It generally afflicts the genitals first of all, and the body is wracked with pain, then boils and blotches break out, chiefly on the head and face but also on other limbs. Tumors and, as it were, lumps appear, at first somewhat hard, later full of blood and pus as well. Thus many people met a miserable end after long torments in almost every limb, and so disfigured by protuberances and ulcers as to be scarcely recognizable. It was impossible to know what medicines were needed against this new and unprecedented pestilence.[33]

And so it raged across Europe, North Africa, and the Middle East, killing many people and leaving others disfigured, blind, or sterile.

* * *

Not surprisingly, Sultan Bayezid II was watching Charles's advance with particular interest. At first he had been worried about the strength and power of King Charles's army and the threat posed by his own brother, Prince Djem. But the subsequent developments had revealed Italy to be weak, disunited, and powerless in the face of a coordinated assault. Europe as a whole suddenly seemed far more vulnerable than it had ever been, and the Turks prepared to take advantage of the opportunity. "Sultan Bayezid had in fact already begun to outfit old galleys and construct new ones as soon as he found out that Charles had entered Florence, and he ordered his infantry and cavalry to get themselves ready for war so that they would be at his disposal when he wanted them," wrote Bembo.[34]

But the brutality of the French invasion of Italy had truly shocked the rest of Europe. The army sent by Ferdinand and Isabella had arrived on the peninsula to resist the French, but now the sovereigns mobilized a group of other rulers, including the leaders of the Republic of Venice, the Holy Roman emperor Maximilian I, and the pope, calling themselves the Holy League. Maximilian was, of course, inclined to join up right away—he had been miffed at King Charles ever since the young French king had jilted his daughter and stolen his own betrothed wife, Anne of Brittany. The Venetians, for their part, had decided by now that things were clearly out of hand; the English were soon persuaded to join the alliance because King Henry VII remained so keen to please the blue-blooded Queen Isabella.

Ferdinand and Isabella used the proposed marriage of Catherine and Arthur, something Henry VII really wanted, to pressure him into sending support for the war against the French in Italy, ideally as soon as possible. This was a point they repeatedly made clear in letters to their ambassador in England. "A single day, now that the war has actually begun, is of greater moment than a year would have been before hostilities between Spain and France had taken place," they wrote in March 1496. "The War is a war for the Pope and the Church."[35]

In 1495 and 1496, around the time the marriage contract between Catherine and Arthur was finalized, Venice, Spain, Pope Alexander VI, and the Holy Roman Empire signed a twenty-five-year treaty to defend and protect the pope. King Henry soon jumped on board as well.

Each of the rulers pledged to contribute to a standing force of 8,000 cavalry and 1,000 infantry, and to the costs of sending a fleet, as needed, to aid in Italy's defense. This alliance formed so quickly and quietly that the French ambassador to Venice, Philippe de Commynes, who had been in constant communication with the ambassadors of the other kingdoms, was entirely blindsided by it. As Bembo recalled, Commynes was "dumbstruck" and stumbled from the Doge's palace, asking for companions to recount what he had just been told, as he was unable to process it all.[36]

Isabella organized Spain's contribution to this force as an army that consisted of "specifically Castilian troops, under a Castilian commander," who was her lifelong friend and stalwart support Gonzalo Fernández de Córdoba. Of the six captains assigned to lead the troops, four had served with the Santa Hermandad during the war with Granada. Some had fought for Isabella ever since the war against Portugal over the Castilian succession. Francisco de Bobadilla was originally assigned to go to Italy as well but was sent to Hispaniola instead to deal with the uprising against Christopher Columbus. About five thousand men went with the first contingent; more followed later. These battle-hardened troops brought to the Italian campaign the techniques they had used to win the war against Granada—siegecraft, light artillery, and the element of surprise—to startling success. Most important, they brought a unique esprit de corps to battles that had been dominated by mercenary soldiers who were fighting for personal gain, not for a greater cause in which they believed.[37]

This Spanish fleet, with some forty ships, joined up with the Neapolitan king Ferrandino, who had twelve ships of his own that had remained faithful to him. When they arrived in Naples, they found that many of the residents had returned their allegiance to Ferrandino and that everywhere people were beginning to fight back against the French.

Despite shortages of food and supplies, Gonzalo Fernández de Córdoba quickly distinguished himself on the Italian battlefields, where he earned the nickname "the Great Captain." The town of Crotone, for example, had shifted its allegiance from Ferrandino to the French, then back to Ferrandino and back to the French; Gonzalo landed in Calabria and put an end to the vacillations by taking the town by storm. The Venetians watched in admiration as Gonzalo, whom Bembo called "a man of great spirit and remarkable courage," broke the French and their supporters in a "pitched battle," killing a number of officers, as well as two hundred infantry and cavalry, and took more than twenty nobles prisoner.[38] Gonzalo similarly turned the tide of battle in the town of Tela.

By July 1496, King Ferrandino was back on the throne of Naples, mostly as a result of the help he got from Spain, specifically from Gonzalo Fernández de Córdoba. He soon died, however, and was replaced on the throne by his uncle Federico. Naples had had four kings in three years, and none of them had been a successful ruler. The Kingdom of Naples, the largest single territory in Italy and the part most exposed to possible invasion, continued drifting in its habitual rudderless manner.

Pope Alexander VI was grateful for the help he had received from the Spanish sovereigns. In December 1496 he conferred on them an impressive new title, the Catholic Kings, as a recognition and reward for helping expel the French from Naples and for their successful conquest of Granada.[39] The sovereigns took enormous pride in this new designation and began to use it as their personal sobriquet. It became the way their subjects referred to them as well. In a letter announcing the new title that had been granted, the pope wrote:

> You serve as a public notice and example to Christian princes, because your strength and arms have not been for the ruin and killing of other Christians out of ambition for territory and dominion but instead for the benefit of Christians and in defense of the Church and faith. . . . Your reverence and devotion to the Holy See, so many times demonstrated, is once again patently clear in the

recent war in Naples. To whom, then, is the title Catholic Monarchs better suited than to your majesties, who continually strive to defend and enlarge the Catholic faith and the Catholic Church?[40]

The instrument of these most recent successes, Gonzalo Fernández de Córdoba, remained in Italy for two more years, engaging in mopping-up operations, including giving some help to the pope in recovering Rome's port city of Ostia. The Great Captain at last returned to Spain in the summer of 1498. He went immediately to Zaragoza, where the royal court was sitting. King Ferdinand embraced him with kisses upon his arrival and conducted him to the presence of the queen. She was sitting on her throne, surrounded by her ladies-in-waiting, but when she saw that Gonzalo had arrived, she arose and walked to the landing to meet him. "He bowed one knee to the ground and kissed her hand; but she raised him up and embraced him, saying, 'Great Captain, you are very welcome.'"[41]

Isabella showed her appreciation for his accomplishment with generous grants of towns, castles, and rents in Granada and Íllora, adding to the properties he already owned in Loja. Gonzalo, a second son, was now a wealthy man in his own right.

In the aftermath of the victory that returned King Ferrandino to his throne, however, Ferdinand and Isabella felt that Naples had not adequately appreciated their contributions, something that proved irritating to them. They stewed over the perceived ingratitude.

King Charles VIII, meanwhile, more or less walked away from Italy, abandoning his soldiers and doing nothing to bring home the survivors; he died a few years later of an injury suffered when he hit his head on a lintel. He may have been suffering from syphilis as well: he may have become infertile, as he left no heirs, and his cousin the Duke of Orléans inherited his throne, taking the title of King Louis XII.

Ironically, according to Commynes, Charles might have actually prevailed in battle against the Turks if he had attacked Bayezid at that particular moment instead of going after Naples. "Millions of Christians" in eastern Europe had taken Charles seriously, Commynes had learned in Venice, and had been preparing an uprising to support him. In Thessaly, for example, more than five thousand men had rallied for battle. "All these countries, Albania, Sclavonia, and Greece, all very populous, all acquainted with the fame and character of our king by their correspondents in Venice and Apulia, to whom they wrote constantly and expected nothing but their direction to rebel," waited fruitlessly. If he had advanced at that time, King Charles could have succeeded, his ambassador sadly concluded.[42]

Instead the Turks remained an implacable reality. With Djem out of the way, Bayezid decided the opportunity was at hand to strike again at Europe, this time at Venice. In 1496 he closed Ottoman ports to Venetian grain merchants, cutting off their trade access. He imprisoned Venetian merchants living in the Ottoman Empire. In 1497 a Venetian ship carrying Christian pilgrims to Jerusalem was captured, and its passengers were killed or enslaved.[43]

By mid-year 1499, Peter Martyr reported, rumors were flying in the Castilian court that the Turks were amassing a "great fleet" in Istanbul and that a "land army is being collected throughout all Greece."[44] More details arrived within a few months: the fleet comprised more than three hundred ships, which was a vast armada for the day, including a number of ships with what Martyr called "sea towers," floating fortresses that could come alongside other ships and allow soldiers in the towers to shoot down onto the crews of their opponents. Much to the relief of the Spanish, the fleet was hit by a storm, destroying some of the ships, but they were disappointed to learn that the Turks saw the loss as only a temporary setback. Bayezid was said to be leading a force of 120,000 warriors.[45]

In August 1499, Bayezid besieged and took Lepanto, one of several trading entrepôts that Venice maintained on the west coast of Greece; they were key parts of the city's Adriatic trading empire. By this point, the Venetians had almost given up hope of seeing reinforcements from western Europe; they had already been disappointed so often when they had asked for help. Financially exhausted and demoralized by the Turkish drubbing that had now lasted more than sixty years, they gave up Lepanto almost without a fight.

That winter, when they recovered their nerve a bit, the Venetians sent an envoy to Istanbul to ask for Lepanto to be restored and for the merchants to be released. Sultan Bayezid instead demanded that they surrender the additional cities of Modon and Coron and begin to pay an annual tribute as well.[46] His intention was clearly to eviscerate the remaining Venetian trading ports on the Greek mainland and to consolidate his control over the entire kingdom. Hearing this, Pope Alexander VI put out a plea to the western European nations to send support to Venice.

Isabella and Ferdinand decided it was time to weigh in. The queen sent a fleet to aid the Venetians, again in the charge of her beloved friend Gonzalo Fernández de Córdoba. She asked other countries to join in. On January 20, 1500, she and Ferdinand told their ambassador, González de Puebla, to plead with the King of England to follow her lead.

> We have received word from Italy of the damage that the Turks have done to the fleet of the Venetians and their lands, and that they have taken the city of Lepanto, as there was very little resistance from the Venetians, which causes us much sadness as you can imagine. Seeing the danger that is coming to the defense of Christianity from these, we have decided to send them our fleet. . . . Please tell the king of England our brother that we are begging him to help as well against these Turks, enemies of our holy Catholic faith. Write soon to tell us what he says and what he can provide.[47]

But Henry VII of England was not inclined to help. In June, González de Puebla responded to the queen. "Henry greatly praised their intention of sending a fleet against the Turks," he wrote, "but added that, although he was on very intimate terms with Venice, the Venetians had said nothing to him about their great need. Henry does not seem to be inclined to take part in the expedition against the Turks."[48]

The French sent some troops to aid the Venetians, but they soon withdrew from the front and were lost at sea.

Gonzalo Fernández de Córdoba's fleet, however, was on the way. He sailed from Málaga with six hundred seasoned knights and about eight thousand foot soldiers. They headed to Sicily, arrived there on July 19, 1500, and stayed for about a month. Gonzalo encountered some delays in his departure due to very high temperatures and difficulty obtaining food for his troops. Ferdinand was ruler there, but officials in Sicily did not seem to feel a sense of urgency in aiding the Castilian troops, despite the marital alliance of the two rulers.

So Gonzalo took his time getting to the eastern Mediterranean. He was also misled into believing the Venetians had the situation under control. On August 13 he learned they did not. He received a desperate message from the pope urging him to go to the relief of the city of Modon. But by the time he arrived in the area, both Modon and Coron had fallen to the Turks.

An unfortunate mistake at Modon had contributed to that fortress's loss on August 9. The Turks had blockaded the port, and the defenders were running low on food and gunpowder. Both sides—the Venetians and the Turks—knew these fresh supplies were essential to the fortress's defense. The Turkish commanders told their soldiers that anyone who allowed goods to get through the blockade would be executed. The Venetians nonetheless managed to get supply ships past the blockade and into the harbor, inspiring a wave of delight among the garrison. The fort's commander, desperate to get the gunpowder up from the ships to the fortress, announced that whoever got the first cask of gunpowder within the walls would be rewarded with a gold drachma, and so a number of soldiers deserted their posts and clambered down to replenish the munitions.

But there were Albanian spies or turncoats inside the fortress, and they signaled by waving their hands and their cloaks to inform the Turks that the stations had been left unguarded. The Turks threw their ladders up against the undefended sections of the walls, and more than ten thousand Turks surged inside. "A lamentable slaughter takes place; no one escaped who was not killed, captured or led as a slave," Martyr wrote. "The Prince of the Turks, joyful with that victory, returns to Byzantium puffed up and insolent."[49]

Another victory soon added to the Turks' satisfaction. On the way back to Istanbul, the Turkish forces passed by the port of Coron, which had already heard what had happened in Modon. Its defenders, "terrified by the calamity of their neighbors and the threats of the Turks, surrendered itself," Martyr concluded. "Thus through our sloth the strength of the enemy increased and ours is weakened."[50]

It was into this unpromising scene, far to the east from his home bases in Castile, that the Great Captain finally arrived with orders to stem the Turkish tide. Gonzalo and his men joined the Venetian fleet at Corfu, an island off the west coast of Greece, south of the Adriatic Sea, on October 2. By November 7, he was pondering an attack on the port of Cephalonia, which the Turks had used as their staging point when they attacked Lepanto. He thought the port "was the best in the world and it is an island that belongs to the Turks," he wrote to the sovereigns.[51] Moreover, only about three hundred Turks were stationed there, with a civilian Christian population of about 3,500. The island had an interesting history: it had once belonged to Leonardo Toco, a close relation of the former Byzantine emperors of Constantinople; the Turks had taken it in revenge for the assistance that it had given to the Christian general Skanderbeg, who had resisted the Turkish advances in the 1460s.

Carrying with him, as he always did into battle, a figure of a baby representing the infant Jesus, Gonzalo Fernández de Córdoba announced himself and his men to the Turks manning the castle at Cephalonia as "the conquerors of the Moors in Spain" and demanded they surrender. The Turks were not permitted to do such a thing and said they would not give up, but they sent him a gift of a golden bow and a golden quiver filled with arrows as a sign of respect. A ferocious battle then began for the castle, known to the Christians as the Fort of Saint George. The Spaniards and Venetians ran low on food and grew "ravenous with hunger," eating whatever was available.[52]

At one point the Turks attempted to tunnel out from under the walls of the fortress, but the Spaniards discovered and blew up the tunnel, killing the men trapped inside. Gonzalo came up with a plan. He ordered a steady bombardment for several days, leaving the defenders exhausted. Then he ordered a coordinated attack. They won the victory on December 24, 1500.

This conquest, although relatively small, brought great glory to Spain. The return of Cephalonia was "a victory very celebrated everywhere," the Aragonese historian Jerónimo Zurita wrote, because it was the only fortress the Christians had recovered from the Turks since the fall of Constantinople almost fifty years before.[53] It was to be the last Christian victory and recovery of land from the Turks for more than one hundred years, but it became a symbol of the possibility of effective resistance. The Turks never reconquered the island, and much later, the Hapsburgs used it as a base when they fought and defeated the Turks at the climactic sea battle off Lepanto.

The unique success at Cephalonia was "achieved only with Spanish help," writes John Julius Norwich in *A History of Venice*.[54] The Venetians recognized that Gonzalo deserved the credit for the victory. They called him to their city, where they gave him the honorary title of Citizen of Venice, and they loaded him with awards and applause. The last, very old descendant of the ruling clan of the Byzantine Empire called Gonzalo the inheritor of the throne of Byzantium.

The victory, to be sure, was limited in what it had accomplished. In December 1502 the Venetians agreed to a treaty that gave the Ottomans everything they had asked for on the mainland. This marked an important turning point in Ottoman-Venetian relations. "From the military standpoint, the 1499–1502 war seems a decisive moment in the construction of a hardening line between the Christian and Islamic Mediterranean worlds," writes the historian Daniel Goffman. "As a result of this conflict, the front between the Ottomans and the Venetians became almost entirely coastal, and thus clearly delineated."[55] But the victory at Cephalonia and the resulting truce helped win the Christian West a two-decade breathing space from Turkish incursions. The period of "Ottoman disengagement from Europe ... was to last until 1521," writes the historian Colin Imber, while the Turks turned their attention to violently squelching religious heresies and schismatic movements inside the Muslim world.[56]

These events in the eastern Mediterranean proved a bittersweet victory for the Great Captain, for Gonzalo soon learned that while he had been fighting the Turks in Greece, the conquered Muslims in Spain had rebelled and killed his brother. With much of the Spanish army away, a revolt had sprung up among the Muslims of Andalusia, and they had killed a number of Castilian soldiers, including Gonzalo's older brother Don Alonso de Aguilar. The Muslims remained furious about the Reconquest and angry that they were being forced to convert to Christianity. Alonso's body was sliced into pieces and rendered almost unrecognizable.

But Gonzalo couldn't go home, and he couldn't go any further against the Turks in eastern Europe either. Instead he was recalled to Sicily, to deal with new hostilities arising in Italy. France, now under King Louis XII, had decided to retake Naples. Ferdinand and Isabella were growing fatigued with the need to repeatedly come to the rescue of their unpopular cousins, who lacked the support of their own people and were under perpetual pressure from the French. They were also still smarting from the sting of the Neapolitan ruling family's ingratitude. "We have never had any gratitude shown us by King Fadrique for what we formerly did for him, nor any amity or brotherhood, but quite the contrary," the Spanish sovereigns wrote their ambassador in England. "Notwithstanding, we have not ceased to travail for him, endeavoring by all possible means to bring about a reconciliation between him and the King of France, in order that he might remain secure in his kingdom, and that the King of France might desist from the enterprise he had in hand."[57]

Faced with flagging support from Castile and a new threat from

France, the Neapolitan ruling family decided to reach out for military reinforcement from an unexpected quarter. They asked for troops from the Turks, or so they told Ferdinand and Isabella. This step went much, much too far, the sovereigns told their ambassador:

> King Fadrique sought aid from the Turks, giving us notice of the same by his ambassadors more than a year ago, and certified us of his determination, notwithstanding that we opposed him, and censured him, and endeavored to turn him away from his purpose. At last we told him that we should be his chiefest enemies if he should persist in his purpose, but we could never prevail upon him to relinquish it. . . . The Turks also, having taken part in the matter, that alone would have been cause sufficient for us not only to refuse to aid King Fadrique, but to oppose him. . . . Seeing that King Fadrique was and still is determined to have recourse to the Turks, it was our duty for the sake of the Christian faith, to unite ourselves with Christian princes.[58]

And so Ferdinand and Isabella decided to ally themselves with their old enemy, France, and to partition Naples between the two kingdoms, which they quickly did. The Neapolitan ruling family left for exile in various places—King Fadrique went to live in France; others, including Ferdinand's sister and the male heir to the throne, Fadrique's son Ferdinand, the Duke of Calabria, went to Spain.

Isabella and Ferdinand were a bit defensive about their action here: they had in effect taken by force a kingdom ruled by their relatives. But they said at the time that they were only being practical about it. They told people at the court that they had accepted the lesser of two evils—that they had, as Peter Martyr explained, opted to take "half of the kingdom lest it should all fall into the hands of the French," and that they hoped in time to gain control of the entire kingdom. This caused some consternation, however, Martyr noted, because King Fadrique was "indeed an excellent man."[59]

Not surprisingly, the two allies in the partition of Naples, Spain and France, found themselves too deeply at odds to be able to share their trophy amicably. They engaged in border disputes that ultimately erupted into war. Under new orders from the Spanish sovereigns, Gonzalo found himself once more engaged in pitched battles with the French. One of these battles, fought at Cerignola on April 28, 1503, is considered by military hisorians to be a turning point in modern warfare. Using small firearms and shooting from trenches, Gonzalo Fernández de Córdoba's military tactics set a model that would be followed by Spaniards all over the world and that established Iberian supremacy on the battlefield for the next two hundred years. He also instituted the battlefield custom, after that battle, of praying for the fallen among the enemy.

Ultimately, Spain emerged as the unquestioned winner against France, ending up in control of Naples. That meant that the Spanish Empire now included the entire southern half of the peninsula of Italy. Gonzalo Fernández de Córdoba became the very popular viceroy of Naples, establishing Spanish rule there so firmly that Spain would retain control of the city and surrounding provinces for the next three hundred years.

Under the administration of the Spanish Hapsburgs, the Neapolitans would not enjoy self-government, and they would suffer from the religious intolerance that by this time was ingrained into the culture. Still, the Neapolitans were somewhat protected from incursions by pirates that were backed and supported by the Turks and, for the most part, from further assault by the French.

More important, Spanish imperial control reduced and eventually eliminated the threat of an Ottoman invasion of the Italian peninsula, at a time when Turkish aggression was approaching its zenith in the Mediterranean. "Until the battle of Lepanto in 1571, Naples remained the bulwark of Christianity against the Turks," writes the historian Tommaso Astarita.[60]

TWENTY

ISRAEL IN EXILE

After the fall of Granada and the forced departure of the Jews in 1492, Jews and Muslims continued to fall victim to the Spanish sovereigns' single-minded pursuit of Catholicism.

Queen Isabella's goal was not actually to expel people but rather to force everyone to convert to Christianity—both for the security of the nation and for the protection, as she saw it, of their immortal souls. But to those Muslims and Jews who were determined to maintain their own faiths, conversion was unacceptable, even unthinkable. Religious hatreds are corrosive and self-perpetuating; what happened in these years would have implications for the centuries ahead.

Queen Isabella did not deny what she was doing. She never questioned it, and in fact, over the years, her views hardened. She believed she had done what was necessary, even while acknowledging that it had caused pain. In the 1480s, for example, some Spaniards, including the bishop of Segovia, had raised criticisms and asked Pope Innocent VIII to intervene and stop the Spanish Inquisition. She admitted to her ambassador in Rome, "I have caused great calamities and depopulated towns, provinces and kingdoms."[1] But she justified it to the pope by saying that she had done so to protect the Christian faith.

Queen Isabella was not alone in that time and at that place in doing what she thought was to her own people's advantage. It was a heartless age. In these years, Muslims justified cruelties to Christians, Christians

justified cruelties to Muslims, and Christians and Muslims justified cruelties to Jews. Some Jews, angry at the injustices they suffered at Christian hands, became enthusiastic supporters of the Ottoman regime.
Elijah Capsali, a rabbi in Venetian-controlled Crete, wrote approvingly of
Turkish aggression against Christians, which he viewed as evidence of a
coming spiritual cataclysm that would produce the Messiah.[2] Many Jews
across Europe and in the Ottoman Empire shared his view.

Moreover, each of the three faiths focused on its own injuries without
exhibiting much compassion for the woes of others. Christians mourned
most for Christians, Muslims for Muslims, and Jews for Jews. Surviving
accounts in which people sympathize with the problems of people from
other faiths are few and far between. Spanish Christians noted the grief-
stricken faces of Jews fleeing Spain but rationalized it. Merchants traveling in the Ottoman Empire noted the slave markets stocked with pitiful
Christian slaves but seldom questioned whether the institution of slavery
was just. It was simply another harsh fact in a hard world.

Very soon after the Reconquest was completed, new problems arose
for the Muslims of Andalusia. At the time when Granada surrendered,
Queen Isabella and King Ferdinand had made several specific pledges
to the Muslims. They could keep their possessions and homes, operate their mosques with freedom from interference, and maintain their
customs, language, and style of dress. In short, they could continue
to observe their faith without hindrance. According to Arab accounts,
the surrender had been made with "tears by all present," but the Muslims had agreed because their lives and their religious beliefs would be
protected. They had had confidence that Isabella and Ferdinand would
adhere to these terms, and their accounts noted that the soldier who had
handled the negotiations on behalf of the sovereigns had been Gonzalo
Fernández de Córdoba, the Great Captain, a respected figure who spoke
Arabic fluently.[3]

Obtaining a peaceful surrender in 1492 had, of course, saved many
lives on both sides, as Queen Isabella was inalterably determined to take
possession of the south of Spain. From her perspective, there was no
other choice.

Almost immediately afterward, however, Isabella began pressuring
Muslims throughout the former emirate to convert, and within ten years,
she and her husband had completely retracted the pledge they had made
to them. In a sense it is not surprising because it was consistent with her

fundamental beliefs. She thought she had a spiritual obligation, both personally and as queen, to evangelize and increase the number of Christians. She could also justify it on the basis that it was dangerous to have a large Muslim population in the south of Spain—they might welcome an Ottoman Turk invasion. But the Muslims of Granada, understandably enough, felt that they had been deceived.

At first the conversion process relied on gentle but persistent persuasion. Queen Isabella's confessor, the converso Hernán de Talavera, was made archbishop of Granada, and he immediately set to work to convert as many people as possible through a gradual process of education about the Christian faith. He studied Arabic and read the Koran to look for common elements that he could use to illustrate the similarities between the two faiths. It was an important post for Talavera, and a loss to Isabella, who had relied on his judgment and good sense for more than a decade. When her daughter Isabel was transferred as a hostage to Portugal at the age of eight, for example, it was Talavera who had been given oversight and responsibility for the girl.[4]

Talavera's close friend, the Count of Tendilla, was put in place as the top Castilian administrator in Andalusia. The count was Inigo López de Mendoza, nephew of Cardinal Mendoza and a scion of a family known for its thoughtful and broad-minded intellectuals. He was the man who had induced the Italian humanist Peter Martyr to move to Castile to introduce classical learning and Renaissance thought. The Count of Tendilla was respectful of the Islamic faith and the customs of the local people, but he was also committed to the work of converting everyone to Christianity.

The two men quietly made inroads among the Muslim population, converting a significant number to Christianity and making many friends among the Muslims of Andalusia, who considered both men trustworthy. But their evangelization efforts nevertheless left many Muslims uneasy, and many reluctantly began to consider moving to North Africa to escape the pressure.

Talavera's move to Granada had left a vacancy in the post of confessor to the queen. To fill it, she had chosen Francisco Jiménez de Cisneros, a fierce, ascetic spiritual warrior who came from a poor family in Torrelaguna, a small town near Madrid. Isabella approved of Cisneros's stringent religious and moral code, and his abstinence suggested his life had a higher purpose than those of people who merely enjoyed pleasures. Many faiths have a long tradition of viewing self-denial as a kind of holiness. Isabella viewed ascetics as holier than ordinary people, and she may have had some reason. Certainly a person who has renounced worldly ambitions has taken a first step toward concentration on spiritual matters, even if the resulting spiritual judgments are not necessarily sound. Moreover, as a result of his renunciation, Cisneros was certainly less likely than others to be personally corrupt; she would not need to worry that he was trying to gather worldly wealth for himself. In choosing Cisneros, she was consciously choosing a spiritual adviser who was the polar opposite of the sensual, pleasure-loving, but also more tolerant Rodrigo Borgia.

Cardinal Pedro Mendoza died in late 1494, leaving a vacancy in the top clerical post in Castile, the archbishopric of Toledo, which he had taken over at the death of Archbishop Carrillo. Isabella then arranged for the position to be transferred to Cisneros. It would make him the most important and powerful cleric in Spain. Cisneros at first rejected the job, preferring a monkish and solitary life, but eventually he was pressured into accepting. This was highly irritating to King Ferdinand, who had wanted his illegitimate son Alonso, the archbishop of Zaragoza, by now the father of a large and growing brood of children, to have the top religious post in Castile, as it would give him both additional wealth and additional prestige. But Isabella was adamant that Cisneros was the man for the job. He was the antithesis of the king's son, who had demonstrated in many ways his unsuitability for a religious calling. But in choosing a spiritual zealot, she also put her kingdom on a more rigid, and less tolerant, religious path. It was clearly a conscious decision and a shift of course. Hardened by war and saddened by life, Queen Isabella was herself becoming more rigid and less tolerant.

* * *

By the late 1490s, Cisneros decided that Talavera's gentle persuasion was not converting Muslims quickly enough to Christianity. He asked for permission to visit and then led a group of hellfire-and-brimstone preachers to Andalusia. They introduced heavy-handed new conversion techniques that included intense preaching sessions, bribes, and threats. He began pursuing with particular intensity people of Muslim descent who had converted but seemed to him insincere in their new faith, provoking fear and anger. Some former Muslims no doubt had reason to be worried that they would fall into the hands of the Inquisition because they remained—or might be accused of remaining—Muslim at heart. But anonymous accusations could be employed in such a way that anyone could be found guilty of heresy. Many Jews who had converted to Christianity had already found that conversion did not offer protection from persecution.

But a number of Muslims still found it expedient to convert to Christianity at this time. Some four thousand accepted baptism on a single day. It was a remarkable event. Why did so many agree to convert? For some, it was probably fairly easy because they were not particularly religious in any case. Some, exposed to Christianity for the first time, may have converted sincerely, possibly convinced by the arguments presented by Talavera and perhaps had come to fear damnation. Others probably saw the writing on the wall, that Christians were now in control and that their lives would be easier if they joined their religion. Some may have responded to a traditional gift offered by Cisneros, who offered a free shirt to anyone willing to be baptized.

The successful evangelization effort filled Cisneros with enthusiasm and propelled him to greater efforts. To him, it was no longer enough to attack the Islamic faith; he began an assault on Islamic culture and literature as well. In Granada in 1499, he presided over a mass burning of rare and precious handwritten, gold-embossed Arabic manuscripts. Only about three hundred tracts on medical treatments were spared from the flames. Cisneros was an erudite man himself, so his single-handed destruction of the surviving jewels of Islamic Andalusian culture was an intentional act that demonstrated flagrant contempt for Islamic learning and scholarship. It was reminiscent of the Turks mindlessly destroying the manuscripts and books of Constantinople in 1453, and it inspired the same simmering rage among Muslims that the Turkish destruction had inspired in Christians.

Many faithful Muslims had been unsettled by the mass conversions, but this destruction by Cisneros sparked true outrage. They believed that his actions were a betrayal of the promises they had been made by the Spanish sovereigns when Granada surrendered. Violence erupted in the city. A mob descended on the place where Cisneros was living; he had to barricade himself inside for safety. One of his employees was killed. It seemed that a general uprising was going to spread.

Pleading for peace, Archbishop Talavera and the Count of Tendilla went together to the center of the storm. They entered a large crowd of angry Muslims, at some considerable personal risk to themselves. It was seen as a gesture of goodwill. Talavera's kindness of spirit was well known; some of the residents even asked to kiss the hem of his garment. As surety that the Moors' concerns would be fully aired, the Count of Tendilla offered his wife and children to them as hostages while they discussed the problems that had led to the uprising. But even as tensions eased in Granada, rebellions spread through the mountainous areas surrounding the city, leading to a renewed civil war, as vicious as the last one.

When King Ferdinand heard what Cardinal Cisneros had done, he taunted the queen for having been so foolish as to select him for his post. "So we are likely to pay dear for your archbishop, whose rashness has lost us in a few hours what we have been years in acquiring," he was heard to tell her.[5] Isabella ordered Cisneros to present himself at court, where she questioned him "in the severest terms"[6] about what he had done. She may have been ambivalent about his strategy. On the other hand, she would have been pleased by the groundswell of conversions he had obtained. And the uprising gave Ferdinand and Isabella the justification they probably wanted for saying that the terms of the surrender had been broken. At the end of January 1500, King Ferdinand told the Muslims in Granada that everyone must convert to Christianity. He offered amnesty from prosecution for anyone who would accept baptism by February 25.

Under this intense pressure, many Muslims agreed to be baptized, and this dubious method of conversion appeared to have produced some results. About fifty thousand people converted to meet the deadline.[7] But Muslims who did not want to convert and did not want to leave rebelled against the edict and reached out for assistance and support from Muslims in North Africa and the Ottoman Empire. That inspired a further crackdown by the Spanish crown, who feared the prospect of a new Islamic invasion into Andalusia. A new cycle of violence erupted in different places at different times. King Ferdinand ruthlessly crushed such opposition. There were atrocities: in one town in the Alpujarras, a mountainous region near the city of Granada, Muslim women and children fled to a mosque for safety, and Spanish soldiers blew up the building.

It was during one of these local uprisings that Alonso de Aguilar, the brother of Gonzalo Fernández de Córdoba, was killed. The Muslims lured Castilian troops into a ravine and slaughtered them. The Muslims rampaged through southern Spain, killing every Christian they encountered. "A vast number were killed, they did not spare anyone they met, they by no means allowed to take or keep any captive," Peter Martyr wrote.[8] In a tense parley between the Castilians and the Muslims, Ferdinand and Isabella were unwilling to compromise in any way. They gave the rebels the choice of converting to Christianity or leaving Spain. The king and queen offered to transport them to North Africa if they chose to go. From this point on, religious tolerance of any kind would be off the table.

Many Muslims decided to depart. "They have chosen to leave their native soil and ancestral homes" to avoid giving up Islam, Peter Martyr wrote. "Their departure was not unpleasing to the Sovereigns. They say that thus by degrees the land is purged of the bad seed."[9]

But later even those who chose to convert found themselves under suspicion. The machinery of the Inquisition now turned in their direction. Much as former Jews had been questioned, persecuted, and killed for their presumed failure to completely convert, the same thing now happened to the Muslims who had converted or who claimed they had. And in fact, some people only did pretend to convert, building cellars under their homes where they taught their children the lessons of the Koran, according to the Barbary corsair Hayreddin Pasha, who transported some of them to safety in North Africa.[10] Those in Spain who were found to be doing this unrepentantly were consigned to the flames by the Inquisition. Queen Isabella supported this inquiry, as she had when it had been applied to people of Jewish heritage or descent. She thought it essential to rid the kingdom of people who were not sincerely Christian, as active Muslims would undermine the faith of people who had been baptized.

Still more Muslims, consequently, left Andalusia to move across the narrow strait to North Africa or to the Ottoman Empire. They were angry at their ejection from a place they had considered their home. Some began engaging in piracy, rationalizing it as a just and commendable response to unfair treatment by the Spanish Christians.

The Turks took advantage of the new interest in piracy and began offering support and encouragement for buccaneering operations. Piracy became a growing problem in the Mediterranean. Corsairs based in North Africa attacked Spanish targets, stealing their possessions, and enslaving Christians, shouting "Allah! Allah," as they did so, according to the reminiscences of Hayreddin Pasha. In one month alone he captured and enslaved 3,800 Christians.[11] His work was seen as so valuable to the Ottomans that in time they made him admiral of their fleet.

Meanwhile, the Jews who had left Spain as a result of the expulsion order of 1492 experienced misery in other countries as well. Many had fled to Portugal, where the ruthless and opportunistic King João had permitted them entry, as long as they paid a hefty entrance tax. But it was a short-term welcome; if they stayed longer than a prescribed time, he told them, they would be enslaved.

Many Jews nevertheless accepted King João's terms and headed west to Portugal, where they were hit with new misfortunes almost immediately. Many were robbed as soon as they crossed the border. Nobody knows for sure how many moved there, but Christian and Jewish chronicles say the numbers were large. The refugees were packed into a string of camps just across the frontier from Castile.[12] Soon these makeshift settlements were swept by disease, and whole families died, which inspired terror and fear among the Portuguese living nearby in long-established towns. They demanded that the Jews be forced to move once more.

Now the Jews realized they had fallen into a trap, because King João also imposed heavy exit taxes, making it very expensive for the people who had arrived in Portugal to legally depart. Moreover, those who wished to leave by ship were forced to travel on vessels owned by the king, which allowed him to profit once again on the plight of the hapless Jews. Ship captains who offered alternative transport were executed.[13]

King João, eager as he was to profit from the plight of the Jews, also wanted to force them to convert to Christianity. In an edict of October 19, 1492, he ordered that any Jew who accepted baptism would be exempted from paying the entry and exit taxes. As the deadline for departure arrived, he announced that anyone who did not have the money to depart Portugal would become a slave. Some number—between one thousand and fifteen thousand people—became captive servants of the king under this provision.

Then the king announced that he would seize Jewish children for nonpayment of taxes. Hundreds and possibly up to two thousand children were transported to the barren island of São Tomé, off the coast of West Africa, where they died of hunger and exposure. There is little or no record of this event in Castilian chronicles of the time. Perhaps it was considered too disturbing to mention. This failure to address the abandonment of the children was, writes François Soyer, "a lapse [that] defies explanation."[14]

However, the timing of these events suggests what may have motivated King João to do something so cruel. The Aragonese historian Jerónimo Zurita, who had access to original archival documents, wrote that Princess Isabel, João's daughter-in-law, was so distraught when her husband Afonso died that she became convinced that the sins of Portugal had caused the young man's death. She was particularly concerned about Portugal's willingness to accept Jews and conversos who were fleeing the Spanish Inquisition, heretics who had angered God, according to Zurita. She had become obsessed with the issue. "And the disaster that had befallen Prince Don Afonso, her first husband, she attributed to the fact that they had favored heretics and apostates who had fled Castile," Zurita wrote. "And she formed a great scruple about it, and it created such a fear of having offended God that she believed it had caused his death."[15]

This dark soul-searching after the young Afonso's death had surely became a topic of much discussion among the Portuguese royal family, who had lost their son and legitimate heir. So it seems possible that King João's vindictiveness toward the Jewish children may have been a twisted kind of revenge on God and the Jewish people for taking his own son.

There is no record of how Isabella reacted when she heard, as she almost certainly did, about João maliciously putting children out to die. But around that time, she issued safe-conducts to Jews who had gone to Portugal and who wanted to come home—but only, again, subject to their pledge to convert to Christianity. Many now drifted back to Castile, reluctantly accepting baptism and conversion.

When King João II finally died in 1495, it was no doubt a relief to the surviving but dwindling number of Jews of Portugal. But their moment of reprieve was short. When King Manuel took the throne in 1495, he initially showed compassion for the captive Jews and ordered them to be released. But within a year, he decided to expel them from Portugal, unless they agreed to convert to Christianity. Princess Isabel—the young widow whom the king sought to marry—had made him promise to compel Jews to accept baptism as a condition of her agreeing to marry him; he was to deport anyone who had been convicted of heresy in Spain. At first King Manuel feared that this was one more pretext for Isabel to avoid marrying him. So, Zurita said, Princess Isabel wrote him a letter in her own hand promising to take an oath "to assent to the marriage, and to go to live with him in his country," if he would ensure that all the people condemned for heresy were made to leave.[16]

According to the Portuguese historian Antonio Enrique de Oliveira Marques, however, this pledge to Isabel simply provided Manuel with a "pretext" to do what he had wanted to do anyway.[17] In expelling the Jews, he was doing the same thing that other rulers in Europe had done, an action that was seen as reducing internal tensions and interreligious conflicts.

But King Manuel, who was devoutly religious himself, came up with a draconian new method of enforcing conversion: he ordered the Jews to leave if they wanted to, but they would be required to leave behind their children under age fourteen, to be parceled out to Portuguese Christian families to raise. This idea was chillingly close to the Turkish *devsirme* concept. To save and keep their children, several thousand Jews in Portugal at last gave in and converted. The familiar pattern repeated itself: some converted to Christianity sincerely, while others only pretended to convert.

Conversion to Christianity did not eliminate the hostility of longtime Christians. In 1506 a Christian mob rampaged in Lisbon and massacred two thousand former Jews. King Manuel executed the mob's leaders, but it had become clear that even conversion did not bring safety.

Soon Jews were flowing not just out of Spain but out of Portugal, too, heading for Amsterdam, North Africa, or, most successfully, the Ottoman Empire. Contrary to a widely reported myth, Bayezid II did not specifically welcome them to Ottoman lands.[18] But he did allow them to enter, subject to obeying the sharia rules that defined the culture: they had to accept second-class status, pay special taxes, and show deference in various ways to Islamic beliefs.

After the ordeals they had experienced, many Jews found the Ottoman lands a safe haven. They could accept the restrictions there. Soon many of them recovered, mentally and emotionally, and began to prosper.

But they didn't forget. The family of Rabbi Elijah Capsali, for example, living on the island of Crete, considered every Ottoman victory a new triumph for God over the evil Christians. Many Jews became secret supporters of the Turks. Some Sephardic Jews became slave traders in Istanbul, peddling Christian captives to harems and as galley slaves. Capsali said the Jews of Spain brought valuable technical information on "the development of firearms," which helped the Turks win more battles against the Christians.[19]

Some came to see the defeats of the Christians by the Turks as ordained by God for their sins. Joseph Ha-Kohen, a contemporaneous Jewish historian in Genoa, saw "the rise of the Ottomans [as] part of a divine plan to punish Christianity for its ongoing oppression of the Jews," writes Martin Jacobs. Ha-Kohen described the sack of the Cathedral of Hagia Sophia as removing Christian "images" and "idols" and called it a "fulfillment of God's prophecy," as spoken through the prophet Jeremiah.[20]

For the next five hundred years, Jews from Spain, known as the Sephardim, and Muslims would harbor painful and bittersweet memories of life in Spain, which in time they came to view as an idyllic paradise lost. "The vanished land of Sepharad provides one of the great themes of Jewish history, somewhat analogous to the destruction of the Temple and the Babylonian Exile," writes the historian Jane Gerber.[21] No Arab or Muslim "has ever visited al-Andalus and viewed its great Islamic monuments without experiencing a mixture of pride and regret," writes another scholar, Salma Khadra Jayyusi.[22]

Isabella had succeeded in making Spain almost monolithically Catholic, but she had lost the industry and artistry of the Jews and Muslims who had lived there for hundreds, even thousands, of years. She made many enemies for the kingdom in doing so. The Inquisition, and the religious intolerance it represented, forms an indelible blot, a dark mark against her legacy that has haunted Spain for generations.

TWENTY-ONE

THREE DAUGHTERS

The pace never relented for Isabella, who reached her early fifties in the years following the half millennium of 1500. As she continued to deal with wars overseas and domestic unrest, there were two remaining children to launch in life, her daughters María and Catherine, and she was in the process of recalling Juana, now the heiress to the thrones of Castile and Aragon, back to Spain so she could be sworn as the next queen. Juana had to be prepared to govern. All three relationships had their own particular problems, and as a mother, Isabella still had much to do.

But the queen was not well. Normally undaunted in her willpower, drive, and energy, she began to suffer periods of debilitating fatigue. She had chills and fevers. She deferred, delayed, or stopped doing the kinds of things that had made her so successful in the past.

When Juana came home in 1502, riding into Toledo with her husband to be recognized as the heir to the thrones of Castile and Aragon, Isabella was unable to ride out to greet her and instead waited at the palace for her daughter's arrival. King Ferdinand and Archduke Philip rode ahead of Juana, taking precedence over her as they entered the city, something that should not have happened to the future queen of Spain. The misstep showed that Isabella, who had so carefully crafted her own succession to the throne, was slipping. She had always used her indomitable will to shape events and how they were perceived, but she no longer had the strength to control things as she once had.

The problems were both physical and psychological. Isabella had some unspecified internal ailment, possibly cancer or perhaps something else. She had also suffered three serious personal blows: the deaths of Juan and Isabel, her two favorite children and the ones she had raised to replace her, and the death of her tiny grandson Miguel de la Paz, who would have inherited Castile, Aragon, and Portugal. Isabella's hopes and plans for the future had been dashed, and now she was having difficulty recovering. In the months following Miguel's death in July 1500, she was so distraught that she could hardly communicate.

Many activities had to be postponed. The humanist scholar Lucio Marineo Siculo, a Sicilian living at the Castilian court, told a friend that the court had virtually ground to a halt. "So great grief has swept over our most Christian princes and the whole court that no one has been able as yet to approach or even address the queen," he told a correspondent, Fadrique Manel. "For the king and queen are bowed down with great distress, as is no wonder since within so brief a time they have lost three renowned princes, all legitimate heirs."[1]

The problems went beyond this most recent tragedy. In public Isabella maintained her stoic demeanor, but pain and ill health ravaged her appearance. The good looks of her youth had faded. She grew overweight. She covered her head with an unflattering cap, perhaps for religious reasons or because her hair was thinning or had turned gray. Portraits capture her increasingly careworn appearance.

In private, her positive outlook had dissipated as well. A young nobleman who had lived in the court described Queen Isabella to Peter Martyr as "sorrowful," something that he struggled to understand. The queen was admired and feared by her subjects, but political clout and status had not made her happy, he told Martyr, who agreed with him.[2]

Soon it became apparent to people throughout Spain that something was seriously amiss with the queen and consequently with the nation as a whole. As her vigor eroded, a great many other things started to disintegrate as well.

Alonso de Hojeda, for example, who had served in the Granada war and then traveled with Columbus, arrived back on the island of Hispaniola with some news: he told the Castilian colonists that Queen Isabella was very ill and was believed to be dying. Everyone knew that Isabella had been hard hit by the deaths in her family, but it was almost impossible to imagine such a strong, indomitable person being struck down. Columbus considered the story a malicious rumor, and his son Ferdinand later recalled it as an attempt by Hojeda to undermine Columbus's administration and oversight of the islands.[3]

But as the reports circulated around the islands, a subtle change in behavior soon became apparent. Isabella had made it clear that she was a protector of the Indians, and that people who hurt them would be chastised and punished. But with her health declining, the colonists gradually became emboldened to behave more aggressively toward the native Americans than they had at first.

Would-be colonist Bartolomé de Las Casas, then a young man seeking to make his fortune in the Americas, arrived in Hispaniola in 1502 and saw this transition firsthand. He had been among the inner circle knowledgeable about the discoveries from the beginning. He came from a converso family from Segovia that had moved to Seville,[4] and his father and three uncles had accompanied Columbus on his second voyage to the Americas. Las Casas had decided to go there himself and later recalled how warmly he had initially been welcomed by the native Americans. Spaniards had been in the islands for a decade by then, and they were still seen as benign forces by many Indians.

But as people internalized the news that Isabella was failing, Las Casas noticed that attitudes toward Indians became much harsher. The Spaniards demanded that the Indians serve and work for them. If the Indians objected or rebelled, the Spaniards responded at times with monstrous cruelty, turning their hunting dogs upon them to disembowel them, or slicing the limbs off men, women, and infants.

Making problems worse was the fact that the class of settler heading to the New World had deteriorated. The first group had been simple seamen. Hordes of promising young men had joined Columbus's second voyage. But so many of these first explorers had died of syphilis or other diseases or had been killed that it was no longer easy to attract explorers and colonists. The crown attracted new entrants by offering amnesty from execution or long-term imprisonment to convicted criminals if they would emigrate to the Americas. Lower-quality people were crossing the Atlantic as emissaries of the Old World to the New. Columbus called the Spaniards living in Hispaniola then "little else but vagabonds."[5]

Las Casas said these cruel practices had erupted because it had become easier to conceal information from the queen. Deeply disturbed by what he had seen, he was becoming a human rights advocate, traveling back and forth between the Americas and Europe trying to get the government in Castile to put a stop to abuses in the New World.

But in these years, trying to conserve her health, Isabella focused primarily on securing Castile. The succession issues were pressing, and the death of Princess Isabel had left the kingdom's left flank, its border with Portugal, vulnerable once again.

With Isabel's death, King Manuel of Portugal, now thirty-one, was a bachelor again. Queen Isabella had tried hard to convince him to accept María instead of Isabel because the older sister had not wanted to remarry, but Manuel had been adamant in insisting on Isabel and rejecting María. Now Queen Isabella had to once again offer him María, who was fifteen years old, and hope that this time he would accept. And he did, in fact, eventually marry her.

This was an immensely awkward situation for María, of course. But as the fourth child, as a twin who had lost her sibling in utero, and as the third sister in the family, she was accustomed to taking what was left over after everyone else got their first choice. There are fewer records of purchases of clothing and finery for María than for her older siblings. Cloth was expensive, and María likely got hand-me-downs tailored to fit her rather than the same number of new garments made to order for her brother and sisters.

So she might be able to accept a hand-me-down husband as well. It must have been excruciating for her, because Manuel turned down the offer several more times. Finally, he reluctantly consented, and in April 1500 the Portuguese and Spanish royal families signed an agreement for the marriage. Her parents made the match a profitable one for Manuel. He would receive a dowry of 200,000 gold doblas, payable in three installments, and María would be comfortably self-supporting thanks to an annual income of 4.5 million maravedis, based on rents from Seville.[6] And María would be well attended, adding to the grandeur of the king's entourage. In May it was decided that María would have a household of forty-seven, including six ladies-in-waiting, a chief of staff, a majordomo, scribes, accountants, footmen, and four pages. In addition, she would be accompanied by "two or three white slaves."[7] They were most likely to have been Russian or Greek slaves captured in war from Muslims but retained as slaves by the Spaniards.

There was one small problem. Manuel would be marrying the sister of his deceased wife, which would be skirting the prohibition in the book of Leviticus against marrying the brother or sister of a previous spouse. Manuel was, of course, a widower, and the ban was probably inapplicable to the situation, but just to be on the safe side, they decided to obtain a papal dispensation—an official religious forgiveness—granting specific approval for the union. Pope Alexander VI wasn't as cooperative as he had been in the past. He was starting to feel that his contributions to Spain's success were underappreciated, which had led to some testy scenes in the Vatican, and this time he required that Ferdinand make his nephew, Pedro Luis de Borja, archbishop of Valencia in return. This had been Cesare's former clerical post, but he had by now left the church. Rodrigo had come to feel that that seat, which had been his before he became pope, belonged to his family as a sort of hereditary right. The pope signed the dispensation on August 24.[8]

The wedding festivities for Manuel and María occurred in October 1500; the chronicler Hernando del Pulgar said that the king and the nobles of Portugal received the princess "with a great reception."[9] Queen Isabella's Portuguese aunt and cousins showered María with attention and helped her make an easy adjustment to life in Portugal.

From the beginning, the reports on the union were favorable. "The Lady Queen dresses very well at all times, and she is plump and very gentle, thanks be to God, and the King shows her much love and is much attached to her, and all the gentlemen and ladies of the court do the same," a courtier in Portugal wrote to Isabella and Ferdinand on November 24, 1500.[10]

Placid and easygoing, willing to let bygones be bygones, María received a warm welcome from her new husband. She was pregnant by the following summer and gave birth to a son, the future King João III, on June 6, 1502. She followed up the next year with a lovely daughter whom they named Isabel. And then she had another baby almost every year for a decade. Eight in all survived to adulthood, leaving the Portuguese succession nicely secured. "Great was the fruit that God gave them," wrote the chronicler Fray Prudencio de Sandoval.[11]

With Queen María at his side, King Manuel's life proceeded in an orderly and extraordinarily successful way. "From 1500 on, during his lifetime, the Portuguese obtained nothing but victories from Arabia to Malaysia, thoroughly controlling the Indian Ocean," writes the Portuguese historian Antonio Henrique de Oliveira Marques.[12] Isabella's daughter was queen over the expanding Portuguese Empire at the time when her family at home in Castile was presiding over the vast and growing Spanish Empire. The explorer Vasco da Gama had rounded the Cape of Good Hope and reached India by sea in 1498 and returned home to

Portugal in a ship loaded with spices. Now the Portuguese had a pathway around the Ottoman bottleneck to Asia, and to its silks, spices, and other trade goods, by cruising around the coastline of Africa. The Portuguese also expanded their dominions in Brazil in South America, which was theirs through the division of the globe in the Treaty of Tordesillas of 1494.

It became apparent now how much that treaty had played into Isabella's hands because now she was queen of Spain, and her daughter was queen of Portugal. Together they ruled over much of the world, and wealth poured into their countries, which gave them the resources to do many things. "Don Manuel was at the height of his royal grandeur. Honours, wealth, all things seemed to vie in laying their offerings at his feet," writes the historian Edward McMurdo. They lived in "truly Oriental luxuriousness and decorations. From all parts of Europe came singers and players to amuse the King, and who performed in his bedchamber to lull him to sleep. Horse races, rides along the Tagus, sumptuous banquets, bull-fights, tilts and tournaments completed the palace life."[13]

Queen María and King Manuel maintained the same focus on religious mission and Christian indoctrination in the New World as did Queen Isabella. The Portuguese sent many missionaries to Africa, South America, and Asia, swelling the number of Christian faithful. The great monastery of Belém, at the entrance to Lisbon, was, as the Cathedral in Seville had been, the starting place and final destination of every Portuguese trip to distant shores. Explorers attended mass there before setting out. Castile, of course, was similarly tying exploration to evangelization. For Queen Isabella and her daughter María, the alliance of Spain with Portugal was in all ways a success, and they attributed it to God's favor resting on them.

María said this explicitly. Friar Hernando Nieto once asked her if she felt grateful to God for the gifts she had received in her life—for her happy marriage, for her children, and for the riches they enjoyed. Queen María fell to her knees and raised up her hands in prayer, saying, "I give you thanks, my great true God, for all the gifts and benefits you have given me."[14]

But Queen Isabella's work wasn't finished yet. There was still one child left at home, Isabella's youngest, Catalina, better known as Catherine of Aragon. During the years of deliberations over the marriage arrangements and the dowry, she had grown up being called the Princess of

Wales. At last she was preparing to make the journey to England. Isabella hated to lose her and gave one excuse after another for delaying Catherine's departure. A proxy marriage ceremony between Catherine and Arthur occurred on May 19, 1499, and in October, Prince Arthur wrote to Catherine asking her when she would arrive in person. In January 1500 the English royal family asked again. In April the Spaniards explained that Catherine's departure had been delayed by an uprising of the Muslims, then was delayed again by stormy weather. In October the English asked once more when Catherine was arriving. In May 1501, Queen Isabella told them the girl's departure had been delayed again because she was waiting to see her father before she left. On May 21 they said she was too ill to travel, and in July they said she was coming slowly because it was very hot in Spain.

The truth was that by 1501, when the travel plans were being finalized, Queen Isabella was widely recognized at home as being "in ill health," and it made her reluctant to let her intelligent and thoughtful daughter out of her sight.[15] The two women were very much alike in temperament and bearing, and both knew that once Catherine left Spain, she would probably never see her mother again.

When Catherine finally departed, in the summer of 1501, two years after the proxy wedding ceremony, her mother was too weak to accompany her to the coast to bid her farewell as she had done when Juana left for Flanders. They said goodbye in Granada. Catherine was fifteen years old when she set sail, on August 15, from Corunna, in the north. Her mother drafted anxious letters in her own hand to the ship's pilots to ensure that Catherine would be protected as much as possible.

The trip was dangerous, as it had been for Juana and for Margaret. Ocean voyages were treacherous because shipbuilding techniques were still primitive, and people traveled aboard tiny vessels that were only marginally safe, even in calm waters. Catherine and her entourage spent six weeks making the voyage from Spain to England, crossing first the Bay of Biscay and then the English Channel. Early in the trip they were hit by a ferocious storm that bore down on them from the Atlantic Ocean. One of the ships in their fleet was lost, causing them to rush back to port to refit before they could set out once again. It was a terrifying ordeal, although Catherine remarkably retained her composure through it all.

Her ship dropped anchor at Plymouth on October 2, 1501. The princess was greeted by cheering crowds; King Henry VII had planned a spectacular arrival reception. He insisted on seeing the princess in person before the marriage ceremony was conducted. She raised the bridal veil covering her face for his inspection. He pronounced himself delighted and shared his exuberant reaction with her parents: "We have much admired her beauty, as well as her agreeable and dignified manners," King Henry wrote to Ferdinand and Isabella on November 28, 1501. " . . . Great and cordial rejoicings have taken place. . . . The union between the two royal families, and the two kingdoms, is now so complete that it is impossible to make any distinction between the interests of England and Spain."[16]

Catherine and Arthur were married at Old St. Paul's Cathedral on November 14. There was a bit of confusion about whether the consummation of the marriage had occurred. The pale, slender young blond prince was said by some to have "swaggered boastfully out of his bride's bedroom demanding beer,"[17] while Doña Elvira Manuel, Catherine's governess, said the young woman had been left "virgo intacta."[18] But Catherine and Arthur were still young, and the problem, if there was one at all, would surely rectify itself.

Now Isabella turned to her most difficult problem. Juana, the third-in-line, the daughter who had never been prepared to be queen, was now heiress to the thrones of Castile and Aragon, an inheritance that included Naples, Sicily, and as they were gradually becoming aware, immense lands across the Atlantic Ocean. She was bright and well-educated but had not been trained to rule, so it had been essential to recall her to Spain to begin preparing her for the huge tasks ahead. That meant she would need to travel back to Castile with her husband, the Archduke Philip.

But something had gone wrong with Juana. Perhaps Isabella had had a premonition of disaster when she stayed with her daughter so long in Laredo before she left for Flanders. It had not been a good sign when Archduke Philip had not been there to greet Juana when she arrived. In fact, the Flemish courtiers surrounding Philip, who were in the pay of the French king, had been trying from the beginning to drive a wedge between the young couple.

Philip's standoffish behavior—leaving her cooling her heels while he slowly made his way to greet her—was a harbinger of worse things to come. It was a mismatch that had quickly become apparent. Juana was attractive, and Philip was quick to consummate the marriage. Soon Juana was pregnant. But the handsome and vain young archduke was accustomed to picking and choosing from among the comeliest women in Flanders and France, and in his eyes, Juana did not really measure up. Moreover, her seriousness and intense love for him left him bored and irritated. "He only cared for pleasure and amusement in his lively court at Brussels," the biographer Christopher Hare wrote, and Juana's "tears and complaints" of his neglect only made him impatient with her.[19]

Juana had been raised in a harmonious court infused with a sense of mission and purpose; she had been an admired and beloved child. But in Flanders she found it difficult to navigate the treacherous shoals of court politics, where people feigned friendship while they secretly maneuvered to undermine each other. The death of Philip's mother when he was a small child had left the archduke open to manipulation by courtiers who learned how to control him through his interests, tastes, and libido.

Philip's predilictions, consequently, were avant-garde verging on dissolute. He was, for example, a patron of Flemish painter Hieronymus Bosch, best known for his *Garden of Earthly Delights*. Bosch's works, ostensibly on religious themes, depict fantastic and lewd humans and animals cavorting in dreamlike pastoral landscapes. The frequently pornographic and sado-masochistic imagery leaves the viewer uncertain whether the paintings are portraying a spiritual lesson or contemptuously mocking conventional morality.

The culture clash between the two kingdoms, Castile and Flanders, the latter dominated by the Burgundians, was immediately obvious, as it had been in the entourages of Princess Margaret and Prince Juan. Castile was sedate, solemn, austere, and religious; Burgundy was rollicking, sensual, and cynical. The companions whom Isabella had sent with her daughter were dismayed by what they considered the "moral corruption" at its court; the Burgundians thought the Spaniards were dowdy and puritanical.[20] Flemish and French courtiers who wanted Philip to discard Juana soon found ways to discredit her and make her look foolish and, even worse, mentally incompetent.

Following the advice of his courtiers, Philip took control of Juana's household by appointing new attendants for her from among the Flemish nobles and deciding how much they would be paid. This created tensions within the court. In some cases, the pay of the Flemings was decreased because the overall size of the royal household had grown, and more people needed to be paid than in the past. Some Spaniards who had traveled with Juana were not paid at all, moreover, and Juana was not given money to pay them herself. The Spaniards, meanwhile, were forced to conform to Burgundian customs and living standards and were treated as unwelcome outsiders.

The change of climate was a shock for the Spaniards as well. Juana's Spanish entourage were chilled to the bone and demoralized by the cold and gloomy weather in northern Europe, and many of those who were able to do so went home, leaving her with a much smaller contingent of supporters. They were replaced by Flemish courtiers who took their orders from Philip, or more precisely, from the advisers who controlled Philip.

Conditions were particularly harsh for the crew of the fleet, who were forced to bide their time over the winter waiting for Margaret's trip to Spain. Juana sought to rush Margaret's departure but was not successful. Philip left the soldiers and sailors who had traveled in the fleet to fend for themselves in the frigid winter on the bitter northern European coast, where nothing had been done to prepare for their arrival or accommodation. Within the next few months, up to nine thousand of them died of cold and hunger.

This degree of intentional callousness stunned the Castilians. It had the effect of intimidating Juana's remaining Castilian attendants and sent an important signal to the Flemings about how Spaniards could and should be treated.

Juana had no money to provide dowries for her ladies-in-waiting, which created a crisis for some of them. At least one Castilian attendant, from the high-ranking Bobadilla family, was consequently summoned back home for a Spanish marriage. The young woman remained loyal to Juana and decided to stay, along with eight other female attendants. But financial conditions were so difficult that the situation was inevitably untenable, and one by one they dropped away from Juana. Ultimately she was left almost entirely surrounded by Flemish courtiers, many of whom were actively working against her interests. Out of the thousands who had accompanied her in her bridal entourage, only the two or three slaves who had accompanied her to Flanders remained by her side. Presumably they had little choice in the matter.

This situation was a betrayal of Juana and a violation of her marriage contract. The accord of 1495, according to the historian Bethany Aram, had stipulated that both Juana and Margaret would receive annual allowances of 20,000 escudos to maintain themselves and their households.[21] In Spain, that amount and more was liberally granted to Margaret, who received many other valuable gifts. But in Flanders, the money was disbursed to Juana through the Chambre des Comptes (House of Accounts) at Lille, which withheld it from her or allowed the money to be diverted to Flemish courtiers.

When Isabella learned about Juana's dire financial situation in Flanders, she pushed her ambassadors there to make sure Juana received the money she was due. They tried to bribe top Flemish officials to make sure some money went to Juana, but other patrons were paying the same officials even more to advance their own ends, and the Spanish efforts were unsuccessful. Even gifts that were given to Juana were taken from her and distributed to others.

Philip seemed to intentionally exacerbate the situation. He refused to give his wife any money even for incidental expenses. In the eyes of her servants and Spanish envoys, she did not fight on their behalf, or did not fight effectively enough. She soon seemed resigned to the intolerable conditions.

A Spanish ambassador who visited the court in Flanders wrote that Juana "lived in such penury" and that her servants were "dying of hunger."[22] He said that Juana desperately needed financial support from her parents. In fact, the ambassador added, Philip was not allowing him to be fed either, for which reason he was pleading for cash to be sent to him from Castile.

Instead of giving Juana regular money, Philip lavished gifts on her, but at his discretion and his choice. He gave her valuable jewelry that had belonged to his family, and occasionally gave gifts and cash to her servants, which had the effect of making them more loyal to Philip than to her. In fact, they soon found they won more favor with Philip by circumventing Juana's authority than by respecting it.

It was a classic abusive marriage, which leaves the subjugated partner confused and disoriented. Philip made Juana feel fearful, intimidated, and publicly humiliated; he withheld necessities and limited her access to money, friends, and family. "Philip . . . honed his sadistic treatment of Juana into a high art through a combination of sexuality, tenderness and intimidation," writes the historian Nancy Rubin.[23]

Philip was himself dominated by one official in particular, François de Busleyden, the archbishop of Besançon, who had attained that same kind of control over the archduke that Álvaro de Luna had developed over Isabella's father and that Juan Pacheco had developed over Isabella's brother Enrique. Even the language used to describe the relationship was remarkably similar. Philip "would not know how to eat without [the archbishop] telling him to," wrote Spanish ambassador Gutierre Gómez de Fuensalida, assigned to the Flemish court.[24]

Philip's advisers controlled him by feeding his vices, as Álvaro de Luna had done with King Juan II of Castile, Isabella's father. Juana was as little able to handle the situation as her grandmother Isabel had been when she found herself in a similar predicament, caught between her husband the king and his favorite.

On one occasion, the Spanish ambassador Fuensalida urged Juana to be more assertive in the relationship and to demand what she needed from her husband when they were alone. Juana shook her head and sadly said that whatever she told Philip in private, he repeated to the archbishop. The latter, she told Fuensalida, was "absolute master of [Philip's] soul."[25]

There were soon signs that Philip had nefarious plans in mind for Juana. When her brother Prince Juan died in 1497, Juana went into mourning, but Philip quickly began calling himself Prince of Asturias, a title that now belonged to Juana's older sister Isabel, who was married to the king of Portugal. Philip also began trying to find ways to get the French to support his claim to the Castilian crown, supplanting his sister-in-law Isabel, then the rightful heiress to the throne. Isabel's death, and then the death of Isabel's son Miguel, opened what appeared to Philip to be a direct route to control of all Spain. He seemed to view Juana's existence as a nuisance. His entry into Toledo ahead of Juana in 1502 had not been accidental. He intended to displace her.

Philip's attitude toward his children was chilling as well. He was controlling and abusive to Juana in connection with the births of their children, who began arriving perfectly on schedule. In late 1498 everyone was waiting with bated breath for the birth of a much-desired son, but on November 15 of that year, Juana instead gave birth to a daughter, Leonor. Juana was strong and healthy, and the delivery went smoothly.

Philip showed himself off after the delivery, dressing up in rich brocade and green silk to participate in jousts to celebrate the safe delivery of the child, earning the applause of the crowd. But he had privately told Juana that he considered the birth of a girl a disappointing failure, and that he would not provide any funds for the child's support. According to the Spanish ambassador, the archduke had said: "Because this child is a girl, let the archduchess provide for the child's keep, and then, when God grants us a son, I will provide it."[26]

Juana nevertheless was soon pregnant again, and this time, in the city of Ghent, she delivered the desired male child. On February 24, 1500, she gave birth to a son, whom they named Charles. This was the child whom Queen Isabella in Castile had predicted, because of his birth on the feast day of Saint Matthias, would eventually become king of Spain.

A third baby, Isabella, was born in 1501 and was named for Juana's mother. Sometime after little Isabella's birth, Philip took the children away from Juana and arranged for them to be raised by others. This further traumatized her.

It is unclear how much Queen Isabella knew about what was happening, and what she could have done about it even if she did. She received only a partial picture from the ambassadors, and nobody seemed able to identify the strange dynamics that had enveloped Juana, although everyone agreed that something seemed badly amiss. The Spanish ambassadors prodded Juana to write to her mother but did not receive much of an answer as to why she did not do so more regularly. Under persistent questioning, she admitted that she missed her mother so deeply that it would hurt too much to try to write. She told a visiting cleric that she "could not think of her mother, and how far she was separated from her forever, without shedding tears."[27]

For a variety of reasons, then, Queen Isabella wanted Juana to come home. She and King Ferdinand urged the young couple to come to Spain as quickly as possible, with their children, to secure their inheritance. Because of continuing tensions with France, the Spanish sovereigns told the young couple to travel by ship. By this point, Spain had been embroiled in a dispute with France for years over its invasion of Italy, and Ferdinand was still deeply aggrieved over continuing French possession of the border city of Roussillon. If the French were to seize the heirs to the throne of Castile and Aragon, Spain would lose any leverage it had, and Juana could potentially be at physical risk.

But Philip insisted on traveling by land through France, nevertheless, where he agreed to give obeisance to King Louis XII in exchange for control of three towns on the frontier between their two countries. Juana refused to defer to the French, ostentatiously dressing in the Spanish style and performing a Spanish dance at a ball, angering their French hosts and embarrassing her husband, who seemed to have reached the point where he could hardly bear her presence.

That was the situation when the young couple arrived in Spain in 1502. To meet them at the border and escort them home to the court, Isabella sent her trusted friend Gutierre de Cárdenas, the man who had held the sword aloft when she had taken the throne in Segovia thirty years earlier. De Cárdenas had been a source of strength and a dependable ally to the queen from her teenage years, and she turned to him again for his counsel in handling the new family dynamics.

Isabella had not been able to stage-manage the initial entry of Juana and Philip into Toledo, but otherwise many other things went according to plan. They had come to the ancient Visigothic city because the Cortes was meeting there, and Isabella arranged for Juana to be sworn as heir apparent to her mother while Philip was given the lesser standing of prince consort. Then the couple went to Zaragoza, where the Cortes of Aragon swore the same oath to Juana, which was the first time they had ever named a woman successor to the realm. Philip was not happy when he realized that he had slipped down a notch in the succession. He did not want to be the king consort. Women had succeeded to the throne in Burgundy before, so he was not unfamiliar with the concept of women in positions of power, but he did not want it to happen to him. He was, in fact, furious.

The king and queen did their best to smooth the tensions. They attempted to get to know Philip better, to influence him, but he clearly cared more for entertainments than instruction. His boorish behavior, so different from his youthful charm, made these events uncomfortable for everyone. At a tournament in Burgos, he thought it was funny to throw leftover sweets into the crowd and watch poor people scramble for the scraps; he liked to masquerade in Turkish clothing and pretend to be a Moor. Isabella and Ferdinand nevertheless organized parties, banquets, and tournaments to keep Philip busy and amused. Pleasing Philip became even more important after the announcement that Juana was pregnant once more. Isabella and Ferdinand wanted Philip and Juana to stay in Castile for good.

But Philip was increasingly eager to leave. His close companion, Archbishop Busleyden, who had traveled to Spain with him, had suddenly died after a short illness, and Philip's aversion to life in Castile became a sort of panic. He seemed to think the archbishop had been poisoned and that the same thing could happen to him. He was in a frenzy to get out of Castile as soon as possible. He announced he was leaving immediately.

Isabella and Ferdinand begged him to stay. It was Christmas. They were at war with France again, over Naples and also over Roussillon. Juana's pregnancy was advanced, and it would be dangerous for her to embark on a long journey.

But Philip insisted, saying that he had promised his subjects he would return to Flanders within one year. It was a humiliating turn of events for Princess Juana to be abandoned by her husband at Christmastime. She still loved him, at least on some level, but his lack of interest in her made it impossible for her to exert any power in the relationship. She wept and sobbed, begging him to stay. He rebuffed her, which became common knowledge in the Castilian court. Peter Martyr was stunned by his intransigence: "Nor is Philip softened by these things, he is more adamant than adamant, he prepares his departure," he wrote to a friend.[28]

Philip set out for Flanders at Christmas. When he crossed the border into France, however, he found plenty of new amusements—the French were masters at finding enjoyable pastimes—and he established himself there for some months, making it clear that his reasons for departing Castile had been merely subterfuge. Juana's parents, who were at war with France over Naples, were appalled by his disloyalty and weakness of character. He was completely dominated by the French, and putting himself in their power created a risk both to himself and to Spanish interests. "So great is the influence of his counselors whom they think to have been corrupted by French bribes that he does not seem to be in his own power," Peter Martyr wrote.[29]

Philip's continuing presence in France exacerbated Juana's sense of abandonment and left her obsessed with jealous suspicion about his sexual activities while they were separated. Her fears were not unfounded. "He was highly susceptible to his counselors, who made him drunk with a licentious life, taking him from banquet to banquet, from woman to woman, until he was owned body and soul by the French, who had made him their satellite," wrote Gutierre Gómez de Fuensalida, the Spanish ambassador to Flanders.[30]

Mortified and hurt, Juana turned her anger on her mother, who had insisted that Juana remain in Spain. Ferdinand had returned to the battlefield to fight the French in Perpignan, and so Isabella was the parent who remained present as a target. She bore the brunt of Juana's quiet fury. The princess "lives with clouded brow, meditating day and night and never utters a word without being urged and if she [does] it is a troublesome one," Peter Martyr wrote.[31]

In March, still simmering with barely suppressed rage, Juana gave birth at Alcalá de Henares to her fourth child, who was her second son. He was named Ferdinand, after his grandfather. It was another easy delivery. Juana had scarcely recovered when she began insisting that she wanted to rejoin her husband, in a frenzy of jealousy to recapture his love and attention. She was willing to leave the baby behind with her parents to get started as quickly as possible. Isabella looked for every means to delay her, because going to Flanders would require her to journey overland in France, a kingdom with which they were now fully at war, or by sea, with all the risks the family by now realized that such voyages entailed.

Isabella persuaded Juana that they should go to their family home, the palace in Segovia, since it was on the route to Burgos and therefore on the way to Flanders. Once there she sent Juana on again, a bit farther along the road, to Medina del Campo, under the care of Juan de Fonseca. It was a sign of Isabella's sense of the delicacy of the job that she recruited Juan de Fonseca, the official who was already busy overseeing expeditions to the New World, but whom she must have viewed as entirely trustworthy.

When Juana got to the castle at La Mota, in Medina del Campo, she received a letter from Philip asking her to rejoin him, and she became vociferously insistent that she depart immediately. She ordered her household staff to begin packing for the trip. This put Juan de Fonseca in a terrible spot, because if he blocked her, he would incur her wrath, and if he didn't, he would be disobeying the queen. Fonseca ordered the doors to the fortress closed to prevent Juana from leaving. She raged at him, threatening him with death when she became queen. And indeed, Isabella's declining health meant that Juana would soon have the means and power to punish those who had displeased her.

Fonseca sent out frantic messages to Isabella telling her what was happening, and then he set to work trying to persuade Juana to wait until her mother arrived to discuss the matter further. Juana, in a fury, tried to rush out of the citadel as though she would run to Flanders herself. Fonseca held his ground and would not allow the gates to be opened. Juana, screaming abuse and crying, refused to go back inside and spent the night outside on the fortress walls in the chilly winter air, her erratic and hysterical behavior drawing the attention of the entire town.

Queen Isabella's health was poor, but she was a fiercely protective mother, and she immediately took to the road to take care of her daughter, the way she had rushed to rescue her eldest daughter Isabel when she had been at risk in Segovia as a child, trapped in the castle in an uprising during the war with the Portuguese. The confrontation between Isabella and Juana was painful for both women. Obsessive love in an abusive relationship is a sorry sight, but when it occurred within the royal family, it became an embarrassing public spectacle.

At last Juana calmed down and went on her way. Isabella, exhausted and drained, could go no further herself and settled into her home in Medina del Campo, a familiar place from her own childhood. The contretemps had left her weakened. Queen Isabella was "very distressed and fatigued by the Señora princesa," one of her secretaries wrote.[32]

Isabella's dreams for Castile, meanwhile, seemed to be crushed—Juana's behavior had made it clear that she lacked the even temper and composure that were essential to establishing herself securely as queen. And she was anchored to a frivolous and venal man who was more interested in his own pleasure than in Spain's interests.

There was more drama when Juana got home to Flanders. Philip had entered an intense love affair with a lady of the court. In a jealous rage, Juana threw herself at her rival and ordered the woman's long blond hair shorn from her head. Philip was furious. "He spoke very cruelly to her, giving her much injury, and they say he put his hands on her," wrote the chronicler Alonso de Santa Cruz. "And as the Princess Doña Juana was a delicate young woman, and raised that way, under the guidance of her mother, she felt very intensely the mistreatment that her husband gave her, and she fell ill on her bed."[33]

To silence Juana, Philip ordered her sealed inside her bedchamber. She pounded on the floor and ceiling of her room and demanded to speak with her husband. He ignored her, and so she began starving herself. Reports from the ambassadors left Isabella even sadder, and she urged her envoys to find ways to foster "love and agreement" between the warring spouses.[34]

Isabella's doctors worried that the emotional turmoil over Juana might precipitate a downward health spiral for the queen and, indeed, her condition steadily worsened from that time, with her fevers becoming almost continual. "The Queen brooded about it, greatly angered by the Prince Don Philip," Santa Cruz wrote, "and it weighed upon her that she had arranged such a marriage."[35]

But Isabella had another family problem to solve as well: another young family member had been struck down in the prime of life. Catherine's husband, Arthur, Prince of Wales, fell dead from a plague on April 2, 1502. Catherine had contracted the ailment at the same time, but she had survived. Once more a royal court was plunged into deepest mourning. And again the question arose of what to do with a widowed princess.

Queen Isabella offered two suggestions to the English king: either send Catherine back home to Spain, or marry her to Arthur's younger brother Henry. That latter option was under consideration in both courts, if only the financial arrangements could be handled smoothly. Of course, that immediately presented problems because of the financial wrangling that had occurred over the dowry when Catherine and Arthur had married, and a portion of that money had not yet been paid.

Grieving for his son and clutching his strongbox, King Henry VII demanded payment of the rest of the dowry. He made life difficult for the young princess by refusing to give her money for her living expenses and those of her attendants. It was bad enough that Catherine was a widow. Now she became a needy one as well, pressed to, in effect, beg for charity from home and from King Henry. Her only consolation was the kindness of her mother-in-law, Elizabeth of York.

And then that source of support was extinguished as well. Elizabeth of York died in childbirth, about ten months after Prince Arthur died. Henry VII shed some tears over the loss of his sweet and long-suffering wife, then began looking around for a new bride. He spied Catherine's fresh young face and body. Perhaps he had been as eager to get a look at her when she arrived for his own interests as for his son's. He wrote to Castile suggesting that Catherine marry him instead.

This idea appalled Queen Isabella, who denounced it in no uncertain terms. "It would be a very terrible thing—one never before seen, and the mere mention of which offends the ears," she told her ambassador in England.[36] The younger Henry was the only possible choice in England, she insisted. It was Prince Henry or home for Catherine.

But for Catherine to marry Henry, they would need yet another dispensation from Pope Alexander VI, this time for Henry to marry his brother Arthur's widow. But was she really his widow? There was that awkward question of whether the marriage had actually been consummated. Some people said it had, some said it hadn't.

King Ferdinand was drafted to make the request to the pope, who was by now a lifetime ally of his king, although their relationship had had some ups and downs. These long-distance deliberations over papal dispensations were time-consuming and complicated and sometimes expensive to procure, so Isabella began leaning on everyone she could to make sure that copies of the official document arrived in the Spanish and English courts as soon as possible.

In 1504 the long-awaited dispensation finally arrived. Isabella breathed a sigh of relief. She knew she was dying, and she was satisfied that she had secured a safe, and possibly even happy, future for Catherine as the wife and queen of the future King Henry VIII.

For with this dispensation in place, and the marriage blessed by the pope, what could possibly go wrong?

❖

TWENTY-TWO

A CHURCH WITHOUT
A SHEPHERD

I n the last two years of her life, Queen Isabella focused her energies on the things that mattered the most to her: her religious faith, her children's well-being, and the security of Spain.

The war with France was dragging on, year after weary year. It had been almost ten years since the French had begun their ill-fated assault on the Italian peninsula. Gonzalo Fernández de Córdoba had left Spain to fight in Greece and Italy in 1499, and now, in 1503, he was engaged in the mop-up operations in Naples. He and his men fought ferociously and tirelessly in the service of the Spanish sovereigns, braving extremes of harsh weather, exhaustion, and even starvation. And the queen had been his most consistent supporter as the war wore on. She wrote to him in her own hand in May 1503, urging him to seek complete victory in Naples. "All the eyes of Christians and infidels are watching what you do," she told him, imploring him to move forward quickly to accomplish as much as possible.[1]

But despite the queen's loyalty to Gonzalo, a whispering campaign was under way against him in Spain, instigated and encouraged by Ferdinand, who criticized him from afar for perceived missteps or mistakes. Those who found fault with Gonzalo, talking about the cost of the campaign or its duration, found favor with the king. "There was much murmuring by all, the nobles and even the king himself saying that el Gran Capitán's run of good fortune had run out," writes the biographer Mary

Purcell. " . . . Queen Isabella was the only one who took his part, saying that they should not judge him until they saw how the war went."[2]

In Italy, however, Gonzalo's bravery was acknowledged by all who witnessed him in battle. "The Spanish fought like devils," wrote one French chronicler, "and the Great Captain ran up and down in the first line of the attack, calling his men-at-arms by their own names and giving them heart."[3] Then, in December 1503, he won the overwhelming victory against the French at Garigliano, through a traditional surprise assault. He attacked the French army during cold and rainy winter weather, when they had left key defensive positions undermanned. The Spanish had built a concealed bridge that allowed their troops to suddenly spring up inside the French cantonments, and in so doing, they "completely destroyed the French army of Italy," writes the military historian Charles Oman.[4]

The Spanish victory was absolute. "Of the French who were led to war," Peter Martyr wrote, "few have escaped who did not perish by the sword or famine, ill health, of the people, scarcely anyone."[5] Back in Castile, Queen Isabella couldn't help but preen with pride over what her longtime friend had managed to achieve. "I was certain he would succeed," she told her courtiers. "What the Great Captain cannot accomplish no other man in our dominions can, and those who go about backbiting him are doing so out of sheer envy."[6]

Then the Great Captain added insult to injury, from the French perspective, by behaving magnanimously in victory. He rounded up the remnants of the French troops, who had been abandoned in Italy by their leaders, and gave them free transportation back home. That was another bitter pill for the French king Louis XII, so he decided to seek revenge by claiming back Roussillon, the province that the French had been feuding over with Ferdinand and his father for five decades. King Ferdinand rushed north with troops to try to run them off. He had been left on the sidelines in Castile during the war over Naples, with the Great Captain getting all the glory, and this was his opportunity to shine.

Back in Castile, Queen Isabella went into action once more. She continued to do what she did best—mobilize troops for war. She had perfected the logistics of battle, gathering troops, supplies, armor, horses, carts, foodstuffs, and hospital equipment and preparing it for transport. She had in fact become what the Spanish historian Tarsicio de Azcona called "the consummate expert" of the quartermaster's art.[7]

But Isabella was not happy about this military campaign, because she had become obsessed with the need to engage the Muslims, not fellow Christians. According to Peter Martyr:

> This our Catholic Queen at no time ever seemed to have derived joy from successes of this sort, nay she clouded her brow whenever it was told that Christian blood had been spilled, wherever it happened. Whether this was with feigned countenance or from the breast let Him inquire who dwells in the hearts of men. She said with sighs she would rather that blood had been preserved against the enemies of our Law. But the King does not refrain from serene face, with open and placid brow he professes that enemies whoever they may be, ought to be shaken off as enemies.[8]

Whether Isabella was sincere or not, Peter Martyr could not be sure. For although he had lived within her court for more than fifteen years and spent much time with her, he still found it difficult to know what she really felt. She was amazingly well schooled at concealing her thoughts and emotions.

While Ferdinand headed off to the battlefield in the north of Spain, and despite the problems with Juana, Isabella made sure the king had all the supplies and armaments he needed. Auxiliary troops, well equipped, were dispatched from all over the kingdom. She was kept constantly abreast of troop movements, with fast horses arriving several times each day with the latest news from the conflict zone. But she wasn't enthusiastic about this new campaign. She feared that the French would foolishly attempt to storm the strong citadel of Salsas, which would expose them to mass slaughter. By this point, after thirty years in which Spain had fought war after war, the Spanish military had become such a well-oiled machine that Isabella could foresee another resounding defeat for the French.

In fact, as the troops advanced, Queen Isabella sent messengers to all the convents and monasteries of Segovia and ordered them to say prayers for the French soldiers. She led a day of prayer and fasting on the day they anticipated the battle would begin. She prayed for the safety of the French. The queen's prayers were answered: the French decided to abandon their positions by night, when Ferdinand and his soldiers were sleeping. When they discovered the retreat was under way, Ferdinand gave chase, but the French had made a clean getaway. Isabella was relieved that very few Christian men had been killed. "Therefore the Most Highest heard the prayers of the Holy Queen and of the Religious and the [ladies of the court]," Peter Martyr wrote in November 1503. "He afforded a way to the French to turn their backs safe. Do you therefore give thanks to the Gods to whom you are thought dear for a victory obtained without much blood."[9]

This outcome, however, did not give Ferdinand the glorious victory he had hoped to achieve, and his criticisms of Gonzalo Fernández de Córdoba continued.

There was one other task, however, that Isabella had to pass to Ferdinand: obtaining the dispensation to permit Catherine to marry Henry. She could not ask the pope for the dispensation herself. She was by now openly feuding with him, sending him letters and personal messages, delivered by emissaries, that criticized his conduct and the way he was leading the church. She believed that the church's failure to reform its ways was putting the institution at risk. Her concerns predated the start of the Protestant movement—Martin Luther was a nineteen-year-old college student in Erfurt, and the Counter-Reformation, the Catholic response to his criticism, was still forty years away.

Queen Isabella was aware of the scandal and criticism swirling around Pope Alexander VI in Italy. The Italian preacher Girolamo Savonarola, with his flashing eyes and hawklike profile, was delivering fiery sermons attacking corruption in the church and in public life. He warned against bad priests and monks, sodomy, pornography, gambling, prostitution, drunkenness, and lascivious dressing. He told the flock that God would bring a scourge upon the land for the sins of the people. At the end of 1492, he had had a vision in the night where he saw a hand in the sky wielding a sword, and he warned that God was angry and would take vengeance. This line of reasoning found receptive listeners in Europe at a time when the Ottoman Turks were so clearly in the ascendancy and vanquishing Christian armies left and right. "The sword of the Lord is coming, swiftly and speedily," Savonarola told his followers. The brutal invasion by the French army in 1495 soon persuaded the crowds in Florence that he had foreseen the future.

His preaching about abuses in the church struck a chord with many people, including Isabella, who was trying to clean up corruption in the church in Spain. "His overriding aim was to reform and renew Catholic Christendom," writes the Savonarola biographer Desmond Seward. Isabella was operating from the same impulse, although unwilling to challenge the church so openly.

As Savonarola gathered more followers, he started to unnerve Pope Alexander VI, who was a practitioner of many of the vices that Savonarola was decrying. The pope decided to try to neutralize Savonarola by offering to make him a cardinal, but the friar publicly rejected the offer as a temptation that would lead the bearer to forget the key tenets of Christ's life.

The events that made Savonarola famous, the Bonfire of the Vanities, occurred during Lent in 1497 and 1498. A vacuum of civic leadership had followed the death of Lorenzo de' Medici, the merchant banker and de facto ruler of the city. Florence had been hard hit by drought and starvation in 1496 and 1497. Children were found dead of hunger in the streets; people were trampled to death in a rush to get free grain offered as charity. Savonarola convinced the crowds that their sybaritic ways had brought on God's wrath, and he called on them to erect a wooden platform and there to burn objects that represented human vices and unnecessary luxuries. Items thrown into the bonfire included rich clothing, mirrors, playing cards, and paintings and books, some of which were pornography but others of which were great works that represented the celebration of sensuality at the heart of the Italian Renaissance.

Soon Savonarola began to openly denounce the pope, something Alexander VI at first tried to ignore. The Florentine friar grew increasingly strident as his phalanx of supporters grew. He compared Alexander to Pharaoh, who enslaved the Israelites, and likened himself to Moses trying to free his people. At last the pope had had enough and decided to get rid of Savonarola permanently: he excommunicated him. But Savonarola retorted that the pope's action was invalid. Soon Alexander concluded that this bothersome priest, whom he called in a letter "this little worm," had to be put to death.[10]

Savonarola realized his days were numbered. He stopped preaching and decided to reach out to the crowned heads of Europe for help. He asked the Holy Roman Emperor, and the rulers of France, Spain, England, and Hungary, to convene a council to overthrow the pope:

> The moment of vengeance has come and the Lord commands me
> to reveal new secrets, making clear to the world the danger that
> threatens the Barque of Peter because of your neglect. The Church

is full of abominations, from the crown of her head to the soles
of her feet, yet not only do you fail to apply any sort of cure but
you even pay homage to the source of the evils that pollute her. In
consequence, the Lord is deeply angered and for a long time has
left the Church without a shepherd.

He went on to specifically attack the pope, referring to Alexander's "all
too obvious vices—I declare that he is not a Christian and does not believe
in the existence of God."[11]

In the letter to Isabella and Ferdinand, he added some particularly
pointed and bruising lines: "What good can come of your victories over
the infidels? You have raised a building that is hollow, for inside the
foundations of the Church are collapsing and the whole edifice is falling
into ruin."[12]

Allies of Savonarola hand-delivered the letters to the various rulers,
including the Spanish sovereigns. A copy of the letter, however, fell into
the hands of the pope, for whom this was the last straw. Soon inquisitors
were challenging Savonarola's orthodoxy, seeking to demonstrate that he
was a treasonous heretic. He was tortured and confessed at last that his
sermons had been acts of "pride" and "for the sake of personal glory."[13]
He signed a confession, and having given the church what it needed, he
was hanged and his body was burned. He had by this point fallen from
popular favor. Florentines in the crowd threw gunpowder into the fire to
make the blaze hotter.

Savonarola's actions nonetheless proved inspirational to Martin
Luther, who admired his words and his courage in defying the power of
the papacy. In 1524 Luther published a book of Savonarola's meditations,
which he praised.

Martin Luther wasn't Savonarola's only fan. In faraway Castile, Queen
Isabella kept among her possessions a commentary by Savonarola, and a
handwritten manuscript that was a book of spiritual meditations, translated into Spanish, called *Sobre el Salmo Miserere mei*.[14]

Isabella privately pressed the pope through her ambassadors for some
of the same kinds of changes that Savonarola had advocated publicly.
She supported the creation of a council that would study the Roman
Catholic Church and make needed reforms. This was something Pope
Alexander VI opposed. He had climbed to the pinnacle of clerical power
under the existing system, and a reform council could threaten everything he had accomplished for himself and for his family.

Isabella and the pope, consequently, had a series of clashes. She sometimes found herself opposing the clerics of Spain, who did not favor the church reforms she was making, and the Vatican, which also complained she was being too hard. Her appointment of Cisneros as archbishop of Toledo was symbolic of the difference between the kind of church apparatus she was molding in Spain and what was customary in Rome.

Many Spanish clerics had grown accustomed to lives of easy prosperity in church-owned properties purchased and supported by God-fearing parishioners who sought to ensure their own salvation through generous bequests of goods and property. But Cisneros, archbishop of Toledo and top cleric in Castile, modeled his behavior on that of Christ and eschewed accoutrements of affluence. He traveled from monastery to monastery, wearing coarse robes, walking barefoot, and begging for his food. This was one of the early points of contention between the Catholic Church in Rome and in Spain. The pope protested Cisneros's failure to maintain ecclesiastical dignity, and he was ordered to dress more regally.

But Cisneros's moral rigidity was undiminished and enjoyed Isabella's full support. At each religious house he visited, he would inspect the account books looking for signs of luxurious living. He ordered the monasteries to cut out all extravagances, serve only simple and inexpensive food, and give away costly garments. Concubines were forced from the premises. A new emphasis was placed on serving the needs of the flock. Priests who protested found themselves locked out of the monasteries where they lived. Some staged a demonstration, parading about in Toledo carrying crosses aloft and chanting *"In exitu Israel,"* a phrase that refers to the time when the Israelites left Egypt, and may have felt themselves exiled from their previous home.[15]

When the pope sent the Portuguese cardinal Jorge da Costa to investigate, the prelate agreed with the Castilian priests that Cisneros's austerity measures were excessive. Da Costa asked for a meeting with the queen and told her that he thought Cisneros's reforms were damaging the monasteries, and that his sanctimoniousness was a pretext to advance his own ambitions. He insisted that Isabella force Cisneros to resign.[16]

The queen listened impassively. When he was finished, she responded, "Are you in your senses? Do you know whom you are addressing?"

Cardinal da Costa coolly responded that Isabella was, like him, little more than a "handful of dust." In other words, he told her, she was as vainglorious in her sanctity as was Cisneros.[17]

But Isabella was adamant in support of Cisneros and his reform program, which she believed the church needed. Pope Alexander VI eventually deferred to Isabella on this issue and gave Cisneros permission to proceed.

The pope, however, won in a confrontation over another zealous prelate, the infamous Tomás de Torquemada, Ferdinand's former confessor who had become the chief inquisitor of Castile and Aragon. In response to concerns that Torquemada had become a dangerous fanatic, the pope decided to quietly depose him in 1494, saying it was out of concern for the prelate's health, noting that he was suffering from gout.[18]

But a few years later Isabella and Ferdinand underscored their gratitude for Torquemada and his work with the Inquisition. When their son Prince Juan died in 1497, his body was placed in Torquemada's religious home, the Royal Monastery of Santo Tomás in Ávila, with a special request that money be set aside for thousands of masses to be said there for the repose of Juan's soul. Burying Juan there made the church a popular pilgrimage site and added to its renown among the faithful, turning it into a memorial to Torquemada and his tactics.

Queen Isabella's differences with the pope led to several fiery confrontations in Rome between Alexander VI and the queen's closest associates. The first caught the pope by surprise.

After the first French invasion of Italy in 1494, the queen had sent Gonzalo Fernández de Córdoba to defend the pope, and he had succeeded in taking back the port city of Ostia for the papacy. In 1497 the pope invited the Great Captain to Rome so he could honor him, expecting the pious Castilian soldier to be giddy with the thrill of it all; but instead Gonzalo took the opportunity to raise his serious concerns about the immorality at the Vatican and the poor example the pope was setting for Christians. According to the Aragonese chronicler Zurita, Gonzalo told the pope that he was creating "scandal and danger" for the church. He asked him to reform his practices and said it was necessary that he do so. The pope was astounded at Gonzalo's eloquence and found himself at a loss for words, "sheepish and ashamed" by the commander's direct talk.[19]

Two years later, another critique from Isabella and her allies arrived. In late 1499 the Spanish sovereigns ordered their ambassador, Garcilasso de la Vega, to read aloud to the pope a reprimand they had written to him about his immorality, his schemes to advance his children, and the scandalous behavior of his son Cesare. The pope flew into a rage and attempted to seize the letter and tear it apart, shouting insults about Isabella and Ferdinand. De la Vega told Isabella about it in a letter and said that the pope's "hypocrisies" were too great to be suffered.[20]

During another, similar confrontation in 1498, Pope Alexander VI threatened to order that Garcilasso de la Vega be thrown to his death in the Tiber River—a strange comment for a man whose son's dead body had been fished out of that same river.[21] Ambassadors who heard this exchange said that the Spaniards had told the pope that his son's death was a punishment for the pope's sins; the pope retorted that the deaths of Prince Juan of Castile and Princess Isabel were caused by Isabella's sin in taking the throne unjustly from King Enrique's daughter, shouting that Isabella and Ferdinand were "intruders and usurpers."[22]

The pope was also miffed because he thought Isabella should have given his family some land in Granada after the Reconquest. He had told his son Juan, Duke of Gandía, who had moved to Spain, to pursue such a gift, which he assumed would be easily granted. But when Juan was stabbed to death and thrown into the Tiber, Juan's widow, who was Ferdinand's cousin, persisted in making a fuss about it and began insisting that she believed that Juan had been killed by his brother, Cesare. She wanted Cesare tried for murder. Instead of making a generous land grant, Ferdinand's family was looking for a prosecution.

The possible motive for that murder was murky. Some believed that Cesare had resented being forced to join the priesthood and envied his brother's pleasure-filled secular life. There was also the possibility of a messy love triangle, as both Cesare and Juan were romantically involved with Sancha of Aragon, who was married to their younger brother, Jofre. Sancha, moreover, was also Ferdinand's cousin. It was an untidy tangle.

Cesare was also widely suspected of having ordered the murder of another of Ferdinand's relatives, Alfonso of Bisceglie, the illegitimate son of the king of Naples. The unfortunate Alfonso had been married to Cesare's sister, the beautiful Lucrezia. To complicate matters further, the murdered young man was the brother of Cesare's mistress Sancha. Another untidy tangle.

Queen Isabella also strongly disapproved of Cesare's motives and methods in stepping down from the cardinalship. Cesare had never wanted to be a priest. Now that his older brother was out of the way, he wanted to leave the church and marry a princess so he could become a prince. He had cast his eye on Carlota, the daughter of the Neapolitan king Fadrique. Carlota did not want to marry Cesare, who was widely known to be infected with syphilis, and her father had not attempted to force her to do so. Neither did Ferdinand and Isabella. By this time, they were all starting to see family ties to Cesare as life-threatening.

So instead, Cesare and his father the pope struck up an alliance with the French. This was a sudden and incongruous turn of events, given that only two years earlier Alexander VI had called on the rulers of Europe to join him in an alliance against the French when they invaded Italy, took control of papal lands, and seized Naples. But the pope had now apparently decided to turn the other cheek, helped along by a generous offer from the French king Louis XII. In exchange for the pope giving Louis XII an annulment of his marriage to homely and devout Joan of Valois so he could marry the wealthy widow Anne of Brittany, Louis gave Cesare his pick of French heiresses to marry. He selected Charlotte of Albret, a French aristocrat who was part of the ruling family in the Kingdom of Navarre. On the day Cesare stepped down from the cardinalship, Louis named him Duke of Valentinois, an interesting play on words given that Cesare's former employment had been as archbishop of Valencia. This gave Cesare the new nickname "Valentino."

Eager to establish a family military dynasty to expand the territories under their control, Pope Alexander VI made Cesare commander of the papal army, and Cesare set off on a rampage through Italy, seizing control of the cities of Imola and Forlì. Cesare went on to command French troops in the sieges of Naples and Capua, which were defended by the Italian condottiere Prospero Colonna. He thereby ended up participating in the destruction of the Aragonese ruling family of Naples once and for all. It was at this point that Ferdinand and Isabella, seeing that their cousins' reign was effectively at an end, threw in with the French and partitioned Naples between them.

Cesare's successes were made possible because of his father's role as pope but were also the result of the son's real genius at duplicity and deceit, combined with flashes of personal charm that disarmed the people who stood in his path and allowed him to gain popular support in unexpected places. For reasons that aren't entirely clear, he won the admiration of his contemporary Machiavelli, who became obsessed with him. But Cesare's victories never led to lasting institutions, and all he left behind was a trail of death and destruction.

For all those reasons, Queen Isabella was not very sad when she was informed of Pope Alexander VI's death in August 1503. She showed little overt reaction at the time. But she fervently rejoiced when she learned of his replacement, a pious man who in fact took the name Pius III.

Isabella did not appear to receive the news of Rodrigo Borgia's passing "grievously," Martyr wrote cautiously. "But when [she heard] that Cardinal of Sienna, the nephew of Pius II who wishes himself to be called Pius III, was put in his place, she gave proofs of joy." She ordered special prayers to be given by the priests of the city, and called residents to the churches to pray for the new pope's health and good leadership of the church. "Then she caused thanks to be given to the Omnipotent with hymns and canticles and psalmody, the Te Deum Laudamus, because he had afforded such a pastor to the Church, for the queen always thought highly of the man."[23] Pope Pius, however, died soon afterward and was replaced by Pope Julius II. It was Julius who issued the needed dispensation for Catherine's marriage, cautiously noting that the previous marriage to Arthur had "perhaps" been consummated.[24]

Like so many other aspects of the lives of the Borgias, the facts of Alexander VI's death were shadowy, contradictory, and complicated. The pope was said to have been dining with Cesare when both became violently ill. Peter Martyr, who had a wide network of correspondents in Italy and within the Vatican, was convinced that the pope and his son had poisoned themselves by accidently consuming a toxic wine mixture they had prepared for a guest. The pope was seventy years old, and after he died, his body quickly began decomposing and became swollen and malodorous. Cesare was only twenty-seven and survived, thanks to being wrapped in a warm muleskin that helped him maintain his body temperature while he fought for his life.

When Cesare recovered, he sought safety among family friends from Spain, who were plentiful in Naples and included, he thought, the master of Naples, Gonzalo Fernández de Córdoba. But when Cesare got to Naples, Gonzalo, under orders from Isabella and Ferdinand, took Cesare prisoner and sent him off to a prison in Spain.

Isabella wanted Cesare Borgia tried for murder. Ultimately, therefore, Cesare Borgia, the cynical man whom Machiavelli called a political genius, was undone by the hyper-righteous Isabella, who had decided it was time to take him out of action once and for all. He was bundled off to the fortress of Chinchilla, near Valencia, but after he attempted to strangle the prison warden and throw him off the ramparts, he was moved to the well-guarded fortress of La Mota in Medina del Campo, under Isabella's watchful eye, with strict limitations on his movements. His hunting falcons became his only companions.

Quietly, and attracting little attention to herself, Isabella had become Cesare's "most relentless enemy,"[25] invisible to everyone, including the astute political observer Machiavelli, who never noticed that his hero's most effective enemy was someone he had not even bothered to mention in his book *The Prince*. Unbeknown to Machiavelli, who missed it entirely, Europe's most strategic and most effective prince of that generation was in fact a princess, for it was Queen Isabella who possessed many of the qualities that Machiavelli most lauded.

Cesare Borgia was delivered into Isabella's custody at the fortress of La Mota by Prospero Colonna, who had become a key ally of Gonzalo Fernández de Córdoba in Naples. When he arrived in Medina del Campo, Colonna asked to see the queen, who was by now virtually housebound in her private apartments in the palace on the edge of the town's central square.

"I want to see the woman who governs the world from her bed," Colonna told Ferdinand.[26] And so he was ushered in to make her acquaintance.

TWENTY-THREE

THE DEATH OF
QUEEN ISABELLA

Between 1502 and 1504, there was no masking Isabella's decline in health, and it was limiting what she could accomplish. She had good days and bad, and she couldn't predict when they would occur. She explained this to her son-in-law, King Manuel, in a letter of November 21, 1502:

> I received your letter brought by Juan de Ferreyra, your ambassador. And I much wanted to dispatch to you [an answer] before now [but could not] because of my bad condition. Then I felt better, but I had two relapses and I am unable to write by hand. . . . Thanks be to God, I am doing better but still am not able to do it. . . . Serene and excellent king, my very dear and very beloved son, may God have you in his special guard and protection.[1]

But in October 1504, Isabella's health suddenly took a turn for the worse. She was swollen with dropsy, burning with fever, gasping for breath, desperately thirsty but unable to eat. Tumors and lumps were visible under her skin. The physicians attending the queen gave up any hope for a possible cure. Queen Isabella, almost completely bedridden, used the final reserves of her strength to compose her last will and testament.

The Castilian court grew hushed and fearful, worried for her but also increasingly worried for itself. The succession seemed troublingly uncertain with Juana and Philip far away in Flanders and King Ferdinand's position uncertain. Everyone was wrestling with the need to pick sides in the coming conflict. "Woe to all Spain!" wrote Peter Martyr to his friends Hernán de Talavera and the Count of Tendilla, describing the queen's worsening symptoms. " . . . We see the faces of the King and the internal servants cloudy. It is already murmured what will come to pass if she departs."[2]

They were fearful about the future of Spain, because Isabella had dispelled the chaos of the past and nobody was certain whether the transfer of power would occur peacefully or through violence. Many Spaniards had come to believe that Isabella alone was the bulwark that kept mayhem at bay, that she had brought peace to a tortured land. Martyr wrote to another courtier:

> You inquired yesterday when we sat together sorrowful in the palace what I think of the sinking Queen. I dread lest virtue and religion should desert us with her. It is to be desired that where she herself goes, we when called from earth may depart to the same place. She has lived having surpassed every human height so that she cannot die; she will finish her mortality with death, not die. Therefore we must grieve but she is to be envied for she will enjoy a double life. For she will leave the world adorned with [her] perpetual fame, but she herself will live for ever with God in heaven.[3]

All over Spain, people went to church to pray for Queen Isabella's survival, pledging to do penance or to make pilgrimages if she were to be spared. They read doom from dark portents—an earthquake that had hit in the spring had caused walls and towers to tumble and crushed people in debris; freakish bad weather that struck unexpectedly in Andalusia, causing famine and then disease. Spaniards had time to weigh all such omens, for Isabella had been sick since 1502 but grew progressively weaker and weaker over about a three-month period in the fall of 1504.

In England Catherine, waiting anxiously for word about her mother's health, wrote to ask how she was doing. Catherine said she had been encouraged to hear from her sister Juana that her mother's attacks of ague were lessening, and she was hoping her mother was improving. She told Isabella to write back soon, because she could not be "satisfied or cheerful" until she received a letter from her letting her know that she had recovered.[4] Frantic for word, she sent multiple copies of the letter on November 26, just to make sure one of them reached her mother.

Queen Isabella, meanwhile, was hanging on, waiting for a particular document to arrive—the dispensation that would allow Catherine to marry Prince Henry. A copy of it was sent to her ahead of its formal release and under a "seal of secrecy," the English bishop of Worcester told King Henry VII, "for her consolation, when on her deathbed."[5]

When that arrived, her work was finished. At last the time came when the queen saw the end was drawing near, and she asked that last rites be administered to her. The Holy Sacraments were performed, including a ceremonial anointing of her eyes, ears, nose, lips, and hands with holy oil blessed by the priest, and with the doctors, family, and close friends gathered round saying prayers.

Ferdinand was there, and Isabella's childhood friend Beatriz de Bobadilla, as well as her confessor Cisneros, the archbishop of Toledo.

She asked King Ferdinand to promise not to marry again. This request may have come from jealousy of a future bride, but it also may have reflected her desire to discourage Ferdinand from remarrying so that their children's inheritances would be protected. Ferdinand swore he would not, according to Zurita, who said that "several people affirmed" that that pledge had been made.[6]

Normally the sacrament of Extreme Unction involved anointing the feet of the person who was dying, but Queen Isabella would not allow anyone in the room to see her feet except the priest, an odd action that chroniclers attributed to her modesty and chastity.

Isabella's last recorded action was making the sign of the cross with her hand across her chest as the priests finished their prayers. She died about noon on November 26, 1504, the same day Catherine was writing to her so frantically. Isabella was fifty-three years old.

"And so ended the days of the Most Excellent Queen Doña Isabella, honor of the Spains and mirror of all women, in Medina del Campo," Santa Cruz wrote. There was a spontaneous outpouring of grief "at the court and in all the cities, and with great reason, for they had lost a queen of such a kind that nature had never before made such a person ever before to rule over a nation."[7]

The sky itself seemed to be weeping, as the most tremendous storms in living memory broke loose from the clouds. King Ferdinand notified rulers throughout Europe of her death and ordered her body transported to Granada, though he did not accompany it himself. And so the entourage, including the loyal Peter Martyr, set out for Andalusia.

The word went out everywhere, and Isabella's passing was deeply grieved in many places. "In all the realms," wrote the historian Jerónimo Zurita,

> her death was mourned with such great pain and sentiment, not just by her subjects and countrymen, but commonly by all, that the least of the praise was that she had been the most excellent and valiant woman seen, not just in her time but for many centuries. This very Christian queen took great account of sacred things and to increasing our Holy Catholic faith, and she did it with such study and care that it served to the advantage of everyone who reigns in all Christendom.[8]

In the *Book of the Courtier,* the Italian Baldessare Castiglione, who had lived in Spain, called Isabella one of the greatest rulers of Europe in recent memory.

> Unless the people of Spain—lords and commoners, men and women, poor and rich—have all conspired to lie in praising her, there has not been in our time anywhere on earth a more shining example of true goodness, of greatness of spirit, of prudence, of piety, of chastity, of courtesy, of liberality—in short of every virtue—than Queen Isabella; and although the fame of that lady is very great everywhere and among all nations, those who lived in her company and who personally witnessed her actions, all affirm that this fame sprang from her virtue and merits. And whoever considers her deeds will easily see that such is the truth. For, leaving beside countless things that bear witness to this, and that could be recounted if it were to our purpose, everyone knows that, when she came to rule, she found the greater part of Castile held by the grandees; nevertheless, she recovered the whole with such justice and in such manner that the very men who were deprived of it remained greatly devoted to her and content to give up what they possessed. Another notable thing is the courage and wisdom she always showed in defending her realms against very power-

ful enemies; and in such a long and hard war against obstinate
enemies—who were fighting for property, for life, for religion, and
(to their way of thinking) for God—she always showed, both in
her counsel and in her very person, such ability that perhaps few
princes in our time have dared, I will not say to imitate her, but
even to envy her.[9]

Castiglione said she had set a new standard for behavior in Spain:

There arose thus among the people a very great veneration for her,
comprised of love and fear, and a veneration still so fixed in the
minds of all that it almost seems that they expect her to be watching them from heaven, and think she might praise or blame them
from up there; and so those realms are still governed by her fame
and by the methods instituted by her, so that, although her life
is ended, her authority lives on—like a wheel which, when spun a
long while by force, continues to turn by itself for a good space,
even though no one impels it any more.[10]

Even her enemies in other countries recognized her merits. Isabella
was "by report, one of the wisest and most honourable persons in the
world," wrote the Frenchman Philippe de Commynes.[11]

She had spent the last two months of her life writing and rewriting
her will, which she left as a blueprint for what she wished to happen in
Spain after her death. She was farsighted in seeing what was likely to go
wrong.

She ordered that the succession go to her daughter, the Princess
Juana, as "Queen Proprietress of these my said Realms, lands and lord-
ships, whom God has allowed me to name head of the kingdom."[12] The
crown was to go directly to Juana. But Isabella added this caveat: that if
Juana were absent or "should prove unwilling or unable to govern," then
Ferdinand should serve as regent until Prince Charles, Juana's oldest son,
was twenty years old and could assume the throne. Isabella specifically
urged Juana and Philip to be "very obedient" to Ferdinand because of
his "eminent virtues." She pointedly excluded Archduke Philip from any
specific role in ruling Spain, a conscious decision on her part.

Isabella made sure to provide comfortably for Ferdinand by ensuring that he would receive the lucrative masterships of the three religious

military orders, as well as half the income each year that came to the throne from the discoveries in the Americas. In her will, she praised him effusively. The vast wealth she was leaving to him was, she said, "less than I could wish and far less than he deserves considering the eminent services he has rendered the state."[13]

She expressed her deep attachment to her husband in words that far exceed the typical pleasantries of legal documents. She was leaving him her jewels "so that, seeing them, he may be reminded of the singular love I always bore him while living, and that I am waiting for him in a better world; by which remembrance he may be encouraged to live the more justly and holy in this."[14]

She asked that the dowries for Catherine and María be paid in full, under the terms of the agreements made for each marriage. This would allow the young women to move ahead in their marriages without financial quarrels.

She asked to be buried in the place that marked her greatest victory—in Granada, in the Church of San Francisco in the Alhambra. People should not wear mourning clothing but instead use the money that would have been spent on such clothes as gifts for the poor. She asked that her debts be paid.

She ordered large sums for charity, including 2 million maravedis to give dowries to poor girls so they could marry or enter religious vocations. She asked that money be provided to buy the freedom of two hundred captives who were being held by what she called the infidels. The money for these bequests should come from selling her personal possessions.

She asked that the kingdom appreciate the valuable contribution made by Andrés de Cabrera and his wife, Beatriz de Bobadilla, so that they would hold their posts as Marqués and Marquesa of Moya for all time, as would their descendants. She also singled out for specific praise Gonzalo Chacón, her childhood tutor and mentor, and Garcilasso de la Vega, who had served as her ambassador to the Vatican. Chacón was one of the men who had impressed upon her the possibility of a female role model in Joan of Arc, all those years ago, back in Arévalo. Garcilasso de la Vega was the courtier who had battled on her behalf with Pope Alexander VI about his corruption.

Her religious principles remained at the forefront of her thoughts. Queen Isabella sought to impress upon her children and grandchildren their obligation to protect and advance the Christian faith, instructing them to follow the commandments of the church and to maintain the Inquisition. She told them to never give up Gibraltar, the rocky outcrop where the North Africans had staged their invasion of Spain back in 711, saying that the city and area should be permanent properties of the crown and part of the royal patrimony.

One of her most interesting gestures was toward her brother Enrique, the king with whom she had so dramatically differed when she married Ferdinand and took the throne. As though to make amends with him, Isabella left her single most valued possession, a relic that she believed to have been owned by Jesus Christ and that she believed had healing powers, to his beloved Church of San Antonio, on the edge of Segovia. The relic was a small piece of bloodied cloth said to be a remnant of Christ's seamless tunic, worn on the day of his crucifixion.

San Antonio, Enrique's boyhood home, had been converted into a monastery and later, under Isabella's reign, into a convent of the Clarissa order. There the nuns performed spiritual and community outreach to workers who eked out their livings scrubbing woolskins under Segovia's Roman aqueduct. In the convent the nuns cared for the infants whose mothers were unable to support them, either because of poverty or illegitimacy.

Living in a cloistered order, the nuns kept the tiny piece of cloth as a sacred object and believed it to have miraculous powers in healing female ailments and diseases. A wisdom tooth was attached to it. The nuns believed the tooth belonged to Isabella, and she left it there so something of herself would always remain in Segovia and would rest next to something that had once belonged to Jesus Christ.

Moreover, Isabella ordered that if it was impossible to transport her body to her intended burial spot in Granada, she should be placed at rest instead in that convent, or at the monastery and church she had ordered built in Toledo called San Juan de los Reyes.

She asked to be buried in a Franciscan habit, with her beloved daughter Princess Isabel brought to rest by her side. She wanted a simple stone to mark her grave, level with the ground.

She later added a codicil that included a number of small items she had overlooked and that set out two more instructions. Both reflected her awareness of the coming ecclesiastical and imperial challenges that her nation would face. She asked that the reform of the monasteries continue, "to avoid damages and scandals." And she specified that the "principal intention" of the discoveries of the new lands across the Atlantic had been "the evangelization and conversion of the natives to the Catholic faith," and the residents of the New World should not be injured but instead should be "justly treated."[15]

After Isabella died, King Ferdinand announced her death to the public and sent out messengers across Spain with the news. He reported that Juana was queen and that he would help her rule. He took responsibility for administration of the government, because Juana was not there. She would need to travel to Spain, and it would take a while.

Ferdinand ordered the funeral cortege to set out for Granada right away. It was pouring rain, and people wondered whether to wait a while for a break in the weather, but Ferdinand insisted, and nobody wanted to question the king. He sent them on their way, hauling the coffin, but did not accompany the casket himself. Peter Martyr was part of the funeral procession, which he recalled later as a terrible ordeal: "We seemed driven by the storms of the sea. . . . We crossed through the valleys and plains, almost swimming, we had perpetual pools and lakes in the way. We were overwhelmed with clay and mud everywhere."[16]

They passed through Isabella's childhood home of Arévalo and continued south. The leaders frequently took counsel among themselves, wondering if it made sense to continue to travel in such difficult conditions. In Toledo they seriously considered stopping until the weather improved, but they were afraid of angering Ferdinand and kept moving forward, slipping, sliding, straining through the freezing rain and mud. People died on the trip, swept away by flood-swollen rivers, and pack animals drowned. "Nothing more dreadful ever happened to me," Martyr wrote. " . . . We did not progress even one mile in which we were safe from the face of death."[17]

At last, after weeks of travel, they reached Granada and placed Isabella's body in a church of the Alhambra, until a more suitable resting place could be constructed.

It was almost as though she was never really destined to be buried in Granada, and that all nature was conspiring to block her passage there. It would have been so much simpler to keep her remains in Segovia, the beautiful city that she and her brother Enrique had loved, but the attendants were fearful of displeasing Ferdinand, and so they had struggled through the mud and mire for weeks until they arrived at the former capital of the Nasrid dynasty. Somehow getting to Granada always turned out to be a terrible and unforgettable ordeal.

She first was buried, in accordance with her instructions, in an austere chapel in a former palace of the Nasrid dynasty that had been converted into a Franciscan convent.[18]

Later, in 1521, Isabella was moved once again: her body was placed beneath an imposing marble effigy in a sumptuous cathedral that was constructed in the center of Granada. She had wanted a simple grave, with a marker level with the ground. She had wanted to be buried next to Princess Isabel, but her daughter's body was never brought there. She lies surrounded by religious symbols, in the same way the Muslims had inscribed ONLY GOD IS VICTORIOUS, over and over, on the walls of the Alhambra.

THE WORLD AFTER ISABELLA

J ust as members of her court had feared, Spain went into a tailspin
at Isabella's death. But within twenty years, building on the foundation she had laid, Spain had become the world's first truly global
superpower—envied, admired, and feared by all. A golden age of Spanish art, literature, and architecture was dawning, with masterpieces being
created by geniuses in their fields—among them the writer Miguel de Cervantes, and the painters El Greco and Velázquez. And as the queen had
hoped, in ways both good and bad, Isabella's grandchildren and great-
grandchildren took up her causes and committed their lives to them.

But all this began with a period of chaos.

Ferdinand's shortcomings became apparent as soon as Isabella died.
That same day he sent letters announcing her death to his peers in other
kingdoms. He told England's Henry VII, for example, that Isabella's death
was "the greatest affliction that could have befallen him."[1] His daughter
Juana was the new queen, he told Henry, but promptly added that he was
now in control of the realm.

He did not accompany Isabella's body on the dreary trek to burial in
Granada, something that even the most estranged of spouses would normally have felt obligated to do. Instead he went into seclusion for a week
with his counselors, then emerged to begin wreaking havoc.

The first thing he did was dispose of her belongings in a most cavalier
way. She had asked that her possessions be sold to benefit the poor and

pay off her debts; seeing little advantage in maximizing their value, he sold them as quickly as possible, amid an unseemly display of "confusion, greed and a lack of transparency."[2] Courtiers and clerics snapped up objects at rock-bottom prices and resold them later. Objects of gold and silver were melted down for the value of the metal. Other items were allowed to deteriorate and were sold for smaller sums than they should have brought.

Within two months, Ferdinand disposed of Isabella's carefully assembled set of paintings of Christ's life, even those that contained portraits of her family, at fire-sale prices of two to six ducados. The pieces did not appear to have been appraised; paintings that contained gold went for the same price as those that did not.[3] Books, tapestries, music scores, and books of hours were scattered to the winds. One of the greatest art collections of the Renaissance was randomly dispersed. It was, wrote the historian Tarsicio de Azcona, as though "a brilliant day had been followed by a gloomy and bitter nightfall."[4]

Ferdinand then turned his focus to finding a way to elbow his daughter and her husband out of power. He quickly proposed that he remarry—initially reaching out to Juana la Beltraneja. This was the young woman, now middle-aged, who had been the child of King Enrique's wife and had possibly been the legitimate heir to the throne, if she were indeed the child of the king. Ferdinand and Isabella, of course, had gone to war with Portugal, asserting that Isabella was the rightful heir, and thousands of people had been killed in the resulting battles.

Now, however, if Ferdinand could convince people that Juana had been the rightful heir, and that the war with Portugal had been an unfortunate mistake, he could restore himself to the same power on the peninsula that he had enjoyed while being married to Isabella. This would mean extracting Juana la Beltraneja from the convent where she had been living, but he might have reasoned that she had embraced religious life only reluctantly in the first place. The proposed marriage, of course, would have had the effect of bumping his children with Isabella out of the line of succession, indeed would question the validity of Isabella's entire reign.

This idea drew stunned silence from all corners. Opposition began to coalesce quickly all over Spain. Ferdinand, it became apparent, was very unpopular, and the love that the people had shown for the sovereigns had been for Isabella, not for him.

In Flanders, meanwhile, Archduke Philip, who had developed what Peter Martyr called "a panting hunger for the scepter," had been kept informed about Isabella's declining health and sought to control the situation by further isolating Juana.[5] In early November 1504, he dismissed twelve of the attendants she had brought back with her from Castile and gave her Dominican confessor forty livres to return home to Spain.[6] Using bribes and threats, he made sure that the people surrounding Juana were loyal to him and not to her. The remaining Spanish attendants, said the Castilian ambassador Fuensalida, were "all relatives of Judas; none of them has stayed faithful; each one is trying to do his best for the king."[7]

Even Fuensalida was intimidated by the attitude at the court. He too was informed that Isabella was dying but did not tell Juana. He was probably hedging his bets, waiting to see who would come out on top in the power struggle that was already beginning.

When Philip learned of Isabella's death, he decided to withhold the news from his wife, the new queen of Castile, whom he maintained in a state of near-incarceration. For a period of time, perhaps a week or more, he plotted what to do but kept his wife in the dark. King Ferdinand sent an official messenger, Juan Rodríguez de Fonseca, who delivered the news officially to the couple on December 12.

Finally Juana learned the truth, which must have been painful to her. Her last meetings with her mother in Medina del Campo had been dreadful, and she had shown little regard for Isabella's failing health when she had been at home in Castile. Now the word hit her hard, and she began emulating the exaggerated mourning rituals that everyone had admired in her sister, Princess Isabel, when she lost her husband Afonso. Juana asked to be left alone to mourn, spurned contact with others, and went into religious seclusion. Funerary customs were less dramatic in pleasure-seeking Flanders, and Juana's behavior became another reason that the Flemings viewed her as odd or ridiculous.

In the meantime, Philip busily planned his own coronation as king of Castile, León, and Granada, giving Juana only a small part in the ceremonies. In mid-January, he was crowned king at the Church of St. Michael and St. Gudula in Brussels, a grand Gothic edifice, with Juana standing at his side. The sword of justice, once famously held aloft for Isabella, was handed to Philip and not to Juana.

After discussing the situation with the Spanish ambassadors at court, Juana wrote her father a letter and entrusted it to a servant to deliver. The servant, who was Aragonese and a subject of Ferdinand's, shared it with Philip, who was unhappy with the contents. Philip ordered one of the envoys, Ferdinand's personal secretary Lope de Conchillos, seized and thrown into jail, where he was tortured. The ferocity of Philip's reaction suggests that Juana had told her father that he should prevent Philip from seizing the Castilian crown for himself. The envoy "was thrust into a foul dungeon as if he had committed a horrible crime," Peter Martyr told his friend Talavera, adding that when Lope de Conchillos finally was released, stumbling into the sunlight, he was temporarily senseless and all the hair had fallen from his head.[8]

After this breach in the wall of secrecy with which he had surrounded Juana, Philip ordered that no one in Flanders was allowed to communicate with anyone in Spain without his knowledge.

Philip's advisers next prepared an alternative letter ostensibly written by Juana that assigned her right to govern to Philip, saying it was because of her "love" for him. She objected to the word *love* and refused to sign the letter, so they forged her signature and sent it anyway, according to biographer Bethany Aram.[9]

Then the bribery started. Philip reached out to Spanish noblemen, offering them lucrative properties, rights, and privileges if they would support his claim to the Castilian throne and repudiate Ferdinand. He began negotiating with the French to support him in seizing power from his father-in-law. That would not have been seen as an idle threat for the Spanish, who had fought with the French over both Roussillon and Naples and who viewed the French as their mortal enemies.

Then the two men—Philip and Ferdinand—engaged in an intense propaganda war about who should rule. Both were angling for the right to the throne, but first Juana had to be shunted aside. Ferdinand and Philip separately and then together asserted that Juana was mentally ill, too mentally ill to be allowed to rule. Removing her from the picture would leave each man with only one competitor—the other man. Juana's father and her husband both circulated rumors about her allegedly insane conduct. Stories of the scene at Medina del Campo, Juana's seclusion, and her jealous attack on her husband's lover, when she had cut off her hair, received wide circulation as examples of female madness. Alleging that women are insane is a time-tested way to discredit them if they contest male power or otherwise cause problems.

In early 1505, according to Aram, Ferdinand called together the Cortes to ask that he be named regent for Juana. He referred to Queen Isabella's will and said that the queen's "modesty and sorrow" had prevented her from disclosing the reasons why Juana might be unable to rule—that Juana's "passions" made her incompetent to govern.[10] That set the ball rolling, and soon many people came to believe that Juana was *"loca."*

Back in Flanders, impartial observers said she looked and acted just fine. The Venetian ambassador Vicenzo Quirini described an evening of festivities with Juana, who was "dressed in black velvet, looking very well"; he thought her "very handsome, her bearing being that of a sensible and discreet woman." He greeted her on behalf of the Venetian Signory, and she made a "loving reply"; then together they strolled to a joust, which took place by torchlight in a spacious hall on the ground floor of the palace.[11]

About six months later, in early 1506, according to Quirini, Philip sent an envoy from his court, Monsieur de la Chau, to Castile to meet with Ferdinand to make sure they had their stories straight—that Juana was "incapable and unfit to rule." Quirini said many Flemish courtiers wanted Philip to do so because they had already begun receiving "pensions" from Castile, ranging from 500 to 3,000 ducats per year, and they feared that Juana would stop those stipends if she were to take the reins of government. They also hoped to find lucrative sinecures for their "children, grandchildren and remotest connections" through the three religious military orders that the monarch of Castile would command.[12] "The ministers also seek to avoid an insurrection," Quirini wrote.

> They fear lest Spaniards, who are turbulent naturally—especially the grandees, who love change and have feuds amongst each other—might rise and make some stir on the plea of choosing to be governed by the Queen, who is their legitimate sovereign. Their object now is, that before the arrival of King Philip, his father-in-law should circulate a report that Queen Juana is unfit to govern, as is generally believed here, and they hope King Ferdinand will accede to their wishes, both as it may prove to his interest, and also because, on the death of Queen Isabella, amongst the other reasons assigned to him for not ceding the government of Castile, he alleged that his daughter was incapable and unfit to rule; an opinion which he seems he retain, according to the last letters of King Philip's ambassadors, who are doing their utmost to arrange this

business, as it affects them personally: Monsier de Verre having an annual pension in Castile of 3,000 ducats, together with a promise of the first vacant bishopric for one of his brothers and Monsieur de la Chau a pension of 1,000 ducats; and all live in hopes that King Philip may provide their children, grandchildren and remotest connections with commanderies of St. James, of Calatrava or of Alcántara; for although King Ferdinand be master of these three orders, and has all the revenues, yet the vacant commanderies are in the alternate gift of either sovereign, and when King Philip's turn comes, King Ferdinand is bound to accept his presentations.[13]

The Flemish courtiers were doing their best to sow discord between Juana and her father. The Spanish ambassador, the Count of Haro, was given a short audience with Juana, although Philip's confederates warned him to make a short stay and to do "good service" to Philip. Juana warmly received him, according to Quirini, and she

very tenderly made many inquiries of him how her father fared, six months having elapsed since she had received any news of him, and whether it was true that he wished her as much harm as she was told he did. . . . The ambassador replied that not one of these things were true; nay, that the King her father loved her and her husband as his very dear children. . . . Thereupon the ambassador took leave as quickly as he could. He told [Quirini] that he knew for certain that King Philip's councilors had given the Queen to understand that her father bears her ill will, and would fain not see her in Spain, in order that on her going thither with this impression, she might, at their first meeting, treat him unbecomingly; whilst Ferdinand, being informed in like manner, that his daughter loved him not, and was such as they described her, would the more readily consent to deprive her of the government.[14]

Whatever Ferdinand knew or did not know, he responded soothingly to Philip in mid-April that he would arrange matters "so as to satisfy all parties."[15] Ferdinand unctuously urged Philip to come to Castile so everything could be handled.

Philip dragged his feet about going there. Still suspicious about how his friend, the archbishop of Besançon, had died so precipitously, he was afraid that Ferdinand would kill him if he set foot in Spain. Others shared his fear: in June 1506 a nobleman living in Rome wrote to Philip urging him to use extreme caution in dealing with Ferdinand to avoid becoming a victim of poisoning or other violence. He specifically urged Philip to avoid eating with Ferdinand at any time.[16]

But to win the rich prize of Spain and its dominions, Philip and Juana had to go there to assert control. They set out to Castile by sea, leaving their children back home in Flanders with Philip's intelligent and kindly sister Margaret, the young widow of Prince Juan of Castile. She established a household with the four children remaining at home—Eleanor, Charles, Isabel, and Juana's youngest, baby Mary—in the small and pretty town of Mechelen, some distance from the large Flemish royal palace in Ghent and its scheming courtiers.

The sea passage was frightening for Juana and Philip. Storms along the way drove them to England, where King Henry VII met and spent time with both of them. Continuing to make their case that Juana was unstable, Philip and his attendants went out of their way to tell the English court that she was unhinged. Henry privately told his courtiers that Juana seemed perfectly sane to him. Envoys from other countries who traveled with the fleet also described Juana as pleasant and appropriate in her behavior, and stoic when others had panicked in the storm.

By the time Philip and Juana arrived in Castile, Ferdinand had remarried, although not, as he had hoped, to Juana la Beltraneja. He had done an end run around his daughter and her husband by making a speedy alliance with Spain's old enemy France. He secured for himself a saucy eighteen-year-old French princess, his grandniece Germana de Foix, the granddaughter of his half sister, in exchange for a promise that he would leave Naples to the children he would have with Germana.[17] This was appealing to King Louis XII because Germana was his niece as well, and this agreement would bring Naples back into the French sphere of influence. Ferdinand also promised to reimburse Louis for his military expenses.

King Ferdinand told his subjects that he needed to marry the young French princess to provide a male heir to the throne of Aragon. In reality, of course, he did it to spite Philip by threatening Juana's children's right to the throne. The justification of needing an heir was absurd: by this time in his life, Ferdinand had three young and fertile daughters, all legitimate, and many grandchildren in line to inherit the throne. (Juana eventually had six children; María already had three, and Catherine was likely to have children in the future too.) This meant that Ferdinand was attempting to produce children who would be rivals to the children he already had.

His announcement was particularly harmful to Juana, whose claim to the throne of Aragon would be jeopardized if another child were born, but also to Catherine, who was twenty years old, alone in England, widowed, and hoping to finalize her marriage with young Prince Henry. Losing her place in the line of succession in Castile would complicate that already difficult task.

Ferdinand's speedy remarriage, though unseemly, was not too surprising, despite the unfortunate promise he had made to Isabella that he would not marry again. He had perhaps grown tired of being married to an ailing woman. By July 1505 he was the subject of leering gossip at the English court, where envoys told Henry VII that Ferdinand was "right lusty for his age," which was fifty-three. Moreover, he still was perceived as having "a goodly personage," despite a lisp he had developed since losing a tooth and a "little cast in the left eye." And finally Ferdinand was "reputed to be very rich, having during his Queen's life spent nothing of his revenues of Aragon and Sicily."[18]

Maximilian, the Holy Roman emperor, who was Philip's father and baby Charles's grandfather, thought the situation could be handled by appealing to Ferdinand's high libido. He tried to lure Ferdinand into making another, politically safer choice by offering to let him select "among the most noble virgin princesses ... the most beautiful in body and face that can be found in Germany."[19]

But Ferdinand rushed to the marital bed with Germana de Foix instead. Their marriage contract was concluded by September 1505, less than a year after Isabella's death.[20] Ferdinand explained that the reason he was taking a French bride was to win French support to his side rather than to Philip's, but this was difficult for the families of men who had died in his many anti-French campaigns to accept.

And it proved impossible to explain his action to the people who had loved and respected Queen Isabella, who could not understand how Ferdinand had been able to replace her so hastily. The new courtship was difficult to watch, particularly because the appreciation for Isabella had only grown since she had died. "It seems hard to all to behold new nuptials so suddenly," Peter Martyr told Talavera, particularly because the kingdom "venerates" Isabella as much in death as it "worshipped her" while she was living.[21]

Ferdinand spent his honeymoon with Germana in the same small town—Duenas—where he had spent the early days of his marriage with Isabella, which struck some people as disrespectful of his former wife's memory. Soon afterward Germana, who liked to dress in the French style, took up her role as the acting queen of Castile.

Ferdinand's popularity in Castile plummeted. Once Philip and Juana arrived in the kingdom, in April 1506, all Spain rallied to their support. Almost the entire nobility deserted Ferdinand, except for a small handful of diehards. Devoted counselors to Isabella, including Garcilasso de la Vega, whom Isabella had honored in her will, turned against her husband.

Only a handful of people, including Archbishop Cisneros and the Duke of Alba, remained loyal to Ferdinand. Within two months of his daughter's arrival, Ferdinand announced he would go back home to Aragon and departed Castile with almost as small an entourage as he had had when he first came to marry Isabella, back in 1469. "Of his blood relations," Peter Martyr wrote to Talavera, almost all "deserted him . . . partly from fear, partly from cupidity."[22]

Whether Ferdinand saw Juana before he left is unclear; if he did, it was only a brief visit. This would not, in any case, have created a very happy leavetaking. Castile was unceremoniously giving Ferdinand the boot.

Ferdinand and his wife left Castile for Aragon and then went to his rich new Kingdom of Naples, where he was greeted as a conquering hero. Gonzalo Fernández de Córdoba, acting as viceroy of Naples since his decisive defeat of the French, honored him upon his arrival with lavish celebrations. Ferdinand was visibly irritated, however, when a number of prominent Italians and even some Frenchmen spoke effusively of their admiration for Gonzalo. Gonzalo was one of those very unusual military leaders who commanded the respect not just of the men he led into battle but also of the men he vanquished. Ferdinand's jealousy of Gonzalo grew increasingly obvious.

Meanwhile, in Castile, Philip sought permission from the Cortes to have Juana imprisoned, but Castilian officials would not permit it. They interviewed Juana and gave her their support. Juana said she wanted Ferdinand to come back and rule, but Philip arranged for their joint coronation in July 1506, himself as king and Juana as queen.

This was the opening Philip needed. He began to do what he wished in Castile. He removed officials whom Isabella had appointed and replaced them with his friends from Flanders. He stripped the rule of the city of Segovia from Beatriz de Bobadilla, although Isabella in her will had expressly pledged it to Beatriz for life and for the life of her descendants. Philip gave the post to his new court favorite, Don Juan Manuel.

Then in September 1506, Philip unexpectedly died. He was attending a party in Burgos thrown for him by Don Juan Manuel and grew thirsty. He took a long draught of cool water—and then fell ill. He died in stomach distress, just as others who had stood in Ferdinand's way had come to sudden ends. Philip was twenty-eight years old.

Did Ferdinand arrange for Philip to be killed? It seems more than possible. By this point, Ferdinand's older half siblings, Charles and Blanca, and Isabella's brother Enrique, had all died under circumstances some thought mysterious, and he had benefited in each case. But in an era without antibiotics or autopsies, it is impossible to determine if the cause of death was poison or something else.

Queen Juana stood vigil over Philip's sickbed but did not cry at his passing. He had been cruel to her, and she most likely had mixed emotions at his death. Her ways of mourning him, and of observing the solemnities of his funeral rites, were odd, however, and added to the already rife speculations about her mental health.

She wanted to bury him in Granada, which was appropriate for his status as her husband and as the father of the future king of Spain, young Charles, who was still in Flanders. But she was conflicted about how to go about transporting his embalmed body, particularly as she simultaneously faced a growing chorus from her Castilian subjects who wanted her to begin presiding over the nation's business, something she had never been trained to do and had never shown any desire to do. The challenges were mounting because the kingdom had endured a vacuum of leadership since Isabella's death two years earlier, and so Queen Juana deferred the burial, moving the corpse from one monastery to another as she pondered how to handle the situation. She had no surviving close family members at hand in Castile to help her make these decisions.

Moreover, she was pregnant again and bore her final child, a little girl she named Catherine, some five months after her husband's death. This almost certainly added to her stress.

* * *

Queen Juana tried to fend off some decisions by maintaining an exaggerated widow's seclusion and mourning period. That behavior would not have seemed unusual for an ordinary woman, but it caused complex and thorny problems when done by a queen who had to address a number of issues of pressing national and international concern. She took one step, however: on December 18, 1506, she signed an order revoking all the rights and lands in Castile that Philip had distributed to his friends.[23] She ordered everyone restored to the rights they had been given by Isabella.

But she didn't seem to take to the responsibility placed in front of her. It requires a great deal of courage for a woman to do what is unusual in society, and makes everyone uncomfortable. Isabella had been praised, but she had also been viewed as an oddity, an aberration. Women continued to be viewed as inferior to men and less likely to play a significant role, despite Isabella's success as a ruler. That very year Juana's brother-in-law, King Manuel of Portugal, spelled that out very clearly when he announced to Ferdinand the birth of his fourth child and second son, Luis:

> If the Queen, my best beloved and cherished wife, had brought forth a daughter, we should have announced this to you more modestly, as befitted the birth of a daughter, but because last night, between two and three hours after midnight, Our Lord delivered her and she gave birth to a son, we wished to let you know this by letter, whereby you may also know that the fear we had lest it should be a daughter like the others, which we felt would shame us both, has increased our pleasure and satisfaction![24]

In that environment, it's not all that surprising that Juana was reluctant to attempt to take control of her tumultuous kingdom. Most people want to be viewed as part of the mainstream of their culture, not as strange outliers, and so Juana decided that her manner of ruling would be not to rule at all.

It had became popular, even desirable, for widows to retreat into seclusion after the deaths of their husbands. The dowager Queen Isabel, Isabella's mother, had done so, and the oldest sister in the family, the young Isabel, had attempted to do so after the death of her husband Afonso, the heir to the Portuguese throne. This "pious enclosure, called recogimiento," became very popular in the sixteenth century, and Juana was at the forefront of the trend, writes the historian Bethany Aram.

"Indeed many of Queen Juana's practices after the death of her mother in 1504—fasting, frugal dress, silence, solitude, and vigils—may be associated with this type of voluntary and/or enforced confinement."[25]

Juana did, however, prove to be a devoted mother to her daughter, Catherine, the only one of her six children she was allowed to keep. The other five had all been taken from her. Philip had insisted the four older children, including the heir Charles, be left behind in Flanders, where they were cared for by Juana's sister-in-law Margaret, Philip's sister. Juana's other child in Spain, her son Ferdinand, who had been born during Juana's ill-fated visit home in 1503, had been cared for by Isabella and King Ferdinand, and Ferdinand ended up keeping the boy with him.

Juana gave Catherine the same excellent education that her own mother had given her daughters, and the girl grew up well versed in Latin and Greek and a good dancer, described as gracious and well mannered. Young Catherine was another exemplar of the high standards for female education that had been set by her grandmother, Queen Isabella, and when she became queen of Portugal in adulthood, she established herself as one of the foremost art collectors of her generation, owning more non-European objects than anyone else on the continent.[26]

In short, Queen Juana embraced the life of a traditional upper-class woman in Castile, pious and a good mother, the kind of woman the devotedly Catholic family was inclined to embrace. When an ordinary woman chose this kind of life, it was viewed as admirable, even saintly. But when a queen did it, rather than display the rights and prerequisites of men in order to rule over them, then perhaps she might be viewed as insane. The rumors about Juana came to be seen as fact, and she did not do enough to establish herself in public life and defend herself.

Soon Juana had a sobriquet of her own. Her husband had been Philip the Fair. She would be known to history as Juana la Loca. Generations of male historians would guffaw in talking about this abused young woman. For them, *crazy* wasn't a strong enough term—some even called her "demented."

Many people, it seemed, had been uncomfortable with a woman ruler, and when Juana moved slowly to assert control, she appeared weak, perhaps too weak to govern. Lacking her mother's fortitude and courage to step outside accepted boundaries of female behavior, she failed to act decisively when she took power, and thus soon all that power was stripped from her.

The de facto regent of the kingdom during this period was the man with the highest ecclesiastical status in Spain, Isabella's former confessor, Cisneros, whom she had elevated to the post of archbishop of Toledo. After surveying the political landscape, he decided to call for Ferdinand to come back to Castile.

* * *

By this time, Ferdinand and Queen Germana were on an extended tour of their possessions, including his new Kingdom of Naples, but they soon began the journey back home. Upon his return, Juana slipped back into a deferential relationship with her father, perhaps in an effort to follow the stricture in her mother's dying request that she be "very obedient" to him. Juana remained at court in pious seclusion for a while more, and then Ferdinand and his friends decided to keep her under armed guard. She was at times physically restrained and was told, untruthfully, that there were plagues and dangers afoot to make her afraid of leaving. She spent the rest of her life in confinement in the castle at Tordesillas, visited by her family but seldom interacting with the outside world.

Now at last Ferdinand was free to rule on his own. He found that he liked Cisneros better than he had at first. Cisneros was a proven ally, willing and eager to abet him in taking power from Queen Juana. Soon after Ferdinand returned from Naples, Cisneros received a red hat from Pope Julius II and became Cardinal Cisneros. Together he and Ferdinand presented the world with an image of Queen Juana as too emotionally frail to rule Spain.

But other people who had been trusted allies of Queen Isabella did not find themselves in a comfortable spot with Ferdinand in charge. When Hernán de Talavera realized that payments to support his work as archbishop of Granada were not being sent promptly, he asked Peter Martyr to inquire what was happening. Martyr found that he could not get a straight answer. It turned out that Talavera himself was falling into the hands of the Inquisition.

A fiendish new inquisitor, Diego Rodríguez Lucero, had been appointed head of the tribunal in Córdoba in 1499, after the man who had previously held the post was found guilty of fraud and extortion. He embarked on an aggressive round of prosecutions of wealthy people in the city, saying that a large nest of pro-Jewish sentiment had taken root. Many of the people he accused said he was using the allegations to seize their property fraudulently. According to the historian Henry Kamen, conversos later testified that they were detained in prison and forced to teach Jewish prayers to longtime Christians so that Lucero could accuse the wealthy Christians of having been converted into secret Judaism. People who protested found themselves targets of the Inquisition as well.

When an investigation called Lucero's methods into question, the executions suddenly increased in number, with 147 people burned at the stake in 1504 and 1505, to silence them. This happened as Isabella was sick and dying, and it is unclear whether she knew it was occurring, although Ferdinand did.

As time wore on, even those who had been closest to Queen Isabella found themselves at risk from the Inquisition. This is what happened to Talavera, who was of converso descent. Lucero found people who were willing to testify that Talavera had been using the archbishop's home in Granada as a secret temple; Talavera's female relatives were alleged to be performing Jewish rituals in the kitchen. Talavera was jailed and beaten and forced to walk barefooted in the streets to prove his penitence. Many furiously protested this treatment of an eighty-year-old cleric widely seen as a great and good man, and at last Talavera was released. But his health had been broken by the ordeal, and he soon died.

Afterward there was a great clamor to bring Lucero to justice, but Ferdinand defended and shielded him. Lucero was ultimately removed from office, but Ferdinand's role in this case makes clear that for him, the Inquisition was purely a political tool to be used to frighten people and take their money. He was willing to allow innocent people to be persecuted, even when many witnesses could testify the charges were concocted.

Talavera's fate makes it obvious that Ferdinand was responsible for some large percentage of the deaths during the first thirty years of the Inquisition. Queen Isabella was certainly not blameless and believed that the Inquisition was needed to root out actual cases of heresy, but in the eyes of her children and grandchildren, it was Ferdinand's initiative that caused the Inquisition to grow and flourish. Years later, when his descendants erected a statue of him to be placed in the Great Hall at the palace at Segovia, the place of their ancestors from Pelayo to their own times, they gave Ferdinand the sole credit—others would say the blame—for creating the Inquisition in Spain.

Once Ferdinand was fully in charge, he was also free to vent his jealousy on Gonzalo Fernández de Córdoba, the soldier who had stood by the monarchs' side when they were young and vulnerable, who had fought for them against the Turks, and who had won one of the first real victories against them in fifty years. He was the man who had secured for Spain the much-coveted realm of Naples, something the French had wanted so badly that they allowed tens of thousands of Frenchmen to die in their bid to obtain it. Gonzalo had always been loyal to Isabella, ever since their childhood together, when Isabella's brother Prince Alfonso died after eating the trout pastry in Cardeñosa. He had once said that his greatest source of pride was knowing that he had her faith and support.

He had been devastated by her death. Two chroniclers called Gonzalo grief-stricken. One noted his "extreme sadness and weeping," while another said that every Spaniard lamented her death, "but none more than Gonzalo Fernández, who from his 14th year, when he began to serve her as a page, had been brought up at her court."[27]

The Great Captain continued to be heaped with accolades from everyone with whom he came in contact. According to the chronicler Hernando del Pulgar:

> Neither lack of sleep nor hunger affected him when on his fighting campaigns, and when need required he took upon himself the hardest tasks and the greatest risks. Although not a man for jesting, being always very much in earnest, in times of danger he would crack jokes with his men to cheer them and raise their spirits. He used to say that kind words from a captain won him the love of his soldiers. He was as competent in perfecting many affairs as he was diligent in bringing one to a successful end. Ability and diligence were so united in him that he not only defeated his foes by his great intelligence and vigorous efforts, but surpassed them by his intelligence and wisdom.[28]

Green with envy, Ferdinand probed for flaws in Gonzalo's management of affairs in Naples and convinced himself that the Great Captain was undermining his authority and had become potentially traitorous. Ferdinand called him back to Spain, telling him he wanted to honor him by making him the Commander of the Order of Santiago. But when Gonzalo returned, that offer was forgotten, and Gonzalo was given the job of holding the reins of the horse when Queen Germana went riding. Gonzalo soon went into seclusion in Loja and was given no further military assignments. When his nephew became involved in the protest against the misconduct of the inquisitor Lucero, Ferdinand said the young man was a traitor and ordered the family homestead, the castle at Montilla, destroyed. This nephew was the son of Gonzalo's brother Alonso de Aguilar, who had been slashed to pieces defending Castile in the uprising in the Alpujarras. The ancestral home of Alonso and Gonzalo was now destroyed so that Ferdinand could assert his dominance.

Ferdinand wasn't all that interested in bringing Cesare Borgia to justice either. Borgia was still imprisoned in the fortress of La Mota in Medina del Campo, where Isabella had wanted him tried for murder. Queen Juana had shared her mother's belief that Cesare Borgia was a dangerous man and had kept him imprisoned. But in 1507 Borgia managed to escape from the castle and made his way to Navarre, where he found work as a mercenary. But he didn't last long: he was killed in a skirmish and his body was found sometime later, with multiple wounds and stripped naked for the value of his clothes and armor. And so Cesare Borgia came to a sorry end, despite the honors and accolades that had been heaped on him by his father, Pope Alexander VI.

King Ferdinand also showed himself careless and callous in his dealings with the Americas. Columbus came back from his fourth and last voyage in 1506, old before his time. He had had a terrible ordeal, having been shipwrecked and abandoned in Jamaica for months before he was rescued. He arrived in Castile right at around the time Isabella died, and he too deeply mourned her death. Columbus knew, his friends later recalled, that Ferdinand would never recognize his accomplishments the way that Isabella had.

Columbus realized his career was over when he heard the queen was dead. "In Seville, the news that Queen Isabella had died filled Columbus with intense grief," the human rights advocate Bartolomé de Las Casas later wrote.

> To him, she represented protection and hope, and no amount of pain, hardship or loss (even loss of his own life) could afflict and sadden him more that such news. . . . She had received his services humbly and with gratitude. As for the Catholic King Ferdinand, I do not know why he was not only ungrateful in words and deeds but actually harmed Columbus whenever possible, although his

actions belied his words. It was believed that if, in good conscience
and without losing face, he could have violated all the articles
of the privileges that he and the Queen had justly granted him
for his services, he would indeed have done so. I have never been
able to ascertain the reason for this dislike and unkingly conduct
toward one whose unparalleled services no other monarch ever
received.[29]

Columbus died in Valladolid in 1506. He was more comfortable in his
old age than he liked to pretend. He had relished creating a perception
of some sort of martyrdom, but in fact he left his two sons very wealthy
men, and his descendants, as he had hoped, became high nobility.

The New World no longer got the same attention it had received from
Isabella, and things on the ground there began to go wildly awry. Ferdinand wasn't interested in discoveries, except as they could provide him
with new sources of cash. Voyages of discovery declined for most of the
first part of his solo reign. They had slowed to a crawl when Isabella first
grew ill. Scholars have described themselves as perplexed by the drop-
off. "For six years after Columbus's departure on his last voyage in 1502,
there is a curious lull in Spain's exploring activities," Roger Merriman
writes. "Only one or two smattering expeditions were undertaken, and
with practically no results."[30]

Unfortunately, abuse of the native Americans grew much worse as a
result of neglect, avarice, cruelty, and poor stewardship. It was Las Casas's
belief that far fewer Indians would have died if Isabella had lived: "Queen
Isabella's holy zeal, intense care, tireless efforts and meritorious will to
save the Indians are attested by the royal decrees she issued in the few
years she lived after the discovery of the Indies, and these years hardly
came to ten when one considers that for quite some time, information
concerning the Indies was a matter of guesses and hearsay."[31]

With her mother dead and unable to intervene when her father
undertook self-serving and callous courses of action, Princess Catherine
of Aragon, living far away in England, suffered as well. In 1509 she finally
married young King Henry VIII. Her father had allowed her to dangle at
the English court for years, almost penniless at times, while he dickered
with Henry VII over the remainder of the dowry. On his deathbed, King
Henry VII acknowledged Catherine's merits and urged his son to marry
her, which he soon did. Then, soon after Catherine and Henry were mar-

ried, Ferdinand entered a pact with Henry VIII to fight together against the French, then betrayed and humiliated him to win some lands for himself in Navarre. That infuriated Henry, who was an ambitious young man trying to establish himself on the world stage, and it caused damage to the young couple's marriage.

This additional strain imposed even greater burdens on Catherine, who endlessly worried about her inability to produce the male heir that her husband desired so ardently. The quarreling between Henry and Ferdinand caused her physical distress and contributed to the loss of a pregnancy in 1514. "The Queen of England has had a miscarriage, brought on by her distress over the discord between the kings, i.e., her husband and her father, owing to her unbearable sorrow she is said to have delivered a premature fetus," Peter Martyr confided to Luis Hurtado de Mendoza. "The husband blamed the innocent queen for the desertion of her father and kept voicing to her his complaints."[32]

The limited horizons of Ferdinand's interests became apparent once Isabella was gone. He spent the rest of his reign bickering over territorial borders, warring with one European power after another. In another effort to remove a rival for public esteem, he did allow Cisneros to lead an expedition into North Africa, assuming the seventy-three-year-old prelate was too aged to make much of an impact. Cisneros squared his shoulders, set out, and conquered the city of Oran. In so doing, he freed about fifteen thousand Christian slaves held captive there.[33]

But this conquest, and a few others made around the same time in North Africa, had the effect of exacerbating tensions with Muslims in North Africa and gave renewed impetus to Muslim pirates attacking the Mediterranean coast. Raiding expeditions led by the corsair Hayreddin on unsuspecting towns, sometimes with the assistance of people who had previously lived in Spain, were so successful that Bayezid's son, known as Selim the Grim, made Hayreddin admiral of the Turkish fleet. The Turks conquered the Mamluk empire of Egypt in 1517 and, as Isabella had feared, moved menacingly ever closer to Spain.

During the years of Ferdinand's regency of Castile, the Christians benefited from a fortuitous outbreak of heresy in the Muslim world that distracted the Turks' attention from further conquests in Europe as they pursued conflicts closer to home. In this case, the wrong thinking involved a mystical order led by Sheikh Safi ad-Din, who claimed descent from a son-in-law of Muhammad. It was called Safawiyya. "The

Ottomans, who were sternly orthodox Muslims, abhorred the teaching of Safawiyya as heretical," writes the historian V. J. Parry. "They rightly regarded the movement, however, as far more than a religious danger; for them it was also a grave political menace."[34]

Spain had a little breathing space during this period, as it had during the infighting between Bayezid and Djem. During these years young Charles, the heir to the throne of Castile, grew to adulthood back in Mechelen in Flanders, under the careful tutelage of Margaret, Isabella's beloved daughter-in-law, who ended up raising Isabella's heirs, just as Isabella had hoped she would. Margaret carried the torch for Isabella's legacy. She even bought from the hurried estate sale of Isabella's possessions many of the paintings of Christ's life, keeping them close at hand. It was there in Mechelen that the artist Albrecht Dürer saw them and famously praised the paintings for their "purity and excellence."[35]

Margaret made sure the paintings were kept as a set and presented as a gift in adulthood, as a final bequest from her, to Isabella's grandchildren. Today most of them remain in Madrid's Royal Palace; the rest are part of the treasured collections of major art museums, including the Metropolitan Museum of Art in New York and the National Gallery of Art in Washington.

Margaret's enthusiasm for art made the family home in Mechelen one of the first great centers of Latin American art in Europe, for the golden masks, obsidian ritual objects, and feathered headdresses that Hernán Cortés collected when he conquered Mexico were sent to Prince Charles but placed in Margaret's care. This was the first glimpse Europeans had of the rich and varied artistic traditions in the Americas.

Gonzalo Fernández de Córdoba lived out the rest of his life in some seclusion and was never sent to battle again by the king. But his military leadership had transformed the Spanish armies, and his influence lasted for generations. He died after suffering a high fever in December 1515, and was greatly mourned by the kingdom. In his deathbed confession, he said he regretted only three sins—betraying the king of Naples and betraying Cesare Borgia, both of whom had come to him in faith of their safety; the third, he said, would be known only to God. He had remarried but was buried in Granada, in the Monastery of San Jerónimo, just a short walk from the final resting place of Queen Isabella. Hanging over his tomb were the one hundred battle pendants he had won in his victories for the Castilian crown.

Peter Martyr, who had managed to retain his place at court by carefully adapting to the political winds, said all Spain grieved at the news of Gonzalo's death. "Woe to thee, All Spain!" Martyr wrote in his characteristically florid style, recounting in a letter all the great successes that Gonzalo had achieved and noting that he had rightly earned the name the Great Commander. King Ferdinand also seemed regretful at the news of Gonzalo's death. "The news was very troublesome to the king, or so it seems to have been, God is the only searcher of hearts," Martyr wrote. "For that man's magnanimity was sometimes suspected: therefore he allowed him to live at leisure in a secluded place."[36]

* * *

King Ferdinand died in 1516, just a few months later. His health had been undermined by the side effects of a concoction made of bull's testicles that he had consumed at his wife's behest to boost his sexual potency. It was puzzling that Ferdinand was never able to produce healthy children with his eager young wife. He had always previously been notably fertile. Ferdinand and Germana had only one child together, and that infant died soon after birth. Of course, given Ferdinand's record of promiscuity, he may have been one of the earliest Europeans to contract syphilis, which was rampant in his kingdom and probably got its start in Barcelona at the time when he was living there. Recent forensic evidence has found that syphilis was widespread among members of the Aragonese royal family; and it was then incurable and caused sterility.

The disease is thought to have traveled from Barcelona to an explosive epicenter in Naples in 1494. Many members of Ferdinand's extended Aragonese family either fell victim to it or were likely exposed, whether they became ill with it or not. His cousins frequently traveled back and forth from Spain to Barcelona and throughout Italy, often with extensive entourages of fawning and flirting courtiers in tow.

Archaeological pathologists who have studied the Neapolitan royal family have discovered that Ferdinand's cousin King Ferrante, who was born in 1431 and died in 1494 at age sixty-three, died of colon cancer and did not appear to have contracted syphilis. But his younger family members most certainly did. Ferrante's granddaughter, the beautiful Isabella of Aragon, born in 1470 and married to the Duke of Milan, had markers for syphilis and is believed to have tried to treat her condition with a course of mercury, which caused her teeth to become blackened. She tried to chisel away the evidence by having the enamel removed from her darkened teeth. A stepsibling of hers, María of Aragon, had deep ulcerated syphilitic lesions on her lower limbs. Sores on the legs and elsewhere on the body were a common marker for syphilis at the time.[37]

Ferdinand had died in a tiny house in a small village, Madrigalejo, while he was traveling. Unlike Isabella's death, however, his passing did not cause enormous sorrow in Spain. He was buried next to her in Granada, in a spectacular mausoleum quite at odds with the simple resting place she had requested. Isabella had asked that her daughter Isabel be buried near her, but her daughter's body was left in Toledo. Instead, it was Ferdinand who was laid to rest next to Queen Isabella, Queen Juana, and King Philip, together for eternity, in a triumph of public relations and a cynical assertion of dynastic harmony.

In the centuries ahead, Ferdinand became a famous man, credited for many of Isabella's achievements. The fact that his name appeared first on official documents—sometimes because she requested that he be added—meant that future historians, sometimes blinded by their own sexism, would cite him as the primary architect of events, even when he played only a minor role in them.

For generations, scholars have looked at the twenty-five-year marriage of Ferdinand and Isabella and tried to deduce the contributions that each made to the success of their reign, which decisions were hers and which his. An easy test for answering those questions is to look at how Ferdinand ruled alone after Queen Isabella's death. He lived until 1516, twelve years after she died. When he ruled with Isabella, he could rank among the great kings of Europe and be viewed as a man of consequence. Without Isabella, he produced almost nothing of significance and frittered his time away in pointless international intrigues.

In the *Book of the Courtier,* Baldassare Castiglione, an Italian who had spent some years in Spain after Isabella's death, pondered the relative significance of their lives. The book recounts a long series of parlor conversations held at the palace of the Duke of Urbino. At one point Castiglione's verbal sparring partner asks him whether Isabella really did what he claims. Wasn't it really Ferdinand? he queries.

Castiglione answers that Ferdinand deserved to be compared with Isabella, but only because she chose to love him. "For since the Queen judged him worthy of being her husband, and loved and respected him so much, we cannot say that he does not deserve to be compared with her," Castiglione wrote. "Yet I believe that the fame he had because of her was a dowry not inferior to the kingdom of Castile."

Love can be inexplicable.

* * *

Isabella's Hapsburg grandchildren, benefiting from their tutelage at Margaret's hands, took on the heavy mantle of responsibility for their holdings, which encircled the world. Charles became king of Spain in 1516 and Holy Roman emperor in 1519, when he was nineteen years old. Under his reign, the Spaniards conquered Mexico and Peru, fabulous empires with wealth beyond reckoning.

Juana's younger son Ferdinand, who had been born in Spain during her visit to Castile with Philip and who had been raised in Spain, was given control of the family's Austrian lands. He took charge of watching over the frontiers with the Ottoman Turks. He halted the Turkish advance by land when he successfully withstood a siege at Vienna in 1529; he became Holy Roman emperor himself in 1558, when his brother retired to a monastery in Spain. A generation later Charles's son Don Juan led the naval force against the Ottomans near the port of Lepanto in 1571, in one of the Christian West's first major naval victories against the Turks. Neither of these victories was in itself decisive, as some have claimed, but both were watershed moments in world history nonetheless. They marked a crucial turning point, and made it clear that the West was going to fight, and fight effectively, and would eventually contain the Turkish expansion.

The baton had been passed to Isabella's male grandchildren, to Charles and his brother Ferdinand, and then to Philip II and Don Juan. They remained the only formidable opposition to the Ottoman Empire, organizing their defenses against an overpowering foe by unifying themselves under a single religious banner, with a single-minded focus on religious orthodoxy. They continued to view themselves as the defenders of Christianity, bringing all their resources from the New World to bear in this struggle. They also expanded their list of enemies to include the new, and to their thinking heretical, branch of Christianity, the Protestant movement. Just as their grandparents had done against others they considered heretical, they used the mechanisms of the Inquisition against wrong-thinking people—in this case, Protestants. But the Protestant threat never materialized in Spain to the same degree as elsewhere in Europe.

The religious reforms that had been undertaken in Spain under Isabella's rule had rooted out many of the worst abuses in the Catholic Church long before the Counter-Reformation swung into action.

Fighting alongside the Hapsburgs in this new Christian army were descendants of the Indians from the New World, including the grandchildren of the Aztec leader Moctezuma and the Extremaduran explorer Hernán Cortés, who had intermingled and had children together. In the New World, in the next 120 years, the Spaniards would build seventy thousand churches, five hundred monasteries, and three thousand church-sponsored schools and hospitals; they would found at least four universities, located in Colombia, Peru, and Mexico. They also extracted some $1.5 billion in gold and silver, used for their enterprises in Europe.[38]

When Isabella was born, Christianity had been a dying religion, weakened from within and under withering assault from without. Today, five hundred years after her death, it is the world's largest religion, encompassing some two billion people in scores of countries. One of them was a man who was born in Latin America, in Argentina, and when he became pope in 2013, he called himself Francis I. The first saints he named were the eight hundred people—whom he called the martyrs—killed at Otranto in 1480.

Isabella's direct descendants remain in positions of power throughout Europe. The ruling families of Spain, Belgium, Luxembourg, the Netherlands, the United Kingdom, Denmark, Norway, Sweden, and Monaco all share a common ancestry from Queen Isabella and King Ferdinand.

AFTERWORD

E very booklover has a favorite place to steal away to read and
dream of distant lands. When I was a girl living in the American-
controlled Panama Canal Zone, my special spot was a concrete
seawall near my house where I could look out over the Caribbean Sea. I
didn't have to travel far in my imagination because the place where I sat,
dangling my legs over the water, had been visited by explorer Christopher
Columbus in 1502, on his last voyage, when he was still desperately eager
to bring back good news to his sponsor, the intense and dynamic Queen
Isabella of Castile.

Isabella's legacy was visible everywhere in Panama, once the hub of
Spain's colonial empire, where tons of gold and silver were transported
to Europe so that the queen's descendants could expand their power and
dominion in the Old World. There were dozens of sites, mostly crumbling, abandoned ruins, covered in jungle vines, where the Spaniards had
lived and worked when they ruled the planet. The derelict Castillo de San
Lorenzo and the tumbled-down walls of Panama Viejo were evidence that
even awesome political power can be fleeting. This made a vivid impression on me, a child of the American empire overseas, then at the apex of
its strength, both admired and resented around the world.

In college I continued to pursue my interest in Spanish history, art,
and literature. When I attended Spain's University of Salamanca, a college favored by its patroness Queen Isabella, I toured the country, visiting

the palaces, castles, and museums that the wealth of the New World had financed. General Francisco Franco had just died, and the country was once again opening itself to the world after a dark phase in its history.

Then one day when I was traveling to Madrid, the train made an unexpected stop at the forlorn hamlet of Madrigal de las Altas Torres. With time on my hands, I wandered about its dusty alleyways and stumbled upon a brick building that caught my eye. A small sign noted that Isabella had been born there. The medieval structure was unprepossessing, not looking at all like a home to monarchs. The sight underscored to me how humble Isabel's beginnings had been, and how unlikely her meteoric rise to power. It seemed almost unbelievable that a young woman from this background, at a time when women seldom wielded power, would pave the way to world domination for her grandchildren. I was fascinated, and I think the idea for the book began percolating in my mind at that time—although I spent some decades in journalism before circling back to my early interest in history. I was curious about Queen Isabella, puzzled by her actions, and I wanted to better understand her, what she did and why she did it. It seemed essential to try to understand her from the context of her own times, which is what I have attempted to do.

Queen Isabella's life is a Rorschach test for her biographers. Everyone brings a point of view, an internal bias, to the subject of her life. Catholics see her one way; Protestants, Muslims, and Jews see her very differently. Some false information about her has circulated widely. Spanish history has been systematically distorted by propagandists, in a process that is known as the Black Legend, and the era of Muslim control has been painted in an inaccurately rosy hue. Moreover, the conquest of the New World is seen differently by Europeans and Native Americans, and by their descendants. Consequently, Isabella is one of the world's most historically controversial rulers, both adored and demonized.

It seems only fitting that I should bare my own particular biases here as well. First, on the issue of faith: I am not religiously active; I am primarily descended from a mix of Protestants, Catholics, and Jews from Europe. I have attempted to be open-minded about the sensitivities of all the participants to the events I am describing, but I have a particular bias in that I think killing or enslaving people is evil, regardless of who the victims are or why the cruelty was rationalized at the time.

On balance, I think the fact that Isabella sent Christopher Columbus to the New World was a good thing. Why? Because I myself am a product of what has been called the Columbian Exchange.

When I was a child, my mother would proudly say that her family first came to the New World at Jamestown, meaning that she hailed from early American stock. And my father, partly of Native American heritage, through the Lenni Lenape tribe, would laughingly respond, "Yes, we met your boat and we greeted you when you arrived."

Consequently, I am sympathetic to the claims of Native Americans that their lands were stolen. And I am also sympathetic to the challenges faced by the Europeans when they arrived, for they suffered hardship and loss, too.

I also bring to the task a profound appreciation for the courage and daring shown by the early explorers to the New World. The first time I saw a Spanish fort in the New World was when I was six years old and visited Fort Saint Augustine in Florida. A few years later, my family moved from the United States to Panama, a trip that then entailed a three-day car ride along modern highways to reach New Orleans, where we embarked on a four-day voyage by sea. It was a long journey even in the 1960s.

One day we drove through the jungles on the Caribbean coast of Panama to Fort San Lorenzo, which I realized with amazement was a sister fortification to the one I had seen in Saint Augustine. I early saw the massive scope and scale of the Spanish empire, how far it had reached across the oceans, and how effectively it had imposed its culture, language, and religion in places thousands of miles apart. Whatever you might think of Spain during this period, its achievements and accomplishments cannot be denied.

Another part of my perspective comes from my life experience as a journalist. I've covered the present manifestations of some of the same issues and problems that were confronted by the Iberians of the fifteenth century. As a reporter, I place great value on primary accounts of events that occurred, and so in researching this book, I always looked first to what had been said from the beginning by people who were there and saw things occur themselves. I have paid attention to later critiques of these sources as well, but generally tend to favor eyewitness reports over later interpretations of events by people who were not there. I was fortunately able to find a great many of these primary resources at the Library of Congress, the world's preeminent library, where dozens of librarians helped me track down titles or provided access to ancient books and manuscripts that allowed me to find the first published accounts of many of the incidents described in this book.

I made a special effort to locate nontraditional or "outsider" accounts to round out the story as clearly as possible. For accounts of the Inquisition and its effects, I sought out Jewish sources and found valuable material in the Judaica Collection at Harvard University's Houghton Library. For accounts of what transpired in the Kingdom of Granada and during the Ottoman advances, I sought Arabic accounts and first-person contemporary reports from Eastern Europe. Some of these accounts have only recently been translated into English. In some cases, I paid for translations of original materials that have not yet been published in English. I traveled to Spain, England, France, Panama, and Puerto Rico in pursuit of the tale, using libraries and archival resources wherever they could be found.

I sometimes quoted older history books rather than more contemporary sources simply because of the beauty of their language. The work of William Hickling Prescott and Benzion Netanyahu, to cite just two examples, has been superseded by other, more contemporary research, but these men's accomplishments remain seminal in the field and have provided the foundation for much that came later.

That means this book is somewhat different from those that are written by most academic historians today. There are a couple of areas where this is most obvious—the topics of cannibalism in the Caribbean and the probable origins of syphilis in the New World. Many modern historians have expressed doubts about the accounts of those things, probably as an overcorrection for the deep-rooted racism and ethnocentrism of some of the original European chroniclers, who were eager to justify seizing land in the Americas. However, numerous first-person accounts agree in describing the same basic sets of facts, and so I have presented them as likely facts myself.

Moreover, cannibalism has had ritual elements or been the result of human desperation a great many times in history. I don't see mentioning it as pejorative to any individual group. New research has found signs of cannibalism in Jamestown, so no culture had a monopoly on the idea that human flesh could be palatable under the right circumstances.

On syphilis, the arrival of the disease in such a virulent form in Europe at that particular time does not seem coincidental to me. Many of the first-person accounts at the time described a terrible new disease spread by sexual intercourse. Moreover, contagion is usually a two-way street. Syphilis may have gone east, but smallpox, the measles, influenza, and the bubonic plague went west at the same time, producing a far greater number of deaths. And it was the Americans and Europeans who introduced syphilis for the first time in the Hawaiian Islands in the 1800s.

The discussion of the distinct possibility of childhood sexual abuse in Isabella's family comes from my own journalistic work and that of my colleagues, and after consultation with psychologists who are experts in the field. Isolated archival records discussing events in Isabella's family, taken together, paint a picture of the kind of predation that has been around forever but that is only now being investigated and exposed. The patterns in the Castilian court in the late 1400s are remarkably similar to those that have been revealed in recent public scandals involving the clergy and other powerful figures.

What I have tried to do is place Isabella within the context of the time and place in which she lived. She was a religiously fervent Catholic, living in an era when the Ottoman Turks seemed on the verge of wiping Christianity off the map. I am convinced that much of what she did was a reaction to this perceived threat, and to her belief that she was being called upon to bolster the faith against a very formidable enemy.

ACKNOWLEDGMENTS

It will be difficult for me to thank everyone who deserves acknowledgment for the completion of this book, because in many ways I have been working on it all my life—whether at the time I knew it or not—and many people gave me guidance, thoughtful perspective, and encouragement along the way.

My mother, Melinda Hoppe Young, is an avid reader and a romantic, and she inspired me to look for the stories everywhere we traveled. And oh the places we went! She loved the jungle, and the ruins, and the history of Panama, and she took us everywhere fearlessly, on expeditions to see what we could find. With her at the wheel, we forged riverbeds in a van, explored deserted tropical beaches, and hiked into the interior to remote villages that were seldom visited by outsiders.

My childhood best friend, Laura Gregg Roa, who was the same age as me, shared our fascination with Panama and its Spanish and Indian heritage. She frequently accompanied us. Then Laura got her driver's license ahead of me, and we two ventured out on our own, this time with Laura at the wheel, sometimes riding a motorcycle and sometimes more sedately in her parents' station wagon.

Laura stayed in Panama when the United States returned the former Canal Zone to the Panamanians in 2000, teaching Spanish and French, and then moved to Belgium to teach in the American military school there. She had hoped to help me research this book about Queen Isabella but died of cancer when she was fifty-two years old, leaving a daughter and two sons behind. I dedicate this book to her.

After I left the Canal Zone to go to college, I studied journalism at Pennsylvania State University, a happy choice that eventually led to my career in the news business. While I was there I indulged my passion for Spanish and Latin American art and history, and took a number of courses in those areas. I spent a semester at the Universidad de Salamanca in Spain, and it was then that this book actually started to take shape in my mind. The professors in both locations, at Penn State and in Salamanca, gave me an excellent foundation in the history of the era, something that formed the basis for the research that I later did on my own.

Once I began researching the book in earnest, several highly respected scholars gave me invaluable assistance in understanding the time period and context within which Isabella lived. First and foremost was the wonderful Teofilo Ruiz, a history professor at UCLA who spoke with me at various points during the research and writing of the book. His brilliant scholarship, personal generosity, and profound humanity have been inspirational to me. He did me the great honor of reading the manuscript in its nearly completed form and making dozens of suggestions for changes and improvements. Professor Ruiz, thank you.

Simon Doubleday, a history professor at Hofstra University, spoke at length with me at the beginning of my work. At the end, although he was traveling in Spain for his own research, he nevertheless took the time to weigh in with some important suggestions for changes in the manuscript.

Theresa Earenfight, a history professor at Seattle University; and Nancy Marino, a professor of Spanish literature at Michigan State University, offered advice and encouragement. I frequently consulted Chiyo Ishikawa's brilliant and beautiful book on Isabella's private devotional art, which contains pictures of remarkable paintings that are otherwise unavailable to the public because they are housed in parts of Madrid's Palacio Real that are closed to visitors. She also discussed my manuscript with me as I reached the final stages of writing. David Hosaflook's pathbreaking research into Albanian history offered the explanations for obscure references I found in Isabella's papers to terrifying events taking place in Eastern Europe.

If there are any errors in fact or interpretation in the book, they are my own.

My wonderful agent and friend, Gail Ross, made this book possible, and her partner at Ross Yoon agency, Howard Yoon, masterfully prepared the proposal so that it appealed to editor Ronit Feldman at Nan A. Talese/Doubleday. Ronit encouraged and guided me throughout the research and writing process and served as a sounding board year after year as we learned new things about Isabella and reflected on what they meant. Ronit is a gifted wordsmith with excellent organizational skills, and she shepherded the book deftly through to production. Nan A. Talese, who is justly famous for her editing genius, did some skillful surgery on the final product. Others on the Doubleday team whom I'd like to thank include interior designer Pei Loi Koay, production editor Nora Reichard, and copyeditor Janet Biehl. I'd also like to express my appreciation to the team at Anchor Books, my friend Keith Goldsmith, and also Kathleen Cook, the production editor, and Mandy Licata, the publicist. I am grateful to them all.

I received assistance from knowledgeable experts at a great many libraries and art museums. There are too many individuals to specify by name. The bulk of my work was done at the Library of Congress, where I began in the Hispanic Reading Room with subject-area experts who set me on the path and directed me toward significant works in both the general collection and in rare books and manuscripts. I would like to specifically thank Juan Manuel Pérez, Everette E. Larson, Barbara A. Tenenbaum, Georgette M. Dorn, Katherine McCann, Tracy North, Eric Frazier, Betty Culpepper, Janice C. Ruth, and Sheridan Harvey.

The people in Spain were unfailingly gracious, submitting yet again to another round of questioning by Americans who come seeking information about their roots. Barbara Minguez Garcia and Jorge Sobredo, at the Spanish embassy in Washington, D.C., paved the way, providing introductions to key archivists who were able to give access to rare and valuable early manuscripts. Severiano Hernandez Vicente, Gonzalo Anes Alvarez, Carlos Martinez Shaw, Manuel Barrios Aguilera, and Gregorio Hernandez Sanchez were particularly helpful. All archives are wonderful places to spend an afternoon or a month, but I owe a particular debt of gratitude to the Real Academia de la Historia and the Biblioteca Nacional, both in Madrid, and public libraries and archives in Segovia, Seville, Simancas, Valladolid, Granada, and at the Escorial. Significant works of art that were referenced in this book are housed at the Prado in Madrid, the National Galley of Art in Washington, D.C., the Metropolitan Museum of Art, and the Monasterio de las Huelgas in Burgos. I traveled all over Spain tracing Isabella's path, and enjoyed many a glass of wine and plate of tapas along the way.

In France, I reviewed the Margaret of Austria papers at the Archives du Nord in Lille. I spent many hours in London at the British Library and National Archives. Wellcome Library in London provided a welcome translation into English of Peter Martyr's *Opus Epistolarum*.

I visited historic sites relevant to the New World chapters of this story in Panama, Puerto Rico, and Mexico. I am grateful to all the people with the vision and foresight to realize that our own hemisphere also has history worth preserving.

In the United States, I consulted collections at Harvard University's Houghton Library, the Huntington Library and Art Collection in San Marino, California, the Chicago Institute of Art, the Cleveland Museum of Art, the Stephen A. Scharzman Building of the New York Public Library, Washington College's Miller Library, McKeldin Library at the University of Maryland, and Georgetown University's Lauinger Library.

The excellent libraries in Alexandria and Arlington, Virginia, provided much material that has been published in the past two decades.

Marta Rueda, of the Segovia office of tourism, spent many hours with me, taking me all over the city and sharing with me her thoughts and perspective about Isabella, gleaned over a lifetime. She became not just a guide but a true friend. The proprietors of San Miguel Hotel gave me a room with a view overlooking the red-tiled roof of the Church of San Miguel, so I could look out at the site where Isabella took the throne. They were unfailingly warm and generous with me.

I also want to thank Andrew Hoppe, Louisa Woodville; Alexis Simendinger; Kim Winfrey; Camille Brilloit in Lille, France; Jesus Ibarra in San Miguel de Allende, Mexico; Luis Chaffo; Holly Hall; Laura Evenson; and Wendy Silverthorne.

The book could not have been written without the scholarship of those who went before me. Some of them are living, and some have gone to their rewards, and I list them in no particular order. I want to especially thank María Isabel del Val Valdivieso, Juan de Mata Carriazo, Jerónimo Zurita, Luis Suárez, Tarsicio Azcona, Peggy Liss, Nancy Rubin, and William Hickling Prescott.

My sister Elizabeth Gately initiated the work on the bibliography when I ran out of steam toward the end, and that was a generous gift of time and love. She's a wonderful sister. My mother-in-law, B. J. Averitt, shared her knowledge and lifelong interest in Islamic art.

My beloved husband, Neil Warner Averitt, assisted me with the research for this book, with his own deep knowledge of world history a valuable resource for drawing connections among far-flung events. As our children like to say, he is the Big Book of Everything. He read the manuscript three times, carefully edited the text, and offered me the benefit of his insight and, most recently, his new interest in early church history and the story of Christ's life. He educated me on many things I did not know about Christianity.

Our five children—John, Elizabeth, Amelia, Alex, and Rachel—all listened to talk about Isabella's life for many hours and retained faith in me that I would get the book done. I want to thank them all once again.

And one of them in particular: My daughter Rachel and I went together to Spain, exploring the countryside, venturing into olive groves, hiking through fields of giant sunflowers to get to unique vantage points to see historic sites that were otherwise hard to access, wandering Roman roads and clambering up crumbling castle ruins. She has the same intrepid spirit as my mother, and she, too, has made my life more of an adventure because she has been there to share the journey.

NOTES

PROLOGUE

1. J. H. Elliott, *Imperial Spain: 1469–1716* (London: Penguin, 1990), p. 103.

ONE: A BIRTH WITHOUT FANFARE

1. Nancy Rubin, *Isabella of Castile: The First Renaissance Queen* (New York: St. Martin's Press, 1991), p. 16.
2. King of Castile Don Juan II to the City of Segovia on the birth of his daughter Isabel, Madrid, April 23, 1451, Archivo Exmo, Ayuntamiento de Segovia.
3. Jerónimo Zurita, *Anales de Aragon* (Zaragoza: Instituto "Fernando el Católico" [C.S.I.C.] de le Exma Diputación Provincial, 1975), vol. 6, p. 33, "that they had been given herbs," poisonous herbs, by Luna.
4. Fernán Pérez de Guzmán, *Comienza la crónica del serenísimo príncipe Don Juan, segundo rey deste nombre* (Madrid: Librería y Casa Editorial Hernando, 1930), p. 633.
5. Peggy K. Liss, *Isabel the Queen: Life and Times* (New York: Oxford University Press, 1992), p. 17.
6. Rubin, *Isabella of Castile*, p. 19.
7. Ibid.
8. Didier T. Jaén, *John II of Castile and the Grand Master Álvaro de Luna* (Madrid: Editorial Castalia, 1978), pp. 189–90.
9. Nicholas Round, *The Greatest Man Uncrowned: A Study of the Fall of Don Álvaro de Luna* (London: Tamesis Books, 1986), p. 42.
10. Rubin, *Isabella of Castile*, p. 19.
11. Jean Descola, *A History of Spain* (New York: Alfred A. Knopf, 1963), pp. 40–42.
12. Townsend Miller, *The Castles and the Crown: Spain, 1451–1555* (New York: Coward-McCann, 1963), p. 17.
13. Descola, *History of Spain*, pp. 32 and 33.

14. *Isidore of Seville's History of the Kings of the Goths, Vandals and Suevi,* trans. Guido Donini and Gordon B. Ford (Leiden: Brill, 1966), p. 1.

15. John L. Esposito, *The Oxford History of Islam* (Oxford, U.K.: Oxford University Press, 1999), p. 13.

16. Bernard Lewis, *Islam: From the Prophet Muhammad to the Capture of Constantinople* (New York: Oxford University Press, 1987), p. 2:xvi.

17. Roger Collins, *The Arab Conquest of Spain: 710–797* (New York: Wiley-Blackwell, 1995), p. 63.

18. Ahmad ibn Muhammad Al-Maqqari, *The History of the Mohammedan Dynasties in Spain,* trans. Pascual de Gayangos, 2 vols. (London: Oriental Translation Fund, 1840–43), p. 1:250, referring to quote from Ayyeshah, widow of the Prophet.

19. Ibid., p. 1:18.

20. Ibid., pp. 1:264–65.

21. Ibid., p. 1:265.

22. Ibid.

23. Ibid., p. 1:267.

24. Lewis, *Islam from the Prophet Muhammad,* p. 2:111.

25. Collins, *Arab Conquest of Spain,* p. 97.

26. Ibid., p. 105.

27. Al-Maqqari, *Mohammedan Dynasties,* p. 1:272.

28. Ibid., p. 1:275.

29. Ibid.

30. Ibid., p. 1:276.

31. Ibid., p. 1:279.

32. Ibid., p. 1:280.

33. Ibid., pp. 1:280–81. Gayangos said he believes this pattern was so consistent because Jews in Iberia may have already been in communication with North Africans. Of the Berbers who came from North Africa, some were of Jewish descent, and allied themselves with the Jews in Spain upon their arrival. Others may have been only superficially Muslim, and retaining Jewish customs and beliefs "felt great sympathy for their former brethren" (pp. 511, 531).

34. Al-Maqqari, *Mohammedan Dynasties,* pp. 1:282–88.

35. Ibid., pp. 1:291, 2:20.

36. Ibid., p. 2:41.

37. Diego de Valera, *Crónica de España* (Salamanca, 1499). Only three copies of this book survive, including one at the Library of Congress in Washington, D.C.

38. Al-Maqqari, *Mohammedan Dynasties,* p. 2:34.

39. Descola, *History of Spain,* p. 82.

40. Jane I. Smith, "Islam and Christendom: Historical, Cultural, and Religious Interaction from the Seventh to the Fifteenth Centuries," in Esposito, ed., *The Oxford History of Islam,* pp. 318–19.

41. Ibid., p. 320.

42. Ibid.

43. Dario Fernández-Morera, "The Myth of the Andalucian Paradise," *Intercollegiate Review* 41, no. 2 (Fall 2006).

44. Smith, "Islam and Christendom," pp. 22, 23, 25, 29.

45. Al-Maqqari, *Mohammedan Dynasties,* p. 2:195.

46. Fernández-Morera, "Myth of Andalusian Paradise," p. 27.

47. Ibid., pp. 27–28.

48. Bradley Smith, *Spain: A History in Art* (Garden City, N.Y.: Doubleday, 1971), pp. 60–62, depicting works held at El Escorial.

49. Al-Maqqari, *Mohammedan Dynasties*, pp. 2:124–25.

50. Nancy Bisaha, *Creating East and West: Renaissance Humanists and the Ottoman Turks* (Philadelphia: University of Pennsylvania Press, 2004), p. 68.

51. Alonso Fernández de Palencia, *Crónica de Enrique IV*, ed. Antonio Paz y Meliá (Madrid: Ediciones Atlas, 1973–75), pp. 50–52.

52. George Sphrantzes, *The Fall of the Byzantine Empire: A Chronicle, 1401–1477*, trans. Marios Philippides (Amherst: University of Massachusetts Press, 1980), p. 70.

53. John McManners, *The Oxford Illustrated History of Christianity* (Oxford, U.K.: Oxford University Press, 1992), p. 166.

TWO: A CHILDHOOD IN THE SHADOWS

1. Ana Sánchez Prieto, *Enrique IV el Impotente* (Madrid: Alderabán Ediciones, 1999), p. 7.

2. Peggy K. Liss, *Isabel the Queen: Life and Times* (New York: Oxford University Press, 1992), p. 18.

3. Ibid., p. 20.

4. Diego de Valera, *Crónicas de los reyes de Castilla: Memorial de diversas hazañas. Crónica del rey Enrique IV*, ed. Juan de Mata Carriazo y Arroquia (Madrid: Espasa-Calpe, 1941), doc. 33, cited ibid., p. 14.

5. Condesa de Yebes, *La Marquesa de Moya: la dama del descubrimiento* (Madrid: Ediciones Cultura Hispánica, 1966), p. 13.

6. *La Poncella de Francia*, cited in Nancy Bradley Warren, *Women of God and Arms: Female Spirituality and Political Conflict, 1380–1600* (Philadelphia: University of Pennsylvania Press, 2005), p. 107.

7. Friar Martín de Córdoba, p. 94, cited ibid.

8. Antonio Blanco Sánchez, *Sobre Medina del Campo y la reina agraviada* (Medina del Campo: Caballeros de la Hispanidad, 1994), pp. 76–77 and 94–99.

9. Jaime Vicens Vives, "The Economies of Catalonia and Castile," in *Spain in the Fifteenth Century, 1369–1516: Essays and Extracts by Historians of Spain*, ed. J. R. L. Highfield, trans. Frances M. López-Morillas (New York: Harper & Row, 1972), p. 43.

10. *Memorias de Don Enrique IV de Castilla*. vol. 2, *La colección diplomática del mismo rey* (Madrid: Real Academia de Historia, 1835–1913), doc. 96, cited in Liss, *Isabel the Queen*, p. 17.

11. "Cierto es que el nuevo monarca, Enrique IV, que subió al trono en 1454, no respetó los deseos paternos y entregó el maestrazgo de Santiago a su favorite Beltra'n de la Cueva y el cargo de condestable a otro de sus fieles, Miguel Lucas de Iranzo."

12. María Isabel del Val Valdivieso, "Isabel, Infanta and Princess of Castile," in *Isabella la Católica, Queen of Castile: Critical Essays*, ed. by David A. Boruchoff (New York: Palgrave Macmillan, 2003), p. 42.

13. Liss, *Isabel the Queen*, p. 13.

14. Alonso Fernández de Palencia, *Crónica de Enrique IV*, ed. Antonio Paz y Meliá (Madrid: Ediciones Atlas, 1973–75), dec. 1, bk. 3, chap. 2, cited in Liss, *Isabel the Queen*, p. 14.

15. Diego Enríquez del Castillo, *Crónica de Enrique IV*, ed. Aureliano Sánchez Martín (Valladolid: Universidad de Valladolid, 1994), pp. 133–35.

16. Ibid., p. 134.

17. Ibid., pp. 138–39.

18. Malcolm Letts, ed. and trans., *The Travels of Leo of Rozmital Through Germany,*

Flanders, England, France, Spain, Portugal and Italy, 1465–1467. Hakluyt Society (Cambridge, U.K.: Cambridge University Press, 1957), p. 96.

19. Enríquez del Castillo, *Crónica de Enrique IV*, p. 248.
20. Ibid., p. 163.
21. Ibid., pp. 146–47.
22. Liss, *Isabel the Queen*, p. 48.
23. Mary Purcell, *The Great Captain: Gonzalo Fernández de Córdoba* (New York: Alvin Redman, 1963), p. 29.
24. Alonso de Palencia, "Fiesta," in *Crónica de Enrique IV*, ed. Antonio Paz y Meliá (Madrid: Atlas, 1973), p. 75.
25. *Crónica incompleta de los Reyes Católicos, 1469–1476,* ed. Julio Puyol (Madrid: Academia de la Historia, 1934), p. 55.
26. Emilio Calderón, "Maleficio," in *Usos y costumbres sexuales de los Reyes de España* (Madrid: Editorial Cirene, 1991), p. 70.
27. *Memorias de Don Enrique IV de Castilla,* vol. 2, p. 638.
28. Eduardo de Oliver-Copóns, *El Alcázar de Segovia* (Valladolid: Imprenta Castellana, 1916), pp. 99–105.
29. Purcell, *Great Captain*, p. 32.
30. Ibid., p. 31.
31. Nancy Rubin, *Isabella of Castile: The First Renaissance Queen* (New York: St. Martin's Press, 1991), p. 25.
32. Felix Grayeff, *Joan of Arc: Legends and Truth* (London: Philip Goodall, 1978).
33. Liss, *Isabel the Queen*, p. 18.
34. Warren, *Women of God and Arms,* pp. 89, 106–18.
35. Nancy Bradley Warren, "La Pucelle, the 'Puzzel,' and La Doncella: Joan of Arc in Early Modern England and Spain," presentation at the 46th International Congress on Medieval Studies, Kalamazoo, Mich., May 12–15, 2011.
36. Liss, *Isabel the Queen*, p. 52.
37. Enríquez del Castillo, *Crónica*, p. 183.
38. Purcell, *Great Captain*, p. 29.
39. Rubin, *Isabella of Castile*, p. 23.
40. Teofilo Ruiz, *The Other 1492: Ferdinand, Isabella and the Making of an Empire* (Teaching Co., 2002).
41. Liss, *Isabel the Queen*, p. 53.
42. *Memorias de Don Enrique IV de Castilla,* vol. 2, p. 638.
43. Isabel I of Castile, letter of March 1471, in *Memorias de Don Enrique IV de Castilla,* vol. 2, cited in Liss, *Isabel the Queen*, p. 60.
44. Liss, *Isabel the Queen*, p. 53.
45. Ibid., p. 47.
46. Nancy F. Marino, *Don Juan Pacheco: Wealth and Power in Late Medieval Spain* (Tempe: Arizona Center for Medieval and Renaissance Studies, 2006), p. 92.
47. Rubin, *Isabella of Castile*, pp. 31–32.
48. Charles Derek Ross, *Edward IV* (Berkeley and Los Angeles: University of California Press, 1974), p. 84.

THREE: FRIGHTENING YEARS

1. James Gairdner, ed., *Letters and Papers Illustrative of the Reigns of Richard III and Henry VII,* p. 1:31, cited in Charles Derek Ross, *Edward IV* (Berkeley and Los Ange-

les: University of California Press, 1974), p. 85; Cora Louise Scofield, *The Life and Reign of Edward the Fourth, King of England and of France and Lord of Ireland* (London: Frank Cass & Co., 1967), p. 1:320.

2. Ross, *Edward IV*, p. 10.
3. Scofield, *Life and Reign of Edward the Fourth*, p. 1:154.
4. Ross, *Edward IV*, p. 85.
5. Ibid., p. 90.
6. John Warkworth, *A Chronicle of the First Thirteen Years of the Reign of King Edward the Fourth*, ed. James Orchard Halliwell (London: Camden Society, 1839), p. 3.
7. Ross, *Edward IV*, p. 89.
8. Scofield, *Life and Reign of Edward the Fourth*, p. 1:320; Henry Ellis, ed., *Original Letters, Illustrative of English History, Including Numerous Royal Letters* (London: Richard Bentley, 1846), series 2, p. 1:152; Gairdner, *Letters and Papers Illustrative*, p. 1:31; Cora Louise Scofield, "The Movements of the Earl of Warwick in the Summer of 1464," *English Historical Review* (October 1906), pp. 732–33.
9. Alonso Fernández de Palencia, *Crónica de Enrique IV*, ed. Antonio Paz y Meliá (Madrid: Ediciones Atlas, 1975), dec. I, bk. 5, chap. 2, cited in Peggy K. Liss, *Isabel the Queen: Life and Times* (New York: Oxford University Press, 1992), p. 54.
10. Ibid., p. 56.
11. Townsend Miller, *The Castles and the Crown: Spain 1451–1555* (New York: Coward-McCann, 1963), pp. 40–41.
12. Ibid., p. 41.
13. Josef Miguel de Flores, *Crónica de Don Alvaro de Luna, condestable de los reynos de Castilla y de León* (Madrid: Imprenta de Antonio de Sancha, 1784), p. 15.
14. Teofilo F. Ruiz, *Spain's Centuries of Crisis: 1300–1474* (West Sussex, U.K.: Wiley-Blackwell, 2011), p. 89.
15. Ana Sánchez Prieto, *Enrique IV el Impotente* (Madrid: Alderaban Ediciones, 1999), p. 13.
16. Gregorio Marañón, *Ensayo biólogico sobre Enrique IV de Castilla y su tiempo* (Madrid: Colección Austral, 1997), pp. 30–31.
17. Ibid., p. 33.
18. Fray Gerónimo de la Cruz, an eighteenth-century historian who based his account on a fifteenth-century Castilian chronicle, cited in Nancy F. Marino, *Don Juan Pacheco: Wealth and Power in Late Medieval Spain* (Tempe: Arizona Center for Medieval and Renaissance Studies, 2006), p. 51.
19. Barbara Weissberger, "Alfonso de Palencia," in *Queer Iberia*, ed. Josiah Blackmore and Gregory S. Hutcheson (Durham, N.C.: Duke University Press, 1999), p. 315.
20. Miller, *Castles and Crown*, p. 42.
21. Ibid., p. 45.
22. William Prescott, *History of the Reign of Ferdinand and Isabella* (Philadelphia: J. B. Lippincott, 1873), p. 181–82.
23. Diego de Colmenares, *Historia de la insigne ciudad de Segovia,* revised by Gabriel María Vergara (Segovia: Imprenta de la Tierra de Segovia, 1931), p. 276.
24. Mary Purcell, *The Great Captain: Gonzalo Fernández de Córdoba* (New York: Alvin Redman, 1963), p. 35.
25. Ibid., p. 34.
26. Ibid., p. 42.
27. Ibid., p. 41.
28. Ibid., p. 42.
29. Ibid., pp. 42–43.

30. Liss, *Isabel the Queen*, p. 63.
31. María Dolores Cabanas González, Carmelo Luis López, and Gregorio del Ser Quijano, *Isabel de Castilla y su época: Estudios y selección de textos* (Alcalá de Henares: Universidad de Alcalá, 2007), pp. 22–23.
32. Purcell, *Great Captain*, p. 37.

FOUR: ISABELLA FACES THE FUTURE ALONE

1. Serita Deborah Stevens and Anne Klarner, *Deadly Doses: A Writer's Guide to Poisons* (Cincinnati: Writers Digest Books, 1990).
2. Charles Thompson, and John Samuel, *Poisons and Poisoners* (London: Harold Shaylor, 1931), p. 83.
3. María Dolores Carmen Morales Muñiz, *Alfonso de Ávila, Rey de Castilla* (Ávila: Diputación Provincial de Ávila, Institución Gran Duque de Alba, 1988), p. 363.
4. Nancy Rubin, *Isabella of Castile: The First Renaissance Queen* (New York: St. Martin's Press, 1991), p. 50.
5. Peggy K. Liss, *Isabel the Queen: Life and Times* (New York: Oxford University Press, 1992), p. 68.
6. John Edwards, *The Spain of the Catholic Monarchs, 1474–1520* (Oxford, U.K.: Blackwell, 2000), p. 8.
7. Rubin, *Isabella of Castile*, p. 50.
8. Townsend Miller, *The Castles and the Crown: Spain 1451–1555* (New York: Coward-McCann, 1963), p. 52.
9. Diego de Valera, *Memorial de diversas hazañas*, ed. Juan de Mata Carriazo (Madrid: 1941), p. 139, cited in Warren H. Carroll, *Isabel of Spain: The Catholic Queen* (Front Royal, Va.: Christendom Press, 1991), p. 35.
10. Miller, *Castles and Crown*, pp. 51 and 52.
11. Liss, *Isabel the Queen*, p. 68.
12. María Dolores Cabanas González, Carmelo Luis López, and Gregorio del Ser Quijano, *Isabel de Castilla y su época: Estudios y selección de textos* (Alcalá de Henares: Universidad de Alcalá, 2007), p. 27.
13. Edwards, *Spain of the Catholic Monarchs*, pp. 8, 9.
14. Archivo General de Simancas, Patrimonio Real, 7-112, leg. 738, cited in Rubin, *Isabella of Castile*, p. 57.
15. *Crónica incompleta de los Reyes Católicos, 1469–1476*, ed. Julio Puyol (Madrid: Academia de la Historia, 1934), p. 69.
16. Liss, *Isabel the Queen*, p. 69.
17. Rubin, *Isabella of Castile*, p. 59.
18. *Crónica incompleta*, p. 70.
19. Salvador de Madariaga, *Christopher Columbus: Being the Life of the Very Magnificent Lord Don Cristóbal Colón* (New York: Macmillan, 1940), p. 5.
20. Vivien B. Lamb, *The Betrayal of Richard III: An Introduction to the Controversy* (London: Mitre Press, 1968), p. 43.
21. María Isabel del Val Valdivieso, "Isabel, Infanta and Princess of Castile," in *Isabella la Católica, Queen of Castile: Critical Essays*, ed. David A. Boruchoff (New York: Palgrave Macmillan, 2003), p. 49.
22. Lamb, *Betrayal*, p. 43.
23. Ibid., p. 57.
24. Liss, *Isabel the Queen*, p. 73.
25. María Isabel del Val Valdivieso, ibid., p. 50.

26. *Crónica incompleta*, p. 70.
27. Edwards, *Spain of Catholic Monarchs*, p. 12.
28. Juan Ferrer to Juan II of Aragon, January 30, 1469, cited in Carroll, p. 47.

FIVE: MARRIAGE

1. Félix de Llanos e Torriglia, *Así llegó a reinar Isabel la Católica* (Madrid, 1927), p. 163, cited in Peggy K. Liss, *Isabel the Queen: Life and Times* (New York: Oxford University Press, 1992), p. 73.
2. John Edwards, *The Spain of the Catholic Monarchs, 1474–1520* (Oxford, U.K.: Blackwell, 2000), pp. 11, 13.
3. Liss, *Isabel the Queen*, p. 71.
4. Ibid., p. 75.
5. Ibid.
6. *Crónica incompleta de los Reyes Católicos, 1469–1476*, ed. Julio Puyol (Madrid: Academia de la Historia, 1934), p. 90.
7. Salvador de Madariaga, *Christopher Columbus: Being the Life of the Very Magnificent Lord Don Cristóbal Colón* (New York: Macmillan, 1940), p. 8.
8. J. H. Elliott, *Imperial Spain, 1469–1716* (London: Penguin, 1990), p. 15.
9. Liss, *Isabel the Queen*, p. 79.

SIX: FERDINAND AND HIS FAMILY

1. Alan Ryder, *The Wreck of Catalonia: Civil War in the Fifteenth Century* (New York: Oxford University Press, 2007), p. 77.
2. William Prescott, *History of the Reign of Ferdinand and Isabella* (Philadelphia: J. B. Lippincott, 1873), p. 63.
3. "El dicho Rey Don Juan . . . ," order granted by Blanca de Navarre, April 30, 1462, Real Academia de la Historia, p. 19, A-7, folio 16 to 20, cited in *Indice de la colección de don Luis Salazar y Castro, formado por Antonio de Vargas-Zúñiga y Montero de Espinosa y Baltasar Cuartero y Huerta*, vol. 1 (Madrid: Real Academia de la Historia: 1949).
4. Joan Margarit, bishop of Elna, addressing the Cortes of Barcelona, Oct. 6, 1454; published in R. Albert and J. Gassiot, *Parlaments a les corts catalanes* (Barcelona: Editorial Barcino, 1928), pp. 209–10; cited in Ryder, *Wreck of Catalonia*, p. 29.
5. Paul H. Freedman, *Origins of Peasant Servitude in Medieval Catalonia* (Cambridge, U.K.: Cambridge University Press, 1991), p. 46.
6. Ryder, *Wreck of Catalonia*, pp. 156, 163.
7. Ibid., p, 183.
8. Ibid., p. 193.
9. Ibid., p. 186.
10. Ibid.
11. Jerónimo Zurita, *Anales de Aragón* (Zaragoza: Instituto "Fernando el Católico" [C.S.I.C.] de le Excma Diputación Provincial, 1977), vol. 8, p. 242.
12. Ibid., p. 281.
13. Ryder, *Wreck of Catalonia*, p. 83.
14. Ibid., p. 87.
15. Ibid., pp. 88 and 89.
16. Ibid., p. 92.

17. Ibid., pp. 94–95.
18. Ibid., p. 104.
19. Ibid., p. 105.
20. Ibid., p. 124.
21. Henry John Chaytor, *A History of Aragon and Catalonia* (London: Methuen, 1933).

SEVEN: THE NEWLYWEDS

1. Townsend Miller, *The Castles and the Crown: Spain, 1451–1555* (New York: Coward-McCann, 1963), p. 69.
2. Jerónimo Zurita, *Anales de Aragón* (Zaragoza: Instituto "Fernando el Católico" [C.S.I.C.] de le Excma Diputación Provincial, 1975 and 1977), p. 7:620.
3. Miller, *Castles and Crown,* p. 69.
4. Aureliano Sánchez Martín, *Crónica de Enrique IV de Diego Enríquez del Castillo* (Valladolid: Secretariado de Publicaciones, Universidad de Valladolid, 1994), Chapter 137, p. 335.
5. Isabella to the Countess of Palencia, October 30, 1469, in María Isabel del Val Valdivieso, *Isabella la Católica, Princesa, 1468–1474* (Valladolid: Instituto Isabel la Católica de Historia Eclesiástica, 1974), citing Real Academia de la Historia, 9-30-7-6483, folios 485–486.
6. Peggy K. Liss, *Isabel the Queen: Life and Times* (New York: Oxford University Press, 1992), p. 40.
7. Ibid., p. 83.
8. Tarsicio de Azcona, *Isabella la Católica: Estudio crítico de su vida y su reinado* (Madrid: Biblioteca de Autores Cristianos, 1993), p. 162.
9. William Prescott, *History of the Reign of Ferdinand and Isabella* (London: Richard Bentley, 1838), p. 225.
10. William D. Phillips, Jr. *Enrique IV and the Crisis of Fifteenth-Century Castile, 1425–1480* (Cambridge, Mass.: Medieval Academy of America, 1978), p. 113.
11. Nancy Rubin, *Isabella of Castile: The First Renaissance Queen* (New York: St. Martin's Press, 1991), p. 92.
12. Jaime Vicens Vives, *Historia crítica de la vida y reinado de Ferdinand II de Aragón* (Zaragoza: Instituto Fernando el Católico, 1962), p. 279, no. 912.
13. Rubin, *Isabella of Castile,* p. 93.
14. Diego Clemencin, *Elogio de la reina Católica Doña Isabella* (Madrid: Imprenta de Sancha, 1820), p. 6:100.
15. Archivo General de Simancas, Diversos de Castilla, leg. 9, number 65, folio 2v, cited in María Isabel del Val Valdivieso, *Isabel la Católica, Princesa,* p. 497.
16. Vicens Vives, *Historia crítica,* p. 288.
17. Rubin, *Isabella of Castile,* p. 97.
18. Liss, *Isabel the Queen,* p. 85.
19. Fernando del Pulgar, *Crónica de los Señores Reyes Católicos,* ed. Juan de Mata Carriazo (Madrid: Espasa-Calpe, 1943), p. 75.
20. Peggy K. Liss, *Isabel the Queen: Life and Times* (Philadelphia: University of Pennsylvania Press, 2004), p. 74.
21. Isabella to Juan II of Aragon, April 29, 1473, in Antonio Paz y Meliá, *El cronista Alonso de Palencia, su vida y obras, sus decadas y las crónicas contemporáneas* (Madrid: Hispanic Society of America, 1914), p. 127, cited in Warren H. Carroll, *Isabel of Spain: The Catholic Queen* (Front Royal, Va.: Christendom Press, 1991), p. 65.

22. Vicente Rodríguez Valencia, *Isabella la Católica en la opinión de españoles y extranjeros, siglos XV al XX* (Valladolid: Instituto "Isabel la Católica" de Historia Eclesiástica, 1970), p. 3: 74, trans. Warren Carroll and Maria Barone, *Isabel of Spain,* p. 72.

23. Fusero Clemente, *The Borgias,* trans. by Peter Green (New York: G. P. Putnam's Sons, 1913), p. 16.

24. Mary Purcell, *The Great Captain: Gonzalo Fernández de Córdoba* (New York: Alvin Redman, 1963), p. 41.

25. Ibid., p. 43.

26. Ibid., pp. 46–47.

27. Ibid., p. 46.

28. Ibid., pp. 48–49.

29. Ibid., p. 49.

EIGHT: THE BORGIA CONNECTION

1. Marion Johnson, *The Borgias* (New York: Holt, Rinehart & Winston, 1981), p. 74.

2. Clemente Fusero, *The Borgias,* trans. Peter Green (New York: Praeger, 1972), p. 75.

3. Ibid., p. 77.

4. Ibid., p. 78.

5. Ibid., p. 79.

6. T. C. F. Hopkins, *Empires, Wars and Battles: The Middle East from Antiquity to the Rise of the New World* (New York: Forge Books, 2006), p. 213.

7. Fusero, *Borgias,* p. 119.

8. Ferdinand to Juan II, August 1472, Biblioteca Nacional, *Índice de la colección de don Luis Salazar y Castro, formado por Antonio de Vargas-Zúñiga y Montero de Espinosa y Baltasar Cuartero y Huerta,* vol.1 (Madrid: Real Academia de la Historia: 1949), appendix letter 55.

9. Ferdinand to Juan II, March 1473, ibid., appendix letter 65.

10. José Sanchis y Sivera, "El cardenal Rodrigo de Borgia en Valencia," *Boletín del Real Academia de Historia* 84 (1924), p. 149.

11. Peggy K. Liss, *Isabel the Queen: Life and Times* (New York: Oxford University Press, 1992),p. 91.

12. John Edwards, *The Spain of the Catholic Monarchs, 1474–1520* (Oxford, U.K.: Blackwell, 2000), p. 18.

13. William D. Phillips, Jr., *Enrique IV and the Crisis of Fifteenth-Century Castile, 1425–1480* (Cambridge, Mass.: Medieval Academy of America, 1978), p. 117.

14. Richard P. McBrien, *Lives of the Popes: The Pontiffs from St. Peter to John Paul II* (New York: HarperCollins, 1997), p. 182.

15. Tarcisio de Azcona, *Isabel la Católica: Estudio crítico de su vida y su reinado* (Madrid: Biblioteca de Autores Cristianos, 1993), p. 186, cited in Rubin, *Isabella of Castile: The First Renaissance Queen* (New York: St. Martin's Press, 1991), p. 108.

NINE: PREPARING TO RULE

1. María Isabel del Val Valdivieso, "Isabel, Infanta and Princess," in Boruchoff, 53.

2. Benzion Netanyahu, *The Origins of the Inquisition in Fifteenth-Century Spain* (New York: Random House, 1995), p. 804.

3. Conde Brotardi, in Trento, February 7, 1474, Real Academia de la Historia, A-7, folio 158, S&Z, p. 164, cited in Biblioteca Nacional, *Índice de la colección de don Luis Salazar y Castro, formado por Antonio de Vargas-Zúñiga y Montero de Espinosa y Baltasar Cuartero y Huerta,* vol. 1 (Madrid: Real Academia de la Historia: 1949), letter 632.

4. George Merula, "The Siege of Shkodra" (1474), trans. George Elsie, in *Texts and Documents of Albanian History,* http://www.albanianhistory.net/en/texts1000-1799/AH1474.html.

5. Karolus Vitalus Caurell to unknown person, "remitiendo el juramento que se menciona en la ficha siguiente y el gran temor que había sobre una invasion de los turcos en Ragusa y Venecia." Real Academia de la Historia, October 27, 1474. A-7, folio 158, p. 164, cited in *Índice de la colección de don Luis Salazar y Castro,* vol. 1, letter 631.

6. Gonzalo de Oviedo y Valdés, cited in Don Eduardo de Oliver-Copóns, *El Alcázar de Segovia* (Valladolid: Imprenta Castellana, 1916), p. 129.

7. Andrés de Cabrera, June 15, 1473, A-7, folio 89–91, in *Índice de la colección de don Luis Salazar y Castro,* vol. 1, letter 617.

8. *Crónica incompleta de los Reyes Católicos, 1469–1476, según un manuscript anónimo de la época,* ed. Julio Puyol (Madrid: Tipografía de Archivos, 1934), pp. 113–21.

9. Ibid.

10. Diego de Colmenares, *Historia de la insigne ciudad de Segovia,* revised by Gabriel María Vergara (Segovia: Imprenta de la Tierra de Segovia, 1931), p. 319.

11. Ibid., p. 320.

12. Ibid.

13. Peggy K. Liss, *Isabel the Queen: Life and Times* (New York: Oxford University Press, 1992), p. 93.

14. Ibid., p. 93.

15. Ibid., p. 94.

16. Ibid., p. 95.

17. Ibid.

18. Nancy F. Marino, *Don Juan Pacheco: Wealth and Power in Late Medieval Spain* (Tempe: Arizona Center for Medieval and Renaissance Studies, 2006), pp. 163–64.

19. Liss, *Isabel the Queen,* p. 95.

20. María Isabel del Val Valdivieso, *Isabel la Católica, Princesa,* pp. 506–8, Real Academia de la Historia, Colección Salazar, M-26, folio 92–92v.

21. Diego Enríquez del Castillo, *Crónica de Enrique IV,* ed. Aureliano Sánchez Martín (Valladolid: Universidad de Valladolid, 1994), p. 398.

22. Ibid., p. 96.

23. Townsend Miller, *The Castles and the Crown: Spain, 1451–1555* (New York: Coward-McCann, 1963), p. 79.

24. Liss, *Isabel the Queen,* p. 96.

TEN: ISABELLA TAKES THE THRONE

1. María Isabel del Val Valdivieso, "Isabel, Infanta and Princessa," in *Isabella la Católica, Queen of Castile: Critical Essays,* ed. David A. Boruchoff (New York: Palgrave Macmillan, 2003), p. 54.

2. Peggy K. Liss, *Isabel the Queen: Life and Times* (New York: Oxford University Press, 1992), p. 96.

3. Ibid., p. 97.

4. Liss, *Isabel the Queen*, pp. 97, 98.

5. Diego de Colmenares, *Historia de la insigne ciudad de Segovia*, revised by Gabriel María Vergara (Segovia: Imprenta de la Tierra de Segovia, 1931), p. 330.

6. John Edwards, *The Spain of the Catholic Monarchs, 1474–1520* (Oxford, U.K.: Blackwell, 2000), p. 21.

7. Ibid.

8. Ibid., pp. 21, 22.

9. Alonso Fernández de Palencia, *Crónica de Enrique IV*, ed. Antonio Paz y Meliá (Madrid: Ediciones Atlas, 1975), pp. 160–61.

10. *Crónica incompleta de los Reyes Católicos, 1469–1476*, ed. Julio Puyol (Madrid: Academia de la Historia, 1934), p. 145.

11. *Memorias de Don Enrique IV de Castilla*, vol. 2, *La colección diplomática del mismo rey* (Madrid: Real Academia de Historia, 1835–1913), doc. 206.

12. M. Grau Sanz, "Así fue coronado Isabel la Católica," *Estudios Segovianos* I (1949), pp. 24–39.

13. Nuria Silleras-Fernández, *Power, Piety and Patronage in Late Medieval Queenship* (New York: Palgrave Macmillan, 2008), p. 5.

14. Theresa Earenfight, ed., *Queenship and Political Power in Medieval and Early Modern Spain* (Hampshire, U.K.: Ashgate Publishing Limited, 2005), p. xiv.

15. Liss, *Isabel the Queen*, p. 105.

16. William Prescott, *History of the Reign of Ferdinand and Isabella* (Philadelphia: J. B. Lippincott, 1896), p. 118.

17. Janna Bianchini, *The Queens Hand, Power and Authority in the Reign of Berenguela of Castile* (Philadelphia: University of Pennsylvania Press, 2012), p. 21.

18. Miriam Shadis, *Berenguela of Castile (1180–1246) and Political Women in the High Middle Ages* (New York: Palgrave Macmillan, 2009), p. 23.

19. Edwards, *Spain of Catholic Monarchs*, p. 22.

20. Ibid., p. 22.

21. Peggy K. Liss, "Isabel, Myth and History," in Boruchoff, p. 60.

22. Barbara F. Weissberger, "Tanto monta: The Catholic Monarchs' Nuptial Fiction and the Power of Isabel I of Castile," *The Rule of Women in Early Modern Europe*, eds. Anne J. Cruz and Mihoko Suzuki (Urbana: University of Illinois Press, 2009), pp. 43, 46.

23. Ruy de Pina, 1902, ch. 165, cited in Miguel Ángel de Bunes Ibarra et al., *The Invention of Glory: Afonso V and the Pastrana Tapestries* (Madrid: Fundación Carlos de Amberes, 2011), p. 75.

24. Edwards, *Spain of the Catholic Monarchs*, p. 5.

25. Ibid., p. 1.

26. Andrés Bernáldez, *Historia de los Reyes Católicos Don Fernando y Doña Isabel: Crónica inedita del siglo XV* (Granada: Imprenta y Librería de Don José María Zamora, 1856), p. 51.

27. Queen Isabella, June 21, 1475, from Àvila, in *Documentos referentes a las relaciones con Portugal durante el reinado de los Reyes Católicos*, ed. Antonio de la Torre and Luis Suárez Fernández (1858; Valladolid: Consejo Superior de Investigaciones Científicas, Patronato Menéndez Pelayo, 1963), letter 524, pp. 1:85–87.

28. Fernando del Pulgar to Obispo de Osma, in *Letras: Glosa a las coplas de Mingo Revulgo* (Madrid: Ediciones de la Lectura, 1929), letter 5, pp. 27–29.

29. Luis Suárez Fernández, Juan de Mata Carriazo y Arroquia, and Manuel Fernández Álvarez, *La Espana de los Reyes Católicos, 1474–1516* (Madrid: Espasa-Calpe, 1969), p. 163.

30. Cora Louise Scofield, *The Life and Reign of Edward the Fourth, King of England and of France and Lord of Ireland* (London: Frank Cass & Co., 1967), p. 1:195.

31. Nancy F. Marino, *Don Juan Pacheco: Wealth and Power in Late Medieval Spain* (Tempe: Arizona Center for Medieval and Renaissance Studies, 2006), p. 172.

32. Fernando del Pulgar to Obsipo de Osma, in Fernando del Pulgar, *Letras: Glosa a las coplas de Mingo Revulgo* (Madrid: Ediciones de la Lectura, 1929), letter 5, pp. 27–29.

ELEVEN: THE TRIBE OF ISABEL

1. Tarsicio Azcona, cited in Peggy K. Liss, *Isabel the Queen: Life and Times* (New York: Oxford University Press, 1992), p. 153.

2. Andrés Bernáldez, *Historia de los Reyes Católicos Don Fernando y Doña Isabel: Crónica inedita del siglo XV* (Granada: Imprenta y Libreria de Don José Maria Zamora, 1856), p. 459.

3. Ibid., chap. 33, cited in María Isabel del Val Valdivieso, *Isabel I de Castilla, 1451–1504* (Madrid: Ediciones del Orto, 2004), p. 75.

4. Hernando del Pulgar, *Letras: Glosa a las coplas de Mingo Revulgo* (Madrid: Ediciones de La Lectura, 1929), letter 9, in Liss, *Isabel the Queen,* pp. 154–55.

5. Vicente Rodríguez Valencia, *Isabel la Católica en la opinión de españoles y extranjeros, siglos XV al XX* (Valladolid: Instituto "Isabel la Católica" de Historia Eclesiástica, 1970), vol. 3, pp. 75–79.

6. Giles Tremlett, *Catherine of Aragon: The Spanish Queen of Henry VIII* (New York: Walker & Co, 2010), p. 24.

7. *Crónica incompleta de los Reyes Católicos, 1469–1476,* ed. Julio Puyol (Madrid: Academia de la Historia, 1934), p. 239.

8. Ibid., pp. 243–45.

9. Baldesar Castiglione, *The Book of the Courtier,* trans. Charles S. Singleton (New York: Anchor Books, 1959), p. 191.

10. Don Ferdinand to King Juan II, November 23, 1475, Burgos: Biblioteca Nacional, cited in Biblioteca Nacional, *Índice de la colección de don Luis Salazar y Castro, formado por Antonio de Vargas-Zúñiga y Montero de Espinosa y Baltasar Cuartero y Huerta,* vol. 1 (Madrid: Real Academia de la Historia: 1949), letter 126.

11. Ludwig Pastor, *The History of the Popes from the Close of the Middle Ages,* trans. E. F. Peeler (St. Louis, Mo.: B. Herder, 1898), p. 4:397.

12. Sergio L. Sanabria, "A Late Gothic Drawing of San Juan de los Reyes in Toledo at the Prado Museum in Madrid," *Journal of the Society of Architectural Historians* 51, no. 2 (June 1992), pp. 161–73.

13. Jack Freiberg, *Bramante's Tempietto and the Spanish Crown* (Rome: American Academy in Rome, 2005), p. 1:154.

14. Ibid., p. 1:155.

15. John Julius Norwich, *The World Atlas of Architecture* (New York: Portland House, 1988), p. 276.

16. Bethany Aram, *Juana the Mad: Sovereignty and Destiny in Renaissance Europe* (Baltimore: Johns Hopkins University Press, 2005), p. 15.

17. Tremlett, *Catherine of Aragon,* pp. 26–27.

18. María del Cristo González Marrero, *La casa de Isabel la Católica: espacios domésticos y vida cotidiana* (Ávila: Diputación de Ávila, Institución Gran Duque de Alba, 2004), p. 40.

19. Ibid., pp. 42, 43.

20. Malcolm Letts, ed. and trans., *The Travels of Leo of Rozmital through Germany, Flanders, England, France, Spain, Portugal and Italy, 1465–1467* (Cambridge, U.K.: Cambridge University Press, 1957).

21. Erasmus, *Opus Epistolarum* (Oxford, U.K.: Oxford University Press).

22. Mark P. McDonald, *Ferdinand Columbus: Renaissance Collector* (London: British Museum Press, 2000), p. 35.

23. Ibid., p. 36.

24. Gonzalo Fernández de Oviedo y Valdés, *Historia general y natural de las Indias* (Madrid: Imprenta de la Real Academia de la Historia, 1851), part 1, p. 71.

25. McDonald, *Ferdinand Columbus*, p. 42.

26. Ferdinand Columbus, *The Life of the Admiral Christopher Columbus: By His Son Ferdinand*, trans. Benjamin Keen (New Brunswick, N.J.: Rutgers University Press, 1959), p. vii.

27. Antonia Fraser, *The Wives of Henry VIII* (New York: Alfred A. Knopf, 1992), p. 11.

28. Aram, *Juana the Mad*, p. 21.

29. Ibid., pp. 18–19.

30. Fraser, *Wives of Henry VIII*, p. 11.

31. Ibid., p. 16.

32. James Gairdner, ed., "Journals of Roger Machado," in *Historia Regis Henrici Septimi* (London: Longman, Brown, Green, Longmans, and Roberts, 1858), pp. 157–99.

TWELVE: THE WHOLE WORLD TREMBLED

1. John Freely, *The Grand Turk* (New York: Overlook Press, 2009).

2. Mark Mazower, *Salonica, City of Ghosts: Christians, Muslims, and Jews, 1430–1950* (New York: Alfred A. Knopf, 2005), p. 30.

3. Ibid.

4. Marios Philippides, *Emperors, Patriarchs and Sultans of Constantinople: A Short Chronicle of the Sixteenth Century* (Brookline, Mass.: Hellenic College Press, 1990), p. 31. Translation from an anonymous Greek chronicle of the sixteenth century.

5. Freely, *The Grand Turk*, p. 20.

6. Ibid., p. 12.

7. Ibid., p. 21.

8. Franz Babinger, *Mehmed the Conqueror and His Time* (Princeton, N.J.: Princeton University Press, 1992), p. 430.

9. Giacomo de Langushi, cited in Freely, *Grand Turk*, p. 59.

10. Halil İnalcık, *The Ottoman Empire: The Classical Age 1300–1600* (London: Phoenix Press, 2000), p. 26.

11. Marios Philippides, ed., *Mehmed II the Conquerer: And the Fall of the Franco-Byzantine Levant to the Ottoman Turks: Some Western Views and Testimonies* (Tempe: Arizona Center for Medieval and Renaissance Studies, 2007), p. 171.

12. Babinger, *Mehmed the Conqueror*, p. 93.

13. Ibid.

14. Kritoboulos quoted in Freely, *Grand Turk*, p. 43.

15. Evlyia Celebi quoted in Freely, *Grand Turk*, p. 46.

16. Philippides, *Mehmed II the Conquerer*, pp. 37–40.

17. Freely, *Grand Turk*, p. 48.

18. Ibid., p. 49.

19. Inalcik, *The Ottoman Empire*, p. 29.

20. Freely, *Grand Turk,* p. 60.
21. Ibid., p. 69.
22. Babinger, *Mehmed the Conqueror,* p. 280.
23. Marin Barleti, *The Siege of Shkodra: Albania's Courageous Stand Against the Ottoman Conquest 1478,* trans. David Hosaflook (Tirana, Albania: Onufri, 2012), p. 184.
24. Ibid., p. 51.
25. Freely, *Grand Turk,* p. 181.
26. Babinger, *Mehmed the Conqueror,* p. 390.
27. Ibid., pp. 390–92.
28. Carta de Reina de Sicilia al Conde de Cardona, Sitio de Otranto, 1481, in Antonio Paz y Meliá, *El cronista Alonso de Palencia, su vida y sus obras, sus decadas y las crónicas contemporáneas* (Madrid: Hispanic Society of America, 1914), pp. 310–11.
29. Freely, *Grand Turk,* p. 170.
30. Hernando del Pulgar, *Crónica de los Señores Reyes Católicos por su secretario Fernando del Pulgar,* ed. Juan de Mata Carriazo (Madrid: Espasa-Calpe, 1943), vol. 1, p. 435.
31. Ibid.

THIRTEEN: THE QUEEN'S WAR

1. Salma Khadra Jayyusi, ed., *The Legacy of Muslim Spain* (Leiden: Brill, 1994), p. 1:83.
2. José Antonio Conde, *Historia de la dominación de los Arabes en España, sacada de varios manuscritos y memorias arábigas* (Madrid: Biblioteca de Historiadores Españoles, Marín y Compañía, 1874), p. 309.
3. Ibid.
4. Ibid., p. 310.
5. Peter Martyr, *Opus Epistolarum: The Work of the Letters of Peter Martyr* (London: Wellcome Library), epistle 32, August 13, 1488.
6. L. P. Harvey, *Islamic Spain, 1250 to 1500* (Chicago: University of Chicago Press, 1992), p. 268.
7. Alonso Fernández de Palencia, *Guerra de Granada* (Barcelona: Linkgua Ediciones, 2009) bk. 1, pp. 13–14.
8. Don Jose Antonio Conde, *Historia de la dominación de los Arabes en Espana: sacada de varios manuscritos y memorias arábigas* (Madrid: Marin y Co., 1874), p. 310.
9. Ibid.
10. Ibid., p. 310.
11. Condesa de Yebes, *La marquesa de Moya: la dama del descubrimiento, 1440–1511* (Madrid: Ediciones Cultura Hispánica, 1966), p. 58.
12. Jerónimo Zurita, *Anales de Aragón,* vol. 8, p. 406.
13. Conde, p. 310.
14. Palencia, *Guerra de Granada,* p. 33.
15. Hernando del Pulgar, *Crónica de Los Señores Reyes Católicos, Don Fernando y Doña Isabel de Castilla y de Aragón* (Valencia: Imprenta de Benito Monfort, 1780), p. 173.
16. Zurita, *Anales de Aragón,* vol. 8, pp. 414–15.
17. Ibid., pp. 406–10.
18. Harvey, *Islamic Spain,* p. 268.
19. Juan Mata Carriazo y Arroquia, *Los relieves de la guerra de Granada en la sillería del coro de la Catedral de Toledo* (Granada: Universidad de Granada, 1985), p. 33.
20. Peggy Liss, *Isabel the Queen: Life and Times* (New York: Oxford University Press, 1992), p. 194.
21. Harvey, *Islamic Spain,* p. 273.

22. Ibid., p. 312.
23. Jerónimo Münzer, *Viaje por España y Portugal, 1494–1495* (Madrid: Ediciones Polifemo, 1991), pp. 117-19.
24. Harvey, *Islamic Spain*, p. 309.
25. Conde, *Historia de la dominación*, p. 310.
26. Ibid., p. 311.
27. Ibid., p. 274.
28. Ibid., p. 313.
29. Ibid., p. 312.
30. Ibid., p. 315.
31. Ibid., p. 288.
32. Isabella to Ferdinand, May 18, 1486, *Cartas autógrafas de los reyes católicos de Espana, Don Fernando and Doña Isabel que conservan en el archivo de Simancas, 1474–1502*, ed. Amalia Prieto Cantara (Valladolid: Instituto "Isabel la Católica" de Historia Eclesiástica, 1971), letter 9, p. 57.
33. Ibid.
34. Ibid.
35. Mata Carriazo y Arroquia, *Los relieves de la guerra de Granada*, p. 58.
36. Liss, *Isabel the Queen*, p. 216.
37. Harvey, *Islamic Spain*, p. 301.
38. Liss, *Isabel the Queen*, p. 218.
39. Ibid., pp. 219-20.
40. Peter Martyr to Sforza, August 14, 1489, in Martyr, *Opus Epistolarum*.
41. Ibid.
42. Ibid.
43. Harvey, *Islamic Spain*, p. 301.
44. Mata Carriazo y Arroquia, *Los relieves de la guerra de Granada*, p. 112.
45. Marilyn Yalom, *Birth of the Chess Queen* (New York: Harper Perennial, 2005), p. 195.
46. Harvey, *Islamic Spain*, p. 310.
47. Harvey, *Islamic Spain*, p. 312.
48. Ibid.
49. Ibid., p. 322.
50. Zurita, *Anales de Aragón*, vol. 8, p. 602.
51. Bernarndo Del Roi to Italy, January 7, 1492, cited in Arnold Harris Mathew, *The Diary of John Burchard of Strasburg* (London: Francis Griffiths, 1910), pp. 1:407-8.
52. Hieronymus Münzer, *Viaje por España y Portugal* (Granada: Asociación Cultural Hispano Alemana, 1981), pp. 19-20.
53. Mathew, *Diary of Burchard*, pp. 1:407-8.
54. Münzer, *Viaje por España y Portugal*, p. 95.
55. Zurita, *Anales de Aragón*, vol. 8, p. 603.
56. Mathew, *Diary of Burchard*, pp. 1:317-18.

FOURTEEN: ARCHITECTS OF THE INQUISITION

1. Henry Kamen, *The Spanish Inquisition: A Historical Revision* (London: Weidenfeld & Nicolson, 1997), p. 82.
2. Archivo Histórico Nacional, *Catálogo de las causas contra la fe seguidas ante el tribunal de Santo Oficio de la Inquisición de Toledo* (Madrid, 1903).
3. Lu Ann Homza, ed. and trans., *The Spanish Inquisition, 1478–1614: An Anthology of Sources* (Indianapolis: Hackett, 2006), p. xi.

4. Benzion Netanyahu, *Don Isaac Abravanel: Statesman and Philosopher* (Philadelphia: Jewish Publication Society of America, 1982), p. 3.

5. Elias Hiam Lindo, *The History of the Jews of Spain and Portugal* (1848; repr. New York: Burt Franklin, 1970), p. 6.

6. Ibid., p. 51.

7. Netanyahu, *Don Isaac Abravanel*, p. 6.

8. Kamen, *Spanish Inquisition*, p. 30.

9. Netanyahu, *Don Isaac Abravanel*, p. 52.

10. Yolanda Moreno Koch, *El judaísmo hispano, según la crónica hebrea de Rabi Eliyahu Capsali* (Granada: Universidad de Granada, 2005), pp. 133-35.

11. Jerónimo Zurita, *Crónica de los Reyes Católicos*, ed. Juan de Mata Carriazo y Arroquia (1927), p. 1:127, cited in Netanyahu, *Origins of the Inquisition*, p. 899.

12. Ian MacPherson and Angus MacKay, *Love, Religion and Politics in Fifteenth-Century Spain* (Leiden: Brill, 1998), p. 183.

13. Ibid., p. 184.

14. Charles Berlin, *Elijah Capsali's Seder Eliyyahu Zuta*, Ph.D. dissertation, Harvard University, September 1962, p. 82.

15. Charles Berlin, "A Sixteenth Century Hebrew Chronicle of the Ottoman Empire: The Seder Eliyahu Zuta of Elijah Capsali and Its Message," in *Studies in Jewish Bibliography, History, and Literature,* ed. Charles Berlin (New York: KTAV Publishing, 1971), pp. 23-31.

16. Hernando del Pulgar, *Crónica de los Reyes Católicos,* ed. Juan de Mata Carriazo y Arroquia (Madrid: Espasa-Calpe, 1943), p. 1:309.

17. Ibid., pp. 1:310-11.

18. Ibid., p. 1:314.

19. Ibid., p. 1:313.

20. Rafael Sabatini, *Torquemada and the Spanish Inquisition: A History* (London: Stanley Paul, 1924), p. 98.

21. Ibid., pp. 98-99.

22. Ibid., pp. 102-3.

23. Ibid., p. 108.

24. Peggy Liss, *Isabel the Queen: Life and Times* (New York: Oxford University Press, 1992), p. 196.

25. Henry Charles Lea, *History of the Inquisition in Spain* (London: Macmillan, 1906), p. 1:587.

26. Kamen, *Spanish Inquisition*, pp. 49-50.

27. Sabatini, *Torquemada*, pp. 120-21.

28. Ibid., pp. 121-24.

29. Ibid., p. 125.

30. Benzion Netanyahu, *The Origins of the Inquisition in Fifteenth-Century Spain* (New York: Random House, 1995), p. 1035.

31. José Martínez Millán, "Structures of Inquisitorial Finance," in *The Spanish Inquisition and the Inquisitorial Mind,* ed. Ángel Alcalá (New York: Columbia University Press, 1987).

32. Netanyahu, *Origins of Inquisition*, p. 898.

33. Ibid., p. 972.

34. Ibid., p. 930.

35. Renée Levine Melammed, *Heretics or Daughters of Israel? The Crypto-Jewish Women of Castile* (New York: Oxford University Press, 1999), p. 174.

36. Archivo Histórico Nacional, Catálogo, pp. 198, 228, 239.

37. David Martin Gitlitz, *Secrecy and Deceit: The Religion of the Crypto-Jews* (Albuquerque: University of New Mexico Press, 2002), p. 576.
38. Ibid.
39. Gretchen D. Starr-LeBeau, *In the Shadow of the Virgin: Inquisitors, Friars, and Conversos in Guadalupe, Spain* (Princeton, N.J.: Princeton University Press, 2003), p. 39.
40. Ibid., p. 172.
41. Ibid., p. 217.
42. Kamen, *Spanish Inquisition*, p. 42.
43. Ibid.
44. Netanyahu, *Origins of Inquisition*, p. 1010.
45. Ibid., p. 795.
46. Ibid., p. 903.
47. Ibid., p. 921.
48. Ibid., p. 1032.
49. Ibid., p. 918.
50. Netanyahu, *Don Isaac Abravanel*, p. 56.
51. Lindo, *History of Jews of Spain*, p. 284.
52. Charles Berlin, *Elijah Capsali's Seder Eliyyahu Zuta*, p. 154.
53. Andrés Bernáldez, *Historia de los Reyes Católicos Don Fernando y Doña Isabel: crónica inedita del siglo XV* (Granada: Imprenta y Librería de Don José María Zamora, 1856), quoted in Lindo, *History of Jews of Spain*, p. 285.
54. Ibid.
55. Ibid., p. 290.
56. Ibid., p. 291.

FIFTEEN: LANDING IN PARADISE

1. Felipe Fernández-Armesto, *Columbus* (Oxford, U.K.: Oxford University Press, 1991), p. 20.
2. Bartolomé de Las Casas, *History of the Indies,* trans. and ed. Andrée Collard (New York: Harper & Row, 1971), p. 19.
3. Ibid.
4. Fernández-Armesto, *Columbus,* p. 4.
5. Las Casas, *History of the Indies,* p. 22.
6. Capitan Gonzalo Fernández de Oviedo y Valdés, *Historia general y natural de las Indias* (Madrid: Imprenta de la Real Academia de la Historia, 1851), pt. 1, p. 19.
7. Samuel Eliot Morison, *Admiral of the Ocean Sea: A Life of Christopher Columbus,* vol. 1 (Boston: Little, Brown & Co., 1942), p. 118.
8. Ibid., p. 130.
9. Duke of Medina Celi to Grand Cardinal of Spain, March 19, 1493, in *Journals and Other Documents on the Life and Voyages of Christopher Columbus,* ed. and trans. Samuel Eliot Morison (New York: Limited Editions Club, 1963), p. 20.
10. Fernández-Armesto, *Columbus,* p. 41.
11. Ferdinand Columbus, *The Life of the Admiral Christopher Columbus: By His Son Ferdinand,* trans. Benjamin Keen (New Brunswick, N.J.: Rutgers University Press, 1959), p. 9.
12. Ibid., p. 284.
13. Morison, *Admiral of the Ocean Sea,* vol. 1, p. 133.
14. Ibid., p. 135.

15. Ibid., p. 136.
16. Columbus, *Life of Columbus,* p. 42.
17. Morison, *Admiral of the Ocean Sea,* vol. 1, p. 137. Morison calculated that 2 million maravedis would be $14,000 in 1942 dollars (when he performed the calculation); that would be $195,000 in 2012.
18. Fernández-Armesto, *Columbus,* p. 62.
19. Alice Bache Gould, cited in Samuel Eliot Morison, *Admiral of the Ocean Sea: A Life of Christopher Columbus* (Boston: Little, Brown & Co., 1949), pp. 141–42.
20. Royal decree requiring the people of Palos to provide Columbus with caravels *Pinta* and *Niña,* April 30, 1492, Archives of the Indies, in Samuel Eliot Morison, ed. and trans., *Journals and Other Documents,* pp. 31–32.
21. Fernández-Armesto, *Columbus,* p. 62.
22. Las Casas, *History of the Indies,* p. 23.
23. Alice Bache Gould, cited in Morison, *Journals and Other Documents,* pp. 33 and 34.
24. Morison, *Admiral of the Ocean Sea,* one-volume edition (Boston: Little, Brown & Co., 1949), pp. 158–59.
25. Oviedo, *Historia general y natural,* pp. 22, 23.
26. Fernández-Armesto, *Columbus,* p. 80.
27. Oviedo, *Historia general y natural,* p. 24.
28. Morison, *Admiral of the Ocean Sea,* one-volume edition, p. 229.
29. Morison, trans., *Journals and Other Documents,* pp. 65, 67, 68.
30. Ibid., p. 142.
31. Ibid., p. 146.
32. Morison, *Admiral of the Ocean Sea,* one-volume edition, p. 2:7.
33. Ibid., p. 2:8.
34. Las Casas, *History of the Indies,* p. 37.
35. Columbus, *Life of Columbus,* p. 100.
36. Oviedo, *Historia general y natural,* p. 29.
37. Ibid.
38. Las Casas, *History of the Indies,* p. 38–39 (book 1, chapter 78).
39. Ibid., p. 42 (book 1, chapter 80).
40. Oviedo, *Historia general y natural,* p. 71.
41. Fernández-Armesto, *Columbus,* p. 61.
42. Columbus's Letter to the Sovereigns on His First Voyage, February 15 to March 4, 1493, New York Public Library, in Morison, ed. and trans., *Journals and Other Documents,* pp. 180–86.
43. Ibid.
44. Morison, ed. and trans., *Journals and Other Documents,* p. 181.

SIXTEEN: BORGIA GIVES HER THE WORLD

1. Michael Mallett, *The Borgias: The Rise and Fall of a Renaissance Dynasty* (New York: Barnes & Noble, 1969), p. 120.
2. John Fyvie, *The Story of the Borgias* (New York: G.P. Putnam's Sons, 1913), p. 29.
3. Paul Strathern, *The Artist, the Philosopher and the Warrior: The Intersecting Lives of Da Vinci, Machiavelli, and Borgia and the World They Shaped* (New York: Bantam Books, 2009), p. 69.
4. Mary Hollingsworth, *The Cardinal's Hat: Money, Ambition and Everyday Life in the Court of a Borgia Prince* (Woodstock, N.Y.: Overlook Press, 2005), p. 230.

5. Peter Martyr to Count of Tendilla, September 23, 1492, in *Opus Epistolarum: The Work of the Letters of Peter Martyr* (London: Wellcome Library).

6. Peter Martyr to Franciscus Pratensis Griolanus, September 18, 1492, ibid.

7. Peter Martyr to Ascanio Sforza, September 27, 1492, ibid.

8. Peter de Roo, *Material for a History of Pope Alexander VI, His Relatives and His Time,* vol. 2 (New York: Universal Knowledge Foundation, 1924). pp. 308–14.

9. Vatican Secret Records, ASV, A.A. ARM I-XVIII, 5023, ff 61v–64r, cited in Sarah Bradford, *Lucrezia Borgia* (New York: Viking, 2004), pp. 22 and 23.

10. Ibid., p. 24.

11. Jean Lucas-Dubreton, *The Borgias* (New York: E. P. Dutton & Co., 1955), pp. 82–83.

12. Samuel Eliot Morison, *Admiral of the Ocean Sea: A Life of Christopher Columbus,* one-volume edition (Boston: Little, Brown, 1949), p. 2:22.

13. Paul Gottschalk, *The Earliest Diplomatic Documents on America: The Papal Bulls of 1493 and the Treaty of Tordesillas* (Berlin: Paul Gottschalk, 1927), p. 35.

14. Ibid., p. 21.

15. Ibid.

16. Mallett, p. 97.

17. Bradford, *Lucrezia Borgia,* p. 30.

18. Ibid., p. 31.

19. Miquel Batllori, *La Família Borja,* Luzio, p. 120, July 13, 1493, cited ibid., p. 31.

20. Marion Johnson, *The Borgias* (New York: Holt, Rinehart & Winston, 1981), p. 116.

21. Christopher Hibbert, *The Borgias and Their Enemies, 1439–1513* (New York: Harcourt, 2008), p. 51.

22. Peter Martyr to Count of Tendilla and Archbishop of Granada, September 28, 1492, in *Opus Epistolarum.*

23. Morison, *Admiral of the Ocean Sea,* p. 224.

24. Antonio de la Torre, *Documentos,* pp. 142–43; Jack Freiberg, *Bramante's Tempietto and the Spanish Crown.*

25. Hugh Thomas, *The Conquest of Mexico* (London: Pimlico, 1993), p. 72.

SEVENTEEN: LANDS OF VANITY AND ILLUSION

1. Andrés Reséndez, *A Land So Strange: The Epic Journey of Cabeza de Vaca* (New York: Basic Books, 2007).

2. Roger Bigelow Merriman, *The Rise of the Spanish Empire in the Old World and the New* (New York: Cooper Square, 1962), p. 2:205.

3. Samuel Eliot Morison, *Admiral of the Ocean Sea: A Life of Christopher Columbus* (Boston: Little, Brown, 1949), p. 390.

4. Laurence Bergreen, *Columbus: The Four Voyages, 1492–1504* (New York: Viking, 2011), pp. 129–30.

5. Bartolomé de Las Casas, *History of the Indies,* trans. and ed. Andrée Collard (1875; repr., New York: Harper & Row, 1971, originally circulated between 1560 and 1600), p. 43 (original chapter 84).

6. Samuel Eliot Morison, *Journals and Other Documents on the Life and Voyages of Christopher Columbus* (New York: Limited Editions Club, 1963), p. 211.

7. Peter Martyr to Pomponius Letus, December 5, 1494, in *The Discovery of the New World in the Writings of Peter Martyr of Anghiera,* ed. Ernest Lunardi, Elisa Magioncalda, and Rosanna Mazzacane (Rome: Istituto Poligrafico e Zecca dello Stato, 1992), p. 57.

8. Capitan Gonzalo Fernández de Oviedo y Valdés, *Historia general y natural de las Indias* (Madrid: Imprenta de la Real Academia de la Historia, 1851), pt. 1, pp. 30–35.

9. Las Casas, *History of the Indies,* pp. 48–50 (chaps. 88 and 92).

10. Oviedo, *Historia general y natural,* p. 49.

11. Morison, *Journals and Other Documents,* p. 213.

12. Ibid., p. 212.

13. Las Casas, *History of the Indies,* p. 52 (chapter 92).

14. Ibid., pp. 52–53 (chapter 92).

15. Ibid., p. 49.

16. Morison, *Journals and Other Documents,* p. 226.

17. Andrés Bernáldez, *Historia de los Reyes Católicos, Don Fernando y Doña Isabel: Crónica inedita del siglo XV* (Granada: Imprenta y Libreria de Don José María Zamora, 1856), pp. 1:331–32.

18. Andrés Bernáldez, *Historia de los Reyes Católicos,* Tomo I (Granada: Imprenta y Librería de José María Zamora, 1856).

19. Salvador de Madariaga, *Christopher Columbus: Being the Life of the Very Magnificent Lord Don Cristóbal Colón* (New York: Macmillan, 1940), p. 304.

20. Ibid., p. 306.

21. Oviedo, *Historia general y natural,* p. 88.

22. Bartolomé de Las Casas, *Apologética historia,* ch. 19, p. 44, ed. Serrano y Sanz (Madrid: Bailly y Baillière, 1909) [this citation is in the book, which is in the Hispanic Reading room], cited in Samuel Eliot Morison, *Admiral of the Ocean Sea: A Life of Christopher Columbus,* vol. 2 (Boston: Little, Brown & Co., 1942), p. 196.

23. Ibid., p. 2:204.

24. Karl Sudhoff, *Earliest Printed Literature on Syphilis,* p. xxxii, 190, cited ibid., p. 2:198.

25. Oviedo, cited ibid., pp. 201–2.

26. Tom Mueller, "CSI: Italian Renaissance," in *Smithsonian Magazine,* July–August 2013.

27. Morison, *Journals and Other Documents,* p. 202.

28. Ferdinand Columbus, *The Life of the Admiral Christopher Columbus: By His Son Ferdinand,* trans. Benjamin Keen (New Brunswick, N.J.: Rutgers University Press, 1959), pp. 221–22.

29. Madariaga, *Christopher Columbus,* p. 305.

30. Morison, *Journals and Other Documents,* p. 212.

31. Morison, *Admiral of the Ocean Sea,* p. 2:301.

32. Hugh Thomas, *Rivers of Gold: The Rise of the Spanish Empire from Columbus to Magellan* (New York: Random House, 2003), pp. 201–2.

33. Ibid., p. 205.

34. Oviedo, *Historia general y natural,* p. 84.

EIGHTEEN: FAITH AND FAMILY

1. Ruth Mathilda Anderson, *Hispanic Costume, 1480–1530* (New York: Hispanic Society of America, 1979), p. 135.

2. Ibid.

3. Teresa de Castro, ed., "El tratado sobre el vestir, calzar y comer del Arzobispo Hernando de Talavera," *Espacio, tiempo, forma,* Serie III, *Historia medieval,* no. 14 (2001), pp. 11–92.

4. Nancy Rubin, *Isabella of Castile: The First Renaissance Queen* (New York: St. Martin's Press, 1991), p. 261.

5. Chiyo Ishikawa, *The retablo of Isabel la Católica* (Brussels: Brepols, 2004), p. 1.

6. *Miracle of the Loaves and Fishes,* Patrimonio Nacional, Palacio Real, Madrid.

7. *Marriage of Cana,* Metropolitan Museum of Art, New York City.

8. *Mocking of Christ,* Palacio Real, Madrid.

9. Ignacio Omaechevarría, *Orígenes de La Concepción de Toledo* (Burgos: Aldecoa, 1976), pp. 8–10.

10. Peter Martyr to Count of Tendilla and Archbishop of Granada, November 8, 1492, in *Opus Epistolarum: The Work of the Letters of Peter Martyr* (London: Wellcome Library).

11. Peter Martyr to Count of Tendilla, December 23, 1492, ibid.

12. *Crónica de Felipe Primero, llamado El Hermoso,* Lorenzo de Padilla y Dirijida to Emperador Carlos V, in *Colección de documentos inéditos para la historia de España* ed. Miguel Salvá y Munar and Pedro Sainz de Baranda (Madrid: Imprenta de la Viuda de Calero, 1846), p. 8:20.

13. Rodrigo González de Puebla to Ferdinand and Isabella, July 15, 1488, *Calendar of Letters, Despatches, and State Papers, Relating to the Negotiations Between England and Spain, Preserved in the Archives of Simancas and Elsewhere.* vol. 1, *Henry VII: 1485–1509,* ed. Gustav Bergenroth (London: Lords Commissioners of Her Majesty's Treasury, 1862).

14. Letters of December 1497 and December 1502, ibid.

15. Isabella to De Puebla, September 12, 1496, ibid.

16. Ibid.

17. Ruy de Pina, *Crónica de el-rei D. Affonso V* (Lisbon: Escriptorio, 1901), pp. 1:147–48.

18. Elaine Sanceau, *The Perfect Prince: A Biography of the King Dom João II* (Porto and Lisbon: Livraria Civilizacão, 1959), p. 318.

19. Ibid., p. 377.

20. Philippe de Commynes, *The Memoirs of Philippe de Commynes, Lord of Argenton* (London: G. and W. B. Whittaker, 1823), p. 2:402.

21. Ruy de Pina, *Croniqua Delrey Dom Joham II* (Coimbra: Atlantida, 1950), p. 113.

22. Ibid., p. 123.

23. Ibid., p. 125.

24. Ruy de Pina, cited in Antonio Henrique de Oliveira Marques, *Daily Life in Portugal in the Late Middle Ages,* trans. S. S. Wyatt (Madison: University of Wisconsin Press, 1971), pp. 264–65.

25. Ruy de Pina, *Croniqua Delrey Dom Joham II,* p. 130.

26. Antonio Henrique de Oliveira Marques, *History of Portugal,* vol. 1, *From Lusitania to Empire* (New York: Columbia University Press, 1972), p. 1:179.

27. Commynes, *Memoirs of Comines,* p. 2:402.

28. Peter Martyr to Alfonso Carrillo, bishop of Pamplona, March 18, 1492, in *Opus Epistolarum.*

29. Ruy de Pina, cited in Oliveira Marques, *Daily Life in Portugal,* pp. 274–75.

30. Ibid., pp. 277–79.

31. José-Luis Martín, *Isabel la Católica: sus hijas y las damas de su corte, modelos de doncellas, casadas y viudas, en el Carro de Las Doñas. 1542* (Ávila: Diputación Provincial de Ávila, Institución "Gran Duque de Alba," 2001), pp. 102–5.

32. Jerónimo Zurita, *Historia del rey Don Hernando el Católica: De las empresas y ligas de Italia,* vol. 2 (Zaragoza: Diputación General de Aragón, 1989–1994), p. 26–29.

33. Peter Martyr to Pomponius Laetus, December 7, 1494, in *Opus Epistolarum.*

34. Peter Martyr to Archbishop of Braga, September 1, 1492, ibid.

35. Peter Martyr to Ludovidus Torres, March 30, 1492, ibid.
36. Dagmar Eichberger, *Women of Distinction: Margaret of York, Margaret of Austria* (Turnhout, Belgium: Brepols, 2005), pp. 139–40.
37. Peter Martyr to Cardinal Carvajal, October 3, 1496, in *Opus Epistolarum*.
38. Peter Martyr to Cardinal Santa Croce, December 10, 1496, ibid.
39. Ibid.
40. Ibid.
41. Christopher Hare, *The High and Puissant Princess Marguerite of Austria, Princess Dowager of Spain, Duchess Dowager of Savoy, Regent of the Netherlands* (New York: Charles Scribner & Sons, 1907), p. 66.
42. Jacobo Stuart Fitz-James and Falcó Alba, *Correspondencia de Gutierre Gómez de Fuensalida* (Madrid: Imprenta Alemana, 1907), p. xxii.
43. Bethany Aram, *Juana the Mad: Sovereignty and Dynasty in Renaissance Europe* (Baltimore: Johns Hopkins University Press, 2005), pp. 37–38.
44. Dagmar Eichberger, *Women at the Burgundian Court: Presence and Influence* (Turnhout, Belgium: Brepols, 2010), p. 46.
45. The Sub-prior of Santa Cruz to Ferdinand and Isabella, August 16, 1498, in *Calendar of Letters, Despatches, and State Papers, Relating to the Negotiations Between England and Spain, Preserved in the Archives of Simancas and Elsewhere*, vol. 1, Henry VII: 1485–1509, ed. Gustav Bergenroth (London: Lords Commissioners of Her Majesty's Treasury, 1862).
46. Peter Martyr to Cardinal Santa Croce, June 13, 1497, in *Opus Epistolarum*.
47. Fernando Díaz-Plaja, *Historia de España en sus documentos, siglo XV* (Madrid: Ediciones Catedra, 1984), p. 346.
48. Thomas P. Campbell, *Tapestry in the Renaissance: Art and Magnificence* (New York: Metropolitan Museum of Art, 2002), pp. 4, 138.
49. Eichberger, *Women of Distinction*, pp. 195–96.
50. Ibid., pp. 184–85.
51. Peter Martyr to Cardinal Santa Croce, June 13, 1497, in *Opus Epistolarum*.
52. Biblioteca de la Academia Real, Volumen ms. en folio, rotulado, "Varios de Historia y Marina," E 132, p. 89; Fray Diego de Deza to Ferdinand and Isabella, 1497, in Gonzalo Fernández de Oviedo y Valdés, *Libro de la Camara Real del principe Don Juan e officios de su casa e servicio ordinaro* (Madrid: La Sociedad de Bibliofilos Españoles, 1870), pp. 232–33.
53. Peggy Liss, *Isabel the Queen: Life and Times* (New York: Oxford University Press, 1992), pp. 324–25.
54. Jerónimo Zurita, *Historia del rey Don Hernando el Católico: De las empresas y ligas de Italia*, ed. Angel Canellas López (Zaragoza: Diputación General de Aragón, 1989), p. 2:67.
55. Peter Martyr to Archbishop of Granada, October 30, 1497, in *Opus Epistolarum*.
56. Philippe de Commynes, *The Memoirs of Philip de Comines, Lord of Argenton* (London: G. and W. B. Whittaker, 1823), p. 2:400.
57. Ibid., p. 2:400–1.
58. Ibid., p. 2:401.
59. Zurita, *Historia del rey Don Hernando*, pp. 2:120–21.
60. Alonso de Santa Cruz, *Crónica de los Reyes Católicos*, ed. Juan de Mata Carriazo y Arroquia (Seville: Escuela de Estudios Hispano-Americanos de Sevilla, 1951), p. 2:215; a similar account appears in *La Crónica del emperador Carlos V*.
61. Bethany Aram, *Juana the Mad: Sovereignty and Dynasty in Renaissance Europe* (Baltimore: Johns Hopkins University Press, 2005), pp. 53–54.

NINETEEN: TURKS AT THE DOOR

1. Halil İnalcık, *The Ottoman Empire*, p. 6.
2. Jason Goodwin, *Lords of the Horizon: A History of the Ottoman Empire* (New York: Henry Holt, 1998), p. 69.
3. Ibid., p. 65.
4. Pietro Bembo, *History of Venice*, ed. and trans. Robert W. Ulery, Jr. (Cambridge, Mass.: Harvard University Press, 2007–9), p. 1:39.
5. V. J. Parry, *A History of the Ottoman Empire to 1730* (London: Cambridge University Press, 1976), pp. 57, 58.
6. Marin Barleti, *The Siege of Shkodra: Albania's Courageous Stand Against Ottoman Conquest 1478*, trans. David Hosaflook (Tirana, Albania: Onufri, 2012), p. 194.
7. Ibid., p. 233.
8. Ibid., p. 241.
9. Miguel A. de Bunes Ibarra and Emilio Sola, *La vida y historia de Hayradin, llamado Barbarroja* (Granada: Universidad de Granada, 1997), p. 33.
10. Press Department, Ministry of the Interior, *The Turkish Woman in History* (Ankara, Turkey, 1937), p. 10.
11. Robert Dankoff and Sooyoung Kim, *An Ottoman Traveler: Selections from the Book of Travels of Evliya Celebi* (London: Eland, 2010), p. 231.
12. Halil İnalcık, *Studies in Ottoman Social and Economic History* (London: Variorum Reprints, 1985), p. 39.
13. Klemen Pust, "Slavery, Childhood and the Border: The Ethics and Economics of Child Displacement Along the Triplex Confinium in the Sixteenth Century," presented at the 15th World Economic History Congress, Stellenbosch University, South Africa, July 9–13, 2012.
14. Halil İnalcık, *Studies in Ottoman Social and Economic History* (London: Variorum Imprints, 1985), p. 35.
15. Geza Palffy, "Ransom Slavery Along the Ottoman-Hungarian Frontier in the Sixteenth and Seventeenth Centuries," in Suraiya Faroqhi and Halil İnalcık, eds., *The Ottoman Empire and Its Heritage* (Leiden: Brill, 2007), p. 37.
16. Halil İnalcık, *Studies in Ottoman Social and Economic History*, p. 27.
17. Georgius de Hungaria, *Libellus de Ritu et Moribus Turcorum* (1530); digitized version provided by Göttingen State and University Library, Germany, translated by Paul A. Healy, ch. 6.
18. Ibid., chapter 7.
19. Ibid., chapter 12.
20. Inalcik, *Studies in Ottoman Social and Economic History*, p. 26.
21. Ekmeleddin Ihsanoglu, *The History of the Ottoman State, Society and Civilization* (Istanbul: Research Centre for Islamic History, Art and Culture, 2001), pp. 1:352–55.
22. King James IV, in Edinburgh, May 21, 1490, in "Venice 1486–1490," in *Calendar of State Papers Relating to English Affairs in the Archives of Venice*, ed. Rawdon Brown (Great Britain: National Archives, 1864).
23. Henry VII to Pope Alexander VI, January 12, 1493, ibid.
24. Philippe de Commynes, *The Memoirs of Philip de Comines, Lord of Argenton* (London: G. and W. B. Whittaker, 1823), pp. 2:363–64.
25. Pope Alexander VI to Isabella and Ferdinand, March 20, 1494, Archivo General de Simancas, Patronato Real, leg. 60, folio 34, cited in Luis Suárez Fernández, *Política internacional de Isabel la Católica, estudio y documentos* (Valladolid: Universidad de Valladolid, 1971), pp. 189–90.

26. Archivo General de Simancas, Patronato Real, leg. 60, fol. 35, cited in Suárez Fernández, *Política internacional de Isabel la Católica*, pp. 192–94.

27. Commynes, *Memoirs of Philip de Comines*, pp. 2:159–60.

28. John Addington Symonds, *A Short History of the Renaissance in Italy* (New York: Henry Holt & Co., 1894), p. 105.

29. Bembo, *History of Venice*, p. 1:79.

30. Memoir of what has taken place between Ferdinand and Isabella and the King of France, July 20, 1495, in *Calendar of Letters, Despatches, and State Papers, Relating to the Negotiations Between England and Spain, preserved in the Archives of Simancas and Elsewhere*, vol. 1, *Henry VII: 1485–1509*, ed. Gustav Bergenroth (London: Lords Commissioners of Her Majesty's Treasury, 1862).

31. Peter Martyr to archbishops of Braga and Pamplona, October 31, 1494, in *Opus Epistolarum: The Work of the Letters of Peter Martyr* (London: Wellcome Library).

32. Birsen Bulmus, *Plagues, Quarantines and Geopolitics in the Ottoman Empire* (Edinburgh: Edinburgh University Press, 2012), p. 45.

33. Bembo, *History of Venice*, p. 1:219.

34. Ibid., p. 1:115.

35. Ferdinand and Isabella to De Puebla, March 28, 1496, in Bergenroth, ed., *Calendar of Letters, Despatches, and State Papers*, vol. 1.

36. Bembo, *History of Venice*, p. 1:121.

37. Paul Stewart, "The Santa Hermandad and the First Italian Campaign of Gonzalo de Córdoba, 1495–1498," *Renaissance Quarterly* 28, no. 1 (Spring 1975), pp. 29–37.

38. Bembo, *History of Venice*, p. 1:203.

39. Miguel Ángel Ladero Quesada, *La España de los Reyes Católicos* (Madrid: Alianza Editorial, 1999), p. 276.

40. Alison Caplan, "The World of Isabel la Católica," in David Boruchoff, ed., *Isabel la Católica, Queen of Castile: Critical Essays* (New York: Palgrave Macmillan, 2003), p. 29.

41. Mary Purcell, *The Great Captain: Gonzalo Fernández de Córdoba* (New York: Alvin Redman, 1963), p. 124.

42. Commynes, *Memoirs of Philip de Comines*, p. 2:251.

43. Stanford Shaw, *History of the Ottoman Empire and Modern Turkey* (Cambridge, U.K.: Cambridge University Press, 1976), p. 1:75.

44. Peter Martyr to Count of Tendilla, April 26, 1499, in *Opus Epistolarum*.

45. Peter Martyr to Archbishop of Granada, September 3, 1499, ibid.

46. Daniel Goffman, *The Ottoman Empire and Early Modern Europe* (Cambridge, U.K.: Cambridge University Press, 2002), p. 143.

47. Archivo General de Simancas, Patronato Real, leg. 52, fol. 70, Bergenroth, cited in Luis Suárez Fernández, *Política internacional de Isabel la Católica: Estudios y documentos* (Valladolid: Universidad de Valladolid, 2002), pp. 6:88–90.

48. De Puebla to Ferdinand and Isabella, June 16, 1500, in Bergenroth, ed., *Calendar of Letters, Despatches, and State Papers*. vol. 1,

49. Peter Martyr to Peter Fagardius, September 2, 1500, in *Opus Epistolarum*.

50. Ibid.

51. Biblioteca Nacional, mss 20.211, folio 12, cited in Suárez Fernández, *Política internacional de Isabel la Católica*, p. 6:180–81.

52. Purcell, *Great Captain*, pp. 136–37.

53. Jerónimo Zurita, *Historia del rey Don Fernando el Católico: De las empresas y ligas de Italia*, ed. Ángel Canellas López (Zaragoza: Diputación General de Aragón, 1989), pp. 2:264–65.

54. John Julius Norwich, *A History of Venice* (New York: Vintage Books, 1988), p. 385.

55. Goffman, *Ottoman Empire*, p. 144.
56. Colin Imber, *The Ottoman Empire, 1300–1650: The Structure of Power* (London: Palgrave Macmillan, 2002), p. 41.
57. Ferdinand and Isabella to De Puebla, July 29, 1501, in Bergenroth, ed., *Calendar of Letters, Despatches, and State Papers.*
58. Ibid.
59. Peter Martyr to Cardinal Santa Croce, February 16, 1501, in *Opus Epistolarum.*
60. Tommaso Astarita, *The Continuity of Feudal Power: The Caracciolo di Brienza in Spanish Naples* (Cambridge, U.K.: Cambridge University Press, 1992), p. 13.

TWENTY: ISRAEL IN EXILE

1. David A. Boruchoff, "Introduction: Instructions for Sainthood and Other Feminine Wiles in the Historiography of Isabel I," in Boruchoff, *Isabel la Católica* (New York: Palgrave Macmillan, 2003), p. 4.
2. Charles Berlin, *Elijah Capsali's Seder Eliyyahu Zuta,* Ph.D. dissertation, Harvard University, September 1962.
3. Don José Antonio Conde, *Historia de la dominación de los Árabes en España, sacada de varios manuscritos y memorias arábigas* (Madrid: Biblioteca de Historiadores Españoles. Marín, y Compañía, 1874), p. 320.
4. Antonio de la Torre and Luis Suárez Fernández, *Documentos referentes a las relaciones con Portugal durante el reinado de los Reyes Católicos* (1858; Valladolid: Consejo Superior de Investigaciones Cientificas, Patronato Menéndez Pelayo, 1963), pp. 2:116–17.
5. William Prescott, *History of the Reign of Ferdinand and Isabella* (New York: Harper & Brothers, 1854), vol. 1, p. 420.
6. Ibid., p. 457.
7. Peggy Liss, *Isabel the Queen: Life and Times* (New York: Oxford University Press, 1992), p. 331.
8. Peter Martyr to Cardinal Santa Croce, June 9, 1501, in *Opus Epistolarum: The Work of the Letters of Peter Martyr* (London: Wellcome Library).
9. Ibid.
10. Miguel Ángel de Bunes Ibarra and Emilio Sola, *La vida, y historia de Hayradin, llamado Barbarroja* (Granada: Universidad de Granada, 1997), p. 43.
11. Ibid., p. 46.
12. François Soyer, "King João II of Portugal, 'O Principe Perfeito,' and the Jews (1481–1495)," *Sefarad* 69, no. 1 (2009).
13. Ibid., p. 91.
14. Ibid., p. 97.
15. Jerónimo Zurita, *Historia del rey Don Hernando el Católico: De las empresas y ligas de Italia,* ed. Angel Canellas López (Zaragoza: Diputación General de Aragón, 1989), pp. 2:26–29.
16. Ibid.
17. Antonio Henrique de Oliveira Marques, *History of Portugal* (New York: Columbia University Press, 1976), vol. I, p. 213.
18. Minna Rozen, *A History of the Jewish Community in Istanbul: The Formative Years, 1453–1566* (Leiden: Brill, 2010), p. 38.
19. Aryeh Shmuelevitz, "Capsali as a Source for Ottoman History, 1450–1523," *International Journal of Middle Eastern Studies* 9 (1978), p. 342.

20. Martin Jacobs, "Joseph ha-Kohen, Paolo Giovio and Sixteenth-Century Historiography," *Cultural Intermediaries, Jewish Intellectuals in Early Modern Italy*, ed. David B. Ruderman and Giuseppe Veltri (Philadelphia: University of Pennsylvania Press, 2004), p. 74.

21. Jane S. Gerber, *The Jews of Spain: A History of the Sephardic Experience* (New York: Free Press, 1994), p. xi.

22. Salma Khadra Jayyusi, ed., *The Legacy of Muslim Spain* (Leiden: Brill, 1994), p. xvii.

TWENTY-ONE: THREE DAUGHTERS

1. Caro Lynn, *A College Professor of the Renaissance: Lucio Marineo Sículo Among the Spanish Humanists* (Chicago: University of Chicago Press, 1937), p. 122.

2. Peter Martyr to Perdro Fagiardo, Lord of Cartagena, December 19, 1494, in *Opus Epistolarum: The Work of the Letters of Peter Martyr* (London: Wellcome Library).

3. Ferdinand Columbus, *The Life of the Admiral Christopher Columbus: By His Son Ferdinand* (New Brunswick, N.J.: Rutgers University Press, 1959), p. 215.

4. Bartolomé de Las Casas, *An Account, Much Abbreviated, of the Destruction of the Indies*, ed. Franklin W. Knight, trans. Andrew Hurley (Indianapolis: Hackett, 2003), p. xvi.

5. Bartolomé de Las Casas, *History of the Indies*, trans. Andrée Collard (New York: Harper & Row, 1971), p. 71.

6. Ruth Mathilda Anderson, *Hispanic Costume, 1480–1530* (New York: Hispanic Society of America, 1979), p. 142.

7. Document from Academia de la Historia Colección Salazar, A-11, fol. 288r-v, cited in Luis Suárez Fernández, *Política internacional de Isabel la Católica: Estudios y documentos* (Valladolid: Universidad de Valladolid, 2002), pp. 6:108–9.

8. Nancy Rubin, *Isabella of Castile: The First Renaissance Queen* (New York: St. Martin's Press, 1991), p. 378.

9. Hernando del Pulgar, *Crónica de los Señores Reyes Católicos Don Fernando y Doña Isabel de Castilla y de Aragón* (Madrid: Biblioteca de Autores Españoles, Librería de los Sucesores de Hernando, 1923), p. 3:65.

10. Ochoa de Isasaga to the Reyes Católicos, November 24, 1500, Estabdo Leg. 3678, fol. 17, cited in Antonio de la Torre, and Luis Suárez Fernández, *Documentos referentes a las relaciones con Portugal durante el reinado de los Reyes Católicos* (1858; Valladolid: Consejo Superior de Investigaciones Científicas, Patronato Menéndez Pelayo, 1963), pp. 66–69.

11. Fray Prudencio de Sandoval, *Historia de la vida y hechos del emperador Carlos V* (Madrid: Biblioteca de Autores Españoles, Atlas, 1955), p. 22.

12. Antonio Henrique de Oliveira Marques, *History of Portugal, vol. 1, From Lusitania to Empire* (New York: Columbia University Press, 1972), p. 2:214.

13. Edward McMurdo, *History of Portugal* (London: St. Dunstan's House, 1889), pp. 3:111–13.

14. José-Luis Martín, *Isabel la Católica: sus hijas y las damas de su corte, modelos de doncellas, casadas y viudas, en el Carro de las Doñas, 1542* (Ávila: Diputación Provincial de Ávila, Institución "Gran Duque de Alba," 2001), p. 109.

15. Sandoval, *Historia de la vida y hechos*, p. 20.

16. King Henry VII to Reyes, November 28, 1501, in *Calendar of Letters, Despatches, and State Papers, Relating to the Negotiations Between England and Spain, preserved in the*

Archives of Simancas and Elsewhere, vol. 1, *Henry VII: 1485–1509*, ed. Gustav Bergenroth (London: Lords Commissioners of Her Majesty's Treasury, 1862).

17. Giles Tremlett, *Catherine of Aragon: The Spanish Queen of Henry VIII* (New York: Walker & Co., 2010), p. 81.

18. Garrett Mattingly, *Catherine of Aragon* (New York: Quality Paperback Books, 1941), p. 55.

19. Christopher Hare, *The High and Puissant Princess Marguerite of Austria, Princess Dowager of Spain, Duchess Dowager of Savoy, Regent of the Netherlands* (New York: Charles Scribner & Sons, 1907), p. 79.

20. Bethany Aram, *Juana the Mad: Sovereignty and Dynasty in Renaissance Europe* (Baltimore: Johns Hopkins University Press, 2005), p. 35.

21. Ibid., p. 47.

22. Subprior of Santa Cruz to Fernando and Isabel, January 15, 1499, Archivo General de Simancas, Patronato Real 52–116, cited ibid., pp. 48, 49.

23. Rubin, *Isabella of Castile*, p. 377.

24. Jacobo Stuart Fitz-James and Falcó Alba, *Correspondencia de Gutierre Gómez de Fuensalida* (Madrid: Imprenta Alemana, 1907), p. xxvii.

25. Ibid., p. xxv.

26. Tomás de Matienzo to Fernando and Isabel, January 15, 1499, Archivo General de Simancas, Patronato Real 52–116, cited in Aram, *Juana the Mad*, p. 52.

27. Subprior of Santa Cruz to Isabella, January 15, 1499, in Bergenroth, ed., *Calendar of Letters, Despatches, and State Papers*.

28. Peter Martyr to Cardinal Santa Croce, September 20, 1502, in *Opus Epistolarum*.

29. Peter Martyr to Cardinal Santa Croce, December 19, 1503, ibid.

30. Stuart Fitz-James and Alba, *Correspondencia de Gómez de Fuensalida*, p. ix.

31. Peter Martyr to Cardinal Santa Croce, March 10, 1503, in *Opus Epistolarum*.

32. Vicente Rodríguez Valencia, *Isabel la Católica en la opinión de españoles y extranjeros, siglos XV al XX* (Valladolid: Instituto "Isabel la Católica" de Historia Eclesiástica, 1970), p. 1:278.

33. Alonso de Santa Cruz, *Crónica de los Reyes Católicos*, ed. Juan de Mata Carriazo y Arroquia (Seville: Escuela de Estudios Hispano-Americanos de Sevilla, 1951), p. 302.

34. Aram, *Juana the Mad*, p. 77.

35. Santa Cruz, *Crónica de los Reyes Católicos*, p. 302.

36. Tremlett, *Catherine of Aragon*, p. 99.

TWENTY-TWO: A CHURCH WITHOUT A SHEPHERD

1. Vicente Rodríguez Valencia, *Isabel la Católica en la opinión de españoles y extranjeros, siglos XV al XX* (Valladolid: Instituto "Isabel la Católica" de Historia Eclesiástica, 1970), p. 1:278.

2. Mary Purcell, *The Great Captain: Gonzalo Fernández de Córdoba* (New York: Alvin Redman, 1963), p. 155.

3. Ibid., p. 158.

4. Charles Oman, *A History of the Art of War in the Sixteenth Century* (New York: E. P. Dutton, 1937), p. 55.

5. Peter Martyr to archbishop and count, January 12, 1504, in *Opus Epistolarum: The Work of the Letters of Peter Martyr* (London: Wellcome Library).

6. Ibid., p. 178.

7. Tarsicio de Azcona, *Juana de Castilla, mal llamada La Beltraneja, 1462–1530* (Madrid: Fundación Universitaria Española, 1998), p. 65.

8. Peter Martyr to archbishop and count, January 12, 1504, in *Opus Epistolarum*.

9. Peter Martyr to archbishop of Granada, November 1, 1503, ibid.

10. Desmond Seward, *The Burning of the Vanities: Savonarola and the Borgia Pope* (Stroud, U.K.: Sutton, 2006), p. 221.

11. Ibid., p. 229.

12. Fray Prudencio de Sandoval, *Historia de la Vida y Hechos del Emperador Carlos V,* Biblioteca de Autores Españoles (Madrid: Atlas, 1955), p. 22.

13. Ibid., pp. 250–51.

14. Francisco Javier Sánchez Cantón, *Libros, tapices y cuadros que collecciónó Isabel la Católica* (Madrid: Consejo Superior de Investigaciones Cientificas, 1950), p. 54.

15. Nancy Rubin, *Isabella of Castile: The First Renaissance Queen* (New York: St. Martin's Press, 1991), pp. 337–38.

16. Ibid., p. 367.

17. Ibid.

18. Ibid., p. 339.

19. Jerónimo Zurita, *Historia del rey Don Hernando el Católico: De las empresas y ligas de Italia* (Zaragoza: Diputacion General de Aragón, 1989), pp. 2:6–7.

20. William Prescott, *History of the Reign of Ferdinand and Isabella* (Philadelphia: J. B. Lippincott, p. 502.

21. Ibid.

22. Jean Lucas-Dubreton, *The Borgias* (New York: E. P. Dutton & Co., 1955), p. 159.

23. Peter Martyr to Count of Tendilla and Archbishop of Granada, November 10, 1503, in *Opus Epistolarum*.

24. Pope Julius II, December 26, 1503, Calendar of State Papers, Spain.

25. Fusero Clemente, *The Borgias,* trans. Peter Green (New York: Praeger Publishers, 1972), p. 278.

26. Prescott, *History of the Reign,* p. 585.

TWENTY-THREE: THE DEATH OF QUEEN ISABELLA

1. Isabel to King Manuel of Portugal, November 21, 1501, in *Documentos referentes a las relaciones con Portugal durante el reinado de los Reyes Católicos,* ed. Antonio de la Torre and Luis Suárez Fernández (1858; Valladolid: Consejo Superior de Investigaciones Científicas, Patronato Menéndez Pelayo, 1963), pp. 3:106–7.

2. Peter Martyr to Count of Tendilla and Archbishop Talavera, October 3, 1504, in *Opus Epistolarum: The Work of the Letters of Peter Martyr* (London: Wellcome Library).

3. Peter Martyr to Licenciate Polancus, Royal Counselor, October 15, 1504, ibid.

4. Catherine, Princess of Wales, to Queen Isabella, November 26, 1504, in *Calendar of Letters, Despatches, and State Papers, Relating to the Negotiations Between England and Spain, preserved in the Archives of Simancas and Elsewhere,* vol. 1, *Henry VII: 1485–1509,* ed. Gustav Bergenroth (London: Lords Commissioners of Her Majesty's Treasury, 1862).

5. Bishop of Worcester to Henry VII, March 15, 1505, ibid.

6. Jerónimo Zurita, *Historia del rey Don Hernando el Católico: De las empresas y ligas de Italia,* ed. Ángel Canellas López (Zaragoza: Diputación General de Aragón, 1989), p. 3:331.

7. Alonso de Santa Cruz, *Crónica de los Reyes Católicos,* ed. Juan de Mata Carriazo y Arroquia (Seville: Escuela de Estudios Hispano-Americanos de Sevilla, 1951), p. 2:303.

8. Zurita, *Historia del Rey,* pp. 328–29.

9. Baldesar Castiglione, *The Book of the Courtier,* trans. Charles S. Singleton (Garden City, N.Y.: Anchor Books, 1959), p. 237.

10. Ibid., p. 238.

11. Philippe de Commynes, *The Memoirs of Philip de Comines, Lord of Argenton* (London: G. and W. B. Whittaker, 1823), p. 2:402.

12. *Testamento de la Reina Isabel la Católica, Publicaciones del quinto centenario, 1504–2004,* Granada, p. 59.

13. Nancy Rubin, *Isabella of Castile: The First Renaissance Queen* (New York: St. Martin's Press, 1991), p. 414.

14. Ibid.

15. *Testamento de la Reina Isabel la Católica,* p. 59.

16. Peter Martyr to Ferdinand of Aragon, December 25, 1504, in *Opus Epistolarum.*

17. Ibid.

18. Juan Antonio Vilar Sánchez, *Los Reyes Católicos en la Alhambra* (Granada: Editorial COMARES, 2007), pp. 135–37; and Juan Manuel Barrios Rozva, *Guía de la Granada Desaparecida* (Granada: Editorial COMARES, 2006), pp. 131–33.

TWENTY-FOUR: THE WORLD AFTER ISABELLA

1. King Ferdinand to King Henry VII, November 26, 1504, in *Calendar of Letters, Despatches, and State Papers, Relating to the Negotiations Between England and Spain, Preserved in the Archives of Simancas and Elsewhere,* vol. 1, *Henry VII: 1485–1509,* ed. Gustav Bergenroth (London: Lords Commissioners of Her Majesty's Treasury, 1862).

2. Tarsicio de Azcona, *Isabel la Católica: Estudio crítico de su vida y su reinado* (Madrid: Biblioteca de Autores Cristianos, 1993), p. 951.

3. Chiyo Ishikawa, *The retablo of Isabel la Católica* (Turnhout, Belgium: Brepols, 2004), pp. 5–8.

4. Azcona, *Isabel la Católica,* p. 951.

5. Peter Martyr, *Opus Epistolarum: The Work of the Letters of Peter Martyr* (London: Wellcome Library), vol. 3, letter 285.

6. Bethany Aram, *Juana the Mad: Sovereignty and Dynasty in Renaissance Europe* (Baltimore: Johns Hopkins University Press, 2005), pp. 77–78.

7. Jacobo Stuart Fitz-James and Falcó Alba, *Correspondencia de Gutierre Gómez de Fuensalida* (Madrid: Imprenta Alemana, 1907), p. 389.

8. Peter Martyr to Archbishop of Granada, August 4, 1505, in *Opus Epistolarum.*

9. Aram, *Juana the Mad,* p. 82.

10. Ibid., p. 80.

11. Vincenzo Quirini to the Signory, September 1505, *Calendar of State Papers Relating to English Affairs in the Archives of Venice,* vol. 1, *1502–1509,* ed. Rawdon Brown (Great Britain: National Archives, 1864), pp. 300–10.

12. Quirini to the Signory, April 4, 1506, ibid.

13. Ibid.

14. Ibid.

15. Quirini to the Sigorny, April 4, 1506, April 16, 1506, ibid.

16. Philibert Naturel to Philip le Beau, June 7, 1506, LM 24195, correspondence of Margaret of Austria, Archives du Nord, Lille, France.

17. King Ferdinand to De Puebla, December 1505, *Calendar of Letters, Despatches, and State Papers, Relating to the Negotiations Between England and Spain, Preserved in the Archives of Simancas and Elsewhere,* vol. 1, *Henry VII: 1485–1509,* ed. Gustav Bergenroth (London: Lords Commissioners of Her Majesty's Treasury, 1862).

18. James Braybroke to Henry VII, July 1505, ibid.

19. Maximilian de Austria, 1505, in Fernando Díaz-Plaja, *Historia de España en sus documentos, siglo XVI* (Madrid: Ediciones Catedra, 1988).

20. April 4, 1506, Brussels, September 9, 1505, in Brown, ed., *Calendar of State Papers Relating to English Affairs,* vol. 1.

21. Peter Martyr, in *Opus Epistolarum,* vol. 3, letter 300.

22. Ibid., letter 311.

23. Aram, *Juana the Mad,* p. 88.

24. Elaine Sanceau, *The Reign of the Fortunate King, 1495–1521* (New York: Archon Books, 1970), p. 140.

25. Aram, *Juana the Mad,* p. 10.

26. Annemarie Jordan, *The Development of Catherine of Austria's Collection in the Queen's Household: Its Character and Cost* (London: Simon & Schuster, 2010).

27. Mary Purcell, *The Great Captain: Gonzalo Fernández de Córdoba* (New York: Alvin Redman, 1963), p. 190.

28. Ibid., p. 159.

29. Bartolomé de Las Casas, *History of the Indies,* trans. and ed. Andrée Collard (New York: Harper & Row, 1971), pp. 138–39.

30. Roger Bigelow Merriman, *The Rise of the Spanish Empire in the Old World and the New* (New York: Cooper Square, 1962), vol. 1, p. 213.

31. Las Casas, *History of the Indies,* p. 35.

32. Peter Martyr to Luis Hurtado de Mendoza, December 31, 1514, in *Opus Epistolarum,* epistle 542.

33. Robert C. Davis, *Christian Slaves, Muslim Masters: White Slavery in the Mediterranean, the Barbary Coast, and Italy, 1500–1800* (New York: Palgrave Macmillan, 2003), p. xiv.

34. V. J. Parry, *A History of the Ottoman Empire to 1730* (Cambridge, U.K.: Cambridge University Press, 1976), p. 64.

35. Ishikawa, *The retablo of Isabel la Católica,* p. 1.

36. Peter Martyr to Marquess of Mondejar, December 5, 1515, in *Opus Epistolarum.*

37. Tom Mueller, "CSI: Italian Renaissance," *Smithsonian,* July–August 2013.

38. G. González Dávila, *Teatro de Las Grandeza de la Villa de Madrid* (Madrid, 1623), quoted in Clarence Henry Haring, *Trade and Navigation Between Spain and the Indies* (Cambridge, Mass.: Harvard University Press, 1964), pp. xii and xiii.

BIBLIOGRAPHY

Abenia, C., and R. Bágueña. *Catálogo de una serie de cartas de los Reyes Católicos (1479–1502)*. Valencia: Universidad de Valencia, 1945.

Abulafia, David. *The Great Sea: A Human History of the Mediterranean*. London: Allen Lane, 2011.

Ady, Cecilia M. *A History of Milan Under the Sforza*. London: Methuen, 1907.

Ahmad, Jalal Al-E. *Plagued by the West*. Translated from the Persian by Paul Sprachman. Bibliotheca Persica, Center for Iranian Studies. New York: Columbia University, 1961.

Aksan, Virgina H., and Daniel Goffman. *The Early Modern Ottomans: Remapping the Empire*. Cambridge: Cambridge University Press, 2007.

Alcala, Angel. *The Spanish Inquisition and the Inquisitorial Mind*. Symposium internacional sobre la inquisición en Española. Newark, N.Y., 1983.

Allen, Peter Lewis. *The Wages of Sin: Sex and Disease, Past and Present*. Chicago: University of Chicago Press, 2000.

Al-Maqqari, Ahmad ibn Muhammad. *The History of the Mohammedan Dynasties in Spain*. Translated by Pascual de Gayangos. 2 vols. London: Oriental Translation Fund, 1840–43.

Álvarez Palenzuela, Vicente Ángel. "Relations Between Portugal and Castile in the Late Middle Ages—13th to 16th Centuries." *e-JPH* 1, no. 1 (Summer 2003).

Anderson, Ruth Mathilda. *Hispanic Costume, 1480–1530*. New York: Hispanic Society of America, 1979.

Andrés Díaz, Rosana de. *El último decenio del reinado de Isabel I, a través de la tesorería de Alonso de Morales (1495–1504)*. Valladolid: Universidad de Valladolid, Instituto de Historia Simancas, 2004.

Anes y Álvarez de Castrillón, Gonzalo. *Isabel la Católica y su tiempo*. Madrid: Real Academia de la Historia, 2005.

Aram, Bethany. *Juana the Mad: Sovereignty and Dynasty in Renaissance Europe*. Baltimore: Johns Hopkins University Press, 2005.

Archivo General de Simancas. *Catálogo V. Patronato Real, 834–1851*. Edited by Amalia

Prieto Cantero. Valladolid: Cuerpo Facultativo de Archiveros, Bibliotecarios y Arqueólogos, 1946–49.

Archivo Histórico Nacional. *Catálogo de las causas contra la fe seguidas ante el Tribunal del Santo Oficio de la Inquisición de Toledo*. Madrid, 1903.

Armas, Antonio Rumeu de. *Itinerario de los reyes católicos, 1474–1516*. Madrid: Raycar, 1974.

Astarita, Tommaso. *The Continuity of Feudal Power: The Caracciolo di Brienza in Spanish Naples*. Cambridge, U.K.: Cambridge University Press, 1992.

Azcona, Tarsicio de. *Isabela la Católica: Estudio crítico de su vida y su reinado*. Madrid: Biblioteca de Autores Cristianos, 1993.

———. *Juana de Castilla, mal llamada La Beltraneja, 1462–1530*. Madrid: Fundación Universitaria Española, 1998.

———. *Isabel la Católica, vida y reinado*. Madrid: La Esfera de los Libros, 2004.

Babinger, Franz. *Mehmed the Conquerer and His Time*. Princeton, N.J.: Princeton University Press, 1992.

Backhouse, Janet. *The Isabella Breviary*. London: British Library, 1993.

Barleti, Marin. *The Siege of Shkodra: Albania's Courageous Stand Against Ottoman Conquest 1478*. Translated by David Hosaflook. Tirana, Albania: Onufri, 2012.

Barrios Aguilera, Manuel. *La convivencia negada: Historia de los moriscos del Reino de Granada*. Granada: Editorial COMARES, 2007.

———. *La suerte de los vencidos*. Granada: Editorial Universidad de Granada, 2009.

Barrios Rozúa, Juan Manuel. *Guía de la Granada desaparecida*. Granada: Editorial COMARES, 2006.

Baumgartner, Frederic. *Louis XII*. New York: St. Martin's Press, 1994.

Beg, Tursun. *The History of Mehmed the Conqueror*. English translation by Halil İnalcık, and Rhoads Murphey. Minneapolis: Bibliotheca Islamica, 1978.

Bembo, Pietro. *History of Venice*. Edited and translated by Robert W. Ulery, Jr. 3 vols. Cambridge, Mass.: Harvard University Press, 2007–9.

Benecke, Gerhard. *Maximilian I, 1459–1519: An Analytical Biography*. London: Routledge and Kegan Paul, 1982.

Benítez, Fray Jesús Miguel. *Madrigal de las Altas Torres: Monasterio de Nuestra Señora de Gracia*. León: Edilesa, undated.

Bergreen, Laurence. *Columbus: The Four Voyages, 1492–1504*. New York: Viking, 2011.

Berlin, Charles. *Elijah Capsali's Seder Eliyyahu Zuta*. Ph.D. dissertation, Harvard University, September 1962.

———. "A Sixteenth Century Hebrew Chronicle of the Ottoman Empire: The Seder Eliyahu Zuta of Elijah Capsali and Its Message." In Berlin, ed., *Studies in Jewish Bibliography History and Literature*. New York: KTAV Publishing, 1971.

Berlin, Charles, ed. *Studies in Jewish Bibliography, History, and Literature in Honor of I. Edward Kiev*. New York: KTAV Publishing, 1971.

Bernáldez, Andrés. *Historia de los Reyes Católicos Don Fernando y Doña Isabel: Crónica inédita del siglo XV*. 2 vols. Granada: Imprenta y Librería de Don José María Zamora, 1856.

———. *Memorias del reinado de los Reyes Católicas, que escriba el bachiller Andrés Bernáldez*. Edited by Manuel Gómez-Moreno and Juan de M. Carriazo. Madrid: Real Academia de la Historia, 1962.

Bianchini, Janna. *The Queens Hand, Power and Authority in the Reign of Berenguela of Castile*. Philadelphia: University of Pennsylvania Press, 2012.

Bisaha, Nancy. *Creating East and West: Renaissance Humanists and the Ottoman Turks*. Philadelphia: University of Pennsylvania Press, 2004.

Bisso, Don José. *Crónica de la Provincia de Sevilla*. In *Crónica general de España, historica illustrada y descriptiva de sus provincias, sus poblaciones más importantes de la peninsula y de ultramar*. Madrid: Rubio, Grilo y Vitturi, 1869.

Blackmore, Josiah, and Gregory S. Hutcheson. *Queer Iberia*. Durham, N.C.: Duke University Press, 1999.

Blanco Sánchez, Antonio. *Sobre Medina del Campo y la reina agraviada*. Medina del Campo: Caballeros de la Hispanidad, 1994.

Blázquez Hernández, Gregorio. "María Vela y Cueto, la mujer fuerte." *Diario de Ávila*, May 14, 2006.

Blumenthal, Debra. *Enemies and Familiars: Slavery and the Mastery in Fifteenth-Century Valencia*. Ithaca, N.Y.: Cornell University Press, 2009.

Boruchoff, David A., ed. *Isabel la Católica, Queen of Castile: Critical Essays*. New York: Palgrave Macmillan, 2003.

Bóscolo, Alberto, ed. *Fernando el Católico e Italia*. Zaragoza: Institución Fernando el Católico (C.S.I.C) de la Excma Diputación Provincial de Zaragoza, 1954.

Boswell, John. *Christianity, Social Tolerance and Homosexuality*. Chicago: University of Chicago Press, 1980.

Bown, Stephen R. *1494: How a Family Feud in Medieval Spain Divided the World in Half*. New York: St. Martin's Press, 2011.

Bradford, Ernie. *The Sultan's Admiral: Barbarossa—Pirate and Empire Builder*. London: Hodder & Stoughton, 1969.

———. *Gibraltar: The History of a Fortress*. New York: Harcourt Brace Jovanich, 1971.

Bradford, Sarah. *Cesare Borgia*. New York: MacMillan Publishing Co., 1976.

———. *Lucrezia Borgia*. New York: Viking, 2004.

Bulmus, Birsen. *Plagues, Quarantines and Geopolitics in the Ottoman Empire*. Edinburgh: Edinburgh University Press, 2012.

Bunes Ibarra, Miguel Ángel de, and Emilio Sola. *La vida, y historia de Hayradin, llamado Barbarroja*. Granada: Universidad de Granada, 1997.

Bunes Ibarra, Miguel Ángel, et al. *The Invention of Glory: Afonso V and the Pastrana Tapestries*. Madrid: Fundación Carlos de Amberes, 2011.

Burke, Ulick Ralph. *The Great Captain; An Eventful Chapter in Spanish History*. London: Society for Promoting Christian Knowledge, 1877.

Cabanas González, María Dolores, Carmelo Luis López, and Gregorio del Ser Quijano. *Isabel de Castilla y su época: Estudios y selección de textos*. Alcalá de Henares: Universidad de Alcalá, 2007.

Calderón, Emilio. *Usos y costumbres sexuales de los Reyes de España*. Madrid: Editorial Cirene, 1991.

Calendar of Letters, Despatches, and State Papers, Relating to the Negotiations Between England and Spain, Preserved in the Archives of Simancas and Elsewhere, vol. 1, *Henry VII: 1485–1509*. Edited by Gustav Bergenroth. London: Lords Commissioners of Her Majesty's Treasury, 1862.

Campbell, Thomas P. *Tapestry in the Renaissance: Art and Magnificence*. New York: Metropolitan Museum of Art, 2002.

Campo, Victoria, and Victor Infantes, eds. *La Poncella de Francia: La historia Castellana de Juana de Arco*. Madrid: Iberoamericana, 2006.

Capponi, Niccolò. *Victory of the West: The Great Christian-Muslim Clash at the Battle of Lepanto*. Cambridge, Mass.: Da Capo Press, 2007.

Caro Baroja, Julio. *Los Mariscos del Reino de Granada*. Madrid: Alianza Editorial, 2010.

Carroll, Warren H. *Isabel of Spain: The Catholic Queen*. Front Royal, Va.: Christendom Press, 1991.

Cartas Autógrafas de los Reyes Católicos de España, Don Fernando y Doña Isabel que conservan en el Archivo de Simancas, 1474–1502. Valladolid: Instituto "Isabel la Católica" de Historia Eclesiástica, 1971.

Castiglione, Baldesar. *The Book of the Courtier.* Translated by Charles S. Singleton. Garden City, N.Y.: Anchor Books, 1959.

Castro, Teresa de, ed. "El tratado sobre el vestir, calzar y comer del Arzobispo Hernando de Talavera." *Espacio, tiempo, y forma.* Serie III. *Historia Medieval,* no. 14 (2001), pp. 11–92.

Cervantes, Miguel de. *"The Bagnios of Algiers" and "The Great Sultana": Two Plays of Captivity.* Edited and translated by Barbara Fuchs and Aaron J. Ilika. Philadelphia: University of Pennsylvania Press, 2010.

Chaytor, Henry John. *A History of Aragon and Catalonia.* London: Methuen, 1933.

Cheetham, Anthony. *The Life and Times of Richard III.* London: Weidenfeld & Nicolson, 1972.

Chesterton, G. K. *Lepanto.* San Francisco: Ignatius Press, 2004.

Chipman, Donald E. *Montezuma's Children: Aztec Royalty Under Spanish Rule, 1520–1700.* Austin: University of Texas Press, 2005.

Chronicles and Memorials of Great Britain and Ireland During the Middle Ages. Oxford University, 1879.

Chueca Goitia, Fernando. *Historica de la arquitectura española: Edad antigua, edad media.* 2 vols. Ávila: Fundación Cultural Santa Teresa, 2001.

Classen, Albrecht. "The World of the Turks Described by an Eyewitness: Georgius de Hungaria's Dialectical Discourse on the Foreign World of the Ottoman Empire." *Journal of Early Modern History.* Leiden: Brill, 2003.

Clemencín, Diego. *Elogio de la Reina Católica Doña Isabella.* Madrid: Imprenta de Sancha, 1820.

Collins, Roger. *The Arab Conquest of Spain: 710–797.* New York: Wiley-Blackwell, 1995.

Collison-Morley, Lacy. *Naples Through the Centuries.* New York: Frederick A. Stokes Co., 1925.

Colmenares, Diego de. *Historia de la insigne ciudad de Segovia.* Revised by Gabriel María Vergara. Segovia: Imprenta de la Tierra de Segovia, 1931.

Columbus, Ferdinand. *The Life of the Admiral Christopher Columbus: By His Son Ferdinand.* Translated and annotated by Benjamin Keen. New Brunswick, N.J.: Rutgers University Press, 1959.

Commynes, Philippe de. *The Memoirs of Philip de Comines, Lord of Argenton.* London: G. and W. B. Whittaker, 1823.

Conde, Don José Antonio. *Historia de la dominación de los Arabes en España, sacada de varios manuscritos y memorias arábigas.* Madrid: Biblioteca de Historiadores Españoles, Marín y Compañía, 1874.

Constable, Olivia Remie. *Medieval Iberia: Readings from Christian, Muslim and Jewish Sources.* Philadelphia: University of Pennsylvania Press, 2011.

Consuelo Díez Bedmar, María del. *Teresa de Torres, (ca. 1442–1521) Condesa de Castilla.* Madrid: Ediciones del Orto, 2004.

Cook, Weston F. "The Cannon Conquest of Nasrid Spain and the End of the Reconquista." *The Journal of Military History,* vol. 57, no. 1 (January 1993).

Cortés Timoner, María del Mar. *Sor María de Santo Domingo (1470/86–1524).* Madrid: Ediciones del Orto, 2004.

Costa-Gomes, Rita. *The Making of a Court Society: Kings and Nobles in Late Medieval Portugal.* Cambridge, U.K.: Cambridge University Press, 2003.

Craig, Leigh Ann. *Wandering Women and Holy Matrons: Women as Pilgrims in the Later Middle Ages.* Leiden: Brill, 2009.

Crónica incompleta de los Reyes Católicos, 1469–1476. Edited by Julio Puyol. Madrid: Academia de la Historia, 1934.

Csukovits, Eniko. "Miraculous Escapes from Ottoman Captivity." In Suraiya Faroqhi and Halil İnalcık, eds., *The Ottoman Empire and Its Heritage*. Leiden: E.J. Brill, 2007.

Da Costa, Isaac. *Noble Families Among the Sephardic Jews by Isaac da Costa (1798–1860). With Some Account of the Capadose Family (Including Their Conversion to Christianity), by Bertram Brewster, and an Excursus on Their Jewish History, by Cecil Roth*. Oxford, U.K.: Oxford University Press, 1936.

Dankoff, Robert, and Sooyoung Kim. *An Ottoman Traveler: Selections from the Book of Travels of Evilya Celebi*. London: Eland, 2010.

Dávid, Géza, and Pál Fodor, eds. *Ransom Slavery Along the Ottoman Borders: Early Fifteenth–Early Eighteenth Centuries*. Leiden: Brill, 2007.

Davis, Robert C. *Christian Slaves, Muslim Masters: White Slavery in the Mediterranean, the Barbary Coast, and Italy, 1500–1800*. New York: Palgrave Macmillan, 2003.

De la Torre, Antonio. *Documentos sobre relaciones internacionales de los Reyes Católicos*, vol. 2. Barcelona: Consejo Superior de Investigaciones Científicas, 1962.

De la Torre, Antonio, and Luis Suárez Fernández. *Documentos a las relaciones en Portugal durante el reinado de los Reyes Católicos*, vol. 3. Valladolid, 1963.

Descola, Jean. *A History of Spain*. New York: Alfred A. Knopf, 1963.

De Winter, Patrick M. "A Book of Hours of Queen Isabel la Católica." *The Bulletin of the Cleveland Museum of Art* 68, no. 10 (December 1981), pp. 342–427.

Díaz del Castillo, Bernal. *The Conquest of New Spain*. Translated by John M. Cohen. London: Penguin Classics, 1963.

Díaz-Plaja, Fernando. *Historia de España en sus documentos, siglo XV*. Madrid: Ediciones Catedra, 1984.

———. *Historia de España en sus documentos, siglo XVI*. Madrid: Ediciones Catedra, 1988.

Donini, Guido, and Gordon B. Ford, trans. *Isidore of Seville's History of the Kings of the Goths, Vandals and Suevi*. Leiden: Brill, 1966.

Doubleday, Simon, and David Coleman, eds. *In the Light of Medieval Spain: Islam, the West, and the Relevance of the Past*. New York: Palgrave Macmillan, 2008.

Drane, Augusta Theodosia. *The Knights of St. John: A History to the Siege of Vienna, 1688*. U.K.: Leonaur, 2009.

Duffy, Eamon. *Marking the Hours: English People and Their Prayers, 1240–1570*. New Haven, Conn.: Yale University Press, 2006.

Earenfight, Theresa. *The King's Other Body: María of Castile and the Crown of Aragon*. Philadelphia: University of Pennsylvania Press, 2010.

Edge, P. Granville. "Pre-Census Population Records of Spain." *Journal of the American Statistical Association* 26, no. 176 (December 1931), pp. 416–23.

Edward IV on May 26th, 1464 (A Contemporary Account Now First Set Forth from a 15th Century Manuscript). London, 1935.

Edwards, John. *The Spain of the Catholic Monarchs, 1474–1520*. Oxford, U.K.: Blackwell, 2000.

Eguílaz Yánguas, Leopoldo de. *Reseña histórica de la conquista del reino de Granada por los Reyes Católicos según las cronistas árabes*. Granada: Tip. Hospital de Santa Cruz, 1894.

Eichberger, Dagmar, ed. *Women of Distinction: Margaret of York, Margaret of Austria*. Turnhout, Belgium: Brepols, 2005.

———. *Women at the Burgundian Court: Presence and Influence*. Belgium: Brepols, 2010.

Eisenberg, Daniel. "Enrique IV and Greogrio Marañón." *Renaissance Quarterly* 29, no. 1 (Spring 1976).

Elbl, Ivana. "Man of His Time (and Peers): A New Look at Henry the Navigator." *Luso-Brazilian Review* 28, no. 2 (Winter 1991), pp. 73–89.

Elliott, J. H. *Spain and Its World, 1500–1700: Selected Essays*. New Haven, Conn.: Yale University, 1989.

———. *Imperial Spain, 1469–1716*. London: Penguin, 1990.

Ellis, Henry, ed. *Original Letters, Illustrative of English History, Including Numerous Royal Letters*. London: Richard Bentley, 1846.

Encinas, Alonso de. *Madrigal de las Altas Torres, cuna de Isabel la Católica*. Madrid: Revista geográfica española, 1955.

Enríquez del Castillo, Diego. *Crónica de Enrique IV*. Edited by Aureliano Sánchez Martín. Valladolid: Universidad de Valladolid, 1994.

Espejo, Cristóbal, and Julián Paz. *Las antiguas ferias de Medina Del Campo: Investigación histórica acerca de ellas*. Valladolid: Maxtor, 2003.

Esposito, John L. *The Oxford History of Islam*. Oxford, U.K.: Oxford University Press, 1999.

Faroqhi, Suraiya, and Halil İnalcık. *The Ottoman Empire and Its Heritage*. Leiden: Brill, 2007.

Faroqhi, Suraiya, and Kate Fleet. *The Cambridge History of Turkey, Volume 2: The Ottoman Empire as a World Power, 1453–1603*. Cambridge, U.K.: Cambridge University Press, 2013.

Fehrenbach, T. R. *Fire and Blood: A History of Mexico*. New York: Da Capo Press, 1995.

Fernández Álvarez, Manuel. *Juana la Loca: la cautiva de Tordesillas*. Spain: Espasa-Calpe, 2008.

———. *Isabel la Católica*. Madrid: Espasa Calpe, 2006.

Fernández Collado, Ángel, et al. *Cathedral of Toledo*. Translated by Surtees Robinson. Toledo: Cabildo Catedral Primada, 2009.

Fernández de Oviedo, Gonzalo. *Natural History of the West Indies*. Translated and edited by Sterling A. Stoudemire. Chapel Hill: University of North Carolina Press, 1959.

Fernández Gómez, Marcos. *El Alcazar y la Atarazanas de Sevilla en el reinado de los Reyes Católicos*. Seville: Patronato del Real Alcázar y de la Casa Consistorial de Sevilla, 2011.

Fernández-Armesto, Felipe. *Columbus*. Oxford, U.K.: Oxford University Press, 1991.

———. *Columbus on Himself*. Indianapolis: Hackett, 2009.

———. *1492: The Year the World Began*. New York: HarperCollins, 2009.

Fernández-Morera, Dario. "The Myth of the Andalusian Paradise." *Intercollegiate Review* 41, no. 2 (Fall 2006).

Fichtner, Paula S. *Ferdinand I of Austria: The Politics of Dynasticism in the Age of the Reformation*. Boulder, Colo.: East European Monographs, 1982.

Finlay, George. *The History of Greece: From Its Conquest by the Crusaders to Its Conquest by the Turks, and the Empire of Trebizond, 1204–1461*. Edinburgh and London: Blackwood, 1851.

———. *The History of Greece Under Othoman and Venetian Domination*. Edinburgh and London: Blackwood, 1861.

Fisher, Sydney Nettleton. "Sultan Bayezit and the Foreign Relations of Turkey." Ph.D. dissertation, University of Illinois, 1935.

———. *Foreign Relations of Turkey, 1481–1512*. Urbana, Ill.: University of Illinois Press, 1948.

Fletcher, Richard. *Moorish Spain*. Berkeley and Los Angeles: University of California Press, 1992.

Flores, Josef Miguel de. *Crónica de Don Alvaro de Luna, condestable de los reynos de Castilla y de León*. Madrid: Imprenta de Antonio de Sancha, 1784.

Fusero, Clemente. *The Borgias*. Translated by Peter Green. New York: Praeger Publishers, 1966.

Francisco, Adam S. *Martin Luther and Islam: A Study in Sixteenth-Century Polemics and Apologetics*. Leiden: Brill, 2007.

Fraser, Antonia. *The Wives of Henry VIII*. New York: Alfred A. Knopf, 1992.

Freedman, Paul H. *Origins of Peasant Servitude in Medieval Catalonia*. Cambridge, U.K.: Cambridge University Press, 1991.

Freely, John. *Ionian Islands: Corfu, Cephalonia, Ithaka and Beyond*. London: I. B. Tauris, 2008.

———. *Aladdin's Lamp, How Greek Science Came to Europe Through the Islamic World*. New York: Alfred A. Knopf, 2009.

———. *The Grand Turk*. New York: Overlook Press, 2009.

———. *Jem Sultan: The Adventures of a Captive Turkish Prince in Renaissance Europe*. New York: HarperCollins, 2013.

Freeman, Charles. *Holy Bones, Holy Dust: How Relics Shaped the History of Medieval Europe*. New Haven: Yale University Press, 2012.

Freiberg, Jack. *Bramante's Tempietto and the Spanish Crown*. Rome: American Academy in Rome, 2005.

Frucht, Richard, ed. *Eastern Europe: An Introduction to the People, Lands and Culture*. Santa Barbara, Calif.: ABC-CLIO, 2004.

Fulin, Rinaldo. *I Diarii di Marino Sanuto*. Venice: M. Visentini, 1880.

Fusero, Clemente. *The Borgias*. Translated by Peter Green. New York: Praeger, 1972.

Fyvie, John. *The Story of the Borgias*. New York: G.P. Putnam's Sons, 1913.

Gairdner, James, ed. "Journals of Roger Machado," in *Historia Regis Henrici Septimi* (London: Longman, Brown, Green, Longmans, and Roberts, 1858), pp. 157–99.

———. *Letters and Papers Illustrative of the Reigns of Richard III and Henry VII*. London: Longman, Green, Longman and Roberts, 1861.

Galíndez Carvajal, Lorenzo. *Crónica de los Reyes de Castilla*. Madrid: Libraría de los sucesores de Hernando, 1923.

Garcés, María Antonia. *Cervantes in Algiers: A Captive's Tale*. Nashville, Tenn.: Vanderbilt University Press, 2002.

García Mercadel, José. *La segunda mujer del Rey Católico, doña Germana de Foix, última reina de Aragón*. Barcelona: Editorial Juventud, SA, 1942.

Gayangos, Pascual de. *The History of the Mohammedan Dynasties in Spain*. London: Oriental Translation Fund, 1843.

Georgius de Hungaria. *Libellus de Ritu et Moribus Turcorum* (1530); digitized version provided by Göttingen State and University Library, Germany.

Gerber, Jane S. *The Jews of Spain: A History of the Sephardic Experience*. New York: Free Press, 1994.

Gerli, E. Michael, "Social Crisis and Conversion: Apostasy and Inquisition in the Chronicles of Fernando del Pulgar and Andrés Bernáldez." *Hispanic Review* 70, no. 2 (Spring 2002), pp. 19–25.

Gitlitz, David Martin. *Secrecy and Deceit: The Religion of the Crypto-Jews*. Albuquerque: University of New Mexico Press, 2002.

Goffman, Daniel. *The Ottoman Empire and Early Modern Europe*. Cambridge, U.K.: Cambridge University Press, 2002.

Gómara, Francisco López de. *Los corsarios Barbarroja*. Madrid: Ediciones Polefemo, 1989.

Gomarez Marín, Antonio. *Documentos de los Reyes Católicos (1492–1504)*. Murcia: Academia Real Alfonso X el Sabio, 2000.

Gómez, María A., Santiago Juan-Navarro, and Phyllis Zatlin, eds. *Juana of Castile: History and Myth of the Mad Queen*. Lewisburg, Pa.: Bucknell University Press, 2008.

González Marrero, María del Cristo. *La casa de Isabel la Católica, espacios domesticos y vida cotidiana*. Ávila: Diputación de Ávila, Institución "Gran Duque de Alba," 2004.

Gonzálo Herrera, Manuel. *Castilla: Negro sobre rojo, de Enrique IV a Isabel la Católica*. Segovia: Ediciones Castellanas, 1993.

Goodwin, Jason. *Lords of the Horizon: A History of the Ottoman Empire*. New York: Henry Holt, 1998.

Gottschalk, Paul. *The Earliest Diplomatic Documents on America, the Papal Bulls of 1493 and the Treaty of Tordesillas*. Berlin: Paul Gottschalk, 1927.

Gould, Alicia Bache. *Nueva lista documentada de los tripulantes de Colón en 1492*. Madrid: Viuda de E. Maestre, 1942–44.

Goury, M. Jules, and Owen Jones. *Plans, Elevations, Sections and Details of the Alhambra: from Drawings Taken on the Spot in 1834*. London: Owen Jones, 1842.

Graña Cid, María del Mar. *Beatriz de Silva (ca. 1426–ca. 1491)*. Madrid: Ediciones del Orto, 2004.

Grayeff, Felix. *Joan of Arc: Legends and Truth*. London: Philip Goodall, 1978.

Green, Mary Anne Everett. *Letters of Royal and Illustrious Ladies of Great Britain, from the Commencement of the Twelfth Century to the Close of the Reign of Queen Mary*. London: Henry Colburn, 1846.

Green, Toby. *Inquisition: The Reign of Fear*. New York: St. Martin's Press, 2009.

Hach, W., J. Dissemod, and V. Hach-Wunderly. "The Long Road to Syphilitic Leg Ulcers." *Phlebogie* 2/2013. Schattauer 2013.

Hare, Christopher (pseudonym for Maria Andrews). *The High and Puissant Princess Marguerite of Austria, Princess Dowager of Spain, Duchess Dowager of Savoy, Regent of the Netherlands*. New York: Charles Scribner & Sons, 1907.

———. *Maximilian the Dreamer: Holy Roman Emperor, 1459–1519*. Germany: S. Paul & Co., 1913.

Haring, Clarence Henry. *Trade and Navigation Between Spain and the Indies*. Cambridge, Mass.: Harvard University Press, 1964.

Harvey, L. P. *Islamic Spain, 1250 to 1500*. Chicago: University of Chicago Press, 1992.

Hayden, Deborah. *Pox: Genius, Madness and the Mysteries of Syphilis*. New York: Basic Books, 2003.

Hefele, Karl Josephon von. *The Life of Cardinal Ximénez*. Translated by John Canon Dalton. London: Catholic Publishing & Bookselling Company, 1860.

Hess, Andrew C. *Forgotten Frontier: A History of the Sixteenth-Century Ibero-African Frontier*. Chicago: University of Chicago Press, 1978.

Heywood, Colin. *Writing Ottoman History: Documents and Interpretations*. Aldershot, Hampshire, U.K.: Ashgate Publishing, 2002.

Hicks, Michael. *Anne Neville, Queen to Richard III*. Gloucestershire, U.K.: Tempus, 2006.

Highfield, Roger, ed. *Spain in the Fifteenth Century, 1369–1516: Essays and Extracts by Historians of Spain*. Translated by Frances M. López-Morillas. New York: Harper & Row, 1972.

Hills, George. *Rock of Contention: A History of Gibraltar*. London: Robert Hale & Co., 1974.

Himmerich y Valencia, Robert. *The Encomenderos of New Spain, 1521–1555*. Austin: University of Texas Press, 1991.

Hollingsworth, Mary. *The Cardinal's Hat: Money, Ambition and Everyday Life in the Court of a Borgia Prince*. Woodstock, N.Y.: Overlook Press, 2005.

Homza, Lu Ann, ed. and trans. *The Spanish Inquisition, 1478–1614: An Anthology of Sources*. Indianapolis: Hackett, 2006.

Hopkins, T. C. F. *Empires, Wars, and Battles: The Middle East from Antiquity to the Rise of the New World*. New York: Forge Books, 2006.

Hutson, James. *Forgotten Features of the Founding: The Recovery of Religious Themes in the Early American Republic.* Lanham, Md: Lexington Books, 2003.

Ihsanoglu, Ekmeleddin. ed. *The History of the Ottoman State, Society, and Civilization.* 2 vols. Istanbul: Research Centre for Islamic History, Art and Culture, 2001.

Imber, Colin. *The Ottoman Empire, 1300–1650: The Structure of Power.* London: Palgrave Macmillan, 2002.

Inalcık, Halil. *Studies in Ottoman Social and Economic History.* London: Variorum Reprints, 1985.

———. *The Ottoman Empire: The Classical Age 1300–1600.* London: Phoenix Press, 2000.

Irizarry, Estelle. *Christopher Columbus's Love Letter to Queen Isabel.* San Juan, Puerto Rico: Ediciones Puerto, 2012.

Irving, Washington. *Chronicle of the Conquest of Granada.* Philadelphia: Carey, Lea & Carey, 1829.

Irwin, Robert. *The Alhambra.* Cambridge, Mass.: Harvard University Press, 2004.

Ishikawa, Chiyo. *The Retablo of Isabel la Católica.* Brussels: Brepols, 2004.

Izbicki, Thomas. *Protector of the Faith: Cardinal Johannes de Turrecremata and the Defense of the Institutional Church.* Washington, D.C.: Catholic University Press, 1981.

Jacobs, Martin. "Joseph ha-Kohen, Paolo Giovio and Sixteenth-Century Historiography." In *Cultural Intermediaries: Jewish Intellectuals in Early Modern Italy.* Edited by David B. Ruderman and Giuseppe Veltri. Philadelphia: University of Pennsylvania Press, 2004.

Jaén, Didier T. *John II of Castile and the Grand Master Álvaro de Luna.* Madrid: Editorial Castalia, 1978.

Jayyusi, Salma Khadra, ed. *The Legacy of Muslim Spain.* Leiden: Brill, 1994.

Jennings, Ronald C. *Studies on Ottoman Social History in the Sixteenth and Seventeenth Centuries: Women, Zimmis and Sharia Courts in Kayseri, Cyprus and Trabzon.* Istanbul: Isis Press, 1999.

Johnson, Marion. *The Borgias.* New York: Holt, Rinehart & Winston, 1981.

Jones, Jonathan. *The Lost Battles: Leonardo, Michelangelo, and the Artistic Duel That Defined the Renaissance.* London: Simon & Schuster, 2010.

Jordan, Annemarie. *The Development of Catherine of Austria's Collection in the Queen's Household: Its Character and Cost.* Providence, R.I.: Brown University, 1994.

Kagan, Richard L. "Prescott's Paradigm: American Historical Scholarship and the Decline of Spain." *The American Historical Review* 101, no. 2 (April 1996), pp. 423–46.

Kagan, Richard L., and Abigail Dyer. *Inquisitorial Inquiries: Brief Lives of Secret Jews and Other Heretics.* Baltimore: John Hopkins University Press, 2011.

Kamen, Henry. *The Spanish Inquisition: A Historical Revision.* London: Weidenfeld & Nicolson, 1997.

———. *Empire: How Spain Became a World Power 1492–1761.* New York: HarperCollins, 2004.

———. *Spain, 1469–1714: A Society of Conflict.* Harlow, U.K.: Pearson Education, 2005.

Kaplan, Gregory B. "In Search of Salvation: The Deification of Isabel la Católica in Converso Poetry." *Hispanic Review* 66, no. 3 (Summer 1998), pp. 289–308.

Kizilov, Mikhail. *Slave Trade in the Early Modern Crimea from the Perspective of Christian, Muslim and Jewish Sources.* Leiden: Koninkijke Brill NV, 2007.

Kleinschmidt, Harald. *Ruling the Waves: Emperor Maximilian I, the Search for Islands, and the Transformation of the European World Picture c. 1500.* Netherlands: Hes & De Graaf, 2008.

Koch, Yolanda Moreno. *El judaísmo hispano, según la crónica hebrea de Rabí Eliyahu Capsali.* Granada: Universidad de Granada, 2005.

Kraus, H. P. *Americana Vetustissima: Fifty Books, Manuscripts, and Maps Relating to America from the First Fifty Years After Its Discovery (1493–1592): In Celebration of the Columbus Quincentenary*. New York: H. P. Kraus, 1990.

Labalme, Patricia H., and Laura Sanguinetti White, eds. *Venice, Città Excelentissima: Selections from the Renaissance Diaries of Marin Sanudo*. Translated by Linda L. Carroll. Baltimore: Johns Hopkins University Press, 2008.

Ladero Quesada, Miguel Ángel. *Castilla y la conquista del reino de Granada*. Granada: Diputacion Provincial de Granada, 1993.

———. *La España de los Reyes Católicos*. Madrid: Alianza Editorial, 1999.

———. *La guerra de Granada, 1482–1491*. Granada: Los Libros de la Estrella, 2001.

———. *Los Reyes Católicos y su tiempo*. Madrid: Centro de Información y Documentación Científica, 2004.

Lamb, Vivien B. *The Betrayal of Richard III: An Introduction to the Controversy*. London: Mitre Press, 1968.

Lanyon, Anna. *The New World of Martin Cortes*. Cambridge, Mass.: Da Capo Press, 2004.

Las Casas, Bartolomé de. *An Account, Much Abbreviated, of the Destruction of the Indies*. Edited by Franklin W. Knight. Translated by Andrew Hurley. Indianapolis: Hackett, 2003.

———. *Apologética historia de las Indias*. Edited by Manuel Serrano y Sanz. Madrid: Bailly y Baillière, 1909.

———. *History of the Indies*. Translated and edited by Andrée Collard. New York: Harper & Row, 1971. Circulated between 1560 and 1600; first published in 1875.

Lea, Henry Charles. "Lucero the Inquisitor." *The American Historical Review* 2, no. 4 (July 1897).

———. *A History of the Inquisition in Spain*. London: Macmillan, 1906.

Letts, Malcolm, ed. and trans. *The Travels of Leo of Rozmital through Germany, Flanders, England, France, Spain, Portugal and Italy, 1465–1467*. Hakluyt Society. Cambridge, U.K.: Cambridge University Press, 1957.

Levack, Brian P. *The Witch-Hunt in Early Modern Europe*. London: Longman Group, 1987.

Levine Melammed, Renée. *Heretics or Daughters of Israel? The Crypto-Jewish Women of Castile*. New York: Oxford University Press, 1999.

Lewis, Bernard. *Islam: From the Prophet Muhammad to the Capture of Constantinople*. New York: Oxford University Press, 1987.

Lindo, Elias Hiam. *The History of the Jews of Spain and Portugal*. 1848. Reprint. New York: Burt Franklin, 1970.

Liss, Peggy K. *Isabel the Queen: Life and Times*. New York: Oxford University Press, 1992.

Liss, Peggy K. *Isabel the Queen: Life and Times*. Philadelphia: University of Pennsylvania Press, 2004.

———. "Isabel of Castille (1451–1504), Her Self-Representation and Its Context." In *Queenship and Political Power in Medieval and Early Modern Spain*. Edited by Theresa Earenfight. Hampshire, England: Ashgate Publishing, 2005.

Llorente, Juan Antonio. *A Critical History of the Inquisition of Spain*. Williamstown, Mass.: The John Lilburne Co., 1967.

Lojendio, Luis-María de. *Gonzalo de Córdoba, El Gran Capitán*. Madrid: Espasa-Calpe, 1942.

López de Coca Castañer, José Enrique. "La Conquista de Granada: El Testimonio de los Vencidos." *Norba: Revista de Historia* 18 (2005).

Lorenzo Arribas, Josemi. *Juana I de Castilla y Aragón, 1479–1555*. Madrid: Ediciones del Orto, 2004.

Lucas-Dubreton, Jean. *The Borgias*. New York: E. P. Dutton, 1955.

Luke, Mary M. *Catherine the Queen*. New York: Coward-McCann, Inc., 1967.

Lunenfeld, Marvin. *Keepers of the City: The Corregidores of Isabella I of Castile, 1474–1504.* Cambridge, U.K.: Cambridge University Press, 1987.

Lynn, Caro. *A College Professor of the Renaissance: Lucio Marineo Siculo Among the Spanish Humanists.* Chicago: University of Chicago Press, 1937.

Machiavelli, Niccolò. *The Prince and the Discourses.* New York: Modern Library, 1950.

MacKay, Angus. "Ritual and Propaganda in Fifteenth Century Spain." *Past & Present,* no. 107. Oxford: Oxford University Press, May 1985.

MacPherson, Ian, and Angus MacKay. *Love, Religion and Politics in Fifteenth Century Spain.* Leiden: Brill, 1998.

Madariaga, Salvador de. *Christopher Columbus: Being the Life of the Very Magnificent Lord Don Cristóbal Colón.* New York: Macmillan, 1940.

Major, Richard Henry. *The Life of Prince Henry of Portugal, Surnamed the Navigator.* London: A. Asher & Co., 1868.

Mallett, Michael. *The Borgias: The Rise and Fall of a Renaissance Dynasty.* New York: Barnes & Noble, 1969.

Mann, Charles C. *1491: New Revelations of the Americas Before Columbus.* New York: Alfred A. Knopf, 2005.

———. *1493: Uncovering the New World Columbus Created.* New York: Alfred A. Knopf, 2011.

———. "Exhibition of Portuguese Art at the Royal Academy." *Burlington Magazine* 97, no. 633 (December 1955), pp. 367–73.

Marañón, Gregorio. *Ensayo biológico sobre Enrique IV de Castilla y su tiempo.* Madrid: Colección Austral, 1997.

Marek, George R. *The Bed and the Throne: The Life of Isabella d'Este.* New York: Harper & Row, 1976.

Marino, Nancy F. *Don Juan Pacheco: Wealth and Power in Late Medieval Spain.* Tempe: Arizona Center for Medieval and Renaissance Studies, 2006.

Márquez de la Plata, Vicenta María. *Mujeres renacentistas en la corte de Isabela la Católica.* Madrid: Editorial Castalia, 2005.

Martín, José Luis. *Isabel la Católica: sus hijas y las damas de su corte, modelos de doncellas, casadas y viudas, en el Carro de las Doñas, 1542.* Ávila: Diputación Provincial de Ávila, Institución "Gran Duque de Alba," 2001.

Martínez Millán, José. "Structures of Inquisitorial Finance." In *The Spanish Inquisition and the Inquisitorial Mind.* Edited by Angel Alcalá. New York: Columbia University Press, 1987.

Martyr, Peter, of Anghiera. *Opus Epistolarum: The Work of the Letters of Peter Martyr.* Letters written between 1457 and 1526, translated into English ca. 1855. London: Wellcome Library.

———. *The Discovery of the New World in the Writings of Peter Martyr of Anghiera.* Edited by Ernest Lunardi, Elisa Magioncalda, and Rosanna Mazzacane. Translated by Felix Azzola. Rome: Istituto Poligráfico e Zecca dello Stato, Libreria dello Stato, 1992.

———. *De Orbo Novo: The Eight Decades of Peter Martyr D'Anghera.* Translated by Francis Augustus MacNutt. Project Gutenberg, 2004.

Mata Carriazo y Arroquia, Juan de. *Crónica de Juan II de Castilla.* Madrid: Real Academia de la Historia, 1982.

———. *Los relieves de la guerra de Granada en la sillería del coro de la Catedral de Toledo.* Granada: Universidad de Granada, 1985.

Mathew, Arnold Harris. *The Diary of John Burchard of Strasburg.* London: Francis Griffiths, 1910.

Mattingly, Garrett. *Catherine of Aragon.* New York: Quality Paperback Books, 1941.

Maxwell-Stuart, P. G. *Chronicles of the Popes.* New York: Thames & Huckon, 1997.

Mazower, Mark. *Salonica, City of Ghosts: Christians, Muslims, and Jews, 1430–1950*. New York: Alfred A. Knopf, 2005.

McBrien, Richard P. *Lives of the Popes: The Pontiffs from St. Peter to John Paul II*. New York: HarperCollins, 1997.

McDonald, Mark P. *Ferdinand Columbus: Renaissance Collector*. London: British Museum Press, 2000.

McManners, John. *The Oxford Illustrated History of Christianity*. Oxford, U.K.: Oxford University Press, 1992.

McMurdo, Edward. *History of Portugal*. London: St. Dunstan's House, 1889.

Memorial Histórico español: colección de documentos, opúsculos, y antigüedades que publica la Real Academia de la Historia, vol. 6. Madrid: Imprenta de la Real Academia de Historia, 1853.

Memorias de Don Enrique IV de Castilla, vol. 2, *La colección diplomática del mismo rey* Madrid: Real Academia de Historia, 1835–1913.

Menocal, María Rosa. *The Ornament of the World: How Muslims, Jews, and Christians Created a Culture of Tolerance in Medieval Spain*. Boston: Little, Brown, 2002.

Menzies, Gavin. *1421: The Year China Discovered America*. New York: HarperCollins, 2002.

Merriman, Roger Bigelow. *The Rise of the Spanish Empire in the Old World and the New*. New York: Cooper Square, 1962.

Merula, George. "The Siege of Shkodra" (1474). Translated by George Elsie. *Texts and Documents of Albanian History*, http://www.albanianhistory.net/en/texts1000-1799/AH1474.html.

Miller, Kathryn A. *Guardians of Islam*. New York: Columbia University Press, 2008.

Miller, Townsend. *The Castles and the Crown: Spain, 1451–1555*. New York: Coward-McCann, 1963.

Monasterio de San Antonio el Real, Segovia.

Morales Muñiz, María Dolores-Carmen. *Alfonso de Ávila, Rey de Castilla*. Ávila: Diputación Provincial de Ávila, Institución "Gran Duque de Alba," 1988.

Morales Muñiz, María Dolores-Carmen, and Luis Caro Dobón. "La muerte del rey Alfonso XII de Castilla." *Revista Hidalguía* 358–59 (2013), p. 293.

Morgan, David. *Medieval Persia, 1040–1797*. Singapore: Longman Singapore Publishers, 1988.

Morgenthau, Henry. *Ambassador Morgenthau's Story*. Detroit: Wayne State University Press, 1999.

Morison, Samuel Eliot. *Admiral of the Ocean Sea: A Life of Christopher Columbus*, vol. 1. Boston: Little, Brown, 1942.

———. *Admiral of the Ocean Sea: A Life of Christopher Columbus*. One-volume edition. Boston: Little, Brown, 1949.

Morison, Samuel Eliot, trans. and ed. *Journals and Other Documents on the Life and Voyages of Christopher Columbus*. New York: Limited Editions Club, 1963.

Mueller, Tom. "CSI: Italian Renaissance." *Smithsonian Magazine*. July–August 2013.

Münzer, Jerónimo. *Viaje por España y Portugal, 1494–1495*. Madrid: Ediciones Polifemo, 1991.

Murphy, Cullen. *God's Jury: The Inquisition and the Making of the Modern World*. Boston: Houghton Mifflin Harcourt, 2012.

Myers, Kathleen Ann. *Fernández de Oviedo's Chronicle of America: A New History for a New World*. Austin: University of Texas Press, 2007.

Nader, Helen. *Power and Gender in Renaissance Spain*. Urbana: University of Illinois Press, 2004.

Netanyahu, Benzion. *Don Isaac Abravanel: Statesman and Philosopher.* Philadelphia: Jewish Publication Society of America, 1982.

———. *The Origins of the Inquisition in Fifteenth Century Spain.* New York: Random House, 1995.

———. *The Marranos of Spain: From Late 14th to the Early 16th Century, According to Contemporary Hebrew Sources.* Ithaca, N.Y.: Cornell University Press, 1999.

Norwich, John Julius. *The World Atlas of Architecture.* New York: Portland House, 1988.

———. *A History of Venice.* New York: Vintage Books, 1989.

O'Callaghan, Joseph P. *A History of Medieval Spain.* Ithaca, N.Y.: Cornell University Press, 1975.

Oliveira Marques, Antonio Henrique de. *Daily Life in Portugal in the Late Middle Ages.* Translated by S. S. Wyatt. Madison: University of Wisconsin Press, 1971.

———. *History of Portugal,* vol. 1, *From Lusitania to Empire.* New York: Columbia University Press, 1976.

Oliver-Copóns, D. Eduardo de. *El Alcázar de Segovia.* Valladolid: Imprenta Castellana, 1916.

Omaechevarría, Ignacio. *Orígenes de La Concepción de Toledo.* Burgos: Aldecoa, 1976.

Oman, Charles. *A History of the Art of War in the Sixteenth Century.* New York: E. P. Dutton, 1937.

Önalp, Ertugrul. *Las Memorias de Barbarroja.* Ankara: Ankara Üniversitesi Basimevi, 1997.

Oviedo y Valdés, Gonzalo Fernández de. *Historia general y natural de las Indias.* Madrid: Imprenta de la Real Academia de la Historia, 1851.

———. *Libro de la Cámara Real del Príncipe Don Juan e officios de su casa e servicio ordinario.* Madrid: La Sociedad de Bibliofilos Españoles, 1870.

———. *Natural History of the West Indies.* Translated by Sterling A. Soutudemire. Chapel Hill: University of North Carolina Press, 1959.

———. *Batallas y quinquagenas.* 2 vols. Madrid: Real Academia de la Historia, 2000.

———. *Writing from the Edge of the World: The Memoirs of Darien, 1514–1527.* Translated by Glen F. Dille. Tuscaloosa: University of Alabama Press, 2006.

Padilla, Lorenzo de. *Crónica de Felipe Primero, llamado El Hermoso.* In *Colección de documentos inéditos para la historia de España.* Edited by Miguel Salvá and Pedro Sainz de Baranda. Madrid: Imprenta de la Viuda de Calero, 1846.

Paez Carrascosa, José. *Ronda and the Serranía.* Translated by Katie Boyle. Ronda, Spain: Publicaciones Ronda, 2000.

Palencia, Alonso Fernández de. *Crónica de Enrique IV.* Edited by Antonio Paz y Meliá. Reprint, Madrid: Ediciones Atlas, 1975.

———. *Guerra de Granada.* Reprint, Barcelona: Linkgua Ediciones, 2009.

Parker, Margaret R. *The Story of a Story Across Cultures: The Case of the Doncella Teodor.* London: Tamesis, 1996.

Parkes, Henry Bamford. *A History of Mexico.* Boston: Houghton Mifflin, 1969.

Parry, V. J. *A History of the Ottoman Empire to 1730.* London: Cambridge University Press, 1976.

Pastor, Ludwig von. *The History of the Popes from the Close of the Middle Ages.* Translated by E. F. Peeler. St. Louis: B. Herder, 1898.

Patterson, Jack E. *Fonseca: Building the New World: How a Controversial Spanish Bishop Helped Find and Settle an Empire in the Americas.* CreateSpace Independent Publishing Platform, 2010.

Paz, Julián. *Catálogo de la colección de documentos inéditos para la historia de España.* 2 vols. Madrid: Instituto de Valencia de Don Juan, 1930–31.

Paz y Meliá, Antonio. *El cronista Alonso de Palencia, su vida y sus obras, sus décadas y las crónicas contemporáneas.* Madrid: Hispanic Society of America, 1914.

Pearson, Andrea G. "Margaret of Austria's Devotional Portrait Diptychs." *Women's Art Journal* 22, no. 2 (Autumn 2001–Winter 2002), pp. 19–25.

Peirce, Leslie P. *The Imperial Harem: Women and Sovereignty in the Ottoman Empire.* New York City: Oxford University Press, 1993.

———. "In Search of the Harem: Sexual Crime and Social Space in Ottoman Royal Law of the 15th and 16th Centuries." *The Ottoman Empire: Myths, Realities and Black Holes.* Istanbul: The Isis Press, 2006.

Penzer, N. M. *The Harem: Inside the Seraglio of the Turkish Sultans.* Mineola, N.Y.: Dover Publications, Inc., 2005.

Pérez de Guzmán, Fernán. *Comienza la crónica del serenísimo Príncipe Don Juan, segundo rey deste nombre.* Madrid: Librería y Casa Editorial Hernando, 1930.

Pérez Samper, María Ángeles. *Isabel la Católica.* Barcelona: Random House Mondadori, 2004.

Peters, Edward. "Jewish History and Gentile Memory." *Jewish History* 9, no. 1 (Spring 1995).

Philippides, Marios. *Patriarchs, Emperors, and Sultans: A Short Chronicle of the Sixteenth Century.* Brookline, Mass.: Hellenic College Press, 1990.

Philippides, Marios, ed. *Mehmed II the Conqueror: And the Fall of the Franco-Byzantine Levant to the Ottoman Turks: Some Western Views and Testimonies.* Tempe: Arizona Center for Medieval and Renaissance Studies, 2007.

Phillips, Carla Rahn, and William D. Phillips. "Christopher Columbus in United States Historiography." *History Teacher* 25, no. 2 (February 1992), pp. 119–35.

Phillips, William D., Jr. *Enrique IV and the Crisis of Fifteenth-Century Castile, 1425–1480.* Cambridge, Mass.: Medieval Academy of America, 1978.

Pina, Ruy de. *Crónica de El-Rei D. Afonso V,* vol. 1. Lisbon: Escritorio, 1901.

———. *Croniqua delrey Dom Joham II.* Coimbra: Atlantida–Livraria Editora, 1950.

Pohl, John, and Charles M. Robinson III. *Aztecs and Conquistadores: The Spanish Invasion and the Collapse of the Aztec Empire.* New York: Osprey, 2005.

Pou, José. "Un monumento de los Reyes Católicos en Roma." *V Congreso de Historia de la Corona de Aragón,* Zaragoza, Oct. 4–11, 1952. Zaragoza: Instituto Fernando el Católico, 1954.

Pratt, Michael. *Britain's Greek Empire: Reflections on the History of the Ionian Islands from the Fall of Byzantium.* n.p.: Rex Collings, 1978.

Prescott, William. *History of the Reign of Ferdinand and Isabella.* London: Richard Bentley, 1838.

———. *History of the Reign of Ferdinand and Isabella.* Philadelphia: J. B. Lippincott, 1896.

Press Department, Ministry of the Interior. *The Turkish Woman in History.* Ankara, Turkey, 1937.

Prieto Cantero, Amalia. *Archivo general de Simancas, catálogo V, Patronato Real (834–1851), tomo II.* Valladolid: Cuerpo Facultativo de Archiveros, Bibliotecarios y Arqueológicos, 1949.

———. *Cartas autografas de los Reyes Católicos de España Don Fernando y Doña Isabel que conservan en el Archivo de Simancas, 1474–1502.* Vallodolid: Insituto Isabel la Católica de Historia Eclesiástica, 1971.

Pulgar, Hernando del. *Crónica de los Señores Reyes Católicos, Don Fernando y Doña Isabel de Castilla y de Aragón.* Valencia: Imprenta de Benito Monfort, 1780.

———. *Crónica de los Señores Reyes Católicos Don Fernando y Doña Isabel de Castilla y de Aragón.* Madrid: Biblioteca de Autores Españoles, Librería de los Sucesores de Hernando, 1923.

——. *Letras: Glosa a las coplas de Mingo Revulgo*. Madrid: Ediciones de la Lectura, 1929.

——. *Crónica de los Reyes Católicos*. Edited by Juan de Mata Carriazo y Arroquia. Madrid: Espasa-Calpe, S.A., 1943.

Purcell, Mary. *The Great Captain: Gonzalo Fernández de Córdoba*. New York: Alvin Redman, 1963.

Pust, Klemen. "Slavery, Childhood and the Border: The Ethics and Economics of Child Displacement Along the Triplex Confinium in the Sixteenth Century." Presented at the 15th World Economic History Congress, Stellenbosch University, South Africa, July 9–13, 2012.

Puyol, Julio. *Crónica incompleta de los Reyes Católicos, 1469–1476: Según un manuscrito anónimo de la época*. Madrid: Tipografía de Archivos, 1934.

Quintana, Manuel José. *Memoirs of Gonzalo Hernández, Styled the Great Captain*. Translated by Joseph Russell. London: Edward Churton, 1851.

Reilly, Bernard F. *The Kingdom of Leon-Castilla Under Queen Urraca, 1109–1125*. Princeton, N.J.: Princeton University Press, 1982.

Reséndez, Andrés. *A Land So Strange: The Epic Journey of Cabeza de Vaca*. New York: Basic Books, 2007.

Reston, James, Jr. *Dogs of God, Columbus, the Inquisition, and the Defeat of the Moors*. New York: Anchor, 2006.

Reyes Ruiz, Manuel. *The Royal Chapel of Granada: The Exchange ("Lonja"), the Church, the Museum: Visitor's Guide*. Translated by Neil McLaren. Granada: Fifth Centenary Publications, 2004.

——. *Testamento de la Reina Isabel la Católica: Testamento del Rey Fernando el Católico*. Granada: Capilla Real de Granada, 2004.

Ribot, Luis, Julio Valdeón, and Elena Maza. *Isabel la Católica y su época. Actas del congreso internacional 2004*. Valladodid: Instituto Universitario de Histórica Simancas, Universidad de Valladolid, 2004.

Rivera Garretas, María-Milagros. *Juana de Mendoza*. Madrid: Ediciones del Orto, 2004.

Rodríguez Valencia, Vicente. *Isabel la Católica en la opinión de españoles y extranjeros, siglos XV al XX*. 3 vols. Valladolid: Instituto "Isabel la Católica" de Historia Eclesiástica, 1970.

Roo, Peter de. *Material for a History of Pope Alexander VI, His Relatives and His Time*, vol. 5. New York: The Universal Knowledge Foundation, 1924.

Rosell, Cayetano, et al. *Crónicas de los Reyes de Castilla: Desde Don Alfonso el sabio hasta las católicos Don Fernando y Doña Isabel*. Madrid: Librería de los Sucesores de Hernando, 1923.

Ross, Charles Derek. *Edward IV*. Berkeley and Los Angeles: University of California Press, 1974.

Rothschild, Bruce M. "History of Syphilis." *Clinical Infectious Diseases*. Oxford Journals, 2005:40 (May 15), pp. 1454–63.

Round, Nicholas. *The Greatest Man Uncrowned: A Study of the Fall of Don Álvaro de Luna*. London: Tamesis Books, 1986.

Rowdon, Maurice. *The Spanish Terror: Spanish Imperialism in the Sixteenth Century*. London: Constable, 1974.

Rozen, Minna. *A History of the Jewish Community in Istanbul: The Formative Years, 1453–1566*. Leiden: Brill, 2010.

Rubin, Nancy. *Isabella of Castile: The First Renaissance Queen*. New York: St. Martin's Press, 1991.

Ruderman, David B., and Giuseppe Veltri, eds., *Cultural Intermediaries: Jewish Intellectuals in Early Modern Italy*. Philadelphia: University of Pennsylvania Press, 2004.

Ruiz, Teofilo. *Spanish Society, 1400–1600*. Essex, U.K.: Pearson Education, 2001.

———. *The Other 1492: Ferdinand, Isabella, and the Making of an Empire*. Chantilly, Va., Teaching Co., 2002.

———. *Spain's Centuries of Crisis: 1300–1474*. West Essex, U.K.: Wiley-Blackwell, 2011.

Ruiz-Domènec, José Enrique. *El Gran Capitán: Retrato de una época*. Barcelona: Ediciones Peninsula, 2002.

Ruy de Pina. *Chronica de el-rei D. Affonso V*. Lisboa: Escriptorio, 1901.

———. *Croniqua Delrey Dom Joham II*. Coimbra: Atlantida, 1950.

Ryder, Alan. *The Wreck of Catalonia: Civil War in the Fifteenth Century*. New York: Oxford University Press, 2007.

Sabatini, Rafael. *Torquemada and the Spanish Inquisition: A History*. London: Stanley Paul, 1924.

Sahagún, Fray Bernardino de. *Florentine Codex: General History of the Things of New Spain*. Translated by Arthur J. O. Anderson and Charles Dibble. Salt Lake City: University of Utah Press, 1982.

Salter, Anna. *Predators, Pedophiles, Rapists and Other Sex Offenders*. New York: Basic Books, 2004.

Sanceau, Elaine. *Henry the Navigator: The Story of a Great Prince and His Time*. New York: W. W. Norton, 1947.

———. *The Perfect Prince: A Biography of the King Dom João II*. Porto and Lisbon: Livraria Civilizacão, 1959.

———. *The Reign of the Fortunate King, 1495–1521*. New York: Archon Books, 1970.

Sánchez Cantón, Francisco Javier. *Libros, tapices y cuadros que colleccionó Isabel la Católica*. Madrid: Consejo Superior de Investigaciones Científicas, 1950.

Sanchez Martín, Aureliano. *Crónica de Enrique IV de Diego Enríquez del Castillo*. Valladolid: Secretariado de Publicaciones, Universidad de Valladolid, 1994.

Sánchez Prieto, Ana. *Enrique IV el Impotente*. Madrid: Alderaban Ediciones, 1999.

Sanchis y Sivera, José. "El Cardenal Rodrigo de Borgia en Valencia." *Boletín de la Real Academia de Historia* 84 (1924), p. 149.

Sandoval, Fray Prudencio de. *Historia de la vida y hechos del Emperador Carlos V*. Madrid: Biblioteca de Autores Españoles, Atlas, 1955.

Santa Cruz, Alonso de. *Crónica de los Reyes Católicos*. Edited by Juan de Mata Carriazo y Arroquia. 2 vols. Seville: Escuela de Estudios Hispano-Americanos de Sevilla, 1951.

Santa María de Miraflores. Burgos: Caja de Ahorros Municipal de Burgos, 1992.

Sanz, M. Grau. "Así fue coronada Isabel la Católica." *Estudios Segovianos* 1 (1949), pp. 24–36.

Saracheck, Joseph. *Don Isaac Abravanel*. New York: Bloch Publishing Co., 1938.

Sarwar, Ghulam. *History of Shah Ismail Safavi*. Aligarh: Muslim University, 1939.

Scofield, Cora Louise, "The Movements of the Earl of Warwick in the Summer of 1464." *English Historical Review* (October 1906).

———. *The Life and Reign of Edward the Fourth, King of England and of France and Lord of Ireland*. London: Frank Cass & Co., 1967.

Seton Watson, R. W. *Maximilian I: Holy Roman Emperor*. Westminster, U.K.: Archibald Constable & Co., 1902.

Seward, Desmond. *The Burning of the Vanities: Savonarola and the Borgia Pope*. Stroud, U.K.: Sutton, 2006.

Shadis, Miriam. *Berenguela of Castile (1180–1246) and Political Women in the High Middle Ages*. New York: Palgrave Macmillan, 2009.

Shaw, Stanford. *History of the Ottoman Empire and Modern Turkey*. Cambridge, U.K.: Cambridge University Press, 1976.

Shmuelevitz, Aryeh. "Capsali as a Source for Ottoman History, 1450–1523." *International Journal of Middle Eastern Studies* 9 (1978), pp. 339–44.

Simpson, Leonard Francis. *Autobiography of Charles V.* London: Longman, Green, Longman Roberts & Green, 1862.

Smith, Bradley. *Spain: A History in Art.* Garden City, N.Y.: Doubleday, 1971.

Smith, George. *The Coronation of Elizabeth Wydeville, Queen Consort of Edward IV, on May 26th, 1465: A Contemporary Account Set Forth from a XV Century Manuscript.* London: Ellis, 1935.

Solé, José María. *Los reyes infieles, amantes y bastardos: De los Reyes Católicos a Alfonso XIII.* Madrid: La Esfera de los Libros, 2005.

Soyer, François. *The Persecution of the Jews and Muslims of Portugal: King Manuel I and the End of Religious Tolerance, 1496–1497.* Leiden: Brill, 2007.

———. "King João II of Portugal, 'O Principe Perfeito,' and the Jews (1481–1495)." *Sefarad* 69, no. 1 (2009).

Sphrantzes, George. *The Fall of the Byzantine Empire: A Chronicle, 1401–1477.* Amherst: University of Massachusetts Press, 1980.

Starr-LeBeau, Gretchen. *In the Shadow of the Virgin: Inquisitors, Friars and Conversos in Guadalupe, Spain.* Princeton, N.J.: Princeton University Press, 2003.

Stevens, Serita Deborah, and Anne Klarner. *Deadly Doses: A Writer's Guide to Poisons.* Cincinnati: Writers Digest Books, 1990.

Stewart, Paul. "The Santa Hermandad and the First Italian Campaign of Gonzalo de Córdoba, 1495–1498." *Renaissance Quarterly* 28, no. 1 (Spring 1975), pp. 29–37.

Strathern, Paul. *The Artist, the Philosopher, and the Warrior: The Intersecting Lives of Da Vinci, Machiavelli, and Borgia and the World They Shaped.* New York: Bantam Books, 2009.

Stuart Fitz-James, Jacobo, and Falcó Alba, eds. *Correspondencia de Gutierre Gómez de Fuensalida.* Madrid: Imprenta Alemana, 1907.

Suárez Fernández, Luis. *Política Internacional de Isabel la Católica: Estudios y documentos.* Vallalodid: Universidad de Valladolid, 1971, 2002.

Suárez Fernández, Luis, Juan de Mata Carriazo y Arroquia, and Manuel Fernández Álvarez. *La España de los Reyes Católicos, 1474–1516.* Madrid: Espasa-Calpe, 1969.

Sudhoff, Karl. *The Earliest Printed Literature on Syphilis, Being Ten Tractates from the Years 1495–1498.* Adapted by Charles Singer. Florence: R. Lier & Co., 1925.

Symonds, John Addington. *A Short History of the Renaissance in Italy.* New York: Henry Holt, 1894.

Tagarelli, Antonio, Giuseppe Tagarelli, Paola Lagonia, and Ann Piro, "A Brief History of Syphilis by Its Symptoms." *History of Medicine* 19, no. 4. Acta Dermatovenerologica Croatia, 2011.

Tanner, Marie. *Jerusalem on the Hill: Rome and the Vision of St. Peter's in the Renaissance.* Belgium: Brepols, 2011.

Thomas, Hugh. *The Conquest of Mexico.* London: Pimlico, 1993.

———. *Rivers of Gold: The Rise of the Spanish Empire from Columbus to Magellan.* New York: Random House, 2003.

———. *The Golden Empire: Spain, Charles V, and the Creation of America.* New York: Random House, 2010.

Thompson, Charles, and John Samuel. *Poisons and Poisoners.* London: Harold Shaylor, 1931.

Thompson, E. A. *The Goths in Spain.* Oxford U.K.: Oxford University Press, 1969.

Tilly, Charles. "The Europe of Columbus and Bayazid." Middle East Research and Information Project, *Middle East Report,* no. 178 (September–October 1992).

Torre, Antonio de la. *Documentos sobre relaciones internacionales de los Reyes Católicos.* Barcelona: Atenas A.G., 1966.

Torre, Antonio de la, and Luis Suárez Fernández. *Documentos referentes a las relaciones con Portugal durante el reinado de los Reyes Católicos.* 1858. Valladolid: Consejo Superior de Investigaciones Científicas, Patronato Menéndez Pelayo, 1963.

Trame, Richard H. *Rodrigo Sánchez de Arévalo, 1404–1470: Spanish Diplomat and Champion of the Papacy.* Washington, D.C.: Catholic University of America Press, 1958.

Tremayne, Eleanor E. *First Governess of the Netherlands: Margaret of Austria.* New York: G. P. Putnam's Sons, 1908.

Tremlett, Giles. *Catherine of Aragon, the Spanish Queen of Henry VIII.* New York: Walker & Co., 2010.

Val Valdivieso, María Isabel del. *Isabel la Católica, princesa (1468–1474).* Valladolid: Instituto "Isabel la Católica" de Historia Eclesiástica, 1974.

———. *Isabel I de Castilla, 1451–1504.* Madrid: Ediciones del Orto, 2004.

Val Valdivieso, María Isabel del, and Julio Valdeón Baruque. *Isabel la Católica, Reina de Castilla.* Valladolid: Ambito Ediciones, 2004.

Valdecasas, Guillermo G. *Fernando el Católico y el Gran Capitán.* Granada: Editorial COMARES, 1988.

Valdeón Baruque, Julio. *Judíos y conversos en la Castilla medieval.* Valladolid: Universidad de Vallodolid, 2000.

Valera, Diego de. *Historia de España.* Salamanca, 1499.

———. *Crónica de los Reyes Católicos.* Madrid: José Molina, 1927.

———. *Crónicas de los reyes de Castilla: Memorial de diversas hazañas. Crónica del Rey Enrique IV.* Edited by Juan de Mata Carriazo y Arroquia. Madrid: Espasa-Calpe, 1941.

Varela, Consuelo. *Cristóbal Colón: Textos y documentos completos.* Madrid: Alianza Editorial, 1992.

Varga, Domokos. *Hungary in Greatness and Decline: The 14th and 15th Centuries.* Translated by Martha Szacsvay Liptak. Atlanta: Hungarian Cultural Foundation, 1982.

Vargas-Zuñiga, Antonio, and Baltasar Cuartero. *Índice de la colección de Don Luis de Salazar y Castro.* Madrid: Imprenta y Editorial Maestre, 1949.

"Venice: 1486–1490." In *Calendar of State Papers Relating to English Affairs in the Archives of Venice,* ed. Rawdon Brown. London: National Archives, 1864.

Vicens Vives, Jaime. *El Príncipe Don Fernando (El Católico), Rey de Sicilia.* Zaragoza: Instituto "Fernando el Católico" (C.S.I.C.) de le Exma Diputación Provincial, 1949.

———. *An Economic History of Spain.* Translated by Frances M. López-Morillas. Princeton, N.J.: Princeton University Press, 1969.

———. *Spain in the Fifteenth Century, 1369–1516: Essays and Extracts by Historians of Spain.* Edited by J. R. L. Highfield and Frances M. López-Morillas. New York: Harper & Row, 1972.

———. *Historia crítica de la vida y reinado de Ferdinand de Aragón.* Zaragoza: Instituto Fernando el Católico, 1962, 2006.

Vickery, Paul S. *Bartolomé de Las Casas: Great Prophet of the Americas.* New York: Paulist Press, 2006.

Vinyoles y Vidal, Teresa-María, and Mireia Comas Vía. *Estefanía Carrós y de Mur, ca. 1455–1511.* Madrid: Ediciones del Orto, 2004.

Walpole, Horace. *Historic Doubts on the Life and Reign of Richard the Third.* Guernsey, U.K.: Guernsey Press Co., 1987.

Warkworth, John. *A Chronicle of the First Thirteen Years of the Reign of King Edward the Fourth.* Edited by James Orchard Halliwell. London: Camden Society, 1839.

Warren, Nancy Bradley. *Women of God and Arms: Female Spirituality and Political Conflict, 1380–1600.* Philadelphia: University of Pennsylvania Press, 2005.

Wass, Glenn Elwood. *The Legendary Character of Kaiser Maximilian.* New York: Columbia University Press, 1941.

Watt, William Montgomery. *A History of Islamic Spain*. Edinburgh: Edinburgh University Press, 1965.

Webb, Diana. *Medieval European Pilgrimage, c. 700 to c. 1500*. Hampshire, U.K.: Palgrave, 2002.

Weber, Alison. "Recent Studies on Women and Early Modern Religion in Spanish." *Renaissance Quarterly* 52 (1999).

Weiss, Jessica. *Inquisitive Objects: Material Culture and Conversos in Early Modern Ciudad Real*. LAII Research Paper Series, University of New Mexico, October 2011.

Weissberger, Barbara F. "Alfonso de Palencia," in *Queer Iberia*, ed. Josiah Blackmore and Gregory S. Hutcheson. Durham, N.C.: Duke University Press, 1999.

——. *Queen Isabel I of Castile: Power, Patronage, Persona*. Rochester, N.Y.: Tamesis, 2008.

——. "Tanto Monta: The Catholic Monarchs' Nuptial Fiction and the Power of Isabel of Castile," in *Rule of Women in Early Modern Europe*. Edited by Anne J. Cruz and Mihoko Suzuki. Urbana: University of Illinois Press, 2009.

Wolf, John B. *Barbary Coast: Algiers Under the Turks, 1500 to 1830*. New York: W.W. Norton, 1979.

Yebes, Condesa de. *La Marquesa de Moya: la dama del descubrimiento, 1440–1511*. Madrid: Ediciones Cultura Hispánica, 1966.

Zilfi, Madeline C. *Women in the Ottoman Empire: Middle Eastern Women in the Early Modern Era*. Leiden: Brill, 1997.

Zurita, Jerónimo. *Anales de Aragón*. Zaragoza: Instituto "Fernando el Católico" (C.S.I.C.) de la Excma Diputación Provincial, 1975 and 1977.

——. *Historia del Rey Don Hernando el Católico: De las empresas y ligas de Italia*. Edited by Ángel Canellas López. Zaragoza: Diputación General de Aragón, 1989.

INDEX